T0338614

Handbook of Research on Digital Transformation and Challenges to Data Security and Privacy

Pedro Fernandes Anunciação
Polytechnic Institute of Setúbal, Portugal

Cláudio Roberto Magalhães Pessoa
Escola de Engenharia de Minas Gerais, Brazil

George Leal Jamil
Informações em Rede Consultoria e Treinamento, Brazil

A volume in the Advances in Information Security,
Privacy, and Ethics (AISPE) Book Series

Published in the United States of America by
IGI Global
Information Science Reference (an imprint of IGI Global)
701 E. Chocolate Avenue
Hershey PA, USA 17033
Tel: 717-533-8845
Fax: 717-533-8661
E-mail: cust@igi-global.com
Web site: http://www.igi-global.com

Copyright © 2021 by IGI Global. All rights reserved. No part of this publication may be reproduced, stored or distributed in
any form or by any means, electronic or mechanical, including photocopying, without written permission from the publisher.
Product or company names used in this set are for identification purposes only. Inclusion of the names of the products or
companies does not indicate a claim of ownership by IGI Global of the trademark or registered trademark.

Library of Congress Cataloging-in-Publication Data

Names: Anunciação, Pedro Fernandes, 1967- editor. | Pessoa, Cláudio
    Roberto Magalhães, editor. | Jamil, George Leal, 1959- editor.
Title: Handbook of Research on digital transformation and challenges to data security and privacy /
    Pedro Fernandes Anunciação, Cláudio Roberto Magalhães Pessoa, George
    Leal Jamil, editors.
Description: Hershey, PA : Business Science Reference, an imprint of IGI
    Global, [2021] | Includes bibliographical references and index. |
    Summary: "This book provides relevant theoretical frameworks and the
    latest empirical research findings for professionals who want to improve
    their understanding of the digital transformation, information
    management, information security, information system reliability, and
    business continuity in a business environment aimed at data
    protection"-- Provided by publisher.
Identifiers: LCCN 2020033494 (print) | LCCN 2020033495 (ebook) | ISBN
    9781799842019 (hardcover) | ISBN 9781799858485 (paperback) | ISBN
    9781799842026 (ebook)
Subjects: LCSH: Database security. | Computer security. | Information
    commons.
Classification: LCC QA76.9.D314 D54 2021 (print) | LCC QA76.9.D314
    (ebook) | DDC 005.8--dc23
LC record available at https://lccn.loc.gov/2020033494
LC ebook record available at https://lccn.loc.gov/2020033495

This book is published in the IGI Global book series Advances in Information Security, Privacy, and Ethics (AISPE) (ISSN:
1948-9730; eISSN: 1948-9749)

British Cataloguing in Publication Data
A Cataloguing in Publication record for this book is available from the British Library.

All work contributed to this book is new, previously-unpublished material. The views expressed in this book are those of the
authors, but not necessarily of the publisher.

For electronic access to this publication, please contact: eresources@igi-global.com.

Advances in Information Security, Privacy, and Ethics (AISPE) Book Series

Manish Gupta
State University of New York, USA

ISSN:1948-9730
EISSN:1948-9749

MISSION

As digital technologies become more pervasive in everyday life and the Internet is utilized in ever increasing ways by both private and public entities, concern over digital threats becomes more prevalent.

The **Advances in Information Security, Privacy, & Ethics (AISPE) Book Series** provides cutting-edge research on the protection and misuse of information and technology across various industries and settings. Comprised of scholarly research on topics such as identity management, cryptography, system security, authentication, and data protection, this book series is ideal for reference by IT professionals, academicians, and upper-level students.

COVERAGE

- Risk Management
- Network Security Services
- Security Classifications
- CIA Triad of Information Security
- Information Security Standards
- Telecommunications Regulations
- Technoethics
- Security Information Management
- Device Fingerprinting
- Tracking Cookies

IGI Global is currently accepting manuscripts for publication within this series. To submit a proposal for a volume in this series, please contact our Acquisition Editors at Acquisitions@igi-global.com or visit: http://www.igi-global.com/publish/.

The Advances in Information Security, Privacy, and Ethics (AISPE) Book Series (ISSN 1948-9730) is published by IGI Global, 701 E. Chocolate Avenue, Hershey, PA 17033-1240, USA, www.igi-global.com. This series is composed of titles available for purchase individually; each title is edited to be contextually exclusive from any other title within the series. For pricing and ordering information please visit http://www.igi-global.com/book-series/advances-information-security-privacy-ethics/37157. Postmaster: Send all address changes to above address. Copyright © 2021 IGI Global. All rights, including translation in other languages reserved by the publisher. No part of this series may be reproduced or used in any form or by any means – graphics, electronic, or mechanical, including photocopying, recording, taping, or information and retrieval systems – without written permission from the publisher, except for non commercial, educational use, including classroom teaching purposes. The views expressed in this series are those of the authors, but not necessarily of IGI Global.

Titles in this Series

For a list of additional titles in this series, please visit: http://www.igi-global.com/book-series/advances-information-security-privacy-ethics/37157

Limitations and Future Applications of Quantum Cryptography
Neeraj Kumar (Babasaheb Bhimrao Ambedkar University, Lucknow, India) Alka Agrawal (Babasaheb Bhimrao Ambedkar University, Lucknow, India) Brijesh K. Chaurasia (Indian Institute of Information Technology, India) and Raees Ahmad Khan (Independent Researcher, India)
Information Science Reference • © 2021 • 335pp • H/C (ISBN: 9781799866770) • US $225.00

Advancements in Security and Privacy Initiatives for Multimedia Images
Ashwani Kumar (Vardhaman College of Engineering, India) and Seelam Sai Satyanarayana Reddy (Vardhaman College of Engineering, India)
Information Science Reference • © 2021 • 278pp • H/C (ISBN: 9781799827955) • US $215.00

Blockchain Applications in IoT Security
Harshita Patel (Vellore Institute of Technology, India) and Ghanshyam Singh Thakur (Maulana Azad National Institute of Technology, India)
Information Science Reference • © 2021 • 275pp • H/C (ISBN: 9781799824145) • US $215.00

Real-Time and Retrospective Analyses of Cyber Security
David Anthony Bird (British Computer Society, UK)
Information Science Reference • © 2021 • 267pp • H/C (ISBN: 9781799839798) • US $195.00

Transdisciplinary Perspectives on Risk Management and Cyber Intelligence
Luisa Dall'Acqua (University of Bologna, Italy & LS TCO, Italy) and Irene Maria Gironacci (Swinburne University of Technology, Australia)
Information Science Reference • © 2021 • 273pp • H/C (ISBN: 9781799843399) • US $195.00

Handbook of Research on Cyber Crime and Information Privacy
Maria Manuela Cruz-Cunha (Polytechnic Institute of Cávado and Ave, Portugal) and Nuno Ricardo Mateus-Coelho (Polytechnic Institute of Management and Technology, Portugal)
Information Science Reference • © 2021 • 753pp • H/C (ISBN: 9781799857280) • US $425.00

Large-Scale Data Streaming, Processing, and Blockchain Security
Hemraj Saini (Jaypee University of Information Technology, India) Geetanjali Rathee (Jaypee University of Information Technology, India) and Dinesh Kumar Saini (Sohar University, Oman)
Information Science Reference • © 2021 • 285pp • H/C (ISBN: 9781799834441) • US $225.00

701 East Chocolate Avenue, Hershey, PA 17033, USA
Tel: 717-533-8845 x100 • Fax: 717-533-8661
E-Mail: cust@igi-global.com • www.igi-global.com

George Leal Jamil and Pedro Fernandes da Anunciação dedicate this book to all healthcare profession-als who sacrificed their lives under dramatic threat on saving us from the Covid-19 Pandemic.

Cláudio Pessoa dedicates this book to his wife Patrícia for always being by his side at all times of their lives. Your fight is my inspiration. Thanks!

List of Reviewers

Juan Andres Bernal Conesa, *Centro Universitario de la Defesa de San Javier, UPCT, Cartagena, Spain*
Antonio Juan Briones-Peñalver, *Technological University of Cartagena, Spain*
José Manuel Carvalho Vieira, *ISMAI, Portugal*
Mario Chong, *Universidad del Pacífico, Lima, Peru*
Marco Elisio Marques, *Universidade Fumec, Brazil*
Liliana Esteves Gomes, *Universidade de Coimbra, Portugal*
Manuel da Rocha Fiúza Branco Júnior, *Universidade Fumec, Brazil*
Mario Franco, *Universidade da Beira Interior, Portugal*
Nuno Geada, *Instituto Politécnico de Setúbal, Portugal*
Leonardo Grandinetti Chaves, *Prodemge, Brazil*
Llarina Gonzalez, *Universidade da Coruña, Spain & General Secretariat of the Council of the European Union, Belgium*
Jesus Gonzalez-Feliu, *Excelia Business School, La Rochelle, France*
Beatriz Leal Jamil, *Pontifícia Universidade Católica, Brazil*
Jorge Lima de Magalhães, *FioCruz, Brazil*
Sérgio Maravilhas Lopes, *SENAI/CIMATEC, UNIFACS, Salvador University, Brazil*
Dele Odunlami, *Olabisi Onabanjo University, Nigeria*
Volkan Polat, *Yalova University, Turkey*
Maria José Sousa, *Instituto Universitário de Lisboa, Portugal*
Anna Svirina, *Kazan National Technica University, Russia*
Dušan Vujošević, *Union University School of Computing, Serbia*

List of Contributors

Table of Contents

Section 2
Practical Cases, Application Reflections Over Digital Transformation, Security, and Privacy

Detailed Table of Contents

Section 1
Conceptual Views for Digital Transformation, Data Security, and Privacy

Users' personal, highly sensitive data such as photos and voice recordings are kept indefinitely by the companies that collect it. Users can neither delete nor restrict the purposes for which it is used. Learning how to machine learning that protects privacy, we can make a huge difference in solving many social issues like curing disease, etc. Deep neural networks are susceptible to various inference attacks as they remember information about their training data. In this chapter, the authors introduce differential privacy, which ensures that different kinds of statistical analysis don't compromise privacy and federated learning, training a machine learning model on a data to which we do not have access to.

Ethics is an important social and technological issue. The powerful computer capabilities provide new frontiers of economic and social human activities. Information, about employees, consumers, and markets, becomes more relevant when it enables economic decisions and impacts on the organization's competitiveness. Recent examples such as fake news show a necessity of a comprehensive and multidimensional economic and social approach to frame the use of algorithms and technologies to guarantee suitable ethical patterns in the information society. It is important to analyze the sensibility of economic stakeholders to the ethical limits of information collection and treatment about consumers and technology users. The aim of the present study was to evaluate the proposed model for ethical analysis through a proof of concept applied to a Portuguese energy operator, framing the identification and mitigation of the ethical risks associated with the continuous digital transformation process.

Chapter 3

In the contemporary organizational context, the sharing and transfer of knowledge play a significant role, and therefore, it is important to overcome internal and external barriers for them to be processed. This can be facilitated by the implementation of data governance (GovD). The problem is that, in addition to being a new construct and still little studied, conceptual divergences are fed by the amplitude the possible dimensions of analysis. In this context, the objective of this study arises in identifying the conceptualization of the construct governance and data proposed in the scientific literature to support its better understanding and perspective of future investigations. A theoretical research was conducted through a systematic literature review, followed by an analysis of the most relevant publications on the subject. The discussions about this subject are considered in the context of contemporary organizations; however, it signals the importance of future studies of empirical and theoretical order to foster discussions on the subject today.

The role of the internet of things (IoT) and cyberspace in a digital society is well recognized, and they have become tremendously popular due to certain features like the ability to ease the operational process of businesses and instant communication. Recent developments in the fields of wireless communication networks like 4G, 5G, and 6G with IoT applications have greatly benefited human welfare. Still, the rapid growth of various IoT applications focuses on automating different tasks and are trying to empower the inanimate physical objects to act without any human intervention. It has also contributed to unethical practices by hackers who use new tools and techniques to penetrate more complex or well-controlled environments and produce increased damage and even remain under the cover. The main objective of this chapter is to improve understanding of the challenges to secure future digital infrastructure while it is still evolving. In this context, a detailed review of the security-related issues, challenges, threats, and countermeasures in the IoT applications is presented.

Chapter 5

Digitization is currently radically and exponentially changing business across all sectors. Organizations are facing the challenge of managing all rapid and repetitive adaptation in the face of changing infrastructures in order to correspond with the needs of the digital age, so organizations must be aware to avoid unnecessary disruptions to business. The digital economy shows great growth potential in the scope of transactions between companies. Today, consumers have a huge impact on the economy, as we are in a society that is always "online" and well informed.

Chapter 6

Felipe Palhares, Barbosa Müssnich Aragão Advogados, Brazil

After several years discussing the creation of a comprehensive data protection law, Brazil finally has its first law that specifically addresses this area -and that will be a game-changer on regulating data processing activities in the country and abroad – in force. Although Brazil's data protection law bears many similarities with the European Union General Data Protection Regulation, it also deviates from its European counterpart in several aspects. This chapter intends to provide an overview of the background relating to laws that carry privacy and data protection provisions in their core and to thoroughly analyze Brazil's new data protection law.

Chapter 7

Kamalkumar Macwan, Sardar Vallabhbhai National Institute of Technology, India
Sankita Patel, Sardar Vallabhbhai National Institute of Technology, India

Recently, the social network platforms have gained the attention of people worldwide. People post, share, and update their views freely on such platforms. The huge data contained on social networks are utilized for various purposes like research, market analysis, product popularity, prediction, etc. Although it provides so much useful information, it raises the issue regarding user privacy. This chapter discusses the various privacy preservation methods applied to the original social network dataset to preserve privacy against attacks. The two areas for privacy preservation approaches addressed in this chapter are anonymization in social network data publication and differential privacy in node degree publishing.

Chapter 8

Sofia Sousa, Polytechnic Institute of Setúbal, Portugal

Fast and accurate information is essential so that managers can analyze and structure their decisions, ensuring the good performance of logistics processes. Thus, in a constantly evolving world, it is increasingly important for the organization to keep up with consumer needs, adapting and investing in information systems and technologies (ITS) that appear on the market. Within the supply chain, warehouses and their management are often seen only as an inevitable cost for the organization, ending up being left aside when it comes to high investment implementations and changes. However, currently they have proven to be a relevant component that, if well managed and with the appropriate technology, can eliminate costs for the organization while also providing profits, allowing to maintain a perfect balance between demand and supply.

Chapter 9

Jose P. Rascao, Polytechnic Institute of Setúbal, Portugal

In the contemporary organizational context, the sharing and transfer of knowledge plays a significant role, and therefore, it is important to overcome internal and external barriers for them to be processed. This can be facilitated by the implementation of information and knowledge governance (GovIC), an emerging interdisciplinary approach that crosses the fields of information sciences, business sciences, and human resources sciences. The problem is that, in addition to being a new construct and still little studied, conceptual divergences are fed by the amplitude the possible dimensions of analysis. In this context, the objective of this study emerges in identifying the conceptualization of the construct of information governance and knowledge proposed in the scientific literature to support its better understanding and perspective of future investigations. A theoretical research was conducted through a systematic literature review, followed by an analysis of the most relevant publications on the subject.

Chapter 10

We are experiencing a time of intense change in human relations with great exposure and with this the need for governments and companies to be prepared to ensure the protection of personal data of their users and customers. The purpose of this chapter is to provide clear evidence of the impacts that arbitration and arbitration chambers will be subject to by changes imposed by data protection laws. The arbitral chambers shall prepare and adapt their procedures to this new reality under penalty of its extinction.

Chapter 11

The world scenario is changing when we talk about personal data protection. Not that long ago, it was common to find companies that sell databases, and other companies that work with the information contained into these databases, aimed to create profiles and generate solutions, using technologies such as big data and artificial intelligence, among others, looking to be attractive and get more customers. In order to protect the privacy of citizens across the world, laws have been created and/or expanded to reinforce this protection. In Brazil, specifically, the Lei de Proteção de Dados Pessoais – LGPD [General Data Protection Law] was created. This research aims to analyze this law, as well as other laws that orbit around it. The goal is to know the impact of law enforcement on business routine and, as a specific objective, what the role of DPO (Data Protection Officer) in organizations will be.

Chapter 12

In an increasingly complex and competitive world, information is a valuable asset and a difference maker. It contributes to better government through supporting efficient business, assisting decision-making, mitigating risks, and adding economic value. This case study reviews Portuguese military information security requirements and its potential application on business company's crucial information protection. It's a military security policy, procedures, and measures approach to commercial environment. It's defined a security checklist to be applied by companies which want to achieve success. The explosive growth of information and communication technologies and their global dissemination and penetration have been a special impact on commercial activities, making them an attractive target to competitors and other agents. Cybersecurity is an organization's top priority. It's necessary to build an increasingly effective security policy in order to protect critical information. Keeping safe business competitive information advantages will be the key to success.

Chapter 13

Moisés Rockembach, Federal University of Rio Grande do Sul, Brazil
Armando Malheiro da Silva, University of Porto, Portugal

From the consolidation of the application of European data protection regulations and the recent adoption of Brazilian data protection regulations, we are faced with a scenario that crosses borders. In a world marked by companies whose business model is the analysis and commercialization of personal data and of governments that use their citizens' data for control and surveillance, it is imperative to discuss the necessary characteristics to foster a society that respects ethical and legal values regarding data privacy and consented uses there; the authors address concepts and cases that they consider important for the establishment of reflections on the use of web data. They also take into account ethical issues and regulatory instruments in Europe and Brazil, analyzing the strongness and weaknesses in the implementation of data protection and privacy.

Chapter 14

Maria José Sousa, Instituto Universitário de Lisboa, Portugal
Gabriel Osório de Barros, Ministério da Economia e Transição Digital, Portugal
Nuno Tavares, Ministério da Economia e Transição Digital, Portugal

Artificial intelligence is reconfiguring the economy and redefining the product and service market. It is a disruptive technology that leads to the creation of multiple more efficient activities, new business models, and industrial processes. The literature stresses that AI should be used in all aspects of the personal lives of organisations and individuals, and such complexities are still largely unstudied. The aim of this study is to highlight AI's innovations and applications to the organisation's digital transformation.

Section 2
Practical Cases, Application Reflections Over Digital Transformation, Security, and Privacy

Chapter 15

Bruno de Lacerda, Chess Consultoria, Brazil
George Leal Jamil, Informações em rede Consultoria e Treinamento, Brazil

Digital transformation landed on organizational daily lives, whether businesspeople understand it or not. Adaptations and flexibility became strategic principles, along with new ways to comprehend how technology can really position a competitive advantage. Examining some open reflections and based on experiences, the authors of this chapter elaborate some scenarios, questions, and problems, which will motivate the reader on evaluating the actual turbulent context and understand precisely the achievements of their decisions regarding technology and novelty management contexts.

Chapter 16

In Brazil, organized crime, unfortunately, finds a fertile field that allows its growth and development due to several different aspects. Also, the vast and continental dimension of the Brazilian territory, the evident social inequality, and in many cases, the lack of synergy and collaboration among municipal, provincial, and federal levels are problems. It is important to mention that, in recent times, via its main institutions—executive, legislative, and judiciary—Brazil has been organizing itself and trying to tackle corruption on different fronts, with the use of advanced technology, new procedures of criminal investigation, an increased collaboration between different players and internal cooperation, the celerity in the process of penal persecution, and the revision of laws related to the theme. This chapter aims at displaying technological innovations that have helped law enforcement to act with rigor, speed, and assertiveness in the production of evidence from digital evidence, while respecting the Brazilian Constitution, individual rights, and guarantees of every citizen.

This exploratory and descriptive study aims to analyze the impacts and effectiveness of a public innovation policy promoted by a city hall in a Brazilian state capital involving startups, large companies, and a scientific and technological institution between 2017 and 2019; the purpose of this study is to promote economic development and address urban problems common to large metropolises. The strategy adopted, inspired by the propositions of the Triple Helix, was able to bring together startups, large companies, a city hall, and an important representative of academia. The results indicate the evolution of indicators of entrepreneurship in the city and present important lessons for the formulation of municipal innovation policies in Brazil.

Chapter 18

In an economy that tends to operate in real time, where companies reduce stocks and value the customization of products and services according to the needs of their customers, information systems and technologies assume a predominant role. Equipment maintenance proves to be critical in supplying markets and meeting consumer needs. Regarding the maintenance of equipment, most managers are faced with the technical indications of suppliers, serving as a reference for the respective interventions. However, these indications often do not contemplate the contingency of certain situations, excessive hours of operation, or temperatures higher than those indicated. Preventive maintenance assumes an important role in the maintenance area by allowing interventions that are more appropriate to the wear and tear of the equipment. The technological potential associated with the internet of things or analytics allows the generation of economic value by guaranteeing the adequate conditions of the equipment and by avoiding disruptions in supply to the markets.

Chapter 19

Bhimavarapu Usharani, Koneru Lakshmaiah Education Foundation, India
Raju Anitha, Koneru Lakshmaiah Education Foundation, India

Due to the advancement in internet technology, everyone can connect to anyone living anywhere in this world who is far away from us by using social media. Social media became a public place to share everyone's personal photos and videos. These photos or videos are viewed, shared, and even downloaded by their respective friends, someone from their friends' profiles, and even unrelated persons also without their permission. One of the risks from the social media is the cyber bullying or online harassment. Cyber bullies perpetrate either through denigration or doxing. The cyber bullies are anonymous, and it is very difficult for us to catch and punish them. The main aim of this chapter is to provide the privacy and security to the photos that are sharing on social media. This chapter proposes a novel algorithm to keep the photos safe that are uploading on social media and the extension of the novel algorithm to reveal the details of the cyber bullies those who performed morphing on the photos that were downloaded from social media.

Chapter 20

Maria Tereza Sousa Silva, Bio-Manguinhos, Fiocruz, Brazil
Erica Louro da Fonseca, Bio-Manguinhos, Fiocruz, Brazil
Zulmira Hartz, Institute of Hygiene and Tropical Medicine (IHMT), Global Health and
    Tropical Medicine (GHMT), University NOVA of Lisbon, Portugal
Jorge Magalhães, Institute of Hygiene and Tropical Medicine (IHMT), Global Health and
    Tropical Medicine (GHMT), University NOVA of Lisbon, Portugal

The informational and digital era of big data brings with it the challenge of knowledge management. There is a need for better management, protection, and security of these data, as well as the respective validation. It is imperative to develop new technologies for data security and their respective implementation in any organizations. In this way, this chapter presents a blueprint in a pharmaceutical industry with the aim at proposing a risk analysis of digital data use during quality control. It is worth mentioning the age of knowledge, the intellectual capital plays an important role in economics and business. A key to competitiveness and, therefore, to economic development in technology runs through a robust process that demonstrates perpetual security for its digital transformation and the respective control in a process ensured by quality assurance. Thus, this implies that time and human resources in organizations are not infinite.

Chapter 21

Luciano Barbosa, UFPE, Brazil
Sérgio Ricardo Goes Oliveira, UFBA, Brazil
Joao Rocha Jr., UEFS, Brazil
Emanuele Marques, UFC, Brazil
Sérgio Maravilhas, SENAI CIMATEC, Brazil & UNIFACS, Salvador University, Brazil

In this chapter, the birth of a Brazilian start-up is analyzed against the background of the digital transformation of the real estate segment. First, the authors describe the economic importance of the sector and its operation. Then they present the platform that makes use of advanced techniques in the areas of artificial intelligence, visualization, management, and data processing. This platform helps to capture wealth and amount of data in real-time, demonstrating the revolutionary potential of the era of big data and consumer analytics. The text explores the changes that the platform imposes on the traditional real estate model while detailing how the decision-making process in this sector is impacted.

Chapter 22

Gustavo Vinicius Duarte Barbosa, Faculdade Pitágoras, Brazil
José Ronaldo Tavares Santos, Centro Universitário UNA, Brazil

Electrical power systems are susceptible to faults caused, for example, by storm, pollution, vandalism, lightning, salt spray, etc. The unscheduled interruption in the supply of electricity to consumers, whether industrial, residential, or commercial, entails severe fines for the transmission utility and/or electricity distributor, imposed by the regulatory agency. Thus, the EPS must have a well-dimensioned protection system, capable of identifying the fault, which is characterized by a single-phase, two-phase, three-phase short circuit, among others, and interrupt the missing section in the minimum time so that the effects of this lack are as small as possible for the SEP, especially with regard to its integrity and operational security.

Chapter 23

Miraldina Ximenes Duarte, Escola Superior de Ciências Empresariais, Instituto Politécnico
de Setúbal, Portugal

Information disseminated through digital networks has a fundamental impact on social welfare, given the range of opportunities offered by the digital economy and the new information and communication technologies, with profound impacts in several areas, namely work, education,and increase the quality and efficiency of public services.The creation of a more efficient, effective, more transparent public administration capable of providing public services with a higher quality level and in an integrated way to the citizen is one of the great objectives and at the same time one of the great challenges that the professionals of public administration face. The state has the social role of avoiding info-exclusion by applying measures directed at the population at risk. Such measures should be able to be applied in the governmental organs closest to the target population. The objective of this study will focus on the analysis of the transition of municipalities to the digital society.

    Igor Oliveira, Brazilian Navy, Brazil & UNIFACS, Salvador University, Brazil
    Sérgio Maravilhas, SENAI CIMATEC, Brazil & UNIFACS, Salvador University, Brazil
    Sérgio Ricardo Goes Oliveira, UFBA, Brazil

The Brazilian Navy encourages the adoption of active learning methodologies aiming the development of competencies in the military. This research aims to analyze the contributions of the game Simulador para Treinamento em Administração (Simulator for Training in Administration) in the development of competencies of the Supply Officers who accomplished the Curso de Aperfeiçoamento em Intendência para Oficiais (CAIO). This research has a qualitative approach and an exploratory-descriptive nature. A questionnaire was used to investigate the participants' perception and semi-structured interviews were conducted to understand the expectation of the Centro de Instrução Almirante Newton Braga (CIANB) regarding the application of business games for the development of competencies. The results show that the participants positively perceive the use of business games as a teaching-learning strategy. Finally, it was possible to map the competencies developed with the application of the STA and verify that the intended objectives with the use of the methodology were met.

    Marta Lamelas Costa, Polytechnic Institute of Setúbal, Portugal
    João Loureiro, Tecnovia Sociedade de Empreitadas S.A., Portugal
    Catarina Gata, Tecnovia Sociedade de Empreitadas S.A., Portugal

The transition from a traditional organizational logic to a digital one is not immediate as it forces a readjustment of processes, Information Systems and even organizational structures. The company selected for analysis belongs to the civil construction sector. The case study consists of identifying and detailing operational procedures in the field of information systems and consequent diagnosis of the transition to a digital scenario, preparing it for new global competitiveness scenarios, as well as analyzing the intra and extra-organizational dimensions that should be considered in the process of transformation. The operational management of the company is based on traditional procedures, where data recording is mostly handwritten. It would be beneficial to use knowledge management systems, preparing the company for an increasingly widespread trend, such as the digital economy. This would allow an increase in the efficiency and productivity of processes, through the improvement of production, archive, and knowledge management in the scope of its operations.

    Sofia Carujo, Plátano Editora, Portugal

Digital transformation is a current challenge for all companies; it cannot be seen as a trend but as a necessity. Normally, when we hear about digital transformation, we associate it with a technological integration in the processes. But its scope is more comprehensive, as it implies a dematerialization of all resources and processes, a redesign of the material processes hitherto practiced that requires a structural transformation of the company with direct repercussions on its culture. We can even talk about digital literacy. The impact of this transformation in companies can be comparable to the impact of the industrial revolution, which will bring companies greater competitiveness; however, not all of them are qualified for this process because, in addition to financial capacity, there must be capable human capital.

Chapter 27

One of the great mistakes some companies or business leaders do when thinking about their digital transformation is to start by technology. Frequently, it is common to hear from companies that they would like to do a project using artificial intelligence (AI), or they would like to have a blockchain or even use internet of things (IoT). There is nothing wrong on thinking and knowing about technologies and their potential. However, the digital transformation is broader than it. So, the question that comes immediately is: How to start? What should organizations think about when planning a digital journey? There are several frameworks to help to start.

Preface

Challenging times. No doubt about it. We composed this book, in another opportunity offered by IGI Global, during the Covid-19 Pandemic. A continuous torrent of worrisome news, troubles in all places of the world, sometimes showing a dramatic situation of unprecedent fashion for mankind.

In the middle of that, we choose to approach complex, intricated issues together: Digital Transformation (DT), its motivation, implications, fundamentals, concepts and, mainly, data production and usage, observed by the aspects of privacy and security. A topic so implicative that deserved specific regulatory negotiations and laws in countries and continents, from businesses to governments, corporations, institutions, universities, and research groups, attempting to determine how DT can be delimited, understood, and implemented.

Emerging technologies and their associated resources are motivating people around the world on developing implementations which produce innovative solutions, such as new business models, devices and, overall, changes in our lives, altering the way we work, entertain, relate to each other, and not forget, survive to this immense difficulty we face during the Pandemic. This is an undeniable digital transformation phenomenon, which will mark humanity forever.

But, to accomplish such a successful goal, on improving mankind´s future, technological application, through projects and processes suitably designed to use these new resources, we face thorough problems regarding Security and Privacy. Security produced by data, security of data, security threats posed with data usage and because of it also. Privacy is another critical factor, as people can be exposed, just as simple, individual users, but also as employees, entrepreneurs, decision-makers, and governmental authorities. Various degrees of exposition, protection, requirements affect Privacy, provoking our interest on aiming these two topics relating it to digital transformation projects.

This way, we managed to receive and developed Twenty-Seven chapters which approached theoretical and practical aspects of safety and privacy when observed in the digital transformation studies, analysis, and implementations in real solutions. An interesting front of discussion emerged as we proposed the book project, which, finally, reaches our readers with the main message of continuous study about DT related to security and privacy.

The first section of our book, comprised of the first fourteen chapters, focuses more on theoretical fundamentals, social, ethical, and managerial impacts of digital transformation, producing a better understanding on its conceptual definitions and relating it to privacy and security essential aspects, also observing the contextual associations. Second section, which presents the final thirteen chapters, was produced with the contribution of cases, implementation studies, relationship of data and information management in market platforms, ensuring a level of understanding on how digital transformation occurs in practice and implicates in privacy and security issues. This way, the book, analyzed as whole, provides to our reader a context where he or she can develop understanding, conceptual definitions, advances and examine the state-of-the-art implementations, perceiving how these always demanded market solutions face privacy and security issues.

Chapter One, authored by George Jamil and Alexis da Silva, conceptualize, and describe some of the most successful emerging technologies available today, both from theoretical and practical aspects, producing a leveled overview of these resources and tools. As an overture chapter, it aimed to promote comprehension and improved book reading. Technology conceptualization is always pressured by markets phenomena, which distort these essential definitions, creating a risky condition for projects planning and theoretical discussion. This chapter enables our reader to take advantage of the remaining book coverage, avoiding common misconceptions about technology.

As a remarkable formal connection about privacy, security and technology adoption, ethical and social responsibility on its usage are critical aspects to be observed. Pedro Fernandes da Anunciação approached this context in Chapter Two, where the author also addressed questions around the belief of technological reliability and moral issues regarding its application and overall data and information management. This chapter brings a provocative level around technology adoption itself, not restricting only to computing resources.

From a top-level managerial aspect, the Data Governance construct (GovD) construct also proposes a way professionals and organizations can deal, handle, and develop their businesses, markets and social relationships when producing knowledge. Calling attention about the need to promote more studies around GovD, renowned author José Poças Rascão brings his usually fundamental contribution, in Chapter Three, working with a systematic literature review, producing a consistent base for further studies and practices towards Data Governance implementation and comprehension.

Emerging technologies permanent pressures security and privacy. It is possible to understand it when cases of cyberattacks are examined, as it was addressed by authors Alimul Haque, Shameemul Haque, Kailash Kumar and Narendra Kumar Singh on Chapter Four. They explore this topic, observing the immense diffusion of IoT devices and their usage over telecommunications networks, eventually becoming a definite solution for daily routine environments. Approaching in an introductory level, this chapter enables the reader for a basic comprehension, when technologies are still in an average level of maturity for adoption.

Author Nuno Geada, on Chapter Five, proposes a model for change management construct, applying and examining fundamentals from ITIL framework and observing it when applied to information technology projects. In these cases, effectively, changes are not well perceived by managers and business teams. The critical observation produced by the author, regarding his proposed framework model, brings an opportune view even for those readers who already implemented controls and risk management for their IT projects, becoming a perspective for improved management.

As privacy and security issues started to occupy a main scenario about digital transformation, especially data and information treatment, regulatory codes and laws needed to be established and implemented, assuring rights to their owners and mandatory conduct recommendations for those who process these valuable contents. Felipe Palhares studies, on Chapter Six, the Brazilian law code, comparing it to the European Union similar definition, producing an important presentation for this relevant legal conception. He also reflects about its implementation and overall adoption in the dynamic Brazilian economic context, pressured by market and social developments. As an ethical and technical base, regulatory law codes will be also addressed by other authors, as it is a significant topic for the book proposition, starting with this study.

Social networks, undeniably, changed the way we communicate and live. They offer an easy channel of social inclusion, content sharing and publication, becoming one of the *de facto* digital transformation faces for modern societies. But, on the other hand, also turned out to be a difficult arena for privacy and security issues, mainly when misused or criminally managed. Authors Kamalkumar Macwan and Sankita Patel analyzed various aspects of this important social and technological phenomenon in Chapter Seven. Concepts, methods, and parameters for social networks adoption were addressed by authors, promoting a better understanding around this relevant arena.

Author Sofia Sousa brings an additional light to another opportune concept, related to digital transformation management: information systems. In Chapter Eight she studies its typical adoption, in one supply chain operation, were these tools, methods and processes offered perspectives of optimized knowledge production, application of emerging technologies – as a frontline Digital Transformation trend – eventually also presenting challenges for privacy and security when treating data. She also calls our attention for the conceptual approach, where IS concept becomes a standard on how to relate several concepts around data and information management.

José Poças Rascão also authored the Chapter Nine, were he extended his reputable view about Governance concept to information and knowledge management. Observing Governance from the literature, the author develops an additional fundamental, called GovIC, where he motivates organizations as to expand their views around ethical and social administration, bringing more transparency to their market exposure, exactly in the moment when we face a huge advance of emerging technologies, under digital transformation projects.

Thiago Costa, on Chapter Ten, advances the analysis about regulatory codes, such as Brazilian LGPD and European Union GDPR, observing their approaches in the moment we face an astonishing data production and new technologies implementations. As the author mentions, concepts such as privacy, security, protection, and reputation are continuously being discussed and practiced, demanding regulation. He defines the role of Arbitration Chambers as mature, legally supported institutions to be socially adopted to reinforce these law codes and successfully implement it in our daily digitally transformed routines.

Reflecting about implementation factors for these law codes, authors Claudio Pessoa, Marco Elísio Marques, Bruna Cardoso Nunes and Camila Oliveira analyzed, in Chapter Eleven, the role of the Joint Controller, one of the most important professional activities which will define how these codes are practically adopted in organizations. Sometimes not well evaluated by managers, entrepreneurs, and even governmental authorities, works such as those essentially held by the Joint Controller, as it is defined by the Brazilian LGPD law code, must be understood and effectively defined, as to guarantee essentials of security and privacy for digital transformation adoption in every project.

Ricardo Correia brings, in Chapter Twelve, the important view from military studies and practices for information and knowledge management, with a focus on intelligence coordination. As data and information contents are massively produced, from different aspects, sources and methods, critical analysis becomes more essential, as to understand if these contents are useful, real, well produced, and managed, not offering additional risks in digital transformation cases. Additionally, projects must overlook if these implementations do not present security and privacy severe issues. Clearly, this is one of the most expected points of view for our intended analysis in this book.

On Chapter Thirteen, authors Moisés Rockembach and Armando Malheiro conclude our approach on studying main aspects regarding Brazilian and European Union data protection law codes, analyzing it for a perspective oriented to understand organizational proposition – for example, when defining a global business model for a competitive design by one company – and operation, enabling a connected view for different, although similar, laws. The chapter also presents a reflection about tools, methods and instrumental codes used to reinforce and keep these law codes as necessary parameters to conduct any commercial activity.

Finishing the first section of our book, in the Chapter Fourteen, authors Maria José Souza, Gabriel Osorio de Barros and Nuno Tavares studied artificial intelligence, as one of the most influential emerging technologies (and its associated methods and processes) which impact our lives today. Observed in the context of this book project, the power to propose digital transformation solutions from AI implementations are analyzed by these authors, enabling readers to understand its implications and impacts for routinely resources we all have access and adopt for daily tasks.

Chapter Fifteen opens the second section of this book, aiming to bring cases of digital transformation, observing and researching about data privacy and security. Authors Bruno de Lacerda and George Jamil evaluated how organizations face structural and cultural implications regarding digital transformation. Thinking from the strategic level, a perception from various relevant sources was developed to understand how DT is creating new propositions, advances, possibilities, perspectives and continuously changing pace for our society. This chapter brings a specific contribution for entrepreneurs, as to promote a better conception on digital transformation projects impacts and developments.

In Chapter Sixteen, a critical global scenario regarding worries about data privacy and security is approached by authors Rafael da Silva and Matheus da Silva: Corruption and frauds prevention and detection. Experienced professionals, authors develop an opportune observation on how legal authorities are organized and supported by their formal structures and technologies to attack such challenges. It is also interesting to notice that, potentially, this chapter also motivates on understand how digital transformation can be applied to assure data and privacy just on DT projects, from the legal authorities working place.

Chapter Seventeen presents an interesting study which encompasses principles of innovation management and digital transformation, applied in the context of a challenging Brazilian metropole, the city of Salvador, in the state of Bahia. Authors Ivan Euler Paiva, Sérgio Maravilhas, Flavio Souza Marinho and Renelson Ribeiro Sampaio discussed how these implementations and associated methods resulted in a triple helix modeling when adopted for public policies plans and execution. Several implied concepts regarding these major and dynamic scientific fields were also explored, producing a deep understanding for digital transformation as the way to innovate and strategically offer new perspectives for citizens.

Considering the Industry 4.0 author and editor Pedro Fernandes da Anunciação approached, in chapter Eighteen, Maintenance as a significant factor for real implementations, system configurations and project planning. As this framework becomes more and more incorporated to our lives, it is important to consider disciplines and topics like Maintenance when thinking about their competitive application. With managed lifecycles, these solutions offer a perspective of being used and adapted for longer periods, enabling more profitability for digital transformation projects.

Chapter Nineteen presents a recommendation, by authors Bhimavarapu Usharani and Raju Anitha for a framework model, called Ripple and cyber bullies information reveal - RACYBDD – which aims to address matters of security and privacy of social media usage. These authors recognize the complexity around the massive adoption of social media tools and how it poses security and privacy issues, as they became platforms for definite digital transformation. Thinking on how these digital environments show an increasing usage every day, risk management is tackled by authors, with the detail approach resulting in a conceptualization for a framework model definition.

Authors Maria Tereza Sousa Silva, Erica Louro da Fonseca, Zulmira Hartz, and Jorge Magalhães, analyze additional privacy and safety implications for Healthcare sector when defining models and plans for action, based on data management. As a fundamental sector, extremally exposed to market events, such as now happening with the Covid-19 Pandemic, Healthcare deals with sensitive data, large contents (Big data) of information, analysis methods and other processes which need to address a continuous pressure for digital transformation. As a demanded sector, Chapter Twenty presents an opportune background for decision-makers and researchers to a better comprehension towards real problems faced by its institutions and organizations.

This way, we can affirm that it is always opportune to understand demands from market sectors, when analyzing factors and cases such as those about privacy and safety of data and information. This way, authors Luciano Barbosa, Sérgio Ricardo Goes Oliveira, Joao Rocha Jr., Emanuele Marques, and Sérgio Maravilhas, promoted an interesting study about the real estate market, as an example of a market industry where big data and analytics are adopted for scenario modeling and decisions, regarding new business dynamics and needed customer attraction and retention. As a sector which presents a continuous challenge by customers and entrepreneurs, data and information management abilities, along with undeniable digital transformation trend, Chapter Twenty-One advances its analysis, on how these facts can result in expressive competitive advantage, from digital transformation projects.

One interesting practical case of digital transformation, where a critical operation for an electrical power system is potentially automated, is shown in Chapter Twenty-two. Formerly manual and intensive power operations, just conducted by human operators with immediate and risky interventions, through semi-automatic maneuvers, faced a significant change by the introduction of technological contexts. Now, supported by the software platform which perform calculation methods presented by authors Gustavo Barbosa and José Ronaldo dos Santos, these operations can be planned, proposed, intervened, and executed in a progressive digital transformation fashion, as a typical information system for a modern usage.

Miraldina Duarte discusses, in chapter Twenty-Three, how information and communication technologies (ICT) can be the pilar for digital transformation projects which will enable public management to advance into a new era, offering more services and resources for citizens. The author chose the case of Setúbal, in Portugal, to illustrate how experiences can be produced, replicated and, effectively, produce knowledge for public planning, facing the risks of privacy, safety and change in this modern fast-changing scenario, when proposing a new level for citizenship principles.

Authors Igor Oliveira, Sérgio Maravilhas and Sérgio Ricardo Goes Oliveira studied how business games, as a source for knowledge generation for projects, are successfully applied in the context of military formation in the Brazilian Navy. Among ideas and propositions regarding these powerful and intricated simulations, Chapter Twenty-Four enable the reader to understand in a more comprehensive way, how technological decisions can be formulated, planned (played as business game) to produce robust project decisions, allowing optimal implementation for projects, an essential approach when dealing with dynamic contexts such as digital transformation.

For a big company, changing from a traditional, cultural impacted way to plan, design and work can be desirable, but it is always a challenging path. In Chapter Twenty-Five, author Marta Costa reflects about a real case of a Civil Construction company, referential for its sector, which decided to invest in digital transformation, profoundly modifying their way of planning and executing their projects. For this case, it is remarkably understood the practical view for several concepts, related to this main objective, like, for example, information systems, organizational culture, structure and knowledge management. The chapter produces an interesting approach on the overall impacts of a real digital transformation intention and strategic change.

Another case of real change is studied by author Sofia Carujo, approaching, in this case, a company which the tradition relies on age and image, resulting in some of the aspects that bring severe challenges for any change, especially if a digital transformation project is approached. The oldest Editorial company of Portugal, a country always reputed as a historical reference on literary production for several centuries, was observed by the author, when they decided to bring decision-making, logistics, financial and editorial operations to a new level of automation and technological perspectives. Chapter Twenty-Six, this way, produces another way to understand the real problems in the transformation towards a digital perspective.

Finally, Chapter Twenty-Seven, authored by experienced IT manager Luciano da Silva analyzes how agile principles and modern trends of management, can be applied, and developed as to promote scalability for digital transformation projects, aiming to reduce time and costs to obtain results, becoming a fast track on achieving strategic goals. He also evaluates a business case where one company adopted agile methods, performance squads, indicators and metrics management related to strategic performance and various other aspects, tools, and processes towards becoming a real digital transformation factory, delivering its projects with leadership and quality.

Looking back at this project we are glad about the results obtained. Authors from different countries, cultures, formations, and experiences studied dynamic themes, cases, and applications. Conceptualization in a fast-moving scenario was also attempted, producing a base to advance these studies, in other works and implementations. These results provide a substantial benefit for us, editors, for our authors and, obviously, for our readers in these unprecedent difficult times, where mankind is addressing a terrible disease.

Let us expect for advances such as those potentially proposed by this remarkable work! Let us develop our knowledge towards a better future for us, with digital transformation, respecting culture, privacy, safety, security and, mainly, our humanity!

George Leal Jamil

Section 1
Conceptual Views for Digital Transformation, Data Security, and Privacy

Chapter 1
Emerging Technologies in a Modern Competitive Scenario:
Understanding the Panorama for Security and Privacy Requirements

George Leal Jamil

Informações em Rede Consultoria e Treinamento Ltda, Brazil

Alexis Rocha da Silva

IBM Software Engineering, Brazil

ABSTRACT

Users' personal, highly sensitive data such as photos and voice recordings are kept indefinitely by the companies that collect it. Users can neither delete nor restrict the purposes for which it is used. Learning how to machine learning that protects privacy, we can make a huge difference in solving many social issues like curing disease, etc. Deep neural networks are susceptible to various inference attacks as they remember information about their training data. In this chapter, the authors introduce differential privacy, which ensures that different kinds of statistical analysis don't compromise privacy and federated learning, training a machine learning model on a data to which we do not have access to.

INTRODUCTION

In this chapter, the authors will begin by discussing an applied view for theoretical concepts of emerging technologies like Big Data, Cloud Computing, Internet of Things, Blockchain and Cognitive Computing. In the realm of this book project, this chapter aims to present a leverage of comprehension of these technologies, allowing our reader to improve the overall perception of the problems addressing modern technologies, regarding security and privacy.

To approach in this view, relationships between these technologies are also offered, relating how Big Data and Cloud Computing, Big Data and Internet of Things and Big Data and Cognitive Computing

DOI: 10.4018/978-1-7998-4201-9.ch001

Copyright © 2021, IGI Global. Copying or distributing in print or electronic forms without written permission of IGI Global is prohibited.

and Blockchain perspectives regarding all other technologies can be adopted and what are their perspectives and business capabilities.

At the end, authors will present examples and practical applications of each of the concepts presented previously, regarding emerging technologies, as well as examples of how the relationships between these tools and their associated usage methods, reaching a comprehension on how they can motivate and produce digital transformation journey for governments and corporations of all sizes and corporations.

After reading the chapter, the reader should:

- Understand, conceptually and in practice, the concepts of Cloud Computing, IoT, Cognitive Computing and Blockchain and how they relate to Big Data.
- Understand how these concepts and their relationships can foster innovation in areas of knowledge that interact with technology.
- Apply the concepts learned in practice, in the development of applications that implement these concepts and their relationships.

The chapter starts with individual conceptual definitions, advances towards an analysis on how these tools and resources can be understood when observed, planned and adopted together, and, finally, a comprehensive development on their perspectives – analyzed in a superficial, introductory way – about privacy and security, to be contemplated compared to its costs and maintenance.

BIG DATA

According to Davenport (2014):

Big Data refers to data that is too big to fit on a single server, too unstructured to fit into a row-and-column database, or too continuously flowing to fit into a static data warehouse. While the seize receives all attention, the most difficult aspect of big data really involves its lack of structure.

Data such as text, voice and video messages from chat applications, videos and images from social media, data from various types of sensors, read at every millisecond and from other sources, composing an enormous volume on size, are produced every day in all world. These data is also presented in different formats, sizes, and ways of storing and processing. This way, although an opportune context for analysis, data massively produced and collected, without any treatment or preparation, can be useless, as we cannot relate it for an objective interpretation, as to produce a problem solution or answer. This scenario illustrates this as the most difficult aspect of handling this flood of data, as production and collection are, nowadays, with technological support, widely available.

Big Data now plays such an important role in the Information Technology world that even the prestigious Oxford English Dictionary, in its latest editions, has come up with a definition for it as: *"Data of a very large size, typically to the extent that its manipulation and management present significant logistical challenges."*. Ohata and Kumar (2012) pointed out several perspectives and applications for Big Data tools, methods and strategies, relating it do decision-making processes and, moreover, to traditional techniques and IT-related environments like business intelligence.

This way, we can define this technological environment to a valuable agent of data analysis, supported by analytical tools and modelling perspectives (Jamil and Magalhães, 2015). As a powerful and versatile concept, together with stable and solid scientific background, Big Data nowadays associate with several other technologies and tools, as to provide better decision-making for companies, professionals, but also implementing modern and foreseeable processes, such as artificial intelligence algorithms and analytics (Park *et. al,* 2012; Jamil, Rocha and Jamil, 2018). Another interesting perspective on understanding Big Data potentialities, is to comprehend this technology as a component of modern revisions of classical topics around data management, like, for example, information systems (Jamil, Vieira and Xavier, 2018).

Big data, conceived as a support to join contexts of structured and unstructured data, from massive information and data collection tools, aimed to produce knowledge for phenomena interpretation and subsequent modelling, is positioned as one stable component for modern entrepreneurship, resulting in ways to review business conceptions already been practiced by industries and market sectors (McAfee & Brynjolfsson, 2012). Its association with analytics is a remarkable factor in nowadays business propositions, composed around data, information and knowledge management (Delloite, 2017; Google, 2020).

In a common overview, Big Data projects can be accomplished not only to "gather data" wherever it is and produce an objective result. In addition to this particular view, Big Data structures, mapping, study, analytical and prospective functions and capabilities can result in data modelling, a valuable result where one can perceive a complete model from the real world, obtained and expressed after data analysis, composing interpretative scenarios, conception for new businesses and organizational structures, perceiving human reactions, among several other results (Al-Jarrah *et al.,* 2015).

Another prospective association of Big Data is a tool which supports artificial intelligence (AI) – both from machine learning and deep learning ways – as the first data collection and conceptual technique to be applied in some "training" and "learning" phases of an IA strategy. Composing consistent scenarios from data, Big Data models allow analysts to create robust models that were born connected to the real world from facts to conception. This way, automated machines, algorithms and appliances will tend to adjust easier to user´s final perceptions, resulting in a well-defined potential for artificial intelligence systems to be useful since its operational start, developing a scenario of optimization through IA implementation earlier, at a more reasonable costs and related performance (McKinsey, 2011, Qiu *et al.,* 2016).

CLOUD COMPUTING

Cloud computing has evolved from the simple conception of being a "backup shared storage" to a smart, efficient, sustainable and integrated technology, provided to improve systems design and implementation. Nowadays, as a context solution, cloud computing involves dynamic and rational functions such as those from storage and its associated management, data loads balance and overall architectural designs, virtualization for computing systems and networks – optimally implementing sophisticated solutions at manageable costs – and associated governance techniques (Kathuria, 2018; Aiyebelehin *et al.,* 2020).

Aggressively offered in the market, by heavy players of information technology and consulting services, like Microsoft, IBM, Oracle, Amazon, among several others, cloud computing became an attractive solution for systems implementation, computing sites and performance design, information systems architecture and mobile systems distributions. As a technology trend, it is estimated that cloud computing will become not an innovative tool or infrastructure in the becoming years, but an integrated and indispensable resource for any computational service being published for users (Gartner, 2020; Welsh & Benkhelifa, 2020).

One of the simplest and most direct definitions of Cloud Computing is: A cloud computing service is a dedicated online machinery with the capability to host and store data, simulate and virtualize environments. Additionally, it has software needed installed, as an emulation package and subsystem and ready to be utilized over the internet (IBM, 2020; AWS, 2020; Microsoft Azure, 2020).

Initially thought as a backbone service for storage, cloud computing, nowadays, comprises several powerful resources, which allow a computing systems designer to implement architectural features for an information management solution, such as:

- Dynamic storage and mapping for data contents, associated with management resources, which allow optimal management, distribution, safety and privacy implementations (Welsh & Benkhelifa, 2020);
- Virtual computing definition, management, implementation and offer, enabling techniques of a complete computational site specification, configuration and installing, replacing the need for physical devices and infrastructure (Alnajrani, Norman, Ahmed, 2020);
- Virtual network definitions, as to gather and optimally arrange virtual machines in powerful, versatile and safe arrays for distributed computing, implementing networking services without demanding physical arrangements (Kathuria, 2018);
- Management tools to direct, define, install, configure, test, prepare, offer and share these resources, allowing users around the world to use "apps", internet services and information systems without perceiving these tools as "installed", locally-consuming resources implementations (Stein, Campitelli and Mezzio, 2020).

In one additional view, cloud computing can be understood as the delivery of on-demand computing resources, from hardware (servers, network, storage, etc), to software, to services, over the internet with a pay-per-use model. This characteristic translates into a modifiable, flexible and adaptive resource for technological solutions, with wide applications for business and other institutions. Using the cloud computing model, users can store data (photos, videos, text, audio, messages, etc), test and develop applications, host websites, analyze large amounts of data (For example, Big Data), compose simulated networks, installations, server-based installations, connect to other clouds, among many other architectural configurations.

The National Institute of Standard and Technology (NIST), in the United States, defines the Cloud Computing model using the figure bellow (NIST, 2020):

Figure 1. Cloud Computing definition, according to NIST
(NIST, 2020)

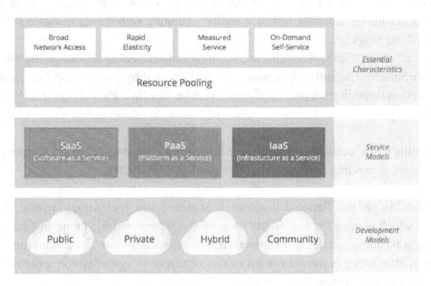

In the Fig. 01, above, it is possible to understand how a cloud implementation, from the technological base, can occur, resulting in powerful adaptations and different solutions for any customer. First, among Essential characteristics we can verify aspects of performance such as:

- Broad network access – Cloud services can be accessed from any device or system, connected through programming code segments, etc. in a versatile way.
- Rapid elasticity – A configuration of cloud services can extend its services horizontally – as reproducing one characteristic or service several times, in identical fashion for several users – or vertically – as adding functions and sophistication or complexity towards new levels of implementation.
- Measured service – All commercial and institutional implementations of cloud services allow wide and detailed ways to measure performance, costs and resources used, allowing plenty of accountability, which results in optimal management ways, such as "pay only for what you use".
- On-demand self-service – Available cloud services can be requested as demanded, avoiding needs to have huge client terminals, such as expensive configuration for workstations, only loading and starting functions and services needed by a customer.

The same diagram shows the "resource polling" feature which, dynamically, researches user demands, tuning performance and requirements suitably, optimizing performance and the cost management strategies.

Cloud Computing offers three different service models that can be used, depending on the needs of its users (NIST, 2020; Welsh & Benkhelifa, 2020; Stein, Campitelli and Mezzio, 2020):

- Infrastructure as a Service (IaaS): Provides the hardware layer including networking, storage, and computing components. Examples: Virtual Servers Instances, Bare Metal Servers, Network Components provisioned in a traditional Cloud provider such as IBM Cloud, AWS, Azure or Google Cloud.

- Platform as a Service (PaaS): Provides the necessary hardware and software needed to develop, run and host applications.Examples: An operating system, a programming language execution environment, a running database instance and/or a running web server instance provisioned in a traditional Cloud provider.
- Software as a Service (SaaS): Provides applications and services available on the internet through a cloud environment. Examples: business models supported by cloud computing, where any customer can access through a simple "app" or internet service, like PayPal, Google Apps, Drop Box, Gmail, etc.

Cloud Computing is also available through three different and most widely used development models, that can also be used, depending on the needs of its users (NIST, 2020):

- Public Cloud: As per the National Institute of Standard and Technology, public cloud is an infrastructure which is open for use by any user, by the general public, being owned, managed and operated by a business, academic or governmental organization or a combination of them. This way, a designer or user can use this cloud infrastructure in an open fashion, eventually free or associative in terms of payment and access.
- Private Cloud: This is the way where a cloud infrastructure is provisioned for exclusive use by a single organization comprising multiple consumers (e.g., business units). It may be owned, managed and operated by the organization, a third party, or some combination of them, and it may exist on or off premises. In this offer, a cloud is usually configured and implemented by a commercial agent, a company, which, in general, will restrict its usage for their employees, agents and partners, becoming an informational infrastructure for its own services.
- Hybrid cloud: Conceptualized as an infrastructure which is a composition of two or more distinct cloud infrastructures (private, community, or public), resulting in unique manageable and configurable entities, but are bound together by standardized or proprietary technology that enables data and application portability (e.g., *cloud bursting,* used for load balancing between clouds).
- Community Cloud: NIST finally conceive this type as that implementation where the cloud infrastructure is implemented for exclusive usage by a specific community of consumers from organizations that have shared concerns (e.g., special and tactical missions, security requirements, policy, and compliance considerations). It may be owned, managed and operated by one or more of the organizations in the community, a third party, or some combination of them, also implementing a somewhat dedicated hybrid environment, and it may exist on or off premises.

These definitions where based strictly on the NIST Special Publication 800-45, as cited in our references. Cloud services can be associated to all of the other technologies discussed in this chapter, serving as both as a conceptual background of digital transformation infrastructure as also a resource to be adopted in modern arrangements that will allow designers and implementors to configure flexible, strategic alternatives for any firm or institution.

INTERNET OF THINGS (IoT)

Internet of thins is an evolutionary implementation which aims to put available a connection for any device, if it is a computer or note, to Internet. This way, any device becomes "addressable", offering a possibility of interconnection implementation and configuration (Evans, 2011).

The Internet of Things can additionally be conceptualized in the following terms: (1) The concept of connecting physical objects to the Internet to transmit and gather data, including control signals, demands and answers by devices; (2) These physical objects can be, essentially, anything which can be addressed. (3) From personal items, such as laptop and clothes to electronic appliances, such as a TV set and a refrigerator; or enterprise assets, such as a bridge, a traffic light, etc (Collina, *et al*, 2014;Pessoa, Batista and Marques, 2018).

These objects are connected to the Internet, and the data they produce, as they are usually operated, can be communicated, stored and analyzed so that a decision or insight can be derived. An arrangement of functions and systemic connections can be conceived, implementing a way where any operator or integrator can command and monitor these devices. For example, automatically decide when an action can be triggered from this insight and when this action has a result that is meaningful.

Usually, during Internet of Things projects, experiments or other kind of work, there are five phases (IBM, 2020b; Kurnia, Mulyanti & Widiaty, 2020):

- Connect: In this phase sensors are connected to objects of the domain in which project is intended to cover, where systemic functions are to be held, and these sensors are also connected to some network appliances (usually Internet gateways) capable of sending data through the Internet. Most of the time, this data is sent using regular Internet protocols such as https, https, udp, and tcp, enabling integrative applications.
- Gather: For this phase, the data collected from sensors and sent through the Internet backbone are gathered by, typically, a Cloud computing platform. Most of the Cloud providers have specific platforms for dealing with Internet of Things data gathering, showing the potential for integration of these technologies for any purpose, as a system platform.
- Store: Data generated and communicated can be stored in a regular storage mechanism like a SQL Database, a Non-SQL database, Text files, Cloud storage mechanisms, among others. With this simple architectural approach, data can also be collected and referred, for another function, as analytics or big data analysis.
- Analysis: Now that all data collected is stored, any mechanism of analytics can be applied to analyze the data and produce meaningful information and knowledge on top of it. Automated systems, robots and artificial intelligence-based web integrated solutions are among many potential implementations.
- Create solutions: Any kind of software solution can be created to display the insights to the final user. Nowadays, even modern business models, such as marketplaces and platforms can be benefitted from IoT integration to other technologies.

Interestingly, the simple automation provided by IoT implementation, allows from simple functions, like those related to utilities and domestic devices – for example, when some domestic apparatus communicate to each other and, using rules specified in one algorithm, proportionate comfort and easiness for a user – to complex, industrial services, when connecting robotic assembly lines.

IoT can also be considered from an application side, as a massive data generator, serving as a data collector or producer, regarding usual functionalities. For example, in a naïve approach, one can understand air conditioning demands, analyzing the daily frequency of door and windows opening in one room of a house. Automatic adjustments in this ventilation system can be adopted by machines correctly programmed and configured, without further human intervention (Pessoa, Batista and Marques, 2018).

COGNITIVE COMPUTING

Cognitive computing comes from a combination of cognitive science (which studies the human brain and its functioning) and computer science. Cognitive computing has the objective to simulate the process of how human beings think using computational models.

Using algorithms that learn on their own, and use data mining, pattern recognition and natural language processing, the computer can mimic the way the human brain works. The more these algorithms are exposed to data from a particular problem domain, the more they learn about that domain, and the more accurate they become.

It can also be said that Cognitive computing would be the simulation of the human cognition process defined and implemented in a computer model. As a text extract from the Stanford University states: *"Cognitive computing is a technology platform based on the scientific disciplines of artificial intelligence and signal processing. In summary, a cognitive computer ploughs through structured and unstructured data, to find hidden knowledge and present data in an actionable form. It is worth noting that Cognitive computing is an iterative process, with humans verifying or discarding any new discoveries. This allows the system to 'learn' over time, and become better at identifying patterns."* (Jaykishen Gokani, Stanford University)

The aim of the cognitive computing is not to replace the humans or the way human thinks, in any field it accts, but to assist humans with data intensive analysis that can be performed by computers in matter of minutes instead of days or months.

BLOCKCHAIN

Blockchain can be understood as a digital record of transactions. It is based in a distributed ledger technology. This ledger is shared among various peers in a network and it is immutable. Data is distributed but not copied, and this data is usually reconciled frequently to the database, that is stored in multiple locations and updated instantly. Blockchain is used for recording transactions, tracking assets, reaching consensus, building trust, etc. Blockchain is being used for supply chain management, smart contracts, digital identity, voting, healthcare, food safety, food tracking, intellectual property, real estate, among others and it is one of the fastest growing areas in Information Technology nowadays (INVESTOPEDIA, 2020; IBM Blockchain, 2020c).

Blockchain support is easy to understand, based on simple principles, structured basically in the fact that each user's transaction - as simple money transfer operation, or a commercial purchase - can be recorded in one block, and this specific action will be inserted, through this block, in the list, the chain of blocks. This insertion operation is, indeed, done with some rigour, which gives the security and stability to the whole operation.

For example, each block insertion is done with coding of that specific transaction, using a hashing algorithm, which will be assigned to that block as an address. After this hashing codification, the block where the transaction is registered can be inserted in the chain. This hash will be calculated depending on the last insertions, resulting in a situation where the insertion itself cannot be reproduced easily, as one who is interested in doing so, must calculate this hashing code for every insertion produced for that specific chain.

Blockchain is kept by an array of redundant computers, where chains are copied and operations, such as insertion, copy, deletion are easily validated by several machines, creating a required agreement, which also imposes another level of security to the whole chain operation and maintenance. However, this does not mean that this infrastructure is free from criminal actions and attack attempts.

As a distributed ledger, blockchain can be regarded as an easy structure to record data, allowing its manipulation as records in a database, a basic process which is completely known and considered by software engineers, designers and developers. So, blockchain is now becoming a real alternative - simple, cheap and safe - as a computer-based structure to store records and allow its manipulation, serving as a file or database structure for apps, internet based systems and connection through old and new software applications and programs (Mearian, 2020).

Its usage is continuously spreading and, in one of the most remarkable applications, blockchains serves as the base for cryptocurrency implementations, such as bitcoin, ethereum, among many others, proposing, simply, to create an independent monetary system, without banking and governmental bureaucracy, costs and time. Additionally, logistics and supply chain is another powerful area where blockchain is being applied. In one interesting application, ideally each product, like agricultural food, for example apples, peers, coffee seeds, etc., can be traced from the producer to the supermarket. When a consumer reaches the package with that product stored - let us consider a pack of apples - he or she can check, through an app, installed in his or her smartphone, through a QR code scanning, the path which was used to supply that product, understanding why it can be valuable regarding its production and storage. All the supporting information can be stored in blockchain structures, accessed by the app and associated software. All communication done through simple and available mobile devices, from the producing site to the commercial shop (Jebran, 2018; IBM, 2020c).

Taken as a fundamental infrastructure, emerging as a technology base, blockchain has also, as it was cited for cloud computing services, public and private ways of usage. One company can, for example, mount its own blockchain services, or use a public resource to implement their blockchain-based systems, even interconnecting both environments through software coding.

As a final remark, it is interesting also to perceive that, a formerly untrusted platform and infrastructure, as Blockchain is, nowadays, related to corporative governance in value aggregated chains, like those from sectors such as food, agriculture, mining, finance, oil, gas, information technology among many others. Offering an open, safe and well understood structure and implementation for additional higher-level apps and internet portals, Blockchain implemented a secure and up-to-date technological infrastructure which is becoming a *de facto* standard for information interchange in managerial platforms and software services, easily integrating to other emerging technologies described in this introductory text. This will, probably, be remembered in the years to come as a market factor which arose from practical and implementation levels, turning out to be a standard for governance, firms reliability and transparence.

EMERGING TECHNOLOGIES ASSOCIATIONS

In the following subsections, we explore associations of some emerging technologies, both to improve comprehension about their specific usage and its conceptual application. With these examples in mind, we can advance the understanding on how these technologies could foster modern business models, promote additional levels of negotiation spaces and, overall, define new markets.

Big Data and Cloud Computing

Cloud Computing relates to Big Data as Cloud it is an enabler to Big Data as well as used as a means to store this big amount of data. As an enabler, Cloud acts as a repository for new applications, software, systems, integration points and others that can gather or enable users to gather data from the outside world in different formats. As a means to store the amount of data generated today, usually, Cloud providers offer a great variety of data store mechanisms, such as SQL Databases, NonSQL Databases, and also more reliable, robust and long term storage mechanisms such as:

- File Storage: File storage is a type of cloud computing storage that provides a persistent, fast and flexible storage that is network-attached and is based on NFS (Network File System). In this model, users have total control over their file shares and performance. These file shares can be connected to up to tens of authorized devices over a TCP/IP based network for resiliency.
- Block Storage: Block storage is a type of cloud computing storage that provides persistent and high-performance storage that is provisioned and managed independent of their computer resources. With block storage, data is broken into blocks and these blocks are stored as separate pieces on Storage Area Networks (SANs) or cloud-based storage environments. When this data is requested by a user, the storage system reassembles the data from the blocks before presenting it.
- Object Storage: Object storage can, virtually, store infinite amounts of structured and unstructured data in a simple and cheap way. Usually, object storage is used for long term backup and data archiving, but it can also be used as a scalable storage mechanism for applications. Data is stored in objects, each object typically includes the data itself, a variable amount of metadata, and a globally unique identifier.

These choices allow a system designer to develop a project definition with several technology alternatives, tuning from performance to interactivity, widening the scope and complexity of any implementation.

Big Data and the Internet of Things

The Internet of Things relates to Big Data as it serves as one of the main data generators that feeds the Big Data concept. The number of "things" connected to the Internet have grown exponentially in the last decades. From around 50.000 in 1950´s, to an estimated number of more than 30 billion in 2020. Some predictions say that around 2050, there will be over 100 billion "things" connected to the Internet.

These "things", as was mentioned before, can be anything like a refrigerator, an oven, a smart television, a temperature sensor, or an automobile. These sensors have become cheap, capable of handling more data with some embedded logic and store these data for some time, until they can be connected to the Internet to transmit this data. These factors were the enablers for this exponential growth. An example of some common sensors or "things" that are seen nowadays are: Carbon dioxide sensor, turbine speed sensor, luminosity sensor, parking sensor, tire pressure monitoring sensor, accelerometer, GPS, motion detector sensor, air flow sensor, smoke detector, a car speed sensor, a vibration sensor, presence sensor, a mobile phone camera, among others.

The exponential growth on the number of "things" or sensors connected to the Internet, in conjunction with these "things" being able to connect more data, do some processing within themselves and store some of this data for some time, until this data can be transferred to the Internet, were some very important factors for Big Data become one of the most important topics not only in Technology, but in our day to day lives nowadays.

The amount of data generated has also seen an exponential growth in the last decades. It is said that 90% of all the data generated in the world, during human existence, has been generated in the last 2 years. Most of this data is unstructured data, which is data that does not have a predefined organization model or that is not organized in a predefined manner, such as video, audio and images.

Having most of the data generated being unstructured also contributes for the exponential growth in size of this data. Unstructured data such as videos, audio recordings, an airplane turbine function logs, among others can achieve massive size, in terms of gigabytes or even terabytes, in a relatively small fraction of time, depending on the details set during its generation.

Data collection and transmission are responsibility of these "things" or sensors. But collecting and transmitting the data could be said as just the tip of the Iceberg for the relationship between Big Data and Internet of Things. After this data is collected and transmitted to the Internet, it needs to be stored, then it needs to be analyzed for better insights and, finally, solutions can be developed and presented to the final users.

Data without proper analysis can be, most of the times, useless. And it is said, in a commonsense overview, that over 60% of the data that is collected is never used in any sense.

Big Data and Cognitive Computing

Cognitive Computing relates to Big Data as Big Data is one of the concepts that contributes most for its success. Besides having well developed algorithms, based on optimal machine learning, artificial intelligence, or other concepts, and running on top of large computing capacity, the amount of data is what makes cognitive computing to work more and more precisely. As more and more data are fed to any cognitive computing technique, more this technique can be trained and more precise and meaningful the outcome will be.

As with the human learning process; in which the most one person reads and studies (or is exposed to data), the most it will learn and the most it will use this knowledge for some purpose; the computer can only "learn" if it is exposed to data related to the subject it needs to "learn" and build outcome about.

However, the analysis of data by humans can be a time-consuming activity, so the use of sophisticated cognitive systems can help to tackle this enormous amount of data. Cognitive computing can be utilized to reduce the shortcomings of the concerns faced during big data analysis. Take as an example the use of cognitive computing in the field of medicine. While a doctor can read and absorb dozens of new papers related to cancer research, the Alzheimer disease or drug discovery per week, a computer would be fed with the same amount of information and "learn" in a matter of minutes. Then, this very same cognitive computer would be able to recommend the best approach to the doctor or even to support the doctor with the results of its analysis.

Cognitive Computing is being used in various data intensive or Big Data related subject, such as medicine (for diagnosis help, drug and vaccine discovery, examination analysis, etc), fraud detection, risk assessment, image recognition for various purposes, weather forecasting and prediction, predictive maintenance, customer service, supply change management, targeted marketing, genomics and other researches, chemical materials studies and discoveries, among others.

Since training the algorithms and understanding data are especially important steps in the Cognitive Computing field, nowadays, the data scientist is a kind of professional in high demand. The data scientist is an interdisciplinary professional that is focused on the study and analysis of data (economic, financial, and social data, structured and unstructured). The data scientist, then, extracts knowledge, detects patterns and obtains variables to support decision making. Besides that, the knowledge obtained from data analysis can be refitted in the system itself, this way, helping it learn from this data.

REAL CASE: THE INTERNET OF THINGS IS HELPING THE INSURANCE INDUSTRY TO REDUCE CLAIMS AND ACCIDENTS

One of the major insurance companies in Europe, with the goal of cutting down theft and fraud by knowing where the vehicles were at all times, began deploying smart sensors to cars and trucks from its customers, four years ago. Besides the benefits for the insurance company, customers that opted into this Internet of Things system, known in the industry as telematics, could have a reduction in their annual premium of 15 percent to 25 percent.

After some months and many sensors installed on the first customers vehicles, this insurance company discovered that knowing the location, speed and acceleration of the vehicles could also reveal crashes in real time. If one appeared serious enough (50 points or higher on a 100-point impact scale), dispatchers would contact the customer. If no one answered, emergency services could be immediately sent. On hundreds of occurrences each month, first responders are sent, according to the European Insurance Company, arriving faster than they otherwise might have. This has helped prevent some injuries from becoming serious or even fatal. Saving lives was only the beginning of the surprises from this insurance company Internet of Things telematics program.

The telematics services are also helping the insurance company´s customers navigate safer, to use more direct routes, to reduce reckless driving, to protect their vehicles from criminals and even to keep an eye on their families. As one of the insurance company´s executive states: "Usually, when customers are reaching out to insurers, it is because something unfortunate has happened, now, we can ease their trouble, or even prevent it."

As it can be imagined, this kind of telematics service can generate great amounts of data: vehicle GPS position minute by minute, or even second by second, vehicle acceleration, vehicle braking, weather data, map data (static or live), traffic information and many more. As the service grew in data collected and stored, new services could also be launched to customers. The insurance company can now help customers navigate their routes based on weather patterns or road closures, and there is even a hope this could prevent crashes at some point. If its algorithm knows a certain driver likes to speed through a particularly crash-prone section of some busy highway, which is especially treacherous in the rain, the system could encourage the driver to slow down or even take a different route. This data is also helping the general society, since data is being collected on potholes and other infrastructure problems, which the insurance company plans to share with local governments. Such repairs both improve rides and prevent damage to vehicles.

All of these is already showing benefits, for customers and also for the insurance company. Since good driving behavior is rewarded by lower rates, the insurance company has shown a very good impact on aggressive driving, with speeding and dangerous braking significantly reduced: according to this data, at least 800 crashes have been avoided a year among its drivers. The insurance company also states that it is on track to reduce its claim expenses by as much as 15 percent annually.

The next phase of the telematics services will also rely a lot on Cognitive Computing. The aim of the insurance company is to create a platform that is as much lifestyle concierge as driving assistant.

This caso also bring concerns related to data sharing, unwanted customer data use, data leaking and others. However, the company says data is never shared with third parties that may use it for marketing or sales and it is kept protected at all times (Strong encryption is used at all time, during data transit and also during data storage).

REAL CASE: BLOCKCHAIN IS BOOSTING SALES OF SOME PRODUCTS IN A LARGE SUPERMARKET CHAIN

A large supermarket retailer has seen a boost in sales by the use of the blockchain ledger technology to track chicken, eggs, raw milk, oranges, pork, cheese, and other fruits from farms to stores and it will extend it to more products to increase customer trust. The total number of products tracked are said to be over a hundred and the supermarket chain does not want to stop at this number.

Blockchain is a shared record of data kept by a network of individual computers rather than a single party. Blockchain digital tracking technology allows customers to see very detailed information related to the products mentioned above. Information such as when it was planted, what kind of seed was used, when it was harvested, who harvested it, how long it took to be harvested, the weather in all of the steps just mentioned, when it was packed, when the transport began, what was the transporter route can be easily seen. This can confirm to the customers the quality of items they buy and allow them to avoid products with genetically modified organisms, antibiotics, or pesticides if they want.

One clear benefit for customer is the simplicity and quickness all the information can be accessed. Customers can scan a QR barcode on a pomelo grapefruit, for instance, with their phone and find out the date of harvest, location of cultivation, the owner of the plot, when it was packed, how long it took to transport to Europe and tips on how to prepare it.

For the supermarket chain, one of the benefits is the "halo effect". If the customer can trust them on chicken quality, why they would not trust them for their apples or cheese?

Another benefit for the supermarket chain is the granularity and the amount of data it has about its products and its customers behavior. One executive of the supermarket chain said: "The pomelo sold faster than the year before due to blockchain,". "We had a positive impact on the chicken versus the non-blockchain chicken." Customers in countries like China and most of Europe are interested in information about the origin of products and how animals are cared for.

However, there are still some challenges to be overcome, such tracking fruit and vegetables sold loose that come from different farms, and resistance from farmers to sharing too much information, or how to add the possibility for the customer to check product information in a product that a QR Code cannot be printed.

CONCLUSION

Emerging technologies studies are needed, in a remarkably fast way. This is provoked by its adoption for several, sometimes imprecise, purposes. It is not rare to identify these tools and their associated methods applied in contexts they were not suited to or even to replace older technologies, without any project management supporting design.

In these chapter, aiming to contribute to the initial reader, or those who are not from the information technology, computing science, information systems sectors, or others related to these, we produced an introductory text, a fundamental base to promote our book reading with a leverage for technological conceptual view. As our reader advance the book browsing, it is always possible to clarify and identify the approached technologies, reviewing both from conceptual to practical aspects, allowing a better comprehension for all book chapters.

REFERENCES

Aiyebelehin, A. J., Makinde, B., Odiachi, R., & Mbakwe, C. C. (2020). Awareness and Use of Cloud Computing Services and Technologies by Librarians in Selected Universities in Edo State. *International Journal of Knowledge Content Development & Technology*, *10*(3), 7–20.

Al-Jarrah, O. Y., Al-Jarrah, P. D., Yoo, S. M., Karagiannidis, G. K., & Taha, K. (2015). *Efficient Machine Learning for Big Data: A Review. In Big Data Research*. Elsevier. doi:10.1016/j.bdr.2015.04.001

Alnajrani, H. M., Norman, A. A., & Ahmed, B. H. (2020). Privacy and data protection in mobile cloud computing: A systematic mapping study. *PLoS One*, *15*(6). doi:10.1371/journal.pone.0234312 PMID:32525944

AWS – Amazon Web Cloud services. (2020). *Free Tier for cloud computing services*. Available at https://aws.amazon.com/products/storage/?nc2=h_ql_prod_st

Collina, M., Bartolucci, M., Vanelli-Coralli, A., & Corazza, G. E. (2014). Internet of Things application layer protocol analysis over error and delay prone links. *2014 7th Advanced Satellite Multimedia Systems Conference and the 13th Signal Processing for Space Communications Workshop (ASMS/SPSC)*, 398-404. doi: 10.1109/ASMS-SPSC.2014.6934573

Davenport, T. (2014). *Big data @ work: Dispelling the myths, uncovering opportunities*. Harvard Press Review. doi:10.15358/9783800648153

Deloitte. (2017). *Five questions about applying analytics to risk management*. Available at https://www2.deloitte.com/content/dam/Deloitte/au/Documents/risk/deloitte-au-risk-risk-angles-applying-analyticsrisk-management-250215.pdf

Evans, D. (2011). *Internet of things: How the next Internet evolution changes everything*. Cisco Computers report. Available at https://www.cisco.com/c/dam/en_us/about/ac79/docs/innov/IoT_IBSG_0411FINAL.pdf

Gartner Group. (2020). *Four trends impacting cloud adoption in 2020*. Available at https://www.gartner.com/smarterwithgartner/4-trends-impacting-cloud-adoption-in-2020/

Google. (2020). *Google Analytics*. Available at https://www.google.com/analytics/

IBM – International Business Machines – Blockchain. (2020c). *What is Blockchain technology?* Available at https://www.ibm.com/br-pt/blockchain/what-is-blockchain

IBM – International Business Machines – Cloud services. (2020). Available at https://www.ibm.com/br-pt/cloud

IBM – International Business Machines – Internet of Things. (2020b). Available at https://www.ibm.com/br-pt/cloud/internet-of-things

Investopedia. (n.d.). *Blockchain explained*. Available at https://www.investopedia.com/terms/b/blockchain.asp

Jamil, G. L., & Magalhães, L. F. C. (2015). Perspectives for big data analysis for knowledge generation in project management contexts. In *Handbook of research on effective project management research through the integration of knowledge and innovation*. IGI Global. doi:10.4018/978-1-4666-7536-0.ch001

Jamil, G. L., Santos, L. H. R., & Jamil, C. C. (2018). Market Intelligence as an Information System Element: Delivering Knowledge for Decisions in a Continuous Process. In *Handbook of Research on Expanding Business Opportunities With Information Systems and Analytics*. IGI Global.

Jamil, L. C., Vieira, A. A. P., & Xavier, A. J. D. (2018). Reflecting on Analytics Impacts on Information Architecture Contexts as a Source of Business Modelling for Healthcare Services. In *Handbook of Research on Expanding Business Opportunities With Information Systems and Analytics*. IGI Global.

Jebran, L. (n.d.). *Learning about Internet governance, blockchain and cryptocurrency*. Available at the Internet Society information portal at https://www.internetsociety.org/blog/2018/08/blockchain-technologies-internet-governance/

Kathuria, A., Mann, A., Khuntia, J., Saldanha, T. J. V., & Kauffman, R. J. (2018). A Strategic Value Appropriation Path for Cloud Computing. *Journal of Management Information Systems*, *35*(3), 740–775. doi:10.1080/07421222.2018.1481635

Kurnia, R., Mulyanti, B., & Widiaty, I. (2020) *IOP Conference on Services Materials for Science Engineering*. doi:10.1088/1757-899X/830/4/042098

Mc Kinsey. (2011). *Big Data: the next frontier for innovation, competition, and productivity*. Accessed at https://www.mckinsey.com/insights/business_technology/big_data_the_next_frontier_for_innovation

McAfee, A., & Brynjolfsson, E. (2012). Big data: The management revolution. *Harvard Business Review*, *90*(10), 60–68. PMID:23074865

Mearian, L. (2020). *Computerworld – What is Blockchain: A complete guide*. Available at https://www.computerworld.com/article/3191077/what-is-blockchain-the-complete-guide.html

Microsoft Azure. (2020). Available at https://azure.microsoft.com/pt-br/

National Institute for Standards and Technology. (n.d.). *The NIST definition of cloud computing*. Available at https://csrc.nist.gov/publications/detail/sp/800-145

Ohata, M. & Kumar, A. (2012, Sept.). Big Data: A Boom for Business Intelligence. *Financial Executive*.

Park, S. H., Huh, S. Y., Oh, W., & Han, S. P. (2012). A social network-based inference model for validating customer profile data. MIS Quarterly, 36(4), 1217-1237.

Pessoa, C. R. M., Batista, C. L., & Marques, M. E. (n.d.). Internet of Things and Internet of All Things. In *Handbook of Research on Expanding Business Opportunities With Information Systems and Analytics*. IGI Global.

Qiu, J., Wu, Q., Ding, G., Yuhua, X., & Feng, S. (2016). A survey of machine learning for big data processing. *EURASIP Journal on Advances in Signal Processing, 67*. Advance online publication. doi:10.118613634-016-0355-x

Stein, M., Campitelli, V., & Mezzio, S. (2020). Managing the Impact of Cloud Computing. *The CPA Journal, 90*(6), 20–27. Retrieved October 2020, from http://search.ebscohost.com/login.aspx?direct=true&db=bsu&AN=144364480&lang=pt-br&site=ehost-live

Welsh T., Benkhelifa E. (2020). On Resilience in Cloud Computing: A Survey of Techniques across the Cloud Domain. *ACM Computing Surveys, 53*(3), 59-59. doi:10.1145/3388922

Chapter 2
Ethics and Social Responsibility:
Critical Success Factors in Digital Transformation Processes

Pedro Fernandes da Anunciação
https://orcid.org/0000-0001-7116-5249
Instituto Politécnico de Setúbal, Setúbal, Portugal

Antonio Juan Briones-Peñalver
https://orcid.org/0000-0002-2893-007X
Universidad Politécnica de Cartagena, Spain

Juan Andres Bernal-Conesa
Centro Universitario de La Defensa, Spain

Francisco Madeira Esteves
Instituto Politécnico de Setúbal, Setúbal, Portugal

ABSTRACT

Ethics is an important social and technological issue. The powerful computer capabilities provide new frontiers of economic and social human activities. Information, about employees, consumers, and markets, becomes more relevant when it enables economic decisions and impacts on the organization's competitiveness. Recent examples such as fake news show a necessity of a comprehensive and multidimensional economic and social approach to frame the use of algorithms and technologies to guarantee suitable ethical patterns in the information society. It is important to analyze the sensibility of economic stakeholders to the ethical limits of information collection and treatment about consumers and technology users. The aim of the present study was to evaluate the proposed model for ethical analysis through a proof of concept applied to a Portuguese energy operator, framing the identification and mitigation of the ethical risks associated with the continuous digital transformation process.

DOI: 10.4018/978-1-7998-4201-9.ch002

Copyright © 2021, IGI Global. Copying or distributing in print or electronic forms without written permission of IGI Global is prohibited.

INTRODUCTION

Information technologies are not 100% reliable. They are insecure because they are vulnerable to attackers. They can either be attacked directly, to disrupt their services, or they can be abused in clever ways to do the bidding of an attacker as a dysfunctional user (Bronk et al., 2013). Because of this, among other reasons, the ethics issue has taken a clear economic and social dominance. Various news associated with easy access, availability of data and information about consumers and economic organizations or the generation of fake news in the economic context are examples of situations that have justified the importance of ethics and social responsibility as two dimensions of increasingly relevant in the economy and society.

Eric Schmidt, Chief Executive of Google, has issued a stark warning over the amount of personal data people leave on the Internet and suggested that many of them will be forced one day to change their names in order to escape their cyber past. The Internet is the first thing that humanity has built that humanity doesn't understand, the largest experiment in anarchy we've ever had (Taylor, 2010).

The theme of ethics and social responsibility in this technological context of the digital economy and society, is currently a topic of study and research extremely opportune and relevant in the sociological and economic domain. Moral economy is thus an ethical and political as well as a scientific approach, and as such it would seem to complement the social quality approach (Elder-Vass, 2015). Each new information technology, for sure, takes a step forward in the history of human civilization (Maggiolini, 2014). The great challenge focuses on the balance between opportunities for technological innovation, the behavior of society and confidence in economic transactions. The recent report entitled «People, Power and Technology: The 2018 Digital Attitudes Report» shows the general feeling of people regarding some aspects of today's society, namely (Doteveryone, 2018):

- The Internet has had a strongly positive impact on our lives as individuals, but people are less convinced it has been beneficial for society. 50% say it has made life a lot better for people like themselves and only 12% say it's had a very positive impact on society;
- There is a major understanding gap around the technologies. Only a third of people are aware that the data they have not actively chosen to share has been collected. A quarter has no idea how Internet companies make their money;
- People feel disempowered by a lack of transparency in how online products and services operate. 89% want clearer terms and conditions and half would like to know how their data is used but can't find out;
- There is a public demand for greater accountability from technology companies. Two-thirds say that government should be helping ensure companies treat their customers, staff and society fairly.

The disruption of democracy is a reality, arising from the technological revolution. The treatment of massive amounts of information associated with digital platforms gives individuals and organizations, in an easy way, instruments to circumvent the democratic principles on which our societies have traditionally sustained (Vergílio, 2019). The strong technological context and the lack of a broad consensus regarding the relevance of this topic, in the professional and social conduct of most information technology users, has resulted in a regulatory vacuum of principles, rules, and values essential to the framing of postures and practices in a digital context. Democracies are being gamed (Moore, 2018).

Let us specify the scope of the concept of ethics for further reflection. Ethics is a science whose study focuses on the analysis of human conduct. Ethics can be understood as the set of rules of conduct considered generally absolute and universally valid, which allows us to analyse and evaluate the conduct and behaviour of people. Ethics must distinguish between good and evil, right, and wrong. Ethics aims to frame, regulate, and guide human practices, values and conduct in their personal, professional, and social life, to live in compliance with the laws of nature (Anunciação, 2014). The concepts of good and evil fall into the domain of morals and constitute the elements that take on full significance in the context of freedom and respect for human beings, whether the author of the actions or all those who are directly or indirectly conditioned by them.

If in the past ethical scope was conditioned, in form and content, by personal and face-to-face relationships, the current technological context of society and economy has changed the form and content of it. Technological relations between people and between them and economic agents have justified the need for new foundational principles. The new digital support of economic and social activities, due to the intangibility and the loss of control that users have over technologies, refers to the necessity of the new context of the ethics on the relationships that cannot be confined to the discretion of each part.

Given the loss of dominance and control over the technological resources and infrastructures used by most users, the relationships established in the digital context must necessarily be based on values such as trust. It is important to note that the interlocutors can be people and institutions, on the one hand, or people and machines (algorithms, intelligent machines, or any other non-human form), on the other. In this sense, the well-being of humanity and markets stability depends on the consolidation of trust and security in the relationships between economic stakeholders. This confidence, as a critical success factor for digital operation, results from the following factors (Vergílio, 2019):

- The new technological realities of cyberspace and artificial intelligence (AI) create new personal, social, business and political contexts, for which society is not prepared;
- Internet-based businesses are not understood by most people and given the lack of regulation and adequate control they aggravate the feeling of distrust;
- The media and opinion-makers are more concerned with speculating about the moment when AI will become more intelligent than humans, than the immediate impacts on our lives;
- Crises of confidence generate significant ethical risks for people and companies.

Social and economic changes in society are deep and most of the technological fans do not realize it. In the same way, everything that is achieved, economically and socially, outside the ethical framework is unlikely to be able to recover within this scope. Although information technologies currently lead to this issue, the focus of ethical problems is on data/information. In this context, we can mention the case of social networks and other electronic business platforms, as an example, where the business is often carried out in a non-transparent manner and which discredit the digital economy presenting a significant ethical impact on the digital economy. The business model of social networks mixes social relationships with the opportunity to access and process personal information, which is often collected without the consent or even knowledge of users.

This has long been a "gold mine" for companies in the digital economy. Through them, advertising is offered or sold based on the capture and analysis of the personal information they collect. When you research or buy, they are collecting our personal data. Isn't a conflict of interest in the commercial approach based on our information without the protection of our privacy or our well-being to achieve economic value?

As stated by Chris Hughes, co-founder of Facebook, "We pay for Facebook, with our data and our attention, and by either measure, it doesn't come cheap" (Taylor, 2010). The change is economic and, above all, social. And this is so relevant that the problems associated with it have long gone beyond the boundaries of people or companies, presenting itself as a global problem. The use of digital technologies in an unethical and not transparent way by countries, enterprises, and citizens, accentuates the uncertainty between operators, consumers, and citizens.

Russia, for example, is preparing to temporarily disconnect the entire country from the global Internet. The information exchanged between Internet users in Russia is expected to remain within the country, instead of being transmitted through international servers. The objective of the exercise is to understand if the country is already able to guarantee the uninterrupted functioning of the Internet in case of threats and unforeseen blockages from abroad (Expresso, 2019).

India is in the process of building the world's largest digital biometric identification system (Biometric, 2020). Scanning fingerprints, recording iris', and linking demographic information, Aadhaar connects 1.3 billion residents to all public and many private services" (Biometric, 2020).

In China, facial recognition cameras have already become part of daily life. In conjunction with AI algorithms, facial scanners are being used for everything from recommending a personalized KFC order to police tracking persons of interest (Hawkins, 2017).

Countries and global companies compete to create a growing sense of insecurity. We live in a world with unbalanced access to information, in which the risk of unauthorized or authorized exposure has grown exponentially. As stated by Garry Kasparov (Naughton, 2017) "We don't need less technology, we need better humans".

The future harmony in digital society will only exist within an ethical framework that aims a model of trust and justice between people, institutions, and machines, be they more or less intelligent. The focus of technologies must be limited to improving the quality of life and solving problems that people's physical and intellectual limitations do not allow. In the field of information systems, suppliers of products or services supported on digital platforms that assume a posture based on ethics, safety, and sustainability will be rewarded in the future with less litigation and greater commercial credibility. Customers of digital products and services will tend to make and justify their choices for technological solutions (development and operation) based on the safety of organizations, people's ethics, and environmental and social sustainability.

It is a long-term social and economic investment and a shared responsibility. All stakeholders, from suppliers to customers, from governments to citizens, are irreplaceable in the identification and specification of rules that allow an institutionalization of relationships of trust. This involves individual and, at the same time, collective responsibility for each and for all of us as professionals. In the field of information systems, everyone who participates in the respective analysis, development, and construction, from analysts to architects, from programmers to users, will have to ask themselves about the ethical perspective of their professional performance and responsibilities. Is what they do right or wrong? Do your activities respect people or violate their autonomy and freedom? These and other issues should guide the ethical attitude of information systems professionals, minimizing personal and, consequently, business risk.

The awareness of an ethical and responsible posture results from the fact that the decisions made by technologists are implicitly decisions made on behalf of other people, those we usually refer to as "end-users". At the ethical level, the assumption of challenges by these professionals, whether at a personal or business level, will always have a strong impact on organizations, markets, and users. The postures marked by conscience or negligence will have, as a result, a positive or negative reflection on the individuals and organizations where they work.

New solutions are needed, both individually and collectively. At the collective level, it is important an inclusive digital society, where citizens have the right skills to seize the opportunities of the digital world and boost their chance of getting a job (European Commission, 2019). In global organizations, acting at the level of technological innovation means increasing the capacity for intervention, as is the case of the United Nations (UN) that will be opening a Centre on Artificial Intelligence and Robotics. The office will help focus expertise on AI throughout the UN in a single agency, which will be organized under the UN Interregional Crime and Justice Research Institute (UNICRI). On October 2015, the 70th Session of the UN General Assembly held the event, "Rising to the Challenges of International Security and the Emergence of Artificial Intelligence" (UNICRI, w.d.).

At the individual, organizational or professional level, it appears relevant, among other examples, the creation and establishment of codes of ethics as self-regulatory mechanisms representative of the professional or organizational class, the choice of qualified technology suppliers, the adoption of honest postures and transparent regarding the personal data collected from customers, the purposes of collection and processing, the retention times, etc. In this area, economic organizations should be more proactive and defining policies related to technologies and information. But, as stated by Katharine Schwab (2019) "there's a problem with codes of ethics–they don't work. A 2018 study from North Carolina State University found that the software engineering professional organization Association for Computing Machinery's newly issued code of ethics had no measurable impact on the decisions of its members in questionable situations involving technology".

However, the recommendations to organizational ethical dimensions in the digital context are the followers (Biometric, 2020):

- Unified, not uniform;
- Solutions should create and coexist with diverse solutions on shared infrastructure;
- Unbundle by creating smaller digital infrastructure can be applied successfully to multi-dimensional challenges;
- Design interoperability using specifications that connect and combine microservices which can build solutions;
- Adopt open standards and open source;
- Design built-in retractability and observability telemetry;
- Plan scalability at the outset of the design phase by building in resilience for failure contingencies in every microservice;
- Aim at maintaining "data minimalism" and construct privacy and security "by design";
- Build trust by design through registries, attestations, and signatures;
- The employment of nearly acute automation in which every repeated task and API testing shall be automated; and
- Simplicity or the "elimination of feature creep," unless required, and then "layer them."

Analytics and Artificial Intelligence the New Frontiers of Ethics

It seems uncontroversial the importance of ethics. The digital economy has grown at an unprecedented pace, both in scale and in its influence over our lives (Elder-Vass, 2018). Today, technology and values are mutually important. Many aspects of technology are reflected, or not, in society dimensions, such as politics, economic impacts or environmental issues. Ethics are well recognized in the academic debate, just as technology is an important topic, within the disciplines relating to these topics (Albrechtslund, 2007).

The computerization of the economic and social environment has created entirely new realities. It made possible unprecedented human phenomena of virtual experiences, provided a wealth of extremely powerful tools and methodologies, raised a wide range of unique problems and conceptual issues, and opened endless possibilities hitherto unimaginable (Floridi, 2009). The technological developments and the associated behaviour of the users become relevant to the analysis of traditional legal and ethical standards and assess whether they will be enough to fit the new realities that are technologically supported (Anunciação, Esteves & Gonçalves, 2019).

Ethics is a characteristic of the human domain and has always been associated with everything that concerns people. It is not a new subject or a recent social problem. However, the speed of technological innovations and the potential of extending people's actions, leaving users with the possibility to define their own freedom to use the technologies according to individual objectives or interests. This ethical gap, concerned with total individual autonomy and the collective absence, is reinforced in each innovation because represents a new opportunity of freedom of action in the economic or social domain. So, in each innovation, the degrees of ethical freedom of the people should be questioned with the new possibilities for action. For this reason, we believe that the current technological paradigm of society and the economy constitutes an excellent opportunity for a deep reflection on this theme.

Several economic, political, social, and technological facts show the emergence of ethical importance and stimulate the reflection on the apparent or real loss of relevance that this issue has been in the context of today's society. Since the current paradigm does not correspond to a new phase in social development, the challenges of analytics and intelligence cannot leave us indifferent to the change of traditional paradigms assumed in the information society context. There are many facts that stress and show the depreciation of this social dimension (Anunciação, Esteves & Gonçalves, 2019).

The new paradigms open always new social and economic perspectives on several aspects of the economy and society. Ethics is not an exception. The recent concept of AI that offers new possibilities to social and economic systems, propose to the human being new diverse environmental analysis possibilities, decision making scenarios and levels of intelligent behavior to achieve new and specific objectives (European Commission, 2020). As a new reality that is consolidated in society, artificial intelligence continues to find its way into our daily lives, its propensity to interfere with human rights only gets more severe (Accessnow, 2018). Reflecting on a dystopian future, we move away from the immediate impacts of AI-based systems, namely the ability to be autonomous in the decision-making process, a fact that differentiates them from other machines and systems.

The development of artificial intelligent comes out the fact that machines may have responsibility, so the machines should have ethical attributes (Chao, 2019). Therefore, the development of an automated machine with ethical features to implement decisions such as scenario analysis and judgment, has become the focus of current research in the field of artificial intelligence (Piteira, Aparicio & Costa, 2019) (Anderson, Anderson & Armen, 2004).

Ethics in artificial intelligence focuses on the behavioral consequences that machines bring to human and other machines. The analysis carried out under the Stanford One Hundred Year Study of Artificial Intelligence shows the following general observations (Grosz, & Stone, 2018):

- Like other technologies, AI has the potential to be used for good or nefarious purposes. A vigorous and informed debate about how to best steer AI in ways that enrich our lives and our society is an urgent and vital need;
- As a society, we are not investing resources in research on the social implications of AI technologies. Private and public financial resources should be directed toward interdisciplinary teams capable of analyzing AI from multiple angles;
- Misunderstandings about what AI is and is not could fuel opposition to technologies with the potential to benefit everyone. Poorly informed regulation that stifles innovation would be a tragic mistake.

Still in this study, the main societal concerns are the <u>following</u>:

- Predictive policing tools raise the specter of innocent people being unjustifiably targeted. But well-deployed AI prediction tools have the potential to actually remove or reduce human bias;
- AI will likely replace tasks rather than jobs in the near term and will also create new kinds of jobs. But the new jobs that will emerge are harder to imagine in advance than the existing jobs that will likely be lost;
- As AI applications engage in behavior that, were it done by a human, would constitute a crime, courts and other legal actors will have to puzzle through whom to hold accountable and on what theory.

The ethical dimensions that can be analyzed considering the economic and social impacts are several. Floridi (2009) points out, the scope of information ethics and business and social ethics goes through the moral nature of the various agents (Floridi & Sanders, 2004): the moral nature of the receivers (Floridi, 2003), the nature of the environment, and the moral nature of relationships and interactions. Anunciação (2014) states that the ethical dimension in information systems can also be evidenced by:

- The vulnerability of the organization and the information resulting from the integration of the different information systems;
- The weakness of architectures and the difficulties of implementing and operating information systems;
- The benefits or losses obtained according to the nature of the relationships established and the information shared between organizations;
- The need to extend the network and systems to other stakeholders;
- The need to integrate information systems and the existence of high levels of reliability, security, privacy, and integrity; and,
- In the exercise of control and urban planning responsibility of the shared system.

This author also presents, through an expression, some of the foundations that must be considered and stimulated when framed the ethics in the scope of the information society:

- Information Society = Values (Competencies (Responsibilities (Behaviours (Freedom)))).

This is an issue in the agenda of the European Commission. The lack of ethical, economic behaviour leads this government entity to reinforce legal regulation. The European Commission force of the General Regulation on Data Protection (GDPR) to regulate the share and treatment of personal data or information and share it with third parties. GDPR establishes the legal basis for data processing, storage period and transfer. Now the legal basis includes the direct consent of the individual to the establishment of a contract for processing their personal data, in accordance with legal obligations, protecting their legitimate interests in the economic relationship with your suppliers.

The regulation made it compulsory, to guarantee the exercise of the rights of data owners, monitoring and documenting the exercise of this right. In addition, the regulation has also defined the right to data portability, the elimination of data and the notification of third parties on the rectification or erasure or limitation of treatment requested by the holders.

This European regulation goes a step further and defines the concept of sensitive data, forcing economic entities to ensure specific conditions for their treatment, such as for example, biometric data. Economic organizations must now demonstrate that the applicability of the regulation is in conformity with specific technical and organizational measures that they are able to assess their robustness and suitability.

This demonstration of compliance includes the definition of data protection policies under control, an up-to-date assessment of risks to personal data (access privileges), technical measures implemented to enhance protection (e.g., encryption), rules on data transfer to other countries, internal training programs on data protection, means to identify and investigate data breaches, and the means to respond promptly to requests for access to personal data of each individual, among others.

With analytics and artificial intelligence, this opportunity, depth and reach in the analysis of information, structured and unstructured, grow significantly, opening new perspectives in the modus operandi of current and future society. We believe that ethics will be a sensitive issue in the future. It should be noted that it is not only the emergence and comprehensiveness of problems associated with computer crime, viruses, spyware, espionage, among others related to the technological context. These problems are also relevant, and their impacts are significant. But we speak of a deeper dimension, associated with a new human paradigm, strongly marked by knowledge, intangibility, connection, and relationship.

It is important to continue to safeguard feelings close and important to the human person such as the feeling of security, integrity, privacy, confidence, trust, or freedom. Ethics probably comprises society's greatest challenge today, and analytics and intelligence are here to accelerate the opportunity for collective reflection in this sociological domain.

Objectives and metodology

The main objective of this study is to make an evaluation of a proposed model to assess organizational different ethical dimensions through information systems. Anunciação (2014) proposed a model with four structural factors and eight dimensions that economic organizations must consider when reflecting about ethics and social responsibility in the context of information society.

This assessment will be effectuated through the adoption of proof of concept. The proof of concept has as main objective to show clear evidence of the relevance of an instrument or model by analyzing its applicability in a real context. This methodology aims to test and evaluate a conceptual idea or a proposal. In this case, the proof of concept aims in a simple and focused way to analyze the utility of the proposed model, allowing if necessary, identify eventual adjustments to be made.

The motivation for this study was essentially due to two reasons. The first reason was due to news associated with the practices, unethical, of many companies corresponding to the availability of data from third parties, the vulnerabilities in the security of systems and technologies are the vulnerabilities in privacy in the established economic relations, among other examples. And the second reason was to validate the model presented at the largest Portuguese energy production company. In this case, the main reasons for the choice of this company were three. The first concerns the economic and social impact of the company, as it is inserted in a vital sector for the functioning of companies and the Portuguese State. The second refers to the high volume of data and information that it deals with and that is refreshing to citizens across the country, which allows it the opportunity to have high levels of economic knowledge about them. The third refers to the development of artificial intelligence projects with a high impact on the community in the short term.

So, the present study is based on the identification of how the largest energy operator in Portugal identifies and seeks to mitigate the ethical risks associated with the continuous digital transformation process and by their comparison with the theoretical model proposed.

Although the proposed model respects a more general analysis of ethics and social responsibility in economic organizations, from an information society perspective, we believe that the integration of this model in this case study associated with AI, although more specific, can provide an opportunity for possible adjustments that are needed for the future.

Through the analysis of the similarity of the dimensions present in the theoretical model and the dimensions considered in the artificial intelligence project of this company, an attempt will be made to assess the usefulness and pragmatism of the presented proposal.

The largest national electricity company has been taking on the theme of ethics as a structural factor in the digital transformation process to which it has undergone.

Ethics and Social Responsibility Structural vectors

Anunciação (2014) proposed a model with four structural vectors for the analysis of the ethical dimension and social responsibility in the information economy and society: market (economic perspective), commercial offer (perspective of products and economic goods), consumers (perspective of users) and information and communication technologies (perspective of technological infrastructure). The actual economy and markets have a pronounced characteristic of intangibility and automation. It emphasizes the intangibility of entities and operations through positioning on technological platforms, the ubiquity of activities through the opening of new forms and possibilities of transaction and communication channels, and the immateriality of structures through the unification and integration of technological information and communication platforms.

Economic agents are positioned in a new commercial space that is virtually enlarged, attractive, easy to access and of high wealth and scope. The unlimited and easy access to raw materials (information and knowledge), the growing dominance of productive means (since production to distribution) and the high performance made available by technologies (from processing to storage) reveal the preponderance of ethics and social responsibility as a primary determinant condition for the proper functioning of the markets. In this commercial context, strongly marketed by technological interface, real-time and difficulty of returning the decisions made, it is important to identify the players, to trust transparency of economic activities and respect the commercial needs and purposes.

The relevance of the commercial offer and the new preponderance that most customers have over the market, results from the possibilities of action and economic intervention and from the openness that ICTs provide in analysis and simulation of commercial decisions or the customization of relationships established with suppliers. The possibility of access to information, the generation of knowledge and the ability to make decisions, among other aspects, provides a scenario for action and value generation that greatly attracts the generality of technology users. Customers stopped assuming a passive economic behavior, associated with traditional commerce and started to adopt an active, interventionist and partnership-based role, to increase the value in establishing relationships.

This new role of the customer/user expresses a new logic of income or commercial value that corresponds to a win-win result for both parties. This will be possible if ethics and social responsibility support a relationship of trust between customer and supplier, based on a clear commercial offer, an objective transaction process, and management of commercial timing appropriate to the needs of customers. In addition, it is also important to guarantee confidentiality and security in commercial transactions, observation, and compliance with legal standards and the protection of treatment, storage, and information distribution.

The last vector integrates the production and distribution systems (Information Systems and Technologies – IST). The proximity between buyers and sellers, the establishment of partnerships between both, the articulation of respective dynamics requires integration of IST. This proximity seeks essentially to obtain gains in efficiency and commercial effectiveness materialized in the insertion and automatic and immediate treatment, by suppliers, of orders or instructions from customers, reducing the possibility of errors and delays associated with their manual treatment.

Transparency of IST and operations guaranty credibility to the digital economy. The digital commerce development depends on the quality of its operation, and its input, treatment, and availability functions.

Table 1 – Structural vectors and critical commercial axes

Structural Vectors	Critical Commercial Axes
Markets	· Player identification · Commercial activities transparency · Respect for business needs and purposes
Commercial offer (Products and services)	· Commercial offer identification · Execution and distribution process knowledge · Commercial timing management
Consumers (users)	· Confidentiality, privacy, and security · Legal and contractual rules knowledge · System understanding and operation
Information Systems and technologies	· Record data transactions · Technological infrastructure management of volume and transactions complexity · Interfaces and back-office systems adequacy to business needs.

Ethics and social responsibility assume, in the context of the information society, an important collective and relational dimension that must be covered through the set of aspects that encompass the purpose and usefulness of information systems in an economic or social relationship. Some dimensions of analysis must correspond to these aspects to improve the specification and understanding of the ethical, quality and responsibility aspects that are associated with the digital economy. These are the dimensions that must be administered to guarantee the necessary efficiency and effectiveness of economic and commercial activities. Anunciação (2014) systematizes the dimensions and user expected results in table 2.

Table 2 – Ethical and social responsibility core dimensions and user expected results in the Digital Economy (Anunciação, 2014)

Dimensions		User Expected Results
System *(Architecture, Functionality, Performance, Goals, and Objectives)*	→	**Reliability** *(Trust and Reliability of Information Processing, Storage, and Availability)*
User *(Human dimension associated with users' needs, expectations, and desires)*	→	**Confidentiality** *(Security and privacy execution of operations, and information sharing)*
Exploration *(Usefulness, operation utility, and system enjoyment)*	→	**Simplicity** *(Ease of use, and intuitive operating system)*
Commercial *(Commercial offer clarity, and carry out economic transactions)*	→	**Opportunity** *(System, products and services availability to customer needs, and commercial execution)*
Decision *(Information objectivity to decision making, and commercial option)*	→	**Velocity** *(System performance expectations, responsiveness in user interaction, and outputs consistency to the instructions made)*
Product and Service *(Trade purpose, and economic transaction)*	→	**Integrity** *(Clarity of the Product/Service identification, regarding its structure, and quality)*
Ubiquity *(Commercial opportunity without geographical or temporal limitations or constraints)*	→	**Mobility** *(System portability and access through different channels)*
Governance *(Policies for the administration of needs, content, information, and information systems and technologies in economic and organizational context)*	→	**Universality** *(Opportunity to an integrated user access to any commercial offer or institution, regardless of the operator, place, time, and channel used)*

Portuguese largest energy operator Case Study

The Portuguese largest energy operator has been taking the theme of ethics as a structuring factor in the digital transformation process to which it has undergone. Currently, this company is going through a process of reflection on several topics, namely:

- The impacts of AI systems and other digital innovations;
- Science and engineering expectations for the near future;
- What are the purposes of using AI in the company and what are the real ethical impacts;
- What model of governance should be adopted in the company for AI;
- Who should control and be responsible for AI technologies;
- How the impact of AI should be assessed;

- How to articulate individual and business responsibilities in the construction and manipulation of intelligent systems and what their respective ethical impact is;
- How the company should adapt to regulatory and other data manipulation and other AI-related responsibilities.

This company adopts nine themes, as central subjects to the introduction of intelligent systems and the analysis of associated ethical risks, namely: Trust, Inclusion and Social Responsibility, Privacy, Transparency, Collaboration, Regulation, Competency, Diversity, Safety, and Sustainability. A proposal for each of these themes is presented with the respective description, the identification of associated risks and their mitigation with different proposals for identifying ways to minimize them. These central themes were defined as follows (Vergílio, 2019):

- **Trust:**
  - Description – the absence of clear and verifiable relationships of trust between the autonomous systems and the company (operators and management).
  - Risk – the lack of clear, transparent, observable, and enforceable relationships of trust creates uncertainty and risk for companies and people, with potential economic, social, and personal impacts.
  - Mitigation – ensure in advance the establishment of limits and boundaries adjusted to the level of technological maturity, experience, and degree of impact on organizations and people, which should, whenever possible, be incorporated into the machine code and algorithms.
- **Inclusion and Social Responsibility:**
  - Description – insufficiently validated algorithms can generate bias with a potential impact on social exclusion and fragmentation.
  - Risk – use of software and algorithms of insufficient quality, can cause bias in the analysis, generating potential discrimination between groups and people, with potential negative impacts on people and society.
  - Mitigation – the adoption of software from credible and eventually certified sources, as well as algorithms, made public or available for analysis by customers.
- **Privacy:**
  - Description – the absence of privacy, in addition to being illegitimate and illegal, as it violates a democratic right, inhibits creativity and autonomy.
  - Risk – the erosion of privacy results from the massive use of data, without prior knowledge and authorization of users, in all AI techniques. Older systems, poorly designed systems, or systems deliberately designed to capture data illegitimately, do not guarantee privacy "by design".
  - Mitigation – implementation of legal requirements (type GDPR), with sensitivity and intelligence, through projects aimed at respecting individual privacy.
- **Transparency:**
  - Description – opacity in algorithms, or any other type of code, or associated business models, creates risks and mistrust, which are dangerous for the stability of society and business.
  - Risk – the lack of transparency, due to proprietary code, prevents independent verification and knowledge of its real and potential impacts, which can generate distrust and fear. It is potentially negative for the use of technology, with an impact on its creators, sellers, and us-

ers. Prevents third-party verification of the value and accuracy of automatic and intelligent processing.

- ○ Mitigation – implementation of certifying entities for the code, and algorithms, explanation and advertising of system objects, certificates of conformity, etc.

- **Collaboration:**
  - ○ Description – the absence of collaboration adds risk and removes importance to the processes that enhance the use of technology as a transforming and positive element of human action and decision.
  - ○ Risk – it is not the competition between humans and machines that enhances the use of technology, but on the contrary, it is the design of technology as an enhancer of human skills and abilities that makes the maximum benefit. Collaboration is understood as an alignment of technology and human capacity around a well-designed process.
  - ○ Mitigation – never forget the incorporation of the process in the construction of the man-machine binomial and the importance of the alignment between the Product Owner and ScrumMaster.

- **Regulation:**
  - ○ Description – its absence that accentuates the risks of less ethical use of the technology and its incorrect operation generates inefficiency.
  - ○ Risk – regulation cannot inhibit innovation, but its absence generates a lack of ethically dangerous social control. The idea that regulation prevents innovation is perverse and easy to demonstrate to be wrong, because nowadays, the countries where more regulation exists, are also the most innovative. The digital literacy of people and organizations is crucial for the correct implementation of regulatory frameworks, preventing bureaucratization that only destroys confidence in new processes.
  - ○ Mitigation – promoting the intelligent use of existing regulation and participation in the creation and promotion of efficient regulation.

- **Competency:**
  - ○ Description – incompetence and ignorance, digital illiteracy, is the source of most of the ethical problems we experience, as it prevents the perception of risks and the identification of the best solutions to problems.
  - ○ Risk – ignorance of the limits and characteristics of the available technologies, ignorance about the real capabilities of the technologies, generates new risks, false expectations, impossible goals and is a perfect breeding ground for overcoming ethical limits.
  - ○ Mitigation – education and training and use only of qualified or open source suppliers.

- **Diversity:**
  - ○ Description – its absence and the intensive use of data manipulation that promotes uniformity, limits creativity and progress.
  - ○ Risk – it is not from the excess of information or from the processing of «gigantic» amounts of information that creativity is born. This requires reserve, privacy, and the ability to question the obvious. The analytical capacity or AI, performed by machines and with pre-existing data, create solutions that generate uniformity.
  - ○ Mitigation – do not reduce all action to the manipulation of algorithms, valuing human intervention and creativity, valuing to guarantee the diversity of human resources, in its various aspects, as a central concern of companies.

- **Security:**
  - ○ Description – insecurity stems from inadequate, fraudulent, or criminal use of technologies that operate in cyberspace. It generates significant economic and ethical risks.
  - ○ Risk – the malicious use of cyberspace generates distrust in the associated technologies, in the people and organizations that develop it, in the results obtained, and is an excellent stage for social disruption, crime and the misuse of advantages by states and organizations.
  - ○ Mitigation – security of systems design, increased resilience to security risks through training and promotion of security risk, resilience indicators, such as Bit Sighy's rating, demonstrating the progress made in this area.
- **Sustainability:**
  - ○ Description – a negative impact of technology on the sustainability of the planet, it is dangerous and ethically reprehensible.
  - ○ Risk – the impact of digital transformation on sustainability can be significant, facilitating, accelerating, or hindering that same sustainability. It is also expected that the most advanced digital technologies can make a fundamental contribution to the control and reversal of climate change and the depletion of the planet's resources.
  - ○ Mitigation – incorporating the criterion of sustainability and environmental impact in the process of evaluating the goodness of technological projects and monitoring the environmental impact of digital projects.

Main Results

As we said before, the proposed model respects a more general analysis of ethics and social responsibility in economic organizations from an information society perspective. We believe that, although the domain of AI is more specific, it will be possible to carry out a comparative analysis between them and, consequently, provide an opportunity for possible adjustments that are needed for the future.

The main results showed, as we can see in table 3, that the themes adopted by the electrical company fall within the structural vectors of the proposed model. The relationship of these themes with the market, the offer of products and services, consumers and information technologies are clear. However, the themes considered relevant do not correspond exactly to those stated in the model, possibly due to the specificity of the IA theme. This difference may constitute a line of analysis and investigation in the future.

Another interesting aspect refers to the finding of a different number of themes in each vector of the model. The issues related to the market or to consumers are greater in number than the rest. This observation is also, in our opinion, an interesting finding for future analysis.

The approach stated by Anunciação (2014) expresses a sequence of dimensions that could integrate a lifecycle for the analysis of ethics compliance through information systems. The approach followed by the studied organization has a focus with a greater preponderance in the dimension of the consumer, which can be explained by the specificity of its activity.

It is important to note that there are no universal recipes or prescriptions for this theme. The ethics theme is universal. However, the approach may present specificities resulting from the sector of activity, the proximity of the organization to its customers, the internal and external culture of the organization, among other examples.

It should be noted the evident concern of this great company with the theme of ethics regarding its economic activity. And above all, it is worth highlighting the human aspect, from the consumer's perspective, when referring to dimensions such as Inclusion and Social Responsibility, Privacy, Collaboration or Competences.

Table 3 – Dimensions of different approaches

Structural Vectors	Dimensions	Central Electrical Themes
Markets	· Decision · Ubiquity	· Trust · Regulation · Sustainability
Commercial offer (Products and services)	· Commercial · Product and Service	· Transparency
Consumers (users)	· User · Exploration	· Inclusion and Social Responsibility · Privacy · Collaboration · Competence
Information and communication technologies	· System · Governance	· Diversity · Security

Only an ethical commitment, individually assumed and collectively observed, can guarantee that aspects as diverse as the lack of quality in products and services, the lack of information, the breach of contracts, breach of confidentiality or commitments, communication difficulties, relationship inaccuracies, the inability to respond commercially, the impossibility of solving problems, among other countless situations, do not constitute serious gaps in economic responsibility towards the market and society.

Conclusions

This is a topic of enormous relevance that reflect how companies and people immerse themselves in the technological context of the economy and society. It is important to promote responsible ethical approaches in companies' digital transformation processes. The main objective is respect for customers and the community, minimizing the risks associated with the respective information and communication technologies. Ethics and the respective practices must cover the entire organization. Ethics must be assumed at the Top Management level.

Due to the relevance and urgency to control the impacts of information technologies regarding organizational security and customer privacy risks, it is important to ensure the opportunities to create organizational areas dedicated to observing the set of policies, rules and procedures related to ethics, and social responsibility. This is justified as a way of monitoring organizational commitment to customers and economic community well-being.

We are convinced that the link between people and the information society will increasingly be based on an ethical language and that it will tend to demand critical attention to the activities developed. It will also be normal and natural that, on the strictly economic level, we assist the tendency to a growing legitimacy of brands, products, and services, systems and technologies, regarding the advantages or disadvantages, security or insecurity in their use.

The market, as can be seen from the example studied, will tend to demand, in the near future, new requirements for organizational conduct, perfectly inserted in the parameters of the information and knowledge society, which express active and exemplary participation of the civic responsibility of each one of the stakeholders.

References

Accessnow. (2018). *Human Rights in the Age of Artificial Intelligence*. Retrieved Mar 13, from https://www.accessnow.org/cms/assets/uploads/2018/11/AI-and-Human-Rights.pdf

Albrechtslund, A. (2007). Ethics and technology design. *Ethics and Information Technology, 9*, 63–72. Retrieved Mar 22, from https://www.researchgate.net/publication/225493059_Ethics_and_technology_design

Anderson, M., Anderson, S., & Armen, C. (2004). *Towards machine ethics*. AAAL-04 workshop on agent organizations: theory and practice, San Jose, CA.

Anunciação, P. F. (2014). *Ethics, Sustainability and the Information and Knowledge Society*. Chiado Publishing.

Anunciação, P. F., Esteves, F. M., & Gonçalves, F. M. (2019). Analytics, Intelligence and Ethics. In Business Intelligence (BI): Advances in Research and Applications. Nova Publishers.

Biometric. (2020). *Aadhaar's architect discusses what went into world's biggest biometric repository*. Retrieved Mar 18, from https://www.biometricupdate.com/202003/aadhaars-architect-discusses-what-went-into-worlds-biggest-biometric-repository

Bronk, C., Krüger, J., Nickolay, B., & Gaycken, S. (2013). *The secure information society: ethical, legal and political challenges*. Spinger.

Chao, C. H. (2019). Ethics Issues in Artificial Intelligence. *2019 International Conference on Technologies and Applications of Artiðcial Intelligence (TAAI) Technologies and Applications of Artiðcial Intelligence (TAAI), 2019 International Conference on*.

Doteveryone. (2018). *People, Power and Technology*. The 2018 Digital Attitudes Report. Retrieved Feb 18, from https://www.doteveryone.org.uk/report/digital-attitudes/

Elder-Vass, D. (2015, Summer). The Moral Economy of Digital Gifts. *International Journal of Social Quality, 5*(1), 35–50.

Elder-Vass, D. (2018). Moral economies of the digital. *European Journal of Social Theory, 21*(2), 141–147.

European Commission. (2019). *REGIOSTARS, Guide for applicants*. Retrieved Mar 21, from https://ec.europa.eu/regional_policy/sources/projects/regiostars/doc/regiostars/2019/regiostars2019_guide_applicants_en.pdf

European Commission. (2020). *Shaping Europe`s digital future, Economy & Policy, Dc Connect*. Retrieved Mar 22, from https://ec.europa.eu/digital-single-market/en/economy-society

Expresso. (2019). *Russia ponders 'temporarily disconnecting' from the world Internet.* Retrieved Mar 19, from https://expresso.pt/internacional/2019-02-11-Russia-pondera-desligar-se-temporariamente-da-Internet-mundial

Floridi, L. (2003). On the Intrinsic Value of Information Objects and the Infosphere. *Ethics and Information Technology, 4*(4), 287–304.

Floridi, L. (2009). Network Ethics: Information and Business Ethics in a Networked Society. *Journal of Business Ethics, 90,* 649–659.

Floridi, L., & Sanders, J. W. (2004). On the Morality of Artiðcial Agents. *Minds and Machines, 14*(3), 349–379.

Grosz, B. J. & Stone, P. (2018). A century-long commitment to assessing artificial intelligence and its impact on society. *Communications of the ACM, 61*(12), 68-73.

Hawkins, A. (2017). KFC China is using facial recognition tech to serve customers - but are they buying it? *The Guardian.* Retrieved Mar 17, from https://www.theguardian.com/technology/2017/jan/11/china-beijing-first-smart-restaurant-kfc-facial-recognition

Maggiolini, P. (2014, September-October). Deepening for the Concept of Digital Ethics. *PENSATA, Business Administration Journal, 54*(5), 585–591.

Moore, M. (2018). *Democracy Hacked. How Technology is Destabilising Global Politics.* Oneworld Publications.

Naughton, J. (2017). Deep Thinking: Where Machine Intelligence Ends and Human Creativity Begins by Garry Kasparov – review. *The Guardian.* Retrieved Mar 17, from https://www.theguardian.com/books/2017/jun/04/deep-thinking-where-machine-intelligence-ends-human-creativity-begins-garry-kasparov-review

Piteira, M., Aparicio, M., & Costa, C. (2019). Ethics of Artificial Intelligence: Challenges. *2019 14th Iberian Conference on Information Systems and Technologies (CISTI) Information Systems and Technologies (CISTI), 2019 14th Iberian Conference.*

Schwab, K. (2019). *2019 is the year to stop talking about ethics and start taking action.* Retrieved Mar 22, from https://www.fastcompany.com/90279512/2019-is-the-year-to-stop-talking-about-ethics-and-start-taking-action

Taylor, J. (2010). Google chief: My fears for Generation Facebook. *Independent.* Retrieved Mar 18, from https://www.independent.co.uk/life-style/gadgets-and-tech/news/google-chief-my-fears-for-generation-facebook-2055390.html

UNICRI. (n.d.). *UNICRI Centre for Artificial Intelligence and Robotics.* Retrieved Mar 19, from http://www.unicri.it/in_focus/on/UNICRI_Centre_Artificial_Robotics

Vergílio, R. (2019). *Main ethical risks arising from the digital transformation of an energy company.* ISGec – Information System Governance European Clube.

Chapter 3
Data Governance in the Digital Age

Jose P. Rascao
https://orcid.org/0000-0003-2448-2713
Polytechnic Institute of Setúbal, Portugal

ABSTRACT

In the contemporary organizational context, the sharing and transfer of knowledge play a significant role, and therefore, it is important to overcome internal and external barriers for them to be processed. This can be facilitated by the implementation of data governance (GovD). The problem is that, in addition to being a new construct and still little studied, conceptual divergences are fed by the amplitude the possible dimensions of analysis. In this context, the objective of this study arises in identifying the conceptualization of the construct governance and data proposed in the scientific literature to support its better understanding and perspective of future investigations. A theoretical research was conducted through a systematic literature review, followed by an analysis of the most relevant publications on the subject. The discussions about this subject are considered in the context of contemporary organizations; however, it signals the importance of future studies of empirical and theoretical order to foster discussions on the subject today.

1. THEME AND SEARCH PROBLEM

In the world of ICT's, the term "ICT governance" is well definedand is known, (Weill and Ross, 2004). It is a discipline of the subset of corporate governance focused on information and communication technologies, their performance and risk management. The growing interest in ICT governance is partly due to compliance (quality) initiatives as well as the recognition that ICT is a resource of increasing importance in products, services and in the implementation and optimization of processes. It consists of "organizational structures and processes that ensure that ICT's support the strategy of organizations and their objectives, (Governance Institute, 2003). ICT governance is therefore an instrument of the alignment of ICT's with the business, according to (Hirschheim and Sabherwal, 2001).

DOI: 10.4018/978-1-7998-4201-9.ch003

Copyright © 2021, IGI Global. Copying or distributing in print or electronic forms without written permission of IGI Global is prohibited.

Therefore, the proper use of information (and not only its production) is of vital importance and is adequately a candidate for governance. We believe (it is our premise) that organizations that have an implemented process of information governance are more effective in identifying sources, collecting, processing, and using information and increasingly creating value for other sources of information. Information governance involves defining the global and immediate or transactional environment, identifying new opportunities, rules and decision-making power for the evaluation, creation, collection, analysis, distribution, storage, use and control of information, which answers the question:

"What is the information that managers need for support in decision making and how they make use of it and who is responsible for it?"

Research into current practice reveals that in many organizations, if not all, a comprehensive information governance policy, (Economist Intelligence Unit, 2008), especially for external and free information, and often the policies and processes they have are not effective.

2. INTRODUCTION

Data is valuable organizational assets and, therefore, must be professionally managed to maximize its value. Governance and management are complementary functions. In the public sector, governance is a response of the State to the external environment, based on the various interactions between public and private actors that influence or are influenced by the activities of public institutions, taking into account the social, political and legal arrangements that structure relations between government institutions and their public.

Governance defines mechanisms to ensure good management, with an emphasis on strait participation, transparency, integrity, and accountability. One of the mechanisms of governance is the implementation of policies, which are formal instruments where the principles to be adopted are defined, as well as the guidelines, responsibilities and how the organizational structure will conduct and monitor, (Ladley governance, 2012; Stumpf, 2016).

From a scientific perspective, public research, development and innovation (R&D) institutions have strived to find new ways to manage data, generating them in their internal activities, in research networks, in interinstitutional relations and in interactions with society in general. This effort aims to ensure the proper management and preservation of these assets, especially research data, to achieve sustainability and competitiveness in the modern scientific and technological system.

Data management has become a major challenge for these institutions, as the global information environment moves towards new phenomena, paradigms, and movements, such as Big Data, e-Science, Open Government and Open Science.

Big Data is defined as the set of "informational assets of great volume, variety and speed, which require innovative formats of adequate cost and benefit for data processing, enabling knowledge and decision-making" (Gartner, 2015). In addition to volume, variety and speed, the phenomenon is also dedicated to the veracity and value of the data, (Mcafee; Brynjolfsson, 2012; Kitchin, 2013).

About value, research institutions generate large volume of data, which are underutilized, little explored or even lost. E-Science – data-intensive science – is the new paradigm of science that is based on the exploration of large amounts of data that are generated throughout research projects and activities, collaborative research and the use of shared resources for data exploration, (Appel, 2014; Borgman,

2007; Gray, 2009). In e-Science, efficient and effective management of search data throughout the life click is one of the key points for accessing, using, and sharing this data.

Open Science encourages science and technology institutions to make available to society the scientific data resulting from publicly funded research projects. The concept of Open Science is still under construction, according to (Albagli, 2015, p. 14). The movement reflects "new ways of thinking and exercising scientificity, with direct repercussions on the commitments, norms and institutional frameworks that directly interfere in scientific practice and in its relations with society".

This movement benefits the increase in the efficiency and effectiveness of the research system, as it reduces duplication and creation costs, through the transfer and reuse of data, accelerating the process of further investigations from the same data, and multiplying opportunities for national and global participationin the research process. Open Science is, therefore, a new way of generating knowledge to address global challenges and promote citizens' participation in science.

Open Government is a new vision of public administration that has as principles transparency, accountability and accountability, citizen participation, technology, and innovation. One of the main benefits of open government is transparency and social control, based on the provision of public data, to monitor and benefit from the opportunities of the digital economy and strengthen the new global scientific paradigm.

3. GOALS

This article aims to reflect on the process of construction of the Data Governance Policy, based on the aggregation of existing literature. The first steps were taken in defining such policies and processes from a compliance perspective, (Donaldson, and Walker, 2004), in a more exploratory way. Finally, to reflect on the inadequacy of ICT governance, in dealing with the decisive role of information in organizations.

The value of information is used, and also aspects of governance are discussed to optimize the use of information. We continue with a discussion on the aspects of governance and the various mechanisms that have been explored so far. We conclude with clues to new Data Governance investigations. This research is, by definition, a full and unconditional attempt to combine rigor (academically speaking) and relevance (from the point of view of practice). Data Governance is "strictly relevant" in both theory and practice.

4. FOCUS AND APPROACH METHODOLOGY

As for its nature, the research is qualitative since it does not claim to quantify events or privilege the statistical study. Its focus is on obtaining descriptive data, i.e. the incidence of topics of interest in two fields, ICT and Business Sciences. Consequently, with regard to the extremities, the research is exploratory in nature and descriptive in nature, to the extent that the technique used is categorized, consensually, as a study of direct documentation, which provides for the consultation of sources related to the study in different media, printed or electronic.

The complexity and turbulence of the information and knowledge society have led to consideration of interdisciplinarity and transdisciplinarity as essential processes for the development and innovation of science and technology. The implementation of these concepts in some areas faces challenges that go not only through the polysemy of these concepts itself, but also by the hardened views departing from the disciplinary formation and tradition itself, still dominant.

The research method is likely to cause two or more sciences to interact with each other. This interaction can go from simple communication of ideas to the mutual integration of concepts, epistemology, terminology, methodology, procedures, data, and research organization.

This is an exploratory study that seeks to clarify and organize the concepts presented in the literature of ICT's and Business Sciences. It is not a proposal of new terms and concepts, but an organization that allows identifying a common denominator, among the different concepts already indicated in the literature. So, it allows its grouping by identity, application / use and pertinence / aggregation of value in the context in which the terms are inserted. Data collection is characterized by bibliographical research on terms and concepts.

It is necessary to understand, through a theoretical review of the concepts, through the historical reference documents; of a psychosocial analysis of the concepts of Data Governance, applied to ICT's and business sciences; the normative framework in which they fall; the Internet as a platform for the exercise of political action and the problems associated with it; digital data, citizen surveillance; social engineering of Power; online social networks and spaces of trust and conflict.

It is a descriptive and analytical approach seeking to know and analyze existing cultural and/or scientific contributions on this subject, from the review of existing literature. The research was structured based on the systemic approach to understanding the problems of Data Governance inthis Complex and Turbulent Society. We represent this conceptual network, as follows:

It presents the model of approach to intervention in information, i.e., actions in the academic space with the purpose of production and sharing information and knowledge among the participants, besides and promote the development of skills of search, recovery, organization, appropriation, production and dissemination of information relevant to scientific researchers,managers and other interest society groups.

2. FUNDAMENTAL CONCEPTS

A. Data, Information and Knowledge

Information is not the same as data, although the two words are often confused. So, it is understood that the subtle distinction between these concepts is essential. The data do not convey sense or meaning of the facts, images, or sounds, since they lack relational elements essential to the establishment of a complete meaning, lacking an internal relational structure for a cognitive purpose.

This structure is one of the attributes of the information. Data is transformed into information when its creator adds meaning to it, (Davenport and Prusak, 1998. Wiliam G. Zikmund, 2000, p.19) defines knowledge as "the mixture of information, experience and understanding that provide a structure that can be applied in the evaluation of new information or new situations". Information "feeds" knowledge. Knowledge can thus be defined as a person's ability to relate complex information structures to a new context.

New contexts imply change, action, and dynamism. Knowledge cannot be shared, although the technique and components of information can be shared. When a person internalizes information to the point that he can use it, we call it knowledge, (Zikmund, 2000). This is a fluid mix of experiences, values, contextual information, and expert judgment, structured that provide a framework for evaluating and incorporating new experiences and information. Organizations are found not only in documents and reports, but also in organization routines, processes, practices, and standards.

Figure 1. Data Governance Model

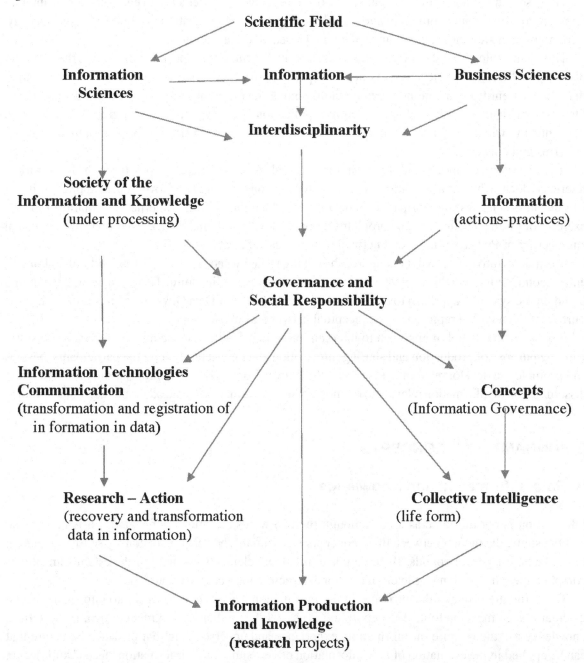

Knowledge has its origin and is applied in the minds of connoisseurs, (Davenport and Prusak, 1998, William Zikmund, 2000). Knowledge is information as valid and accepted, integrating data, acts, information and sometimes hypotheses. Knowledge needs someone to filter, combine and interpret information. Information can be considered as a "substance" that can be acquired, stored, and owned by a person or group and transmitted from person to person or from group to group.

Information has a certain stability and it may be better viewed as existing at the level of society, (Davenport and Prusak, 1998). Although we can store it using various physical supports. The information itself is not physical, but rather abstract and neither purely mental. Knowledge is stored in people's memory, but information is out there in the world. Whatever it is, there is somewhere between the physical world around people and the mental of human thought.

Knowledge = Internalized information + ability to use it in new situations.

Knowledge is found, fundamentally and intrinsically, within people. These are more complex and unpredictable at the individual level than an entire society. So, it is not surprising that knowledge is much more difficult to obtain than information. Knowledge exists mainly within people; it is an integral part of human complexity and unpredictability.

Knowledge has a fundamental duality: it is something storable (at least sometimes we intend to do it) and something that flows (something that communicates from person to person). It is possibly the duality of knowledge (something that flows and storage process) that makes its treatment and management difficult. According to (Dahlberg, 2006), knowledge is organized into units of knowledge (concepts) according to its characteristics (objects / subjects / subjects). The organization of knowledge is related to a process of conceptual analysis of a domain of knowledge and from there, it is structured / architected generating a representation of knowledge about that domain that will be used for the organization of information about that domain of knowledge.

Matrix 1. Data, Knowledge, and Information.

Data	Information	Knowledge
Simple observations on the state of the world: · easily structured. · easily obtained by machines. · often quantified. · easily transferable	Data with relevance and purpose: · requires unit of analysis. · requires consensus on meaning. · necessarily requires human mediation.	Valuable information from the human mind. Includes reflection, synthesis, context. · difficult to structure. · difficult to capture on machines. · often tacit. · difficult to transfer.

Source: (Davenport, 1998).

Data, information and knowledge should be seen and analyzed from the continuing perspective of values and fundamentally marked by the growing human contribution – processing, management, action, result, learning and feedback, that is, human empowerment for actions that generate the desired results at the organizational level.

Matrix 2. Data, Information, Knowledge, Actions / Results

	Data Processing	**Information Management**	**Knowledge Management**	**Stocks/Results**
Activities	· Data capture · Data definition · Data Storage · Data Modeling.	· Information Needs · Acquisition of information · Information Organization · Distribution of Information	· Knowledge Creation · Sharing of Knowledge · Use of Knowledge	· Strategies, alliances and initiatives · Products and Services · Processes · Systems · Structures · Values
Values	· Precision · Efficiency	· Access · Relevance	· Enables action · Value generation	· Innovation · Learning
	"Once we have the data, we can analyze it"	"Bringing the right information to the right person"	"If only we knew what we know"	The ability to learn is the only sustainable advantage"

Source: Adapted from (Choo, 2002, p.258).

b. Information and Communication Technologies (ICT's)

Information and Communication Technologies (also known by the acronym TIC's) are an area of knowledge that uses computing to produce, transmit, store, access and use various data. Because Information and Communication Technologies can cover and be used in various contexts, their definition can be quite complex and broad. However, it is used to **process the data,** helping the user achieve a certain goal. **Information and Communication Technologies can** be divided according to the following areas::

- Programming.
- Database.
- Technical support.
- Data security.
- Tests.

A professional can work in the various **areas of Information and Communication Technologies.** Among them, programming, database, technical support, data security and quality tests.

Security Analysts work primarily **to maintain and improve the data security of a company / institution,** whether public orprivate, creating "barriers" that safeguard the security of equipment and data. In addition, to working with operating systems and company/organization servers, it avoids intrusion attempts. In the event of an invasion of the data, these professionals are also responsible for combating threats and developing more efficient ways, so that it does not occur again.

Technical support is guaranteed by professionals who **work** in the maintenance *of hardware* (physical equipment), working in the repair of computers, problems with access to operating systems and / or applications (**software),** among other issues that appear in the daily life of a company /organization. To work in this area, it is necessary to understand the technical part of the architecture of computers.

The professionals of the programming languages can work in several fields because this is one of the most comprehensive areas of information and communication technologies and, which is more subdivided into other areas. This is because **there are several programming**languages, and professionals can focus on only one. There is, for example, programming for database, for *web,* mobile and even games. Usually, an ICT professional who chooses an area of programming, seeks to specialize even more in this programming language.

Quality professionals work in the verification and analysis of *software and applications* before they even reach the market or the end customer of a company / organization. The professional who works with quality tests does the verification of the **usability of an** application or software *to* know if its operation is, as promised or with what the company / organization expects and do.

Network Administrators are the professionals who are responsible for managing all communication networks that exist within a company/organization, be it their computers or other equipment, such as printers and the like. It is one of the areas of ICT's that requires *technical knowledge of hardware and software (base),* since these professionals deal daily with the infrastructure of the company / organization, the installation and maintenance of the technological systems of the local network. Therefore, generally the professional in this area has a lot of experience in ICT's in general, understanding a little programming, technical support, and database to perform its function effectively.

c. Governance

In 2001, Anna Grandori published an article titled "Neither hierarchy nor identity: Knowledge-governance mechanisms and the theory of the firm", in the Journal of Management and Governance. In this article, the author rescues the term that coined and deepens her studies on principles and mechanisms of intraand inter-organizations knowledge by presenting different cases related to knowledge transfer. On the principles, (Grandori, 2001) cites that governance (Gov) must be continuous, in addition to seeking to balance and combine the organization's systems.

As for the mechanisms, the author believes that the mechanisms of Gov can be evaluated based on two criteria: the first. focused on the cognitive possibility of sustaining certain exchanges of knowledge, and the second, consists of the costs attributed to the mechanisms, especially in cases where more than one is applicable. That is, skills and structures for the sharing and transfer of knowledge, as well as the costs for this to occur.

d. Data Governance

Data governance is a management method used by companies, based on the digital information (data) captured. Software and technological solutions are responsible for capturing data and allow managers to obtain relevant information about the performance of organizations and the direction of their product and /or service to the correct niche market.

However, to deal efficiently with the information generated, it is necessary to have a data governance that aims at structuring, organization, and use. The management model involves company policies, production processes, human resources and, of course, the use of technologies. Data governance describes:

- Who acts with data?
- At what point?
- Using what methods?
- Under what circumstances?

In addition, to enabling a better decision-making process, investor information protection, more efficient processes, cost reduction and transparency, data governance can be implemented from agile methodologies.

The implementation of data governance assists the organization in managing insights, promotes less resource utilization, enabling greater productivity of ICT's teams, and strengthening the security of intellectual property. Data reaches organizations from a variety of sources: internet, mobile devices, internal network, transaction systems, operating software, smart meters, inbound and outbound processes, points of contact with stakeholders, among numerous other forms. For all this to be protected, organized and used in the best possible way by everyone, it is necessary to make a well planned and executed management.

Data management is a discipline that aims to manage and watch over organizations data, treating it as a valuable resource. So, that information can be transformed into business value. For this, data management uses processes, professionals, methodologies, and tools.

Today, in the context of digital transformation, intelligent information management becomes even more important. As organizations are increasingly driven by digital processes, the amount of data grows exponentially. It has never been easier to capture market information, but on the other hand, it has never been more crucial to protect it. Today, data security is a priority..

In addition, companies that fail to organize their large amounts of information end up spending unnecessarily on storage. They also tend to bear extra expenses with compliance and human resources—the time spent searching for information, managing processes, and fulfilling tasks increases dramatically.

However, more than all of this, data management is a foundation of Digital Transformation. As we know, it goes far beyond technology: it is directly linked to organizational culture and operations.

Therefore, this discipline is shown to be the key to the success of this change. What an organization does with its most important information will determine its ability to achieve the results of innovation, productivity, and growth.

3. THEORETICAL-METHODOLOGICAL FRAMEWORK FOR RESEARCH

a. Open Access to Information

The new information and communication technologies allow researchers in the Information Sciences an environment conducive to the development of new forms of scientific communication and the provision of materials that include institutional documents. In Costa's concept (2008, pp. 219-220), "the term openaccess to scientific literature was consensually defined, such as access to literature that is digital, online, free of cost and free from unnecessary copyright restrictions and use licenses. Open Access must remove both pricebarriers and permission to use, i.e. respect the authorship of intellectual production, information must be shared, broadly and unrestricted.

According to (Alves, 2009, p. 12), "these technological advances, like the digital library and institutional reps, offer a range of opportunities for the dissemination of information, especially scientific information, produced in institutions, universities and higher schools", in the provision of knowledge to society. This scenario was based, within the scope of the Budapest Declaration, (Budapest Open Access Initiative, 2002, Weitzel, 2018, p. 106).

b. Data Science

The term resource can be considered as any element used to achieve a particular purpose. Thus, for example, it is possible to speak of economic resources, human resources, technological resources, intellectual resources, renewable resources. From this perspective, the whole resource is an element or set of elements that serves to achieve a goal. Given the breadth of the definition, it is obvious that this term isused in various areas of knowledge and circumstances. However, there are some areas where their use has well-defined limits, due to the importance that this resource means.

One type of resource with attendance and of great importance in the economy is the so-called natural resource. This expression refers to all the element extracted from nature that serves for the production of goods and services. Occasionally, these resources may have a limited obtaining in some cases, already in others, unlimited. In fact, on certain occasions there are resources that, because of natural processes, are constantly renewed: this is the case of natural resources. For the latter case, some energy sources such as energy, wind, solar, water, etc. may be mentioned.

In the area of psychology, the term resource refers to a person's ability to deal with the difficulties of the environment. They can consist of work skills, attitudes, ability to relate to others, etc. In this sense, resources have the function of keeping the person healthy from the, psychic point of view. In fact, when people are overwhelmed by external circumstances, when problems are impossible to solve with the internal tools they have, it is quite possible to fall into depression or some stressful situation.

Finally, it is worth highlighting the economic resources. They are the ones who guarantee the development of a company / organization, family, or person. On some occasions, these resources may become scarce and it is appropriate to assess the possibility of having access to external funding. The relationship between the economic resources produced and those consumed, shows to a large extent the health panorama and the proper functioning of the agents inquestion, from the economic point of view.

Economic resources are those material or immaterial means that offer the possibility of satisfying some needs of the production process or the economic activity of a company / organization. Therefore, economic resources are essential to carry out financial, commercial, or industrial operations.

To have access to an economic resource, it is necessary that there is an investment in advance. In the process of being profitable, it must be recovered through the use or exploitation of the activity itself. Let's examine this general idea through a concrete example: the field is an economic resource that allows the development of agriculture, but this resource may be unfeasible from an economic point of view. If the field is situated in a geographical area that requires a large amount of money in its exploitation. Economic resources allow individuals to meet their material needs and face life.

The process of creating features is called resource engineering (or attribute engineering), which is a complicated but critical component for any process apprenticing to machines/equipment's Better features mean better models, resulting in better business results.

Generating a new resource requires a huge amount of work and creating the pipeline to build the resource is just one aspect. To reach this stage, it probably takes a long process of trial and error, with a wide variety of resources, until you reach a point where you are satisfied with the new unique feature. Then you need to calculate and store it as part of an operational pipeline, which differs, depending on whether the resource is online or offline.

Figure 2. Feature Store data
Source: Microsoft Industry Blogs

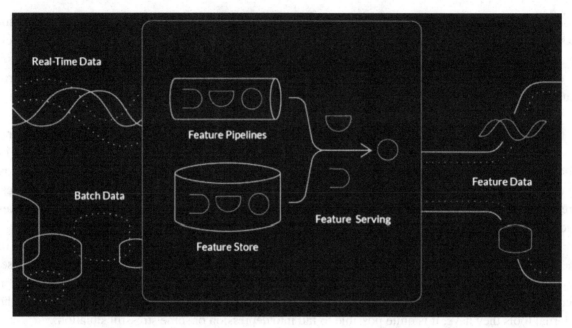

In addition, the entire data science project begins with the search for the right data. The problem is that most of the time, there is no single, centralized place to search; the data is hosted everywhere. Therefore, first, data storage provides a single pane of glass to share all available data. When a Data Scientist starts a new project, you can access this catalog and easily find the data you're looking for. But data on storage is also a data transformation service that allows users to manipulate the raw data and store it, ready to be used by any model of apprentice of the machine (computer). There are two types of data: online and offline

Offline data – some data is calculated as part of a batch job. For example, average monthly spend. They are mainly used by offline processes. Given its nature, creating this type of data can take time. Typically, offline data is calculated through structures such as Spark or simply running SQL queries in given database, and then using a batch inference process.

Online data – it is a bit more complicated data because it needs to be calculated very quickly and is usually displayed in milliseconds. For example, calculate a score for detection of a fraud in real time. In this case, the pipeline is constructed by calculating the mean and standard deviation, in real-time sliding window. These calculations are much more challenging, requiring fast computing as well as fast access to data. **The data can be stored in memory or database** of fast key values. The process itself can be performed on multiple cloud services or a platform.

Here is an example of an online data and offline pipeline using Data Storage (Feature Store). It was designed by Uber, as part of its Michelangelo platform:

Figure 3. Platform Michelangelo of Uber Project
Source: Microsoft Industry Blogs

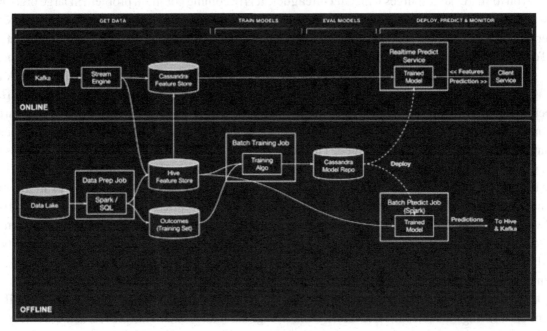

Ideally, data scientists should focus on what they have studied to do and what is best: building models. However, they often spend most of their time in data engineering configurations. Some features are expensive to compute and require aggregation, while others are quite straight forward. But that is not something that should worry data scientists or stop them from leveraging the best features for their model. Therefore, the concept of data storage is to abstract all engineering layers and provide easy access to read and write them..

As mentioned earlier, online, and offline data have different characteristics. Behind the scenes, offline data is built primarily on structures such as Spark or SQL, where actual data is stored in database or files. While online data may require access to data using APIs for streaming engines such as Kafka, Kinesis, or databases of key values in memory, such as Redis or Cassandra.

Working with a data store abstracts this layer, so that when a Data Scientist is looking for a data instead of writing engineering code, he can use a simple API to retrieve the data he needs.

One of the main challenges in data implementing the machine (computer) in production arises from the fact that the data being used to be a model in the software development environment (programs) is not the same as the data in the production service a layer. Therefore, enabling a consistent set of features (computer, and software) across the service layer enables a smoother deployment process, ensuring that the model really reflects the way things work in production.

In addition to the actual data, the data store maintains additional **meta** data for each resource. For example, a metric that shows the impact of the resource on the model it is associated with. This information can help Data Scientists tremendously select resources for a new model, allowing them to focus on those who have achieved a better impact on similar existing models.

The reality today is that almost all businesses are based on Machine Learning, so the number of projects and resources is growing exponentially. This reduces our ability to have a good comprehensive overview of the resources available, since there are so many. Instead of developing in silos, data storage allows you to share our resources with our **colleagues**. It is becoming common problem in large organizations that different teams end up developing similar solutions simply because they are not aware of each other's tasks. Data storage fills that gap and allows everyone to share their work and avoid duplication.

To meet guidelines and regulations, especially in cases where the Artificial Intelligence (AI) models (IA) generated serve sectors such as health, financial services, and security, it is important to track the lineage of algorithms under development. Achieving this requires visibility into the end-to-end data flow to better, understand how the model is generating its results. Because data is being generated, as part of the process, it is necessary to track the flow of the data generation process. Data storage and the lineage of data and a resource can be maintained. This provides the necessary tracking information, such as the data generated ram and provides the vision and reports needed for regulatory compliance.

MLOps is an extension of DevOps where the idea is to apply the principles of DevOps in machine learning pipelines. The development of a machine (computer) apprentice ship pipeline is different from software development (programs), mainly because of the appearance is different from development of the software data. Model quality is not based solely on code quality. It is also based on the quality of the data and the features that are used to run the model. According to Airbnb, about 60%-80% of data scientists' time is spent on creating, training, and testing.

Data storage scans data scientists to reuse resources rather than rebuilding them repeatedly for different models, saving valuable time and effort. Data storage automates data. This process and resources can be triggered by code changes that are sent to Git or by the arrival of new data. This automated resource engineering is an important part of the MLOps concept.

Some of the largest information, and communication technology companies that deal extensively with AI have created their own Feature Stores (Uber, Twitter, Google, Netflix, Facebook, Airbnb, etc.). This is a good indication for the rest of the industry of how important it is to use data storage as part of an efficient Machine Learning pipeline. Given the growing number of AI projects and the complexities associated with putting these projects into production, the industry needs a way to standardize and automate the core of resource engineering. Therefore, it is fair to assume that data storage is positioned to be a basic component of any machine (computer and software) apprentice) pipeline..

c. Information Sciences and ICT's

The concept of technology is immediately understood by those who serve it and who constantly refer to it. There is unanimity on an implicit concept, but it is indispensable to explain. Technology is a complex set of knowledge, *means and know-how,* organized with a view to production. This can be said about high density and measured integrated circuit production technologies, supported by a worldwide network of design and manufacturing centres connected to each other by satellites (Jean-Michel Ribaut and Bruno Martinet and Daniel Lebidois, 1991, p.13). Any technology covers three components:

- Knowledge – which does not constitute a technology.
- The means – which characterize technology, but which are not reduced to them; in non-specialized hands any technology represents a waste of investment.
- *Know-How* – without means is a specialization but cannot get any results and quickly falls into disuse due to lack of application.

Organizations to improve their competitive position do two ways. On the one hand, they observe and analyse the needs of customers to be met and this can lead to technological innovations or analyse the advantages of replacing one technology with another that allows them to *improve their performance.* Any technology always appeals to various scientific disciplines, such as laser *technology,* brings together knowledge of optics, electronics, fluid mechanics and thermodynamics. Scientific research aims at acquiring or strengthening knowledge (provisional certainties), while the creation of technologies aims at production under industrial conditions. Technology only makes sense because of a guaranteed result: a technology only exists, when it is validated and when it allows production in precise conditions, that is, technology solves a problem.

Information and Communication Technologies can be defined as the set of knowledge, material means *(infrastructure) and know-how* necessary for the production, marketing and/or use of goods and services related to the temporary or permanent storage of data, as well as the processing and communication thereof. The emergence and evolution of technologies represent a decisive impetus for the emergence of new forms and perspectives of addressing issues related to how to compete. The use of information and communication technologies has been expanding progressively, so *the English* expression " Information Systems " represents what in Portuguese can be translated as "Computer *Systems*" which do not represent a systemic, complete and organized form of the collection, selection, treatment, analysis and dissemination of information from organizations.

Information and communication technologies allow the storage, processing, accessibility and transmission of data flows (information), so that process technology (hardware) and product (software) cannot be confused with the product (information). Understanding the difference between what information is for business management and information and communication, technologies are vital for managers for the simple reason that information helps managers make decisions, whatever the support technology. But managers also cannot forget that information and communication technologies, as a support, allow to obtain competitive advantages regardless of market share and the size of the business.

In the reflection on this topic, it is important to distinguish support for the collection, processing and transmission of data (technological infrastructures - hardware, software and communications) and the information resulting from the collection, selection, processing and analysis of information, i.e. the information embodied in the flow system (i.e. between the information resource, i.e. data and the product information).

The Post-Shannon Era in Communications Theory

Claude Shannon's research work (1916-2001) led to the definition of the theory of information and classical communication, whose first publication, in 1948, was one of the pillars of 20th century science. Shannon was compared to Einstein and Darwin in terms of their intellectual impact on a significant number of problems and the applications of digital transmission and information encryption in investment theory. The theoretical concepts of information are now also very rapidly penetrating the field of genetic biology, the transmission of cellular signals and neuroscience. Shannon's theory was seen as a perfect theory, that is, complete, proper to all the appropriate definitions or interesting problems of communications – mathematically rigorous that it is, produces results that are "heavy" in several useful paths and provides a definition of what is possible in particular with respect to the signal capacity of sufficiently unequal communication channels.

Shannon's theory was on the "shelf" for thirty to forty years and was forgotten by the actual practical part of engineering (to be discussed elsewhere). But in the last ten to fifteen years, the scientific method of engineering abruptly broke with the theory and even more surprisingly that has surpassed it in some fields of research. The impulse of the method for many of these fields has emerged in the field of engineering and wireless communications, where the unique feature of the wireless channel has created an interesting number of changes in classical information theory.

The readjustment with the practical problems of the engineering method was clarified, when Shannon's theory stopped on certain key assumptions, since not all were fully defined or explored (or perhaps more properly understood) in the original development of the field of research. While we can understand these assumptions, it also becomes possible to see beyond them and what we are seeing is the emergence of the various concepts of post-Shannon signal architecture in which Shannon's conventional theoretical work is being expanded or even replaced by the latest engineering methods (many examples can be discussed).

d. Data Governance

Currently, the use of Big Data in companies becomes essential for the establishment of their market strategies. Software and technological solutions are responsible for capturing data and allow managers to obtain relevant information about the company's performance and the direction of its product and/or service to the correct niche market.

However, to deal efficiently with the information generated, it is necessary to have a data governance that aims at structuring, organization, and strategic use.

The management model involves company policies, production processes, human resources and, of course, the use of technologies. Data governance describes:

- Who acts with what information?
- At what point?
- Using what methods?
- Under what circumstances?

In addition to enabling a better decision-making process, investor information protection, more efficient processes, cost reduction and transparency, data governance can be implemented from agile methodologies.

Many institutions are looking for ways to take advantage of new technologies, such as AI and blockchain, to develop new services and better meet customer needs. Adopting these technologies, often means a digital transformation and migration to the cloud of locally deployed IT solutions to gain processing and storage capacity and reduce administration. IT and compliance teams may worry that cloud data storage can reduce your control and insights, but that is far from true. Moving to the cloud often helps institutions better understand where their data is and how to manage it, which is essential as industry and government regulations on data management and protection are becoming increasingly stringent.

At Sibos 2018, in Sydney, Australia, Microsoft showed how comprehensive data governance technologies help institutions optimize and automate data governance processes. To learn more about our view of how better data management helps institutions meet rapidly evolving global compliance standards.

Data Governance and the Need to Become Digital

Data governance refers to practices and processes that help institutions manage and protect data. Having an effective approach to data governance has gained importance as institutions face significant data overload. Institutions do not just need to process more data; they need to understand the value of using data to drive innovation and modernize their operations and services.

Without the technology to properly filter, store, and protect data, institutions are unable to differentiate between sensitive data assets that require higher levels of protection and those needed to accurately run customer reports. Unfortunately, most institutions today still use manual approaches to data governance, which are not able to keep pace with modern business. In fact, many institutions do not have procedures in place to ensure the creation of reports with relevant information, especially the lack of knowledge they have about their data. In addition, as institutions store huge amounts of unnecessary data, customers' personal and confidential data, as well as the intellectual property (IP) of the institution/company, are at greater risk of being improperly accessed.

As if data governance was not challenging enough, regulations are putting even more pressure on institutions to take control over their data. Penalties for data breaches are strict and institutions/companies need to be aware as many organizations do not comply with the European Union General Data Protection Regulation (GDPR) and face fines from their annual global revenue. To deal with such a challenging environment and improve the management of your data, institutions are analyzing cloud and digital technologies for answers. The cloud is also able to support the implementation of additional encryption and key management capabilities, which are of utmost importance in such a highly regulated industry.

Smart Governance

To help maintain data integrity and confidentiality, Microsoft offers agile cloud technologies such as Client Lockbox for Azure and Compliance Manager. With Client Lockbox, institutions can maximize data security and privacy by controlling the approval loop if a Microsoft support engineer needs to request access to customer content to resolve an issue. This allows the organization to continue to maintain full visibility and control over the data and meet FedRAMP compliance requirements..

Microsoft and its partners are compliant leaders, and our data governance solutions provide what financial institutions need to be ahead of regulatory changes. To learn more about improving data governance and privacy, access the Microsoft Trust Center for Financial Services..

Corporate Governance

Corporate governance has structures that increase the strength of companies through risk mitigation, transparency generation, but requires discipline and control.

In other words, corporate governance is a system by which organizations and other companies are directed, monitored, and encouraged, and involves the relationship between partners, boards of directors, board of directors, supervisory bodies, and control of other stakeholders.

The agile method, in turn, generates a change of mindset, in addition to allowing:

- Constant view of value deliveries
- Analysis of the importance of the team

- Transparency of management
- Transformation of the project management culture

Among the basic principles of governance are transparency, equity, accountability and corporate responsibility.

e. ICT Governance

Governance is now a well-known term in the business world. It has focused mainly on the role of management in representing and defending the interests of shareholders. The fundamental role of governance is to monitor and control the behavior of managers, who are hired to preside over the day-to-day functioning of organizations. Perhaps the best-known use is at the corporate level: "corporate governance", such as the set of processes, customs, policies, laws that affect how the corporation/company is run, managed, or controlled. Corporate governance also includes the relationships between the stakeholders involved and the objectives for the company. The main stakeholders are shareholders, employees, suppliers, customers, banks and other creditors, regulators, and the community.

In the ICT world, the term "ICT governance" is well defined and is known, (Weill and Ross, 2004). It is a discipline of the subset of corporate governance focused on information and communication technologies, their performance and risk management. The growing interest in ICT governance is partly due to compliance (quality) initiatives, as well as the recognition that ICT is a resource of increasing importance in products, services and in the implementation and optimization of processes. It consists of "organizational structures and processes that ensure that ICT's support the strategy of organizations and their objectives", (IT Governance Institute, 2003). The governance of ICT's is therefore an instrument of the alignment of ICT's with the business, according to (Hirschheim and Sabherwal, 2001).

This article takes a devisable approach to information, built based on the observation that:

- Information is what is lacking in the link between business and ICT.
- Information is a business resource, regardless of ICT's.
- The relevant information is increasingly sourced from external sources.

Therefore, the proper use of information (and not only its production) is of vital importance and therefore adequately a candidate for governance. We believe (it is our premise) that organizations that have an implemented process of information governance are more effective in identifying sources, collecting, processing, and using information and increasingly create value for other sources of information. Information governance involves defining the global and immediate or transactional environment, identifying new opportunities, rules and decision-making power for evaluation, creation, collection, analysis, distribution, storage, use and control of information, which answers the question "What is the information that managers need for support in decision making and how they make use of it and who is responsible for it?" Research into current practice reveals that in many organizations, if not all, a comprehensive information governance policy, (Economist Intelligence Unit, 2008), especially for external and free information, and often the policies and processes they have, are not effective.

The first steps were taken in defining such policies and processes from a compliance perspective, (Donaldson and Walker, 2004), but the objective of this article is to define and discuss information governance in a more exploratory way. To this end, first reflect on the inadequacy of ICT governance in dealing with the decisive role of information in organizations. In point 5, the value of information is explored, and aspects of governance are discussed to optimize the use of information. We continue with a discussion on the aspects of governance and the various mechanisms that have been explored so far. We conclude with clues for further investigations of information governance. This research is, by definition, a full and unconditional attempt to combine rigor (academically speaking) and relevance (from the point of view of practice). Information governance is "strictly relevant" in both theory and practice.

The Inadequacy of IT Governance

Although ICT governance is now widely accepted, it is regarded by many authors as a powerful and necessary tool to improve the added value of ICT investments and risk management, while at the same time we argue that governance, both the bases and the application of ICT's, also suffer so far as serious limitations. Some of these limitations are inherent, which means that they arise logically from the concept of ICT governance. Other limitations are self-imposed, which means they are caused by the way, as in practice, organizations apply the concept of ICT governance. Both and their effects will be described below.

ICT's g governance includes decision structures, alignment processes and communication tools. A definition in line with this is given by, (Van Grembergen, 2004): "ICT governance is the organisational capacity exercised by managers, and ICT managers to control the formulation and implementation of ICT's strategy and thus ensure the alignment of ICT's with business". ICT governance is deprived of a clear and consensual definition and is based on very operational terms such as COBIT and ITIL, (Simonsson and Johnson, 2006).

Despite its operational nature, ICT governance is still considered the main mechanism for linking investments in ICT and business value. However, the concept of aligning the business with ICT's itself has been difficult to master and even harmful and misleading. The concept of governance has been criticized on the side of studies of data systems (software), as being a mechanism developed to manage the uncontrollable, in this case incoherent. All activities of breaking borders, for example, innovation, are discouraged or even discarded from governance. Proving itself in this way, it is essentially an instrument of repression. In addition, (Carr, 2003) has argued that it is no longer of strategic importance and, therefore, is no longer a concern of top managers. Nevertheless, in the business the governance of ICT's and their alignment with the business still score points in many investigations related to information managers and are imperative questions.

Inherent Limitations

The limitations inherent in ICT governance logically consist of two words "ICT''s" and "governance". The first major limitation inherent in ICT governance is that they are not concerned with how information can be created, consumed, treated and exchanged in order to add value to the company, but only focus on the resources that must be implemented to achieve this goal, and the associated risks. In other words, ICT governance addresses how an organization should take care of its technological systems but does not address the mere purpose and right of existence of these systems. As a result, professionals trying to find the simple answers to information-related questions will find no consolation in ICT governance. Examples of such issues are:

- How can information governance be shaped to inform managers in a timely manner about the real value of performance indicators?
- How can communication with all supply chain actors be optimized to minimize stocks and delivery times?
- How can you get a better profile of customers, so that they can make personalized offers?
- How can we make the best use of the rapidly growing communities on the Internet in order to identify potential customers and share information?
- How can we ensure that the revenue stemmed by the sale of online content is quite complete and represented in the financial system?

The current concept of ICT governance will leave this, and many other information related to these questions, unanswered.

The second important limitation of ICT governance is that it is unreachable to "control" the business universe, including management, policies, accountability, authorisation, communication, control, and auditing. ICT governance has the paradigm that investment in ICT and the consequent systems can and must be controlled to be successful. At the same time, ICT governance carefully avoids the other half of the business universe, which welcomes vital elements such as entrepreneurship, innovation, business development, creativity, improvisation, value creation and experience. Proponents of these concepts insist that ICT governance is a valuable tool to ensure that ICT investments are aligned with the organisation's strategy (it remains to be proven), but in our opinion, this only illustrates its top-down in nature's "control." It should be seen that this assumption that investments in ICT should be directly derived from the business strategy (ICT alignment-oriented strategy) implies that the reverse (ICT's – guidance for strategy alignment) should not be possible.

The undesirable effects of these inherent limitations are that information managers who adopt ICT governance:

- They tend to focus on ICT's and lose sight of the information that is important to the business strategy.
- They tend to focus too much on control and spend less time on innovation and business development.

The information manager who reviews technology and control as the domain of ICT governance can quickly lose touch with the company and its vital needs. It cannot be included in the company's innovation projects. Worse, these projects will be hampered by the formal policies and procedures that have been implemented as part of an ICT governance structure, which corresponds to further drive it away from the business. Thus, the conscious implementation of ICT governance can widen the described gap between business and ICT rather than overcoming it.

Another, inherent limitation is that the concept of ICT governance was designed by auditors rather than ICT professionals or business professionals. In fact, the current ICT Governance Institute has published the well-known COBIT, which used to be a branch of the Association of Audit and Control Information Systems (ISACA). As a result, ICT governance has material auditing characteristics and contains a lot of audit "jargon" that can hinder their acceptance by business and ICT managers.

Other inherent limitations were mentioned in the introduction of this point, mainly the lack of clear definitions and the fact that they are mainly operationally based.

Self-Limitations

The limitations of ICT governance come from the way it is currently applied in practice. It turns out that, even for narrow purposes, ICT governance can be difficult to implement. First, many ICT governance implementations focus on compliance, ignoring the part that deals with alignment and value aggregation. One possible reason for this, is that many implementations of ICT governance are for compliance reasons ("because the quality auditor wants"). Secondly, in many cases, the implementation of ICT governance does not cross the boundaries of ICT's organization.

A substantial part of ICT governance cannot be applied by the ICT organisation alone, but can only be applied in conjunction with, or even by, the company. But for the reasons mentioned and adding a lack of knowledge on the specific subject of ICT governance, the business is often found to leave ICT governance intact and goes unpunished. Third, the practice shows that ICT governance, even if it is restricted to the organization of ICT's, often undergoes incomplete or half implementations. Examples include policy documents of dubious operational effectiveness, information security projects that are delayed or aborted completely, service levels that are not yet monitored, and the lack of internal controls that are not found until an incident occurs.

There may be several reasons for this. It has been observed that the added value of ICT governance is not always clear to the organisation and often leads to a formal (bureaucratic) process that is not always appreciated by ICT professionals. Fourth, governance, for some reason, is most often translated into strictly hierarchical approaches. Governance, however, includes a wide variety of solutions. One of these solutions is discussed at the point about the governance approach.

Por all types of self-imposed limitations, which are admittedly aggravated by the limitations inherent in the previous description, ICT governance is not always effective for its original purpose. In fact, there are many examples of organisations that have invested substantially in ICT governance, but which are not as successful from the perspective of ICT's,: flows in ICT implementation projects, networks, and security incidents, are examples. At the same time, there are many examples of successful companies that do not excel in ICT governance. Apparently, ICT governance is neither sufficient nor necessary for success. Clearly, a new approach is needed.

4. FINAL CONSIDERATIONS

A systematic review of the literature, and the respective descriptive respective analyses of the selected publications, it was noticed that the theme Data Governance emergent is an emerging concept in the field of Data Sciences and Business Sciences. There are different views on the term Governance because it is a complex concept that can be explored by distinct visions, and because it is interdisciplinary crosses the fields of business management, the management of ICT's, (Foss, 2003; 2007; Foss E Klein, 2008).

As a conclusion to this research, it can be considered that -se Data Governance (GovD), more than its concept, should consider its main objectives, which are:

- Data Governance, (GovD):

  i Turn information into data that can be stored by ICT's.
  ii Management of data stored by ICT's.

iii Management, control, and security of data stored by ICT's.

With the implementation of GovD, companies / organizations will be able to consolidate collaborative management paradigms to share, exchange and transfer data from the intra-organizational level to the inter-organizational level and in learning networks.

In this line of argument, (Foss, 2003, 2007) points out that in the process of data is generated, it is essential to choose a corporate governance structure that provides collaboration, sharing at multilevel. In addition, there is a need to define "mechanisms of governance and coordination [...], in order to influence favorably the processes of transfer, sharing and creation of knowledge", (Foss, 2003, p.11).

Finally, it is concluded that GovD must be implemented in companies / organizations to promote the balance between dependence and power through a set of formal and relational mechanisms for the optimization of economic results. And, as there is not yet a data governance model to be followed, this study provides contributions to the development of a model that recognizes the data, as a critical value for the success of the companies/organization, offering you support as to the principles and mechanisms to be respected.

REFERENCES

Acha, V., & Brusoni, S. (2008). The changing governance of knowledge in avionics. *Economics of Innovation and New Technology*, *17*(1-2), 43–57. doi:10.1080/10438590701279284

Adams, P., Brusoni, S., & Malerba, F. (2010). The long-term evolution of the knowledge boundaries of firms: Supply and demand perspectives. *The Third Industrial Revolution in Global Business*.

Alves, A., & Barbosa, R. R. (2010). Influences and barriers to information sharing: A theoretical perspective. *Ciência da Informação*.

Amin, A., & Cohendet, P. (2011). *Architectures of Knowledge: Firms, Capabilities, and Communities*. *Architectures of Knowledge: Firms*. Capabilities, and Communities.

Antonelli, C. (2006). The business governance of localized knowledge: An information economics approach for the economics of knowledge. *Industry and Innovation*, *13*(3), 2006. doi:10.1080/13662710600858118

Antonelli, C. (2007). Technological knowledge as an essential facility. *Journal of Evolutionary Economics*, *17*(4), 451–471. doi:10.100700191-007-0058-4

Antonelli, C. (2008). The new economics of the university: A knowledge governance approach. *The Journal of Technology Transfer*, *33*(1), 1–22. doi:10.100710961-007-9064-9

Antonelli, C. (2013). Knowledge Governance: Pecuniary Knowledge Externalities and Total FactorProductivity Growth. *Economic Development Quarterly*, *27*(1), 62–70. doi:10.1177/0891242412473178

Antonelli, C., & Amidei, F.B. (2011). *The dynamics of knowledge externalities: Localized technological change in Italy*. Academic Press.

Antonelli, C., Amidei, F.B., & Fassio, C. (2014). The mechanisms of knowledge governance: State owned enterprises and Italian economic growth, 1950-1994. *Structural Change and Economic Dynamics*.

Antonelli, C., Amidei, F.B., & Fassio, C. (2015). Corrigendum to "The mechanisms of knowledge governance: State owned enterprises and Italian economic growth, 1950-1994". *Structural Change and Economic Dynamics.*

Antonelli, C., & Calderini, M. (2008). The governance of knowledge compositeness and technological performance: The case of the automotive industry in Europe. *Economics of Innovation and New Technology, 17*(1-2), 23–41. doi:10.1080/10438590701279243

Antonelli, C., & Fassio, C. (2014). The heterogeneity of knowledge and the academic mode of knowledge governance: Italian evidence in the first part of the 20th century. *Science & Public Policy, 41*(1), 15–28. doi:10.1093cipolct030

Antonelli, C., & Fassio, C. (2016). Globalization and the Knowledge-Driven Economy. *Economic Development Quarterly, 30*(1), 3–14. doi:10.1177/0891242415617239

Antonelli, C., Patrucco, P. P., & Quatraro, F. (2008). The governance of localized knowledge externalities. *International Review of Applied Economics, 22*(4), 479–498. doi:10.1080/02692170802137661

Antonelli, C., & Teubal, M. (2010). Venture capitalism as a mechanism for knowledge governance. *The Capitalization of Knowledge: A Triple Helix of University-Industry-Government.*

Antonelli, C. A. (2016). Schumpeterian growth model: Wealth and directed technological change. *The Journal of Technology Transfer, 41*(3), 395–406. doi:10.100710961-015-9410-2

Assumpção, T. (2008). *Visão sistêmica relaciona conhecimento e ativos intangíveis.* FNQ. Disponível em: www.fnq.org.br/site/ItemID=1032/369/default.aspx

Bianchi, M., Casalino, N., Draoli, M., & Gambosi, G. (2012). *An innovative approach to the governance of E-government knowledge management systems. Information Systems: Crossroads for Organization, Management, Accounting and Engineering: ItAIS.* The Italian Association for Information Systems.

Bianchi, M., Casalino, N., Draoli, M., & Gambosi, G. (2013). *An innovative approach to the governance of e-government knowledge management systems. Information Systems: Crossroads for Organization, Management, Accounting and Engineering: ItAIS.* The Italian Association for Information Systems.

Borghi, V. (2006). Tra cittadini e istituzioni. Riflessioni sull'introduzione di dispositivi partecipativi nelle pratiche istituzionali locali. In *Rivista delle politiche sociali, n°2.* Ediesse.

Burlamaqui, L. (2010). *Knowledge Governance Innovation and Development. Revista de Economia Política* (Vol. 30). Impresso.

Burlamaqui, L. (2011), Knowledge Governance: An Analytical Approach and its Policy Implications. In Knowledge Governance -Reasserting the Public Interest. Anthem Press.

Burlamaqui, L., Castro, A. C., & Kattel, R. (2011). *Knowledge Governance –Reasserting the Public Interest.* Anthem Press.

Byrd, T.A., Markland, R.E., Karwan, K.R., & Philipoom, P.R. (1966). *An object-oriented rule-based design structure for a maintenance management system.* Academic Press.

Cabrita, R. (2004). *O capital intelectual: a nova riqueza das organizações. Revista Digital do Instituto de Formação Bancária.* European Distance Education Network. Disponível em: www.ifb.pt/publicacoes/info_57/artigo03_57.htm

Cadbury, A. (1992). *The Financial Aspects of Corporate Governance. The Committee on the Financial Aspects of Corporate Governance and Gee and Co. Ltd.* Committee on the Financial Aspects of Corporate Governance.

Carr, N. (2003). IT does not matter anymore. *Harvard Business Review*, (5), 41–49. PMID:12747161

Carver, J. (2001). *On Board Leadership. Jossey-Bass Wiley.*

Castells, M. (1996). *The Rise of the Network society, the Information Age: Economy, society and Culture* (Vol. 1). Blackwell Publishers.

Chan, L. (2002). Why Haven't we mastered alignment? The importance of the informal organization structure. *MIS Quarterly Executive*, *1*(2), 97–112.

Chen, L., & Fong, P. S. W. (2012). Revealing Performance Heterogeneity Through Knowledge Management Maturity Evaluation: A Capability-Based Approach. *Expert Systems with Applications*, *39*(18), 13523–13539. doi:10.1016/j.eswa.2012.07.005

Chen, L., & Fong, P. S. W. (2013). Visualizing Evolution of Knowledge Management Capability in Construction Firms. *Journal of Construction Engineering and Management*, *139*(7), 839–851. doi:10.1061/(ASCE)CO.1943-7862.0000649

Choo, C. W. (1998). *The knowing organization, how organizations use information to construct meaning, create knowledge and make decisions.* Oxford University Press.

Choo, C. W. (2008). *Social use of information in organizational groups, information management: Setting the scene* (A. Huizing & E. J. De Vries, Eds.). Elsevier.

Ciborra, C. (1997). From Profundis? Deconstructing the Concept of Strategic Alignment. *Scandinavian Journal of Information Systems*, *9*(1), 67–82.

Curty, R. G. (2005). *O Fluxo Da Informação Tecnológica No Projeto De Produtos Em Indústrias De Alimentos.* 249 F. Dissertação (Mestrado Em Ciência Da Informação) –Programa De Pós-Graduação Em Ciência Da Informação, Universidade Federal De Santa Catarina. Florianópolis.

Davenport, T. H., & Prusak, L. (1997). *Information Ecology: Mastering The information and Knowledge Environment.* Oxford UniversityPress.

Donaldson, A., & Walker, P. (2004). Information Governance – a view from the NHS. *International Journal of Medical Informatics*, *73*(3), 281–284. doi:10.1016/j.ijmedinf.2003.11.009 PMID:15066559

Drahos, P. (2010). The Global Governance of Knowledge: Patent Offices and Their Clients. The Global Governance of Knowledge: Patent Offices and Their Clients.

Economist Intelligence Unit. (2008). *The Future of enterprise information Governance.* The Economist Intelligence Unit Limited.

Fama, E. F., & Jensen, M. C. (1983). Separation of ownership and control. *The Journal of Law & Economics*, *26*(2), 1983. doi:10.1086/467037

Fong, P. S. W., & Chen, L. (2012). Governance Of Learning Mechanisms: Evidence From Construction Firms. *Journal of Construction Engineering and Management*, *138*(9), 1053–1064. doi:10.1061/(ASCE) CO.1943-7862.0000521

Foss, K., & Foss, N.J. (2009). Managerial Authority When Knowledge Is Distributed: A Knowledge Governance Perspective. *Knowledge Governance: Processes and perspectives*.

Foss, N.J. (2005). *The Knowledge Governance Approach*. Academic Press.

Foss, N. J. (2007). The Emerging Knowledge Governance Approach: Challenges And Characteristics. *Organization*, *14*(1), 29–52. doi:10.1177/1350508407071859

Foss, N. J., Husted, K., Michailova, S., & Pedersen, T. (2003). *Governing knowledge Processes: Theoretical Foundations And Research Opportunities*. Working paper No. 1, Center for Knowledge Governance, Copenhagen Business School.

Foss, N.J., & Klein, P.G., (2008). The Theory of The Firm and Its Critics: A Stocktaking And Assessment. *New Institutional Economics: A Guidebook*.

Foss, N.J., & Michailova, S. (2009). Knowledge Governance: What Have We Learned? And Where Are We Heading? *Knowledge Governance: Processes and perspectives*.

Freire, P. S. (2013). *Aumente a Qualidade e Quantidade de Suas Publicações Científicas: Manual Para Projetos E Artigos Científicos*. Editora Crv. doi:10.24824/978858042815.5

Freire, P. S. (2014). *Aumente A Qualidade E Quantidade De Suas Publicações Científicas: Manual Para Projetos E Artigos Científicos*. Editora Crv.

Freire, P. S., Nakayama, K. M., & Spanhol, F. J. (2010). Compartilhamento Do Conhecimento: Grupo Colaborativo Um Caminho Para O Processo De Aprendizagem Organizacional. In *Gestão De Pessoas* (1st ed.). Pandion.

Freire, P. S., Soares, A. P., Nakayama, K. M., & Spanhol, F. J. (2008). Processo de Profissionalização Com A Implantação De Boas Práticas De Governança Corporativa Para A Abertura de Capital (Ipo) Em Empresa Brasileira com Gestão de Tipo Familiar. In XXVIII Encontro Nacional de Engenharia de Produção, Rio de Janeiro.

Galbraith, J. (1997). Projetando a Organização Inovadora. In Como As Organizações Aprendem: Relatos De Sucesso Da Grandes Organizações. Studies In Health Technology And Informatics.

Garde, S., Knaup, P., Hovenga, E. J. S., & Heard, S. (2007). Towards Semantic Interoperability For Electronic Health Records: Domain Knowledge Governance For Openehr Archetypes. *Methods of Information in Medicine*.

Giebels, D., & De Jonge, V. N. (2014). Making Ecosystem-Based Management Effective: Identifying and Evaluating Empirical Approaches to The Governance Of Knowledge. *Emergence*.

Giebels, D., & Teisman, G.R. (2015). Towards Ecosystem-Based Management for Mainports: A Historical Analysis of The Role of Knowledge in The Development of The Rotterdam Harbor from 1827 To 2008. *Ocean and Coastal Management*.

Giebels, D., Van Buuren, A., & Edelenbos, J. (2013). Ecosystem-Based Management in The Wadden Sea: Principles for The Governance of Knowledge. *Journal of Sea Research, 82*, 176–187. doi:10.1016/j.seares.2012.11.002

Giebels, D., Van Buuren, A., & Edelenbos, J. (2015). Using Knowledge in A Complex Decision-Making Process -Evidence and Principles from The Danish Hooting Project's Ecosystem-Based Management Approach. *Environmental Science & Policy, 47*, 53–67. doi:10.1016/j.envsci.2014.10.015

Giebels, D., Van Buuren, A., & Edelenbos, J. (2016). Knowledge Governance for Ecosystem-Based Management: Understanding Its Context-Dependency. *Environmental Science & Policy, 55*, 424–435. doi:10.1016/j.envsci.2015.08.019

Ginneken, J. Van (2009). The power of the Swarm, self Governance in an organization. *Business Contact*.

Goldman, F. (2010). Governança Do Conhecimento E Gestão Do Conhecimento Organizacional. *Revista Gestão & Tecnologia, Pedro Leopoldo*.

Gooderham, P., Minbaeva, D. B., & Pedersen, T. (2011). Governance Mechanisms for The Promotion of Social Capital for Knowledge Transfer in Multinational Corporations. *Journal of Management Studies, 48*(1), 123–150. doi:10.1111/j.1467-6486.2009.00910.x

Goshal, S., & Bartlett, C. (2000). *A Organização Individualizada. Rj*. Campus.

Governança Corporativa & Ética Nas Organizações. (2008). Saber Acadêmico. In *Revista Multidisciplinar Da Uniesp*. São Paulo: Uniesp.

Grandori, A. (1997). Governance Structures, Coordination Mechanisms And Cognitive Models. *The Journal of Management and Governance, 1*(1), 29–42. doi:10.1023/A:1009977627870

Grandori, A. (2001). Neither Hierarchy nor Identity: Knowledge Governance Mechanisms And The Theory of the Firm. *The Journal of Management and Governance, 5*(3/4), 381–399. doi:10.1023/A:1014055213456

Grandori, A. (2009). *Poliarchic Governance and The Growth of Knowledge. Knowledge Governance: Processes and Perspectives*. Academic Press.

Grandori, A. (2013). *Epistemic Economics and Organization: Forms of Rationality and Governance for a Wiser Economy*. Academic Press.

Grandori, A. F., & Ut Facias, M. F. (2009). Associational Contracts for Innovation. *International Studies of Management & Organization*. Advance online publication. doi:10.2753/IMO0020-8825390405

Griffith, T. L., Sawyer, J. E., & Neale, M. A. (n.d.). Virtualness and knowledge in teams: Managing the Lover triangle of organizations, individuals, and information technology. MIS Quarterly, 27(2), 265-287.

Helou, A. R. H. A. (2009). *Método De Gestão Integrada De Riscos No Contexto Da Administração Pública. Dissertação* (Dissertação De Mestrado). 208 F. Programa De Pós-Graduação Em Engenharia E Gestão Do Conhecimento Da Universidade Federal De Santa Catarina. Santa Catarina: Ufsc.

Henderson, J. C., & Venkatraman, N. (1993). Strategic Alignment: Leveraging Information Technology for Transforming Organizations. *IBM Systems Journal, 32*(1), 4–16. doi:10.1147j.382.0472

Hirschheim, R., & Sabherwal, R. (2001). Detours in the Path toward Strategic Information Systems Alignment. *California Management Review, 44*(1), 87–108. doi:10.2307/41166112

Hoebeke, L. (1990). Measuring in organizations. *Journal of Applied Systems Analysis, 117*, 115–122.

Hoebeke, L. (2006). Identity: The paradoxical nature of organizational closure. *Kybernetes, 35*(1/2), 65–75. doi:10.1108/03684920610640236

Holsapple, S.W., & Singh, M. (2001). The Knowledge Chain Model: Activities For Competitiveness. *Expert Systems with Application.*

Hovenga, E., Garde, S., & Heard, S. (2005). Nursing Constraint Models for Electronic Health Records: A Vision for Domain Knowledge Governance. *International Journal of Medical Informatics, 74*(11-12), 886–898. doi:10.1016/j.ijmedinf.2005.07.013 PMID:16115795

Huizing & Bouman. (2002). Knowledge and Learning, Markets and Organizations: Managing the information transaction space. In The strategic management of intellectual capital and organizational Knowledge. Oxford University Press.

Huizing, A. (2007). The value of a rose: rising above Objectivism and subjectivism. In Information Management: Setting the Scene. London: Elsevier.

Husted, K., Michailova, S., Minbaeva, D. B., & Pedersen, T. (2012). Knowledge-Sharing Hostility and Governance Mechanisms: An Empirical Test. *Journal of Knowledge Management, 16*(5), 754–773. doi:10.1108/13673271211262790

Ibgc. (2014). *Introdução Às Boas Práticas De Governança Corporativa Para Organizações De Capital Fechado.* Disponível. Em: Http://Www.Ibgc.Org.Br/Userfiles/Files/Audpub.Pdf?__Akacao=1793926&__Akcnt=98ff2d07&__Akvkey=9c99&Utm_Source=Akna&Utm_Medium=Email&Utm_Campaign=Ibgc%3a+Audi%Eancia+P%Fablica+-+Caderno+De+Governan%E7a+Para+Empresa+De+Capital+Fechado

IT Governance Institute. (2003). *Board Briefing on IT Governance* (2nd ed.). Retrieved from: https://www.isaca.org/Content/ContentGroups/ITGI3/Resources1/Board_Briefing_on_IT_Governance/26904_Board_Briefing_final.pdf

Julien, Cuadra, William, Luke, & Harris. (2009). SECTION III-Information Use-Chapter 7-Information Behavior. Annual Review of Information Science and Technology, 43, 317-358.

Kahn & Blair. (2004). *Information Nation-seven keys to information management compliance.* AIIM.

Kooiman, J. (Ed.). (2005). Fish for life, interactive governance for fisheries. Amsterdam University Press.

Kooiman, J. (2007). *Governing as governance.* Sage Publications.

Löffer, E., & Bovair, A.G. (2009). Public Managemente And Governance (2nd ed.). Nuc: Routledge.

Maes, R. (2007). Information Management: An integrative perspective. In A. Huizing & E. De Vries (Eds.), Information Management: Setting the Scene. London: Elsevier.

Mahnke, V., & Pedersen, T. (2003a). Knowledge Flows, Governance and The Multinational Enterprise: Frontiers in International Management Research. Knowledge Flows. *Governance and The Multinational Enterprise: Frontiers in International Management Research.*

Mahnke, V., & Pedersen, T. (2003b). Knowledge Governance and Value Creation. Knowledge Flows. *Governance and the Multinational Enterprise: Frontiers in International Management Research.*

Marconi, M. A., & Lakatos, E. M. (2009). *Fundamentos de Metodologia Científica*. Atlas.

Mayer, K. J. (2006). Spillovers and Governance: An Analysis of Knowledge and Reputational Spillovers in Information Technology. *Academy of Management Journal.*

Michailova, S., & Foss, N.J. (2009). Knowledge Governance: Themes and Questions. *Knowledge Governance: Processes and Perspectives.*

Michailova, S., & Sidorova, E. (2011). From Group-Based Work to Organizational Learning: The Role of Communication Forms and Knowledge Sharing. *Knowledge Management Research and Practice*, *9*(1), 73–83. doi:10.1057/kmrp.2011.4

Mitroff, I., Mason, R., & Pearson, C. (1994). *Frame break: The Radical Redesign Of American Business*. Jossey-Bass.

Müller, R., Glückler, J., Aubry, M., & Shao, J. (2013). Project Management Knowledge Flows In Networks Of Project Managers and Project Management Offices: A Case Study in the Pharmaceutical industry. *Project Management Journal*, *44*(2), 4–19. doi:10.1002/pmj.21326

Nadai, F. C., & Calado, L. R. (2005). O Conhecimento Como Recurso Estratégico: Caracterizando Uma Organização Intensiva. In *Viii Semead-Seminários Em Administração, 2005. São Paulo. Anais....* Fea-Usp.

Nonaka, I., & Takeuchi, H. (1997). *Criação de Conhecimento na Empresa* (5th ed.). Campus.

Nonaka, I., Toyama, R., & Hirata, T. (2008). *Managing Flow: A Process Theory Of The Knowledge-Based Firm*. Palgrave Macmillan. doi:10.1057/9780230583702

Nooteboom, B. (2000). Learning by Interaction: Absorptive Capacity, Cognitive Distance and Governance. *Journal of Management and Governance.*

OCDE. (2016). *Princípios De Governo Das Sociedades Do G20 E Da Ocde*. Éditions OCDE. Http://Dx.Doi.Org/10.1787/9789264259195-Ptpai

Overbeek, P. (2005). *Information Security under control: Ground rules, management, organization and technique*. FT Prentice Hall Financial Times.

Peltokorpi, V., & Tsuyuki, E. (2007). Organizational Governance in Internal Hybrids: A Case Study of Maekawa Manufacturing Ltd. *Corporate Governance*, *7*(2), 123–135. doi:10.1108/14720700710739778

Pemsel, S., & Müller, R. (2012). The Governance of Knowledge in Project-Based Organizations. *International Journal of Project Management*, *30*(8), 865–876. doi:10.1016/j.ijproman.2012.02.002

Pemsel, S., Müller, R., & Söderlund, J. (2016). Knowledge Governance Strategies in Project-Based Organizations. *Long Range Planning, 49*(6), 648–660. doi:10.1016/j.lrp.2016.01.001

Pemsel, S., Wiewiora, A., Müller, R., Aubry, M., & Brown, K. (2014). A Conceptualization of Knowledge Governance in Project-Based Organizations. *International Journal of Project Management, 32*(8), 1411–1422. doi:10.1016/j.ijproman.2014.01.010

Peppard, J., & Ward, J. (1999). Mind the GAP: Diagnosing the relationship between THE IT Organisation and the rest of the business. *The Journal of Strategic Information Systems, 8*(1), 29–60. doi:10.1016/S0963-8687(99)00013-X

Pijpers, G. (2006). *Information usage behavior theory and practice*. Academic Service.

Provan, K. G., & Kenis, P. (2008). Modes of network governance: Structure, management, and effectiveness. *Journal of Public Administration: Research and Theory, 18*(2), 229–252. doi:10.1093/jopart/mum015

Putnam, L. L. (1983). The Interpretative Perspective: An Alternative to Functionalism. In L. L. Putnam & M. E. Pacanowsky (Eds.), *Communication and Organizations: An Interpretative Approach* (pp. 31–54). Sage Publications.

Raban, D. R., & Rafael, S. (2003). *Subjective Value of Information: The Endowment Effect*. IADIS International Conference: E-Society 2003, Lisbon, Portugal

Rafaeli, S., & Raban, D. (2003). Experimental Investigation of the Subjective Value of information in Trading. *Journal of the Association for Information Systems, 4*(1), 119–139. doi:10.17705/1jais.00032

Ritta, C. O., & Ensslin, S. R. (2010), Investigação Sobre A Relação Entre Ativos Intangíveis E Variáveis Financeiras: Um Estudo Nas Organizações Brasileiras Pertencentes Ao Índice Ibovespa Nos Anos De 2007 E 2008. *10º Congresso Usp De Controladoria E Contabilidade, 2010*.

Santiso. (2001). International Co-Operation for Democracy and Good Governance: Moving Towards a Second Generation? *European Journal of Development Research*.

Senge, P. (2006). The fifth discipline, the art and practice of the Learning Organization. Random House.

Shapiro, C., & Varian, H. R. (1999). *Information rules*. Harvard Business School Press.

Simonsson, M., & Johnson, P. (2006). Assessment of IT Governance-A Prioritization of Cobit. KTH, Royal Institute of Technology, Stockholm, Research report # 151.

Sveiby, K. E. (1998). *A nova riqueza das organizações: gerenciando e avaliando patrimônios de conhecimento*. Campus.

Vale, M. (2004). Innovation, and knowledge driven by a focal corporation: The case of the Autoeuropa supply chain. *European Urban and Regional Studies, 11*(2), 124–140. doi:10.1177/0969776404036252

Vale, M., & Caldeira, J. (2007). Proximity and knowledge governance in localized production systems: The footwear industry in the north region of Portugal. *European Planning Studies, 15*(4), 531–548. doi:10.1080/09654310601134854

Vale, M., & Caldeira, J. (2008). Fashion and the governance of knowledge in a traditional industry: The case of the footwear sectoral innovation system in the northern region of Portugal. *Economics of Innovation and New Technology, 17*(1-2), 61–78. doi:10.1080/10438590701279318

Van Buuren, A. (2009). Knowledge for governance, governance of knowledge: Inclusive knowledge management in collaborative governance processes. *International Public Management Journal, 12*(2), 208–235. doi:10.1080/10967490902868523

Van Grembergen, W. (2004). *Strategies for Information Technology Governance*. IDEA Group Publishing. doi:10.4018/978-1-59140-140-7

Van Grembergen, W., & De Haes, S. (2007). *Implementing IT governance: models, practices and cases*. IGI Global.

Weill, P., & Ross, J. W. (2004). *It Governance – How top Performers Manage it Decision Rights for Superior Results*. Harvard Business SchoolPress.

World Bank. (1992). *Governance and development*. Oxford University Press.

Zyngier, S. (2010). Governance of knowledge management. Encyclopedia of Knowledge Management.

Zyngier, S., Burstein, F., & Mckay, J. (2005). *Governance of strategies to manage organizational knowledge: A mechanism to oversee knowledge needs*. Case Studies in Knowledge Management. doi:10.4018/978-1-59140-351-7.ch006

Chapter 4
A Comprehensive Study of Cyber Security Attacks, Classification, and Countermeasures in the Internet of Things

Md Alimul Haque
https://orcid.org/0000-0002-0744-0784
Department of Computer Science, Veer Kunwar Singh University, Ara, India

Kailash Kumar
https://orcid.org/0000-0003-2916-719X
College of Computing and Informatics, Saudi Electronic University, Riyadh, Saudi Arabia

Shameemul Haque
https://orcid.org/0000-0001-8078-8499
Al-Hafeez College, Ara, India

Narendra Kumar Singh
Department of Physics, V. K. S. University, Ara, India

ABSTRACT

The role of the internet of things (IoT) and cyberspace in a digital society is well recognized, and they have become tremendously popular due to certain features like the ability to ease the operational process of businesses and instant communication. Recent developments in the fields of wireless communication networks like 4G, 5G, and 6G with IoT applications have greatly benefited human welfare. Still, the rapid growth of various IoT applications focuses on automating different tasks and are trying to empower the inanimate physical objects to act without any human intervention. It has also contributed to unethical practices by hackers who use new tools and techniques to penetrate more complex or well-controlled environments and produce increased damage and even remain under the cover. The main objective of this chapter is to improve understanding of the challenges to secure future digital infrastructure while it is still evolving. In this context, a detailed review of the security-related issues, challenges, threats, and countermeasures in the IoT applications is presented.

DOI: 10.4018/978-1-7998-4201-9.ch004

Copyright © 2021, IGI Global. Copying or distributing in print or electronic forms without written permission of IGI Global is prohibited.

1. INTRODUCTION

The recent development of IoT has facilitated diversity in their functions, and they are now widely used in various fields. Networks of objects, devices or items that are embedded with sensors are referred to as the Internet of Things (IoT). These devices can communicate with one another for data exchange. IoT creates various ways of direct integration between the physical world and computer-based systems by remote sensing and controlling of objects across current network infrastructures. The significant benefits obtained are improved efficiency, accuracy and economic-related factors.

In 1999, Kevin Ashton formally introduced the Massachusetts Institute of Technology (MIT) Auto-ID centre (IoT) 'Internet of Things' (Liu & Lu, 2012). For the first time, the IoT applications were used for communication between other objects or a server without human interaction. The IoT applications used Radio Frequency Identification (RFID) system (Ashton, 2009), and Walmart 24 utilized RFID tags in all retailer stores around the world in 2003 (Suresh, Daniel, Parthasarathy, & Aswathy, 2014). European Commission offered a proposal to initiate considerable government-sponsored research in the field of IoT and its application for prospects in 2009 (Reding, 2009). There has been rapid growth in the number of devices connected to the internet in the age of 5G wireless technology. It is predicted to be fifty billion devices connected to the internet by the end of 2020 due to key features of IoT. It is due to the emergence of Machine Type Communication (MTC), which refers to automated data communications between devices to a central MTC server or a set of MTC servers (Agiwal, Roy, & Saxena, 2016). By 2024, Machine-2-Machine (M2M) connection will reach from 5.6 billion in 2016 to 27 billion, and the use of IoT applications is growing globally all over the top countries like USA, UK, China, North America and Western Europe (Hassija et al., 2019). The IoT firms are supposed to increase its revenue from $892 billion in 2018 to $4 trillion by 2025 (Emami-Naeini, Dixon, Agarwal, & Cranor, 2019). According to the Machine report, the total number of M2M connections will increase from 5 billion in 2014 to 27 billion in 2024 (Kasem-Madani & Meier, 2015). It covers a wide range of applications like smart healthcare, smart agriculture, smart cities, smart supply chain and retail, smart grids, smart homes and smart environments etc. (Fernández-Caramés & Fraga-Lamas, 2018). Figure 1 shows the architecture of present and future IoT.

With all this vast spectrum and the arrival of the 5G network, IoT applications will become the most powerful network technology. They will start to change the face of technology like never before. IoT applications have great features like increased efficiency and effectiveness. But with all the positives, the most significant challenges to IoT are security threat in terms of computer hacking, data forgings, financial information theft, online bullying/stalking, denial of services and much more. Cybersecurity Ventures announce that cybercrime damages will cost the world about $6 trillion annually by 2021, up from $3 trillion in 2015. Surprisingly, India has experienced identity theft in four of ten consumers, with 10% impacted in the past year (Rashid, Hossain, & Bhargava, 2009). Therefore, the main objective of the study is to understand the associated cybersecurity threats of IoT as well as their potential solutions.

This chapter is organized as follows: Section 2 discusses the detailed literature review. Section 3 describes the motivation behind writing this chapter and contribution. The overview of the IoT architecture is explored in section 4. Section 5 deals with IoT and its applications, where high security is required. Section 6 describes multiple sources of attacks in IoT enabled applications and proposed countermeasures are discussed in Section 7. Security solutions based on Machine Learning for IoT are explored in section 8. Finally, section 9 discusses the conclusion and future directions for the researchers.

2. BACKGROUND AND RELATED WORKS

As IoT applications combine with diverse systems, these are expected to be rapidly developed in the future, and more in-depth studies are being conducted for the same. In this literature review, we emphasize the importance of security requirements that clarified the relationship of security-related factors of Wireless Sensor Networks (WSNs) through a detailed analysis of the existing studies.

There are various existing surveys on IoT security issues. (Babar, Mahalle, Stango, Prasad, & Prasad, 2010) provided numerous security challenges in the IoT applications and finally discussed security, privacy and trust issues for both devices and information in IoT. (Suo, Wan, Zou, & Liu, 2012) presented security issues in the IoT by analyzing security properties and requirements for the network layer, perceptual layer, support layer and application layer. (Jing, Vasilakos, Wan, Lu, & Qiu, 2014) investigated the cross-layer heterogeneous security issues and the respective solution for IoT. The authors discussed the security issue for the IoT architecture layer and analyzed authentication, confidentiality related challenges in IoT.

(Cooper, 2015) discussed vital challenges such as authentication, authorization, confidentiality and integrity for the IoT environment. (Oriwoh, al-Khateeb, & Conrad, 2016) target the particular problem related to digital forensics and cybercrime investigations and pointed out that basic security principles and resource constraints for authentication in IoT. (Khairi, Farooq, Waseem, & Mazhar, 2015) in their study, reviewed the security and privacy challenges for each architectural layer and mainly focused on the requirement for integrity, confidentiality and availability of data. (Pongle & Chavan, 2015) discussed the wormhole and real-time intrusion attack detection in IoT. The authors proposed a novel method for detecting wormhole threats and attackers. (Mathur, Newe, & Rao, 2016) analyzed selective forwarding and black hole attacks in health applications of IoT. The authors proposed cryptographic hash techniques to detect and correct neighbourhood attacks. (Mishra, Tripathy, Puthal, & Yang, 2018) discussed the Sybil attack in the IoT environment with various schemes, including social graph-based Sybil detection, mobile Sybil detection and behaviour classification based Sybil detection. (Kaur & Gurm, 2016) focused the attack in wireless sensor networks to detect and prevent HELLO FLOOD attacks. (Stephen & Arockiam, 2017) summarized an intrusion detection system in wireless sensor networks to detect Sinkhole attacks in the IoT environment.

(Yang, Wu, Yin, Li, & Zhao, 2017) analyzed some critical security issues in IoT applications. (Yang et al., 2017) targeted the security issues specific to location-based services in IoT devices. (Ngu, Gutierrez, Metsis, Nepal, & Sheng, 2016) discussed the security issues in concern with the IoT middleware and presented a survey of concerned existing protocols. (Din, Guizani, Kim, Hassan, & Khan, 2018) summarized trust management techniques for IoT, along with their advantages and disadvantages. (Farris, Taleb, Khettab, & Song, 2018) discussed Software-defined networking (SDN) and network function virtualization (NFV) techniques to resolve cybersecurity issues in IoT applications. (Yu et al., 2017) differentiated between edge computing and traditional cloud computing to secure IoT technologies. (Lin et al., 2017) mainly focused on the relationship between IoT and fog computing with security issues. (Mosenia & Jha, 2016) discussed various vulnerabilities in IoT applications.

3. MOTIVATION AND CONTRIBUTION

To the best of our knowledge, there is not even a single survey that addresses a broader range of IoT applications by considering all of the critical security issues and challenges. This paper provides a clear idea and a general understanding of the field of IoT security issues to readers and researchers.

The main contributions of the chapter are listed below.

1. Compared to other survey papers in the field of security issues in IoT, this survey provides more profound and most relevant standard specifications.
2. This survey provides a detailed explanation of different attacks in IoT enabled applications.
3. Review the current countermeasures and proposed Machine Learning techniques to overcome the security threats in IoT.
4. Last but not least, the challenges and future research direction of IoT security are summarized.

The method of the comparative study is based on an empirical review of the available literature studies in connection with security issues and possible countermeasures to the security threats of IoT enabled applications.

4. OVERVIEW OF THE IoT ARCHITECTURE

This section provides an overview of the IoT systems. The implementation of a flawless IoT system is crucial in the academe and industry due to the wide range of applications that can enable the execution of smart city concepts through billions of connected smart devices. The IoT architecture generally comprises four layers, namely, the Perception layer, Network Layer, Middleware Layer and Application Layer. This architecture can be further taxonomized for simplicity and improved analysis, as shown in Figure 1.

4.1 Perception Layer

The perception layer is the standard layer in the IoT system and is like the physical layer of the Open System Interface (OSI) model. This layer consists of various nodes, especially actuators and sensors, which gather and process information from the environment. Sensors are selected according to the specifications of the applications. The information obtained by these sensors can involve position, changes in weather, atmosphere, motion, vibration, etc. This layer has some crucial technologies such as sensor technology, intelligence embedded technology, nanotechnology and tagging technology.

Figure 1. IoT Layer Architecture

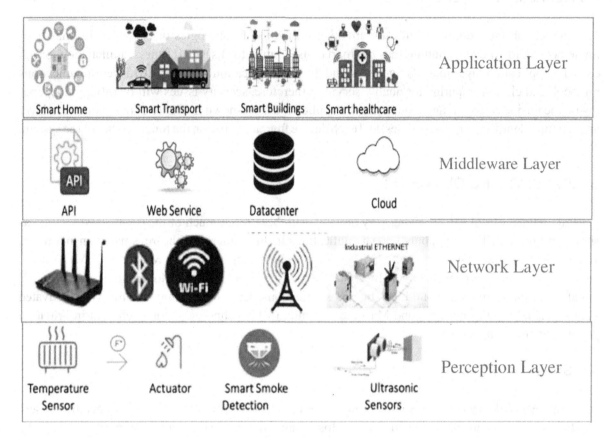

4.2 Network Layer

The Network Layer is responsible for connecting to other smart things, network devices and servers and managing the data transmission among the other layers. Network gateways are the points that serve as a filter for data transmission between different nodes. This layer mainly transmits the data collected from the perception layer to subsequent layers, and all features of this layer are used to transmit and process sensor data. This layer needs a high-security mechanism such as Block-chain technology and Intelligence Intrusion Detection Systems.

4.3 Middleware Layer

Middle-ware is the gateway between the network layer and the application layer and is responsible for communicating with machines and managing data (Ashton, 2009). The function of middleware is to provide a single programming model that interacts with tools. It can also provide powerful computing and storage capabilities (Mosenia & Jha, 2016). Middle-ware is part of the system that facilitates net-working for massive amounts of different items by offering a layer of networking for sensors as well as for application layers that provide utilities that maintain efficient communication between applications.

4.4 Application Layer

The application layer describes all programs that utilize IoT technologies or on which IoT has been implemented. IoT implementations may be smart houses, smart towns, smart fitness, animal monitoring, etc. The application layer may also act as a middleware application (Cooper, 2015), communications protocol, and cloud computing for quality services; therefore, security issues will be different depending on the business context and industry of the applications. As shown in Figure 1, the application layer architecture identifies various modules, and each device function relies on the functionality of the system.

5. APPLICATIONS OF THE IoT

Several applications of IoT are rising very quickly, and these reach much of the established sectors, as shown in Figure 2. The commonly known applications include smart healthcare, smart transportation, smart grid and smart building. Azure IoT package, International Business Machine (IBM) Watson, Amazon Web Services (AWS), Oracle IoT, Kaa, Bevywise IoT platform used for smart grid and IoTIFY cloud-based platform used to build scalable IoT applications. Many open-source platforms are activated with Artificial Intelligence (AI) and Machine Learning (ML) technologies for intelligent information processing and computation.

5.1 Smart Healthcare

In recent years IoT devices have gained prominence in health applications. It is used in healthcare sectors to track and document patient conditions closely and, in crucial situations, send alert signals to the healthcare system concerned to provide patients with a fast and timely treatment. Internet of Medical Things (IoMT) has been implemented in over 60 per cent of the healthcare sector.

Unlike other applications, however, IoT in healthcare systems must be protected while providing universal access to devices to save lives in emergencies. Also, IoT sensors are commonly used for tracking everyday activities related to health. Typically a smartphone is used to track health-related actions such as day-to-day activity and sleep analysis. IoT has prodigious potential for improving healthcare systems and a wide variety of applications. The IoT system can further enhance the advancement of conventional medical devices towards interactive medical devices for the environment by collaboratively integrating embedded, wearable and environmental sensors inside the IoT system to accurately monitor the health of users and ensure real-time health support. Securing IoT systems, however, remains a critical issue, and more research is needed to deploy IoT devices in the healthcare sector securely.

Figure 2. Applications of IoT

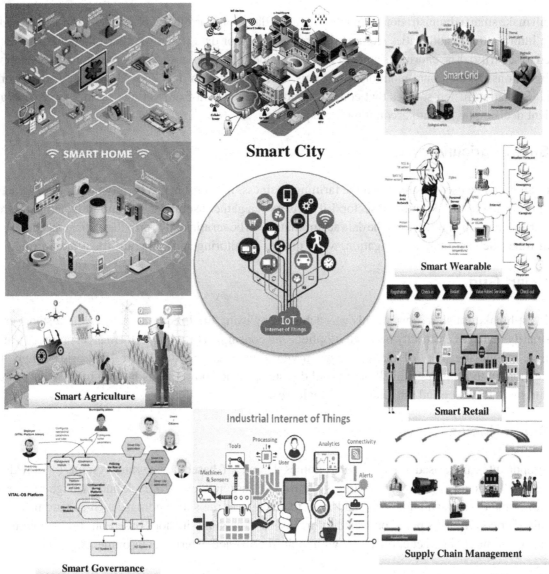

5.2 Smart Transportation

With the help of IoT systems, smart transport systems have become attainable. The main objective of smart transport is to intelligently control everyday traffic in cities by analyzing data from well-connected sensors located in various locations and by introducing data. Besides, the smart transport data analytics will indirectly boost shipping schedules, advance road safety and increase delivery times.

5.3 Smart Governance

IoT will make smart administration simpler. Integrating data from various government sectors can provide ample information to authorities from a wide range of sensor data (from weather-related data to data related to security). The enormous amount of data produced by IoT sensors will exceptionally overcome the limitations of traditional monitoring systems. The presentation of a knowledge-based framework from information fusion sources that compiles and compares data from various sectors to provide an efficient decision taking into account multiple perspectives.

5.4 Smart Agriculture

IoT systems can be used to strengthen the farming business. IoT sensors can be mounted to enable real-time monitoring of the agricultural sector. IoT sensors can gather useful data on humidity, temperature, weather and humidity levels. Then the data accumulated can be scrutinized to provide critical mechanisms in real-time, such as automatic irrigation, water quality monitoring and soil constituent monitoring.

5.5 Smart Grid

The latest breakthrough in power grids was achieved by using the IoT platform to create a smart grid that smartly manages electricity between suppliers and consumers to boost performance, protection and real-time monitoring. The IoT platform plays a vital role in successfully controlling grids. Applying IoT technology to a smart grid will help avoid disasters, reduce power transmission to increase power transmission efficiency and mitigate economic losses.

5.6 Smart Homes

IoT components can be used to realize smart homes. Home IoT-based devices and systems (e.g., fridge, Television, doors, air conditioner, heating systems, etc.) are now easy to track and manage remotely. A smart home device can understand and react to changes in the surroundings, such as automatically switching air conditioners based on weather forecasts and opening the door based on face recognition. Smart homes should interact consistently with their internal and external environments.

5.7 Smart Supply Chain

A significant application of IoT technology in real life is to build business processes that are simpler and more versatile than before. The development of IoT-embedded sensors, such as RFID and Near Field Communication (NFC), allows for the interaction between IoT sensors embedded in the goods and business overseers. Thus, these goods can be tracked during the phases of manufacture and transport before they reach the customer.

Figure 3. Taxonomy of Security attacks in IoT

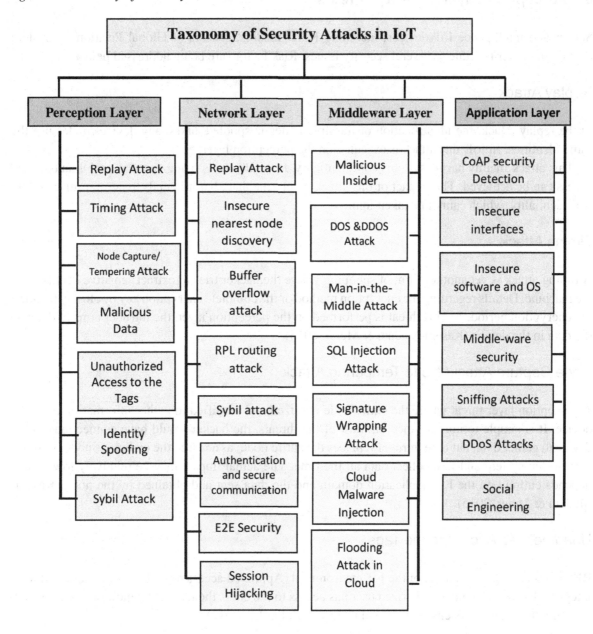

6. SECURITY ATTACKS IN THE INTERNET OF THINGS (IOT)

As discussed in the previous section, IoT architecture can be divided into four layers: (1) Perception Layer; (2) Network Layer; (3) Middleware Layer; and (4) Application Layer. Each of these layers in an IoT application uses diverse technologies that bring several issues and security threats. In this part of the chapter presents some possible attacks in IoT applications of these four layers. Figure 3 shows the potential attacks on these four layers. The particular security issues associated with the gateways that connect these layers are also discussed in this section.

6.1 Perception Layer Security Threats

Sensor and intelligence IoT devices, including RFID readers, sensors or Global Positioning System (GPS), are under risk due to several security issues. Risk factors are being addressed below:

Replay Attack

In the replay attack, the identification of multiple nodes is spoofed, and many devices/nodes use the same identities. In IoT, this attack is executed on the perception layer.

This attack mainly harms systems confidentiality as the device is being spoofed, and unauthorized access can be achieved. The impact of this attack is intermediate, but it intends to compromise system confidentiality, which cannot be taken lightly.

Timing Attack

A timing attack is yet another form of snooping where the hacker tries to extract sensitive details from the machine. Details regarding the encryption method or the complete encryption key by closely tracking the encryption period. As this threat is performed on the perception layer, the intruder aims to damage the data in the device (Kasem-Madani & Meier, 2015).

Node Capture Attack/ Node Tempering Attack

A perception layer threat where the entire node is seized and modified to gather information from the device. It is simple to initiate since, in most of the threats, the hacker would have connections to the device to gather data, but here intruder replaces the entire node; as a result, the malicious node becomes part of that system and will collect data all the time. The actual impact may be relatively low, which depends entirely on the IoT application domain and the data sent and obtained by the node (Kasem-Madani & Meier, 2015).

Unauthorized Access to the Tags

RFID tags are part and parcel of the IoT environment. Approved access to such tags guarantees device integrity. However, if an unauthorized user has access to the code, the tag can be modified or removed, resulting in a lack of system security and integrity (Liu & Lu, 2012).

Malicious Data

Perception and application layer are vulnerable to malicious data attacks where an attacker injects malicious data into the system; the intention is either to get access to the system by doing so or to replace standard data with malicious data. In all cases, device data confidentiality is explicitly violated by the attacker. This threat is possible at that time when the hacker can completely control the node first. This attack affects data from the device, and its impact can differ from low to medium, depending on the IoT application domain (Liu & Lu, 2012).

Identity Spoofing

It begins with a false transmitted message sent to the sensor network by an unauthorized person. Spoofing could be used to obtain access to the victim's data, install malicious software though the highly infectious links or attachments, deactivate network access control mechanisms, or redistribute traffic for a denial-of-service attack. Spoofing is often a way for a malicious person to obtain access to a broader security breach, such as an advanced persistent threat or a man-in-the-middle attack. It is quite often that this scenario results in the attacker obtaining full access to the system, making it vulnerable (Mitrokotsa, Rieback, & Tanenbaum, 2010).

Sybil Attack

The use of Sybil nodes causes this threat, and these are nodes that clone and use the identification of many other nodes to transmit data. The node is located at one site, but digitally at more than one site. Sybil can also be considered as masquerade when it may look like an average user, but it is not. In a typical network, each node has to vote for once, but during a Sybil attack, one node may vote multiple times (Ashton, 2009).

6.2 Network Layer Security Threats

Protected connectivity, routing and sessions control related to IoT network layer specifications, and protocols (e.g. transport layer) is a primary issue for network layer threats. We are providing security threats taxonomy in the network layer that has been derived from the most current articles researching this dimension.

Replay Attack

Reconstruction of fragmented packets in the destination system is necessary due to the fragmentation of IPv6 packets in connected devices in the IoT paradigm for mapping into pre-defined tiny frame size in IEEE802.15.x format. Not only will this phenomenon contribute to buffer overflows and system restarting on the recipient side (Kim, 2008), but it may even be converted into Replay Attack if malicious devices seek to transmit overlapped fragmented packets (Hummen et al., 2013).

Insecure Nearest Node Discovery

Neighbour Discovery Protocol (NDP) was used in IPv6 for locating the closest devices in the same operating IoT area network. NDP identifies the usable routers Medium Access Control (MAC) addresses, preserves address resolution, and detects replication of addresses. This procedure will lead to a Distributed Denial of Service (DDoS) attack without an effective authorization mechanism (B. Park, 2011).

Buffer Overflow Attack

The receiving nodes in the network layer would need to allocate a volume of space for assembling of incoming packets. In certain instances, an attacker can misuse this method by submitting missing packets; this behaviour can result in a DoS attack by removing other packets due to occupying buffer space (Hummen et al., 2013).

Routing Protocol for Low-Power and Lossy Networks (RPL) Routing Attack

The IoT system routing protocol in IPv6 is one ineffective Weak Power and Lossy Networks (RPL) protocol (Dvir & Buttyan, 2011). A malicious system aims to demonstrate the best route to Base Station in the Sinkhole attack. Through doing so, fraudulent devices may exploit other network data and have the required packet payload changed or even lose the message that can trigger delay (Pu & Hajjar, 2018).

Sybil Attack on the Network Layer

False nodes in the network layer will strike Sybil attack through their false network layer identities and also breach user data protection, spamming, malware intrusion or phishing attacks on some other nodes (K. Zhang, Liang, Lu, & Shen, 2014).

Authentication and Secure Communication

Both IoT devices and the associated users require a key management system to authorize them. But often, computational overhead from cryptographic algorithms contributes to vulnerability in security (Raza, Duquennoy, Höglund, Roedig, & Voigt, 2014). For example, the overhead Datagram Transport Layer Security (DTLS) needs to be reduced due to resource constraints.

E2E Security

End-to-End encryption includes a security mechanism to ensure the transfer of data between senders and receivers is carried out successfully. Data security intrusion would be the vital security issue for the IoT network layer to accomplish this aim (Granjal, Monteiro, & Silva, 2013).

Session Hijacking

False messages created by hackers (N. Park & Kang, 2016) will lead to denial of service in the IoT system. The attacker is attempting to hold the connection faked while the other nodes are trying to re-transmit the changed packet sequence number.

6.3 Middleware Layer Security Threats

In IoT, the middleware's function is to construct an abstraction between the application layer and the Network layer. Middleware also can offer efficient computing and storage resources (Mosenia & Jha, 2016). This layer includes APIs to fill up the Application layer needs. Application Middle-ware contains permanent storage warehouses, machine queuing services. Even though the middleware layer is useful for providing a robust and reliable IoT program, which is also vulnerable to numerous threats, these threats may take full control of infecting the middleware of the whole IoT program. The significant challenges in the middleware layer are cloud security and database security. Some possible threats of the middleware layer are discussed as follows.

Malicious Insider

People within the firm are known to be the lowest link in the chain whenever it comes to security. They need access to information depending on the level of numerous access controls. Additionally, insiders can end up removing or tempering actual data for the advantage of personal. This security problem could be solved by implementing new network security mechanisms where not all data would be accessible to all employees, but rather selective access according to the position of the individual in the enterprise. Malicious insiders typically conduct attacks on the middleware layer, and the effect can differ from low to high. (Tuna et al., 2017) .

Denial of Service (DOS) Attack and Distributed Senial of Service (DDOS) Attack

It is one of the most primitive and still widely practised attacks in IoT. In this attack, the attacker transmits data streams to the attacked node and keeps on transmitting until it exhausts. It also keeps network traffic high, and ultimately the authorized nodes cannot communicate with each other. While in DDOS, the attack is launched by continuous flooding of data streams from multiple malicious nodes(Ngu et al., 2016). All these nodes keep the network traffic high by sending multiple data streams and keep the node busy by responding. Here some legitimate nodes also try to communicate with the node under attack, but due to heavy traffic load, their requests are never entertained. This attack can be launched at all layers, but the attack at the perception layer causes tremendous damage to the system (Din et al., 2018).

Man-in-the-Middle Attack

MiTM attacks on an IoT system have important impacts an attacker can take charge of an intellectual in an industrial IoT environment Sensor. In this situation, an attacker is able to spy or track communication between two iot nodes and access their personal information or manipulate the messages in an unprotected channel during transmission.

Standard Query Language (SQL) Injection Attack

Often vulnerable to middleware through attacks of SQL injection (SQLi). In such threats, these attackers may inject malicious SQL statements into the program (Q. Zhang & Wang, 2009) (Dorai & Kannan, 2011). The attackers would then acquire private connections of any user information and can also change documents from the database (Razzaque, Milojevic-Jevric, Palade, & Clarke, 2015). Enable Protection Framework for Web Application Open Web Application Security Project (OWASP) has described SQLi as a significant challenge to web security top 10 in the 2018 OWASP paper.

Signature Wrapping Attack

In the web services used in the middleware, eXtensible Markup Language (XML) signatures are used (Kumar, Rajendran, Bindhumadhava, & Babu, 2017). In a signature wrapping attack, the attacker breaks the signature algorithm and can execute operations or modify the eavesdropped message by exploiting vulnerabilities in Simple Object Access Protocol (SOAP).

Cloud Malware Injection

In malware injection in the cloud, an intruder can get hold and insert maliciously coding or virtual machine into the cloud. The intruder pretends to be a legitimate service. Build an instance of a virtual computer or a malicious application of operation. In this way, the intruder can gain Links to the victim's support demands, and It is possible to collect confidential data that can be changed as per the case.

Flooding Attack in Cloud

This intrusion is just the same as the DoS attack in the cloud and affects the quality of service (QoS). To deplete cloud services, an intruder regularly sends several requests to an opponent. These attacks may have a considerable effect on cloud computing by growing the demand for cloud data centres.

6.4 Application Layer Security Threats

CoAP Security

The use of the Constrained Application Protocol (CoAP) is quite similar to Hypertext Transfer Protocol (HTTP), although using DTLS gives end-to-end encryption. The CoAP messages adopt a pre-defined framework presented in Request for Comments-7252 (RFC-7252) which is necessary for such a proto-col to use encryption mechanisms for protected communications (Shelby, Hartke, & Bormann, 2014).

Insecure Interfaces

Unprotected interfaces are the main security threats to the application layer. Customers of the IoT service typically access suitable resources via web interfaces, and these interfaces are treated as a failure point in their hosting environments.

Insecure Software and Operating System

IoT System Software/Firmware can host a malicious application due to misconfiguration (Alaba, Oth-man, Hashem, & Alotaibi, 2017). As a consequence, several security problems can occur due to weekly code testing or misconfiguration.

Middleware Security

The main goal of IoT middleware is to provide safe connectivity between various types of IoT modules and interfaces. Hence, different IoT framework for interacting with other applications utilizing middle-wares (Conzon et al., 2012).

Sniffing Attacks

Sniffer apps can be used by attackers to track network traffic in IoT apps. It enables the intruder to access sensitive user data if inadequate protection measures are enforced to prevent it (Swamy, Jadhav, & Kulkarni, 2017).

DDoS (Distributed Denial of Service)

Its principle of operation is much like conventional Denial of Service threat. It is therefore executed concurrently by several attackers.

Social Engineering

A significant challenge to the application layer is to access personal information through chatting, understanding each other etc.

7. COUNTERMEASURES AGAINST IoT THREATS

Security challenges in each layer of IoT architecture involved with all perception-based, network-based, middleware-based and application-based. In this section, we present a taxonomy based on state-of-art countermeasures for each security threats. All countermeasures against IoT attacks are shown in Table 1.

Most of the perception-layer safety concerns in IoT environments occur due to a lack of precise control to operate and manage linked devices. Also, the distribution of the implementation of perception layer devices in each IoT application setting creates essential security risks, as shown in Table 1. However, we can mitigate the risk of security challenges by applying an appropriate mechanism. Timestamp and nonce options are using against replay attacks, and timing attacks can be protected by bit checking. Key distribution protocol for node addition and revocation will provide a better solution to avoid risk issues in Node capture and node tempering attack. Randomized Watermarking Filtering Scheme (RWFS) is providing a solution for IoT malicious data threats. Localization or channel based detection can protect from identity spoofing and Sybil attacks.

As mentioned in Table 1, we discuss the proposed countermeasures; the network layer of IoT is facing a lot of threats most of the time. In the network layer of the IoT system, Replay Attack is a pervasive security issue, but with the help of checksum by a hash value, threats can be prevented. Using a lighter model of encryption schemes will significantly minimize the majority of severe attacks in the network layer. Checksum and encryption system can prevent from high- risk issues such as RPL routing threat, Session Hijacking, preserving privacy and secure authentication.

Installing a protection function system such as a network firewall and Intrusion Detection System (IDS) will still minimize the level of the security risks. Intrusion Detection System is beneficial to protect the Sinkhole and wormhole attack. In current times, the use of AI techniques in the IDS will have led to increased detection rates and lower false alarms (Pajouh, Javidan, Khayami, Ali, & Choo, 2016). In summary, there three key solutions for the network layer security and privacy challenges in the IoT environments: (a) Implementing appropriate (lightweight) encryption systems to maintain conventionality and integrity of the data based on the domain application of the IoT (b) Installing suitable tracing parameters like a timestamp for the authorizing the transferred packets (c) Implementing an appropriate threat hunting module for detecting threats and mitigating destructive propagation.

The middleware layer is essential for providing an accurate and stable IoT application and is also vulnerable to common threats. By attacking middleware, these threats can take control over the entire IoT application. Server safety and cloud safety are several other significant security challenges in the middleware layer. Role-Based Access Control (RBAC) is used for avoiding malicious insider attacks, and CEPIDS is the best-proposed solution for the DOS & DDOS threats. Table 1 summarizes the middleware layer threats with its impacts and the countermeasures proposed.

The security issues in the IoT application layer placed existing subscribers to a question of whether or not to implement IoT systems in their workplaces. Luckily, substantial research has been carried out to resolve the common security challenges in this layer. As mentioned in Table 1, we discuss the proposed countermeasures; this is taken from the latest studies for any security threats that occur in the application layer. We also have a propagation column to display the effect of the issues and the corresponding solutions. CoAP security challenges are resolved with the help of the DTLS and Proxy Mirroring mechanism. Secure Coding and Transport Layer Security (TLS) are powerful techniques to fight against Cross-Site Scripting (XSS) and SQL injection challenges. As we described earlier, because of the low computing capability of IoT machines, the firmware and operating system (OS) runs under the compact system design, and this challenge is raising security issues. Security threats between IoT systems (connected things) are also a common problem in most IoT domain applications, especially in transport and mobility environments. In the application layer, middleware security challenges are solved by secure communication channels with authentication, which provides secure policy, gateway and key management. Finally, we can say that application-layer security problems will be handled by secure communication and secure techniques in the IoT environment.

8. MACHINE LEARNING EMPOWERED IoT SECURITY

Machine learning is an essential technique of artificial intelligence, which prepares systems using various algorithms and allows systems to learn from their experiences instead of directly programming them. Last few years, these ML technologies have been widely used for IoT security. So, these ML methods can easily detect various IoT threats at the first stage by analyzing the behaviour of the machines. And correct countermeasures also be provided using multiple ML algorithms for resource-limited IoT devices. In this section, first, we discuss ML technologies and then ML-based solutions for IoT security.

Most popular ML techniques like supervised techniques and unsupervised techniques would be used to find threats in IoT devices and to implement the most effective security policy. Figure 4 presents some ML algorithms used for the security of the IoT network.

Table 1. Taxonomy of Attacks and Countermeasures in IoT Layers

Attacks	Security Impact	Countermeasures
Affected Layer: Perception Layer		
Replay Attack	Medium	Introduction of timestamp and nonce options for protecting against replay attacks
Timing Attack	Low to Medium	Bit checking to remove branches in additive modulus operator
Node Capture attack/ Node tempering attack	Low to Medium	Key distribution protocol for node addition and revocation
Unauthorized Access to the Tags	Medium to High	A Spatial Variant Apodization (SVA) algorithm is implemented at three layers to ensure secure tag generation and authentication.
Malicious Data	Low to Medium	Randomized Watermarking Filtering Scheme (RWFS) for IoT
Identity Spoofing	Medium to High	Localization or channel based detection
Sybil Attack	Low	Sybil attack detection using one-time localization
Affected Layer: Network Layer		
Replay Attack	Medium to High	define timestamp and authentication parameter for packets verification, define checksum by the hash value
Insecure nearest node discovery	Medium to High	Authentication by encrypted Elliptic Curve Cryptography (ECC) based signatures
Buffer Overflow attack	Medium to High	installing threat hunting modules like IDS
RPL routing attack	Medium to High	authentication via the lightweight encryption system, and monitoring connected devices
Sinkhole and Wormhole attacks	Medium to High	verification using hash systems, trust level management, device communication analysis, anomaly detection via IDS, using encrypted key management, signal strength monitoring
Sybil attacks	Medium to High	Graph analysis, user interaction analysis, Applying access control list
Authentication and secure communication	Medium to High	lightweight ticket granting system, applying symmetric and asymmetric encryption system for encrypting packet payload dispatch type values with, collecting logs
end-to-end security	Medium to High	installing IPSec, applying advance encryption system for authentication and authorization
Session Hijacking	Medium to High	using the secret key for the long-time session, the lightweight encryption system
Affected Layer: Middleware Layer		
Malicious Insider	Medium to High	RBAC based authorization model
DOS & DDOS Attack	Medium to High	CUPIDS for attack detection
Affected Layer: Application Layer		
CoAP security with internet	Medium to High	Using DTLS, secure application Proxy and Resource Directory
Insecure interfaces	Medium to High	Password strength verification, secure coding (SQLi and XSS), and installing application gateway firewalls
Insecure Firmware/OS	Medium to High	Regular secure updates of software/firmware, use of file signatures, and encryption with validation
Middleware security	Medium to High	Secure communication channel with authentication, define security policies, key management and distribution, install secure gateways & M2M components, lightweight encryption systems

Figure 4. Machine Learning Classification

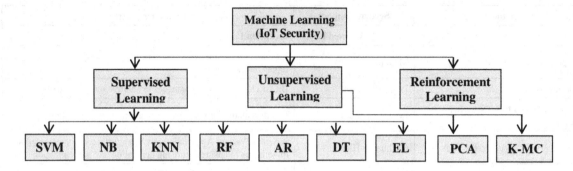

8.1 Supervised Machine Learning

The supervised learning method is a learning method, where output is categorized based on input parameters (features). So it is essential to train the algorithms at the initial phase of supervised learning, which are then used to simulate or identify the new input (Chang, Li, & Yang, 2017). We will discuss the supervised learning algorithms, i.e., Support Vector Machines (SVM), Bayesian Theorem, K-Nearest Neighbor, Random Forest, and Association Rule with their advantages, disadvantages and applications in IoT security.

Figure 5. Pictorial illustration of SVM Learning Techniques

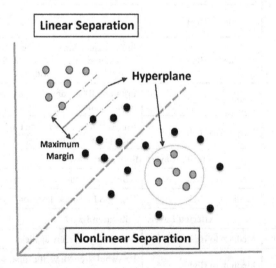

8.1.1 Support Vector Machine (SVM)

SVM is a discriminative classifier that is formally designed by a separated hyperplane. It is a representation of examples as points in space that are mapped so that points of different categories are separated by a gap as wide as possible. The objective of the hyperplane is to minimize error at the maximum margin by increasing the distance between the hyperplane and the most adjacent sample points of each class. When you have a hyperplane after analysis, it becomes nonlinear, and then SVM Uses the kernel function to create it linearly by adding an extra one feature. Even it's very tough to use optimal kernel function on the SVM. The strengths of SVMs are their high accuracy level, which makes it easy for security applications in IoT such as intrusion detection, malware detection and smart grid attacks etc. (Anandakumar & Umamaheswari, 2017). It's tough to choose a kernel optimally. Understanding and interpreting SVM-based models are also challenging. Figure 5 shows the pictorial illustration of SVM learning techniques.

Figure 6. Illustration of KNN Learning

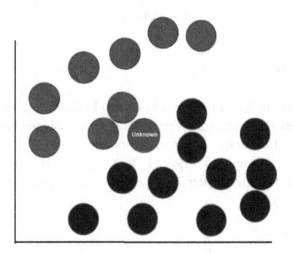

8.1.2 Bayesian Theorem

This theorem is one of the most popular, faster and simplest ML algorithms. It is based on the probability of statistics theorem for learning distribution. This type of ML method creates new results based on current information using Bayesian probability. It is called Naïve Bayes (NB). This method is used to detect anomaly and Intrusion detection in the network layer of IoT (Li, Zhang, Peng, & Yang, 2018). Easy to implementation and understanding, robustness and requiring very low data for classification are the advantages of NB. It controls features independent so can't track important clues from the relationship.

8.1.3 K-Nearest Neighbor (KNN)

KNN algorithm is a type of supervised Ml algorithm, which can be used Euclidian distance. It is a non-parametric statistical method. Figure 6 presents the KNN classes in which new input samples are grouped. The green circles are malicious activities, and the red circles are the regular activities of the device. The currently unidentified sample (orange circle) must be identified as malicious or normal activities. KNN method is a popular and effective ML algorithm for intrusion detection in IoT. KNN algorithm is easy to implement with low cost (Tsai, Hsu, Lin, & Lin, 2009). But KNN is a little bit time-consuming process to search the missing nodes, which is a big issue in terms of accurateness.

Figure 7. Basic Construction of Random Forest Learning Method

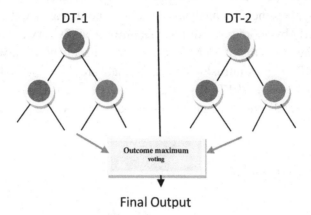

8.1.4 Random Forest (RF)

RF is a unique supervised ML method which develops lots of Decision Tree based on a random selection of data and random selection variables to get correct and suitable estimation model for clients, as shown in Figure 7. RF considered the average the average output and needs less inputs (Cutler et al., 2007). RF is normally used for detecting anomaly attacks, DDoD attacks and illegal IoT devices verification in network surface threats. RF is slightly better classification results in comparison of SVM and KNN to detect DDoS threats in IoT system.

Figure 8. Association Rules between Unknown Variables

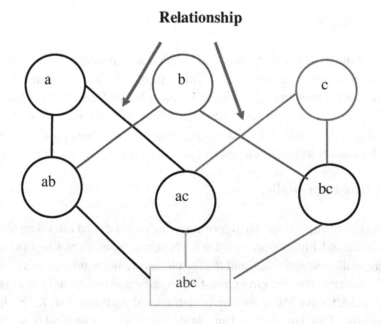

8.1.5 Association Rule (AR)

AR algorithm is also a type of supervised machine learning technique. It is commonly used in the IoT system as it has very high time complexity and produces outputs on expectations that may not be accurately results for the massive and complex model (S. Kotsiantis & Kanellopoulos, 2006). Figure 8 shows that unknown variables depend on mutual relationship them in a given data set. This model is used to detect intrusion in the IoT environment. This algorithm is easy to use, but the major disadvantages of the AR method are time complexity.

8.1.6 Decision Tree

DT algorithm belongs to the family of supervised learning algorithms. In comparison to all other supervised learning algorithms, the decision tree algorithm could also be used to solve classification and regression challenges. DT method uses a prediction model to learn from training samples by representing them as branches and leaves, as shown in Figure 9. The main strengths of the DT- based method are such as easy to implement, handling the massive volume of data samples and straightforward structure. DT needs a large storage capacity of its construction nature; it is a drawback of this ML-based model. It makes the learning algorithm more complicated if some DTs are considered to remove problems. DTs are commonly used as classifiers in security applications such as DDoS and ID (S. B. Kotsiantis, Zaharakis, & Pintelas, 2007).

Figure 9. Simple Constructor of Decision Tree-based Learning

Decision Tree

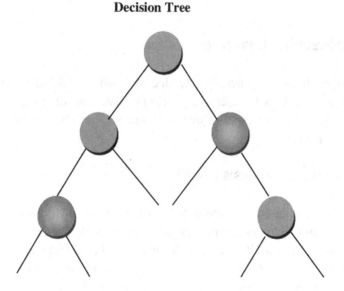

8.1.7 Ensemble Learning

The main objective of EL is a combination of heterogeneous or omogeneous multi-classifiers to achieve an accurate result. In the first stage of Machine Learning development, all learning algorithms have their benefits and achievements in specific applications or dataset. Since EL uses multiple learning algorithms, the approach is well suited for most of the significant problems. However, EL has a high level of difficulty over time, compared with any other single classifier technique. EL eliminates differences and is over-fitting to be robust. This method is widely used to detect an anomaly, malware and intrusion detection (Reddy, Murali, & Rajeshwar, 2019).

Figure 10. K-mean Clustering Learning Algorithm

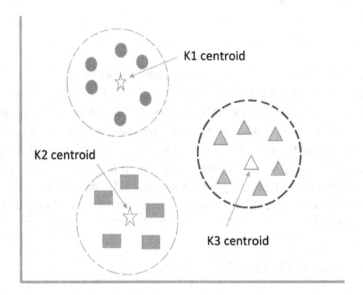

8.2 Unsupervised Machine Learning

Unsupervised learning methods are generally intended to examine unlabeled data. The main g of an unsupervised learning algorithm is to categories the input data into distinctive groups by observing the similarity between them. Various types of unsupervised ML have been used for the security of IoT systems to detect DoS attacks.

8.2.1 Principal Component Analysis (PCA)

PCA, also known as the technique of feature reduction conversion of a massive volume of data into small yet has almost the same quantity of information as in the main package. So, the complexity of a structure is thereby reduced by PCA. This approach can be used to detect real-time intrusion threats in the IoT environment (Candès, Li, Ma, & Wright, 2011). The combination of PCA and other Machine Learning algorithms can be deployed to provide better security protocols.

8.2.2 K-Mean Clustering

It is a type of unsupervised learning method. It produces tiny groups for the categorization of the data samples like a cluster. This is a well-known algorithm that uses clustering techniques as present in Figure 10. These methods are implemented easily. This ML method is best for smart city to search suitable place for living. But this unsupervised algorithm is less efficient with comparison of other supervised algorithm. K-mean Clustering is specially used in Sybill threats detection and anomaly detection (Muniyandi, Rajeswari, & Rajaram, 2012).

8.3 ML Based Solutions for IoT Security

ML-based security solutions for the IoT system become an important area of research, and most of the researchers are getting attention, particularly the IoT system, with security challenges and their solutions last few years. Various ML algorithms in this segment were suggested as critical remedies to secure IoT systems. Mainly these solutions have been found based on the architectural layer of the IoT environment.

General authentication methods are not up to the mark for security point of view in the Physical surface. But Machine Learning methods may be a substitute for authentication in the Perception layer. (Xiao, Li, Han, Liu, & Zhuang, 2016) presented that Q-learning based ML methods decrease the error rate of authentication by about 64.3% and also give much better performance besides standard authentication methods in the perception layer. The authors (Shi, Liu, Liu, & Chen, 2017) presented that the Reinforcement Learning (RL) method, which is very significant to avoid jamming attacks in the IoT network. The authors proposed a centralized system scheme for the aggressive jamming attack in IoT. An intelligent power distribution scheme and Access point of IoT is used to fight against jamming attacks together. In another research (Han, Xiao, & Poor, 2017), RL and deep CNN have been used to prevent jamming signals for cognitive radios that improve RL accuracy. Cognitive radio (CR) tools have dynamic capabilities that change depending on the working environment (Bkassiny, Li, & Jayaweera, 2012).

SVM, NN, and K-NN ML methods are used to identify the intrusion threat in the IoT environment of the Network layer (Raza, Chung, Duquennoy, Voigt, & Roedig, 2010). NN is used to detect DoS attacks in the IoT system by the control system, which is following multilayer perception. The authors presented an ANN algorithm-based model to detect a DDoS attack. (Kulkarni, Pino, & Mohsenin, 2016) demonstrated that the SVM-based ML model in the IoT system was able to obtain a high number of attack detection rate (99.4 percent).

Accordingly, various ML-based models such as K-NN, RF, Q-learning, Dyna-Q are being used to protect the IoT system from web-based malware detection threats (Kulkarni et al., 2016). The authors proposed a supervised K-NN and RF ML model to find malware attacks. In the study, Q-learning shows better performance to detect latency and accuracy than the Dyna-Q-based detection learning method.

9. CONCLUSION AND FUTURE RESEARCH

IoT has been at the forefront of every field of life for the last couple of years; smart home, smart grid, smart agricultural, smart health care in Corona Virus Disease-19 (COVID-19) protection and travel. This change has made it easier for IoT to reach from anywhere else in the world via smartphones or website. The attackers were conscious of these progressions, and every day there are many attacks. In this chapter, numerous security challenges and threats in the different layers of an IoT system are discussed. The issues with perception layer, network layer, middleware layer and application layer are discussed with proposed solutions. The current and future countermeasures for IoT security vulnerabilities, including machine learning, were also discussed. Different open challenges and problems derived from the solution have also been addressed. This study provides feedback on the security requirements of the IoT system and their effect as a priority factor for dealing with these issues. IoT security has already been addressed at the state-of-the-art with so many of the future key research avenues to boost IoT security standards. It is expected that this survey will act as a valuable resource to ensure protection for future IoT applications. It is clear that promising development is being made, but there is still a long way to go in the area of security to secure the IoT systems. In addition, ML algorithms were presented with potential challenges which may enable future researchers to achieve their ultimate goals and set their aim in the field of IoT.

REFERENCES

Agiwal, M., Roy, A., & Saxena, N. (2016). Next generation 5G wireless networks: A comprehensive survey. *IEEE Communications Surveys and Tutorials*, *18*(3), 1617–1655. doi:10.1109/COMST.2016.2532458

Alaba, F. A., Othman, M., Hashem, I. A. T., & Alotaibi, F. (2017). Internet of Things security: A survey. *Journal of Network and Computer Applications*, *88*, 10–28. doi:10.1016/j.jnca.2017.04.002

Anandakumar, H., & Umamaheswari, K. (2017). Supervised machine learning techniques in cognitive radio networks during cooperative spectrum handovers. *Cluster Computing*, *20*(2), 1505–1515. doi:10.100710586-017-0798-3

Ashton, K. (2009). That 'internet of things' thing. *RFID Journal, 22*(7), 97-114.

Babar, S., Mahalle, P., Stango, A., Prasad, N., & Prasad, R. (2010). *Proposed security model and threat taxonomy for the Internet of Things (IoT)*. Paper presented at the International Conference on Network Security and Applications. 10.1007/978-3-642-14478-3_42

Bkassiny, M., Li, Y., & Jayaweera, S. K. (2012). A survey on machine-learning techniques in cognitive radios. *IEEE Communications Surveys and Tutorials, 15*(3), 1136–1159. doi:10.1109/SURV.2012.100412.00017

Candès, E. J., Li, X., Ma, Y., & Wright, J. (2011). Robust principal component analysis? [JACM]. *Journal of the Association for Computing Machinery*, *58*(3), 1–37. doi:10.1145/1970392.1970395

Chang, Y., Li, W., & Yang, Z. (2017). *Network intrusion detection based on random forest and support vector machine*. Paper presented at the 2017 IEEE international conference on computational science and engineering (CSE) and IEEE international conference on embedded and ubiquitous computing (EUC). 10.1109/CSE-EUC.2017.118

Conzon, D., Bolognesi, T., Brizzi, P., Lotito, A., Tomasi, R., & Spirito, M. A. (2012). *The virtus middleware: An xmpp based architecture for secure iot communications*. Paper presented at the 2012 21st International Conference on Computer Communications and Networks (ICCCN). 10.1109/ICCCN.2012.6289309

Cooper, K. A. (2015). *Security for the Internet of Things*. Academic Press.

Cutler, D. R., Edwards, T. C. Jr, Beard, K. H., Cutler, A., Hess, K. T., Gibson, J., & Lawler, J. J. (2007). Random forests for classification in ecology. *Ecology*, *88*(11), 2783–2792. doi:10.1890/07-0539.1 PMID:18051647

Din, I. U., Guizani, M., Kim, B.-S., Hassan, S., & Khan, M. K. (2018). Trust management techniques for the Internet of Things: A survey. *IEEE Access: Practical Innovations, Open Solutions*, *7*, 29763–29787. doi:10.1109/ACCESS.2018.2880838

Dorai, R., & Kannan, V. (2011). SQL injection-database attack revolution and prevention. *J. Int'l Com. L. & Tech.*, *6*, 224.

Dvir, A., & Buttyan, L. (2011). *VeRA-version number and rank authentication in RPL*. Paper presented at the 2011 IEEE Eighth International Conference on Mobile Ad-Hoc and Sensor Systems. 10.1109/MASS.2011.76

Emami-Naeini, P., Dixon, H., Agarwal, Y., & Cranor, L. F. (2019). Exploring how privacy and security factor into IoT device purchase behavior. *Proceedings of the 2019 CHI Conference on Human Factors in Computing Systems*. 10.1145/3290605.3300764

Farris, I., Taleb, T., Khettab, Y., & Song, J. (2018). A survey on emerging SDN and NFV security mechanisms for IoT systems. *IEEE Communications Surveys and Tutorials*, *21*(1), 812–837. doi:10.1109/COMST.2018.2862350

Fernández-Caramés, T. M., & Fraga-Lamas, P. (2018). A Review on the Use of Blockchain for the Internet of Things. *IEEE Access: Practical Innovations, Open Solutions*, *6*, 32979–33001. doi:10.1109/ACCESS.2018.2842685

Granjal, J., Monteiro, E., & Silva, J. S. (2013). *Application-layer security for the WoT: Extending CoAP to support end-to-end message security for Internet-integrated sensing applications*. Paper presented at the International Conference on Wired/Wireless Internet Communication. 10.1007/978-3-642-38401-1_11

Han, G., Xiao, L., & Poor, H. V. (2017). *Two-dimensional anti-jamming communication based on deep reinforcement learning*. Paper presented at the 2017 IEEE International Conference on Acoustics, Speech and Signal Processing (ICASSP). 10.1109/ICASSP.2017.7952524

Hassija, V., Chamola, V., Saxena, V., Jain, D., Goyal, P., & Sikdar, B. (2019). A survey on IoT security: Application areas, security threats, and solution architectures. *IEEE Access: Practical Innovations, Open Solutions*, *7*, 82721–82743. doi:10.1109/ACCESS.2019.2924045

Hummen, R., Hiller, J., Wirtz, H., Henze, M., Shafagh, H., & Wehrle, K. (2013). 6LoWPAN fragmentation attacks and mitigation mechanisms. *Proceedings of the sixth ACM conference on security and privacy in wireless and mobile networks*. 10.1145/2462096.2462107

Jing, Q., Vasilakos, A. V., Wan, J., Lu, J., & Qiu, D. (2014). Security of the Internet of Things: Perspectives and challenges. *Wireless Networks*, *20*(8), 2481–2501. doi:10.100711276-014-0761-7

Kasem-Madani, S., & Meier, M. (2015). *Security and privacy policy languages: A survey, categorization and gap identification*. arXiv preprint arXiv:1512.00201.

Kaur, P., & Gurm, J. (2016). Detect and prevent HELLO FLOOD attack using centralized technique in WSN. *International Journal of Computer Science and Engineering Technology, 7*(8), 379–381.

Khairi, A., Farooq, M., Waseem, M., & Mazhar, S. (2015). A Critical Analysis on the Security Concerns of Internet of Things (IoT). *Perception*, 111.

Kim, H. (2008). *Protection against packet fragmentation attacks at 6LoWPAN adaptation layer.* Paper presented at the 2008 International Conference on Convergence and Hybrid Information Technology. 10.1109/ICHIT.2008.261

Kotsiantis, S., & Kanellopoulos, D. (2006). Association rules mining: A recent overview. *GESTS International Transactions on Computer Science and Engineering, 32*(1), 71–82.

Kotsiantis, S. B., Zaharakis, I., & Pintelas, P. (2007). Supervised machine learning: A review of classification techniques. *Emerging Artificial Intelligence Applications in Computer Engineering, 160*(1), 3-24.

Kulkarni, A., Pino, Y., & Mohsenin, T. (2016). *SVM-based real-time hardware Trojan detection for many-core platform.* Paper presented at the 2016 17th International Symposium on Quality Electronic Design (ISQED). 10.1109/ISQED.2016.7479228

Kumar, J., Rajendran, B., Bindhumadhava, B., & Babu, N. S. C. (2017). *XML wrapping attack mitigation using positional token.* Paper presented at the 2017 International Conference on Public Key Infrastructure and its Applications (PKIA). 10.1109/PKIA.2017.8278958

Li, L., Zhang, H., Peng, H., & Yang, Y. (2018). Nearest neighbors based density peaks approach to intrusion detection. *Chaos, Solitons, and Fractals, 110*, 33–40. doi:10.1016/j.chaos.2018.03.010

Lin, J., Yu, W., Zhang, N., Yang, X., Zhang, H., & Zhao, W. (2017). A survey on internet of things: Architecture, enabling technologies, security and privacy, and applications. *IEEE Internet of Things Journal, 4*(5), 1125–1142. doi:10.1109/JIOT.2017.2683200

Liu, T., & Lu, D. (2012). *The application and development of IoT.* Paper presented at the 2012 International Symposium on Information Technologies in Medicine and Education.

Mathur, A., Newe, T., & Rao, M. (2016). Defence against black hole and selective forwarding attacks for medical WSNs in the IoT. *Sensors (Basel), 16*(1), 118. doi:10.339016010118 PMID:26797620

Mishra, A. K., Tripathy, A. K., Puthal, D., & Yang, L. T. (2018). Analytical model for sybil attack phases in internet of things. *IEEE Internet of Things Journal, 6*(1), 379–387. doi:10.1109/JIOT.2018.2843769

Mitrokotsa, A., Rieback, M. R., & Tanenbaum, A. S. (2010). Classifying RFID attacks and defenses. *Information Systems Frontiers, 12*(5), 491–505. doi:10.100710796-009-9210-z

Mosenia, A., & Jha, N. K. (2016). A comprehensive study of security of internet-of-things. *IEEE Transactions on Emerging Topics in Computing, 5*(4), 586–602. doi:10.1109/TETC.2016.2606384

Muniyandi, A. P., Rajeswari, R., & Rajaram, R. (2012). Network anomaly detection by cascading k-Means clustering and C4. 5 decision tree algorithm. *Procedia Engineering, 30*, 174–182. doi:10.1016/j.proeng.2012.01.849

Ngu, A. H., Gutierrez, M., Metsis, V., Nepal, S., & Sheng, Q. Z. (2016). IoT middleware: A survey on issues and enabling technologies. *IEEE Internet of Things Journal, 4*(1), 1–20. doi:10.1109/JIOT.2016.2615180

Oriwoh, E., al-Khateeb, H., & Conrad, M. (2016). *Responsibility and Non-repudiation in resource-constrained Internet of Things scenarios.* Academic Press.

Pajouh, H. H., Javidan, R., Khayami, R., Ali, D., & Choo, K.-K. R. (2016). A two-layer dimension reduction and two-tier classification model for anomaly-based intrusion detection in IoT backbone networks. *IEEE Transactions on Emerging Topics in Computing.*

Park, B. (2011). Threats and security analysis for enhanced secure neighbor discovery protocol (SEND) of IPv6 NDP security. *International Journal of Control and Automation, 4*(4).

Park, N., & Kang, N. (2016). Mutual authentication scheme in secure internet of things technology for comfortable lifestyle. *Sensors (Basel), 16*(1), 20. doi:10.339016010020 PMID:26712759

Pongle, P., & Chavan, G. (2015). Real time intrusion and wormhole attack detection in internet of things. *International Journal of Computers and Applications, 121*(9).

Pu, C., & Hajjar, S. (2018). *Mitigating Forwarding misbehaviors in RPL-based low power and lossy networks.* Paper presented at the 2018 15th IEEE Annual Consumer Communications & Networking Conference (CCNC). 10.1109/CCNC.2018.8319164

Rashid, M. M., Hossain, E., & Bhargava, V. K. (2009). Cross-layer analysis of downlink V-BLAST MIMO transmission exploiting multiuser diversity. *IEEE Transactions on Wireless Communications, 8*(9), 4568–4579. doi:10.1109/TWC.2009.080513

Raza, S., Chung, T., Duquennoy, S., Voigt, T., & Roedig, U. (2010). *Securing internet of things with lightweight ipsec.* Academic Press.

Raza, S., Duquennoy, S., Höglund, J., Roedig, U., & Voigt, T. (2014). Secure communication for the Internet of Things—A comparison of link-layer security and IPsec for 6LoWPAN. *Security and Communication Networks, 7*(12), 2654–2668. doi:10.1002ec.406

Razzaque, M. A., Milojevic-Jevric, M., Palade, A., & Clarke, S. (2015). Middleware for internet of things: A survey. *IEEE Internet of Things Journal, 3*(1), 70–95. doi:10.1109/JIOT.2015.2498900

Reddy, R. V., Murali, D., & Rajeshwar, J. (2019). Context-aware middleware architecture for IoT-based smart healthcare applications. In *Innovations in Computer Science and Engineering* (pp. 557–567). Springer. doi:10.1007/978-981-13-7082-3_64

Reding, V. (2009). *Internet of the future: Europe must be a key player.* Speech to the Lisbon Council.

Shelby, Z., Hartke, K., & Bormann, C. (2014). *The constrained application protocol (coap)(rfc 7252).* Available online. http://www. rfc-editor. org/info/rfc7252

Shi, C., Liu, J., Liu, H., & Chen, Y. (2017). Smart user authentication through actuation of daily activities leveraging WiFi-enabled IoT. *Proceedings of the 18th ACM International Symposium on Mobile Ad Hoc Networking and Computing.* 10.1145/3084041.3084061

Stephen, R., & Arockiam, L. (2017). Intrusion detection system to detect sinkhole attack on RPL protocol in Internet of Things. *International Journal of Electrical Electronics and Computer Science*, *4*(4), 16–20.

Suo, H., Wan, J., Zou, C., & Liu, J. (2012). *Security in the internet of things: a review.* Paper presented at the 2012 international conference on computer science and electronics engineering. 10.1109/ICC-SEE.2012.373

Suresh, P., Daniel, J. V., Parthasarathy, V., & Aswathy, R. (2014). *A state of the art review on the Internet of Things (IoT) history, technology and fields of deployment.* Paper presented at the 2014 International conference on science engineering and management research (ICSEMR). 10.1109/ICSEMR.2014.7043637

Swamy, S. N., Jadhav, D., & Kulkarni, N. (2017). *Security threats in the application layer in IOT applications.* Paper presented at the 2017 International Conference on I-SMAC (IoT in Social, Mobile, Analytics and Cloud)(I-SMAC). 10.1109/I-SMAC.2017.8058395

Tsai, C.-F., Hsu, Y.-F., Lin, C.-Y., & Lin, W.-Y. (2009). Intrusion detection by machine learning: A review. *Expert Systems With Applications, 36*(10), 11994-12000.

Tuna, G., Kogias, D. G., Gungor, V. C., Gezer, C., Taşkın, E., & Ayday, E. (2017). A survey on information security threats and solutions for Machine to Machine (M2M) communications. *Journal of Parallel and Distributed Computing, 109*, 142–154. doi:10.1016/j.jpdc.2017.05.021

Xiao, L., Li, Y., Han, G., Liu, G., & Zhuang, W. (2016). PHY-layer spoofing detection with reinforcement learning in wireless networks. *IEEE Transactions on Vehicular Technology*, *65*(12), 10037–10047. doi:10.1109/TVT.2016.2524258

Yang, Y., Wu, L., Yin, G., Li, L., & Zhao, H. (2017). A survey on security and privacy issues in Internet-of-Things. *IEEE Internet of Things Journal, 4*(5), 1250–1258. doi:10.1109/JIOT.2017.2694844

Yu, W., Liang, F., He, X., Hatcher, W. G., Lu, C., Lin, J., & Yang, X. (2017). A survey on the edge computing for the Internet of Things. *IEEE Access: Practical Innovations, Open Solutions*, *6*, 6900–6919. doi:10.1109/ACCESS.2017.2778504

Zhang, K., Liang, X., Lu, R., & Shen, X. (2014). Sybil attacks and their defenses in the internet of things. *IEEE Internet of Things Journal, 1*(5), 372–383. doi:10.1109/JIOT.2014.2344013

Zhang, Q., & Wang, X. (2009). *SQL injections through back-end of RFID system.* Paper presented at the 2009 International Symposium on Computer Network and Multimedia Technology. 10.1109/CNMT.2009.5374533

Chapter 5
Change Management in the Digital Transformation Projects:
Process Control Challenge

Nuno Geada

https://orcid.org/0000-0003-3755-0711

Polytechnic Institute of Setúbal, Portugal

ABSTRACT

Digitization is currently radically and exponentially changing business across all sectors. Organizations are facing the challenge of managing all rapid and repetitive adaptation in the face of changing infrastructures in order to correspond with the needs of the digital age, so organizations must be aware to avoid unnecessary disruptions to business. The digital economy shows great growth potential in the scope of transactions between companies. Today, consumers have a huge impact on the economy, as we are in a society that is always "online" and well informed.

INTRODUCTION

Digitization is currently radically and exponentially changing business across all sectors. Organizations are facing the challenge of managing all rapid and repetitive adaptation in the face of changing infrastructures to correspond with the needs of the digital age, so organizations must be aware to avoid unnecessary disruptions to business. The Digital Economy shows great growth potential, in the scope of transactions between companies. Today, consumers have a huge impact on the economy, as we are in a society that is always "online" and well informed.

Regarding digital transformation, it integrates digital technology covering all areas of organizations, triggering changes fundamentally in the way the value chains to be delivered to customers are generated and triggered. There is also a cultural shift that requires organizations to continually challenge the status quo, which can sometimes fail when they apply the changes. Most companies fail to implement change projects in view of the "fears" generated by the "myths" surrounding the processes. It is a constant challenge to be able to control or predict the variables, because for this there are methodologies, such as

DOI: 10.4018/978-1-7998-4201-9.ch005

Copyright © 2021, IGI Global. Copying or distributing in print or electronic forms without written permission of IGI Global is prohibited.

ITIL, that allow managers using tools for the purpose, to apply good practices. ITIL allows the creation of procedural management models, in order to avoid waste and repetition of tasks, which constantly consume resources for organizations. Although to avoid the constantly consuming process resources it can be optimized with a suggested model.

MYTHS EMBRACING CHANGE IN DIGITAL TRANSFORMATION

To remain competitive, businesses around the world are increasingly investing in digital transformation. According to Andriole (2017), there are 5 Myths to overthrow that increase the path to the "unknown" world:

MYTH #1: *Every company should digitally transform*

Not every company, process, or business model requires digital transformation. Digital transformation is not a software upgrade or a supply chain improvement project. It is a planned digital shock to what may be a reasonably functioning system. For an example, to launch a digital transformation of business processes, it is necessary to purposefully model those processes with tools that enable creative, empirical simulations. For instance, the software programs that enable business process modelling and business simulations. So, as a first step to digitally transforming your processes, you need to honestly assess if your company can create digital models that simulate the nuances inherent in its procedures.

MYTH #2: *Digital transformation leverages emerging or disruptive technologies*

Most short-term transformational impact comes from "conventional" operational and strategic technology not from emerging or so-called "disruptive" technology. Most transformational leverage comes from tried-and-true operational technology (for example, networking and databases) and strategic technology (such as enterprise resource planning or customer relationship management software).

MYTH #3: *Profitable companies are the most likely to launch successful digital transformation projects*

If things are going well defined crassly as employee and shareholder wealth creation, then the chances of transforming anything meaningful are quite low. Failing companies are much more motivated to transform themselves, simply because they need to change something, if not everything quickly. Successful companies, especially if they are public companies, are understandably cautious about change. So, how many succeed companies without market duress have truly transformed their business models? Change is expensive, time-consuming, inexact, and painful. It is this sort makes the leaders who suggest it easy targets for in-house politics, especially when the change initiatives move slowly or stumble.

MYTH #4: *We need to disrupt our industry before someone else does*

Disruptive transformation seldom begins with market leaders whose business models have defined their industry categories for years. While market leaders pay lip service to their role as innovators and disruptors, they are usually unlikely champions of change until their profits begin to fall and their shareholders scream for transformation. Historically, industry disruptors have often been start-ups making bold bets on old industries.

Examples include Airbnb (hospitality), Uber and Lyft (transportation), Amazon (books, retail), and Netflix (entertainment).

MYTH #5: *Executives are hungry for digital transformation*

The number of executives who really want to transform their companies is relatively small, especially in public companies. Digital transformation requires strong support from upper management. And while the concept of digital transformation can be sold up the management chain, simply selling the concept is not enough. Transformations require overt, continuous support from the senior management team to succeed. And it is this sort of support public, persistent, enduring, and unwavering that is more difficult to secure than one might assume. Many executives are suspicious of risky change efforts that might affect their status in the company. Many executives are also challenged by the sheer complexity of digital transformation projects, especially when they learn how long they take.

MYTH AND INNOVATION STABILITY

Within a transformation program, you must take a combination of ITIL with good practices. The bigger picture approach that ITIL brings means starting with your problem for example, if you need to transform and touch every part of the business, how will you engage the business and what approaches in ITIL. The real goal needs to be sync with organizational strategy, therefore, pick up ITIL's Service Strategy to apply the best practice approach through the organization.

In fact, ITIL's Guiding Principles come of age with the demands of digital transformation: having a Focus on Value ensures the business is the driver of change, not IT; Design for Experience is all about organizations transforming based on user-centric design and experience, while to progress iteratively, involves sprints and continual feedback loops (Ferris, 2018).

How Control the Impact Triggered by Myth's?

So, how to control and prevent myths from becoming real and disrupting, avoiding the *"Management Obsession by process control"*? Organizations Top Management Administration acquires to control the change's process to avoid disruption. So, myths are directly related to fears because most of the time when idealizing to trigger a change. Myths are first created, derived from fears that coexist in the managers minds. This can be controlled with a methodology that applies good practices. It is possible to control the triggered impacts with a model created based on a methodology, such as ITIL.

ITIL (Cartlidge, et al., 2007) is a methodology created in the late 1980's (initially called the Central Computer and Telecommunications Agency (CCTA), which is based on the management of information technology (IT) services, applying the best practices to help companies achieve their business objectives, with the support of the Information Systems Services. This resulted in the synergy of the best processes and practices for the management of IT services, since from the 90's, several companies in Europe started to adopt these practices based on this methodology.

The ITIL (Cartlidge, et al., 2007) consists of the following items:

- **Service Strategy:** Defining business requirements and requirements;
- **Service Design**: Definition of the solution to be adopted;
- **Service Transition***: Related to the management of the changes made*;
- **Service Operation**: Ensures that services are managed based on *SLAs (Service Level Agreement)*;
- **Continual Service Improvement:** Maintain the constant improvement of services based on the PDCA cycle *(Plan, Do, Check, Act)*.

ITIL is a process control. So, it is possible to say that it can manage digital transformation in organizations, it's based on processes, and since any change or transformation must be controlled and managed, as it always presents risks. Change management focuses on the constant need for adaptation in the most varied application scenarios, as well as its structured control. There are personal, organizational or project changes. The change is present in several methodologies, standards, and standards, such as in the Information Technology Infrastructure Library - ITIL. Therefore, the implementation of the ITIL methodology emerged as a differentiating element in terms of efficiency and effectiveness gains, with implications for cost reduction, that is, the creation of good preventive maintenance, avoiding many difficulties in the future. So, the secret is in control the scope of change barriers to an opportunity, like communication, people, financial resources.

According to Anand (2018), ITSM Product Ambassador, the best practice guidance such as ITIL is there to guide organizations rather than compelling them to do something in a prescribed way. Sometime, when things need to be more prescriptive but, other times, it is necessary to be less focused on specific processes and procedures and to adopt and adapt at the right level. It is about understanding and achieving the goal/objective of each process area. So, the ITIL guidance focuses on the basic things that need to happen while not offering an implementation guide.

Instead, ITIL helps organization:

- Change the way they design and operate services;
- Communicate with and manage expectations of multiple stakeholders;
- Measure and improve the right things;
- Put in place a system that continually improves.

Digital Transformation Can Be an Organizational Challenge?

According to Ferris (2018), organizations that have recognized the value of frameworks and best practice approaches are picking the right ingredients from each of them for the job at hand. Among them, ITIL has absolutely helped organizations in taking a big picture view and adapting its guidance to their circumstances and requirements. Any organization transforming needs a solid foundation on which to build and ITIL provides that foundation if they pick the right building blocks: this means using processes that suit the organization rather than slavishly following the letter of the guidance. But what is vital to understand is that real digital transformation is an organizational change.

Therefore, Business Relationship Management (BRM) is absolutely core to this in helping communicate what transformation means to the organization. The same goes for using the Continual Service Improvement and Organizational Change Management approaches in ITIL.

An organization might understand its strategy, but the IT goals are often not aligned with the strategy equally. There may not be a holistic view across the business and IT. One of the reasons why negative resistance occurs is a lack of clarity on the goals and vision of a project and, likewise, an absence of leadership and governance at the top. A project implemented without clear, well-communicated goals and vision is the equivalent of throwing a dead cat over the neighbour's wall.

MODEL PROPOSAL

The suggestion of this model aims to support managers to manage change minimizing possible impacts. Nowadays there are still organizations, like hospitals, that do not adopt practices associated with ITIL. According to the results from the survey, 46.1% still do not apply these practices, however, 92.3% consider that ITIL has an associated change process. The origin of the creation of this model is based on the combination of procedural variables that constitute the ITIL cycle (Geada & Anunciação, 2020).

It should be noted that the word "change" is a resistance to the implementation from change. However, any necessary to create methodologies using tools to minimize the associated impacts. A methodology is not a definitive solution, but an impact minimizing agent, as there are no magic recipes to eliminate the least good impacts that arise from change, since any change or, as mentioned earlier, change or the idea of improvement will always have impact as we are changing very important variables, such as environment and routines (Geada, 2020).

Therefore, to minimize the less good impact generated by the need to make changes or changes, a methodology called "Improvement Idea Implementation Methodology (IIIM)" is used:

This model is designed to support managers in managing change and predicting possible impacts, as corroborating the data returned by the applied survey all change projects must be managed. The origin of the creation of this model is based on the combination of procedural variables that constitute the ITIL cycle versus the Plan-Do-Check-Act (PDCA) and Standardize-Do-Check-Act (SDCA) cycle (Geada, 2020).

CONCLUSION

The impact of investments, or the introduction of technological innovations in the context of the functioning of organizations creates the need to adapt the modus operandi of economic institutions. The literature warns of managers' lack of planning, technological and market pressure for innovation on change management.

There is a comfortable relationship between ITIL and change, but this evidence is not general as expected from the knowledge of the methodology. The ITIL methodology is very dynamic and can adapt very easily to any reality, so we just need to know what services we want from Information Systems, how we want them, and how they should be made available. It should be noted that the topic of change has no general "revenue" for any type of organization or economic sector. It is necessary to define an object, which should include a path that presents the steps considered core to the management of change. On the other hand, change need not be radical.

It is necessary to consolidate what is well done or considered appropriate to the organizational functioning and market demands, building a path of continuous improvement towards adapting to market evolution and customer needs, since most of the products and services of information Technology. The advantage of applying these methodologies lies in the possibility of developing an integrated vision in models, seeking greater competitive efficiency in business and efficiency in organizational functioning, ensuring a quality assurance strategy in service delivery, process optimization, productivity, customer satisfaction and growth and contributing to the stability and survival of an organization.

Figure 1. Implementation Methodology Improvement Ideas Scheme (Geada, 2020)

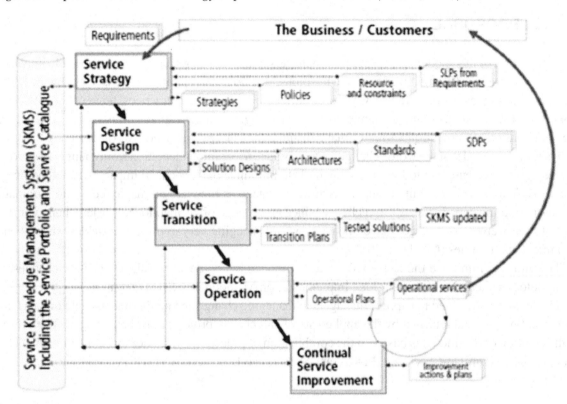

It is possible to consolidate control and management models of change such as IIIM which, when applied, allows to control and manage the impacts that are triggered by the processes, minimizing them. Namely, transforming inefficiencies into opportunities for improvement, generating value with structure and organization so that it can be maintained.

REFERENCES

Alaerds, R., Grove, S., Besteman, S., & Bilderbeek, P. (2017). *The Foundations of our Digital Economy*. Wouter Pegtel & Splend.

Anand, A. (2018, May 31). *ITIL in a world of digital transformation*. Retrieved from Axelos Global Best Practice: https://www.axelos.com/news/blogs/may-2018/itil-in-a-world-of-digital-transformation

Andriole, S. (2017). Five Myths About Digital Transformation Vol58 No 3. *MIT Sloan Management Review*, 1–5.

Axelos. (n.d.). Retrieved from https://www.axelos.com/: https://www.axelos.com/

Bell, S. C., & Orzen, M. A. (2012). *Lean IT: Enabling and Sustaining Your Lean Transformation*. BP Trends.

Burnes, B. (2017). *Managing Change* (7th ed.). Pearson Education Limited.

Cartlidge, A., Hanna, A., Rudd, C., Macfarlane, I., Windebank, J., & Rance, S. (2007). *An Introductory overview of ITIL*. The UK Chapter of the itSMF.

de Ven, A. V., & Hargrave, T. (2000). *Social*. Technical, and Institutional Change.

Ferris, K. (2018, October 8). Built on ITIL. *Digital Transformation*.

Galpin, T. J. (1996). *The Human Side of Change: A Practical Guide to Organization Redesign*. Academic Press.

Geada, N. (2020). Change Management in the Digital Economy. *International Journal of Innovation in the Digital Economy, 11*(3).

Geada, N., & Anunciação, P. (2020, March). Change Management Perceptions in Portuguese Hospital Institutions through ITIL. *International Journal of Healthcare Information Systems and Informatics*.

Hammer, M., & Champy, J. (1994). *Reengineering the Corporation: A manifesto for business revolution*. Nicholas Brealy.

Imai, M. (2006). *Gemba Kaizen*. MT Biznes.

Kling, R., & Lamb, R. (1999, Setembro). IT and Organiacional Change in Digital Economies. *A Socio-Technical Approach*, 17-25.

Laudon, K. C., & Laudon, J. P. (2014). Managment Information Systems - Managing the Digital Firm (13th ed.). Pearson.

O'Brien, J., & Marakas, G. M. (2011). *Management Information Systems*. Mcgraw-Hill.

Requeijo, J. F., & Pereira, Z. L. (2008). *QUALIDADE: Planeamento e Controlo Estatístico de Processos*. Prefácio.

Van Haren Publishing. (2011). *ITIL Foundations - Best Practice*. Author.

Weick, K., & Quinn, R. (1999). *Organizational Change and Development*. Annual Revision Psychology.

Womark, J. P., Jones, D., & Ros, D. (1990). *The Machine that Changed the World*. Macmillan Publishing Company.

Chapter 6
Brazil's Data Protection Law:
Putting Brazil on the Map of Data Privacy Frameworks

Felipe Palhares

Barbosa Müssnich Aragão Advogados, Brazil

ABSTRACT

After several years discussing the creation of a comprehensive data protection law, Brazil finally has its first law that specifically addresses this area -and that will be a game-changer on regulating data processing activities in the country and abroad – in force. Although Brazil's data protection law bears many similarities with the European Union General Data Protection Regulation, it also deviates from its European counterpart in several aspects. This chapter intends to provide an overview of the background relating to laws that carry privacy and data protection provisions in their core and to thoroughly analyze Brazil's new data protection law.

INTRODUCTION

Over the last few years, privacy laws have been arising all around the globe. As personal data becomes more and more a valuable asset for companies to explore and to better understand their customers and the market itself, countries have been trying to regulate data processing activities and to create a set of rules not only to protect data subjects but also to avoid curtailing international data transfers and creating barriers to international commercial relations.

Brazil is one of the latest countries to enact a data protection law, specifically focused on data processing activities, both online and offline, which follows the structure of other international laws such as the GDPR as it has an extraterritorial scope and it is a comprehensive law with a broad reach, being applicable to all data controllers or processors irrespective of their size or of their field of activity.

Although Brazil's Data Protection Law (usually referred to as the 'LGPD', its acronym in Portuguese) is set to deeply change the landscape of data processing activities in the country, it is not the first privacy law enacted in Brazil.

DOI: 10.4018/978-1-7998-4201-9.ch006

Copyright © 2021, IGI Global. Copying or distributing in print or electronic forms without written permission of IGI Global is prohibited.

This chapter intends to explore the privacy legal framework in Brazil in order to provide a better understanding of how the LGPD came to light. It will do this by first diving into the previous laws enacted in the country that carried privacy and data protection concepts and provisions and that are still in effect. Some of them had a huge importance on Brazil's legal system while others rested in the shadows until now but could have larger relevance from this moment on.

Later in the chapter, the author will focus on the LGPD itself: its principles, legal bases, data subjects' rights, rules for international data transfers, the sanctions provided by the law and Brazil's Data Protection Authority.

The main objective of this chapter is to bring awareness regarding Brazil's privacy framework and more specifically regarding its new Data Protection Law. As compliance with the LGPD is mandatory as of September 2020, learning the road that needs to be traveled and the steps toward compliance is fundamental.

BACKGROUND

Prior to enacting the LGPD, Brazil had (and still has considering that these other laws were not superseded) a huge array of laws that directly or indirectly handled issues related to privacy.

As a brief example, the following list include some of the laws with privacy provisions in Brazil:

- Brazil's Constitution
- The Consumer Defense Code
- The Civil Code
- The Criminal Code
- The Good Payers' Registry Act
- The Freedom of Information Act
- The Civil Framework for the Internet
- The Anticorruption Act
- Law No. 7,232/84
- Law No. 8,443/92
- Law No. 9,100/95
- Law No. 9,296/96
- Law No. 9,472/96
- Law No. 9,504/97
- Law No. 9,507/97
- Law No. 9,983/2000
- Law No. 10,703/2003
- Decree No. 3,505/2000
- Decree No. 6,029/2007
- Decree No. 6,425/2008
- Decree No. 6.523/2008
- Decree No. 7,962/2013
- Decree No. 8,771/2016
- Decree No. 8,777/2017

For the purposes of this chapter, the author will address the most relevant pieces of legislation related to privacy rights in this paper which includes the Constitution, the Civil Code, the Consumer Defense Code, the Good Payer Act, the Freedom of Information Act and the Civil Rights Framework for the Internet.

PRIVACY LAWS IN BRAZIL

The Constitution

All of the Constitutions enacted in Brazil have always established some sort of privacy rights. Since its first one, the Constitution of 1824, when Brazil was still an Empire, there were rules defining that an individual's house was his inviolable asylum and that no one could enter there at night without his consent except where necessary to defend it against fire or flooding. The content of letters was also deemed as secret and inviolable by the Constitution and violations of this right would result in severe sanctions.

Throughout the years the following Constitutions repeated these rights that were only suspended in 1942 when a state of war was declared in Brazil due to the ongoing conflicts of the Second World War. Privacy rights were again reestablished in the 1946 Constitution and remained appearing in every constitutional text since then, even in the Constitution of 1967, that was enacted during the military regime. As a matter of fact, the Constitution of 1967 expanded some privacy rights according to the emergence of new technologies as it determined that not only the content of correspondence was inviolable but also the secrecy of phone calls or any telegraphic communications.

The current Brazilian Constitution was enacted in 1988 after the end of the military regime in Brazil and is renowned by its large amplification of civil liberties and fundamental rights and freedoms. For the first time, the constitutional text brought explicit rights related to privacy, setting forth that intimacy, the private life, honor and image are all inviolable and that an award for damages can be pursued when a violation to these rights occurs.

The 1988 Constitution also renewed the protections for an individual's house establishing that entering into the property is prohibited at any time of the day except where the individual consents or in case of blatant offense, disaster or when necessary to provide help to someone, or during the day upon a court order. Moreover, it further broaden the scope of the protections granted to correspondence, phone calls and telegraphic communication, setting forth that data were also included in such provision and that intercepting telephone communications would only be allowed upon a court order and with specific purposes of investigating criminal offenses or assisting the criminal procedure.

The Civil Code

Brazil's current Civil Code was enacted in 2002 and brings a specific section to address personality rights, which states that using someone's name for commercial advertisement is only allowed upon the individual's authorization and this protection is extended to any aliases used for lawful activities by that individual.

The law also prescribes that the private life is inviolable and that the publication or use of someone's image, words or written documents may be prohibited at his request if they can inflict damages to his honor, good fame, respectability or if they are intended for commercial uses. This last part was heavily litigated in the country in connection with the publication of non-authorized biographical books by third parties.

Recently, the Supreme Court has ruled that consent from the subject of the biography or from any third parties relevant to the biographical work (such as family members of the subject or anyone else that played a supporting role in the life of the subject) is not required due to the fundamental right of freedom of speech and expression. However, any abuse from the author of the biography, such as reporting false facts or offending the honor or the image of the subject, could be raised by the affected parties as ground for an indemnification claim.

The Consumer Defense Code

Law No. 8,078/1990 (also known as the Consumer Defense Code) was a groundbreaking piece of legislation for its time and one of the most relevant laws in Brazil due to its impact on the relationship of businesses and consumers around the country.

As its name suggests, the Consumer Defense Code is aimed at providing better assurances and protections to the consumers and created several new rights that changed the landscape for all sectors of the economy in Brazil. The law recognized the consumer as the weaker party in any consumer relationship and set forth that the consumer should have basic rights such as the protection of his life and well-being, fair information, easy access to the judicial courts and administrative organizations, full compensation for any material damages or pain and suffering damages and protection against abusive and misleading advertising.

Among the rights created by the Consumer Defense Code are some related to privacy. The law established that the consumer would have access to the information about him existing in records, files, consumption data and personal data, as well as the sources of that information. It also defined that any records and data on the consumer should be objective, clear, true and written in plain language, easily understandable, and that data which had a negative impact on the consumer related to these facts occurred more than 5 years ago should not be held (Doneda, 2019).

Besides this right of access, the Consumer Defense Code also prescribed a right of being informed – whenever a record, file or personal data on the consumer would be opened by an organization without his prior request, the organization should promptly inform him in writing – and a right of rectification – to demand correction of any incorrect data or record – which should be addressed immediately by the organization responsible for processing the data and should be communicated to recipients of the incorrect information within 5 business days.

Another provision from the Consumer Defense Code that could have some impacts related to data protection is the one that sets forth that a supplier of products or services that becomes aware of the dangerousness of its products or services after they are made available to the market should immediately communicate the fact to the authorities and to the consumers through advertising campaigns. This could be interpreted as an obligation to notify a data breach – as this can potentially harm the consumer as is related to the provision of a product or service – to the authorities and consumers.

In some cases, the State Public Prosecutors' Office have concluded that an organization had an obligation to communicate a data breach to it and the failure to do it resulted in a violation to the Consumer Defense Code.

The Good Payers' Registry Act

In 2011, Congress passed Law No. 12,414/2011 (also known as the Good Payers' Registry Act) which had the goal to create a registry of all individuals that timely fulfilled their payment obligations and did not have late payment or default records. This registry would be used by banks and financial institutions in order to grant loans with lower interest rates to the good payers, considering the higher probability of such institutions getting repaid and the lower probability of defaults on these loans (Bessa, 2019).

The Good Payers' Registry Act has many provisions related to privacy, including relevant principles such as that personal data should be processed for specific purposes, that processing should be transparent and the data subject informed about the identity of the data base owner and the purposes of the proposing, and that data should be accurate, relevant, true, clear and necessary for those purposes. The law established that both excessive data – not relevant for the assessment of the credit risk of the data subject – and sensitive data – referred to as data related to the ethnical and social origin, to political, religious or philosophical beliefs, health data, genetic data and sexual orientation data – should not be processed.

The Good Payers' Registry Act had a huge caveat that prevented it from being largely applied: it presented an opt-in system, in which consumers had to decide to enroll in the registry in order for the banks and financial institutions to be allowed to process their personal data related to fulfillment of payment obligations. The number of individuals that decided to enroll in the registry was quite low, thus the law failed to provide the benefits that were expected – both to consumers at large, that were not able to obtain better loans with betters interest rates, and to the banks and financial institutions, that were eager to create a large database of payment history (Bessa, 2019).

In 2019, due to the low number of opt-ins and the lobby from banks and financial institutions, the Good Payers' Registry Act was amended to change the system from opt-in to opt-out and thus making all individuals subject to the registry unless they expressly inform they do not desire to be a part of such record. Consumers should be notified within 30 days of their profile creation by the organizations that manage such databases.

The right to opt-out can be exercised at any time and database managers should honor the request within 2 business days, revoking or suspending access to the consumers' credit history and communicating such request to third parties that have received the personal data.

There is also a data breach notification requirement under the Decree No. 9,936/2019 (which regulates the Good Payers' Registry Act) which requires database managers to notify both the Data Protection Authority, the Brazilian Central Bank and the Consumer National Secretariat within 2 business days of being aware of the breach or security incident. The notification should include at least a description of the personal data affected, information on the data subjects involved, a description of the security measures used for the protection of the personal data, the risks related to the incident and the measures taken or that will be taken to revert or mitigate the risks.

The Freedom of Information Act

Law No. 12,527/2011 (also known as the Freedom of Information Act) was enacted in late 2011 and aimed at providing greater transparency to the information related to the public administration, especially the expenses incurred by the Treasury and the management of public resources.

The Freedom of Information Act brought a definition of personal data as they are related to an identified or identifiable natural person and set forth that the public bodies and agencies should ensure the protection of the triad confidentiality, integrity and authenticity (Mendes, 2014).

The law prescribes that access to personal data should be restricted to authorized public agents and to the data subject but sets forth that in some circumstances the data could be disclosed to third parties without the consent of the data subject, such as where is necessary to comply with a court order, to the defense of human rights, to the protection of the public interest, to scientific research and statistical purposes in the public interest and to obtain a medical diagnoses where the data subject physically or legally incapable.

The Civil Rights Framework for the Internet

Law No. 12,965/2014 (also known as the Civil Rights Framework for the Internet) is responsible for regulating the online realm and its use by connection providers and providers of internet applications, which includes e-mail providers, hosting services, content providers and information providers. Any organization that has an online presence, such as a website, must comply with the law.

This is one of the first laws in Brazil that explicit includes the word "privacy" in its text, although it does not set aside the expression "private life" adopted by other legislations such as the Constitution and the Civil Code. It is also innovative in defining as its principles the protection of personal data, the assurance of free speech and expression of thoughts, the net neutrality, the accountability of the agents and the protection of the stability, safety and functionality of the Internet.

The Civil Rights Framework for the Internet set forth a range of rights to users of the Internet, which includes the right to obtain clear and complete information on the contract for the provision of services, and also information on the collection, use, storage and processing of personal data, that can only be processed for purposes that justified its collection, that are not prohibited by the legislation and that are specified in contracts, terms of use and privacy notices. In that sense, all connection providers or providers of Internet applications should have policies in place and made available to users (Longhi, 2019).

A right of erasure was first introduced by this piece of legislation. According to the law, users have a right to request the deletion of personal data that were provided to an application upon the termination of the relationship between the parties, respected the obligations of mandatory storage of records set forth by the law. In that regard, the Civil Rights Framework for the Internet establishes that connection providers shall keep records of the connection under a controlled and safe environment for 1 year, while providers of Internet applications shall keep records of access to the application for 6 months. These obligations must be abided by any organizations that perform any processing activity in Brazil, or if it provides services to the Brazilian public or if any company of the same economic group is established in Brazil.

Under the Civil Rights Framework for the Internet, consent was the only legal basis available for the processing of personal data and its requirements were already stringent: it had to be freely given, expressed and informed and made available apart from any other contractual clauses in the provision of services agreement. Although said requirements are hard to achieve, the reality is that there was a lack of enforcement of this part of the law.

On the other hand, the Civil Rights Framework for the Internet was the focus of attention for disputes related to the liability of connection providers and application providers in regard to the content generated by third parties (Leonardi, 2019). According to the law connection providers are not liable for such content while application providers can only be held liable if they fail to remove the content after receiving a court order clearly identifying the location of the content that should be made unavailable. Even though the application provider can remove content that does not comply with its policies and terms of use, it is not up to the application provider to exercise any censorship and decide which non-prohibited content should be removed. The only instance where the application provider will be held responsible for content posted on its application is where it fails to remove images, videos or any other materials that portrait nudity or sexual acts of private nature after receiving a notification from one of the participants of the act or his legal representative.

The Civil Rights Framework for the Internet was further regulated by the enactment of the Decree No. 8,771/2016, which defined personal data as any data related to an identified or identifiable natural person including ID numbers, locational data or electronic tags, and defined processing of personal data as any operation performed on personal data such as collection, reception, production, classification, usage, transmission, reproduction, distribution, store, exclusion, evaluation, and the like.

The Decree also established some guidelines for security standards that should be adopted by organization, as the following: i) establishing a strict access control to the data according to the privileges defined by the company; ii) implementing authentication systems to ensure the adequate identification of the person responsible for the processing, such as two-factor authentication; iii) creating a detailed inventory of the access to the records containing the time, duration and identity of the individual that accessed the file; iv) adopting records' management solutions through methods that guarantee the confidentiality, integrity and availability of the records, such as using encryption. The organization should ensure that information on the security standards adopted by it is made available to everyone, preferably published on its website. Finally, the Decree states that data should be kept in a structured and interoperable standard to facilitate compliance with any court order that requests access to it.

BRAZIL'S DATA PROTECTION LAW – LGPD

Background

Brazil's Data Protection Law was enacted on August 14th, 2018, after being debated by Congress for several years. Back in 2010, the Ministry of Justice launched a public consultation regarding a data protection bill, welcoming ideas for regulating data processing activities. It was the first step towards what would later be the LGPD.

Over the following years three different proposals emerged in Congress: the House Bill No. 4,060/2012, the Senate Bill No. 330/2013 and the Executive Bill No. 5,276/2016. They had distinct approaches to data protection, some more detailed, some more vague, but were discussed by Congress at the same time. The House Bill and the Executive Bill ended up being merged and later became the text of the data protection law, with several amendments and relevant changes to the original text.

The Bill that became the LGPD passed both in the House and in the Senate by a unanimous vote, which is quite remarkable in Brazil considering that Congress encompasses representatives from more than 35 political parties and there is almost always a dissent regarding any legislative proposals.

Two outside factors were relevant and helped steering Congress for passing the Bill: i) the scandal involving Cambridge Analytica and Facebook and the alleged use of personal data for the exploitation of targeted advertising in the election of the United States President Donald Trump and the approval of

Brexit was constantly in the news and called the attention of many politicians in Brazil as well; and, ii) the entering into force of the EU General Data Protection Regulation and its extraterritorial scope that made Brazilian organizations subject to the Regulation even where they did not have an establishment in the European Union. Together, these factors made the Brazilian Congress more aware of the discussions regarding personal data and allowed it to realize the importance of having a data protection legislation right away otherwise international data transfers with countries from the EU could be in danger or demand additional safeguards that were not easy to implement in all cases.

Even after being approved by Congress and sanctioned by the President, the LGPD went through several amendments since its enactment date. On December 27th, 2018, the President issued Provisional Measure No. 869/2018 creating the Data Protection Authority and changing some provisions of the LGPD. Under Brazil's legal system, a Provisional Measure is similar to an Executive Order in the US as it is a law issued directly by the President, with immediate effects, but that needs to be approved by Congress within 120 days otherwise it becomes null and void. Congress also has the power to promote changes to the language of a Provisional Measure as it seems fit before putting it to a vote and this was the case with the Provisional Measure No. 869/2018, that had its text significantly altered by Congress resulting in the Conversion Bill No. 7/2019.

The Conversion Bill No. 7/2019 was approved by Congress and submitted to the President for his approval. Although the bulk of the Bill was approved by President Jair Bolsonaro, some of its provisions related to the penalties set forth by the law, the data protection officer and decisions based solely on automated processing were vetoed (Sombra, 2019). The vetoes were discussed by Congress and the ones regarding the penalties prescribed by the law were overturned. In the end, the LGPD already went through 4 rounds of changes to its language before the date it finally came into force, on September 18, 2020.

Main Definitions

Brazil's Data Protection Law was greatly inspired by the GDPR thus many of its main definitions are closely tied to the concepts of the EU Regulation. Controllers are defined as the public or private organizations that decide the means and purposes of the processing while processors are defined as the public or private organizations that conduct processing activities on behalf of controllers. Personal data is defined as any information related to an identified or identifiable natural person while sensitive personal data is the one related to ethnic and racial origin, religious, political or philosophical beliefs, filiation to trade unions, data related to sexual life, health data, genetic and biometric data when linked to a natural person.

Processing activity is any operation performed on personal data including, but not limited to, collection, production, classification, reception, access, transmission, distribution, communication, modification, storage, exclusion, extraction, and the like. The concept of anonymization under the LGPD differs from the one set forth by other legislations around the world. The LGPD defines anonymization as the procedure using reasonable technical means available at the time of the processing through which the data loses the possibility of being linked, directly or indirectly, to a natural person. The law goes on to say that data will not be deemed anonymous when the process is reverted by an organization using its own means or when it can be reverted through reasonable efforts.

Consent is defined as the freely given, informed and unambiguous manifestation from the data subject agreeing with the processing of his personal data for a specific purpose. The law also defines a research body as a public or private not-for-profit organization legally constituted under the Brazilian laws, with headquarters in the country, that has as its institutional mission or its social objective the performance of basic or applied research of historical, scientific, technological or statistical nature.

Material Scope

The LGPD applies to any processing of personal data, online or offline, carried out both by public bodies or private entities, regardless of their size or field. There is no distinction under the law from processing activities of structured data or unstructured data or of processing by automated means or non-automated means, which means that even where the GDPR would not apply because the data was processed manually and does not form or is intended to form part of a filling system, **the** LGPD would apply (Siqueira, 2019).

There are four major exceptions where the LGPD does not apply: i) when processing is performed by an individual exclusively for private and non-economic purposes; ii) when processing is performed exclusively for journalistic, artistic or academic purposes; iii) when processing is performed exclusively for purposes of public safety, national defense, State security or activities related to the investigation and persecution of criminal offenses; iv) when the personal data originated abroad and is not communicated to or shared with a Brazilian controller or processor, or is transferred internationally to a third country that not the originating one, provided that the country where the data was originated provides the same level of data protection as the one set forth in the LGPD.

The LGPD also does not apply to the processing of anonymized data, which, by definition, is not deemed as personal data thus is exempted from complying with the law.

Territorial Scope

As it occurs with the GDPR, the LGPD also has an extra-territorial scope which might be deemed even wider than the EU Regulation in some cases. A controller or a processor must comply with the LGPD in three scenarios: i) when processing of personal data occurred in Brazil; ii) when processing of personal data is related to the offering of goods or services to data subjects located in Brazil; iii) when the personal data being processed was collected in Brazil (Frazão, 2019). For this last case, it becomes relevant to understand where the data has originated from even, for instance, where a US company processes personal data for a EU controller, considering that if the data was first collected in Brazil, the US company would also be subject to the LGPD notwithstanding the fact that it does not process data in Brazil nor offers goods or services to data subjects located in Brazil.

Whether a company has an establishment in Brazil, where the data is stored or whether the data subjects are Brazilian citizens or foreigners are all irrelevant criteria in assessing if the LGPD applies or not. If any of the above cases occurs, the controller or processor is subject to the Brazilian law.

Differently from the GDPR, the LGPD does not set forth any provision that demands compliance with the law where controllers are monitoring the behavior of data subjects located in Brazil if no data is processed in Brazil or was initially collected in Brazil.

Principles

The LGPD is a legislation based on principles, that are guidelines for any personal data processing activities regardless of the legal basis used for the processing in any particular case. In this regard, all processing activities must abide by the following 10 principles:

1. Purpose – processing should be performed for lawful, specific and explicit purposes, that are informed to the data subject, being prohibited further processing that is incompatible with those purposes;
2. Adequacy – processing should be adequate to the purposes informed to the data subject according to the context of the processing activities;
3. Necessity – processing should be limited to the minimum necessary (data minimization) to fulfill the purposes, restricting the personal data being processed to what is proportional and non-excessive for those purposes;
4. Free access – data subjects should be able to access their data at no cost and through an easy way that allow them to learn the method and period of processing and about the integrity of the personal data;
5. Accuracy – personal data should be accurate, clear, relevant and updated according to what is necessary for the purposes of processing;
6. Transparency – data subjects should receive clear, precise and easily accessible information on the processing activities and on the controller and processor of the data, being respected the commercial secrets;
7. Security – controllers and processors should implement administrative and technical measures to protect personal data from unauthorized access, loss, destruction, modification, communication or diffusion;
8. Prevention – controllers and processors should implement measures to prevent damages to the data subjects arising out of their processing activities;
9. Non-discrimination – personal data should not be processed for illicit or abusive discrimination purposes;
10. Accountability – controllers and processors should implement efficient measures to prove their compliance with the law and the regulations on data protection.

Although there are more principles in the LGPD when compared to the GDPR, most of them are quite similar to the 6 principles presented by the GDPR. The only one that stands out is the non-discrimination principle which is clearly relevant to the social reality in Brazil.

Legal Bases

The LGPD gives controllers a broader lawful capability of processing personal data compared to the GDPR. There are 10 legal bases that could be used to process personal data under the LGPD:

1. Upon consent from the data subject;
2. When necessary to comply with a legal or regulatory obligation;

3. By the public administration, where processing is necessary to fulfill public policies set forth in laws, regulations, contracts, or similar legal documents;
4. By research organizations (as defined by the law), where necessary to conduct research (data should be anonymized where possible);
5. When necessary to perform a contract or any preliminary procedures related to the contract, provided it is upon the request of the data subject;
6. When necessary for the exercise of a legal right in any judicial, administrative or arbitration proceedings;
7. When necessary to protect the life and physical well-being of the data subject or a third party;
8. When necessary for health protection, in procedures performed by health professionals, health services, or by health entities;
9. When necessary to meet the legitimate interests of the controller or of a third party except where the fundamental rights and freedoms of the data subjects related to data protection should prevail;
10. When necessary for credit protection.

Such as under the GDPR, consent requirements in the LGPD are set at a high standard: it must be freely given, specific, informed and unambiguous, by a statement in writing or a clear affirmative action by the data subject. When it is in writing, it should be separate from other contractual clauses and the controller bears the burden of proving that consent was obtained according to the requirements of the law. It could be revoked by the data subject at any time, in a manner equally as simple as the way it was used to obtain it. Therefore, obtaining valid consent could be a challenge thus making this one of the last legal bases to be considered by controllers when assessing the lawful grounds for processing personal data.

The LGPD explicitly includes some cases where the legitimate interest base might be used for processing personal data, which are: i) to support the promotion of the controller's activities (marketing activities); and, ii) to protect the exercise of its legal rights and the provisions of its services, being respected the legitimate expectations from the data subject. Sending an email or postal direct marketing could be deemed as a legitimate interest of the controller as long as it does not override the fundamental rights and freedoms of data subjects in this context.

Processing of sensitive personal data requires specific lawful grounds that might differ from the legal bases available for processing regular data. There are 8 legal bases for processing sensitive personal data set forth in the LGPD:

1. Upon consent from the data subject or his/her legal representative, which has to be specific and separate from other clauses;
2. When necessary to comply with a legal or regulatory obligation;
3. By the public administration, where processing is necessary to fulfill public policies set forth in laws or regulations;
4. By research organizations (as defined by the law), where necessary to conduct research (data should be anonymized where possible);
5. When necessary for the exercise of legal rights in contracts or any judicial, administrative or arbitration proceedings;
6. When necessary to protect the life and physical well-being of the data subject or a third party;
7. When necessary for health protection, in procedures performed by health professionals or by health entities;

8.   When necessary to prevent fraud or guarantee the safety of the data subject, in procedures of authentication and identification of electronic records systems except when the fundamental rights and freedoms of the data subjects related to data protection should prevail.

Even though many of the legal bases available under the LGPD are also available under the GDPR, Brazil's Data Protection Law has some unique lawful grounds such as the processing of personal data where necessary for the credit protection. The creation of this specific provisions was largely sponsored by banks and financial institutions, that needed greater assurances that they would still be able to process personal data after the enactment of the law.

The legal bases for processing sensitive personal data differ more significantly between the LGPD and the GDPR. While the GDPR has more bases for processing special categories of data and they are more detailed, molded for specific situations such as the processing carried out by a foundation, association or any other not-for-profit body, the LGPD mostly repeats some of the bases for processing regular personal data with a few adjustments.

Children's Personal Data

Processing personal data from children and teenagers also require special attention and a greater degree of care in Brazil. All the information regarding the processing must be conveyed in a simple, clear and accessible manner, taking into consideration the physical, perceptive, sensorial, mental and intellectual characteristics of the young data subjects. Under Brazilian law, there is a distinction between the legal definition of children and teenagers. Children are considered those that are under 12-years old while teenagers are defined as those that are 12-years old or older.

According to the LGPD, data from children and teenagers should be processed in their best interest. Processing data from children is only lawful upon specific consent from a parent or legal guardian and the controller is obliged to employ reasonable efforts, according to the available technologies, to verify that consent was given by a parent or legal guardian (Lima, 2019).

Controllers must keep publicly available information on the data collected, the methods of collection, purposes of processing and the procedures to exercise the rights set forth in the law. It is prohibited to condition the participation of children in games, internet applications or other activities upon the provision of personal information beyond what is strictly necessary to the activity.

Children's personal data might be collected without consent only when is necessary to contact their parents or legal guardians and it might be processed only a single time to that specific purpose with no further storing, or when necessary to protect the children. In any case, the personal data must not be shared with third parties without consent.

Data Subjects' Rights

The LGPD sets forth several rights that are available to data subjects and that might be exercised at any given time, at no cost to the data subject, upon a written or oral request made by the data subject or his legal representative. These rights are generally equivalent to those provided in the GDPR and contemplate:

1.   Right of confirming the existence of processing activities;
2.   Right of access;

3.   Right of rectification of incomplete, inaccurate or outdated data;
4.   Right of anonymization, restriction or erasure of unnecessary or excessive data, or of data processed in violation to the law;
5.   Right of portability;
6.   Right of erasing data processed based on the data subject's consent;
7.   Right of being informed about which public and private entities the personal data was shared with;
8.   Right of being informed about the possibility of not giving consent and the negative consequences this might have;
9.   Right of revoking consent at any given time;
10.   Right of lodging a complaint before the controller, the Data Protection Authority or the consumer defense agencies;
11.   Right of requesting a review of any decisions taken solely based on automated processing of personal data, including profiling.

Upon receipt of any requests from the data subject to exercise his rights under the LGPD, the controller must immediately adopt all necessary measures to fulfill the request or, if it is unable to, it must answer to the request asserting that it is not the controller of the processing activities indicated by the data subject (if that is the case) or explaining the reasons and legal grounds for not being able to immediately perform the measures requested (Maldonado, 2019).

In case the data subject exercises his right of rectification, anonymization, restriction or erasure, the controller must also inform all third parties with whom the personal data was shared with to perform the same procedures on their end.

Where the data subject submits a request for confirming the existence of processing activities related to his personal data or a request for accessing the data, the request must be either responded immediately, in a simple manner, or within 15 days as of the date the request was submitted, through a complete and clear report that, at least, states the origin of the data, the criteria used for processing and the purposes of processing. The data should be made available to the data subject through electronic means or via a physical copy, according to the data subject's preference.

Regarding data subject's right of requesting a review of the decisions taken solely based on automated processing, the review can be conducted by a second run of the same algorithm that made the decision in the first place thus there is no need to have human intervention at any time. This was the most controversial points of the law, that was changed several times since its enactment. At first, the review of the decisions taken solely based on automated processing had to be performed by a natural person but it was later altered by the Provisional Measure No. 869/2018 to also allow the review by an algorithm. The language brought by the Conversion Bill No. 7/2019 once again said that the review had to be performed by an individual. However, this provision was vetoed by the President and ended up stating that no human intervention is needed in responding to the request of a review.

International Data Transfers

In order to ensure that data subjects' rights are respected on any personal data processing activities, transferring data internationally is only allow under certain specific circumstances, according to one of the following 9 grounds:

1. When a third country's level of data protection is deemed adequate by Brazil's Data Protection Authority – this assessment is made based on the existence of legislation from the third country that is equal or at least similar to the LGPD, ensuring the same level of protection as the one in place in Brazil, which should take into account the existing laws of the third country, the nature of the data, the compliance with the principles and the rights set forth by the LGPD, the adoption of safety measures and the existence of judicial or institutional guarantees;
2. When the controller provides assurances that the principles of the law, the data subject's rights and the data protection regime set by the LGPD will be complied with through specific documents such as standard contractual clauses, specific contractual clauses, binding corporate rules, seals, certifications or codes of conduct;
3. When the transfer is necessary for legal international cooperation between public entities of intelligence, investigation and persecution, according to international agreements;
4. When is necessary to protect the life and physical well-being of the data subject or a third party;
5. When the Brazilian Data Protection Authority authorizes the transfer;
6. When the transfer is a result of a commitment assumed in an international cooperation agreement;
7. When the transfer is necessary to fulfill public policies or legal attributions of the public service;
8. When specific and separate consent from the data subject was obtained, after being informed of the international transfer and its distinction from other purposes;
9. When the transfer is necessary to comply with a legal or regulatory obligation, to perform a contract or any preliminary procedures requested by the data subject, or for the exercise of legal rights in judicial, administrative or arbitration proceedings.

At this time, there are no adequacy decisions already in place nor standard contractual clauses that have been approved by the Data Protection Authority. However, it is expected that the European Union will be one of the first jurisdictions to receive an adequacy decision issued by Brazil's Data Protection Authority considering the similarity of both legislations. There are no timelines of when this should occur though.

Another controversial issue is how transfers between Brazil and the United States will take place, especially taking into consideration that the US currently has a different data protection framework than Brazil, the European Union and some other third countries. While the US has sectoral-based privacy laws, Brazil will now have a general data protection rule, quite different from the Federal and State laws in place in the United States, thus making it difficult for the US to be deemed as an adequate jurisdiction by Brazil's Data Protection Authority. In light of these critical distinctions, it is possible to foresee that Brazil and the US will try to find contractual arrangements to allow international data transfers, such as the EU-US Privacy Shield.

On the other hand, the LGPD will be an asset for Brazil in allowing the country to continue receiving data from other nations, especially those that have comprehensive privacy laws. Because of the LGPD, Brazil has the chance of being considered as an adequate jurisdiction by the European Commission, provided that some other criteria are also met. This would be a great competitive advantage as it would ensure international data transfers between the country and any Member State of the European Union without the need for companies to implement additional safeguards such as binding corporate rules.

Documentation

The LGPD mandates that both controllers and processors shall keep records of their personal data processing activities, which should be presented to the Data Protection Authority in case of an audit. However, there are no specific requirements of what kind of information those records should encompass or what is the format of such records. The law is silent in prescribing more details on the form of the records and only states they are required, especially when processing is based on the legitimate interest of the controller or a third party. Nonetheless, this obligation of keeping records is applicable to all controllers and processor, regardless of their size or the nature of their processing activities, and differently from the GDPR there are no exceptions to this rule at this moment although the Data Protection Authority could regulate this point lately.

Furthermore, processors should only process personal data on behalf of the controller and on instructions from the controller. The responsibility of verifying that processors are complying with the instructions and with the provisions of the law relies on the controller, making records keeping a relevant task. Here, the LGPD once again stands miles away from the prescriptions of the GDPR as there are no specific requirements of having a contract in place for the processor to be able to process data on behalf of the controller, nor any specific language that must be included in such contract. This means that instructions from the controller to the processor could be transmitted orally without the need of a written agreement between the parties.

Even if a written contract between the controller and the processor is not required by law, it is quite common to have one in place prior to begin any processing activities in order to clearly establish the responsibilities and obligations of each party, how processing should be conducted, and the penalties in case of non-compliance with the law or with the agreement itself.

The LGPD also defines that a data protection impact assessment is the documentation from the controller that contains the description of the processing activities that might create risks to the fundamental rights and freedoms of data subjects and that describes the measures, safeguards and mechanisms to mitigate these risks. Although it brings this definition that clearly resembles the standard provided by the GDPR, the LGPD fails to establish when conducting a data protection impact assessment is mandatory.

As a matter of fact, the law sets forth that a data protection impact assessment may be requested by the Data Protection Authority when processing is based on the legitimate interest, or that the Data Protection Authority is entitled to order the controller to conduct a data protection impact assessment. This assessment must, at least, include a description of the data collected, the method used for collecting the data and for ensuring the safety of the information and the analyzes of the controller, regarding the measures and safeguards adopted to mitigate the risk. Neither of these provisions make conducting a DPIA mandatory prior to a request or order from the Data Protection Authority, although performing one would be a best practice in many situations (Gomes, 2019).

The only provision of the law that seems to indicate that a DPIA has to be conducted is the one specifically addressing processing activities carried out by public entities, when the LGPD establishes that the Data Protection Authority may request that public bodies publish a DPIA. Considering that is impossible to publish something that does not exist, the language used by the law in this instance suggests that a DPIA had to be already performed prior to the publishing request (Cots and Oliveira, 2019).

Moreover, there are no defined criteria for when private entities should perform a data protection impact assessment. While the GDPR states that a DPIA must be conducted when the processing activity is likely to result in a high risk to the rights and freedoms of natural persons, the LGPD is silent and does not mention any of these thresholds for the performance of a DPIA. And, in any case, regardless of the result of the DPIA, there is no requirement of prior consultation with the Data Protection Authority.

Data Protection Officer

All controllers must appoint a Data Protection Officer, regardless of their size or the volume of their processing activities or the nature of the processing activities, and his contact details should be published preferably on the controller's website. As it stands right now, this is a general obligation with no current exceptions, which could be later reviewed by the Data Protection Authority. Processors do not currently have an obligation to appoint a Data Protection Officer but they might be required to appoint one upon further regulation to be issued by the Data Protection Authority, especially considering that the LGPD defines the Data Protection Officer as the person appointed by the controller and the processor. This person will be responsible for being the communication channel between the controller, the data subjects and the Data Protection Authority.

The Data Protection Officer could be either a natural or legal person and could also be the same person for companies of the same economic group, provided that the Data Protection Officer is easily accessible at all times to all companies. There are no specific legal requirements relating to the knowledge of the person that will be appointed as DPO, nor any provisions that guarantee that the DPO will not be fired for exercising his duties.

Data Breaches

The LGPD sets forth that the controller must notify both the Data Protection Authority and the affected data subjects of any security incident that might cause either a risk or a relevant damage to the data subjects.

This provision carries some uncertainty that will need to be resolved later by the Data Protection Authority or the Brazilian courts when they review claims for violations of the law. The first one is related to the idea of reporting a security incident, a concept that is broader than an actual data breach. Any kind of violations to the company's information security policy could be viewed as a security incident, in the sense that it could be a violation to the triad of confidentiality, integrity and availability of the data. However, not every security incident is a data breach.

From what could be interpreted out of the debates carried by Congress when it was discussing the law, the legislative intent behind this provision was to address only data breaches not all security incidents. Nevertheless, the language of the law remains vague and taking a cautious approach would result in reporting all kinds of security incidents if there is a risk or relevant damage to the data subjects.

The second uncertain condition is the level of risk which requires a notification to be made. As the law stands right now, there is no specific threshold of risk that would trigger the notification obligation, which means that a data breach that involves even a low level of risk to the data subjects would have to be informed. As evaluating risk is subjective, this could result in a scenario where almost all data breaches would trigger a notification requirement, considering that is hard to imagine a data breach that carries no risk at all to the data subjects.

When the notification requirement is triggered, the notification should be made within a reasonable period of time – another uncertain criterion - and should at least include:

1.   A description of the nature of the personal data affected;

2.   Information on the data subjects affected;

3.   A description of the technical and security measures implemented to protect the data;

4.   The risks related to the incident;

5.   The reasons for the delay in notifying the Data Protection Authority and the data subjects (if applicable); and

6.   The measures adopted to revert or mitigate the damages to the data subjects.

After verifying the severity of the incident, the Data Protection Authority may order the controller to adopt certain measures such as publicizing the occurrence in the media or even implementing specific actions to revert or mitigate the damages.

Private Right of Action

Brazil's Data Protection Law provides for a private right of action that allows individuals to file claims against controllers and processors for actual damages and pain and suffering damages (moral damages) before the courts. Lawsuits can be brought by sole individuals as well as by groups of individuals. Although Brazil does not have class actions such as those in place in other parts of the world (i.e. the United States of America), the Brazilian legal system allows collective claims and complaints brought by the Public Prosecutors' Office, associations and others pleading damages on behalf of a large group of individuals.

As there are no statutory damages, the amount of the awards that could be granted to data subjects could vary a lot. Actual damages will usually be granted if they are proved and limited to the amount lost by the complainant while moral damages are calculated arbitrarily by the courts according to the pain and suffering caused to the complainant as a result of the violation to the law.

Processors are jointly liable with controllers for damages caused when they failed to comply with the controllers' instructions or with the provisions of the LGPD. Joint controllers are also jointly liable when they are both involved in the personal data processing activities.

Both controllers and processors will only be exempted from liability if they can prove that:

1.   They did not perform the processing activities that the data subject claims; or

2.   Although they performed the processing activities, there were no violations to the LGPD arising out of these processing activities; or

3.   Damages are exclusively a result of an act of the data subject or of a third party and could not be deemed as the controller's or processor's fault.

This last scenario raises a good defense for cases involving cyber-attacks or malicious acts performed by a third party. If the controller or processor can prove that they had implemented state of the art technical and security measures to protect personal data, adopting the best systems and procedures known and available at the time, and that a data breach was only possible because of innovative techniques used by the third party and that could not be anticipated, there might be a chance of avoiding liability for the damages caused by this third party.

Sanctions

The LGPD establishes that the Data Protection Authority can impose several sanctions against controllers and processors, such as the following:

1. Warnings, with a timeframe for the adoption of corrective measures;
2. A fine of up to 2% of the revenue of the last fiscal year of the private legal entity, group or conglomerate in Brazil, excluded taxes, limited to a maximum amount of BRL 50,000,000.00 per infraction;
3. A daily fine, limited to the amounts above-mentioned;
4. Publicizing the infraction after its occurrence is confirmed;
5. Blocking the personal data related to the infraction until it is cured;
6. Erasing the personal data related to the infraction;
7. Partially suspending the database related to the infraction for a maximum period of 6 months, which could be extended for another 6 months until the processing activity becomes compliant with the law;
8. Suspending data processing activities for a maximum period of 6 months, which could be extended for another 6 months;
9. A total or partial ban on carrying out any data processing activities.

Those sanctions could be applied solely or cumulatively according to the nature and extent of the infraction. The most severe sanctions (suspension of the database, suspension of processing activities or a partial or full ban on data processing activities) can only be imposed in case of reoccurring violations, after other sanctions have already been imposed. The pecuniary fines may not be imposed on public entities or bodies.

In respect to the due process principle, sanctions can only be imposed after an administrative proceeding is carried out where the controller or processor have the chance to present a defense. Certain criteria should be assessed in order to decide which sanctions are adequate, such as the severity and nature of the infraction, the level of damages, the cooperation of the controller/processor, the existence of internal procedures to reduce or mitigate damages, the adoption of a privacy program, the prompt adoption of mitigating measures and the reoccurrence of the conduct.

Data Protection Authority

As the LGPD is the first comprehensive data protection law in Brazil, the country did not have a Data Protection Authority prior to the enactment of the law. The Authority was recently created but it is not yet staffed or structured. Right now, it is an empty shell waiting for the President to appoint the members of its board of directors and to assign public servants to work for this new government agency.

The lack of a fully functional Data Protection Authority is concerning as there is no way to predict what kind of regulations and guidelines will be issued by the Authority and if it will follow some interpretations given by European Data Protection Authorities or if it will create a whole new and different regime.

Furthermore, there are more than 50 provisions in the LGPD that mention that the Data Protection Authority has the power to issue regulations that could potentially alter the content of those provisions to a great extent.

The Data Protection Authority will be composed of a board of directors - comprised of 5 directors nominated by the President and confirmed by the Senate – and the National Council of Personal Data Protection and Privacy – comprised of 23 members, appointed by several institutions – and each of these bodies have distinct attributions. While the board of directors is responsible for the major decisions related to the LGPD, as the regulations that need to be issued to solve many pending situations, the Council has an advisory role and will propose guidelines, suggest actions and prepare studies to be presented to the board.

At first, the Data Protection Authority will be linked to the President's Office but its nature can be altered during the first two years after the date the law enters into force. Although the LGPD states that the Data Protection Authority has technical and decision making autonomy, being linked to the Presidential Office has provoked a huge debate on the real independence of the Data Protection Authority. Considering that this is one of the criterion evaluated on the assessments from the European Commission prior to issuing an adequacy decision, it is expected that the Data Protection Authority loses this close ties with the Presidential Office in the near future.

Effective Date

The LGPD entered into force on September 18, 2020, after a series of twists. The first version of the law was set to be enforced 18 months after being published in the Official Gazette, which would be February 16, 2020. However, the deadline was extended by the Provisional Measure 869/2018, thus resulting in August of the present year.

On April 29, 2020, the President issued Provisional Measure 959/2020, which aimed at postponing the effective of the LGPD to May 3, 2021. However, this Provisional Measure was not approved by Congress (at least not in regard to the further extension of the LGPD). Nonetheless, the administrative sanctions prescribed under the LGPD have been delayed to August 1, 2021, due to a bill passed by Congress.

At this time, the LGPD is already in force and can be enforced by regulators, such as the Public Prosecutors' Offices and consumer defense agencies, or by data subjects, upon the exercise of their private right of action.

CONCLUSION

Privacy is not a new subject in Brazil's legal system history. As discussed above, every Brazilian Constitution had some provisions related to protecting the privacy of the individual's home and his mail, since 1824. And throughout the years more protections were raised with important sectoral laws that regulate other areas but also contained privacy and data protection prescriptions such as the Consumer Defense Code and the Civil Rights Framework for the Internet. However, none had the impact that Brazil's Data Protection Law will have on both private entities and public bodies.

The LGPD will inevitably alter the landscape for privacy and data protection in Brazil and will require all organizations to review their data processing activities in order to assess how to implement all the new obligations and responsibilities brought by the law. This groundbreaking effect will be felt not only in Brazil but also abroad as international companies that do business in Brazil, or desire to target people located in Brazil will have to adapt their practices as well.

The law should also create a new practice of law in the country. As the LGPD create several new rights and also provides for a private right of action, violations to the law should be a common issue being discussed in administrative procedures or in lawsuits before the courts. Furthermore, Brazil is well-known by its huge level of litigation due to the low (if any) cost of bringing a lawsuit and the ability of individuals to represent themselves before some specific courts.

In a way, there is still much about the LGPD that remains uncertain. The law is heavily dependent on the existence of a Data Protection Authority and on the regulations that it must issue to fill the voids purposely left by the legislator. For a country that does not have a culture of really caring for privacy in its roots – notwithstanding the existence of provisions related to privacy in a huge array of laws – leaving such an essential task for a body that is still not constituted is a daring move.

Regardless of how the future Data Protection Authority will decide to act, one thing is certain: the consequences of the LGPD will be felt for a long time as this will probably become one of the most relevant laws in Brazil.

REFERENCES

Bessa, L. R. (2019). *Nova Lei do Cadastro Positivo*. Thomson Reuters.

Cots, M., & Oliveira, R. (2019). *Lei Geral de Proteção de Dados Pessoais Comentada*. Thomson Reuters.

Doneda, D. (2019). *Da Privacidade à Proteção de Dados Pessoais – Elementos de Formação da Lei Geral de Proteção de Dados*. Thomson Reuters.

Frazão, A. (2019). Capítulo 4 – Objetivos e Alcance da Lei Geral de Proteção de Dados. In G. Tepedino, A. Frazão, & M. D. Olivera (Eds.), *Lei Geral de Proteção de Dados Pessoais e Suas Repercussões no Direito Brasileiro* (pp. 99–130). Thomson Reuters.

Gomes, M. C. O. (2019). Para Além de uma "Obrigação Legal": o que a Metodologia de Benefícios nos Ensina Sobre o Papel dos Relatórios de Impacto à Proteção de Dados. In A. P. M. C. Lima, C. B. Hissa, & P. M. Saldanha (Eds.), *Direito Digital Debates Contemporâneos* (pp. 141–154). Thomson Reuters.

Leonardi, M. (2019). *Fundamentos de Direito Digital*. Thomson Reuters.

Lima, C. C. C. (2019). Capítulo II – Do Tratamento de Dados Pessoais. In V. N. Maldonado & R. O. Blum (Eds.), *LGPD Lei Geral de Proteção de Dados Comentada* (pp. 179–219). Thomson Reuters.

Longhi, J. V. R. (2019). Marco Civil da Internet no Brasil: Breves Considerações Sobre Seus Fundamentos, Princípios e Análise Crítica do Regime de Responsabilidade Civil dos Provedores. In G. M. Martins & J. V. R. Longhi (Eds.), *Direito Digital Direito Privado e Internet* (pp. 123–154). Foco Jurídico.

Maldonado, V. N. (2019). Capítulo III – Dos Direitos do Titular. In V. N. Maldonado & R. O. Blum (Eds.), *LGPD Lei Geral de Proteção de Dados Comentada* (pp. 220–244). Thomson Reuters.

Mendes, L. S. (2014). *Privacidade, Proteção de Dados e Defesa do Consumidor: Linhas Gerais de um Novo Direito Fundamental*. Saraiva.

Siqueira, A. H. A. (2019). Capítulo I – Disposições preliminares. In B. Feigelson & A. H. A. Siqueira (Eds.), *Comentários à Lei Geral de Proteção de Dados Lei 13.709/2018* (pp. 15–58). Thomson Reuters.

Sombra, T. L. S. (2019). Fundamentos da Regulação da Privacidade e Proteção de Dados Pessoais: Pluralismo Jurídico e Transparência em Perspectiva. São Paulo: Thomson Reuters.

ADDITIONAL READING

Bioni, B. R. (2019). *Proteção de Dados Pessoais: a Função e os Limites do Consentimento*. Forense.

Cagnoni, A. C. (2019, Oct 29). *How Brazil Regulates Children's Privacy and What to Expect Under the New Data Protection Law*. Retrieved from https://iapp.org/news/a/how-brazil-regulates-childrens-privacy-and-what-to-expect-under-the-new-data-protection-law/

Frazão, A., & Mulholland, C. (2019). *Inteligência Artificial e Direito: Ética, Regulação e Responsabilidade*. Thomson Reuters.

Maldonado, V. N. (2017). *Direito ao Esquecimento*. Novo Século.

Marineli, M. R. (2019). *Privacidade e Redes Sociais Virtuais: Sob a Égide da Lei 12.965/2014 – Marco Civil da Internet e da Lei 13.709/2018 – Lei Geral de Proteção de Dados Pessoais*. Thomson Reuters.

Nehemy, A. T. (2019, Aug 23). *Recapping the Latest Updates to Brazil's General Data Protection Law*. Retrieved from https://iapp.org/news/a/brazils-general-data-protection-law-goes-into-effect/

Palhares, F. (2019, Jan 16). *Brazil's DPA has arrived: is it a Blessing or Curse in Disguise?* Retrieved from https://iapp.org/news/a/brazils-dpa-has-arrived-is-it-a-blessing-or-curse-in-disguise/

Palhares, F. (2019). O Relatório de Impacto à Proteção de Dados Pessoais. In V. N. Maldonado (Ed.), *LGPD Lei Geral de Proteção de Dados Pessoais Manual de Implementação* (pp. 247–288). Thomson Reuters.

Palhares, F. (2020). *Temas Atuais de Proteção de Dados*. Thomson Reuters.

Thomaz, A. C. E., & Sombra, T. L. S. (2019, Jun 11). *Congress Approves Creation of Brazilian Data Protection Authority, Amends LGPD*. Retrieved from https://iapp.org/news/a/congress-approves-creation-of-brazilian-data-protection-authority-amends-lgpd/

Chapter 7
Privacy Preserving Approaches for Online Social Network Data Publishing

Kamalkumar Macwan

Sardar Vallabhbhai National Institute of Technology, India

Sankita Patel

Sardar Vallabhbhai National Institute of Technology, India

ABSTRACT

Recently, the social network platforms have gained the attention of people worldwide. People post, share, and update their views freely on such platforms. The huge data contained on social networks are utilized for various purposes like research, market analysis, product popularity, prediction, etc. Although it provides so much useful information, it raises the issue regarding user privacy. This chapter discusses the various privacy preservation methods applied to the original social network dataset to preserve privacy against attacks. The two areas for privacy preservation approaches addressed in this chapter are anonymization in social network data publication and differential privacy in node degree publishing.

INTRODUCTION

The online social network has become popular among thousands of users worldwide and has become the most popular on the internet(Alon,2006; Wu, and Zhu, 2014). The different social networking sites provide a platform for users to create their profile and to maintain their connections with other users. Nowadays, business entities are also very active on social media. Business companies post their specific content to target the audiences more effectively. In recent years, such types of activities have collected a huge amount of data. This data contains personal information like name, address, educational background, employment. It also includes profile information like music taste, shopping habits, locations, etc.

The data collected from these online social media platforms are much helpful for research and analysis. It can be explicitly used for data mining and information extraction. The social data also have

DOI: 10.4018/978-1-7998-4201-9.ch007

Copyright © 2021, IGI Global. Copying or distributing in print or electronic forms without written permission of IGI Global is prohibited.

unspoken information that can be very much useful for market prediction, analysis(Arnaboldi,Conti, Passarella,&Pezzoni, 2012), recommendation(Fields, Jacobson, Rhodes, d'Inverno, Sandler,& Casey, 2011)and for various purposes(Frikken, & Golle, 2006;Zhou, Pei, & Luk, 2008). Researchers in organizations have also gained interest in social network data mining to know user's habits for security purposes(Rosenblum, 2007).

The service providers, who manage the data, may be interested to do a specific analysis of the collected social data. But, due to a lack of internal expertise to perform the analysis, the data is outsourced to external parties. Sometimes, the owner of the data shares the data to third parties as support over the demand. However, releasing social network data in its raw form raises privacy issues(Acquisti,&Gross, 2007;Srivastava, Ahmad, Pathak, Hsu, &David Kuo-Wei, 2008). An adversary may try for documented threats like identity theft, digital stalking, and personalized spam(Wu, Ying, Liu, &Chen, 2010). The publicly available information is also used to train predictive models that can violate user's privacy.

SOCIAL NETWORK DATA PUBLISHING

The social network data publishing components are shown in Figure 1. The architecture contains users, social media applications, service providers, social network data and data recipients. Social network platforms ask users to provide personal information to create a user profile. This information is categorized into three parts: a unique identifier, quasi-identifiers, and sensitive data. The unique identifier is a set of attributes, such as name, mobile number contains data that explicitly identifies a user from the entire social dataset. The quasi-identifier is a set of semi-identifiable attributes like age, current city, educational background, a former company that could identify record owner. Sensitive attributes contain sensitive person-specific information like current location, shopping habit, religion, political opinion, etc.

Social media applications provide a platform to meet up with other people on the internet. These applications are handled by the owner itself and/or by the operator, called service providers. They provide services to achieve the revenue in terms of data generated through social media users. The social network data are being analyzed in various areas for research purposes. The various domains which use the social network data are biology, sociology, psychology, epidemiology and criminology(Alon, 2006; Granovetter, 2005; Wang, Chakrabarti, Wang, &Faloutsos, 2003). The generated large scale social graphs are also useful as a customer-product connection tool where the information related to the product can be used for better social targeting of advertisements. In many cases, social network service providers do not have the in-house expertise to perform analysis. So, the data are outsourced to third parties to generate useful information.

The social network data is represented as graph $G(V, E)$, where V represents user or entities and E defines the relationship between the individuals. The labels are attached to vertices and edges to provide additional information about them. The vertex label contains personal information such as name, gender, birth date, location, education and so on. The edge label represents the information about friendship, co-authorship, and weight of friendship (number of mutual friends, frequency of emails and messages). Figure 2(a) shows the original social network represented as a graph. The service provider releases a graph where the actual identity of a user is replaced by an anonymous identity. Figure 2(b) represents the same social network with an anonymous identity, called a naively anonymized social network.

Figure 1. Social Network Data Publishing Scenario

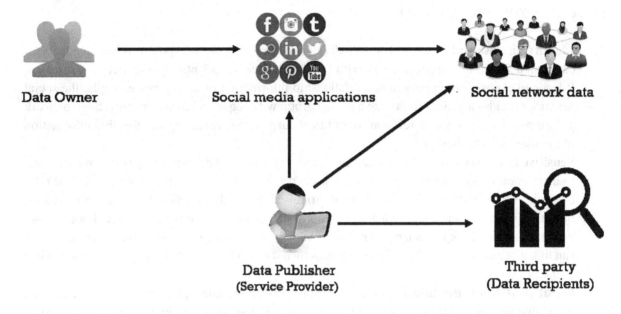

Figure 2. Publishing original social network: (a) Original social network, (b) Naively anonymized social network

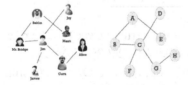

As the social network dataset represents ample information, an adversary can use some extra information to reveal the hidden one. For example, consider the publicly available social network shown in Figure 2(b). Now, an adversary has some information from other sources that one user, named Jim who is part of this dataset has exactly four friends. With the use of this information, user Jim is easily mapped to vertex C in the published dataset. Even though the available dataset itself does not reveal the actual identity of the nodes, available background knowledge helps one to know the users represented as nodes, known as privacy attack. The issue of privacy in social network data publishing has been heightened in recent years(Backstrom, Dwork,& Kleinberg, 2007;Wang,Liau,&Hsu, 2006). The research in this field focuses on to study the privacy-preserving approaches. The approach should be efficient enough to publish the social network data with the desired level of privacy and adequate for useful analysis.

Privacy Breaches

A privacy breach occurs when some sensitive information about an individual is disclosed to an adversary. It poses various threats and it also damages the image and reputation of an individual. Therefore, published data should ensure privacy before it gets released to the third party. Privacy breaches in social networks can be categorized into threetypes (Evfimievski, Gehrke, &Srikant, 2003; Liu, Wang, Liu, Zhang, 2008; Zheleva, & Getoor, 2008):

1. **Identity disclosure:** It occurs when an individual behind a record is exposed. When an adversary can map a victim to a specific query with full confidence, the identity of the victim is revealed. It leads to exposing the personal and relationship information of a user. For example, the social network provides a feature to initiate a closed group with requested members only. Such network groups may have a common religious or political purpose. So, revealing membership information of the users violate their privacy.

2. **Sensitive link disclosure:** The link among vertices represents the relationship between individual users or communities. In some cases, some users do not want to reveal the existence of their relationship. A third party may have high interest to reveal the level of relationship between two users. Sensitive link disclosure occurs when the relationship between two entities is exposed. For example, a user has decided not to declare his religious view in a social network. However, if an adversary can link that user with specific religious groups then it could be possible to infer the religious view of the person.

3. **Sensitive attribute disclosure:** Sensitive attribute disclosure takes place when an adversary can determine the true value of a sensitive user attribute. The sensitive attribute may be related to an entity and also to a link that exists between entities. People usually keep some information visible to everyone, such as a hobby, sports and movies. But, some applications demand extra information from the user to execute the function properly. The data owner expects to keep such information hidden from the third user (Samarati, & Sweeney, 1998).

Existing work focus on to preserve the vertex privacy in the released social network against various attacks(Hay, Miklau, Jensen, Towsley, &Weis, 2008; He, Vaidya, Shafiq, Adam, &Atluri, 2009;Gehrke, Lui, &Pass, 2011; Zhou, &Pei, 2008; Zou, Chen, &Ozsu, 2009)that expose the sensitive link between two users(Backstrom, Dwork, &Kleinberg, 2007,Bhagat, Cormode, Krishnamurthy, &Srivastava, 2009; Duan, Wang, Kam, &Canny, 2005; Korolova, Motwani, Nabar, &Xu, 2008; Zheleva, & Getoor, 2008) and study on how attributes can be predicted to provide security model against sensitive attribute disc losure(Lindamood,Heatherly,Kantarcioglu, &Thuraisingham, 2009; Narayanan, & Shmatikov, 2008). Social network anonymization methods are basically divided into three categories: graph modification approach, clustering based approach(Samarati, & Sweeney, 1998; Blocki, Blum, Datta, & Sheffet, 2013) and differentially private approach (Dwork, 2008). Different techniques that provide vertex and link privacy, are discussed in next sections.

PRIVACY PRESERVATION APPROACHES

The major goal of privacy preservation is to hide sensitive information of an individual. Privacy attacks re-identify the individual user or relationship between two users by joining a published dataset with some external dataset to model the background knowledge of users. There are three main categories of anonymization methods on social network data:

1. Graph modification approach: This type of approach brings a change in the original social network by performing modification (addition and/or deletion) operation on edges or nodes. The approach suggested by Ying and Wu(Ying,& Wu, 2011)is to add randomly k edges followed by deleting k original edges. But, it does not guarantee to achieve k-anonymization for all users(Sweeney, 2002). To overcome this limitation, the k-anonymization concept was introduced. It provides anonymity through specific graph modification operations. The k-anonymization approach considers the extra information available to an adversary and provide the privacy model accordingly.

2. Clustering-based approach: It is also known as a generalization, which divides the nodes and edges into different groups. Each group is substituted by a super-vertex that contains the aggregate information regarding the properties of that group. The generalization approach(Hay, Miklau, Jensen, Towsley, & Weis, 2008)for an unlabeled graph was proposed by Hay. This proposed method tries to find out an optimal super-node by considering a maximum-likelihood approach. Campan and Truta(Campan, & Truta, 2008)extend the generalization approach for labeled graph. Here, the nodes are selected to create a super-node based on attributes and neighborhood similarity.The iterative selection of the nodes continues until all nodes are covered. The proposed approach by Tassa and Cohen(Tassa,& Cohen, 2011)gives higher utility than(Campan, & Truta, 2008). The idea is to initially divide the nodes randomly into different partitions. Then, the nodes are moved from one cluster to the other to achieve smaller information loss. Although these methods resist the identity disclosure attack, the utility of the anonymized graph is significantly low. The super-nodes contain so many self-loop edges. So, the sampling procedure considers all the acceptable super-nodes which leads to sampling errors.

3. Differentially private approach: Differential privacy(DP) model offers strong privacy guarantees regardless of the adversary's background knowledge. It assures that each user is protected under this mechanism (Dwork, 2006). This approach targets the releasing strategy instead of the original data. Here, the objective is to release statistical information about the data. The algorithms used for DP relate the amount of noise to the global sensitivity. Lower sensitivity implies smaller added noise. For the social graph, the DP methods are categorized into node-DP and edge-DP approaches.

The most widely adopted approach in anonymization is k-anonymity principle(Sweeney, 2002). k-Anonymization concept for privacy preservation suggests achieving at least k entities who possess similar property/structure. In order to obtain k-anonymity, social graph connection is modified so that any vertex in the network is structurally indistinguishable with other k-1 vertices. A larger value of k provides better user privacy. While the privacy models ensure user privacy, the usefulness of anonymized datasets also plays an important role. The anonymized dataset stand against the vertex re-identification attack. This modification is done by adding or deleting edge as well as vertices and generalizing the labels of vertices. The following sections explain the method to achieve the k-anonymization to provide privacy against different attacks.

k-DEGREE ANONYMIZATION APPROACH

The k-degree anonymization approach is used to achieve the same degree value among at least k nodes. In order to obtain this, the degree of some nodes is required to be increased or decreased. In other words, the anonymization method contains edges as well as nodes insertion and/or deletion operations. The *k*-anonymized social dataset has at least *k* nodes who holds the same degree value. Thus, the resultant dataset stands against the vertex re-identification attack.

The anonymization concept for privacy preservation has been widely adopted. Liu and Terzi(2008) proposed a privacy model against an attack which identifies the vertices using structural properties. Some attacks also consider the 1-neighborhood connectivity of a vertex and try to disclose that vertex identity. Zhou, Pei(2008)and Zou, Lei and Ozsu (2009)proposed methods that insert new vertices and edges to have a similar pattern of 1-neighborhood among *k* vertices. Some proposed work(Hay, Miklau, Jensen,Towsley, &Weis, 2008; He, Vaidya, Shafiq, Adam, & Atluri, 2009)considers a group of vertices as a single super-vertex or partitions the graph into the local substructure and treats each substructure as a single unit to be anonymized. Although it provides more privacy, it has very low data utility.

The general idea for *k*-degree anonymization method is to achieve at least *k* users presents in published dataset who contains same degree value. Consider a graph G having n vertices, a tuple d_G is defined as $d_G = (d_1, d_2, d_3, ..., d_n)$ where d_i represents the degree of vertex V_i. According to definition in (Rosenblum, 2007), Graph is *k*-degree anonymized if each value in tuple d_G occurs at least *k* times and such degree sequences is called as *k*-anonymized degree sequence.

Figure 3. Flow of the proposed k-degree anonymization approach

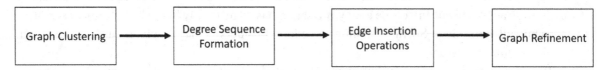

The *k*-anonymity model aims to sanitize the original graph, resulting in a compromise of the data utility. There are different possible options to anonymize a social graph. Although the *k*-anonymized graphs provide the same level of privacy, they differ by the data originality they retain in their respective published dataset. The data utility of the social graph is measured in terms of different graph structural properties (Singh, & Zhan, 2007)like average path length (APL), average betweenness (BW) and clustering coefficient (CC). These properties highlight the relationship among the users of a social network. The deviation in these properties highlights the transformation within the social graph. The data originality can be retained in the anonymized graph by modifying the data in such a way that brings less deviation in the properties. Therefore, in social network data publishing, the trade-off between the individual's privacy and the data utility has become a major concern. The general approach of *k*-anonymity is to achieve degree sequence anonymization by edge modification operations. An efficient approach for *k*-degree anonymization is presented by Macwan and Patel(2017). The entire workflow is represented in Figure 3. Graph clustering is applied as a pre-processing step to partition the entire graph into different clusters. The second step includes dividing the degree sequence into different groups that have low graph anonymization cost. This step decides the target degree for each vertex. Now, the edge insertion operations take place to achieve the target degree value. At last, graph refinement also includes the edge modification operation to incorporate any change in estimated anonymized degree sequence.

k-NMF ANONYMIZATION APPROACH

Social networking sites like Facebook, LinkedIn provide a feature to establish their connection with people. To verify new user identity, they provide a facility to see the list of friends(connections) and mutual friends. Such information is very useful to find people on the social network platform. As shown in Figure 4, one can directly see the list of mutual friends shared with one of his friends on Facebook. Now, one can easily count the number of mutual connections between two vertices from the published social graph. If two users have a unique value of a number of mutual friends, an adversary can identify them by using background knowledge.

Figure 4. Friend list of friend in Facebook

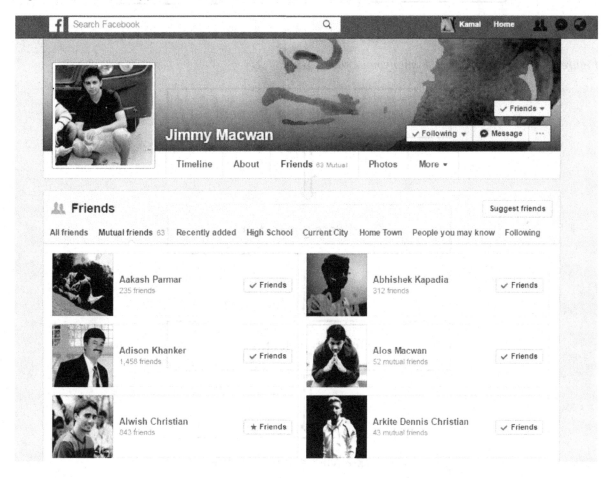

The attacks based on the degree of two vertices are also mentioned in literature (Tai, Yu, Yang, &Chen, 2011;Wu, Zhu, Wu, Gong-Qing & Ding, 2013). An adversary uses the degree of two vertices to breach user privacy, called a friendship attack. The counter method for this attack was introduced by Tai, Yu, Yang, &Chen (2011)that focuses on vertex degree. Then, the mutual friend attack was addressed in(Wu, Zhu, Wu, Gong-Qing & Ding, 2013). The author also suggested *k*-NMF(Number of Mutual Friends) anonymization method to prevent that attack. But, as the anonymization step handles one edge at a time, it performs more edge insertion operations. Thus, the statistical results obtained from the anonymized social dataset has more deviation compared to the original result. However, Macwan and Patel (2018) presented an efficient approach to achieve *k*-NMF anonymization to prevent mutual friend attack. In this section, we present a brief description of the proposed *k*-NMF anonymization method in (Macwan & Patel, 2008) .

Figure 5.NMF sequence partition for k=4

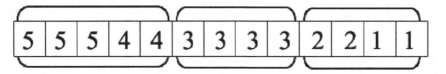

Figure 6. Work-flow for k-NMF anonymous social graph

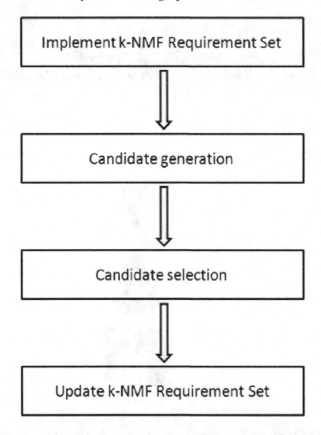

The original graph can be converted to *k*-NMF anonymized graph by acquiring anonymity in mutual friend sequence. Mutual friend sequence is a vector that contains mutual friend value for each edge. The first step towards this anonymization operation is to organize the entire NMF sequence into different groups. The purpose of this step is to decide the target mutual friend value for all the elements of the group. Here, we consider that elements of mutual friend sequence are placed in decreasing order. Initially, *k* elements are placed in one group. After that, for each element, it decides either to start a new group or to merge in the current group. The estimated total cost for the entire group helps to make this decision. Figure 5 shows the partition of the given mutual friend sequence for *k*=4.

Now, the generated partition result indicates the required increment in different NMF values. So, a table named "*k*-NMF requirement set" is maintained to highlight that. It contains <*key,value*> fields where *key* refers to the NMF value of an edge and *value* represents the requirement for that *key* to confirm *k*-NMF anonymity. The next step lists out edges for that NMF value and possible options for increment. It generates a candidate set of vertices for edge insertion. Now, the one node who has a favorable impact on requirement is selected for edge insertion. The "*k*-NMF requirement set" is updated after each edge insertion operation to display revised demand. The entire workflow to achieve *k*-NMF anonymized social graph based on the NMF sequence partition is shown in Figure 6. A separate requirement table helps to perform minimum edge insertion operations. So, it results in very small deviations in graph topological properties.

DIFFERENTIAL PRIVACY APPROACH

The published statistics of the social dataset also contain useful information, such as the number of connections, public opinion poll, or the number of active users in any community/group. Although it does not include the user identity, an adversary may try to disclose some private information with the help of two neighboring datasets. Two datasets distinct from each other by just information about a single user are called neighboring datasets. DP tries to generate the close results for a neighboring set so that the impact of the inclusion of an individual's data does not highlight the difference. Thus, it ensures to produce a similar distribution for two neighboring datasets. The main idea behind this technique is to inject randomized noise into query results to hide the impact of an individual user of the published dataset.

ε-Differential privacy(ε-DP) depends on some query and result perturbation to provide privacy guarantee. This can be achieved in DP by adding some random noise to the query output. This is realized by using the methods such as Laplace distribution and the Normal distribution with variance depending on ε and the query's sensitivity. The notion of ε-differential privacy (Dwork, 2008)is defined based on the concept of a neighboring dataset. A randomized algorithm *A* satisfies ε-DP when for any two neighboring databases, D and D', denoted by D ≅ D', where SÍ Range(A)$ and ε is a parameter for privacy level.

$$Pr\big[A(D) \in S\big] \le \exp(\varepsilon) \times Pr\big[A(D') \in S\big] \tag{1}$$

DP is considered as a capable method for privacy preservation(Dwork, 2006). It produces the most secure privacy model for interactive data analysis(Dwork, 2008; Dwork & Smith, 2010).Initially, Nissim. Raskhodnikova,& Smith(2007) proposed the DP approach for a graph to calculate the cost of a minimum spanning tree by applying edge-DP. This approach was again considered by Karwa, Raskhodnikova, Smith, & Yaroslavtsev(2011) and Hay, Li, Miklau, & Jesen(2009) to show that the post-processing technique can be performed to remove noise. Gehrke, Lui, & Pass(2011) suggest a stronger notion than node-DP called zero-knowledge privacy and demonstrate that this stronger notion can be achieved for several tasks in extremely dense graphs. Kifer and Machanavajjhala (2011) criticize DP in the context of social networks, highlighting that individual users can have a greater effect on a social network than their own relationships. Blocki, Blum, Datta, & Sheffet(2013) also considers a node-DP algorithm to analyze sparse graphs. The assumption was made regarding the dataset that queries should be evaluated on a defined class of datasets.

The node-DP method injects noise in the generated result. This noise function depends on the maximum desirable change in query results because of the inclusion or elimination of a user. Thus, achieving node-DP is much difficult as removal of one node may cause the removal of $|V|$-1 edges, where $|V|$ is the total number of nodes. So, there is a requirement for keeping some limit for the degree value. The "Graph Projection Method" considered as a key technique for node-DP which remodels the original graph to θ-degree bounded graph $G^θ$(degree of all vertices must be less than θ)(Day, Li, & Lyu, 2016).

An advanced approach to achieve θ-degree bounded graph is discussed in(Macwan & Patel, 2018). The proposed approach starts with edge insertion operations for the nodes having a lower degree. The neighboring node having a minimum degree is considered as candidate node for edge insertion operation. This helps to retain edge-set for lower degree nodes. The proposed graph projection approach in (Macwan & Patel, 2018). generates a maximal graph in the manner that a single edge insertion operation increases the degree of at least node above θ. So, it preserves as much information about a graph as possible.

CONCLUSION

Emerging growth of social network data publication has also raised privacy concern of the users. The identity disclosure attack is recognized as the fundamental privacy violation as it reveals more information about any user and relationship among users. The most common approach to preserve user identity is the *k*-anonymization technique. In this chapter, we discussed the *k*-anonymization methods for degree and mutual friend based attacks. In some cases, the statistics related to the social network are also being published. The differential privacy method hides the presence of a user by injecting noise into the generated result. The discussion of the algorithms presented in this chapter helps to understand various privacy attacks and preserving approaches.

REFERENCES

Acquisti, A., & Gross, R. (2007). *Privacy risks for mining online social networks*. In *NSF Symposium on Next Generation of Data Mining and Cyber-Enabled Discovery for Innovation (NGDM'07)*, Baltimore, MD.

Alexa. (2018). *The top 500 sites on the web*. Retrieved from https://www.alexa.com/topsites

Alon, U. (2006). *An introduction to systems biology: design principles of biological circuits*. Chapman and Hall/CRC. doi:10.1201/9781420011432

Arnaboldi, V., Conti, M., Passarella, A., & Pezzoni, F. (2012). Analysis of ego network structure in online social networks. In *2012 International Conference on Privacy, Security, Risk and Trust and 2012 International Conference on Social Computing* (pp. 31–40). IEEE. 10.1109/SocialCom-PASSAT.2012.41

Backstrom, L., Dwork, C., & Kleinberg, J. (2007). Wherefore art thou r3579x?: anonymized social networks, hidden patterns, and structural steganography. In *Proceedings of the 16th international conference on World Wide Web* (pp. 181–190). ACM. 10.1145/1242572.1242598

Bhagat, S., Cormode, G., Krishnamurthy, B., & Srivastava, D. (2009). Class-based graph anonymization for social network data. *Proceedings of the VLDB Endowment International Conference on Very Large Data Bases*, 2(1), 766–777. doi:10.14778/1687627.1687714

Blocki, J., Blum, A., Datta, A., & Sheffet, O. (2013). Differentially private data analysis of social networks via restricted sensitivity. In *Proceedings of the 4th conference on Innovations in Theoretical Computer Science* (pp. 87–96). ACM. 10.1145/2422436.2422449

Campan, A., & Truta, T. M. (2008). Data and structural k-anonymity in social networks. In *International Workshop on Privacy, Security, and Trust in KDD* (pp. 33–54). Springer.

Day, W. Y., Li, N., & Lyu, M. (2016). Publishing graph degree distribution with node differential privacy. In *Proceedings of the 2016 International Conference on Management of Data* (pp. 123–138). ACM. 10.1145/2882903.2926745

Duan, Y., Wang, J., Kam, M., & Canny, J. (2005). Privacy preserving link analysis on dynamic weighted graph. *Computational & Mathematical Organization Theory*, 11(2), 141–159. doi:10.100710588-005-3941-2

Dwork, C. (2006). Differential privacy. automata, languages and programming. *33rd International Colloquium on Automata, Languages and Programming JUL*, 10–14.

Dwork, C. (2008). Differential privacy: A survey of results. In *International Conference on Theory and Applications of Models of Computation* (pp. 1–19). Springer.

Dwork, C., McSherry, F., Nissim, K., & Smith, A. (2006). Calibrating noise to sensitivity in private data analysis. TCC, 3876, 265–284. doi:10.1007/11681878_14

Dwork, C., & Smith, A. (2010). Differential privacy for statistics: What we know and what we want to learn. *Journal of Privacy and Confidentiality*, 1(2), 2. doi:10.29012/jpc.v1i2.570

Evfimievski, A., Gehrke, J., & Srikant, R. (2003). Limiting privacy breaches in privacy preserving data mining. In *Proceedings of the twenty-second ACM SIGMODSIGACT-SIGART symposium on Principles of database systems* (pp. 211–222). ACM. 10.1145/773153.773174

Fields, B., Jacobson, K., Rhodes, C., d'Inverno, M., Sandler, M., & Casey, M. (2011). Analysis and exploitation of musician social networks for recommendation and discovery. *IEEE Transactions on Multimedia*, 13(4), 674–686. doi:10.1109/TMM.2011.2111365

Frikken, K. B., & Golle, P. (2006). Private social network analysis: How to assemble pieces of a graph privately. In *Proceedings of the 5th ACM workshop on Privacy in electronic society* (pp. 89–98). ACM. 10.1145/1179601.1179619

Gehrke, J., Lui, E., & Pass, R. (2011). Towards privacy for social networks: A zero-knowledge based definition of privacy. In *Theory of Cryptography Conference* (pp. 432–449). Springer. doi:10.1007/978-3-642-19571-6_26

Granovetter, M. (2005). The impact of social structure on economic outcomes. *The Journal of Economic Perspectives, 19*(1), 33–50. doi:10.1257/0895330053147958

Hay, M., Li, C., Miklau, G., & Jensen, D. (2009). Accurate estimation of the degree distribution of private networks. In *Data Mining, 2009. ICDM'09. Ninth IEEE International Conference on* (pp. 169–178). IEEE. 10.1109/ICDM.2009.11

Hay, M., Miklau, G., Jensen, D., Towsley, D., & Weis, P. (2008). Resisting structural reidentification in anonymized social networks. *Proceedings of the VLDB Endowment International Conference on Very Large Data Bases, 1*(1), 102–114. doi:10.14778/1453856.1453873

He, X., Vaidya, J., Shafiq, B., Adam, N., & Atluri, V. (2009) Preserving privacy in social networks: A structure-aware approach. In *Web Intelligence and Intelligent Agent Technologies, 2009. WI-IAT'09. IEEE/ WIC/ACM International Joint Conferences on* (vol. 1, pp. 647–654). IET. 10.1109/WI-IAT.2009.108

Karwa, V., Raskhodnikova, S., Smith, A., & Yaroslavtsev, G. (2011). Private analysis of graph structure. *Proceedings of the VLDB Endowment International Conference on Very Large Data Bases, 4*(11), 1146–1157. doi:10.14778/3402707.3402749

Kifer, D., & Machanavajjhala, A. (2011). No free lunch in data privacy. In *Proceedings of the 2011 ACM SIGMOD International Conference on Management of data* (pp. 193–204). ACM. 10.1145/1989323.1989345

Kleinberg, J. M. (2007). Challenges in mining social network data: processes, privacy, and paradoxes. In *Proceedings of the 13th ACM SIGKDD international conference on Knowledge discovery and data mining* (pp. 4–5). ACM. 10.1145/1281192.1281195

Korolova, A., Motwani, R., Nabar, S. U., & Xu, Y. (2008). Link privacy in social networks. In *Proceedings of the 17th ACM conference on Information and knowledge management* (pp. 289–298). ACM. 10.1145/1458082.1458123

Lindamood, J., Heatherly, R., Kantarcioglu, M., & Thuraisingham, B. (2009). Inferring private information using social network data. In *Proceedings of the 18th international conference on World wide web* (pp. 1145–1146). ACM. 10.1145/1526709.1526899

Liu, K., & Terzi, E. (2008). Towards identity anonymization on graphs. In *Proceedings of the 2008 ACM SIGMOD international conference on Management of data* (pp. 93–106). ACM. 10.1145/1376616.1376629

Liu, L., Wang, J., Liu, J., & Zhang, J. (2008). *Privacy preserving in social networks against sensitive edge disclosure. Tech. rep., Technical Report Technical Report CMIDAHiPSCCS 006-08.* Department of Computer Science, University of Kentucky.

Macwan, K. R., & Patel, S. J. (2017). k-degree anonymity model for social network data publishing. *Advances in Electrical and Computer Engineering, 17*(4), 117–224. doi:10.4316/AECE.2017.04014

Macwan, K. R., & Patel, S. J. (2018). k-NMF anonymization in social network data publishing. *The Computer Journal, 61*(4), 601–613. doi:10.1093/comjnl/bxy012

Macwan, K. R., & Patel, S. J. (2018). Node differential privacy in social graph degree publishing. *Procedia Computer Science, 143*, 786–793. doi:10.1016/j.procs.2018.10.388

Narayanan, A., & Shmatikov, V. (2008). Robust de-anonymization of large sparse datasets. In *2008 IEEE Symposium on Security and Privacy* (pp. 111–125). IEEE. 10.1109/SP.2008.33

Nissim, K., Raskhodnikova, S., & Smith, A. (2007). Smooth sensitivity and sampling in private data analysis. In *Proceedings of the thirty-ninth annual ACM symposium on Theory of computing* (pp. 75–84). ACM. 10.1145/1250790.1250803

Rosenblum, D. (2007). What anyone can know: The privacy risks of social networking sites. *IEEE Security and Privacy, 5*(3), 40–49. doi:10.1109/MSP.2007.75

Samarati, P., & Sweeney, L. (1998). Generalizing data to provide anonymity when disclosing information. PODS, 98, 188. doi:10.1145/275487.275508

Samarati, P., & Sweeney, L. (1998). *Protecting privacy when disclosing information: k-anonymity and its enforcement through generalization and suppression. Tech. rep., technical report.* SRI International.

Singh, L., & Zhan, J. (2007). Measuring topological anonymity in social networks. In *2007 IEEE International Conference on Granular Computing (GRC 2007)* (pp. 770–770). IEEE. 10.1109/GrC.2007.31

Srivastava, J., Ahmad, M. A., Pathak, N., & Hsu, D. K. W. (2008). Data mining based social network analysis from online behavior. *Tutorial at the 8th SIAM International Conference on Data Mining (SDM'08).*

Sweeney, L. (2002). k-anonymity: A model for protecting privacy. *International Journal of Uncertainty, Fuzziness and Knowledge-based Systems, 10*(05), 557–570. doi:10.1142/S0218488502001648

Tai, C. H., Yu, P. S., Yang, D. N., & Chen, M. S. (2011). Privacy-preserving social network publication against friendship attacks. In *Proceedings of the 17th ACM SIGKDD international conference on Knowledge discovery and data mining* (pp. 1262–1270). ACM. 10.1145/2020408.2020599

Tassa, T., & Cohen, D. J. (2011). Anonymization of centralized and distributed social networks by sequential clustering. *IEEE Transactions on Knowledge and Data Engineering, 25*(2), 311–324. doi:10.1109/TKDE.2011.232

Wang, D. W., Liau, C. J., & Hsu, T. (2006) Privacy protection in social network data disclosure based on granular computing. In *2006 IEEE International Conference on Fuzzy Systems* (pp. 997–1003). IEEE. 10.1109/FUZZY.2006.1681832

Wang, Y., Chakrabarti, D., Wang, C., & Faloutsos, C. (2003). Epidemic spreading in real networks: An eigenvalue viewpoint. In *22nd International Symposium on Reliable Distributed Systems, 2003. Proceedings* (pp. 25–34). IEEE.

Wellman, B. (1996). For a social network analysis of computer networks: a sociological perspective on collaborative work and virtual community. In *Proceedings of the 1996 ACM SIGCPR/SIGMIS conference on Computer personnel research* (pp. 1– 11). ACM. 10.1145/238857.238860

Wu, X., Ying, X., Liu, K., & Chen, L. (2010). A survey of privacy-preservation of graphs and social networks. In *Managing and mining graph data* (pp. 421–453). Springer. doi:10.1007/978-1-4419-6045-0_14

Wu, X., Zhu, X., Wu, G.Q., & Ding, W. (2014). Privacy preserving social network publication against mutual friend attacks. *IEEE Transactions on Data Privacy, 7*(2), 71–97.

Ying, X., & Wu, X. (2011). On link privacy in randomizing social networks. *Knowledge and Information Systems, 28*(3), 645–663. doi:10.100710115-010-0353-5

Zheleva, E., & Getoor, L. (2008). Preserving the privacy of sensitive relationships in graph data. In *Privacy, security, and trust in KDD* (pp. 153–171). Springer. doi:10.1007/978-3-540-78478-4_9

Zhou, B., & Pei, J. (2008). Preserving privacy in social networks against neighborhood attacks. In *Data Engineering, 2008. ICDE 2008. IEEE 24th International Conference on* (pp. 506–515). IEEE. 10.1109/ICDE.2008.4497459

Zhou, B., Pei, J., & Luk, W. (2008). A brief survey on anonymization techniques for privacy preserving publishing of social network data. *SIGKDD Explorations, 10*(2), 12–22. doi:10.1145/1540276.1540279

Zou, L., Chen, L., & Ozsu, M. T. (2009). K-automorphism: A general framework for privacy preserving network publication. *Proceedings of the VLDB Endowment International Conference on Very Large Data Bases, 2*(1), 946–957. doi:10.14778/1687627.1687734

Chapter 8
The Importance of Information Systems and Technologies (ITS) in the Supply Chain

Sofia Sousa

Polytechnic Institute of Setúbal, Portugal

ABSTRACT

Fast and accurate information is essential so that managers can analyze and structure their decisions, ensuring the good performance of logistics processes. Thus, in a constantly evolving world, it is increasingly important for the organization to keep up with consumer needs, adapting and investing in information systems and technologies (ITS) that appear on the market. Within the supply chain, warehouses and their management are often seen only as an inevitable cost for the organization, ending up being left aside when it comes to high investment implementations and changes. However, currently they have proven to be a relevant component that, if well managed and with the appropriate technology, can eliminate costs for the organization while also providing profits, allowing to maintain a perfect balance between demand and supply.

Nowadays there is a greater need on the part of organizations to reduce costs, increase speed, efficiency, effectiveness and obtain greater competitiveness and offer a wider variety of products and services suitable to the consumer's expectation, taking into account the environment and the footprint ecological (Dr. B. Neerajaa, 2014). Thus, logistics appears to be increasingly technologically integrated, being interconnected with all the organization's operations, being part of the entire process, from the supply of raw material to the delivery of the final product to the consumer (Shiau, Chen, & Tsai, 2015).

The application of information systems (IS) aims at the collection, selection, treatment and analysis of data, transforming it into useful information for decision making, providing the operational information necessary for the normal functioning of day-to-day operations (Ragowsky, SeevNeumann, & NivAhituv, 1996). These add value to the organization that uses them, allowing the connection between the company and the external environment (suppliers/ customers/ among others), thus generating better communication between them. It is important to emphasize that in an organization it is necessary to guarantee the

DOI: 10.4018/978-1-7998-4201-9.ch008

Copyright © 2021, IGI Global. Copying or distributing in print or electronic forms without written permission of IGI Global is prohibited.

existence of an information system suitable to the needs of the organization in which the management of information systems must be responsible for the planning, architecture, management and control of the activities necessary for its operationalization, considering all the elements or resources that integrate it, taking into account the relationship with the organization and the environment (Land, Farbey, & Targett, 1993). In short, the management of information systems should be seen as the management of the information resource and all other resources involved in the planning, development, operation and maintenance of an information system (Varajão, 2007).

A logistics system aims to create value for the customer, with various activities being performed in order to provide the consumer with the right product, in the right place, at the right time, in the right quantity and at the lowest possible cost (Moura, 2006) (Dr. B. Neerajaa, 2014). We can then state that logistics is vital for the consumers, organizations and the economy in general. Due to the fact that there is a wide geographical dispersion of suppliers and customers and, consequently, the need to match supply with demand, providing customers the goods and the services they need, ensuring the flow of their products to organizations, ensuring the supply of raw materials and other inputs used in production operations (Moura, 2006).

In logistics it is possible to find several phases, processes and functions, each with its importance and objective, in which all connected make the product delivered to the final consumer at the lowest possible cost and with the best quality (Dr. B. Neerajaa, 2014). Within logistics, we find the warehouse. Alone, will not bring any value to the product, which is the same when entering and leaving the warehouse. Sometime, its value may even decrease due to the possibility of obsolescence, rupture, deterioration, loss or any other anomaly (Carvalho, 2017).

However, the use of a warehouse, together with transport, allows the fulfillment by the logistic system of the value proposal previously defined to the consumer, due to the ability to make the product available. In this way, storage came to fill the gap between production and consumption, as there is no reliable transport with a short delivery time and at a reasonable cost for constant and direct delivery to the customer. Therefore, the use of a warehouse reduces the total costs of the logistics system and allows the organization that uses them to bring the product closer to the market, responding more quickly to the consumer, improving the service. The existence of a logistical system without the use of storage would require a perfect synchronization between production and consumption, together with the existence of a means of rapid and adapted transport to carry small quantities to the consumer (Carvalho, 2017).

The use of warehouses comes from the need to create stock, due to the existence of differences between supply and consumption over time, meaning, consumption occurs continuously while supply/ production occurs through lots of order. In addition to the discrepancy between demand and production, there are also situations where demand is unknown, with the creation of stock combating unforeseen demand fluctuations (Smith, 1998).

Finally, it is important to note that the topics of information systems, supply chain and warehouses are interconnected. Information systems emerged to globally optimize supply chain processes, where warehouses are one of the main components of the same.

Millar and Porter (1985) claim that the use of IS in value chain activities allows organizations to improve their competitive differentiation, achieve cost leadership and, consequently, obtain sustainable competitive advantage.

Earl (1989) says that IS should be considered a "strategic weapon" in, at least, one of following items: gaining competitive advantage; improve productivity and performance; enable new ways of managing and organizing; develop new business.

Millar and Porter (1985) concluded that the proper use of ITS minimizes costs and maximizes the value of an organization, optimizing value activities and guaranteeing competitive advantages (Kim & Narasimhan, 2002). After analysis and investigation on the topic, it is possible to state that the IS has a high degree of importance for the optimization of the supply chain, as well as also having a significant impact on the performance of the warehouses, being necessary and important to apply it, so that warehouses can be as efficient and effective as possible in carrying out their processes (O'Byrne, 2017).

EVOLUTION OF IS IN THE SUPPLY CHAIN

Schultheis and Sumner (1998) identify the increasing need for managers to resort to the use of information systems to support value-generating activities in the supply chain, both at the level of support activities and at the level of primary activities, namely:

- **Support activities:**
  - Organization in general – Using office automation solutions;
  - Human Resources – Through competence databases;
  - Technology – Through the use of computer-aided design and production;
  - Purchasing – Through online connections with Suppliers.
- **Primary activities:**
  - Inbound Logistics – Through warehouse automation systems;
  - Operations – Through the control of production control processes and systems;
  - Outbound Logistics – Monitoring online orders with incoming systems;
  - Service – Through remote diagnostics.

Logistics should contribute to cost reduction and margin creation, especially through the primary activities of inbound logistics, outbound logistics operations and, in relation to secondary activities, through procurement activity (Ivanov & Sokolov, 2010). The use of ITS logistics has been, more and more frequently, derived from the need to obtain greater competitive advantage, possible to obtain through the increase of efficiency, the reduction of operational costs and the greater capacity of response in systems transactions, these being just some of the advantages of using IS (Carvalho, 2017) (O'Byrne, 2017). Table 1 presents a summary of the evolution of the models, systems and information technologies used in Supply Chain.

Table 1 shows that, due to the advancement of information and communication systems and technologies (ICST), there is a great evolution in the development new application solutions, softwares, programs and platforms that allow organizations to monitor and identify opportunities and redefine processes in a continuous improvement approach throughout the supply chain (O'Byrne, 2017). Finally, it is certain that ITS are quickly overcome by the evolution of the technological market and by the constant creation of new needs by the consumer. It is possible to state that, in the near future, there will be countless new changes that will bring greater complexity and new challenges, testing the creative and innovative capacity of supply chain managers.

Table 1. Evolution of ITS used in Supply Chains

Barcode - 50's, 20th Century
° System Functions: Allows you to identify a product. After reading the code with the reader, the product information is automatically inserted in a database, allowing to keep the *stock* updated.
EDI (Electronic Data Interchange) - Between the 60s and 70s
° System Functions: Allows the exchange of electronic data between business partners.
MRP (Materials Requirements Planning) – Decade of 70
° System Functions: This is an inventory and production control system. It allows the optimization of inventories by reducing costs by calculating the exact quantities, the precise and estimated dates for each component. This system uses as input information the orders in the portfolio and the sales forecasts transmitted by the commercial area.
MRPII (Manufacturing Resource Planning) - 1980s
° System Functions: Provides information as a basis in the production plan for all functional areas, to assist in better management of the organization's resources. It also allows testing through simulations of various scenarios. The information is useful for several functional areas, such as purchasing, production and finance.
WMS (Warehouse Management System) - 1980s
° System Functions: It allows to control in real time the movement and storage of products in the warehouse, processing all transactions associated with their movement such as ordering, delivery, storage and picking. It is a system based on a database that allows to improve the efficiency of the warehouse keeping the stock updated and accurate.
BPO (Business Process Optimization) - 1980s
° System Functions: It allows to optimize the multi-company resources and their integration. This system uses the current infrastructure to collect data from ERP systems or any other source.
PDS (Parallel Distributed Simulation) - Between the 80s and 90s
° System Functions: This is a model for running a simulation program on computer platforms that contain multiple processors. Each simulation model can be run in its own environment, as there is a common protocol that ensures data exchange and synchronization with other distributed simulation models.
ERP (Enterprise Resource Planning) - 90's
° System Functions: Integrates information processes related to the functional areas of an organization spread over multiple locations. Exp of software: SAP, Primavera, Microsoft Dynamics.
SCM Systems (Supply Chain Management Systems) – Decade of 90
° System Functions: This is a system that provides analytical tools for advanced planning and strategic decision making in the Supply Chain.
RFID (Radio Frequency Identification Device) - 90's
° System Functions: This system allows objects to be identified automatically, communicating through radio waves. This consists of an electronic tag or microchip that is placed on an article, it also consists of an antenna that communicates through radio frequency and a receiver/transmitter (reader) that registers the article when it passes through the reading area.
APS (Advanced Planning and Scheduling) – Decade of 90
° System Functions: This is a system that helps to match supply with demand and to forecast demand with the help of complex statistical models and techniques. Integrates with modules for customer relationship management and product lifecycle management.
B2B (Business to Business) & B2C (Business to Consumer) - End of decade 90
° System Functions: It is an electronic market that allows you to carry out commercial transactions with customers and suppliers using the internet.
CPFR (Collaborative Planning, Forecasting and Replenishment) - End of decade 90
° System Functions: This is an approach to SCM between a network of business partners, allowing to share forecasts and results.

Source: Adapted from José Carvalho (2017) and Jain, Wadhwa & Deshmukh (2009)

THE FUTURE CHALLENGES OF STORAGE

Automation of logistical processes and industry 4.0 are themes that are increasingly explored by both researchers and organizations.

Automation of Logistic Processes

The automation of logistical processes is characterized by the application of industrial technologies, such as robots in factories and warehouses, to guarantee the optimization of logistical processes and, consequently, optimize the internal flows of materials (Echelmeyer, Kirchheim, & Wellbrock, 2008) (O'Byrne, 2017).

From 1950 onwards, the application of automated processes in logistics started to be more and more frequent. The processes were applied to various internal tasks such as transport, handling, storage, packaging and palletizing, repetitive and simple tasks that did not require intelligence or thought (Echelmeyer, Kirchheim, & Wellbrock, 2008).

With the development of technology and markets and the growing need to be more competitive, automated processes have quickly expanded to the manufacturing process, an example being the automotive industry that started using industrial robots in various functions such as handling, placing parts and welding (O'Byrne, 2017). This decision, in addition of being beneficial to the employee's ergonomics, as it stopped performing heavy, repetitive and sometimes dangerous tasks, allowed the mass production, the reduction of waste and, consequently, the redistribution of resources (Echelmeyer, Kirchheim, & Wellbrock, 2008) (Sunol, 2020).

Currently, automated processes and robots are found in almost all phases of the logistics process, which has brought about an improvement in tasks and a constant optimization of the entire logistics network (Sunol, 2020).

Table 2 shows some examples of types of process automation in different areas of logistics.

Industry 4.0

In recent years, the complexity and requirements of the manufacturing industry have been constantly and significantly increasing. This increase is due to the growing international competition, the constant fluctuation of the markets, the greater demand for customized products and the increasingly sharp reduction in the product's life cycle, bringing great and complex challenges to organizations. Common value creation approaches are no longer effective or adequate to address the main factors of a business: cost efficiency; flexibility; adaptability; stability and sustainability (Sunol, 2020). It appears that, on the one hand, the requirements of the industry have been increasing significantly, on the other hand, there is a rapid increase in technological progress that has brought with it new potentials and a series of business opportunities (Hofmann & Rüsch, 2017).

The WEF (World Economic Forum) launched, in 2015, a report based on the opinion of around 800 executives and specialists in the information and communication technologies sector, entitled "Deep Shift Technology Tipping Points and Societal Impact", where they are asked to locate 21 critical points of change in time, according to their perception. Figure 1 shows the result of this analysis.

As we can see from Figure 1, it is expected that, from 2022, the sector of information and communication technologies will undergo a significant evolution. However, as can be seen in Figure 2, the

Table 2. Automatic Logistic Processes

By Nature:	Function:
Movement:	
AGV:	They are automatic cars, powered by navigation software, that transport small/large dimension goods over short/ medium distances. They walk on an electric (laser) line (rail) (Williams, 2016).
Power and Free Conveyor:	They are rectilinear or curvilinear metallic structures formed by a single beam in which the electric gutters move. They serve to transport loads that require a continuous process line (Ultimation Industries, 2018).
Roller Conveyors:	They are steel structures, placed along the factory in order to transport materials from a production line from one side to the other (Systems, sd).
Sorters:	It is a system that performs the classification of products according to their destinations. It encompasses several functions in one (receives the goods, transports and distributes them to the correct channel, where they will later be sent to the chosen destination).This process is done through the continuous reading of a bar code inserted in each box/product (BV, 2015) (Consultoria).
Picking:	
Voice Picking:	It is the capture of voice via microphone, by which the employee indicates certain commands that, when processed, generate data. These will be stored by a System in a database (Zetes).
Pick to light:	It allows to quickly and intuitively know the location and the exact amount that the operator must collect for the operation, through luminous LEDs and displays. These shows the amount needed to be collected and obliges the employee to confirm each product collection (Srl, 2015).
Stacker Cranes for pallets:	They are machines created for the automatic storage of pallets. These move along the aisles and perform the functions of entry, storage and exit of goods, guided by management *software* that coordinates all movements (Mecalux, 2020).
Horizontal and vertical carousel:	It is a storage modality for small and medium loads, based on a strategy of delivering the product to the employee (Mecalux, 2020).
Handling and Packaging:	

continued on following page

Table 2. Continued

By Nature:	Function:
Handling robots: 	They are electromechanical devices capable of carrying out work in an autonomous or pre-programmed manner (Fanuc, sd)
Palletizing system: 	It is an automatic electromechanical device that consolidates the packages/boxes by palletizing them, that is, securely joins the packages and packs them for later transport (Solutions D. F., 2020).
Pallet packing system: 	Automatic device that packs pallets with x packaging with plastic tape (Embalagem, 2020).

data was also analyzed in order to identify the percentage of the critical point that would be expected to reach in the year 2025.

It is possible to verify, through the answers in Figure 2, that more and more individuals are looking for devices that allow them to be constantly connected to the internet. In which the objective is for the individual to be able to access any service, physical asset or tool, whenever they need it, to be able to predict a serious health problem before it happens and obtain the necessary service in order to make the best decisions in the shortest space of the time and thus mitigate to the worst consequences of any unforeseen situation, is to be able to predict an event and get a solution before the problem.

For Erik Hofmann and Marco Rüsch (2017), one of the key factors for Europe's growth is the performance of the industrial sector, which brings, in addition to investment, the creation of new jobs. This sector is responsible for 75% of world exports and 80% of the development of innovations. However, within Europe, while Germany and Eastern Europe show a growing industrial sector, several Western European countries have shown a low rate of development in recent decades. In the past 20 years, Europe has lost about 10% of its share in the industrial sector, while certain emerging countries have strengthened around 40% (Hofmann & Rüsch, 2017). In order to regain its power in the sector, Germany introduced the term "Industry 4.0" in 2011, which refers to the introduction of high technology, not only in the manufacturing process, but throughout the industry.

Figure 1. Expected average year for each critical point
Source: (Forum, 2015)

2018	2021	2022	2023	2024	2025	2026	2027
– Storage for All	– Robot and Services	– The Internet of and for Things – Wearable Internet – 3D Printing and Manufacturing	– Implantable Technologies – Big Data for Decisions – Vision as the New Interface – Our Digital Presence – Governments and the Blockchain – A Supercomputer in Your Pocket	– Ubiquitous Computing – 3D Printing and Human Health – The Connected Home	– 3D Printing and Consumer Products – AI and White-Collar Jobs – The Sharing Economy	– Driverless Cars – AI and Decision-Making – Smart Cities	– Bitcoin and the Blockchain

Figure 2. Critical points expected to occur by 2025
Source: (Forum, 2015)

10% of people wearing clothes connected to the internet	91.2
90% of people having unlimited and free (advertising-supported) storage	91.0
1 trillion sensors connected to the internet	89.2
The first robotic pharmacist in the US	86.5
10% of reading glasses connected to the internet	85.5
80% of people with a digital presence on the internet	84.4
The first 3D-printed car in production	84.1
The first government to replace its census with big-data sources	82.9
The first implantable mobile phone available commercially	81.7
5% of consumer products printed in 3D	81.1
90% of the population using smartphones	80.7
90% of the population with regular access to the internet	78.8
Driverless cars equalling 10% of all cars on US roads	78.2
The first transplant of a 3D-printed liver	76.4
30% of corporate audits performed by AI	75.4
Tax collected for the first time by a government via a blockchain	73.1
Over 50% of internet traffic to homes for appliances and devices	69.9
Globally more trips/journeys via car sharing than in private cars	67.2
The first city with more than 50,000 people and no traffic lights	63.7
10% of global gross domestic product stored on blockchain technology	57.9
The first AI machine on a corporate board of directors	45.2

Industry 4.0 brings several opportunities and benefits, such as highly flexible mass production, real-time coordination and optimization of the value chain, reduction of costs derived from complexity and the creation of completely new services and business models. In relation to logistics, there are visible benefits in the possibility of tracking the flow of materials in real time, allowing for optimization and efficiency in transport and bringing the possibility of managing risks more effectively, accurately and in a timely manner. Some experts on the subject say that it will only be possible to have industry 4.0 if logistics is able to supply production systems at the right time, in the exact quantity, with the precise quality and in the right place (Sunol, 2020). Thus, however promising the "Fourth Industrial Revolution" may be, there are still several challenges, risks and barriers to overcome for its implementation. It will be necessary to deconstruct traditional management approaches, reorganize value creation processes, make changes within and between companies, define appropriate infrastructures and standards, ensure data security and educate employees so that it is possible to obtain a positive result from this change (Hofmann & Rüsch, 2017).

Finally, the idea of industry 4.0 includes six components: cyber-physical systems, big date analytics, internet of things (IoT), internet of services (IoS), additive manufacturing (3D printing) and artificial intelligence (AI) (Forum, 2015). These six components combined with logistics bring the possibility of creating a whole new industry, making the industrial sector more competitive, sustainable and safe (Sunol, 2020).

CASE STUDY

Organization Characterization

The organization chosen for the application of the case study is in the food retail business and is considered one of the largest companies in the sector in Portugal, market leader, presenting 6,435 million euros in 2019, data updated in March 2020.

Figure 3. Turnover
Source: (Documentação Interna a., 2020)

The organization is a multinational that has been present in the national market since 1959, with a main focus on food retail, health and well-being, presenting a set of different formats where it offers a wide range of products. By 2019, the organization has 709 stores across the country, employing around 53,000 employees, collaborates with a producer club with more than 200 members with 12,000 jobs and supports 1,175 institutions by performing 6,383 volunteer hours. It also has 100% brand awareness, with around 85% of Portuguese families using the loyalty card. In addition, the organization also manages a diversified business portfolio in several areas, such as clothing (100%), electronics retail (100%), sports retail (30%), financial services (100%), investment management (26% to 89.9%), shopping centers (70%) and telecommunications (23.4%), as a whole it participates in about 90 brands. In addition to Portugal, the organization is still present on all continents, with a team of professionals in all parts of the world, being present in 74 countries, carrying out operations, rendering services to third parties, representative offices, franchising and partnerships (Documentação Interna b., 2019).

The organization's mission is to create long-term economic and social value, bringing the benefits of progress and innovation to an increasing number of individuals. Thus, innovation is present in all business areas of the organization, being an integral part of all the functions and activities of the business, where it is important to create experiment and implement new ideas and solutions for the development of competitive businesses, creating value for stakeholders (Documentação Interna b., 2019).

The financial investment in research, development and innovation on the part of the organization has registered a double-digit annual growth rate since 2005, higher than the average registered by the total of the 1000 largest companies in the world regarding expenses with R&D+I. To this end, the organization relies on the active participation of representatives from different areas and levels of the organization, and there is also an internal team dedicated to innovation, with the collaboration of an international open innovation network in which more than 150 partners are included throughout the World (Documentação Interna a., 2020).

Figure 4. Innovation in numbers
Source: (Documentação Interna a., 2020)

The creation of innovation in the organization consists of three stages. The process begins with the vision of "what could be", provided by an anticipation of what the future may bring and by understanding the client's needs and preferences. Then, there is the experimentation and learning stage that ends in the implementation. The participation of all employees in this flow of innovation is absolutely crucial. In this sense, the organization makes all conditions available and implements several initiatives to encourage the acquisition, development and retention of internal professionals, thus ensuring their contribution. At the same time, the external dimension of the innovation ecosystem is also of paramount importance, in which the organization is dedicated to enriching and consolidating a very prolific, eclectic and international network of partners that represents, in addition to its customers, the areas of science, technology, business and entrepreneurship. This set of aspects makes it possible to fulfil the entire virtuous circle in which the organization converts knowledge into economic value (Documentação Interna a., 2020) .

The organization works in a collaborative ecosystem that acts as a powerful innovation enabler. Its network of partners for innovation includes the academic world, R&D entities, *startups*, business incubators and accelerators, and other organizations, namely international retailers. Joint innovation initiatives cover a wide range of topics and challenges, from applied research to *co-design* and product or service development. By combining knowledge, skills and technologies, they make it possible to accelerate the pace at which the latest discoveries and technologies are brought to the market, while optimizing commercial agility and driving innovation in the retail industry (Documentação Interna a., 2020) .

The organization's activity has, as its main ambition, to promote a culture of learning and openness to change, creating ecosystems of knowledge and innovation. The organization believes that, by recognizing unique and distinctive initiatives, it promotes innovation as a catalyst for its own success. Thus, they organize two awards in this area, one that distinguishes the best and most innovative projects developed throughout the year. The finalist projects are chosen from dozens of applications, reflecting the importance of innovation for the Group's Companies which, annually, invest millions of euros in research, development and innovation (R&D+ I). The second prize is based on the investment of open innovation, involving not only internal teams, but also business partners, universities and other *players* and companies from the most varied sectors of activity. As a result of this focus and the implementation of innovative initiatives, new products, solutions and services are developed every year, as well as new processes and business models, which contribute to reinforce the commercial dynamics and obtain efficiency gains (Documentação Interna a., 2020)

Case Analysis

Following the interviews, it was possible to obtain a general knowledge about the organization, as well as its evolution and current information systems and technologies applied in the warehouses of the Food Retailer warehouses.

With regard to the first interview, it was possible to ascertain that, in the conceptual domain, there is an identity, the warehouse director, with knowledge of the presented concepts of IS and IS management, considering that information systems that gather, store, process and provide relevant information to a specific individual or function, guiding decision making at the three levels of responsibility: operational, tactical and strategic. The role of IS in logistics is assumed in the company, when considered that it allows it to improve its competitive differentiation, establish better prices and, consequently, obtain sustainable competitive advantage.

The director considers that the application of information systems and technologies in organizations has marked the market, allowing to differentiate activities. However, in his opinion, there are still some needs, namely, the reduction of labor costs, greater efficiency in carrying out day-to-day tasks, optimization of the picking process, more rigorous stocks/inventories and optimization warehouses. It is foreseeable that some of these will be filled through the introduction of sorters, handling robots or palletizing systems. It also considers that the biggest obstacles in the implementation of new information systems are the high initial costs and the compatibility of the new systems with the current ones. With regard to the vision of the future of storage, it is envisaged that significant upgrades will be carried out in the warehouses, which can be completely autonomous and free of waste.

The first interview was reinforced by a second one, conducted by e*mail, to* clarify some aspects necessary to understand the history of the company's evolution in the field of warehouse support systems.

It is possible to conclude that, over the years, the food Retailer has made several changes in relation to the information systems used to manage its business. The different investment sought to find solutions that support the business and the activity performed by the organization.

The Organization started the activity with the use of InfoLog 3.0 in 1989, which was later upgraded to InfoLog 5.0. From 1995 to 1999, they resorted to the use of the WCSS system – Worldwide Chain Store Systems, from 1999 to 2019 to the EXE and, finally, in 2019 and until 2021, they will be implementing the Manhattan system, being that they still use the EXE until completing the implementation.

Figure 5. Evolution of Food Retailer Information Systems
Source: Own elaboration

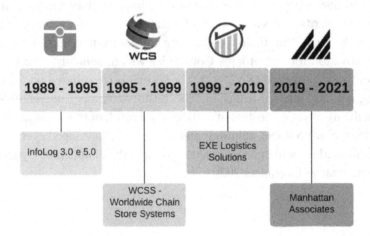

InfoLog

InfoLog is an organization that provides simplified omnichannel software solutions, exclusively for the distribution, logistics and supply chain sectors. This organization specializes in productivity-enhancing solutions, providing material handling and robotics equipment, automated storage, pick/put to light, voice technology and radio frequency scanners. Its solutions contribute to reducing indirect costs, increasing productivity and maximizing the efficiency of daily operations (Infolog Ptd, 2020).

In the organization, Infolog 3.0 was implemented in 1989, directed to the integrated management of warehouses and incorporated into the Logistics Department. An upgrade to InfoLog 5.0 was subsequently made.

Table 3. Information Systems and Technologies: Summary Table

IS	Application Area
° SAP	Applied in the departments of Finance, Accounting and Human Resources
° ICE	Used to manage store orders
° RETEK	Used to carry out provisioning and replenishment operations.
° ROUTYN	Applied to transport
° MAXPRO	It counts the hours worked by employees. It is interconnected with SAP.
° Success factors ° Improving our People	Used for career assessment and management.

WCSS

WCSS is a technology, service and solution provider focused on supply chain performance, providing warehouse management, billing, purchasing, labor management, assent management and analysis software (Stores, 2020).

In the Food Retailer, WCSS was substituted for Infolog 5.0, in which its implementation began, in 1995. This included two aspects: central inventory management, including store and warehouse supply and the integrated warehouse management component, including since receiving the material until the tasks of provisioning, replenishing, picking and shipping. Subsequently, with the WCSS, a labor management module was implemented to measure working times and productivity, being incorporated into the inventory management department and the logistics department.

EXE

EXE Logistics is a logistics solution provider focused on warehousing services, transportation management, supply chain management, order fulfilment and labor requirements. They allow you to optimize the various warehouse operations by providing cutting-edge equipment and tools (Solutions E. L., 2020).

In the organization, EXE was implemented in 1999 with the objective of implementing an integrated warehouse management system prepared to manage the internal flows of the warehouse and its respective tasks. In this way, the stock management component is no longer integrated into the logistical system, moving to the Retek Merchandising System (RMS) system. The EXE also had a Labor Management module, and the Department responsible for its implementation was the Supply Chain Development Department integrated in the organization's Logistics Department. Simultaneously with this implementation, a process of implementing the voice system called "Voice picking" was also started.

Manhattan

The Manhattan Warehouse Management System (WMS) sets the standard for supply chain innovation. The warehouse management software is a flexible WMS that uses advanced AI, machine learning technology and algorithms (Associates, 2019).

In the organization, Manhattan is currently being implemented in the Food Retailer warehouses, its implementation began in 2019 and will be completed in 2021.

Table 4. Information systems and technologies for Warehouses

ITS	Warehouse Director	SI Director
AGVs	Important	Important
Power and Free Conveyors	Not important	Nothing important
Roller Conveyors	Important	Nothing important
Sorters	Very important	Not important
Voice Picking	Very important	Very important
Pick to light	Very important	Important
Trans-lifts for pallets	Important	Important
Horizontal/Vertical carousels	Important	Not important
Handling robots	Very important	Not important
Palletizing system	Very important	Not important
Pallet packing system	Very important	Very important
Cyber-Physical System	Very important	Not important
Big Data Analytics	Very important	Important
IoT (internet of things)	Very important	Not important
IoS (Internet of Services)	Important	Ns/Nr
Additive Manufacturing (3D printing)	Very important	Nothing important
Artificial intelligence	Very important	Ns/Nr

It is an integrated warehouse management system, also incorporating a labor management module, in which its implementation is the responsibility of the Logistics Development Department in conjunction with the information systems area. Currently, the organization, as it is still in the rollout phase, works with both realities, EXE and WMS.

All the aforementioned systems operate in the management of the warehouses, managing all the tasks associated with their operations, with the exception of WCSS, which had a central *stock* management aspect. All the systems referred to are "*order takers*", that is, they are characterized by being performers of tasks performing the same according to the information given by the "*host*" system.

These systems receive two types of information:

- Reference data including store orders and purchase orders from suppliers.
- Transactional data including store orders, store returns, transfers between warehouses, purchase orders from suppliers and ASN (Advance shipment notice)

In relation to the tasks performed by the warehouse, supported for both flows, with and without stock in general are:

Table 5. ITS present in warehouses

ITS	Warehouse Director	SI Director
Current ITS in warehouses	° WMS; ° Voice Picking; ° Robots for packing pallets.	° WMS; ° Picking Voice picking; ° Storax system; ° Drive-in with shuttle

Table 6. ITS that have a greater potential for the organization

ITS	Warehouse Director	SI Director
Technologies with greater impact for the IS and for the respective management	° Sorters; ° Handling robots; ° Palletizing system.	° Big Data Analytics; ° IoT; ° Artificial Intelligence

- Yard Management (inbound / outbound): This is the management of wharves and schedules in the component of entry and exit of goods;
- Receiving: This is the receipt of Merchandise;
- Put Away: This refers to the allocation of the goods to the respective reservation and / or picking locations from the reception;
- Replenishment: This is the replenishment of the picking locations;
- Waving: This involves creating picking tasks with allocation of stocks to store orders, with allocation criteria and sequences;
- Loading: This is the process of associating orders produced with the defined transport plan and, consequently, the loading process;
- Shipping: This is the "billing" process for orders to stores. It is not actually a billing, it is just the confirmation of the shipment (Shipment) sending the information to the host system for later billing to stores.

In addition to these systems, the Food Retailer has also been applying systems and technologies, over the years, in different areas such as:

With regard to the second phase of the study, application of two questionnaires, the following stands out: in relation to the classification of the importance of the technologies mentioned in the management of the warehouses, it is evident that, as can be seen in Table 4, there is a difference in perception between the Director of warehouses and the Director of SI.

Table 7. Impacts of the application of the identified IT

ITS	Warehouse Director	SI Director
What are the possible impacts of the application of the technologies selected in the previous question?	° Reduction of labor costs; ° Greater efficiency; ° Optimization in the picking process; ° More rigorous stocks/inventories; ° Optimization of warehouses.	° Ability to analyze in real time; ° Reduction of time to perform tasks; ° Reduced labor costs.

The Director of warehouses considers sorters, voice picking, pick to light, handling robots, the system for palletizing, the system for packaging pallets, the Cyber-Physical system, Big Data Analytics, IoT, Additive Manufacturing, and Artificial Intelligence

On the other hand, the IS Director considers only voice picking and the system to pack pallets as very relevant.

This reality highlights the importance of the dimension of the architecture of information systems, namely with regard to what Carol O'Rourke, Neal Fishman and Warren Selkow (2003) point out, when they mention the importance of the participation of different organizational actors in the design of IS.

We can infer that, by assigning the classification of very relevant to the indicated technologies, these would be the main strategic and investment options of the company under study.

Regarding the second dimension analyzed, the current technological degree of the warehouses, both respondents are in agreement when considering the current state of the warehouses as little technological.

With regard to the third dimension analyzed, the information systems and technologies currently present in the warehouses, there is also a difference in the responses, as shown in Table 5, which may possibly be justified by the different knowledge of the area under analysis, being that the Director of information systems indicates a future investment in drive-in with shuttle not mentioned by the warehouse director.

Regarding the technologies that present a greater potential for the organization (Table 6), in the domain of the warehouse and the IS, it appears that the person in charge of the warehouse refers to the Sorters, Handling Robots, Palletizing system, while the person in charge of the IS mentions Big Data Analytics, IoT (internet of things), Artificial Intelligence. It is evident in the analysis the specificity of the areas of responsibility and performance.

With regard to the last dimension analyzed, impacts of the application of the identified technologies (Table 7), it appears that the person in charge of the warehouse emphasizes the reduction of labor costs, greater efficiency, optimization in the picking process, the greater rigor of stocks / inventories, and the optimization of warehouses, while the SI director emphasizes the ability to analyze in real time, the reduction of time to perform tasks, and the reduction of labor costs.

Considering the differences in the appreciation of the same reality by the two responsible and given that there was no opportunity to deepen them, it would be interesting, in future works, to investigate the respective reason.

CONCLUSION

The organization under study is one of the largest food retail companies, being the market leader. It has a turnover of around 6,435 million euros. It has been working in Portugal since 1959, constantly showing positive annual results. This multinational systematically seeks to optimize all of its strengths, betting in particular on the evolution of information systems and the application of prizes to innovative projects developed by the group's companies and by internal teams, business partners, universities, players and companies of the most varied sectors.

The results obtained show the relevance of information technologies in the management of warehouses, and it can be said that the organization, over the years, has been making several changes regarding the information systems used. It started its activity with the Infolog 3.0 system and, from this point on, it adjusted according to its needs and the market, going through Infolog 5.0, WCSS, EXE and, finally, Manhattan which it is currently implementing.

Analyzing the data from both interviews and questionnaires, we can conclude that the organization is not technologically developed enough to be able to consider a 4.0 warehouse, however it does present some technologies in the warehouses to assist day-to-day tasks, such as voice picking, robots to pack pallets, a storax system and is currently implementing a drive-in system with shuttle. In addition to these, it also presents some information systems to control and streamline tasks related to different departments, such as SAP and WMS applied to warehouses and the entire supply chain in general.

Although it is recurrent to talk about the importance of the application of information systems and technologies, it is also necessary to take into account the high investments that the application of these requires, as well as the complexity of their entire implementation. It is necessary to carry out several studies, both on the organization itself and on the market, in order to know which path to follow so that there is no failure or unnecessary expenses.

Thus, the success of information systems and technologies in supply chain management depends on the fact that the organization knows how to choose the most appropriate, that is, the one that best adapts to its needs and its logistical principles.

However, in order to start a change process, it is necessary for the company to recognize, as quickly as possible, the existing need for adequate logistical management and an integrated supply chain. This perception is accentuated when organizations feel the incentive and motivation to make the change, often derived from demanding and complex competitive environments that combine high levels of simultaneous pressure in terms of efficiency levels, response time, complexity and service levels (Beth, David N. Burt, & et al, 2003).

The successful implementation of an information system or technology in the management of the Supply Chain does not come only from the purchase of the same. This also includes, for example, the organization's culture, that is, it is important to recognize the importance of integrated planning and the analysis of performance evaluation indicators, as well as the entire flow and needs of the organization, in order to give visibility and greater weight to the established parameters (Beth, David N. Burt, & et al, 2003) .

Finally, we can conclude through questionnaires and interviews, that there is a significant interest on the part of the organization in acquiring more technology and information systems integrated with the entire value chain, being presented as possible investments by the director of the warehouses sorters, manipulation robots and palletizing systems, on the part of the information systems director, this suggests the application of big data analytics, IoT and artificial intelligence, however they do not seem to be for immediate implementation due to the quotation given in question regarding the relevance of information systems and technologies

REFERENCES

Associates, M. (2019). *Manhattan Associates*. Retrieved from https://www.manh.com/

Beth, S., David, N., & Burt, W. C. (2003). Supply Chain Challenges: Building Relationships. *Harvard Business Review*.

BV. O. S. (2015). *Optimus Sorter*. Retrieved 2020, from http://www.optimussorters.com/en/sorters/optisorter-horizontal

Carvalho, J. C. (2017). *Logística e Gestão da Cadeia de Abastecimento.* Edições Sílabo.

Consultoria, I. (n.d.). Fundamentos sobre classificadores ("sorters"). *Revista intraLOGÍSTICA.* Retrieved 2020, from https://www.imam.com.br/consultoria/artigo/pdf/fundamentos_sobre_classificadores_sorters.pdf

Earl, M. J. (1989). *Management Strategies for Information Technology.* Prentice Hall.

Echelmeyer, W., Kirchheim, A., & Wellbrock, E. (2008). International Conference on Automation and Logistics. *Robotics-Logistics: Challenges for Automation of Logistic Processes.*

Embalagem, E.-S. (2020). *Envolvimento com Filme Estirável.* Retrieved 2020, from https://www.embalcer.pt/pt/Categorias/Envolvimento-com-Filme-Estiravel

Fanuc. (n.d.). *Robôs industriais.* Retrieved 2020, from https://www.fanuc.eu/pt/pt/rob%C3%B4s

Forum, W. E. (2015, Setembro). *Deep Shift Technology Tipping Points and Societal Impact.* Retrieved from http://www3.weforum.org/docs/WEF_GAC15_Technological_Tipping_Points_report_2015.pdf

Hofmann, E., & Rüsch, M. (2017, April 13). Computers in Industry. Industry 4.0 and the current status as well as future prospects on logistics, 23-34.

Infolog Ptd, L. (2020). *Infolog Simplifying Logistics & Supply Chain.* Retrieved from https://www.infolog.com.sg/en/

Jain, V., Wadhwa, S., & Deshmukh, S. (2009). Production Planning & Control: The Management of Operations. *Revisiting information systems to support a dynamic supply chain: issues and perspectives, 20*(1), 17–29.

Kim, S. W., & Narasimhan, R. (2002). Information System Utilization in Supply Chain Integration Efforts. *International Journal of Production Research,* 4585–4609. doi:10.1080/00207540210000022203

Mecalux, S. (2020). *Armazéns verticais e carrosséis verticais ou horizontais.* Retrieved 2020, from https://www.mecalux.com.br/manual-de-armazenagem/sistemas-de-armazenagem/armazem-vertical-carrossel-horizontal

Millar, V. E., & Porter, M. E. (1985). *How Information Gives You Competitive Advantage.*

Moura, B. d. (2006). *Logística – Conceitos e Tendências.* V. N. Famalicão: Centro Atlântico.

O'Rourke, C., Fishman, N., & Selkow, W. (2003). Enterprise Architecture Using the Zachman Framework. Pennsylvania State University: Course Technology.

Robert, A., & Schultheis, M. S. (1998). Management Information Systems: The Manager's View. Irwin/McGraw Hill.

Smith, J. A. (1998). *The Warehouse Management Handbook.* Tompkins Press.

Solutions, D. F. (2020). *Paletizador Automático.* Retrieved 2020, from https://dsifreezing.com/pt/produtos/automacao/paletizador-automatico/

Solutions, E. L. (2020). *EXE Logistics Solutions LLC - Excellence in Execution*. Retrieved from https://exelogisticssolutions.com/

SrlC. (2015). *Pick to Light*. Retrieved from https://www.cassioli.com.br/todos-os-produtos/pick-to-light/

Stores, W. C. (2020). *WCS - Supply Chain Expertise. Delivered*. Retrieved from https://www.wwchain-stores.com/

Systems, E. (n.d.). *Roller conveyors*. Retrieved 2020, from Roller conveyors: internal transport according to a modular design: https://easy-systems.eu/en/products/roller-conveyors/

Ultimation Industries. (2018). *Ultimation*. Retrieved from POWER AND FREE CONVEYORS: https://www.ultimationinc.com/products-conveyor-systems/power-and-free-conveyors/

Varajão, L. A. (2007). *Planeamento de Sistemas de Informação*. FCA - Editora de Informática.

Williams, A. (2016). AMS - automotive manufacturing solutions. *AGVs encontram o seu caminho*. Retrieved 2020, from https://www.automotivemanufacturingsolutions.com/agvs-encontram-o-seu-caminho/35024.article

Zetes. (n.d.). *The benefits of voice picking*. Retrieved 2020, from https://www.zetes.com/pt/solucoes-para-armazem/picking-a-encomenda/vantagens-de-voice-picking

Chapter 9
Information and Knowledge Governance in the Digital Age

Jose P. Rascao

(iD) https://orcid.org/0000-0003-2448-2713

Polytechnic Institute of Setúbal, Portugal

ABSTRACT

In the contemporary organizational context, the sharing and transfer of knowledge plays a significant role, and therefore, it is important to overcome internal and external barriers for them to be processed. This can be facilitated by the implementation of information and knowledge governance (GovIC), an emerging interdisciplinary approach that crosses the fields of information sciences, business sciences, and human resources sciences. The problem is that, in addition to being a new construct and still little studied, conceptual divergences are fed by the amplitude the possible dimensions of analysis. In this context, the objective of this study emerges in identifying the conceptualization of the construct of information governance and knowledge proposed in the scientific literature to support its better understanding and perspective of future investigations. A theoretical research was conducted through a systematic literature review, followed by an analysis of the most relevant publications on the subject.

1. THEME AND SEARCH PROBLEM

"Governance" is a well-known term in the business world. It has been focused mainly on the role of management in representing and defending the interests of shareholders. The fundamental role of governance is to monitor and control the behavior of managers, who are hired to preside over the day-to-day functioning of organizations. Perhaps the best-known use is at the corporate level: "corporate governance", such as the set of processes, customs, policies, laws that affect the way the corporation/company is run, managed, or controlled. Corporate governance also includes the relationships between the stakeholders involved and the objectives for the company. The main stakeholders are shareholders, employees, suppliers, customers, banks and other creditors, regulators, and the community.

Therefore, the proper use of information (and not only its production) is of vital importance and, therefore, adequately a candidate for governance. We believe (it is our premise) that organizations that

DOI: 10.4018/978-1-7998-4201-9.ch009

Copyright © 2021, IGI Global. Copying or distributing in print or electronic forms without written permission of IGI Global is prohibited.

have an implemented process of information governance are more effective in identifying sources, collecting, processing, and using information and increase created values for other sources of information. Information governance involves defining the global and immediate or transactional environment, identifying new opportunities, rules and decision-making power for the evaluation, creation, collection, analysis, distribution, storage, use and control of information, which answers the question:

"What is the information that managers need for support in decision making, how they make use of it and who is responsible for it?"

Research into current practice reveals that in many organizations, if not all, a comprehensive information governance policy, Economist Intelligence Unit, (2008), especially for external and free information, and often the policies and processes they have, are not effective.

2. INTRODUCTION

Information and knowledge are valuable organizational assets and, therefore, must be professionally managed to maximize their value. Governance and management are complementary functions. In the public sector, governance is a response of the State to the external environment, based on the various interactions between public and private actors that influence or are influenced by the activities of public institutions, taking into account the social, political and legal arrangements that structure relations between government institutions and their public.

Governance defines mechanisms to ensure good management, with an emphasis on strait participation, transparency, integrity, and accountability (2006). One of the mechanisms of governance is the implementation of policies, which are formal instruments where the principles to be adopted are defined, as well as the guidelines, responsibilities and how the organizational structure will conduct and monitor governance, (Ladley 2012; Stumpf, 2016).

From a scientific perspective, public research, development and innovation (R&I) institutions have strived to find new ways to manage the information and knowledge generated in their internal activities, research networks, interinstitutional relations and interactions with society in general. This effort aims to ensure the proper management and preservation of these assets, especially research data, to achieve sustainability and competitiveness in the modern scientific and technological system.

3. GOALS

This article aims to reflect on the process of construction of the Information and Knowledge Governance Policy, based on the aggregation of existing literature. The first steps were taken in defining such policies and processes from a compliance perspective, in a more exploratory way, (Donaldson, and Walker, 2004).

The value of information is used, and aspects of governance are discussed to optimize the use of information. We continue with a discussion on the aspects of governance and the various mechanisms that have been explored so far. We conclude with clues for new investigations of information and knowledge governance. This research is, by definition, a full and unconditional attempt to combine rigor (academically speaking) and relevance (from the point of view of practice). The governance of Information and Knowledge is "strictly relevant" in both theory and practice.

4. FOCUS AND APPROACH METHODOLOGY

As for its nature, the research is qualitative since it does not claim to quantify events or privilege the statistical study. Its focus is on obtaining descriptive data, i.e., the incidence of topics of interest in two fields, the Sciences of Informação and the Business Sciences. Consequently, with regard to the extremities, the research is exploratory in nature and descriptive in nature, to the extent that the technique used is categorized, consensually, as a study of direct documentation, which provides for the consultants of sources related to the study in different media, printed or electronic.

The complexity and turbulence of the information and knowledge society have led to consideration of interdisciplinarity and transdisciplinarity as essential processes for the development and innovation of science and technology. The implementation of these concepts in some areas faces challenges that go not only through the polysemy of these concepts itself, but also by the hardened views departing from the disciplinary formation and tradition itself, still dominant.

The research method is likely to cause two or more sciences to interact with each other. This interaction can go from simple communication of ideas to the mutual integration of concepts, epistemology, terminology, methodology, procedures, data, and research organization.

This is an exploratory study that seeks to clarify and organize the concepts presented in the literature of Information Sciences and Business Sciences. It is not a proposal of new terms and concepts, but an organization that allows identifying a common denominator, among the different concepts already indicated in the literature. So that it allows its grouping by identity, application / use and pertinence / aggregation of value in the context, in which the terms are inserted. Data collection is characterized by bibliographical research on terms and concepts.

It is necessary to understand, through a theoretical review of the concepts, through the historical documents, a psychosocial analysis of the concepts of Information Governance and Knowledge applied to Information Sciences and Business Sciences, the normative framework in which they fall..

It is a descriptive and analytical approach seeking to know and analyze existing cultural and/or scientific contributions on this subject, from the review of existing literature. So, the research was structured based on the systemic approach to understanding the problems of Governance of Information and Knowledge in this Complex and Turbulent Society. We represent this conceptual network, as follows:

It presents the model of approach to intervention in information actions in the academic space with the purpose of product and sharing information and knowledge, among the participants. Besides to promote the development of skills of search, recovery, organization, appropriation, production, and dissemination of information relevant to scientific researchers, managers, and other interest groups in society.

Figure 1. Information and Knowledge Governance Model

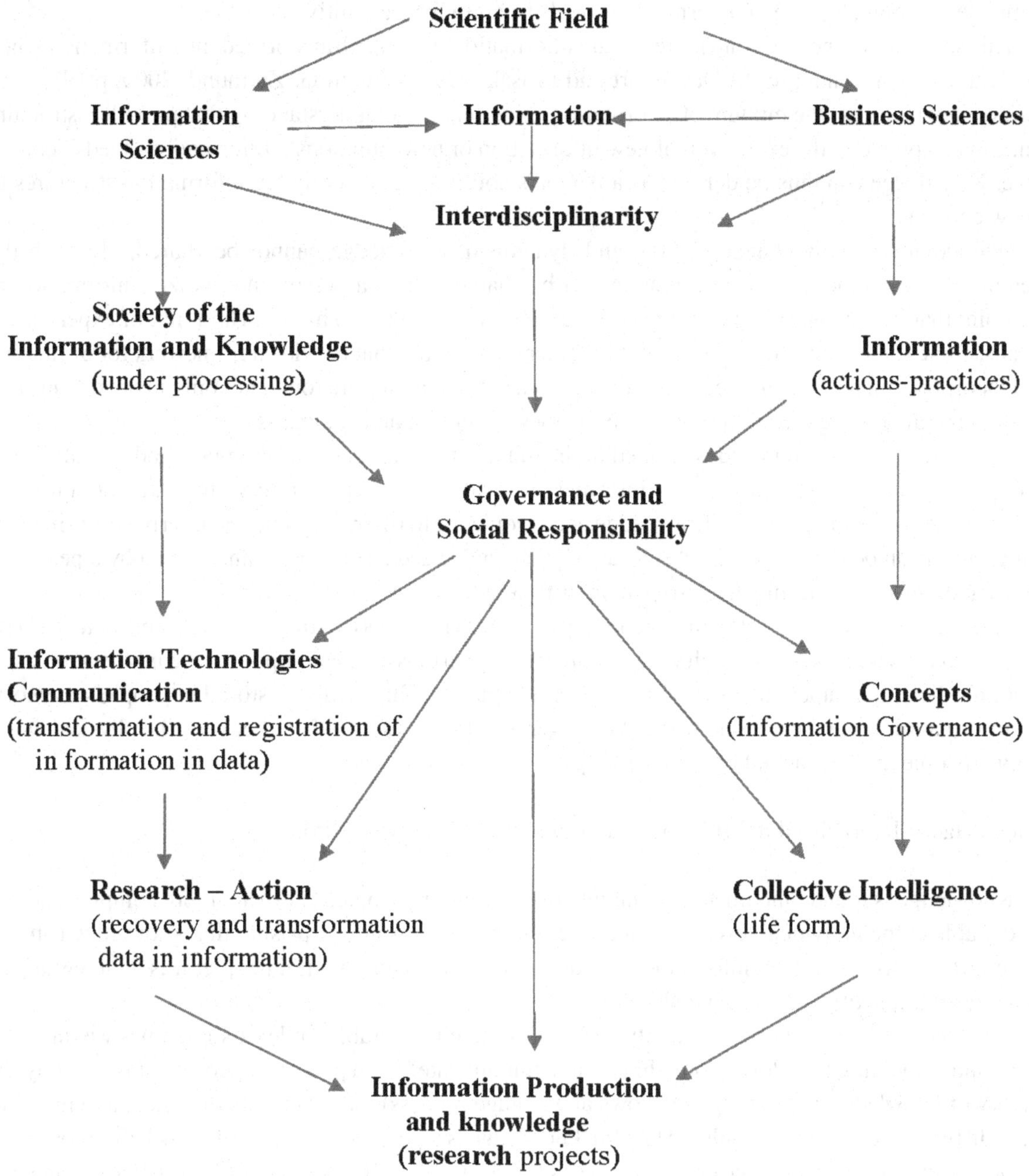

Scientific Field

Information Sciences → **Information** ← **Business Sciences**

Interdisciplinarity

Society of the Information and Knowledge
(under processing)

Information
(actions-practices)

Governance and Social Responsibility

Information Technologies Communication
(transformation and registration of in formation in data)

Concepts
(Information Governance)

Research – Action
(recovery and transformation data in information)

Collective Intelligence
(life form)

Information Production and knowledge
(**research** projects)

5. FUNDAMENTAL CONCEPTS

a. Information and Knowledge

Information is not the same as data, although the two words are often confused. So, it is understood that the subtle distinction between these concepts is essential. The data do not convey sense or meaning of the facts, images, or sounds, since they lack relational elements essential to the establishment of a complete meaning, lacking an internal relational structure for a cognitive purpose.

This structure is one of the attributes of the information. Data are transformed into information when its creator adds meaning to it, (Davenport and Prusak, 1998. Wiliam G. Zikmund, 2000, p.19). They define knowledge as "the mixture of information, experience and understanding that provide a structure that can be applied in the evaluation of new information or new situations". Information "feeds" knowledge. Knowledge can thus be defined as a person's ability to relate complex information structures to a new context.

New contexts imply change, action, and dynamism. Knowledge cannot be shared, although the technique and components of information can be shared. When a person internalizes information to the point that he can use it, we call it knowledge, Zikmund, (2000). This is a fluid mix of experiences, values, contextual information, and expert judgment, structured that provide a framework for evaluating and incorporating new experiences and information. Organizations are found not only in documents and reports, but also in organization routines, processes, practices, and standards.

Knowledge has its origin and is applied in the minds of connoisseurs, (Davenport and Prusak, 1998, William Zikmund, 2000). Knowledge is information as valid and accepted, integrating data, acts, information and, sometimes, hypotheses. Knowledge needs someone to filter, combine and interpret information. Information can be considered as a "substance" that can be acquired, stored, and owned by a person or group and transmitted from person to person or from group to group.

Information has a certain stability and it may be better viewed as existing at the level of society, (Davenport and Prusak, 1998). Although we can store it using various physical supports, the information itself is not physical, but rather abstract and neither purely mental. Knowledge is stored in people's memory, but information is out there in the world. Whatever it is, there is somewhere between the physical world around people and the mental of human thought.

Knowledge = Internalized information + ability to use it in new situations.

Knowledge is found fundamentally and intrinsically within people. These are more complex and unpredictable at the individual level than an entire society. So, it is not surprising that knowledge is much more difficult to obtain than information. Knowledge exists mainly within people; it is an integral part of human complexity and unpredictability.

Knowledge has a fundamental duality: at least, something storable (at least sometimes we intend to do it) and something that flows (something that communicates from person to person). It is possibly the duality of knowledge (something that flows and storage process) that makes its treatment and management difficult. According to Dahlberg (2006), knowledge is organized into units of knowledge (concepts) according to its characteristics (objects / subjects / subjects). The organization of knowledge is related to a process of conceptual analysis of a domain of knowledge and from there. It is structured / architected generating a representation of knowledge about that domain that will be used for the organization of information about that domain of knowledge.

Data, information and knowledge should be seen and analyzed from the continuing perspective of values and fundamentally marked by the growing human contribution – processing, management, action, result, learning and feedback, that is, human empowerment for actions that generate the desired results at the organizational level.

Matrix 1. Data, Knowledge, and Information.

Data	Information	Knowledge
Simple observations on the state of the world: · easily structured. · easily obtained by machines. · often quantified. · easily transferable	Data with relevance and purpose: · requires unit of analysis. · requires consensus on meaning. · necessarily requires human mediation.	Valuable information from the human mind. Includes reflection, synthesis, context. · difficult to structure. · difficult to capture on machines. · often tacit. · difficult to transfer.

Source: Davenport, (1998).

Matrix 2. Data, Information, Knowledge, Actions / Results

	Data Processing	Information Management	Knowledge Management	Stocks/Results
Activities	· Data capture · Data definition · Data Storage · Data Modeling.	· Information Needs · Acquisition of information · Information Organization · Distribution of Information	· Knowledge Creation · Sharing of Knowledge · Use of Knowledge	· Strategies, alliances, and initiatives · Products and Services · Processes · Systems · Structures · Values
Values	· Precision · Efficiency	· Access · Relevance	· Enables action · Value generation	· Innovation · Learning
	"Once we have the data, we can analyze it"	"Bringing the right information to the right person"	"If only we knew what we know"	The ability to learn is the only sustainable advantage"

Source: Adapted from Choo, (2002, p.258).

b. Governance

In 2001, Anna Grandori published an article titled "Neither hierarchy nor identity: Knowledge-governance mechanisms and the theory of the firm" in the Journal of Management and Governance. In this article, the author rescues the term that coined and deepens her studies on principles and mechanisms of intra and inter organizations knowledge by presenting different cases related to knowledge transfer. On the principles, Grandori (2001) cites that governance (Gov) must be continuous, in addition to seeking to balance and combine the organization's systems.

As for the mechanisms, the author believes that the mechanisms of Gov can be evaluated based on two criteria: the first focused on the cognitive possibility of sustaining certain exchanges of knowledge, and the second, consists of the costs attributed to the mechanisms, especially in cases where more than one is applicable. That is, skills and structures for the sharing and transfer of knowledge, as well as the costs for this to occur.

c. Information Governance

It is important to define information governance as a logical alternative, with emphasis on the use of information and not only on its production (systems). Information governance is not a new term, but the proposal for definition in this article is different from the approach in the existing literature. Information governance was introduced scientifically by (Donaldson and Walker, 2004) as a framework to support the work in the National Health Service on the security and confidentiality of information, at various levels, in electronic information services. A report was published by the Economist Intelligence Unit (EIU, 2008) on the use of information governance in companies. Information governance, in these approaches, generally includes record management, privacy regulation, information security, data and ownership flows, and information lifecycle management.

The explorations, so far, point to the possible trap of relying on age principles by introducing a hierarchical control framework, without exploring the possibilities of alternative governance approaches. Let us explore a broader view of information governance as a basis for future investigations. Like the previous points, we divided our approach into one part "information" and another "governance".

The information has unique characteristics, which make it difficult to evaluate. But regardless of its content (financial, commercial information, etc.), the generic principles of understanding the value of information can be defined.

Information is a production of an unusual good in many respects, distribution, cost and consumption. Information is a product, an instrument, or an entry in the production of other goods, decisions, and information, Rafaeli, (2003). It is expensive to be produced and inexpensive to be reproduced, (Shapiro and Varian, 1999).

The value of information is subjective, since it can be more useful to satisfy the desires of one person than another, or of great use to one person, and from little to another. Huizing, (2007), describes in his article that the main difference between ICT and information is the human aspect. Giving means of information is a human element and, by definition, subjective, since objectivism cannot deal with the human feeling of decisions. Information governance should be considered with the inclusion of the human element to understand and use information of value to the business.

Information has many definitions and by itself, has no value. It is necessary to give meaning to information so that it has value for a person. Any "actor", when receiving new information, will give meaning to this information (the information feeds the knowledge). At the same time, the information that the "consumer" or the "receiver", finds is always produced by some "actor", (the producer) in some format, which implies that the production of information cannot be seen without any subjectivism. Information governance should include human interaction with the underlying data and systems.

Finally, information should always be seen within its context. According to Pijpers, information can only be evaluated with awareness of the context in which it is being interpreted. Context is an element of the information environment, which incorporates all the factors that affect the way an organization deals with information, (Davenport and Prusak, 1997). Like the information environment, Huizing and Bouman (2002) describe the information space in transactions, which "represents all possible exchanges of information - economists say in operations - available to any actor at any time".

If an organization intends to influence these exchanges, if possible in all, in some way governance must be introduced and, therefore, an "actor" who governs the keeping of those principles. Therefore, introducing the concepts of "actor and governing", the actor of the third parties involved, as a representative of an organization is a determining factor of the information space in transactions, being able to influence the interaction between the producer and the receiver of information.

In short, information governance be a way for an organization to deal with the use of information among agents involved in the transaction information space. Based on these considerations, we propose the following definition for information governance is the totality of interactions between agents who achieve their objectives using the information they have in common, with the establishment of a normative basis for all activities. Information governance: it is the totality of theoretical conceptions and the principles that govern related information. With this definition, we follow the approach proposed by Kooiman (2007), dividing our definition in governance and information governance, highlighting the various designs and principles applicable to the information manager.

d. Knowledge Governance (GovC)

The state of the art over the term,, even though it does not have many publications on the term or not being one of the most cited in the Scopus database, brings a definition of governance that is worth sharing, Borghi (2006). For the author, governance is a set of transformations interrelated with the intensification and dissemination of participatory practices for the optimization of exchange processes between the various actors.

Peltokorpi and Tsuyuki (2006) describe the importance of corporate governance taking over the coordination of the mechanisms that influence knowledge processes because their non-integration can hinder the sharing of knowledge leading the organization not to achieve the desired strategic objectives. Fleeing the instance of knowledge management, which seems to be the analysis of these authors, (Peltokorpi and Tsuyuki, 2006), this concept is applied to the GovC based on Mayer (2006), which describes that governance mechanisms are responsible for decisions that affect the creation and protection of organizational knowledge.

One of the main references on GovC is the researcher (Nicolai Foss, 2007; 2011), and his collaborators, who analyze the term by the view of the economy. One of his most cited publications (139) is: "The emerging knowledge governance approach: Challenges and characteristics". For Foss, (2010), Knowledge Governance is the result of the interaction of the implementation of corporate governance mechanisms and the management of knowledge processes for the optimization of the economic results of the organization. In an economic approach, the author has been examining the interrelations of corporate governance mechanisms and the organization's capabilities in dealing with knowledge-based transactions, such as no sharing, maintaining, and creating this phenomenon.

Grandori (2007) adds to the concept that this can be understood as a collaborative organizational system oriented to the aggregation of distinctive values to the products, services and brands of the company / organization, creating organizational structures that enable the managementof intangible assets generated in intra and inter organizational interrelations, consisting of people, processes and technologies. The article "The governance of knowledge in project-based organizations" prepared by authors, (Pemsel and Müller, 2012) studies GovC practices more deeply, recording the investigation of patterns of these practices in project-based organizations (PBOs).

The results of companies and organizations are thatGovC practices in PBO's are impacted by structural and situational factors and that the mechanisms of "informal governance" are, as useful as formal mechanisms when it comes to knowledge creation processes. The authors believe that these formal mechanisms seem to be complex for executives, which results in the formation of barriers to productive governance practices. Garde et. al. (2007) the question, whether the author was referring to knowledge management or its governance, since it relates knowledge governance to a set of processes that enable the creation, development, organization, sharing, dissemination, use and continuous maintenance of archetypes. A definition closes to what is meant by knowledge management.

6. THEORETICAL-METHODOLOGICAL FRAMEWORK FOR RESEARCH

a. Sources of Information

To rulers, it is important to know the source of information, a politic an internal and external, which involve the worldwide policy in which the country is inserted because these sources vary in formats, in nationality and content, not the process of using these sources in the strategic political decision-making. Choo (1994, 2006) classifies sources of information into four categories: external, personal, and impersonal, personal, and impersonal interns. The author of the company / organization relates that information is an intrinsic component of almost everything a government does.

The primary sources express the direct interference of the author; secondary sources facilitate the use of knowledge from primary sources, since there is a differentiated treatment for them, according to their function; tertiary sources allow primary and secondary sources to be found. Ribeiro, (20013, p. 44), groups the sources of information into: external personal sources - governance colleagues,experts, other rulers or ex., consultants, partners, international studies state fairs, congresses or lectures (face-to-face or telephone interaction); personal and internal sources – publicservants, co-workers, hierarchical superiors, partners (face-to-face or telephone interaction); electronic personal sources: e-mail (personalorstate), forums, web discussion groups, Messenger, Skype and the like; external impersonal sources - documents produced outside the country, such as magazines, newspapers, books, technical reports, regulations, government publications, radio or television broadcasts; internal impersonal sources - documents produced within the state, such as reports, studies, memos, paper files and work notes; and electronic impersonal sources - electronic documents in general, intranet, electronic databases of the state, on line government websites, various Internet sites, news portals.

b. Creation of Organizational Knowledge

Nonaka (2005, p. 1) says that knowledge has been a new factor of production, joining the classic factors: land, labor, and capital. More than that, different researchers have proposed knowledge as the main source of wealth today of increasing importance of intangible assets. (For Nonaka and Von Krogh, 2009, p. 636), the articles of Winter (1987) and Kogut and Zander (1992) initiated a line of investigations into strategic management often called "vision of the company / knowledge-based organization" (knowledge-based view of the firm).

Grant (2006, p. 203) explains that this line of research that includes the analysis of the resources and capabilities of institutions/companies, epistemology, and organizational learning – is not a theory of the company/organizationin any formal sense. According to Tigre (2005, p. 187): The analysis of the evolution of the ories of the company / organization and its relationship with organizational paradigms shows that there is no single and coherent theoretical body because theories are conditioned by different methodological-theoretical affiliations, focus on different aspects (production or transaction) and are based on diverse institutional, historical and sectoral contexts.

The vision of the company / organization based on knowledge is actually an emerging set of ideas about the existence and role of the company / organization,which seeks to emphasize the role of knowledge, seeking to identify strategies to manage intangible assets, based on a series of assumptions and observations about the nature of knowledge and its participation in production. It is worth noting that the various translations for Portuguese enshrined by the use the expression "vision of the company /

organization based on knowledge". It perhaps diminishes the impact of thinking about a vision based,not only based on knowledge or even prevent are ordering of the terms, which could result in something, such as a "vision based on the knowledge of the company /organization".

Parallel to the works of the "vision of the company / organization based on knowledge"and VBR (Barney, 2007), (Teece, Pisano and Shuen, 1997) developed the theory of Dynamic Capacities which highlights the importance of dynamic processes. In this theory, the competitive benefits based on processes of coordination and combination of assets knowledge. The theory of the Creation of Organizational Knowledge, especially the SECI model, gains another dimension, when viewed, not as an explanation for the world, but as a supporting element, a lantern, to delvedeeper into other broader theories.

Nonaka and Von Krogh (2009, p. 636), consider that: The Theory of Organizational Knowledge Creation aims not only to explain the nature of the assets ofo knowledge and strategies, but also to complement the vision of the company / organization, based on knowledge and the theory of dynamic capabilities by explaining the dynamic processes of organizational knowledge creation, (Nonaka, 1987, 1991, 1994; Nonaka et al., 2006).

The importance that the Theory of The Creationem of Organizational Knowledge can have to better understand the dynamic skillsand achieve a vision of the company / organization based on knowledge, is very clear in the image of the lantern, applicable to all the theory that functions as a lantern that illuminates aspects and dimensions of life and phenomena that before do not see. But like all the lantern pointed into the darkness (here, our ignorance), it illuminates some aspects and leaves others out, Migueles, (2003, p. 50).

c. Informations Science

Origin

It is difficult to specify the emergence of a new science even if it is a recent scientific discipline such as information sciences. However, Foskett (1969) and Ingwersen (1992) mark the date of 1958 as one of the milestones in the formalization of the new discipline when the Institute of Information Cientists (IIS) was founded in the United Kingdom. Meadows (1990) describes the origin of the new discipline from specialized libraries (in industries and other organizations). According to Meadows, (1990), the discipline underwent a sharp development after World War II due to the emergence of the Mathematical Theory of Information described by Shanon and Weaver in the late 1940s. This theory was adopted by many other areas because it explains the problems of transmitting messages through mechanical communication channels. The industrialization of the commercial press promoted the bibliographic explosion, a phenomenon no less important than the advent of the Gutenberg press around 1450. The effects of which became more evident after World War II.

His contribution to the development of information sciences was small but important for the history of the area, as it attracted attention to two needs. The first to clearly define the character of the information with which professionals in the area cared and, the second, to define the conceptual structure to be applied in the organization of that type of information. According to Dias, (2002), there is consensus amongthe authors of the area that The Information Sciences appears in the middle of the twentieth century.". (Claude Shannon e Warren Weaver in 1949), in the book "*The mathematical theory of communication* also according to the authors, it was in definitions are elaborated and the debate began on the origin and theoretical foundations of the new area of knowledge" (Pinheiro & Loureiro, 1995, p.

42). The authors point out several facts that occurred in the 1960s that signified the real milestones of the formation of a new disciplinary field:

- The conference held at *the Georgia Institute of Technology* in 1962,
- The *Weinberg Report* in 1963,
- Mikhailov's Computer Work in 1966
- The study by Rees and Saracevic in 1967 and,
- Borko's definition, *in Information Science: what is it?,* in 1968.

Borko (1968) defined Information Sciences as a discipline that investigates the properties and behavior of information, the forces that govern its flow and the means of processing to optimize its accessibility and use. It referred to the body of knowledge related to the production, collection, organization, storage, retrieval, interpretation, transmission, transformation and use of information. This includes the investigation of the representation of information in natural and artificial systems (...). It has a pure science component that investigates the essence of the subject without considering its application and another component of applied science that develops services and products (...). For Goffman (1970), the goal of Information Sciences is to establish a unified scientific approach to study the various phenomena that involve the notion of information, whether such phenomena are found in biological processes in human existence or in machines created by humans. Consequently, the subject matter should be related to the establishment of a set of fundamental principles governing the behavior of the entire communication process and its associated information systems.

Griffith (1980) proposed a similar definition that establishes The Information Sciences as a discipline that seeks the creation and structuring of a body of scientific, technological, and systemic knowledge related to the transfer of information.

The Information Sciences was born after the Second World War to solve a major problem which was also the great concern of both documentation and information retrieval. This retrieval was to gather, organize and make accessible the cultural, scientific, and technological knowledge produced worldwide. The Information Sciences is a recent science and was born from the exact sciences, that is, seeking to achieve an exact knowledge from the inspiration of mathematical and quantitative models. Bronowski, (1977, p. 47), based on objectivity, sought to formulate universal laws of the "behavior" of information. Strongly influenced by empirical sciences, it was intended to establish universal laws that represented the informational phenomenon and hence the need to resort to mathematical (information theory), physical (entropy) or biological (epidemiological theory) models.

In the seventies, a character comes into play who redirects the focus of information sciences: "man (decision-makers) and as such the human and social sciences also start to contribute with their methods and practices, to the composition of this emerging science", Cardoso, (1996: 73-74). Initially, it was closely linked to computing and automatic information retrieval, according to Gonzalez de Gomez, (2000, p. 6). After the 70s, he effectively enrolled in the social sciences as a "symptom of the ongoing changes that would affect the production and direction of knowledge in the West", González de Gomez, (2000, p. 2). It is, from that decade on, that we can refer to the "social foundations of information". However, some relevant questions are being raised to us right now: what is the branch of science that Information Sciences is closest to? What theories, concepts and methods feed The Information Sciences?

The first studies in information sciences as social science were to study social reality from a statistical perspective, that is, quantitative. Berger & Luckmann (1985) presented reality as something that is socially constructed and not as an existence in itself and pave the way for the understanding of information not as a given, something that would have *meaning and an importance per itself,*but as aprocess. That is, something that will be perceived and understood in various ways by people, which according to Borko's definition (1968) about behavior and information flows. It is something that is outside people and with the definition of Buckland, (1991), that sees information as "thing" outside people.

The subjectivity of information becomes fundamental for the understanding of the different planes of reality and the distinction between the different forms of knowledge and the mechanisms of its configuration and legitimation. People need to be included in studies on information and in their daily interactions, forms of expression and language, rites, and social processes. Several studies can be presented as an example of the incorporation of these concepts in the context of information science studies, such as the *"do sensemaking approach"*, inaugurated by Dervin, Atwood & Palmour, MacMullin & Taylor's studies on people's values, cognitive nature studies inspired by Maturana's theory & Varela of the hermeneutic approach of Information Sciences, the studies of Capurro (2003) on information networks based on the theoretical framework of Bourdieu (1983. p. 46-81), as well as bibliometric studies and scientific communication and the contributions of Foucault's Archaeology of knowledge and sociology of science (Latour, Knorr-Cetina, among others).

The Information Sciences is a discipline that has an overly broad field of practices but does not yet have a theoretical field defined as is the case of other areas of knowledge such as Linguistics, Anthropology and others. It has not yet reached a theoretical construction that integrates all its concepts and practices. Therefore, it operates based on fragmented theoretical constructions, for example, the Representation of Information would be a construct, among others etc. The most important characteristic of information sciences is its interdisciplinary nature in which the magnitude of the problems faced (ecological, ethnic and demographic) is demanding innovative solutions. The Information Sciences have been consolidating from "borrowed" elements among others, by mathematics, physics, biology, psychology, sociology, anthropology, semiology and the theory of communication and other sciences that contributed to its foundation and applicability, Cardoso, (1996, p. 74). *"Information science is not to be looked at as a classical discipline, but as a prototype of the new kind of science"*, Wersig, *(1993, p. 235)..*

Information Sciences evolves into new stages of dialogue and insertion in the social sciences. The reflection on the evolution of information sciences, its relations with the social sciences and as a model of science, is fundamental for research to continue and to incorporate all the knowledge accumulated in this process. Since scientific research is one of the main ways for the formulation of theories of an area, what is perceived is that research in Information Sciences, it has been consolidating and opening new horizons of discussions. Great contribution has been made by professors and researchers at various international universities.

Some important steps have been taken to theoretically strengthen the area of Information Sciences and that research in Information Sciences is expanding and has a Scientific Community that over the years has been consolidating internationally. There are many different challenges that present themselves today besides Information Sciences. As an fapplied science, it needs to respond to the search for information from society and, as an object of research, to the needs of fundamental conceptual esofthes of the area. The realization and sociability of research are the safest ways to create and share new paradigms. Thus, it becomes increasingly important to seek the theoretical, philosophical, and social foundation in the Field of Information Sciences and above all to further strengthen its scientific community.

Interdisciplinarity

There are, at least, four distinct currents of thoughts that reflect on interdisciplinarity in information sciences, (Fernandes and Cendón, 2009). The first places that the Information Sciences, not having a defined theoretical framework, captures concepts from other sciences to be theoretically based, and the interdisciplinary characteristic is born from the unique amalgam established within the Information Sciences. The second, to the company / organization that the object of research of information sciences, **information**, is common to all areas of knowledge, so the Information Sciences is interdisciplinary by nature, being present in the epistemological core of science, as awhole. For the third, there is only interdisciplinarity when conceptual discoveries and practices modify both disciplines involved, at times when concepts and methodologies, shared by both disciplines, merge and change each other. Finally, the fourth current of thought the company / organization that the interdisciplinarity of information sciences, the way it is proposed and discussed does not exist, since there is no mutual influence of the knowledge of both disciplines, occurring a mere juxtaposition of concepts.

Borko (1968), lists the following interdisciplinary areas: Mathematics, Logic, Linguistics, Psychology, Computer Technology, Operations Research, Graphic Arts, Communication, Librarians and Administration. Merta (1968), Cherni and Gilyarevsky (1969) and Mikahilov and al (1969) highlight the following fields of knowledge, in which there is an interdisciplinary dialogue with The Information Sciences, with explanations related to each contribution, among which the methodological: Mathematics and Mathematical Logic; Linguistics and semiotics; Communication, Cognitive Science, Psychology, Librarian economics, Cybernetics and Mathematical Theory of Communication; Reprography and Theory of Automatic Knowledge; Systems Engineering and Computer Science.

Harmon (1971) synthesizes Kitawaga's thinking, from which he identifies the strongest interdisciplinary relationship of the field with behavioral sciences, and all those that have "... a marked common trend for model construction" and concludes that Information Sciences is an "objective, subjective and practical research area". (Wersig and Nevelling, 1975), searched for the "place" of the Information Sciences, the reasons for its emergence and what social needs it meets, considering different orientations: for the phenomenon, for the media, for technologies and for purposes.

According to Japiassou (1976), interdisciplinarity can be understood as the "dialogue between areas of knowledge. For Foskett (1980), the field "... it arises from a cross-fertilization of ideas that include the old art of library economics, the new area of computing, the arts of the new media, and those sciences such as Psychology and Linguistics, which art in their modern form has to do directly with all the problems of communication – the transfer of information".

(Japiassu and Marcondes, 1991), define interdisciplinarity as: "method of research and teaching that can cause two or more disciplines to interact with each other. This interaction can go from simple communication of ideas to the mutual integration of concepts, epistemology, terminology, methodology, procedures, data, and research organization.

Fazenda (1995) explains that the interdisciplinary movement emerged significantly in Europe in the 1960s, a period in which a new university and school status was claimed that broke with education in parts, which was completely alienated from everyday issues. The evolution of the movement towards interdisciplinarity was divided, didactically, by the author, into three periods, including the 1970s, 1980s and 1990s, also presenting information on the context of the development of interdisciplinarity, mainly in education:

- 1st period - 1970: characterized by the search for a philosophical explanation of interdisciplinarity; with the participation of institutions such as UNESCO, in 1961 and the Organization for Economic Cooperation and Development (OECD), in 1972.
- 2nd period – 1980: period of search for a sociological guideline; attempts to explain a method for interdisciplinarity.
- 3rd period – 1990: phase of search for an anthropological project, towards the construction of a theory of interdisciplinarity.

There are two main approaches to studies on interdisciplinarity: the search for the unity of knowledge (objective of constructing a universalizing perspective from the gathering of knowledge around a given situation, especially scientific *knowledge),* and the search for asolution to concrete problems (particular and specific practice to deal more with situations related to everyday existence, especially social problems, than those that are specific to science, with emphasis on the instrumental issue), (Fourez, (1995,apud; Batista, 2007).

According to Cardoso, (1996, p. 74), the interdisciplinarity of Information Sciences is present as a component of current Society Science, in which the magnitude of the problems faced (ecological, ethnic, demographic) are demanding innovative and plural solutions. The Information Sciences are consolidated from the elements "borrowed" by mathematics, physics, biology, psychology, sociology, anthropology, semiology and the theory of communication and many other sciences that contributed to its foundation and applicability.

According to Gomes, (2001), "Information Sciences is a contextual science, that is, it is a science applied to contexts and can be characterized as an interdisciplinary science". Interdisciplinarity is often confused with the mere incorporation of concepts, theories and methods of one discipline on the other, since it uses terms and concepts of a diversity of other sciences, in which it seeks its theoretical bases, such as computer science, business sciences, linguistics, communication, cognitive sciences, education.

Interdisciplinarity is not a simple appropriation of concepts, theories, and methods from one area of knowledge to another. It is only realized from the concrete dialogue between the different areas of knowledge. Effective interdisciplinarity is one that is updated in the field of theoretical abstractions, the establishment of methodologies, but also in the interventions that the different areas of knowledge promote in the social.

For Pinheiro, (2004), it is the "mutual appropriation of methodologies, principles, theories, concepts, and constructs between two or more areas of knowledge, (Pinheiro, 2004). Klein (2004) the company / organization that the concept of interdisciplinarity is linked to complexity. The convergence between these two ideas has significant consequences for understanding the nature of knowledge, the solution of scientific problems and the dialogue between the sciences and the humanities.

According to Klein, (2004), the nature of complex systems offers a comprehensive rationality for interdisciplinary studies, unifies apparently divergent approaches, and serves as a criterion to direct the integration process. The goal of interdisciplinary research is the understanding of the part of the world modeled by a complex system. Interdisciplinarity is characterized by the exchange of knowledge, the transformation of the areas of knowledge and the sharing of objectives.

This author relates that the interdisciplinary approach originates from the need to understand complex objects which a single area of knowledge would be unable to deal with the proper scope. Among these, we can mention the phenomena of the explosion of information and cultural diversity, social and technological problems, or multifaceted concept, such as "body", "mind" and "life". It is perceived the development of a significant number of multi or interdisciplinary areas of knowledge since the mid-20th century and among them, are information sciences.

Interdisciplinary experiences have three basic characteristics, according to Domingues, (2005):

- Approximation of different disciplinary fields for the solution of specific problems.
- Share methodology.
- Generation of new disciplines after cooperation and merger between the fields.

From the many ideas around the term, many taxonomy possibilities have also emerged to better understand how interdisciplinarity occurs. Classifications of interdisciplinarity, individually or collectively, several proposals have been and continue to be presented by scholars. Lenoir, (2003) proposes two categories based on the type of action in which they occur, that is, scientific interdisciplinarity and school interdisciplinarity.

Regarding the scope of scientific interdisciplinarity, the OECD (Klein, 1990) presents two categories: endogenous interdisciplinarity and interdisciplinarity exogenous to the scientific community. The methodology was adopted by internal requirement of the discipline, or it is a requirement of an external character to science. Some authors have a more specific classification, dividing interdisciplinarity according to the way it is found in research.

According to Heinz Heckhausen (1972, 2006), interdisciplinarity can be categorized from the levels of interaction in which they occur. In increasing order, they would be heterogeneous interdisciplinarity; pseudo-interdisciplinarity; auxiliary interdisciplinarity; composite interdisciplinarity; complementary interdisciplinarity; and unifying interdisciplinarity.

For Boisot (1972), the level of interaction presented in interdisciplinarity is divided into: structural interdisciplinarity; linear interdisciplinarity; and restrictive interdisciplinarity. (Huerkamp et al., 1978), propose the following classification: methodological interdisciplinarity; conceptual interdisciplinarity; interdisciplinarity of problems; and border interdisciplinarity, or interdisciplinarity of neighboring disciplines.

The existence and need for information for almost *all professions,* sciences, and cultures, *are* one of the proofs of the interdisciplinarity of the Information Sciences. In any circumstance, information acts as a driving force for the development of the various areas of human knowledge, nations, and peoples and also as an element of unification of inter- and transdisciplinary relations.

On the interdisciplinary fields, the authors highlight part of Mathematics, Logic, Philosophy of Science, Transformational Grammar and Mathematical Theory of Communication and recognize that there is connection of Information Sciences with some traditional areas, including "Psychology (**Information Psychology**), Sociology (Sociology of**information**),Economics (**Information Economy**), Political Science(**Information Policy**) and technology (Information **Technology**)".

Transdisciplinary

It is pertinent to approach some ideas that announce it or converge it to interdisciplinary philosophy, long before the introduction of this concept, such as the notion of system, as well as those that succeed it, as transdisciplinarity. Morin, (1997), rethinks the concept of system, as an organized whole that "... produces or favors the emergence of a certain number of new qualities that are not present in the separate parts", capable of connecting the parts to the whole.

Japiassu, (1976), illustrates the concepts of multidisciplinary, interdisciplinarity and transdisciplinary based on (Jantsch, 1970,72 apud Japiassu). He describes them as systems "... with successive degrees of cooperation and increasing coordination of disciplines." Transdisciplinary is a concept of reciprocity between specialized investigations, but it situates these links within a total system, with no boundaries established between disciplines.

For Pombo, (2004), transdisciplinary is a way to promote the integration of knowledge, to ensure a higher level of interaction, that is, it is a fusion that overcomes disciplinary barriers allowing its transcendence.

The theoretical-methodological approach to transdisciplinary is under construction, being discussed and debated today. Some theories are causally related to the transdisciplinary approach, such as systems theory and information theory, as well as terms related to it, such as passage, transition, change, transformation, complexity, (Nicolescu et al., 2000).

Transdisciplinary, as the prefix "trans" indicates, concerns what is, at the same time, between disciplines, across different disciplines and beyond the whole discipline. Its purpose is the understanding of the current world, and one of the imperatives for this is the unity of knowledge, Project Ciret, Unesco, (1997, p. 4).

Discipline

To understand interdisciplinarity, it is necessary to start from disciplinarity, since the specialties of knowledge are the "foundations on which everything is built", (Clerk apud Klein, 1996). According to Japiassu, (1976), disciplinarily is "... Specialized scientific exploration of a particular homogeneous field of study, that is, the systematic and organized set of knowledge that has its own characteristics in the plans of education, training, methods, and subjects. This exploration consists in the emergence of new knowledge that replaces the old ones". Disciplines have specific focuses and the real of each is always reduced to the angle of view of their specialists, which expands to the extent of interconnections with other disciplines.

For Morin, (2002), the term discipline is related to academic-scientific knowledge that culminated in the emergence of various branches in the field of science, and which developed thanks to the progress of scientific research. In a broader view, Morin, (2002) presents the discipline as a category that organizes scientific knowledge and divides and specializes in the work to respond to the diversity of domains that the sciences cover. A discipline naturally tends to autonomy by the delimitation of its borders, by the language it establishes, by the techniques it is led to elaborate or to use and, eventually, by the theories that are properto it, Morin, (2002, p. 37).

According to Gusdorf (2006), each discipline tries, "an approximation of human reality according to the dimension that is proper to it, with man as a common center", presenting different patterns of formality and organization. Some criteria identified by Heckhausen (2006) help to understand the nature of a discipline, characterizing it or differentiating it from others by aspects that are not always very definitive, as explained by the author himself. They are:

- **Study domain** - specific angle of your material domain. Vaguely defined notion that depends on the constitution of a given discipline.

- **Own methods** – to apprehend and transform phenomena. A discipline becomes autonomous when it has perfected its own methods, which must be adapted to the nature of the field of study, with correspondence between concrete application of methods and general laws at the theoretical level.
- **Instruments of** analysis - they are based on logical strategy, mathematical reasoning, and the construction of process models. They apply to several domains and are neutral criteria.
- **Applications** - guidance for the application and practical use in the field of professional activity.
- **Level of theoretical integration** – construction of the "reality" of its domains in theoretical terms, that is, its fundamental and unifying concepts must be comprehensive, enough to explain and predict the phenomena of its domain of study. Defines the maturity of the discipline and is the most important criterion for identifying a discipline.
- **Historical** – a moment that a discipline goes by in its process of historical evolution, in which both the internal logic of the domain of study and external forces interfere.
- **Material domain** - set of objects they are dealing with. Many disciplines overlap in this area.

The disciplines are made up of groups of researchers who have common intellectual goals. For example, when talking about "physics" or"biology", it is not referring to the representation of knowledge of physics or biology in an epistemic value, but to an organizational structure institutionalized with criteria, interests and objectives of researchers, within the scope of scientific policy.

As a practical example of a disciplinary researches with a scope, the study of sound made in different disciplines: in physics - vibration and amplitude (acoustics); in physiology - production mechanisms (phonator organs); in linguistics - significant and generation of meaning; in music - rhythm, melody, harmony and timbre.

Interactions Between Scientific Disciplines

There is a general recognition, based on various studies and investigations, that the Information Sciences is more debtor than creditor in relation to the contributions of other disciplines. The Information Sciences incorporate a vast body of knowledge from various disciplines, transferring relatively little in return. And many published works establish interdisciplinary relations between the Information Sciences and various disciplines "without explicitness, deepening or theoretical foundation that justifies them", Pinheiro, (2008, p. 29).

Inter and transdisciplinary propose to offer alternatives to the ways of thinking and making of science, providing, in addition to analytical reductionist thinking, forms of scientific research that respond to the needs of understanding facts and phenomena in all their complexity

The levels of integration of the disciplines are classified under different perspectives and formats, starting from simple loans of theories and methodologies to displacement sands or dilution of boundaries between the scientific fields involved, without a very precise distinction of the limits between these levels, within a successive and growing "conceptual chain", as Pinheiro, (2006, p.1), says.

Saracevic, (1999), considers, in the panorama of the development of information sciences, its origin and social role, the nature of its object, information, its structure in terms of problems, evolutionary trends in information retrieval, and the relationship with other areas, issues and educational models.

According to (Wersig and Nevelling, 1975), under the name of Information Sciences (plural), are Systems Theory, Communication Theory, Philosophy, Science of Science, Mathematics, Linguistics, Law, and Information Sciences itself, as well as Librariany, Archiveology, Museology, Communication and Education. This set of disciplines appears linked to information theory, contains areas and theories that are related to the Information Sciences, namely Cybernetics, Semiotics, Computer Science Theory.

The areas are related by theories of a general nature, such as systems theory, applicable to different sciences. The interdisciplinary fields of Information Sciences consist of three levels or hierarchies, where this area appears linked to Philosophy and consists of subareas very similar to those recognized by, (Wersig and Nevelling, 1975), such as Sociology of Information, Information Economics and Information Policy.

Complementarity Between Concepts

In the context of Epistemology, when studying interdisciplinarity, other related concepts emerge, including those that are founders, such as field and area of knowledge, or complementary concepts, including applications related to professional activities. The interaction between disciplines involves different tasks at numerous human levels and categories, so interdisciplinarity needs to be researched in the plurality of its constitution.

Japiassu, (1976), briefly mentions applications, oriented to professions, and, in Information Sciences, this aspect gains importance for another quality of this area, sometimes called horizontality, or rather, the ability of information to go through all fields, on its condition of specialized information.

According to Pinheiro, (1999), "... Applications (contexts, areas, sectors, organisms), that is, scientific, technological, industrial or artistic information, or application in fields of knowledge, such as in economics (economic information are mixed with interdisciplinarity itself) are distinct concepts, although they may present interdisciplinary contributions".

For Amaral, (1990), "... field designates the total territory whose research is intended to operate, such as Medicine, Philosophy, Communication. Area is a subdivision of the field, a cut artificially introduced for reasons of exploratory studies. Theories of Communication and Culture and Image Technologies are areas such as philosophy or surgery."

It complements its explanation of concepts, with the line of research, the company / organization thatthere will be a lineeach time, within an area (which is characterized by a certain informality, in the sense of the absence of a clear individualizing form), certain unifying themes form the cooperation between researchers. They come together to, working together on these themes, deepen the area and develop the field." (Amaral, 1990).

d. Information Sciences and Business Sciences

In the last twenty years, we have seen an important transformation in society, that is, the movement from a society based on industry and transport, to another based on information and knowledge. A great challenge for managers is to understand what information consists of, how it is generated, interpreted and what decision allows us to make, in an era of communications at the globe level, since information is the link that unites us. By being able to transmit it in large quantities quickly from continent to continent, we transform the world into a global metropolis, so in the global economy, information and knowledge can be the greatest competitive advantage of organizations, (*Thomas Davenport & Laurence Prusak, 1998,* p. 13).

Another challenge facing managers is the abundance of information in today's society which their obvious sign of the emergence of this type of society, is the combination of the production of large amounts of information, the intensive use of information and communication technologies and the ongoing learning process. The articulation of these three aspects suggests that from the information society it quickly became the knowledge society. The symbolic culture of this society implies new forms of learning, organisation and management and, consequently, information management. In the information and knowledge society there are several hierarchical levels or progressive stages causally related to the learning process of this knowledge, so we can consider three stages: data, information, and knowledge.

Many people in organizations spend their day-to-day work gathering, analyzing, and processing information. Some industries have developed on the basis of the resource information to produce technologies (process technology – computer, product technology – software and communication technology – communications equipment + software), that is, to store, process, transmit and easily access information. Managers cannot open the newspaper without reading the term information. Many books have the term information. Many people in organizations have as activity the term information. It will be said that it will be easy to say what it consists of. However, when we start thinking about the term information, we have some difficulty in defining it. Part of the difficulty of managers in understanding information is that they are so used to dealing with it, on a day-to-day life, that they do not realize the complexities involved. Managers only realize the difficulties when they face a new language. The potential for misinterpretation is always present.

Given the importance of communication in organizations that are involved in decision making, whether manager or operational, need to find ways to reduce the possibility of error. To do this, it is needed to understand how communication plays out – how information is transmitted from person to person, from computer to computer, and between the person and the computer. The need to understand information – what it is and how it flows – is not limited to large organizations. Whenever one person communicates with another, we have a flow of information because communication is a means to provide information from one person to another.

The information that top managers need is two types: information to identify new business opportunities: internal about the skills and capabilities of the organization and external information about the global and immediate environment. It is not structured and merely consists of data, so to have meaning. It needs to be structured, since not all information makes sense and is important. External information is one that is increasingly important for support in strategic decision-making but needs to be monitored and organized for the work of strategic managers.

e. Information Governance

To define information governance as a logical alternative, with emphasis on the use of information and not only on its production (systems). Information governance is not a new term, but the proposal for definition in this article is different from the approach in the existing literature. Information governance was introduced scientifically by (Donaldson and Walker, 2004) as a framework to support work in the National Health Service on the security and confidentiality of information at various levels in electronic information services. A report was published by the Economist Intelligence Unit (EIU, 2008) on the use of information governance in companies. Information governance in these approaches generally includes record management, privacy regulation, information security, data and ownership flows, and information lifecycle management.

The explorations so far point to the possible trap of relying on age principles by introducing a hierarchical control framework, without exploring the possibilities of alternative governance approaches.

We will explore a broader view of information governance as a basis for future investigations. Like the previous points, we divided our approach into one part "information" and another "governance".

The information has unique characteristics, which make it difficult to evaluate. But regardless of its content (financial, commercial information, etc.), the generic principles of understanding the value of information can be defined.

Information is a production of an unusual good in many aspects, distribution, cost, and consumption. Information is a product, an instrument, or an entry in the production of other goods, decisions, and information, Rafaeli, (2003). It is expensive to be produced and inexpensive to be reproduced, (Shapiro and Varian, 1999).

The value of information is subjective, since it can be more useful to satisfy the desires of one person than another, or of great use to one person and from little to another. Huizing, (2007) describes in his article that the main difference between ICT and information is the human aspect. Giving means of information is a human element and, by definition, subjective, since objectivism cannot deal with the human feeling of decisions. Information governance should be considered with the inclusion of the human element to understand and use information of value to the business.

Information has many definitions and, by itself, has no value, it is necessary to give meaning to information so that it has value for a person. Any "actor", when receiving new information, will give meaning to this information (the information feeds the knowledge). At the same time, the information that the "consumer" or the "receiver" finds is always produced by some "actor" (the producer) in some format, which implies that the production of information cannot be seen without any subjectivism. Information governance should include human interaction with the underlying data and systems.

Finally, information should always be seen within its context. According to Pijpers, information can only be evaluated with awareness of the context in which it is being interpreted. Context is an element of the information environment, which incorporates all the factors that affect the way an organization deals with information, (Davenport and Prusak, 1997). Like the information environment, (Huizing and Bouman, 2002) describe the information space in transactions, which "represents all possible exchanges of information - economists say in operations - at the disposal of any "actor, at any time".

If an organization intends to influence these exchanges, if possible in all, in some way, governance must be introduced and, therefore, an "actor" who governs the keeping of those principles. Therefore, introducing the concepts of "actor and governing", the actor of the third parties involved, as a representative of an organization is a determining factor of the information space in transactions, being able to influence the interaction between the producer and the receiver of information.

In short, information governance is a way for an organization to deal with the use of information among agents involved in the transaction information space. Based on these considerations, we propose the following definition for information governance: the totality of interactions between agents who achieve their objectives using the information they have in common, with the establishment of a normative basis for all activities. Information governance: it is the totality of theoretical conceptions and the principles that govern related information. With this definition, we follow the approach proposed by Kooiman (2007), dividing our definition in governance and information governance, highlighting the various designs and principles applicable to the information manager.

Value Creation and Information Governance

Information governance can be understood as the way to optimize the value of information for the "actors" involved. Does the definition raise the question for whom is the value optimized? What are the dependencies that allow the optimization of the value of information? Gaining a better understanding of the optimization of the value of information and its dependencies, will be the basis for choosing the concept of information governance.

To answer the first question (for whom is the optimized value), we consider the "actors" involved, as discussed in the previous point: the producer, the receiver, and the "actor" of governance. Everyone may refer to one or more people (a single person, group, or group of individuals). The "actor" manages to be seen as the "actor" who is governing the "interaction" between the producer and the receiver within the information transaction space. The three groups will value shared information and for this purpose, value optimization will depend on the value that is given by the three "actors" involved. This leads us to our first hypothesis about the value of information. In the continuation of this point, we will put five hypotheses. They will be indicated here, but not proven. They will serve as the basis for further investigation, as described in the conclusion.

- **Hypothesis 1:** Will a "successful implementation" of an information governance approach lead to a better balance of the value of information for the three groups of "actors" involved?

We use the term "ideal" instead of the maximum because of two reasons: 1st - Maximization would imply that the value of information can be measured. However, this is questionable, since no objective measure can be applied (by definition). Possibly some form of classification can be introduced, which will be useful in the evaluation of information; 2 - Since some information is subjective by definition, information governance can establish an "optimal" point that is acceptable to all "actors" involved. Since they may have different perspectives, it is preferable to consider the "best" rather than the "maximum". To answer the second question, at the beginning of this point ("What are the dependencies to allow the optimization of the value of information"), we propose three hypotheses, each with emphasis on the role of one of the three "actors":

- **Hypothesis 2:** will the optimisation of the value of the information for the "actors" involved depends on the reliability, relevance, and usefulness of the information for the receiver and how the information allows the receiver to make decisions?

For example, a financial report can give value to a financial manager, who is able to interpret it, for example, the "financial health" of a business unit, based on the figures presented. In this case, the report can be prepared by a controller, who is a highly trusted person by the financial manager, and who always provides a report with an extensive list of additional clarifications, in addition to the analysis on the "financial health" of the business unit and ends with an opinion on the actions to be taken by the financial manager. With this approach, the report is relevant to the financial manager due to the controller's approach. The financial manager can decide/act based on the information received. It relies on its controller and the data systems that have been used by the controller, which are the basis of trust, but probably also the controls that have been incorporated (through an audit of the data systems, and a series of system controls). The reliability of the information, in this example, is easy to verify, the relevance and optimization of the value of the information to the financial manager. If none of this applies, the financial manager will not make any decisions. The value of the information for the receiver and the producer would then be useless.

In addition to the reliability and relevance of the information, usability is a factor that can contribute to the optimization of the value of the information for the receiver, as it determines how the receiver makes decisions. The use of information involves the selection and treatment of the information, to answer a question, to solve a problem, to make decisions, to negotiate a position or to understand a situation. People relate the facts to play a role in the process of making use of information, such as the level of subjectivity and intersubjectivity between the producer and the receiver, but also culture, physical context, and mental models.

- **Hypothesis 3:** Will the optimisation of the value of information for the "actors" involved depend on the context in which the information is shared? Can this be influenced by the "actor" who governs governance through information interactions (production and reception), which follows the principles of the economy, political, financial, and / or social mechanisms?

This hypothesis covers the most complex aspects but is the most interesting part of this research. Our definition of information governance aims to go beyond the regular limits of information governance, considering the possibility of influencing the evaluation of information, through governance, interaction, or information flows. This hypothesis is supported by (Huizing and Bouman, 2002), which describe the information space in transactions from the point of view of knowledge management. They developed "a dynamic framework for the management of the information transaction space in economic theory, which integrates the coordination, cost, and learning of perspectives on this topic". In addition, they evaluate four possible governance approaches to transaction space management.

(Raban and Rafaeli, 2003) the company / organization in which: "a vision on the viability of the information society is constructed through the evaluation of the vitality of the exchange of information and the flows within it". In some cases, this may be a one-way issue, but the most frequent is that a flow of information goes from producer to consumer without having reached the same level of understanding, (Griffith et al, 2003).

On the other hand, the governance of the interaction (s) will depend on the objective of the "actor" responsible for managing the interaction. He may want to strictly control the process and the result of the flow of information, independent of the receiver (the value), for example, a Financial Manager wants to control all the information of an annual report. In other cases, governance will be created to facilitate, creating a context where information flows can move freely (e.g. creating a *newsletter* to support workers in knowledge sharing), so that synergy between producers and information receivers can reach its ideal value. A third objective may be to organize flows to optimize the effectiveness for the information receiver.

On the other hand, information flows follow the rules of the economy, the mechanisms of politics, finance, or society. This is clarified through an example in the social mechanism, in some of the police departments in which they are evaluated annually through a series of performance indicators, giving an overview of their policing activities throughout the year. An example of such an indicator is the total number of speeding fines throughout the year. While the number of speeding fines can be measured objectively, it seems that most departments are able to meet the required standard for each year. Taking a closer look reveals a consequent spike in the number of speeding fines in December. Apparently, police departments put more effort into passing speeding fines at the end of the year to get the required standard.

Consequently, other activities may be neglected in that month. It is questionable whether the effectiveness of the police department is ideal because of this behavior. On top of that is the value of the useless performance indicator because it does not give a good perspective of policing activities throughout the year. The value of information for all actors involved is not optimised. This shows that the flow of information relating to performance indicators leads to a desired behavior, a social mechanism. Taking this into account, applying effective information governance would probably lead to a data system where performance indicators are measured at random rather than an annual basis.

Similarly, the economic mechanisms of information flows play an important role, especially as information is expensive to produce, but too cheap to be reproduced, as people are conscious of sharing it without a reward. Can the company/organization in which "useful information" does not come for free. The creation and governance of an information flow will require the attention of these mechanisms.

The optimization of the value of the information that will define a hypothesis about the third "actor", the producer of the information. The producer may want to build the information in yourself, but may also be an aggregator, consolidator, or assimilator of information produced by others. It is not an enviable work; it usually results from the balance between the various information actors. Therefore, the fourth hypothesis focuses on the restrictions of the information producer.

- **Hypothesis 4:** The value of information will be optimized depending on the restrictions of the information producer?

The position of the producer is better understood when considering all possible restrictions:

i Are there legal and regulatory rules that prescribe how information is displayed or restricted in the publication of certain information?
ii The information contained in the information flow can be produced exclusively for this flow, but often the information is based on data for multiple purposes. Can this lead to restrictions on the availability and use of data?
iii If the information is not directly available, the costs must be made to produce the necessary information. Costs can be are striation, (Huizing and Bouman, 2002).
iv The position of the producer in the organization and in the relationship with the other "actors" and / or interested parties will be in determining the ease of obtaining the necessary information for the flow.

In most cases, a flow of information does not have a single meaning, but two ways. In this case, hypotheses 2 and 4 are interchangeable. The last three hypotheses involve exchanging information and optimizing its value is a game between the three groups of "actors". The options for optimising your value will have an impact on the design and organisation of information processes and your underlying data. Focusing only on an "actor", for example, to optimize data systems on the producer side, can lead to sub-optimization. Information governance assumes that it is necessary to consider the three "actors".

Thus, information is closely related to the disciplines of communication. But our research focuses on information-related aspects, not communication-related aspects. We are focused on making sense, for example, of "financial information", but not on how the Financial Manager gives a press conference to explain the figures. Other related disciplines are "information behavior", "information governance", "knowledge management and learning in organizations".

Governance as an Interaction

Governance is generally interpreted as a hierarchical structure of guidelines, policies, responsibilities, and procedures to ensure a certain level of control within an organization. But the definition of information governance does not necessarily mean restricting its use to a specific framework. Information governance can range from a set of policies, a way of working, or creating a space within a predefined agreement (such as an online community), or it may also be applied to an Accounting map, rules within a country (such as IFRS, International Financial Reporting Standards).

As discussed earlier, the governance approach to the use of information is questioned. Other governance work can be more effective in regulating the use of information, provided that the exchange of information is not limited to the boundaries of an organization. In recent years, Kooiman's work has generally been accepted as an important contribution to the approach to governance, both in theory, Kooiman, (2007) and in practice, Kooiman, (2005). At this point, we will discuss the approaches he has proposed and the relationships we anticipated for the use of information.

The basis for governance, according to Kooiman (2005 and 2007), is the concept of interaction. The "actors" within a given context interact, collaborate, and are involved in many relationships. The "actors" alone do not have the knowledge to solve complex, dynamic and diverse social challenges. They need a governance approach to streamline interaction patterns. Kooiman defines three approaches to governance as a way of "governing."

The hierarchical approach can be considered as the "classic" approach. It was defined many years ago and is traditionally the basis for a way to manage an organization or a country. The hierarchical approach is based on management and control, Kooiman, (2007). The key element of management is "direction and control", i.e. it is the way to ensure that the rules are followed. In modern times, this type of governance shifts from regulation to activation, but the basis is composed of a centralized approach directed, including a structuring framework, using structure and concepts.

It is a topic for the discussion of whether this framework is always effective for all forms of information governance, that is, the sharing of formal and informal information, which is not necessarily restricted to organizational boundaries. The leak of the information means that the implementing controls may not sufficiently guarantee the use and sharing of control information.

Because people act in view of the sharing and use of information, they are not based on the belief of information, but on the value they give to information. The predicted hierarchical control probably will not stop them from sharing information the way they prefer. At the top an information is difficult to produce, but easy to reproduce. Therefore, it is easy to share the information uncontrollably.

In his book, Kooiman (2007) he defines two other approaches to governance, known as co-management and self-governance. The essential element of co-management is that the parties that interact have something "in common" to pursue together, that somehow autonomy and identity are at stake. A good example of co-management is network administration. This is a field of research in development, which began with Castells (1996), but with more recent developments on network management by, (Provan and Kenis, 2008).

Co-governance includes the main forms of "horizontalization" that govern actors to, communicate, collaborate, and cooperate without a central or dominant "actor" of government. When the "actors" involved and their relationships are known, these can be the basis for how to share information in an acceptable way. While the formal hierarchical relationship may exist, for example, in a customer-supplier situation, the way to share it can be based on more horizontal governance. Co-governance can lead to a greater willingness to share information, or to ensure a high level of reliability of shared information, because a consensual set of rules has been defined and enclosed.

Auto-governance refers to the capacity of social entities to govern themselves autonomously. Communities created on the Internet self-govern form, where and during the process, but values and standards can be defined in the way information is shared. Kooiman talks about formal agreements, self-application of rules, and the semi-formalization of codes of conduct. Other examples can be found in mass psychology, Van Ginneken (2009). Self-government can be an effective approach to lessening the chance that information sharing will be abused and increase the chances that the use of information will be optimized in some sense.

Kooiman's approaches offer a wide range of possibilities on information governance, each with its own capabilities and flaws. This leads to new research questions about the approach that can contribute to a successful way of sharing information, for example, giving plenty of room to innovate with information, or to mitigate the risks of information abuse. We conclude this point with a hypothesis that relates the "actors" and the approach to governance that can be applied:

- **Hypothesis 5:** is there a direct relationship between the constellation of "actors" involved and the effectiveness of the information governance approach?

As discussed earlier, the optimization of the value of information is related to the three groups of "actors" involved. These "actors" do not necessarily belong to the same organization. For example, the producer and receiver may belong to different organisations and the "governing" actor can be part of any of them. In this case, the "optimal" governance approach can be a form of co-management, such as a network governance approach. Other examples and approaches can be applied as well.

f. Knowledge Governance (GovC)

According to Joskow and Schmalensee (1983 apud Hunt; Shuttleworth, 1997, p. 2), it would theoretically be possible to replace command and control relationships within a given company by contractual relationships between different companies, in order to perform the same functions as the original company. Here, the term "contractual relations" may mean any type of agreement entered into in an attempt to stipulate the terms under which transactions between these different companies would take place. However, these authors highlight the enormous difficulty, if not the impossibility, of specifying in a perfectly complete way all the terms necessary for such contracts, so that all possible situations were covered by them.

All of this could be so laborious and costly to negotiate, litigate and execute that it simply would not be worth it, being much more efficient to maintain activities within a single company, where a manager would take care of all activities. The technical term for the costs of negotiating, litigating and executing the required procurement mechanisms is "transaction costs". According to Hunt and Shuttleworth (1997, p. 3), transaction costs are those associated with making contracts to replace command and control. In fact, the interesting reasoning above originated in a much earlier study.

Ronald H. Coase, winner of the 1991 Nobel Prize in Economics, published in 1937 an article that would become a classic. "The nature of the firm" raised fundamental questions about the concept of enterprise in economic theory. Coase (1937) proposed that the comparative costs of organizing transactions through markets or within companies would be the main determinants of their size and scope.

Coase's article presented a "something primary" question, as Fiani referred to it (2002, p. 267). This question can be presented as follows: "why does a company arise in an economy specializing in trade?"

Coase (1937) used transaction costs as the factor capable of explaining why markets are used in some cases and in other cases the hierarchy, with all its possibility of bureaucratic inefficiency, be chosen. Williamson (1975, 1985, 1996, 2002) laid the foundations of the so-called Transaction Cost Savings (ECA) in several texts. It affirmed the idea that the extent to which companies integrate different activities under direct ownership reflects the comparative costs of transactions between different governance mechanisms, especially "markets" and "hierarchies".

In line with this proposition, Fiani (2002, p. 267-268) says that the ECA deals organizations "with how companies and organizations conduct transactions and protect themselves from the risks arising from them." Also, according to Williamson (1975, 1985), all transactions, whether between people, between companies or between people and companies – both buying and selling, command and subordination – involve costs. These transaction costs are increased by limited rationality and the opportunism of own interests inherent in human nature. The costs of a transaction also depend on the specificity of the assets, the degree of uncertainty and risk involved in the transaction, as well as the frequency with which they are carried out and their duration. The different actors involved in transactions sometimes make mistakes, sometimes cheat.

Thus, in the theoretical framework built by the ECA, the activities will be integrated under a single direct property where it is cheaper to avoid errors and fraud by bureaucratic methods of hierarchy. Managing activities by open markets, on the other hand, will be more appropriate when you can better control unreliable and opportunistic behavior by trading with independent contractors and competitors. According to Williamson (1985, 1996), therefore, vertical integration simply reflects the superior efficiency of hierarchies over markets in the organization of the various transactions involved in a distribution and supply chain. Horizontal integration – or diversification into parallel businesses – takes advantage of hierarchies in the case of synergy management and capital transfers between elements of a corporate portfolio. It is interesting to note that, according to Barney (2007, p. 319), transaction cost savings give very different recommendations regarding the decisions of choice about the vertical integration strategies of those given by the Resource-Based Vision (VBR).).

In the latter, companies should perform only the activities for which they have distinctive skills and hire the other. Meanwhile, the ECA encourages companies to maintain internal activities for which they are vulnerable to error or bad faith. In Whittington's view (2006, p. 99), in Williamson's reasoning it is distrust, not competence, that determines the limits of the company. If as an element of analysis of verticalization strategies in companies and large corporations, the ECA faces other theories that point to different decision-making methodologies, in the field of analysis of how institutions affect economic development, the ECA has proven to be a much more powerful tool.

A group of management researchers, whose largest exponent has been Nicolai Foss, has been collaborating for the vision of the knowledge-based company/organization, from a perspective of the ECA. The Austrian school in which Hayek is part of the basic idea that distributed knowledge is a strong restriction on the use of planned coordination, that is, a problem of the use of knowledge, which is not given to anyone in its entirety. Critical of the concept of routines and training, KGA theorists prefer the use of microfundamentals in management research, pointing out the need for greater emphasis on avoiding regency opportunism and reducing transaction costs, highlighting how property rights concepts and agency theory can help better control the strategic management of knowledge assets.

The KGA criticizes the arguments currently widely disseminated by other lines of analysis, which highlight the importance of knowledge creation and the role of networks, which cross the borders of companies. Do not agree that networks become units of analysis more important than the legal limits of the company / organization (i.e. those that are defined in terms of possession of assets). They question the lack of proof for the argument that the economic organization would be undergoing an important transformation in the knowledge economy that we are living in. The KGA also criticizes the idea that, because of these changes, the relations of authority would be losing importance, as well as that the legal and property definitions based on the limits of companies would be becoming irrelevant. His starting point is that, inspired by Nelson and Winter's seminal work (1982) on the evolutionary economy, a vast literature has emerged, in which organizational routines, resources and skills are fundamental to explain the idiosyncrasies, the differences between company's behavior.

However, according to Foss (2007), most studies aimed at these phenomena do not go deeper into the possible explanations of heterogeneity at the company level. According to him, it is clearly important to understand how individuals and interactional processes allow and/or prevent the development of organizational skills and capabilities. At KGA,the companies are contractual entities focused on transactions, characterized by complementaryassets, employment contracts, authority (concentrated decision rights), and the company/organization limits are defined in terms of asset ownership, and organizational knowledge is seen as collective tacit knowledge, and no evidence demonstrating its existence is recognized.

7. FINAL CONSIDERATIONS

After conducting a systematic review of the literature, and the respective descriptive analyses of the selected publications, it was noticed that the theme of the Information and Knowledge Governance are emerging concepts in the field of Information Sciences, Business Sciences and Data Sciences. And there are different views on the term Governance, because it is a complex concept that can be explored by distinctovisions, and that, by being interdisciplinary crosses the fields of business management, information management, human resources management, (Foss, 2003; 2007; Foss E Klein, 2008).

As a conclusion to this research, it can be considered that Information Governance and Knowledge (GovIC), more than its concept, should consider its main objectives, which are:

- Information Governance, (GovI):
    i How does information influence organizational truth and its meaning?
    ii When can one change the informational meaning of the context?
    iii What is the information relevant to the business?
    iv How can the reciprocity of information between the organization and the ecosystem be allowed?
    v How can passive information consumers become active communicators?
    vi How can organizations profit from the abundance of information?
    vii What information is based on the strategy of companies/organizations?
- Knowledge Governance (GovC):
    i Privilege organizational knowledge in a strategic way.
    ii Ensure the survival and perenity of companies / organizations through the management of knowledge assets.

iii Control and monitor the processes of sharing, exchange and transfer of knowledge and technologies and.

iv Outline GovC strategies, policies, and practices.

With the implementation of GovIC, companies /organizations will be able to consolidate collaborative management paradigms to share, exchange, and transfer knowledge from the intra-organizational level to the inter-organizational level and in learning networks.

In this line of argument, Foss (2003, 2007) points out that in addition to generating knowledge processes, it is essential to choose a corporate governance structure that provides collaboration and sharing at multilevel levels. In addition, there is a need to define "mechanisms of governance and coordination [...], in order to influence favorably the processes of transfer, sharing and creation of knowledge", (Foss, 2003, p.11).

Finally, it is concluded that GovIC must be implemented in companies /organizations to promote the balance between dependence and power through a set of formal and relational mechanisms for optimizing economic results. And, as there is not yet a model of governance of information and knowledge to be followed, this study contributes to the elaboration of a model that recognizes knowledge, as a critical value for the success of companies /organizations,offering support to the principles and mechanisms to be respected.

REFERENCES

Acha, V., & Brusoni, S. (2008). The changing governance of knowledge in avionics. *Economics of Innovation and New Technology*, *17*(1-2), 43–57. doi:10.1080/10438590701279284

Adams, P. Brusoni, S. & Malerba, F. (2010). The long-term evolution of the knowledge boundaries of firms: Supply and demand perspectives. *The Third Industrial Revolution in Global Business*.

Alves, A., & Barbosa, R. R. (2010). Influences and barriers to information sharing: A theoretical perspective. *Information Science*.

Amin, A., & Cohendet, P. (2011). *Architectures of Knowledge: Firms, Capabilities, and Communities. Architectures of Knowledge: Firms*. Capabilities, and Communities.

Antonelli, C. (2006). The business governance of localized knowledge: An information economics approach for the economics of knowledge. *Industry and Innovation*, *13*(3), 2006. doi:10.1080/13662710600858118

Antonelli, C. (2007). Technological knowledge as an essential facility. *Journal of Evolutionary Economics*, *17*(4), 451–471. doi:10.100700191-007-0058-4

Antonelli, C. (2008). The new economics of the university: A knowledge governance approach. *The Journal of Technology Transfer*, *33*(1), 1–22. doi:10.100710961-007-9064-9

Antonelli, C. (2013). Knowledge Governance: Pecuniary Knowledge Externalities and Total FactorProductivity Growth. *Economic Development Quarterly*, *27*(1), 62–70. doi:10.1177/0891242412473178

Antonelli, C., & Amidei, F.B. (2011). *The dynamics of knowledge externalities: Localized technological change in Italy*. Academic Press.

Antonelli, C., Amidei, F.B., & Fassio, C. (2014). The mechanisms of knowledge governance: State owned enterprises and Italian economic growth, 1950-1994. *Structural Change and Economic Dynamics*.

Antonelli, C., Amidei, F.B., & Fassio, C. (2015). Corrigendum to "The mechanisms of knowledge governance: State owned enterprises and Italian economic growth, 1950-1994". *Structural Change and Economic Dynamics*.

Antonelli, C., & Calderini, M. (2008). The governance of knowledge compositeness and technological performance: The case of the automotive industry in Europe. *Economics of Innovation and New Technology, 17*(1-2), 23–41. doi:10.1080/10438590701279243

Antonelli, C., & Fassio, C. (2014). The heterogeneity of knowledge and the academic mode of knowledge governance: Italian evidence in the first part of the 20th century. *Science & Public Policy, 41*(1), 15–28. doi:10.1093cipolct030

Antonelli, C., & Fassio, C. (2016). Globalization and the Knowledge-Driven Economy. *Economic Development Quarterly, 30*(1), 3–14. doi:10.1177/0891242415617239

Antonelli, C., Patrucco, P. P., & Quatraro, F. (2008). The governance of localized knowledge externalities. *International Review of Applied Economics, 22*(4), 479–498. doi:10.1080/02692170802137661

Antonelli, C., & Teubal, M. (2010). Venture capitalism as a mechanism for knowledge governance. *The Capitalization of Knowledge: A Triple Helix of University-Industry-Government*.

Antonelli, C. A. (2016). Schumpeterian growth model: Wealth and directed technological change. *The Journal of Technology Transfer, 41*(3), 395–406. doi:10.100710961-015-9410-2

Assumpção, T. (2008). Systemic vision relates knowledge and intangible assets. *Fnq*. Available from: www.fnq.org.br/site/ItemID=1032/369/default.aspx

Bianchi, M., Casalino, N., Draoli, M., & Gambosi, G. (2012). *An innovative approach to the governance of E-government knowledge management systems. Information Systems: Crossroads for Organization, Management, Accounting and Engineering: ItAIS*. The Italian Association for Information Systems.

Bianchi, M., Casalino, N., Draoli, M., & Gambosi, G. (2013). *An innovative approach to the governance of e-government knowledge management systems. Information Systems: Crossroads for Organization, Management, Accounting and Engineering: ItAIS*. The Italian Association for Information Systems.

Borghi, V. (2006). Tra cittadini e istituzioni. Riflessioni sull'introduzione di dispositivi partecipativi nelle pratiche istituzionali locali. In *Rivista delle politiche sociali, n°2*. Ediesse.

Burlamaqui, L. (2010). *Knowledge Governance Innovation and Development. Political Economics Magazine* (Vol. 30). Printed.

Burlamaqui, L. (2011). Knowledge Governance: An Analytical Approach and its Policy Implications. In Knowledge Governance-Reasserting the Public Interest. Anthem Press.

Burlamaqui, L., Castro, A. C., & Kattel, R. (2011). *Knowledge Governance –Reasserting the Public Interest*. Anthem Press.

Byrd, T.A., Markland, R.E., Karwan, K.R., & Philipoom, P.R. (1966). *An object-oriented rule-based design structure for a maintenance management system*. Academic Press.

Cabrita, R. (2004). Intellectual capital: the new wealth of organizations. *Digital Magazine of the Banking Training Institute*. Available at: www.ifb.pt/publicacoes/info_57/artigo03_57.htm

Cadbury, A. (1992). *The Financial Aspects of Corporate Governance. The Committee on the Financial Aspects of Corporate Governance and Gee and Co. Ltd*. Committee on the Financial Aspects of Corporate Governance.

Carr, N. (2003). IT does not matter anymore. *Harvard Business Review*, (5), 41–49. PMID:12747161

Carver, J. (2001). *On Board Leadership. Jossey-Bass Wiley*.

Castells, M. (1996). *The Rise of the Network society, the Information Age: Economy, society and Culture* (Vol. 1). Blackwell Publishers.

Chan, L. (2002). Why Haven't we mastered alignment? The importance of the informal organization structure. *MIS Quarterly Executive*, *1*(2), 97–112.

Chen, L., & Fong, P. S. W. (2012). Revealing Performance Heterogeneity Through Knowledge Management Maturity Evaluation: A Capability-Based Approach. *Expert Systems with Applications*, *39*(18), 13523–13539. doi:10.1016/j.eswa.2012.07.005

Chen, L., & Fong, P. S. W. (2013). Visualizing Evolution of Knowledge Management Capability in Construction Firms. *Journal of Construction Engineering and Management*, *139*(7), 839–851. doi:10.1061/(ASCE)CO.1943-7862.0000649

Choo, C. W. (1998). *The knowing organization, how organizations use information to construct meaning, create knowledge and make decisions*. Oxford University Press.

Choo, C. W. (2008). *Social use of information in organizational groups, information management: Setting the scene* (A. Huizing & E. J. De Vries, Eds.). Elsevier.

Ciborra, C. (1997). From Profundis? Deconstructing the Concept of Strategic Alignment. *Scandinavian Journal of Information Systems*, *9*(1), 67–82.

Curty, R. G. (2005). *The Flow of Technological Information in the Product Project In Food Industries* (Master's thesis). Graduate Program in Information Science, Federal University of Santa Catarina. Florianopolis.

Davenport, T. H., & Prusak, L. (1997). *Information Ecology: Mastering The information and Knowledge Environment*. Oxford University Press.

Donaldson, A., & Walker, P. (2004). Information Governance – a view from the NHS. *International Journal of Medical Informatics*, *73*(3), 281–284. doi:10.1016/j.ijmedinf.2003.11.009 PMID:15066559

Drahos, P. (2010). The Global Governance of Knowledge: Patent Offices and Their Clients. Academic Press.

Economist Intelligence Unit. (2008). *The Future of enterprise information Governance*. The Economist Intelligence Unit Limited.

Fama, E. F., & Jensen, M. C. (1983). Separation of ownership and control. *The Journal of Law & Economics, 26*(2), 1983. doi:10.1086/467037

Fong, P. S. W., & Chen, L. (2012). Governance of Learning Mechanisms: Evidence from Construction Firms. *Journal of Construction Engineering and Management, 138*(9), 1053–1064. doi:10.1061/(ASCE) CO.1943-7862.0000521

Foss, K., & Foss, N.J. (2009). Managerial Authority When Knowledge Is Distributed: A Knowledge Governance Perspective. *Knowledge Governance: Processes and perspectives*.

Foss, N.J. (2005). *The Knowledge Governance Approach*. Academic Press.

Foss, N. J. (2007). The Emerging Knowledge Governance Approach: Challenges and Characteristics. *Organization, 14*(1), 29–52. doi:10.1177/1350508407071859

Foss, N. J., Husted, K., Michailova, S., & Pedersen, T. (2003). *Governing knowledge Processes: Theoretical Foundations and Research Opportunities*. Working paper No. 1, Center for Knowledge Governance, Copenhagen Business School.

Foss, N.J., & Klein, P.G. (2008). The Theory of The Firm and Its Critics: A Stocktaking and Assessment. *New Institutional Economics: A Guidebook*.

Foss, N.J., & Michailova, S. (2009). Knowledge Governance: What Have We Learned? And Where Are We Heading? *Knowledge Governance: Processes and perspectives*.

Freire, P. S. (2013). *Increase the Quality and Quantity of Its Scientific Publications: Manual for Projects and Scientific Articles*. Crv Publishing House.

Freire, P. S. (2014). *Increase The Quality and Quantity of Your Scientific Publications: Manual for Projects and Scientific Articles*. Crv Publishing House.

Freire, P. S., Nakayama, K. M., & Spanhol, F. J. (2010). Knowledge Sharing: Collaborative Group A Path to The Organizational Learning Process. In *People Management* (1st ed.). Pandion.

Freire, P. S., Soares, A. P., Nakayama, K. M., & Spanhol, F. J. (2008). Professionalization Process With The Implementation of Good Corporate Governance Practices For Ipo in A Brazilian Company with Family Type Management. In *XXVIII National Meeting of Production Engineering*, Rio de Janeiro.

Galbraith, J. (1997). Designing the Innovative Organization. In How Organizations Learn: Successful Reports From Large Organizations. Studies In Health Technology And Informatics.

Garde, S., Knaup, P., Hovenga, E. J. S., & Heard, S. (2007). Towards Semantic Interoperability For Electronic Health Records: Domain Knowledge Governance For Openehr Archetypes. *Methods of Information in Medicine*.

Giebels, D., & De Jonge, V. N. (2014). Making Ecosystem-Based Management Effective: Identifying and Evaluating Empirical Approaches to The Governance Of Knowledge. *Emergence*.

Giebels, D., & Teisman, G.R. (2015). Towards Ecosystem-Based Management for Mainports: A Historical Analysis of The Role of Knowledge in The Development of The Rotterdam Harbor from 1827 To 2008. *Ocean and Coastal Management.*

Giebels, D., Van Buuren, A., & Edelenbos, J. (2013). Ecosystem-Based Management in The Wadden Sea: Principles for The Governance of Knowledge. *Journal of Sea Research, 82,* 176–187. doi:10.1016/j.seares.2012.11.002

Giebels, D., Van Buuren, A., & Edelenbos, J. (2015). Using Knowledge in A Complex Decision-Making Process -Evidence and Principles from The Danish Hooting Project's Ecosystem-Based Management Approach. *Environmental Science & Policy, 47,* 53–67. doi:10.1016/j.envsci.2014.10.015

Giebels, D., Van Buuren, A., & Edelenbos, J. (2016). Knowledge Governance for Ecosystem-Based Management: Understanding Its Context-Dependency. *Environmental Science & Policy, 55,* 424–435. doi:10.1016/j.envsci.2015.08.019

Ginneken, J. Van (2009). The power of the Swarm, self-Governance in an organization. *Business Contact.*

Goldman, F. (2010). Knowledge Governance and Organizational Knowledge Management. *Management & Technology Magazine.*

Gooderham, P., Minbaeva, D. B., & Pedersen, T. (2011). Governance Mechanisms for The Promotion of Social Capital for Knowledge Transfer in Multinational Corporations. *Journal of Management Studies, 48*(1), 123–150. doi:10.1111/j.1467-6486.2009.00910.x

Goshal, S., & Bartlett, C. (2000). *The Individualized Organization.* Rj: Campus. Corporate Governance & Ethics In Organizations. Academic Knowledge. Uniesp São Paulo Multidisciplinary Magazine: Uniesp.

Grandori, A. (1997). Governance Structures, Coordination Mechanisms And Cognitive Models. *The Journal of Management and Governance, 1*(1), 29–42. doi:10.1023/A:1009977627870

Grandori, A. (2001). Neither Hierarchy nor Identity: Knowledge Governance Mechanisms And The Theory of the Firm. *The Journal of Management and Governance, 5*(3/4), 381–399. doi:10.1023/A:1014055213456

Grandori, A. (2009). Poliarchic Governance and The Growth of Knowledge. *Knowledge Governance: Processes and Perspectives.*

Grandori, A. (2013). *Epistemic Economics and Organization: Forms of Rationality and Governance for a Wiser Economy.* Academic Press.

Grandori, A. F., & Ut Facias, M. F. (2009). Associational Contracts for Innovation. *International Studies of Management & Organization.* Advance online publication. doi:10.2753/IMO0020-8825390405

Grembergen, V. W. (2004). *Strategies for Information Technology Governance.* IDEA Group Publishing. doi:10.4018/978-1-59140-140-7

Griffith, T. L., Sawyer, J. E., & Neale, M. A. (n.d.). Virtualness and knowledge in teams: Managing the Lover triangle of organizations, individuals, and information technology. MIS Quarterly, 27(2), 265-287.

Helou, A. R. H. A. (2009). *Integrated Risk Management Method In the Context of Public Administration. Dissertation* (Master's Thesis). Graduate Program in Engineering and Knowledge Management of The Federal University of Santa Catarina. Santa Catarina: Ufsc.

Henderson, J. C., & Venkatraman, N. (1993). Strategic Alignment: Leveraging Information Technology for Transforming Organizations. *IBM Systems Journal, 32*(1), 4–16. doi:10.1147j.382.0472

Hirschheim, R., & Sabherwal, R. (2001). Detours in the Path toward Strategic Information Systems Alignment. *California Management Review, 44*(1), 87–108. doi:10.2307/41166112

Hoebeke, L. (1990). Measuring in organizations. *Journal of Applied Systems Analysis, 117,* 115–122.

Hoebeke, L. (2006). Identity: The paradoxical nature of organizational closure. *Kybernetes, 35*(1/2), 65–75. doi:10.1108/03684920610640236

Holsapple, S.W., & Singh, M. (2001). The Knowledge Chain Model: Activities For Competitiveness. *Expert Systems with Application.*

Hovenga, E., Garde, S., & Heard, S. (2005). Nursing Constraint Models for Electronic Health Records: A Vision for Domain Knowledge Governance. *International Journal of Medical Informatics, 74*(11-12), 886–898. doi:10.1016/j.ijmedinf.2005.07.013 PMID:16115795

Huizing, A. (2007). The value of a rose: rising above Objectivism and subjectivism. In Information Management: Setting the Scene. London: Elsevier.

Huizing, A., & Bouman, W. (2002). Knowledge and Learning, Markets and Organizations: Managing the information transaction space. In The strategic management of intellectual capital and organizational Knowledge. Oxford University Press.

Husted, K., Michailova, S., Minbaeva, D. B., & Pedersen, T. (2012). Knowledge-Sharing Hostility and Governance Mechanisms: An Empirical Test. *Journal of Knowledge Management, 16*(5), 754–773. doi:10.1108/13673271211262790

Ibgc. (2014). *Introduction to Good Corporate Governance Practices for Privately Held Organizations.* Http://Www.Ibgc.Org.Br/Userfiles/Files/Audpub.Pdf?__Akacao=1793926&__Akcnt=98ff2d07&__Akvkey=9c99&Utm_Source=Akna&Utm_Medium=Email&Utm_Campaign=Ibgc%3a+Audi%Eancia+P%Fablica+-+Caderno+De+Governan%E7a+Para+Empresa+De+Capital+Fechado

IT Governance Institute. (2003). *Board Briefing on IT Governance* (2nd ed.). Retrieved from: https://www.isaca.org/Content/ContentGroups/ITGI3/Resources1/Board_Briefing_on_IT_Governance/26904_Board_Briefing_final.pdf

Julien, Cuadra, William, Luke, & Harris. (2009). SECTION III-Information Use-Chapter 7-Information Behavior. Annual Review of Information Science and Technology, 43, 317-358.

Kahn & Blair. (2004). *Information Nation-seven keys to information management compliance.* AIIM.

Kooiman, J. (Ed.). (2005). Fish for life, interactive governance for fisheries. Amsterdam University Press.

Kooiman, J. (2007). Governing as governance. *Information governance: In search of the Forgotten Grail 21.*

Löffer. E., & Bovair, A.G. (2009). Public Management and Governance (2nd ed.). Nuc: Routledge.

Maes, R. (2007). Information Management: An integrative perspective. In Information Management: Setting the Scene. London: Elsevier.

Mahnke, V., & Pedersen, T. (2003). *Knowledge Flows, Governance and The Multinational Enterprise: Frontiers in International Management Research*. Academic Press.

Mahnke, V., & Pedersen, T. (2003). Knowledge Governance and Value Creation. *Knowledge Flows, Governance and the Multinational Enterprise: Frontiers in International Management Research*.

Marconi, M. A., & Lakatos, E. M. (2009). *Fundamentals of Scientific Methodology*. Atlas.

Mayer, K. J. (2006). Spillovers and Governance: An Analysis of Knowledge and Reputational Spillovers in Information Technology. *Academy of Management Journal*.

Michailova, S., & Foss, N.J. (2009). Knowledge Governance: Themes and Questions. *Knowledge Governance: Processes and Perspectives*.

Michailova, S., & Sidorova, E. (2011). From Group-Based Work to Organizational Learning: The Role of Communication Forms and Knowledge Sharing. *Knowledge Management Research and Practice, 9*(1), 73–83. doi:10.1057/kmrp.2011.4

Mitroff, I., Mason, R., & Pearson, C. (1994). *Frame break: The Radical Redesign Of American Business*. Jossey-Bass.

Müller, R., Glückler, J., Aubry, M., & Shao, J. (2013). Project Management Knowledge Flows In Networks Of Project Managers and Project Management Offices: A Case Study in the Pharmaceutical industry. *Project Management Journal, 44*(2), 4–19. doi:10.1002/pmj.21326

Nadai, F. C., & Calado, L. R. (2005). Knowledge as a Strategic Resource: Characterizing a Knowledge-Intensive Organization (oic). In *Viii Sowe-Seminars in Administration, 2005. Sao Paulo. Annals....* Fea-Usp.

Nonaka, I., & Takeuchi, H. (1997). *Creation of Knowledge in the Company* (5th ed.). Campus.

Nonaka, I., Toyama, R., & Hirata, T. (2008). *Managing Flow: A Process Theory Of The Knowledge-Based Firm*. Palgrave Macmillan. doi:10.1057/9780230583702

Nooteboom, B. (2000). Learning by Interaction: Absorptive Capacity, Cognitive Distance and Governance. *Journal of Management and Governance*.

OECD. (2016). *Principles of Government Of Societies Of The G20 And OECD*. Http://Dx.Doi.Org/10.1787/9789264259195-Ptpai

Overbeek, P. (2005). *Information Security under control: Ground rules, management, organization and technique*. FT Prentice Hall Financial Times.

Peltokorpi, V., & Tsuyuki, E. (2007). Organizational Governance in Internal Hybrids: A Case Study of Maekawa Manufacturing Ltd. *Corporate Governance, 7*(2), 123–135. doi:10.1108/14720700710739778

Pemsel, S., & Müller, R. (2012). The Governance of Knowledge in Project-Based Organizations. *International Journal of Project Management, 30*(8), 865–876. doi:10.1016/j.ijproman.2012.02.002

Pemsel, S., Müller, R., & Söderlund, J. (2016). Knowledge Governance Strategies in Project-Based Organizations. *Long Range Planning*, *49*(6), 648–660. doi:10.1016/j.lrp.2016.01.001

Pemsel, S., Wiewiora, A., Müller, R., Aubry, M., & Brown, K. (2014). A Conceptualization of Knowledge Governance in Project-Based Organizations. *International Journal of Project Management*, *32*(8), 1411–1422. doi:10.1016/j.ijproman.2014.01.010

Peppard, J., & Ward, J. (1999). Mind the GAP: Diagnosing the relationship between THE IT Organisation and the rest of the business. *The Journal of Strategic Information Systems*, *8*(1), 29–60. doi:10.1016/S0963-8687(99)00013-X

Pijpers, G. (2006). *Information usage behavior theory and practice*. Academic Service.

Provan, K. G., & Kenis, P. (2008). Modes of network governance: Structure, management, and effectiveness. *Journal of Public Administration: Research and Theory*, *18*(2), 229–252. doi:10.1093/jopart/mum015

Putnam, L. L. (1983). The Interpretative Perspective: An Alternative to Functionalism. In L. L. Putnam & M. E. Pacanowsky (Eds.), *Communication and Organizations: An Interpretative Approach* (pp. 31–54). Sage Publications.

Raban, D. R., & Rafael, S. (2003). *Subjective Value of Information: The Endowment Effect*. In IADIS International Conference: E-Society 2003, Lisbon, Portugal.

Rafaeli, S., & Raban, D. (2003). Experimental Investigation of the Subjective Value of information in Trading. *Journal of the Association for Information Systems*, *4*(1), 119–139. doi:10.17705/1jais.00032

Ritta, C. O., & Ensslin, S. R. (2010). *Research on The Relationship Between Intangible Assets and Financial Variables: A Study In Brazilian Organizations Belonging to the Ibo vespa Index In The Years 2007 and 2008*. In 10th Usp Congress of Comptant and Accounting, 2010.Anais... São Paulo.

Santiso. (2001). International Co-Operation for Democracy and Good Governance: Moving Towards a Second Generation? *European Journal of Development Research*.

Senge, P. (2006). The fifth discipline, the art and practice of the Learning Organization. Random House.

Shapiro, C., & Varian, H. R. (1999). *Information rules*. Harvard Business School Press.

Simonsson, M., & Johnson, P. (2006). Assessment of IT Governance-A Prioritization of Cobit. KTH, Royal Institute of Technology, Stockholm, Research report #151. Information Governance: In search of the Forgotten Grail 22.

Sveiby, K. E. (1998). *The new wealth of organizations: managing and evaluating knowledge assets*. Campus.

Vale, M. (2004). Innovation, and knowledge driven by a focal corporation: The case of the Autoeuropa supply chain. *European Urban and Regional Studies*, *11*(2), 124–140. doi:10.1177/0969776404036252

Vale, M., & Caldeira, J. (2007). Proximity and knowledge governance in localized production systems: The footwear industry in the north region of Portugal. *European Planning Studies*, *15*(4), 531–548. doi:10.1080/09654310601134854

Vale, M., & Caldeira, J. (2008). Fashion and the governance of knowledge in a traditional industry: The case of the footwear sectoral innovation system in the northern region of Portugal. *Economics of Innovation and New Technology, 17*(1-2), 61–78. doi:10.1080/10438590701279318

Van Buuren, A. (2009). Knowledge for governance, governance of knowledge: Inclusive knowledge management in collaborative governance processes. *International Public Management Journal, 12*(2), 208–235. doi:10.1080/10967490902868523

Van Grembergen, W., & De Haes, S. (2007). *Implementing IT governance: models, practices and cases.* IGI Global.

Weill, P., & Ross, J. W. (2004). *It Governance – How top Performers Manage it Decision Rights for Superior Results.* Harvard Business SchoolPress.

World Bank. (1992). *Governance and development.* Oxford University Press.

Zyngier, S. (2010). Governance of knowledge management. Encyclopedia of Knowledge Management.

Zyngier, S., Burstein, F., & Mckay, J. (2005). *Governance of strategies to manage organizational knowledge: A mechanism to knowledge oversee needs.* Case Studies in Knowledge Management. doi:10.4018/978-1-59140-351-7.ch006

Chapter 10
Arbitration Chambers and Data Protection:
Beyond Legal – A Reputational Issue

Thiago R. Veloso Costa
FIA Business School, Brazil

ABSTRACT

We are experiencing a time of intense change in human relations with great exposure and with this the need for governments and companies to be prepared to ensure the protection of personal data of their users and customers. The purpose of this chapter is to provide clear evidence of the impacts that arbitration and arbitration chambers will be subject to by changes imposed by data protection laws. The arbitral chambers shall prepare and adapt their procedures to this new reality under penalty of its extinction.

For some time now, it can be seen that the so-called Information Era, or "Technological Era," which has left such an indelible mark on society because of its exponential exposure to technology and to science and also because of the great mass of information circulating in several platforms – which in theory would lead us to have a greater cognitive autonomy in our judgments and analyses – little by little, and with each society in its own way and in light of constraints and limitations, starts to lose importance, concurrently with the arrival of new historical movements, such as Industry 4.0, to a new era: that of Reputation. As Italian philosopher Gloria Origgi (2019) puts it, it is time to *"say goodbye to the information age: it's all about reputation now"[1]*.

The flood of information, analyses, and opinions calls for some sort of filter, evaluation, and confirmation potentializing one's dependency on agencies, institutions, and individuals who, through their judgments and endowed with a balanced and realistic critical review, allow those submitted to their scrutiny to judge them as trustworthy or not, whereby it can be said that *"reputation has become a central pillar of collective intelligence today. It is the gatekeeper to knowledge, and the keys to the gate are held by others."[2]*

As we seek information credibility, we leave our feet firmly planted in an environment of infinite interconnection, exposure, and in some cases, unwilling exhibitionism of our privacy to public perception,

DOI: 10.4018/978-1-7998-4201-9.ch010

Copyright © 2021, IGI Global. Copying or distributing in print or electronic forms without written permission of IGI Global is prohibited.

interpretation, and judgment. Even if access to social media mostly takes place willingly and consciously, it is virtually impossible to measure how personal data will be treated by companies with platforms in digital media, whether for institutional or commercial purposes. That is because never in history has so much information been recorded and with such great potential to be used commercially to the extent that data can now be considered a particularly valuable class of economic asset, almost like a commodity and, for many, "the new oil³"(The Economist 2017) – most of the times with the unconvincing justification that the adaptation of our consumer habits and interests to the new technologies can more effectively anticipate our own needs.

In an era in which reputation and credibility are judged as quickly as keys are punched in a smartphone, and considering the flagrant fragility of Internet users vis-à-vis the treatment and the manipulation of their data, the preservation of privacy anchored by hitherto fragile informative self-determination, the latter understood here as an individual's faculty to determine the extent of the use of their personal data, gains gradually the state protection. Even if concern for privacy harks back to ancient times, it is in modern society that the fight between technological advancement and invasion of privacy deserves increasingly more protection, making our domestic laws stand out for the treatment of the collection, storage, use, and transmission of personal data.

Resulting from decades of heated arguments, Europe's General Data Protection Regulation (GDPR) became effective on May 25, 2018, and can be considered the most important legal framework on the issue, which, in addition to harmonizing and unifying the requirements for the protection of personal data all across Europe imposed to local citizens and companies, as well as those that somehow do businesses with the European Union, has spawned similar legislation in several countries, including Brazil.

The GDPR defines the term "personal data" as "any information relating to an identified or identifiable natural person". Article IV (1) of the GDPR defines: *"an identifiable natural person is one who can be identified, directly or indirectly, in particular by reference to an identifier such as a name, an identification number, location data, an online identifier or to one or more factors specific to the physical, physiological, genetic, mental, economic, cultural or social identity of that natural person.⁴"(European Union).*

The scope of the GDPR relies on three pillars: the first is the governance of personal data, which is the effective control of the personal data inserted in a company's scope of work or that of its suppliers, as well as the method of communicating any breach; the second is the management of personal data, which has to do with the manner of treatment of such data, from collection, processing, transfer, exclusion, to the appointment of a data protection manager. The third pillar, in turn, is the institution of mechanisms to ensure the transparency of personal data, such as Privacy Policies, consent, and portability. If these guidelines are disregarded, companies are subjected to penalties that can be as high as 2% (two percent) of their annual global sales or 10 (ten) million euros, whichever is the greater. In other cases, such penalties can be as high as 4% (four percent) of their annual global sales or 20 (twenty) million euros, whichever is the greater, irrespective of any other punishments that can be imposed by the authorities.

In Brazil, the General Data Protection Act (LGPD, in the Portuguese acronym), as already mentioned, draws on the regulations and the requirements of the GDPR, which is not to say that it is above criticism. The LGPD was enacted on August 14, 2018 but, effective date had been undefined for a long time, and came into effect, more than two years after, on September 18, 2020, however, there are still some stages to its completely effectivity as the possibility of the administrative sanctions provision set for August 1, 2021, and also the legislators have yet to define the institutional format, the scope and the allocated budget for the National Data Protection Authority (ANPD, in the Portuguese acronym) and for the National Council for Data Protection and Privacy.

Although the legal framework on personal data protection is clearly laid out in both the GDPR and the LGPD, including the hefty penalties for noncompliance – which has been the subject of great debate and discussion – not much has been said about one of the main risks caused by noncompliance, especially considering our historical moment: reputation A Company's method of dealing with personal data, in addition to providing full assurance of its compliance with the law, will be one of its unique selling points, one which will ensure its prosperity and survival.

Now more than ever, companies and institutions will base their activities on their reputation and on the trusts placed in them by their clients or partners, which means that, in addition to governance, confidentiality, and ethics mechanisms, such as those imposed in their compliance programs, they must include in their portfolio of integrity the mechanisms and the control to effectively ensure transparency in governance and in the management of personal data.

In this scenario and considering that it will take a little more than a year until the LGPD goes into effect, it is important to foster discussion on the need for important institutions learn about – and adapt to – this new reality, most notably the Arbitration Chambers. Currently, the chambers' institutional reputation, along with the reputation of their arbitrators, ensures that its technical and independent awards which, under the requirements imposed by the LGPD, especially for dealing with information and personal data set out in contracts and other documents – including information and data from countries that already enjoy the benefit of protection – will effectively guarantee that such information is given adequate treatment. Art. 5 of the LGDP defines personal data as information related to an identified or identifiable natural person, which, therefore, includes name, identification number, address, bank account information, or any other piece of information that whether collectively or in isolation could cause a natural person to be identified.

The transfer of personal data and information derived from commercial contracts and other documents between companies and individuals and the Arbitration Chamber naturally flows out of arbitration proceedings, as well as from documents created after the arbitration proceeding starts, such as minutes, briefs, petitions, documents, technical reports, and even the arbitral award. To that effect, the Arbitration Chambers must have their proceedings reviewed to ensure that the collection, production, receipt, classification, use, access, reproduction, transmission, distribution, processing, filing, storage elimination, evaluation or control of the information, modification, communication, transfer, diffusion, or extraction meet all legal requirements.

Currently, maintaining the parameters of confidentiality and data preservation against the unauthorized use, alteration, processing, distribution, and destruction of said data not only serves to comply with the laws around the world, but in particular ensures the preservation of the Arbitration Chambers' competitiveness, image, and reputation.

In this scenario, in contrast to Hollywoodian plots in which masked figures hide in search of a source code to open doors around the world and act under the false pretext that they are mere transgressors of the system, hackers are now reappearing or undertaking a new "assignment" with new peculiarities or pretexts, albeit with the same destructive power. Some of these covered by the cloak of social and political activism (*Hacktivists*), others under unacceptable state mandate (*State Actors*), as is the case with the United States accusing the Chinese Government, through its Peoples' Liberation Army (PLA), of allegedly conducting cybernetic attacks against US companies to steal industrial secrets that China considers top priority, and the latter motivated by allegedly get-rich-quick schemes and for the threat of disclosing their victims' sensitive information (*Financially Motivated Criminals*)[5] (Pastore, 2019).

Even if placed in new groups – obviously not limited to them – and even in a scenario that little by little ceases to be a "lawless land", the functional re-adaptation of professionals, entities and organizations is imperative in light of this threat. Thus, obviously the Arbitration Chambers are included in this new reality, in which *"not long ago, having knowledge of cybersecurity was a unique selling point for extremely specialist lawyers, whereas these days knowledge in this area is inherent to the very fabric of professional ethics."[6]* (Moreria, 2019).

The Arbitration Chambers can be seen as especially susceptible to a cyber-attack, notably because they command the transmission of relevant documents made up of personal and commercial data and information, from several platforms, by companies, agencies, and States acting locally or internationally, and because they are increasingly looking to use technological tools, such as videoconferencing, e-filing, and e-certificates. Thus, if there was doubt before as to the possibility of a breach of the security of the Arbitration Chambers' database, the question now is simply when the breach will occur. Certainly not the only case, but to many people the most infamous one, which opens the chapter Hackers x Arbitral Tribunal, is the award by the Permanent Court of Arbitration in the Hague, the Netherlands, of a claim involving China and the Philippines for the control of the South China Sea. The breach of the Tribunal's website ended up allowing access to the computers of the attorneys and diplomats working on the case, affording the Chinese an enormous competitive advantage. This, however, did not prevent the Tribunal from deciding for the Filipinos, an award which was not recognized by the Chinese government on the grounds that the Tribunal allegedly had no jurisdiction over the matter.

Whether it is because we are teetering on the edge of a historical moment ("Reputation Era"), calling for trustworthiness and reputation to be closely associated with the main items of differentiation and competitiveness in today's world regarding the relationship between consumers, companies, agencies, governmental entities, and private entities alike – and, consequently, reputational and financial losses arising out of noncompliance –, or in light of the impositions of a new legal framework accompanied by hefty penalties imposed by regulators in the event of violations, or by the imminent risk of being held hostage to cybernetic blackmail that can signify the loss of trust as well as incalculable losses to the parties in an arbitral dispute, it is imperative that the Arbitration Chambers, important as they are to upholding the Law, especially because of their independence and impartiality, including all professionals that act on this scenario, adapt themselves to these new requirements.

Some institutions have clearly pointed to the need for a profound discussion on the issue, especially the International Council for Commercial Arbitration (ICCA) which, together with the New York Bar Association, and the International Institute for Conflict Prevention and Resolution (CPR), which have debated on – and proposed – the creation of a voluntary protocol wherein some cybersecurity steps could be taken, which has since become one of the most important references on this matter.

There is obviously no preset formula with concrete rules by which the Arbitration Chambers could abide, for even though the adaptation requirements are global, the specificities and the forms of treatment satisfy unique requirements to each concrete case, many times influenced by each country's cultural elements and weaknesses.

It is important to encourage the Arbitration Chambers to discuss cybersecurity and the steps to control the use and transmission of personal data, whether they do so individually – which appears to be taking place, albeit timidly so –, or through a wider discussion between the Chambers to foster the creation of a common protocol, involving not only lawyers and operators of Law but also technology and innovation professionals, class entities, and society.

Based on the current principles of data protection and without prejudice to the necessary discussion on the need for the Arbitration Chambers to adapt and the ensuing creation of a Cybersecurity Protocol and Data Protection, which must be formally accepted by all participants in the arbitration procedure, including not only the Parties, but also the external lawyers, arbitrators and the entire administrative body of the Arbitration Chambers, it would seem clear that some guidelines must be preemptively adopted in light of this new reality, which include:

(i)   IT tools, such as modern and up-to-date firewalls and antivirus software concurrently with backup routines and the storage of data in safe environments by means of cryptography or data anonymization;

(ii)   data minimization, optimizing information collection processes and flows to include that which is deemed absolutely necessary, correct and useful to the arbitral proceeding, maintaining periodical checks, in addition to creating procedures to exclude obsolete personal data or data that has fully reached the end of its useful life, in reliance on the information for legal and procedural purposes – which will depend on analyzing each procedure managed by the Chamber;

(iii)   creation and maintenance of procedures that ensure transparency with respect to the collection of personal data, the complete disclosure to the owners of the transmitted information, and the manner in which the data will be used – which must be done transparently, with fewer terms of art and with the implementation of more effective management and control tools.

To these guidelines, we must add (iv) the review as to the collection and transfer of personal data coming from other countries or international bodies, to which an adequate level of protection of personal data with proof that privacy is being safeguarded in compliance with statutory requirements, whether by bilateral recognition by the States or by valid clauses, regulations, seals, and codes.

Lastly, we must underscore the existence of (v) clear policies, routines, and instructions to detect and treat the leak of personal data, in addition to a dedicated and multidisciplinary team. The existence of a qualified team to that effect is important, for it is necessary that, in the shortest time possible and in accordance with applicable laws, the nature and the categorization of the leaked data can be determined, as well as the potential consequences, setting out when needed the steps to be taken in order to notify the owners of the leaked data and the competent authorities, as well as the institution of effective measures to quell and/or mitigate the leak and the possible negative effect thereof.

The manner in which organizations around the world will be perceived in terms of reputation by their partners or clients, along with transparency and legal compliance, is the tool that will ensure that these organizations remain trustworthy and prosperous. Otherwise, they may submerge into discredit in oblivion. The many elements set out in this article corroborate the need for deeper discussion as to the requirements for the Arbitration Chambers to adapt to the new paradigms as the only way to keep them safe – insofar as possible, considering that the leak of personal data is a risk that can be at best mitigated, but not eliminated –, sustainable and compliant with applicable principles and rules. Thus, the Chambers will become increasingly more solid due to their already renowned technician a, the effective promotion of their procedures, and most of all, the safekeeping of all the data entrusted to them.

REFERENCES

Becker & Mota. (n.d.). *Arbitration leaks: a segurança da informação no procedimento arbitral.* Available at https://www.jota.info/opiniao-e-analise/artigos/arbitration-leaks-a-seguranca-da-informacao-no-procedimento-arbitral-18042018

Brasil. (2018). *Lei 13.709 de 14 de agosto de 2018.* Available at http://www.planalto.gov.br/ccivil_03/_ato2015-2018/2018/Lei/L13709.htm

CyberInsecurity. A New Protocol to Counter Cyberattacks in International Arbitration. (n.d.). Available at https://www.cpradr.org/news-publications/articles/2018-07-05-cyberinsecurity-a-new-protocol-to-counter-cyberattacks-in-international-arbitration

European Union. (n.d.). *EU General Data Protection Regulation (GDPR).* Available at https://eugdpr.org/

ICCA Launches Working Group on Cybersecurity in Arbitration. (n.d.). Available at https://www.arbitration-icca.org/news/2017/361/icca-launches-working-group-on-cybersecurity-in-arbitration.html

Moreira, Becker, & Lameirão. (n.d.). Os incidentes cibernéticos e a advocacia. *Lex Machinæ.* Available at: http://www.lexmachinae.com/2017/09/25/os-incidentes-ciberneticos-e-advocacia/

Origgi. (2017). *Reputation: What It Is and Why It Matters* (Reputação: o que é e por que importa, em tradução livre). Available at https://aeon.co/ideas/say-goodbye-to-the-information-age-its-all-about-reputation-now

Paisley. (2017). It's All About the Data: The Impact of the EU General Data Protection Regulation on International Arbitration. *Fordham International Arbitration & Mediation Conference Issue.* Available at https://ir.lawnet.fordham.edu/cgi/viewcontent.cgi?article=2707&context=ilj

Pastore. (n.d.). Practical approaches to cybersecurity in arbitration. *Fordham International Law Journal.* Available at https://ir.lawnet.fordham.edu/cgi/viewcontent.cgi?referer=https://www.google.com.br/&httpsredir=1&article=2658&context=ilj

Permanent Court of Arbitration website goes offline, with cyber-security firm contending that security flaw was exploited in concert with China-Philippines arbitration. (n.d.). Available at https://www.iareporter.com/articles/permanent-court-of-arbitration-goes-offline-with-cyber-security-firm-contending-that-security-flaw-was-exploited-in-lead-up-to-china-philippines-arbitration

The world's most valuable resource is no longer oil, but data. (n.d.). *The Economist.* Disponível em https://www.economist.com/leaders/2017/05/06/the-worlds-most-valuable-resource-is-no-longer-oil-but-data

ENDNOTE

[1]   ORIGGI, Gloria *"Reputation: What It Is and Why It Matters"* (2017), translated by Stephen Holmes and Noga Arikha. Available at https://aeon.co/ideas/say-goodbye-to-the-information-age-its-all-about-reputation-now. Accessed on March 13, 2019.

[2]   Idem.

[3]   The world's most valuable resource is no longer oil, but data, The Economist. Available at https://www.economist.com/leaders/2017/05/06/the-worlds-most-valuable-resource-is-no-longer-oil-but-data. Accessed on April 1, 2019.

[4]   União Europeia. EU General Data Protection Regulation (GDPR). Disponível em https://eugdpr.org/. Acesso em 20 de abril de 2019.

[5]   PASTORE, Jim. Practical approaches to cybersecurity in arbitration. Fordham International Law Journal. Disponível em https://ir.lawnet.fordham.edu/cgi/viewcontent.cgi?referer=https://www.google.com.br/&httpsredir=1&article=2658&context=ilj. Accessed on April 16, 2019.

[6]   MOREIRA, Amanda; BECKER, Daniel; LAMEIRÃO, Pedro. Os incidentes cibernéticos e a advocacia. LEX MACHINÆ. Disponível em: http://www.lexmachinae.com/2017/09/25/os-incidentes-ciberneticos-e-advocacia/ – Accessed on April 16, 2019 [free translation].

Chapter 11
Effects and Projections of the Brazilian General Data Protection Law (LGPD) Application and the Role of the DPO

Claudio Roberto Pessoa
iD https://orcid.org/0000-0002-9439-0382
EMGE Escola de Engenharia, Brazil

Bruna Cardoso Nunes
Faculdade Dom Helder, Brazil

Camila de Oliveira
Faculdade Dom Helder, Brazil

Marco Elísio Marques
Universidade Fumec, Brazil

ABSTRACT

The world scenario is changing when we talk about personal data protection. Not that long ago, it was common to find companies that sell databases, and other companies that work with the information contained into these databases, aimed to create profiles and generate solutions, using technologies such as big data and artificial intelligence, among others, looking to be attractive and get more customers. In order to protect the privacy of citizens across the world, laws have been created and/or expanded to reinforce this protection. In Brazil, specifically, the Lei de Proteção de Dados Pessoais – LGPD [General Data Protection Law] was created. This research aims to analyze this law, as well as other laws that orbit around it. The goal is to know the impact of law enforcement on business routine and, as a specific objective, what the role of DPO (Data Protection Officer) in organizations will be.

DOI: 10.4018/978-1-7998-4201-9.ch011

Copyright © 2021, IGI Global. Copying or distributing in print or electronic forms without written permission of IGI Global is prohibited.

INTRODUCTION

Today, the protection of personal data is a worldwide concern, especially after some incidents such as the case at Cambridge Analytic, where the company was accused of using personal data, to interfere in the election process of the United States of America in 2016. This company has been accused of using techniques, that today have become commonplace, with the concepts of Big Data and Data Mining, to analyze information, to create profiles and strategically align this information with the interests of some organizations.

These technologies have brought many benefits to companies. However, any technology, when used for evil purposes, can be harmful. In this specific case, as can be seen on the website: *Information is Beautiful*[1], several are the security incidents that have exposed citizens data all around the world. These incidents have happened as a consequence of the lack of security planning, or even the way of use of existing data.

In this context, thinking about the protection of privacy, several countries have promulgated laws with the objective of restraining this type of attitude by companies and malicious people. In Brazil, in August 2018, Law 13.709, called the "Lei Geral de Proteção de Dados – LGPD" (General Law of Personal Data Protection), was enacted, in which the "rules of conduct" that people and companies must follow, If a person, or company does not meet its requirements, sanctions will be imposed, and they can be harsh.

Available at https://informationisbeautiful.net/visualizations/worlds-biggest-data-breaches-hacks/

Implementing compliance with this law should be the work of a multidisciplinary team, taking into account the areas of Management, Information Security, Information and Communications Technology (ICT) and Legal. Each area will have an important contribution to make in terms of adaptation of work procedures. Otherwise, it will be difficult for only one of these areas to meet the organizations demands.

This work makes a study about the connection between the areas of Management and Information Security and the effects and projections on the LGPD enforcement in the Brazilian Legal System. LGPD is directly connected to several other Brazilian laws and, only by knowing its impact, it will be possible to draw up an action plan to mitigate the existing risks in the organization's business.

REGULATORY EVOLUTION: ASPECTS OF THE CONTRIBUTION OF GENERAL DATA PROTECTION REGULATION (GDPR) TO THE FRAMEWORK OF THE BRAZILIAN EQUIVALENT LAW (LGPD)

In the 1970´s some countries at Europe were already engaged in establishing parameters for data protection. Going further, in 1995 Directive 95/46/EC of the European Parliament and of the Council concerning data processing was approved and required each member of the European Union to have:

a data protection agency or commission, the latter should be a government agent that oversees the application of individual privacy protection principles and laws. The directive 95/46/EC also requires that each agency or commission should edit laws on the personal data processing. (REINALDO FILHO, Demócrito, 2013)

For 20 years, Directive 95/46/EC has been one of the most important documents in terms of advances in data protection. However, in view of new needs in an increasingly digital universe where the demand for updates was growing, the ideal scenario has opened up for a more up-to-date and comprehensive law to appear on the European scenario.

It was then that, in the year 2016, the "General Data Protection Regulation – GDPR" was legislated, coming into force two years later, in May of 2018. According to VAINZOF (2019), the 2016/679 regulation (EU) came into force on 05/25/2018, replacing the directive 95/46/EC, as well as the national laws and regulations based on it. For GOMES (2018), GDPR is the "largest set of online privacy protection ever created, since the beginning of the Internet".

In the business field, MOREIRA (2017) highlighted that the European resolution offers a rich substratum for entities/companies to be able to guide their actions with considerable legal certainty.

The regulatory evolution of data protection in Brazil, up to the LGPD milestone, suffered many setbacks and was inspired by the European General Data Protection Regulation (GDPR). According to KINGDOM FILHO (2013):

From the 60's and 70's, with the advent of information technologies, the great power of data processing by computers was the factor responsible for the germination of modern legislation in this area. The increase in the power of data control and data processing promptly triggered the demand for specific legislation to regulate the collection and handling of personal information. (REINALDO FILHO, 2013)

Since then, the growing need in Brazil for a more specific legislation that would meet international laws, such as European GDPR, has favored the development of LGPD. Before LGPD, there were some regulations that dealt with data protection, but the LGPD enactment meant a country historic advance in this subject.

The enactment of the law is a milestone for Brazil since there was previously no specific legislation on data protection. Before that, what existed were some sparse regulations, such as the Consumer Defense Code, the Positive Registration Law and the Law 12.965/14 which became popularly known as the Internet Civil Landmark and was partially amended by LGPD. (SANTIAGO & TAMBA, 2018)

Thinking about a data protection law establishment that is in line with the world scenario is a tool that contributes to the advancement of the economy, favoring the dialogue between countries.

Following the GDPR model, LGPD seeks to create a modern regulatory framework, including Brazil in the list of countries and international bodies that are able to provide an adequate degree of personal data protection according to international standards. (BENTO, 2018)

The LGPD was inspired, in many ways, by the European General Data Protection Regulation, or GDPR, which came into force in May 2018. This influence stems, among other reasons, from the intention to include Brazil in the list of countries that provide an adequate level of personal data protection according to international parameters. (SANTIAGO & TAMBA, 2018).

It is known that LGPD will reach all sectors that deals with the personal data processing. Also is important that the need to understand and adapt the reality of companies to the new legislation is urgent, since, although LGTD has provided an adaptation period of 24 months, it has entered into force in September 2020 drastically changing the way of data collection and storage requirements in the Brazil. And, for the purpose of the law, it is important to note that according to LGPD data processing can be defined as:

any operation carried out with personal data, such as those referring to the collection, production, reception, classification, use, access, reproduction, transmission, distribution, processing, archiving, storage, deletion, evaluation or control of information, modification, communication, transfer, dissemination or extraction. (Art. 5, X, in verbis)

In other words, the simple fact of collecting personal data information already brings to organizations the need to LGPD requirements adaptation.

THE LGPD IN THE LIGHT OF FUNDAMENTAL RIGHTS (CR/88)

The Brazilian General Data Protection (LGPD) has, as one of its main scopes, the protection of the fundamental rights of the citizen foreseen in the Republic Constitution (Constituição da República) of 1988 (CR/88). In CR/88´s Article 1, such scope is outlined by the legislator in the following extract: "with the objective to protect the fundamental rights of freedom and privacy and the free development of the citizen's personality".

It is observed that the above-mentioned citizen's' rights are law 13.709/18 essence. The fundamental right of freedom, according to FERNANDES (2017), "can be understood as autonomy (the capacity to self-manage one's life and choices from reason)".

The CR/88 in its article 5, X, lists several rights related to citizens' protection of the personal life, highlighting in the LGPD the image and private life intimacy. "Thus, the right to privacy is explained as a right that an individual has to stand out (separate himself/herself) from a group, isolating him/herself from the group observation, or as the right to control the information conveyed about him/herself". (FERNANDES, 2017, p. 487)

The Universal Declaration of Human Rights (1948), in its article XII, brings light to the need to protect the right to individual privacy of the citizen by saying that "No one shall be subjected to interference in his private life, family, home or correspondence, nor to attack his honor and reputation. Every human being has the right to the protection of the law against such interference or attacks".

It should be noted that fundamental rights, although not renounced in their entirety, can be limited within proportionality, "for this reason, too, it is necessaire to regulate the right to privacy from an economic perspective, focused (...) on the international flow of data - a fundamental element for the globalized economy of the 20th and 21st centuries" (VAINZOF, 2019, p. 22).

Thus, still according to the aforementioned author the law 13.709/18:

Seeks the protection of citizens' fundamental rights and guarantees, in a balanced manner, by harmonizing and updating concepts in order to mitigate risks and establish well-defined rules on the processing of personal data. (VAINZOF, 2019, p. 23)

THE INNOVATIONS BROUGHT BY LGPD IN THE ADAPTATION OF THE BUSINESS AND LEGAL SCENERY, ALLIED TO THE STABLISHMENT OF NEW FIGURES THAT ARE RESPONSIBLE FOR THE PERSONAL DATA PROCESSING.

LGPD's main function is to ensure that Fundamental Rights, especially those listed by it, are effectively protected. For this, it brings as definition of personal data "information related to identified or identifiable citizen". That brings attention to the "identifiable" term treat because, contrary to what can be imagined, data that even, indirectly, can lead to the identification of the holder, will also be considered as personal data. As examples of personnel data, someone can list car plates, cell phone number, among others, as examples of sensitive personal data, someone can list: personal data on racial or ethnic origin, religious conviction, political opinion, union membership or religious organization, philosophical or political character, data concerning health or sexual life, genetic or biometric data, when linked to a citizen. In other words, everything that can give rise to a discriminatory act will be considered as personal data.

Aiming to take care of the issues, the 5th article of LGPD puts on the scene three important figures that are intrinsically linked to such a guarantee, which are: Controller and Operator – both are classified as processing agents- and the DPO (Art. 5, IX).

Controller is understood as the "natural or legal person, of public or private law, that is responsible for the decisions regarding the personal data processing " (Article 5, VI) and Operator is the "natural or legal person, of public or private law, who performs the personal data processing on behalf of the Controller" (Article 5, VII).

There is also the DPO figure, which is a person indicated by both the Controller and Operator to act as a communication channel between the Controller, the Data Subjects and the National Data Protection Authority (Art. 5, VIII). That is, the Controller, Operator and the DPO form a triad, in which the first is responsible for the processing decisions, the second, directly, performs the processing activities, and the third is the communication channel between the Controller and the Data Subjects.

It is necessary to draw attention to the role of the DPO. Previously, the concept of data processing has been seen and, as mentioned above, it is explicit the need for expertise of professionals who deal with the process of concepts and procedures adequacy. It has become important to information security professionals, as well as others involved in data processing (especially the IT professional), understand that personal data can no longer be used as before, since the law gives the Data Subjects the right to interrupt the processing of their data in the company database. Unless it falls within one of the legal bases listed in the LGPD, specific consent must be given by the Data Subjects (basic rule of data processing), which may be withdrawn at the time the owner deems it is necessary.

A reflection in relation to the DPO functions shows that this will, undoubtedly, is one of the most important and challenging roles in this whole new process. The DPO will lead the process of law adaptation. He will have to know, in depth, the business needs, the processes, the employees involved in data processing and LGPD requirements, to allow him to **create a security policy, that is in compliance with the law, but that do not jeopardize business rules**.

According to Pessoa (2016), this strategic alignment will depend greatly in the vision change of the organizations' Managers. It is necessary, in the first moment, to think about the business, the necessary information, Managers' demands and know the people involved (as well as their level of technical and management expertise). Only then, should someone study the electronic tools that will support the business. According to the author, it is common to find companies that invest first in technology and then try to adapt the business to it. When it comes to personal data processing, in the light of LGPD, this would be a business suicide. This is because LGPD brings, in its genesis, the obligation of transparency. It means that the Data Subject will have the right, at any time, to know his processed data in order to be able to modify it (adding or changing inconsistent data) and even demanding its deletion. Here, arises the treat of modern technologies such as Block chain and Big data, which may create a great challenge to IT Managers when eliminating and/or processing the information aiming, for example, at creating profiles for action in Targeted Marketing.

A multidisciplinary effort will be required from a management team, led by the DPO, otherwise one of the areas: management, information security, IT or legal, will be left helpless, which would lead the compliance process to failure.

THE SECURITY, THE GOOD PRACTICES AND DATA SECRECY, THE LINK BETWEEN COMPLIANCE AND INFORMATION TECHNOLOGY IN THE APPLICATION OF LGPD

LGPD´s Chapter VII deals with safety and good practices. More specifically, in its Article 46, it addresses the legal obligation of processing agents to ensure the above-mentioned safety.

The processing agents must adopt security, technical and administrative measures capable of protect personal data from unauthorized access and from accidental or illicit situations of destruction, loss, alteration, communication or any form of improper or illicit processing. (Article 46, Law 13.709/18).

The processing agents or any other person who intervenes in one of the phases of the processing are obliged to guarantee the security of the information foreseen in this Law in relation to the personal data, even after its termination. (Article 47, Law 13.709/18).

Although the LGTD repeatedly refers to "Information Security", it does not bring its definition, as occurs in other concepts such as "processing agents". It is imperative to clarify this concept in the face of such omission of the Law

Information Security is the discipline aimed to protect information, that is considered a business asset (meaning that it has value for the organization), from different types of internal and external threats (events that can have negative impacts, such as malicious employees, cyber-attacks, espionage, unfair competition, digital frauds, etc.) in order to mitigate risks, increase the return on investments and ensure business continuity. (JIMENE, 2019, p. 339).

In order for information security gain applicability, it is understood that the efforts of the processing agents are of paramount importance. However, a joint effort is necessary to guarantee the effectiveness of security, understood by the LGPD as the "use of technical and administrative measures capable of protecting personal data from unauthorized access and from accidental or illicit situations of destruction, loss, alteration, communication or dissemination" (Article 6, VIII).

Regarding technical measures definition:

technical measures are those adopted in the field of Information Technology, such as the use of computer resources, endowed with functionalities, aimed to ensure the Information security. Examples of these technologies are system access authentication tools, software and hardware security mechanisms, network data traffic control resources, system intrusion detection instruments and cryptography resources. (JIMENE, 2019, p. 329)

With respect to the author's citation above, it is understood that Information Security is not limited only to the technological field, since the LGPD also aims at the protection of data that are in the physical media, for example: paper, when it states, in its article 1, that the law "applies to all information, including paper".

The ISO/IEC ABNT 27.002 (2013, pg. X) states that "information may can be contained in various forms. It can be printed, or written on paper, stored electronically, transmitted by mail or electronic means, presented in films or spoken in conversations". This standard goes beyond, saying that Information Security is "the protection of information from various types of threats, to ensure business continuity, maximize return on investment and business opportunities". It is therefore something that must be analyzed in detail.

LGPD clearly states that there should be investments in the sector, focused on the best information security practices. As seen in the ISO 27.002 concept, Information Security is totally linked to the business.

Therefore, in order to make the implementation of LGPD a success, it is essential to reinforce the need of a multidisciplinary team that covers four major groups of knowledge: Management, Information Security, Information Technology and Communication and Legal. All of this expertise will hardly be found in the role of the DPO (in only one person). This professional will undoubtedly be the leader of a group of professionals that will have this mission in organizations.

Some expertise is essential prior to implement LGPD:

- knowledge of the processes involved in the information processing;
- knowledge the standards and best practices of Information Security and concepts of the information cycle within the organization;
- risk analysis;
- knowledge of the technological tools that will support organizations´ processes and services, and;
- knowledge of all the legislation involved to be in legal compliance.

Only in this way can a planning be stablished that involves all the information of the company, whether electronic or physical (paper). It is never too much to remember that the DPO must have unrestricted support from the organization's Top Management, as he or she must have the necessary autonomy for decision-making.

As far as administrative measures are concerned, they are aimed at the managerial and legal practice of processing agents, such measures being understood as: company policies aimed at data protection, privacy policies, code of ethics and conduct, etc.

In short, for companies to be able to faithfully comply with the obligation emanating from LGPD, it is not enough that the processing agents, as well as the DPO, be aware of their duties. The integration of sectors (and professionals) is necessary in order to achieve the objective of the law, keeping in mind that failure to comply with it can, and will, lead to the application of administrative and civil liability sanctions. According to Cots e Oliveira (2019), "it is not a matter of faculty: it is a legal obligation that, if not fulfilled, may lead to the application of administrative sanctions and civil liability".

The information security policy should be built with concepts from the listed areas, under the risk of, in case one of them is missing, that this policy become useless at the moment of application in the company, or of defense of a possible litigation.

DATA SUBJECT CONSENT

Obeying legal and constitutional principles, LGPD comes to transform the whole context that involves the treatment of personal data of Brazilian citizens. During normative silence, it has been easy for those who collect data, to rely on adhesion contracts that deal with privacy terms in a generic and unintelligible way, leaving the consumer, the Data Subject, with no other way out than consent. LGPD's strength eliminates this possibility, guaranteeing greater transparency and objectivity in consumer consent and in the other nine legal bases that legitimize the treatment of personal data, exhaustively listed in its article 7.

The first aspect to be considered concerns the circumstances in which this acceptance occurs. It is usually formulated from a model of membership, where the user only has to accept the terms presented to him/her, being able to access the service, or reject them, in which he/she will be denied access. Although this model of manifestation of will is not new, it only replicates in electronic media the mass contracts that arose in industrial society, it must be considered that there were already numerous reservations regarding the validity and scope of the manifestation of will in these circumstances. (PAULINO, 2015, p.10)

LGPD´s Article 8 relates that stats that the burden of proof that consent has been obtained, within the legal precepts, stays with the Controller. This consent, which "must be provided in writing or by any other means that demonstrates the Data Subject manifestation of will", will be destined for specific purposes, under penalty of nullity. The law also determines the right to revocation at any time by expressing manifestation of the Data Subject, and that, for this, the procedure will be free and facilitated. It should be noted here that, according to item IV of Article 15, data processing might also be interrupted by determination of the National Authority if the rules of the Law are violated.

Comparing the provisions of Law No. 12,965/14, known as the Internet Civil Framework, in its Article 11, caput, and the provisions of Article 3 of Law No. 13,709/18 (LGPD), it is possible to note the legislator's greatest concern in the Data Subject protection. While the former law is limited to operations with acts performed in the national territory, the latter law applies regardless of the country where the acts are performed, as long as the Data Subject is in the national territory.

LGDP Art. 11. In any operation of collection, storage, custody and processing of records, personal data or communications by connection providers and internet applications in which, at least one of these acts occurs in the national territory, the Brazilian legislation and the rights to privacy, protection of personal data and secrecy of private communications and records must be mandatorily respected. (Law n.12.965 of April 2014)

LGDP Art. 3. This Law applies to any processing operation carried out by a citizen or legal entity of public or private law, regardless of the means, the country of its headquarters or the country where the data are located, provided that

I - the processing operation is carried out in the national territory;
II - the processing activity has as its objective the offer or supply of goods or services or the data processing of individuals located in the national territory; or
III - the personal data object of the treatment has been collected in the national territory. (Law No. 13.709 of August 2018)

It is necessary, however, for a good understanding, to study the Data Subject consent. It is important to observe the waiver of consent for processing "data made manifestly public by the Data Subject", provided for in paragraph four of the Article 3, which does not exclude the other rights and principles recognized by this law.

On the other hand, the Brazilian Superior Court of Justice (Superior Tribunal de Justiça – STJ), in a unanimous decision[2], decided that "data banks that share consumer information must inform them, in advance, about the use of such data, under penalty of having to pay compensation for moral damages" even if the data were made public by a unilateral act of the Data Subject.

The decision goes further by pointing out that, even if the Data Subject has disclosed his data on social networks, it does not mean that specific consent has been given. As a legal basis was used Article 5, item. V, of Law 12.414/2011 which "assures the registered person the right to be informed in advance about the identity of the manager and the storage and processing of personal data. Therefore, it is noted that LGPD reinforces what other rules already had in their content, but did not give the focus and specificities needed.

By providing for transparency of the activity, the law guarantees to the Data Subject easy access of information related to the processing, and, among them, elects four information to be obligatorily communicated to him in case of changes. Listed in clauses I, II, III and V of Article 9, they are: data processing specific purpose, data processing form and duration, controller identification and the shared use of data by the controller. With this, the Data Subject will be aware of what is being done with their data, guaranteed the right to revoke consent once dissatisfied with the changes in the contract or regulation.

[2] Available at: https://www.stj.jus.br/sites/portalp/Paginas/Comunicacao/Noticias/Compartilhamento-de-informacoes-de-banco-de-dados-exige-notificacao-previa-ao-consumidor.aspx

LGPD CIVIL LIABILITY AND ADMINISTRATIVE SANCTIONS

The legislator's concern went far beyond the greater scope of the processing concept. The real highlight, among the innovations inserted by LGPD, is the penalties that go through civil liability for damages caused, then, reaching administrative sanctions. These coercive measures are mechanisms that aim to ensure the effectiveness of the Law. The estimated fine, which may reach the amount of 50 million Reais (R$) for violation, represents a great encouragement to agents and managers to seek compliance with this law.

LGPD Article 42 states of the Controller or Operator must repair the damage caused by any/both of them due to the exercise of the activity of processing personal data in violation of data protection legislation. Such liability expressly encompasses moral, property, individual and collective damage. The responsibility of the Operator is joint with several when he fails to comply with his legal obligations or does not follow the Controller's lawful instructions, in which case he equals the Controller. The Controllers directly involved in the data processing are also jointly and severally liable. It is ensured to who repairs the damage, regressive action to the extent of his responsibility for the harmful event.

§ Paragraph 2 The judge, in civil proceedings, may reverse the burden of proof in favor of the Data Subject when, in his judgment, the allegation is plausible, there is lack of sufficiency for the purpose of producing evidence or when the production of evidence by the holder results in it being excessively onerous. (art. 42, law no. 13.709 of August 2018)

The agent who proves not to have carried out the data processing attributed to him, or that there is no legal defect in the procedure or the exclusive fault of the holder or of a third party for the damages, shall be exempt from liability. Once again, it is necessary to plan LGPD implementation based on effective information management because it will be necessary to create an audit report that can prove, in fact, the non-existence of the data processing or if it exists, how all the data processing is carried out by the organization, in a transparent way.

It is worth emphasizing that the penalty in civil sphere does not exclude the possibility of administrative sanctions applicable by the National Authority after administrative procedure, observing the right to broad defense.

I - warning, with indication of deadline for adoption of corrective measures;
II - simple fine, of up to 2% (two percent) of the revenues of the legal body, group or conglomerate in Brazil in its last exercise, excluding taxes, limited, in total, to R$ 50,000,000.00 (fifty million Reais) per infraction;
III - a daily fine, observing the total limit referred to in item II;
IV - publication of the infraction after duly ascertained and confirmed its occurrence;
V - blocking of the personal data to which the infraction refers until its regularization;
VI - deletion of the personal data to which the infraction refers;

(art. 52, caput, law no. 13.709 of August 2018)

It is also important to emphasize the sanctions established in clauses V and VI, which deal with the blocking and elimination of personal data (database). Although the fines, in the first moment, draws more attention, the sanctions that impede the continuity of the processing determining the blocking and/or elimination of the data can also seriously affect organization´s business. Nowadays, most companies depend on databases as an elementary part of their activities.

It is of fundamental importance to understand that, in order to establish these sanctions, criteria of proportionality will be observed to the degree of damage, the nature of the infraction and the rights violated; as well as the advantage gained or intended and the economic condition of the violator, his good faith, recidivism and cooperation. The adoption of internal mechanisms capable of mitigating the risks and corrective measures will also be considered, remaining proportional to the intensity of the sanction and the seriousness of the fault.

The total revenue of the company or group of companies may be considered for the calculation of the amount of the fine listed in item II above, when not fully, unequivocally and appropriately demonstrated, the value of the revenue in the branch of activity in which the violation occurred (art. 52, paragraph 4). Article 54 requires justification by the National Authority on the value fixed as a daily fine.

Created by Law no. 13.853 of July 2019 which modifies the text of the LGPD, the "Autoridade Nacional de Proteção de Dados – ANPD" (National Data Protection Authority in English) is the federal agency responsible for "watching over the protection of personal data, under the terms of the legislation" (art.55-J, caput, item I), with its powers detailed in a list of 24 items.

Single paragraph. The ANPD shall articulate its scope with other bodies and entities with sanctioning and regulatory powers related to personal data protection and shall be the central body for interpretation of this Law and establishment of rules and guidelines for its implementation (Article 55-K, Law No. 13.853 of July 2019).

Art. 55-C. The ANPD is composed of:

I - Board of Directors, maximum management body;

II - National Council for Personal Data Protection and Privacy;

III - Internal Affairs;

IV - Ombudsman;

V - Its own legal advisory body; and´

VI - administrative units and specialized units necessary for the application of the provisions of this Law. (Law No. 13.853 of July 2019)

THE RIGHTS OF THE DATASUBJCT

As far as management transparency is concerned, LGPD upholds in its chapter III a range of innovative rights, among which it is appropriate to highlight: the right to data portability, forgetfulness and explanation.

The Controller must make the data processed available at the express request of the Data Subject. Such access should be provided in a simplified format, enabling the Data Subject to read the document on his personal computer, for example. More importantly, the Data Subject may forward the processed data to a competing supplier, safeguarding the commercial and industrial secrets arranged in the regulations of the controlling body. This is the right to data portability (article 18, item V), which does not include those already anonymized.

The right to forget consists in the "deletion of personal data processed with the consent of the Data Subject" upon request (art. 18, caput, VI). The deletion of data becomes the rule to be followed at the end of the processing, whether by the purpose achievement, or end of the processing period or Data Subject wish and communication or the determination of the National Authority. There are, however, some exceptions listed on article 16 of the same law. "[...] the core of the protection of the right to oblivion derives from the right to free development of the personality. This right counts as an argument in favor of the dignity of the human person". (TORRES, 2019, p.30)

Finally, the right to explanation is related to decisions taken by automated mechanisms, used to trace the "personal, professional, consumer and credit profile" of the holder. In this sense, the databases are precious for the targeted marketing and credit granting business. The novelty is that, with LGPD's application, the Data Subject will now have the right to request the revision of these automated decisions that affect their interests (art. 20, caput), since the legal provision prohibits the use of data referring to the regular exercise of the rights of the Data Subject at his/her expense (art. 21).

The legislation requires the Controller, at the request of the Data Subject, to provide clear and adequate information on the criteria and procedures used in these decisions. This right does not suppress commercial and industrial secrets, hypotheses in which it is lawful for the National Authority to carry out audits to verify discriminatory aspects in the procedure (art. 20, paragraph 2).

One of the most benefited market economy is by the use and processing of personal data, mainly to enable automated decisions to offer its services, is that the market of consumption. This sector is characterized by the need to understand the consumer and even influence his habits. However, in this scenario, the consumer is in a vulnerable position in his relationship with companies and, therefore, should be protected. Among the protection measures, it should include the provision of adequate information so that they can exercise their rights and avoid abusive and discriminatory practices. (MONTEIRO, 2018, p.6)

FINAL CONSIDERATIONS

Brazil, as many countries, is going through a political fragility context, where serious offenses to fundamental rights and constitutional principles are noted in all Three Powers (executive, legislative and Judiciary). Despite of this unstable scenario, the enactment of LGPD represents a democratic step that aligns Brazil with the more developed countries regarding the new culture of data protection, initially adopted by the European Union and some Mercosur countries. The new legislation is strategic to favor trade relations between Brazil and the rest of the world.

From this study, it is possible to observe the purpose of the legislator to preserve the privacy of Brazilians citizens by giving, each individual, autonomy and control over their own personal and sensitive data. The new legislation relies on preventive and repressive institutional mechanisms that already demonstrate effectiveness in pioneer countries, mainly avoiding, but also punishing and repairing any moral or patrimonial damage caused to the Data Subject by the improper use his personal data. The provisions of the LGPD meet the principles of Consumer Law, protecting the most vulnerable part of the relationship.

The preservation of fundamental rights, as well as personality rights, composes the essence of LGPD, avoiding certain abusive practices against the consumer, which linked with a computerized world side effect. The effectiveness of the Law is promising, to say the least, but what can still generate concern is the legal security that has been mitigated by disrespect for the Brazilian legislative process. Proof of this is the sanctioning of provisional measures dealing with matters that do not meet the requirements of relevance and urgency. LGPD has already been the target of this nonsense by having its text edited a few times by the Congress and the President of the Republic, as well as postponed its effective establishment.

However, the whole legal framework brings with it an obligation for companies to create an effective team that will know how to align their business to legal precepts. It became evident in the analysis the complexity to be faced by the professional who will assume the function created by the Law: The DPO.

This function will align the knowledge of Management Areas (process maps, people management), Information Security (risk maps, compliance with standards, best practices), Information and Communication Technology (tools and infrastructure to support all processes and service) and Legal (compliance with LGPD and other laws of the country). This professional should, therefore, have a strategic vision of the business and the flow of information, so that he can adapt, without technical or financial damage, the needs of the company, the requirements of legislation and technological resources.

This endeavor will be a challenge and a great opportunity for companies' strategic turn, since they should have carried out all this analysis, regardless of legal obligation, but never did. A cultural change will be arduous, but of fundamental importance for the world context.

Finally, it is understood that the advent of the LGPD constitutes a progress milestone towards the Democratic Constitutional State and business strategy improvement. The proper application (and supervision) will bring incalculable benefits to Brazilian society in the personal and organizational spheres, in addition to fostering the image of the Brazilian State, in a worldwide perspective, as a reliable country for the creation of lasting international relations.

REFERENCES

ABNT ISO/IEC 27.001 – Information technology - Security Techniques - Information security management systems — Requirements. 2013

ABNT ISO/IEC 27.002 - Code of Practice for Information Security Controls, 2013.

Bento. (n.d.). *A nova lei de proteção de dados no Brasil e o general data protection regulation da União Europeia* [The Brazilian New Data Protection Law and the General Data Protection Regulation from European Union]. Available at https://www.migalhas.com.br/dePeso/16,MI289555,11049-A+nova+lei+de+protecao+de+dados+no+Brasil+e+o+general+data+protection

Brazil. (n.d.b). *Lei Geral de Proteção de Dados*. Available at: http://www.planalto.gov.br/ccivil_03/_ato2015-2018/2018/lei/L13709.htm

Brazil. (n.d.c). *Lei 8.078 – Código de Defesa do Consumidor*. Available at: http://www.planalto.gov.br/ccivil_03/leis/l8078.htm

Brazil. (n.d.d). *Lei 12.965 - Marco Civil da Internet*. Available at: http://www.planalto.gov.br/ccivil_03/_ato2011-2014/2014/lei/l12965.htm

Brazil. (n.d.a). *Constituição Federal*. Available at: http://www.planalto.gov.br/ccivil_03/constituicao/constituicao.htm

Cots & Oliveira. (2018). *Lei Geral de Proteção de Dados Pessoais Comentada*. Ed. Thomson Reuters Brazil.

Declaração Universal de Direitos Humanos. (n.d.). Available at: https://nacoesunidas.org/wp-content/uploads/2018/10/DUDH.pdf

Fernandes. (2017). *Curso de Direito Constitucional* (9th ed.). Salvador: JusPOIVM.

Filho. (n.d.). *A diretiva europeia sobre proteção de dados pessoais - uma análise de seus Aspectos Gerais.* Available at: http://www.lex.com.br/doutrina_24316822_A_DIRETIVA_EUROPEIA_SOBRE_PRO-TECAO_DE_DADOS_PESSOAIS__UMA_ANALISE_DE_SEUS_ASPECTOS_GERAIS.aspx

Gerhardt, Silveira, & Tolfo. (2009). *Métodos de pesquisa.* Universidade Federal do Rio Grande do Sul. Available at: http://www.ufrgs.br/cursopgdr/downloadsSerie/derad005.pdf

Gomes. (n.d.). *Lei da União Europeia que protege dados pessoais entra em vigor e atinge todo o mundo; entenda.* Available at: https://g1.globo.com/economia/tecnologia/noticia/lei-da-uniao-europeia-que-protege-dados-pessoais-entra-em-vigor-e-atinge-todo-o-mundo-entenda.ghtml

Jimene. (2019). *LGPD: Lei Geral de Proteção de Dados Comentada.* Thomson Reuters Brazil.

Moreira & Schenini. (n.d.). *A lei de proteção de dados pessoais da União Europeia (GDPR) e sua aplicação extraterritorial às entidades e empresas brasileiras.* Available at: https://www.migalhas.com.br/dePeso/16,MI267772,81042-A+lei+de+protecao+de+dados+pessoais+da+Uniao+Europeia+GDPR+e+sua

Pessoa. (2016). *Gestão da informação e do conhecimento no alinhamento estratégico em empresas de engenharia* (PhD thesis). Universidade Federal de Minas Gerais. Available at: https://repositorio.ufmg.br/handle/1843/BUOS-AMXG58?locale=pt_BR

Santiago, Tamba, & Harumi. (n.d.). *Proteção de dados no Brasil: novo marco regulatório.* Available at: https://www.migalhas.com.br/dePeso/16,MI290866,91041-Protecao+de+dados+no+Brasil+novo+marco+regulatorio

STJ. (n.d.). *Compartilhamento de informações de banco de dados exige notificação prévia ao consumidor.* Available at: https://www.stj.jus.br/sites/portalp/Paginas/Comunicacao/Noticias/Compartilhamento-de-informacoes-de-banco-de-dados-exige-notificacao-previa-ao-consumidor.aspx

Vainzof. (2019). *LGPD: Lei Geral de Proteção de Dados Comentada.* Thomson Reuters Brazil.

VAINZOF (n.d.). *World's Biggest Data Breaches & Hacks.* https://informationisbeautiful.net/visualizations/worlds-biggest-data-breaches-hacks/

Chapter 12
Information Security as Digital Economy Critical Success Factor:
A Military Approach

Ricardo de Sousa Correia
Polytechnic Institute of Setúbal, Portugal

ABSTRACT

In an increasingly complex and competitive world, information is a valuable asset and a difference maker. It contributes to better government through supporting efficient business, assisting decision-making, mitigating risks, and adding economic value. This case study reviews Portuguese military information security requirements and its potential application on business company's crucial information protection. It's a military security policy, procedures, and measures approach to commercial environment. It's defined a security checklist to be applied by companies which want to achieve success. The explosive growth of information and communication technologies and their global dissemination and penetration have been a special impact on commercial activities, making them an attractive target to competitors and other agents. Cybersecurity is an organization's top priority. It's necessary to build an increasingly effective security policy in order to protect critical information. Keeping safe business competitive information advantages will be the key to success.

BACKGROUND

In a world in fast and permanent transformation, the geopolitical and geostrategic context is increasingly challenging. Aspects such as information confidentiality, integrity, authenticity and quality have gained greater importance in the security policies. It is essential to reflect on preventive measures and strategies to be adopted by organizations, in order to ensure more and better security for their activity and interests. The implementation of security measures requires the development and adoption of appropriate procedures and standards.

DOI: 10.4018/978-1-7998-4201-9.ch012

Copyright © 2021, IGI Global. Copying or distributing in print or electronic forms without written permission of IGI Global is prohibited.

Since ancient times, the armies' best knowledge and information about their opponent gave them an advantage over the outcome of military operations on battlefield. The power of information has a significant importance in the different phases of military actions, since its domain allows to obtain essential elements that inevitably influence the decision making of the Commanders. The complexity and multidimensional nature of the new threats to information security bring a series of challenges and opportunities in the civil and military spectrum.

The progress of information and communication technologies has elevated the battlefield to the dimensions of cyberspace, characterized by the complexity of the global technological environment. The new risks resulting from the action of non-state actors include threats of a different nature from those that were common previously, without respecting geographic or state boundaries. Characteristics such as the anonymity of its actors (accessing from anywhere in the world) and the low operating costs have given small actors the opportunity to affect large organizations and States in their physical, financial, industrial, economic and military dimensions. This peculiarity enhances the asymmetry and hybrid nature of modern conflicts.

Information management shouldn't be seen as an end itself, but as a mean to provide the necessary support to decision-makers, such as governors, managers or team leaders. The information produced, processed and made available has achieved, in recent years, an increasing importance in the decision-making process at different levels, making it a vital resource.

The explosive growth of information and communication technologies and their global dissemination and penetration have been a special impact on commercial activities, making them an attractive target to competitors and other agents. Today, information security is an organization's top priority. It is vital to build an increasingly effective security policy in order to protect critical information. Keeping safe business sensitive information will be the key to increase organizations competitive advantages.

DIGITAL TRANSFORMATION

The context and complexity of organizations and the market in which they operate lead to the adoption of different strategies that contribute to better results. The way organizations are managed is crucial to their competitiveness. The security measures that each organization adopts should contribute to the good management of its business, revealing the organization's responsibility and transparency, mitigating risks, adding economic value and protecting organizational rights and interests.

According to European Commission (2019), the decrease of computing costs, the emergence of the Internet as a communication platform, the evolution of the mobile Internet, the spread of day-to-day applications and the increasing role of the Internet based on social networks and digital business platforms have a strong impact on the functioning of the economy and deeply affected companies, public organizations and personal life. The growth of digital platforms is directly related to the ability of organizations to collect and analyze digital data. However, their interests and behaviors depend on how they manage the relevant data to make it profitable. Nowadays, digital platforms are increasingly important in the world commerce. The combined value of the platform companies was estimated at more than $7 trillion in 2017 – 67 per cent higher than in 2015 (United Nations, 2019).

Data have become a new economic resource for creating and capturing value. The ability to collect, store, analyze and transform data brings strategic competitive advantages. The digital economy is taking shape and undermining conventional notions about how corporations are structured, how they interact and how consumers get services, information and goods. In the digital economy, the customer takes on a new role, as he agrees to share information about himself, requiring in return, mainly, the customization of products and services and the speed of the processes.

The new business models, based on the digitization of the economy, bring undeniable advantages resulting from the application of innovative technologies. These new technological tools allow transforming multiple simultaneous operations along the value chain, increasing execution speed, efficiency, reliability and flexibility, making companies more agile and competitive in relation to other competitors, seeking to obtain greater economic value. Organizations are transforming their procedures and resources to optimize the full potential of new digital technologies such as the Internet of Things (IoT), artificial intelligence (AI), and Big Data. Certainly it will create new challenges and opportunities.

Companies that want to survive and take advantage from new technological tools should invest in digitization projects of their business models, acting in products or processes portfolio, distribution models or optimization of its internal processes, under penalty of being overcome by new players, digitally more prepared and with greater capacity to adapt to the digital economy globalization. This new paradigm has already entered the agenda of executive committees of organizations that seek to identify opportunities arising from digital transformation in order to diversify markets, products and services, and increase their profits or benefits.

Advances in wireless technology (5G) and the emergence of completely new networks are accelerating the application of IoT. It is the vision of an integrated network value chain with total transparency and traceability. IoT is part of our daily lives, being present whenever we use the mobile phone, home automation, when we consult traffic conditions, when monitoring and controlling production in real time, smart cars and so many other applications. The connectivity and interaction of things, which generates noticeable value services to customers, is one of the strongest supports of the revolution that is coming, opening a new world of challenges and opportunities.

On the military side, the digital transformation of the weapons system is underway and will allow commanders access to actionable intelligence data, with better quality and speed, improving operational decision-making. This ability, due to the interoperability of multi- systems, will bring important advantages in the theatre of operations and can differentiate the success or failure of the operation. 5G could additionally improve intelligence, surveillance, and reconnaissance systems and processing; enable new methods of command and control; and streamline logistics systems for increased efficiency, among other uses (Bhardwaj, 2020; Hoehn & Sayler, 2020).

Managing big data is crucial for many sectors, including the military. It would not be possible to do commercial business or military operations effectively without a complete perspective of the information under analysis. Big data helps leaders making better decisions.

Despite the promising advances of the IoT, there are still several problems related to data security and privacy that can severely jeopardize the interests of organizations. It is not necessary to be a military expert to realize that you cannot expose the flank to the enemy. The methods used today are increasingly sophisticated, enabling sneak attacks from anywhere in the world, being practically undetectable, aiming at the illegal appropriation of information, espionage, sabotage, among other illegal acts. Just as the military go to war, public and private organizations and individuals have to fight their own battles to be successful, taking risks and facing different types of challenges. However, the risks and threats are now asymmetric, with a huge multiplicity of actors, from individuals to organized groups or even states, with different types of motivations that can be ethnic, religious, financial, economic, industrial, political, and military.

Intelligence Services - Trick or Treat?

Military communications and information systems define the operational and technical requirements for command, control and communications inherent in military and contingency defense plans through the implementation of joint information security policies, ensuring autonomy-oriented solutions, survival and interoperability of systems. In the military sphere, these services are responsible for information security, electronic warfare and cyber-defense, adopting measures to combat cybersquatting, cybercrime and cyberterrorism. They also have the function of promoting the interoperability and interconnection of organizations civil telecommunications and operators, with a view to their possible use in exception situations or in war.

According to the Office of the U.S. Director of National Intelligence (2019), cyber threat intelligence is the *"collection, processing, analysis and dissemination of information from all sources of intelligence about foreign actors' cyber programs, intentions, capabilities, research and development, tactics, goals, operational activities and indicators and their impact or potential effects on national security interests"*.

Intelligence services are core elements in a country's defense policy. In ancient times, *"in the case of armies you wish to strike, cities you wish to attack, and people you wish to assassinate, you must know the names of the garrison commander, the staff officers, the ushers, gate keepers, and the bodyguards. You must instruct your agents to inquire into these matters in minute detail"*, (Sun Tzu, chap. XIII, § 16 by Griffith's translation). Military strategic information seeks to identify the military potential of its opponents, which allows it to define the best military strategy for a nation. It covers full knowledge of the potential of other parties, which can influence national strategic decisions.

The modern battlefield environment is increasingly multidimensional, with military operations progressively including the development of operations centered on computer networks and information, bringing cyber space to traditional domains or spaces of action. The formal recognition of cyber space as an operational domain by a state, reflecting the national commitment to protect and safeguard its freedom of action in interest cyberspace. In this context, it raises a shift from the traditional military approach with a focus on information security (defense of communications and information systems) to a posture focused on the impact of cyber incidents and cyber-attacks on military missions.

Disclosure to unauthorized persons or total or partial disclosure, regardless of the form of access, information, fact or document, or destruction, subtraction or falsification of information that jeopardizes the sensitive interests of an organization, constitutes a crime punishable by law. According to the FBI (2014), theft of trade secrets results from the theft or misappropriation of a trade secret intentionally and improperly for the economic benefit of anyone other than the owner. Economic espionage also occurs when a trade secret is stolen for the benefit of a foreign government or foreign agent.

Businesses, academic institutions, cleared defense contractors, and government agencies are increasingly exposed to dishonest practices aimed at the misappropriation of trade secrets, such as theft, unauthorized copying, economic espionage or breach of confidentiality requirements. (European Commission, 2013). A spy no longer needs physical access to a document to steal or copy it; nowadays, the cyber world allows global access and transmission instantly. There is also misinformation, which uses communication and information techniques to deceive or give a false image of reality by removing or hiding information, minimizing its importance or modifying its meaning. Its purpose is to influence public opinion and decision-making and has as its objective the achievement of competitive advantages as political, economic, financial, industrial, and military, among others interests.

It is, therefore, necessary to raise the awareness of users about the importance of information systems security, usually through training actions on the organization's security policy and the adoption of good security practices, in order to protect against potential threats. All organization's employees must know and understand their responsibilities of their duties in order to safeguard organizations security. Good security practices must be applied by everyone regardless of the position or level of responsibility in the organization.

Technological innovations, information about new markets and about competitors, both national and international, are essential elements for maintaining the competitiveness of companies. Commit this knowledge and confidential information of organizations, including innovation processes, research and development, intellectual property, business plans and strategies and other confidential business information, can even endanger the national interest.

Despite growing awareness of cyber threats and improved cyber defenses, almost all information, communication networks and systems will be at risk for years to come. Surprisingly, or not, military, political, industrial and commercial espionage can be beneficial for a country's economic development.

Malicious Cyber Activity Impact

Information and communication technologies have becoming fundamental to economic growth and are a critical resource on which all economic sectors depend. They are currently the heart of the complex systems that make the economies work in key sectors. Many business models are building based on the uninterrupted availability of the network systems. While it has vast benefits, the digital world is also vulnerable.

Cybersecurity incidents, whether intentional or accidental, are increasing at an alarming rate making over a million victims a day worldwide. New technologies and connections represent new threats for some countries and new opportunities for others. A malicious cyber activity can be described as an activity not authorized by law, which aims to compromise or impair the confidentiality, integrity or availability of computers, information or communication systems, networks, physical or virtual infrastructure controlled by computers or information systems, or for information contained thereon (White House, 2018).

Today, cyberspace is a strategic area of potential confrontation in which information and all its constituent devices (infrastructure and network assets, computers and other devices) can be used as a cohesive tool. According to NATO (2020), cyber threats and attacks are becoming more and more sophisticated and destructive. To face an evolving complex threat environment, in 2016 it was recognized cyberspace as the fourth NATO operational domain, such as the sea, land and air.

Cyberspace represents an interdisciplinary and multinational domain, characterized by threats from different players, exposing the vulnerabilities of organizations and requiring a multidimensional response in the civil and military spheres through bilateral and multilateral cooperation. Due to its multidimensional and asymmetric nature and the diffuse and unpredictable character, new threats require a great deal of prospective analysis in order to detect and neutralize its materialization.

Although the total cost of malicious cyber activity is difficult to estimate because many data breaches go undetected, and even when they are detected, they are mostly unreported, or the final cost is unknown. The MacAfee Report (2018) estimate cost of cybercrime worldwide reaches $600 billion in 2017. However, the cost of malicious cyber activity involves more than the loss of financial assets or intellectual property. There are also opportunity costs, damage to image and reputation, loss of customers, interruptions or even breaches of service, and costs of enhancing cybersecurity.

Cyber threats are constantly evolving and can come from different and sophisticated perpetrators. Due to system vulnerabilities and the chameleonic evolution of threats, patterns of security breaches are difficult to predict. The critical infrastructure sectors of the organization can generate particularly large negative side effects for the entire economy.

In particular, health, pharmaceutical and biotechnology institutions and organizations, government agencies and infrastructure and supply chains are the preferred targets for intelligence services. Cybercriminals look for vulnerabilities to benefit from an exceptional situation.

Work computers can contain confidential data from organizations that are sometimes used for private purposes when working from home. This could represent irreparable security risks. According to Stamp (2011), users are surprisingly adept at damaging the best established security plans. Security can be broken due to user error, despite the fact that the cryptography, protocols, access control, and software all performed perfectly. Typically, cybercriminals appeal to people's emotional streak in order to obtain confidential information for the purpose of financial enrichment. Wiggen (2020) considers the growing increase in the use of digital applications and the use of poorly protected private IT devices when working at home, illustrates the risks of digital security during the COVID-19 pandemic and highlights the need to take appropriate measures to protect IT systems in critical infrastructures to prevent cyber espionage in order to obtain information on measures to combat the corona virus, potential vaccines and treatments.

Bada and Nurse (2020) argue that there are other two relevant areas of impact: the social and psychological (emotional and behavioral) impacts. The social impact of a cyber-attack is related to people's social disruption and other widespread problems, such as the loss of confidence in the use of cyberspace or technology. The psychological impact can be caused by the social impact and can include more personal aspects, such as anxiety, worry, anger, indignation, depression, among other pathologies.

Malicious cyber activity can jeopardize national interests and security, its people and property. Intelligence can provide insights that are not normally available elsewhere, warn of potential threats and opportunities, and analyze the expected results of proposed or implemented policy options.

Although all organizations appreciate the enormous benefits of ICTs, there is also a perception that their misuse poses risks to the peace and security of all.

Critical infrastructure sectors are important to the economy and national security, for which cyber protection plays a key role. The United States government considers chemical, commercial facilities, communications, critical manufacturing, dams, defense industrial base, emerging services, energy, financial services, food and agriculture, government facilities, healthcare and public health, IT, nuclear reactors, materials, and waste, transportation systems, and water and wastewater systems as critical factors (White House, 2013).

Although cyber connectivity is an important driver of productivity, innovation and growth in the world economy but, sometimes, it can become a high cost. Companies, individuals and governments will continue to be targets of malicious cyber activities.

The constant evolution of the nature and scope of cyber threats suggests that additional and ongoing efforts will be essential and that cooperation between the public and private sectors is essential. Only concerted action by countries and public and private organizations can mitigate the effects of this scourge. Will it ever be possible to achieve?

CYBERSECURITY COOPERATION

In the scope of cybercrime, economic crime is the fastest growing in the world, it is essential that companies are properly prepared to face digital threats, investing in a good management of vulnerabilities to cyber risks, in safeguarding data and information, but mainly in prevention mechanisms. The global trend towards the adoption of emerging technologies (IoT, 5G, Artificial Intelligence, Quantum Computing or cloud platforms, among others) has contributed to a progressive increase in cyber-attacks in the business and military context.

Seeking a robust response through the exchange of good practices and information, early warning, incident response, risk assessment, cyber security awareness and prioritization, NATO and the EU have made joint efforts to avoid duplicating tasks complementing their efforts, thus seeking to increase the resilience of the critical infrastructures of the Administrations, defense and other IT infrastructures. Since 2008, NATO's Centre for Excellence in Cooperative Cyber Defense has played an important multinational and interdisciplinary cyber role, focusing on various aspects related to cybersecurity, such as education, analysis, consulting, lessons learned, research and development. Even though the Centre does not belong to NATO's direct command line, its mission is to increase the capacity, cooperation and information sharing between NATO, NATO nations and partners in cyber defense (Geers, 2020). In 2013, was established the European Cybercrime Centre (EC3), with the aim of providing analysis and information (Intelligence), supporting investigations, facilitating cooperation and creating channels for sharing information between Member States' security authorities, industry, private sector and others interesting parties (Europol, 2020).

Facing multidimensional threats, it is essential to improve synergies between civil and military partnerships to protect critical IT assets. These efforts must be supported by closer cooperation between governments, the private sector and research and development centers. In view of the disruptive impact of cyber threats and the need to ensure integrated command of operations to be carried out in cyberspace, the United States created a Cyber Command in 2010, clearly assuming cyberspace as a new operational domain, where operations can be carried out military (U.S. Cyber Command, 2020).

For the United Nations (2013), the pursuit of international cooperation will require a set of actions that support cybersecurity in an open and cooperative environment. It considers that the measures to be established must promote international peace, stability and security, and must be achieved through common understandings about the application of international law and the norms, rules and principles derived from responsible behavior by States.

Other initiatives, such as Paris Call for Trust and Security in Cyberspace, seek joint cybersecurity measures to address new threats that endanger citizens and infrastructure with the aim of protect and regulate cyberspace's activities. Other initiatives, such as the Paris Call for Trust and Security in Cyberspace, seek joint cybersecurity measures to protect and regulate cyberspace activities and address new threats that endanger states, public authorities, organizations and businesses through cooperation public and private.

Cybercriminals and cybercrime networks are becoming increasingly sophisticated, and there is an urgent need to develop the right operational tools and the skills to fight them. Cybercrime knows no borders, security authorities must adopt a coordinated and collaborative approach to respond to this growing threat. In order to increase the resilience of the communication and information systems that support the defense policy of countries and their national interests, the development of cyber security capabilities should focus on the detection of sophisticated computer threats, the response to be given and the subsequent recovery. Ensuring cybersecurity is everyone's responsibility. End users play a crucial role in protecting computer systems and networks. They need to know the risks they face online and be able to prevent them.

Modern military operations rely heavily on digital technologies, from command and control, to the operation of weapon systems or logistical services, from the tactical, operational and strategic levels. Irrespective of its nature, civil or military, cybersecurity today extends far behind the scenes to include focused exercises, research and development of advanced cyber security tools and processes, coordination with stakeholders against virtually unlimited cyber security threats and attempts at subterfuge (European Defense Agency, 2019).

Countries should seek to develop a coherent international cyber policy aimed at greater commitment and strengthening of relations with major international partners and organizations, as well as with civil society and the private sector. Although the evolution of technologies is associated with the desire of organizations to become stronger and more competitive, there is a growing complexity and sophistication of cyber-attacks. The need for international cooperation between States, international and regional organizations and other entities is emphasized by the borderless and increasingly sophisticated nature of cyber threats, but the effectiveness of such cooperation depends greatly upon strategically aligned policy goals and bilateral and multilateral relations. Combining civil and military efforts between organizations and countries is crucial to prevent or mitigate the effects of cybercrime. They must become brothers in arms to fight this increasingly asymmetric war.

Areas such as information and intelligence sharing and mutual assistance may become essential in responding to a cyber-crisis, but the effectiveness of such cooperation depends greatly upon strategically aligned policy goals and bilateral and multilateral relations. In many domains, such as international criminal cooperation, there are several preconditions that need to be in place in the cooperating countries, such as substantive national law as well as procedural law and international agreements, before the dialogue on the possibility of any sort of international cooperation can grow into further discussions on the efficiency of such cooperation.

Challenges and Required Actions

Information is an important resource and should be treated as such through careful management throughout its life cycle, regardless of the resource and the format used to support it, according to the principle of the need to know, with security, legality and privacy standards. Information is not all the same, it can be public or restricted, being shared only by some sectors of the organization, or it can be sensitive, only being accessed by the authorized elements of the organization. Any person who has access to sensitive information or materials shall be required to maintain confidentiality. Secrecy duty should be maintained after ending the exercise of functions. Violation of the duty of confidentiality, custody and retention of confidential information will have criminal and disciplinary consequences.

An incident chain or a disastrous interaction of complex systems can severely affect vital systems, such as water and electricity supply, communications, transportation, food, health services, among others. The set of processes and procedures that an organization implements to ensure that essential functions are available after an unplanned disruption is described as the business continuity plan. This plan shall ensure that resources considered critical in an organization are properly identified, defining measures that allow it to be quickly and efficiently restored to its normal functioning.

The adoption of security measures aims to protect sensitive and confidential information, personal and organizational data, critical infrastructures, ensure the internal services operation, protect against viruses and hacker attacks, protect organizations image and reputation and its online presence (NATO, 2015). Depending on activity, size, complexity, operation, value or other characteristics of potential interest to a third party, companies that aspire to be competitive should not neglect security measures, otherwise they are at serious risk of survival.

Decision-making should always be done based on the best quality information possible, in what concerns to content, accuracy, relevance and integrity. Information is power! In terms of the policy of a state or the management of an organization, this means gaining advantages over other states or organizations, which may be political, economic, military, technological, financial, and industrial, among others.

According to the World Economic Forum (2020), the industry and government leadership must conduct a set of political actions that encourage the adoption of security solutions and that sustain greater trust and transparency between the different components of the global economic ecosystem, establishing responsibilities and regulatory models that promote international business and trade in data and digital services.

Mitigating cyber threats requires increasingly demanding prevention strategies and mechanisms. Today's business security can be safeguarded by taking out insurance against cyber risks, allowing protection against loss of profits due to business interruption. There is also ISO/IEC 2700-series, international standards and references for information security management. It is a series of best practices to help organizations improve their information security. The general principle of this standard is to adopt a set of requirements, processes and controls in order to adequately mitigate and manage the organization's risk (International Organization for Standardization, 2018). Certain organizations require their stakeholders to get this certification as a guarantee of compliance with information security principles, thus providing their customers and partners with an extra level of protection.

In turn, the multidimensional articulation of national defense with internal and external security policies requires the preparation of intelligence services to diversify international action scenarios, with a special focus on combating criminal actions affecting countries, their peoples and institutions. Organizations sensitive information should be protected through a balanced set of security measures, respecting the principle of defense in-depth. This is achieved through the application of physical, personnel, cryptographic, information, emission and transmission security measures set, which are the fundamental security pillars of any modern organization, whether they are civilian or military, aimed to maximize organizations profits or for other purposes. It is a designation applied to military tactics, through which layers of defense are implemented to prevent the advance of the enemy. The depth is achieved through the provision of in-depth combat and support units, the organization of complementary and alternative positions and proper location of forces.

Defense in depth enhances resilience and provides redundancy in the event of a security check failure. It defines a set of interoperable operations, based on various procedures and equipment, which constitute several layers of access. An effective defense in depth strategy defines defensive control levels, overlapping and complementary (i.e., a layered defense), designed to identify and mitigate together potential attacks that organizations may suffer. To protect sensitive information, it is necessary to implement security procedures in order to protect information, focused on measures to protect systems against cyber-attacks and prevent unauthorized access to the organization's facilities.

Security management mechanisms and procedures must be well implemented in order to block, prevent, detect, resist and recover from potential negative impacts of incidents that affect the security objectives of organizations. To achieve security objectives, also a set of physical security measures should be implemented to create a safe environment for organizations to develop their activity (NATO, 2008).

According to the U.S. National Institute of Standards and Technology (2018), the following steps must be taken to implement a cybersecurity framework:

Step 1 – Prioritize and Scope
Step 2 – Orient
Step 3 – Create a Current Profile
Step 4 – Conduct a Risk Assessment
Step 5 – Create a Target Profile
Step 6 – Determine, Analyze, and Prioritize Gaps
Step 7 – Implement Action Plan

Organizations must repeat the steps that promote the continuous improvement of their cybersecurity and monitor the progress of the measures implemented. The processes and procedures of this security standard can be adjusted to the reality of each organization according to its technological and organizational specificity.

The development of laws, policies and standards worldwide will be the key to effective cybersecurity. At the political-strategic level, Wiggen (2020) claims that governments must respond to cyber incidents launched by another state by imposing political and economic sanctions or by bringing legal charges to isolate and stigmatize the aggressor in order to achieve a long-term behavior change. On the other hand, Ford (2020) argues that modern cyber threats must be responded to with diplomacy and deterrence.

Here are some security measures that every modern and security concerned organizations should implement:

The greater the volume of digital transactions, the more possibilities for security breaches and the more enticing it becomes for cybercriminals. There are no magic solutions. The complexity of the circumstances and the externalities of the decisions will be crucial factors for the measures to be taken.

CONCLUSION

It is legitimate for companies to want to copy the best models to become more competitive. It is a fact that today great nations have in the past followed the best practices of the reference countries to improve their economic, military or geostrategic condition. The student will always want to surpass the master. But at what price?

Security is not an end in itself, but a critical function supporting organization's management. The security levels, policies, procedures and measures adopted must be appropriate and proportionate to the value and level of trust of organization's assets. In both military and civilian environments, the adoption of security measures and a set of best practices is critical for all organizations in digital economy era. It is a fact that today's threats and risks will be different in the future. Organizations that have the ability to quickly adapt and adjust to the context of the environment will be more likely to succeed.

Cyberattacks have reached levels of sophistication never seen before, with hackers using increasingly advanced and creative techniques and technologies in pursuit of deliberate illicit practices that compromise organizations security, namely through social networks and their vulnerabilities exploitation.

Table 1. Security measures checklist

Standard Security Measures	Yes	No	Partially Implemented
Security Action Plan			
Social Networks Use Policy			
Mobile Devices Use Policy			
Workers Access Control			
Visitors Access Control			
Control of Keys and Combinations			
Guards or Security Officers			
Personnel Security Accreditation for Sensitive Information			
Intrusion Detection Systems			
Closed Circuit Television (CCTV)			
Data Protection Passwords			
Virus, Malware, Worm, Spyware, Adware, Trojan, Ransomware, Bots, Rootkits, and Bugs Protection			
Phishing Protection			
Social Networking Monitoring			
Data Backups			
Blockchain Security			

The contemporary world presents new challenges and opportunities to all organizations. Globalization and its effects have brought new threats that have profoundly transformed the security paradigm. It is imperious to take effective measures to fight them.

No single security measure will provide a complete defense in an organization's. The safeguarding of information and its resources is achieved through the continuous and joint use of security measures and good practices, and involves the commitment of all entities. Responsibility for increasing cyberspace security lies with all actors in the information society worldwide, from citizens to governments.

REFERENCES

Bada, M., & Nurse, J. (2020). The Social and Psychological Impact of Cyber-Attacks. In V. Benson & J. McAlaney (Eds.), *Emerging Cyber Threats and Cognitive Vulnerabilities* (pp. 73–92). Academic Press. doi:10.1016/B978-0-12-816203-3.00004-6

Bhardwaj, A. (2020). 5G for Military Communications. *Procedia Computer Science*, *171*, 2665–2674. doi:10.1016/j.procs.2020.04.289

Defense News. (2016). *Chinese Businessman Pleads Guilty of Spying on F-35 and F-22*. Available at https://www.defensenews.com/breaking-news/2016/03/24/chinese-businessman-pleads-guilty-of-spying-on-f-35-and-f-22/

European Commission. (2013). Protection of Undisclosed Know-how and Business Information (Trade Secrets) Against their Unlawful Acquisition, Use and Disclosure. Brussels: COM (2013) 813.

European Commission. (2019). *Digital Economy*. Retrieved on September, 2020, from https://ec.europa.eu/jrc/en/research-topic/digital-economy

European Defense Agency. (2019). *Inside the Engine Room Checking the EU's Defense Mechanics*. Available at https://eda.europa.eu/docs/default-source/eda-magazine/final-full-magazine-edm18-(pdf).pdf

Europol. (2020). *European Cybercrime Centre - EC3*. Available at https://www.europol.europa.eu/about-europol/european-cybercrime-centre-ec3

FBI – Federal Bureau of Investigation. (2014). *Combating Economic Espionage and Trade Secret Theft*. Retrieved on September, 2020, from https://www.fbi.gov/news/testimony/combating-economic-espionage-and-trade-secret-theft

Ford, C. (2020). *U.S. Department of State: Responding to Modern Cyber Threats with Diplomacy and Deterrence*. Retrieved on November, 2020, from https://www.state.gov/responding-to-modern-cyber-threats-with-diplomacy-and-deterrence/

Geers, K. (2018). *Cyberspace and the Changing Nature of Warfare*. NATO Cooperative Cyber Defense Centre of Excellence. Available at https://ccdcoe.org/library/publications/cyberspace-and-the-changing-nature-of-warfare/

Hoadley, D. (2020). *Artificial Intelligence and National Security Report updated by Kelley M. Sayler*. Congressional Research Service Report. Available at https://fas.org/sgp/crs/natsec/R45178.pdf

Hoehn, J., & Sayler, K. (2020). *National Security Implications of Fifth Generation (5G) Mobile Technologies Report*. Congressional Research Service Report. Available at https://crsreports.congress.gov/product/pdf/IF/IF11251

International Organization for Standardization. (2018). *When it comes to keeping information assets secure, organizations can rely on the ISO/IEC 27000 family*. Available at https://www.iso.org/obp/ui/#iso:std:iso-iec:27000:ed-5:v1:en

INTERPOL. (2020). *Cybercrime: COVID-19 Impact*. Retrieved on October, 2020, from https://www.interpol.int/News-and-Events/News/2020/INTERPOL-report-shows-alarming-rate-of-cyberattacks-during-COVID-19

MacAfee. (2018). *The Economic Impact of Cybercrime – No Slowing Down*. Retrieved on November, 2020, from https://www.mcafee.com/enterprise/en-us/solutions/lp/economics-cybercrime.html

Microsoft. (2020). *New cyberattacks targeting U.S. elections*. Retrieved on November, 2020, from https://blogs.microsoft.com/on-the-issues/2020/09/10/cyberattacks-us-elections-trump-biden/

National Institute of Standards and Technology. (2018). *Framework for Improving Critical Infrastructure Cybersecurity – Version 1.1*. Retrieved on November, 2020, from https://www.nist.gov/publications/framework-improving-critical-infrastructure-cybersecurity-version-11

NATO. (2008). Directive on Physical Security. NATO Security Committee. AC/35-D/2001-REV2, 7 January 2008. [s.l.]

NATO. (2015). Directive on Classified Project and Industrial Security. NATO Security Committee. AC/35-D/2003-REV5, 13 May 2015. [s.l.]

NATO. (2020). *Cyber Defense*. Retrieved on April, 2020, from https://www.nato.int/cps/en/natohq/topics_78170.htm

Paris Call. (2018). *For trust and security in cyberspace: Ensuring international cyberspace security*. Available at https://pariscall.international/en/

Stamp, M. (2011). *Information Security: Principles and Practice* (2nd ed.). John Wiley & Sons. doi:10.1002/9781118027974

Sun Tzu. (1963). *The Art of War* (S. B. Griffith, Trans.). Oxford University Press.

TASS – Russian News Agency. (2020). *Russian citizen sentenced for attempt to hand over classified data to CIA*. Retrieved on November, 2020, from https://tass.com/society/1225813

United Nations. (2013). *Report of the Group of Governmental Experts on Developments in the Field of Information and Telecommunications in the Context of International Security*. Available at https://undocs.org/A/68/98

United Nations. (2019). *United Nations Conference on Trade and Development – Digital Economy Report 2019*. New York: United Nations Publications. Available at https://unctad.org/system/files/official-document/der2019_overview_en.pdf

U.S. Cyber Command. (2020). *U.S. Cyber Command History*. Retrieved on October, 2020, from https://www.cybercom.mil/About/History/

White House. (2013). *Presidential Policy Directive – Critical Infrastructure Security and Resilience*. Available at https://obamawhitehouse.archives.gov/the-press-office/2013/02/12/presidential-policy-directive-critical-infrastructure-security-and-resil

White House. (2018). *The Cost of Malicious Cyber Activity to the U.S. Economy*. Retrieved on November, 2020, from https://www.whitehouse.gov/wp-content/uploads/2018/03/The-Cost-of-Malicious-Cyber-Activity-to-the-U.S.-Economy.pdf

Wiggen, J. (2020). *The Impact of COVID-19 on Cyber Crime and State-Sponsored Cyber Activities*. Retrieved on November, 2020, from https://www.kas.de/documents/252038/7995358/The+impact+of+COVID-19+on+cyber+crime+and+state-sponsored+cyber+activities.pdf/b4354456-994b-5a39-4846-af6a0b b3c378?version=1.0&t=1591354291674

World Economic Forum. (2020). *Cybersecurity, emerging technology and systemic risk*. Available at http://www3.weforum.org/docs/WEF_Future_Series_Cybersecurity_emerging_technology_and_systemic_risk_2020.pdf

Chapter 13

Web Data and the Relationship Between the General Data Protection Regulation in Europe and Brazil

Moisés Rockembach
Federal University of Rio Grande do Sul, Brazil

Armando Malheiro da Silva
University of Porto, Portugal

ABSTRACT

From the consolidation of the application of European data protection regulations and the recent adoption of Brazilian data protection regulations, we are faced with a scenario that crosses borders. In a world marked by companies whose business model is the analysis and commercialization of personal data and of governments that use their citizens' data for control and surveillance, it is imperative to discuss the necessary characteristics to foster a society that respects ethical and legal values regarding data privacy and consented uses there; the authors address concepts and cases that they consider important for the establishment of reflections on the use of web data. They also take into account ethical issues and regulatory instruments in Europe and Brazil, analyzing the strongness and weaknesses in the implementation of data protection and privacy.

1. INTRODUCTION

The current problems in the digital transformation, the convergence of all economic activities to online platforms have implied, above all, a reflection on the concepts and issues that involve privacy. In the European Union, the General Data Protection Regulation (GDPR - 2016/679), since 2016, regulates how the collection, processing and access of personal data should be made, which are some of the main

DOI: 10.4018/978-1-7998-4201-9.ch013

Copyright © 2021, IGI Global. Copying or distributing in print or electronic forms without written permission of IGI Global is prohibited.

issues to be clarified and made transparent . In Brazil, published in 2018 and effective in 2020, we have the publication of the General Data Protection Law (LGPD), which we will address in this chapter.

Web data are considered the great source of information for the 21st century. This work concerns digital privacy issues and data protection needs, where large global corporations are responsible of storing these large data sets, also called Big Data. However, Big Data is not restricted only to the storage and keep of data in large volume, but the ability to use computational processing to gather, analyze, link and compare this data through algorithms (Boyd, Crawford, 2012).

Big Data is provided with various types of data and diverse heterogeneous sources, such as cell phones, sensors, social networks, web pages, among others, collecting, storing and processing data at high speed (Melo, Rockembach 2019). It can be said that nine companies in the technological field lead this informational process: Google, Amazon, Apple, IBM, Facebook, Microsoft, Alibaba, Tencent and Baidu (Webb, 2019).

This work aims to address a very relevant topic for Information Science, Technology, Information Ethics and Digital and Global Economy, since there are still problems, whether in the full implementation of the General European Data Protection Regulation (GDPR), or in the Brazilian General Data Protection Regulation (LGPD). This law is still very recent and, therefore, requires further studies, raising the challenges that observe the ethical and legal issues of data protection. Brazilian law was enacted in 2018 and came into force in 2020, even so, there is still a wide debate in society about data protection, which should still cause many problems in the application and enforcement of the law.

2. THE CONCEPTS AND APPROACHES IN INFORMATION ETHICS

The subject in question necessarily calls for an analysis here enunciated from the ethical plane. And if we place ourselves on this plane, we can begin by emphasizing the importance of Multiculturality or the impossibility of a universal Ethics covering all peoples and continents, because Homo Sapiens is one as a living being, but diverse as a social and cultural being.

Rafael Capurro (Capurro, 2010; 11-51) and Adela Cortina (Cortina, 2009) are authors who emphasize Multicultural Ethics or minimal Ethics, alerting to the presence of a core of values and principles transversal to different environments and contexts, which they weigh heavily in the reconfiguration, adaptation and particularization of the universal and the creation of customs and norms with full meaning and strength at the local (ized) level.

At the top of the problems that are methodologically and instrumentally addressed by Information Science and which are also viewed reflexively by Information Ethics is that of freedom of expression and critical choice of information. A central topic that Information Science investigates by exploring the conditions of production and behavioral use of information; Information Ethics weighs cultural specificities, without losing sight of the fact that freedom is a fundamental right and a central principle of anthropocentric ethics. So, it imposes itself as universal, and this universality brings with it the counterpoint that its exercise is only limited by respect unavoidable equal right of the Other. But the full awareness of the centrality of this principle must be accompanied by the critical sense of each individual, that is, by a medium and, preferably, high level of literacy.

A related topic has to do with oppression, submission, manipulation of people - acts that violate human dignity. They appear evidenced in Information Science research. But it is to the Ethics of Information that the topic matters and, currently, acutely, because it seems to make sense again the concept proposed in the century XVI, by Étienne de la Boétie of "voluntary submission", given the hegemonic and "imperialist" behavior of the falsely called "social networks", that is, the digital platforms Facebook, Instagram, Twiter and Google.

Bruno Patino recently denounced such behavior on social networks in a book entitled "La civilisation du poisson rouge: petit traité sur le marché de l'attention" (Patino, 2019), showing how human beings behave more and more like "redfish" trapped / hypnotized by smartphone screens. The Ethics of Information welcomes the diagnosis and points out the balanced path: the screens connect us to the global world, provide us with all kinds of information, but we always need to be free in the way we receive it, confront it and use it. This is the antidote to the infamous "fake News" or false/untrue information.

Lacking the truth or lying is an age-old ethical flaw, which a researcher/scientist of any domain, including that of Infocommunication, must scrupulously avoid but, which in terms of Information Ethics, deserves all the prominence. Nominalism and relativism went to great lengths to cast doubt on reality outside of language and, consequently, devalued the notion of truth and now, in the face of events, especially political ones, marked by the massive use of digital technology to produce and disseminate the old rumors disguised of "fake news", indignation of some against the recourse by "others" to falsehood grows. Both are trenches of certainty and conviction about the truth. If the latter fails to detach itself and hover above the natural subjectivity, it loses the strength of the ethical principle and the Information Ethics cannot, thus, trigger the debate and propose behavioral solutions.

Lying about the authorship or production / appropriation of information recorded in some medium, especially verbal put on paper or in digital format, has been, since the 18th century, an act that undermines the right of an Author to "own" what he originally writes and advertises. It is the famous "Copyright" or "intellectual property" with roots in individualism and the assumption that intellectual exercise could become a profession, that is, be legitimately remunerated.

The authenticity of information, the brand of the producer, whether or not inserted in an institutional or organizational context, does not escape Information Science, as it receives all the attention from the Ethics of Information and Law. Plagiarism (Satur, Sias, Silva, 2020: 57-87) is criminalized and, currently facilitated by technology. It is practical not only enough, with incredible ease and, even more surprisingly, in degrees of unconsciousness or ignorance of criminal gravity by your practitioners. To claim to be the creator of a document that was not entirely produced by you is to lie and, in this way, it becomes an ethical flaw, although the material dimension of the act is of a more economic and legal order.

At the Law field, there is no way to prove that an individual stole the idea (that is, the information that exists only in his head) and not based on an external material support. There is no way to substantially prove the lie and theft, being certain that people people in distant geographies at the same time can formulate the same ideas. This aspect, however, does not detract from the fact that these ideas actually arise, even if they are not made documents. The theme remains accurate, but it is also certain that it has lent itself to some kind of exaggeration, such as the campaign against self-plagiarism. This consists in not considering it ethical for a person to plagiarize himself: if the information someone repeats it "belongs" originally why can't you repeat it or use it one or more times in full? The position of Information Ethics in the face of this questioning helps us escape absurdity or logical numbness.

In ethical values, we have chained the responsibility for the general conduct that is built day by day, the security of intimacy and trust. Clearly, Ethical Information topics, which are also Information Science and Computer Science, must build reliable technological solutions and understand needs and modes of use. Information Science must consolidate the correctness of responsible behavior, protected from public and credible indiscretion or a generator of trust and respect, the basis of a healthy and solid social relationship.

Information Ethics also explores the justification and limits of privacy, confidentiality and contractual loyalty to those with whom it has made an explicit commitment of this type. A case study, which quickly becomes classic, is that of Edward Snowden, an IT "spy" who participated in a program of "massive surveillance and permanent registration" by the NSA. US government agency ended up denouncing this activity and disclosing information obtained in clear abuse of individual and collective privacy, of thousands of innocent anonymous, but also justified by the need for national protection after the September 11, 2001 terrorist attack in New York City (Snowden, 2019). Or the question, which is now regulated internationally, of the protection of personal data, with emphasis on consumer and health data that can be exploited for purposes that harm citizens' freedom and survival (Mcneil, 1992).

To close a list of topics, it is enough to bring up the dependence on the internet ("internet addiction") and the ethical implications of the critical digital inclusion of children.

Regarding the "addiction to the internet" or the state of dependence on use (abuse of navigation in the info-sphere, there is, here, a problem dealt with in the field of Mental Health and Psychotherapies that help face and overcome addiction, that is, the uncontrolled (pulsional) practice that subjects the person to a loss of freedom, unlimited subjection and a serious risk to life, when their vital functions are jeopardized. Also, in the domain of ethical rationality, where it matters to know how the person manages to keep his conscience operational and manages to remain attached to strong ethical principles, such as his freedom or free will and his respect for his own life.

The worrying fragility of children in the "new world" of the Infoesphere, in which they immerse themselves through smartphones, tablets or computers and for excessively long periods of time, begins to be a problem that Educators and Sociologists recognize it as urgent and serious. Information Science has an analytical and collaborative role in the search for valid answers. And a key aspect is to realize that children from an early age adjust and relate to technological devices in a totally uninhibited way, but, in contrast, deeply inadvertent and ignorant.

Therefore, it is necessary to investigate and deepen the binomial digital inclusion and information literacy, deconstructing false proposals, such as that of the "digital natives" - a perfect mirage contradicted by reality. Children must be literate in language (s) and in technology from an early age to understand the functioning of a computer and the internet, its internal composition, features, advantages and dangers / limitations.

In the field of Information Ethics, it is important to monitor the educational activity for freedom and critical sense, but always reinforcing control and constructive vigilance because, until they reach their maturity, adult must control and security legitimate access to infosphere. This also be accompanied by the intensive process of promoting digital inclusion and the solid transition to the critical capacity for analysis and choice of information, in an expression, of information literacy.

These ethical reflections lead us to think about the flow of web data, capture, treatment and use of personal data and how we should have regulations that protect data and privacy. Therefore, we will deal next with the European and Brazilian context, respectively under the General Data Protection Regulation (GDPR) of the European Union and the Brazilian General Data Protection Law (LGPD).

3. DATA PROTECTION AS REGULATORY ACTS IN THE EUROPEAN UNION AND BRAZIL

In the European Union, since 2016, the General Data Protection Regulation - GDPR - 2016/679 (European Parliament, 2016) regulates how the collection, treatment and access of personal data should be made, which are some of the main topics to be clarified and made transparent. In Brazil, since 2018, there is the General Data Protection Law - LGPD (Brasil, 2018), which is inspired by the European GDPR. In the development of European law, some issues were innovative (De Hert & Papakonstantinou, 2016), such as the right to data portability, the right to be forgotten, privacy from conception, data protection, certification, codes of conduct and assessments of impact.

Our concern in this chapter is to address relations between the European General Data Protection Regulation (GDPR) and the Brazilian General Data Protection Law (LGPD), the strengths and difficulties in the treatment of web data. In Information Science, User Studies and Informational Behavior, for example, have undergone transformations, especially with regard to the possibilities of digital media, since data collection can provide us with relevant information on these subjects. This also applies to all sources of information used in Data Science.

Some events in recent years have led us to pay more attention to how this data is collected and processed. From the Edward Snowden, revelations shown in the documentary CitizenFour (2014) to the famous Cambridge Analytica case of electoral manipulation around the world by the Facebook platform (Cadwalladr, Graham-Harrison, 2018) are some examples to be cited and, in a way, is just the beginning of these ethical discussions.

In this conflict between public and private information and the right to be forgotten, the case of Google Spain versus Agencia Española de Protección de Datos and Mario Costeja González (Lindsay, 2015) is emblematic because, from that situation, a discussion was generated about when the right to privacy supersedes the right to publicity of information. In this specific Spanish case, the plaintiff demanded that his name not appear on the Google search engine, associated with a public debt case that had already been paid.

The shift from Informational Capitalism (Castells, 2000) to a Surveillance Capitalism (Zuboff, 2019) is becoming more evident today. Nowadays, the convergence of different activities for online platforms, digital transformation driven by the pandemic generated by COVID-19 and the consequent need for social withdrawal, demands reflection on issues involving data privacy.

Recent phenomena, such as filter bubble (Pariser, 2011), determine the types of content that each user views and, for this analysis, it is necessary to have access to a large amount of data. According to Pariser (2011), the filter bubble phenomenon brings three new dynamics: the first is that the subjects are alone in the bubble, moving away from each other; in the second dynamic, the bubble is invisible because the criteria that platforms determine to form bubbles are not transparent and, in the third dynamic, the subjects do not choose to enter the bubble and they are directed according to certain choices they make on digital platforms. Finally, the price paid for the customization of the platforms is the data that each person makes available in the interaction with the system that are strategically used by the companies, which can affect us both positively and negatively.

In an interview (Schneider & Saldanha, 2015), Rafael Capurro also raises relevant problems that he currently faces when talking about the ethical-epistemological dilemmas of the information age. The first problem is in the relationship between freedom and security, which generates a tension between the power of the democratic state and the citizen, in the exercise of freedoms versus the systems of mass surveillance and censorship. The second issue refers to the collection of voluminous personal data by the State and private agents, which become Big Data and generate ethical issues, as well as concerns about the validity of the epistemic construction from these large datasets (Rockembach, Silva, 2018).

National States and the Government, in general, are also potential leaders in this process as they naturally acquire data from citizens for the performance of their activities. What kind of data is collected for the exercise of State activities, what are the crossings of that data and who has access to it are important issues that need to be transparent, as well as the establishment of privacy policies. In this sense, It is also necessary to reflect on ethical aspects about the safeguard of information and digital preservation of the web (Rockembach, 2017).

Sartor (2014) argues that, in these ethical conflicts, a dilemma needs to be resolved. On the one hand, among advertising interests, widely recognized, such as interests related to freedom of expression and the right to information, democracy and transparency. On the other hand, privacy interests, widely understood and compensated after the event or phenomenon, such as data protection, reputation, identity, dignity and the right to a new start. Also according to Sartor (2014), at some point after the event, it may happen that the balance of interests changes, so that the information, now published, is no longer distributed to protect legitimate privacy interests.

Currently, there is a lack of consideration for the processing and use of personal data worldwide, represented by government agencies and private companies. Often, confidential data has no protection or transparency regarding its treatment. According to Schomakers et al. (2019), the sensitivity of the data is related to the perception of risk on the part of the user, ranging from risks of breach of health information (medical data) to monetary risk (credit card numbers) and social and psychological risks (data social networks), indicating that the greater the perceived sensitivity of the data, the greater the privacy concerns.

The Brazilian General Data Protection Law (LGPD) was inspired by the European Union's General Data Protection Regulation (GDPR) and has similarities and differences in relation to the reflections proposed in the European information and technological context.

According to the General Data Protection Regulation (GDPR), it is not necessary for Member States to implement national laws, as it is applicable to all countries belonging to the EU. However, since the implementation of the GDPR in the countries of the European Union, laws and government acts have been enacted in each government, called DPA or Data Protection Act, updating the oldest laws on the privacy of citizens, the protection of people in the processing of personal data, the use of data by companies and public institutions and the creation of national data protection authorities[1]. In this sense, many countries have their own data protection act, which complies with the GDPR, as for example, Austria[2] (Data Protection Act - *Datenschutz-Anpassungsgesetz*, 2018), Denmark[3] (Danish Data Protection Act, Law n. 502, 2018), Finland[4] (Data Protection Act - *Tietosuojalaki*, 2018), France[5] (LOI n° 2018-493), Germany[6] (*Bundesdatenschutzgesetz* – BDSG, 2017), Ireland[7] (Irish Data Protection Act, 2018), Italy[8] (Legislative decree n. 101, 2018), Netherlands[9] (Dutch General Data Protection Regulation Implementation Act, 2018), Portugal[10] (Law n. 58, 2019) and Spain[11] (Law n.3/2018).

The laws are similar, as they follow GDPR standards, where the scope addresses provisions associated with the right of access, data processing, disclosure of personal information, designation of a Data Protection Officer (DPO), consent limits and administrative sanctions. Besides that, data processing must be done in a legal and fair manner and the data owner must have the right to know the purpose of using his data.

The search for harmonization of legislation in the European Union is the ideal pursued by the GDPR, however, the opening clauses allow each member state to adapt specific issues. Germany is well known for its privacy culture, having the first data protection law in the world (Hessian Data Protection Act of 1970), this was reflected in the regulation and approval of one of the first national laws in conformity with the GDPR, in 2017. Nationally, Sweden, another country with a tradition in the treatment of privacy, has the first national legislation since 1973, with effect since 1974. Some national laws and government acts have different definitions and use their national discretion to implement these changes. For example, the Finnish law, which comprises consent for services for children from 13 years old (Finland Data Protection Act, §5), as well as Denmark, Portugal and Sweden, instead of 16 years old, as defined in GDPR. This difference also occurs in the data protection law of Austria and Italy (14 years old) and France (15 years old). Meanwhile, Germany, Ireland and the Netherlands follow the GDPR standard (16 years).

Some member states exclude, from administrative fines, state authorities and state enterprises, such as Finland (Finland Data Protection Act, §24) and Spain (Spanish Organic Law 3/2018 for the Protection of Personal Data and for the granting of digital rights, article 77) or limit the amount of fine to be charged to public bodies, such as in Ireland (Irish Data Protection Act, Section 141). This is because, under GDPR, article 83, each member state of the European Union can establish rules regarding administrative fines imposed on public authorities and public bodies. This can become an issue to be debated, as it is a problem of public exemplarity. How can public bodies and authorities charge fines if they are not subject to the same penalties? How to implement a culture of public data protection effectively, if there are no financial consequences for violations?

As in the European Union, data protection does not appear only with the promulgation of the GDPR (that rescues its origins in Directive 95/46/EC, in 1995), in Brazil, data protection has a history of legislation, since Brazil's Federal Constitution (1988), mainly its article 5, Consumer Protection Code (1990), Brazilian Civil Rights Framework for the Internet (2014) and finally the General Data Protection Law (2018). One of the main differences between the GDPR / EU and the Brazilian LGPD is the context of application, as the European Union has 25 years of experience in privacy issues, since Directive 95/46 / EC and Brazil, despite the previous laws, only with LGPD has a specific data protection act and needs to create a culture of privacy in organizations. Many countries in EU have had experience with data privacy since the 1970s, as demonstrated by legislation. As for the security techniques required by GDPR, these include encryption and pseudo-anonymization (article 32), while LGPD does not mention which security techniques need to be applied. In the relationship between processors and controller, in GDPR formalization of a contract or legal act is required (article 28), whereas in LGPD this is not necessary.

The definition of sensitive data is also different between legislations, in the GDPR are approached genetic data, health data and biometric data, while according to the Brazilian General Data Protection Law, sensitive personal data is that referring to racial or ethnic origin, religious belief, political opinion, union membership or religious, philosophical or political organization, regarding health or to sexual, genetic or biometric life, when linked to a natural person.

The European Union can determine the level of data protection for non-EU countries, based on Article 45 of the GDPR, allowing personal data to be transferred to third countries without additional safeguards. Currently, some of the countries with this recognition[12] are Andorra, Argentina, Canada, Faroe Islands, Guernsey, Israel, Isle of Man, Japan, Jersey, New Zealand, Switzerland and Uruguay.

The General Data Protection Law - LGPD, published in 2018 and in force since 2020, brings a series of challenges on how to collect and treat personal data and is based on informational self-determination, the inviolability of intimacy, honor and image, with respect for privacy, freedom of expression, information, communication and opinion, economic and technological development and innovation, human rights, the free development of personality, dignity and the exercise of citizenship by people, free enterprise, free competition and consumer protection. On the one hand, we have the right of access to information and the right to memory and, in conflict with these first two rights, the right to be forgotten, informative self-determination, private life, intimacy, honor and image.

In this regulation, the processing of personal data must have the consent of individuals, including any registration information of the data subject. Two other important agents in this process are the controller, who has responsibility for decisions regarding the use or storage of personal data, and the operator, who is responsible for handling personal data on behalf of the controller. The regulatory body is the National Data Protection Authority of Brazil (ANPD), which is responsible for overseeing the General Data Protection Law, with technical and decision-making autonomy to ensure compliance with fundamental rights of privacy and freedom of natural people.

Crossing of data and uncontrolled access can expose individuals to complicated situations in the personal or professional environment. Several cases, ranging from security breaches, data leakage or even the illegal trade of personal data are frequent news and, therefore, regulations that delimit and act on the organizations that collect and process the data are necessary.

This discussion starts with Law No. 12,965 of April 23, 2014, known as Brazilian Civil Rights Framework for the Internet (*Marco Civil da Internet*) and the debate continues with Law No. 13,709 of August 14, 2018, known as General Data Protection Law or LGPD . Two points are changed in the Brazilian Civil Rights Framework for the Internet in articles 7 and 16, with the publication of the LGPD, in relation to the elimination and storage of personal data. The safekeeping of the data, or its elimination after the fulfillment of the purposes for which it was collected, are governed by the provisions of the LGPD.

In the General Data Protection Law, some points are essential for understanding its application: the data were collected or processed in the national territory, or even the treatment of data, even if it does not occur in the national territory, is related to data from individuals who are in the country or are intended to offer goods or services to these individuals.

In this way, the individual residing in Brazil needs to consent to the use of his personal data, being informed, freely and unequivocally, about the purposes for which this use of data is intended and for how long they will be used. There are some actors in this context: the holder, controller, operator, manager, treatment agents and national authority. Two actors are important in this data processing process, considered to be processing agents: the controller, who is the "natural or legal person, of public or private law, who is responsible for decisions regarding the processing of personal data", and the operator, that "carries out the processing of personal data on behalf of the controller" (Brasil, 2018).

The processing of data by the public administration has a special place in the LGPD, in chapter IV, and they need to be oriented to the appropriate public purpose of the agency, and the shared use of data must also meet the specific purposes of implementing policies and providing public services.

Another point that we emphasize is that it concerns the end of the use of data, which authorizes the elimination of data when the purpose of data processing has been reached, at the end of the period necessary for the processing of data, when communicated by the data owner or determined by the national authority if there is a violation of the provisions of the LGPD.

The first case of the General Data Protection Law in Brazil was about a website that commercialized thousands of data from brazilian citizens, the lawsuit was filed in September 2020. The Public Ministry of the Federal District of Brazil believes that 500 thousand people had their data exposed only in the city of São Paulo, with victims in all states of Brazil (Ministerio Público Federal do Distrito Federal e

Territórios, 2020). Unfortunately, the original website was no longer available online, making the judgment dismissed. This reinforces the need to preserve digital content and web archiving (Rockembach, 2018, Rockembach and Pavão, 2018) as a source of evidence and proof in the case of selling private data.

Strategically, it is important that Brazil has a regulation in the scope of data protection, so that it can easiest reach international, political and economic agreements, besides negotiating commercial contracts between countries, considering the transnational flow of personal information, respecting the privacy of personal data and consent in the treatment of users' information. In this sense, the European Union gains, with Brazil, an important commercial partner in international data transactions and an ally in the discussions of digital privacy in the Society.

4. CONCLUDING REMARKS

Digital ethics becomes an extension of ethics in the real world, with new problems and dilemmas. It is necessary to think, represent and put into practice the virtues on digital platforms, just as individuals do outside the virtual environment. The General Data Protection Law, of both in the European Union and Brazil, come to guarantee a series of rights over information regarding anonymity, also controlling the requirement of excessive data on the part of those who collect the information and which goes beyond the purposes what the data is for.

Therefore, the definition of whether the data has the characteristics of being public or not influences the treatment and uses applied to them. Public data are governed by the principle of transparency, access and the right to information. Otherwise, data not considered public, is based on the right to privacy, intimacy, private life, honor and people's image, as provided in art. 5 of the Brazilian Federal Constitution, as well as considerations of the Brazilian Civil Rights Framework for the Internet and of the General Data Protection Law of Brazil. It is also necessary to guarantee both the effectiveness in the application of data protection regulation and the effectiveness of the National Data Protection Authority's performance.

On the one hand, the digital repositories and organizations that maintain the data aim at long-term preservation, on the other hand, the data protection law imposes the elimination of data after the fulfillment of its main purposes, for which they were created. This can be seen, at first, as a conflict of interest. However, data retention may occur in compliance with regulatory, legal or exclusive use of the controller, for study by a research body or transfer to a third party, in view of the LGPD data processing requirements, and should be eliminated for reuse not authorized by the data owners.

In order to implement the General Data Protection Law, it is necessary to change the organizational culture, to reflect on how we think about the business models in companies - based on a surveillance capitalism - and the conception of information systems, the adoption of digital ethical principles and procedures for collecting, analyzing and dissemination of data.

REFERENCES

Boyd, D., & Crawford, K. (2012). Critical questions for big data: Provocations for a cultural, technological, and scholarly phenomenon. *Information Communication and Society, 15*(5), 662–679. doi:10.1080/1369118X.2012.678878

Brasil. (2018). *Lei Geral de Proteção de Dados Pessoais (LGPD)*. Retrieved from http://www.planalto.gov.br/ccivil_03/_ato2015-2018/2018/lei/L13709.htm

Cadwalladr, C., & Graham-Harrison, E. (2018). Revealed: 50 million Facebook profiles harvested for Cambridge Analytica in major data breach. *The Guardian.*

Capurro, R. (2010). Desafíos téoricos y prácticos de la ética intercultural de la información. In Conferencia inaugural en el I Simpósio Brasileiro de Ética da Informação, João Pessoa (Vol. 18). Academic Press.

Castells, M. (2000). The Rise of the Network Society: Economy. *Society and Culture, 1.*

Danish Data Protection Act. (2018). *Law n. 502 (English version), 2018*. Retrieved from https://www.datatilsynet.dk/media/7753/danish-data-protection-act.pdf

De Hert, P., & Papakonstantinou, V. (2016). The new General Data Protection Regulation: Still a sound system for the protection of individuals? *Computer Law & Security Review, 32*(2), 179–194. doi:10.1016/j.clsr.2016.02.006

Dutch General Data Protection Regulation Implementation Act. (2018). Retrieved from https://zoek.officielebekendmakingen.nl/stb-2018-144.html

European Parliament. (2016). *General Data Protection Regulation*. Retrieved from https://gdpr-info.eu/

Finland Data Protection Act - Tietosuojalaki. (2018). Retrieved from https://finlex.fi/fi/laki/ajantasa/2018/20181050

German Data Protection Act - Bundesdatenschutzgesetz (BDSG). (2017). Retrieved https://www.gesetze-im-internet.de/englisch_bdsg/index.html

Irish Data Protection Act. (2018). Retrieved from http://www.justice.ie/en/JELR/Pages/Data_Protection_Act_2018

Italian Data Protection Code. (2018). Retrieved from https://www.gazzettaufficiale.it/eli/id/2018/09/04/18G00129/sg

Lindsay, D. (2014). The 'right to be forgotten' by search engines under data privacy law: A legal analysis of the Costeja ruling. *Journal of Medicine and Law, 6*(2), 159–179. doi:10.5235/17577632.6.2.159

MacNeil, H. (1992). *Without consent: the ethics of disclosing personal information in public archives.* Academic Press.

Melo, J. F., & Rockembach, M. (2019). Arquivologia e Ciência da Informação na Era do Big Data: Perspectivas de Pesquisa e Atuação Profissional em Arquivos Digitais. *Prisma. com*, (39), 14-28.

Ministerio Público Federal do Distrito Federal e Territórios. (2020). *MPDFT ajuíza 1ª ação civil pública com base na LGPD*. Retrieved from https://www.mpdft.mp.br/portal/index.php/comunicacao-menu/sala-de-imprensa/noticias/noticias-2020/12384-mpdft-ajuiza-1-acao-civil-publica-com-base-na-lgpd

Pariser, E. (2011). The filter bubble: What the Internet is hiding from you. Penguin UK.

Patino, B. (2019). *La civilisation du poisson rouge: petit traité sur le marché de l'attention*. Grasset. doi:10.5771/9783956504211-812

Portugal Data Protection Act. (2019). Retrieved https://dre.pt/application/conteudo/123815982

Rockembach, M. (2017). Inequalities in digital memory: Ethical and geographical aspects of web archiving. *International Journal of Information Ethics, 26*, 26. doi:10.29173/irie286

Rockembach, M. (2018). Arquivamento da Web: Estudos de caso internacionais e o caso brasileiro. *RDBCI: Revista Digital de Biblioteconomia e Ciência da Informação, 16*(1), 7–24.

Rockembach, M., & da Silva, A. M. (2018). Epistemology and Ethics of big data. In *Challenges and Opportunities for Knowledge Organization in the Digital Age* (pp. 812–819). Ergon-Verlag.

Rockembach, M., & Pavão, C. M. G. (2018). Políticas e tecnologias de preservação digital no arquivamento da web. *Revista Ibero-americana de Ciência da Informação. Brasília. UnB., 11*(1), 168–182.

Sartor, G. (2014). The right to be forgotten: dynamics of privacy and publicity. In *Protection of Information and the Right to Privacy-A New Equilibrium?* (pp. 1–15). Springer. doi:10.1007/978-3-319-05720-0_1

Satur, R. V., Dias, G. A., & da Silva, A. M. B. M. (2020). Direito autoral, plágio e coautoria. *Brazilian Journal of Information Science, 14*(1), 57–87. doi:10.36311/1981-1640.2020.v14n1.04.p57

Schneider, M., & Saldanha, G. (2015). Entrevista com Rafael Capurro (07-10-2015)| Interview with Rafael Capurro (10-07-2015). *Liinc em Revista, 11*(2).

Schomakers, E. M., Lidynia, C., Müllmann, D., & Ziefle, M. (2019). Internet users' perceptions of information sensitivity–insights from germany. *International Journal of Information Management, 46*, 142–150. doi:10.1016/j.ijinfomgt.2018.11.018

Snowden, E. (2019). *Permanent record*. Macmillan.

Spanish Organic Law 3/2018 for the Protection of Personal Data and for the granting of digital rights. (2018). Retrieved from https://www.boe.es/buscar/pdf/2018/BOE-A-2018-16673-consolidado.pdf

Webb, A. (2019). The big nine: How the tech titans and their thinking machines could warp humanity. Hachette UK.

Zuboff, S. (2019). *The Age of Surveillance Capitalism: The Fight for a Human Future at the New Frontier of Power: Barack Obama's Books of 2019*. Profile Books.

ENDNOTES

1   A list of the European Data Protection Board can be accessed on the site https://edpb.europa.eu/about-edpb/board/members

2   Austrian Data Protection Act (english version), retrieved from https://www.bmf.gv.at/en/data-protection.html

3   Danish Data Protection Act (english version), retrieved from https://www.datatilsynet.dk/media/7753/danish-data-protection-act.pdf

4   Finnish Data Protection Act (Tietosuojalaki), retrieved from https://finlex.fi/fi/laki/ajantasa/2018/20181050

5   French Data Protection Act, retrieved from https://www.legifrance.gouv.fr/jorf/id/JORFTEXT000037085952?r=5RqrqY09NQ

6   German Data Protection Act (english version), retrieved from https://www.gesetze-im-internet.de/englisch_bdsg/index.html

7   Irish Data Protection Act, retrieved from http://www.justice.ie/en/JELR/Pages/Data_Protection_Act_2018

8   Italian Data Protection Code, retrieved from https://www.gazzettaufficiale.it/eli/id/2018/09/04/18G00129/sg

9   Dutch General Data Protection Regulation Implementation Act, retrieved from https://zoek.officielebekendmakingen.nl/stb-2018-144.html

10   Portuguese Data Protection Act, retrieved from https://dre.pt/application/conteudo/123815982

11   Spanish Organic Law 3/2018 for the Protection of Personal Data and for the granting of digital rights, retrieved from https://www.boe.es/buscar/pdf/2018/BOE-A-2018-16673-consolidado.pdf

12   European Commission website, retrieved from https://ec.europa.eu/info/law/law-topic/data-protection/international-dimension-data-protection/adequacy-decisions_en

Chapter 14
Artificial Intelligence a Driver for Digital Transformation

Maria José Sousa
Instituto Universitário de Lisboa, Portugal

Gabriel Osório de Barros
Ministério da Economia e Transição Digital, Portugal

Nuno Tavares
Ministério da Economia e Transição Digital, Portugal

ABSTRACT

Artificial intelligence is reconfiguring the economy and redefining the product and service market. It is a disruptive technology that leads to the creation of multiple more efficient activities, new business models, and industrial processes. The literature stresses that AI should be used in all aspects of the personal lives of organisations and individuals, and such complexities are still largely unstudied. The aim of this study is to highlight AI's innovations and applications to the organisation's digital transformation.

1. ARTIFICIAL INTELLIGENCE A DRIVER FOR DIGITAL TRANSFORMATION

In recent years, there have been increasing interests about Artificial intelligence (AI) from academics and practitioners (Dwivedi et al, 2019) and concepts, such as machine learning (ML). Artificial intelligence is related to machines' ability to think as human beings (Wang, 2019) - to have the power to learn reason, perceive and decide in a rational and intelligent way. The technologies associated with artificial intelligence are Machine Learning, Deep Learning, Natural Language Processing, among others (Mayo, and Leung, 2018; Montes, and Goertzel, 2019).

Machine Learning involves machines that learn, from the data that are introduced to them and with a minimum of programming, reaching the results autonomously (i.e. the custom recommendations on Amazon). Machine learning makes it possible to construct a mathematical model from data, including many variables that are not known in advance. The parameters are configured along the learning pro-

DOI: 10.4018/978-1-7998-4201-9.ch014

Copyright © 2021, IGI Global. Copying or distributing in print or electronic forms without written permission of IGI Global is prohibited.

cess, with training data sets. The different machine learning methods are classified into 3 categories: human-supervised learning, unsupervised learning, and unsupervised learning by reinforcement. These 3 categories group, together, different methods including neural networks, deep learning, and others (Figure 1).

Figure 1. Machine Learning Dimensions
Source: Council of Europe, 2019

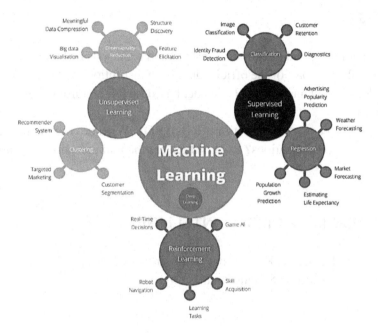

Deep Learning: when machines use complex algorithms to mimic the neural network of the human brain and learn an area of knowledge with virtually no supervision (Schmidhuber, 2015).

Natural Language Processing (PLN): These are machine learning techniques used to find patterns in large data sets and recognize natural language (Huang, and Rust, 2018). For example, the application of PLN to the analysis of feelings, where algorithms can look for patterns in publications in social networks to understand how customers feel about specific brands and products.

Automation, cloud computing and IoT are followed by artificial intelligence, or AI, to enable the smarter machine, the smarter factory and the smarts ecosystem (Wan et al, 2018; Sousa et al. 2019).

AI is driven by the combination of almost limitless computing power in the cloud, the digitization of our world (Huang, and Rust, 2018), and breakthroughs in how computers can use this information to learn and reason much like people do.

By applying advanced AI technologies, such as machine learning and cognitive services (Huang, and Rust, 2018) against the data coming in from the manufacturing process, you now have a value-added layer of insight into your data. This allows you to improve operational efficiencies, speed production, optimize equipment performance, minimize waste, and reduce maintenance costs.

Advancements in AI are also opening a hybrid workforce where people and machines work together (Jarrahi, 2018). According to IDC, by 2020, 60 percent of plant floor workers at G2000 manufacturers will work alongside assistance technologies that enable automation, such as robotics, 3D printing, AI, and AR/VR.

Artificial intelligence is a technology which has been improving the performance of manufacturing and services sectors (Li et al, 2017). This study presents a holistic analysis of AI, namely theoretical frameworks and practical experiences. It provides a broad review of recent developments within the field of AI and its applications (Murdoch, et al, 2019).

2. METHODOLOGY

The methodology is qualitative and quantitative, based on the analysis of secondary data from official sources. The data in analysis is part of the official data from institutions as OECD, European Commission, and others. A documental analysis is also made, based on a literature review of scientific articles and official documents.

The study focuses on three research questions (RQs): RQ1: What are the main AI research Trends? RQ2: Which are the main AI applications? RQ3: Which are the main technologies, and patents associated to AI?

3. OFFICIAL TRENDS IN ARTIFICIAL INTELLIGENCE

To reply to the first research question RQ1: What are the main AI research Trends? an analysis is made on the scientific publishing based on Scopus database (figure 2).

Figure 2. Trends in scientific publishing related to AI, 2006-2016

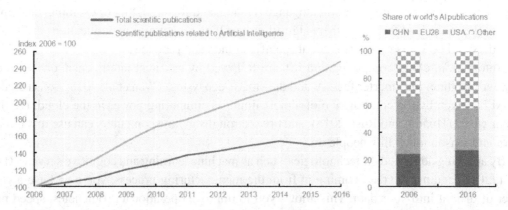

Source: OECD calculations based on Scopus Custom Data, Elsevier, Version 1.2018, January 2019.

Regarding the scientific publications related to machine learning the United States and China are the main countries investing in research (figure 3).

Figure 3. Trends in scientific publishing related to Machine Learning, 2003-2016

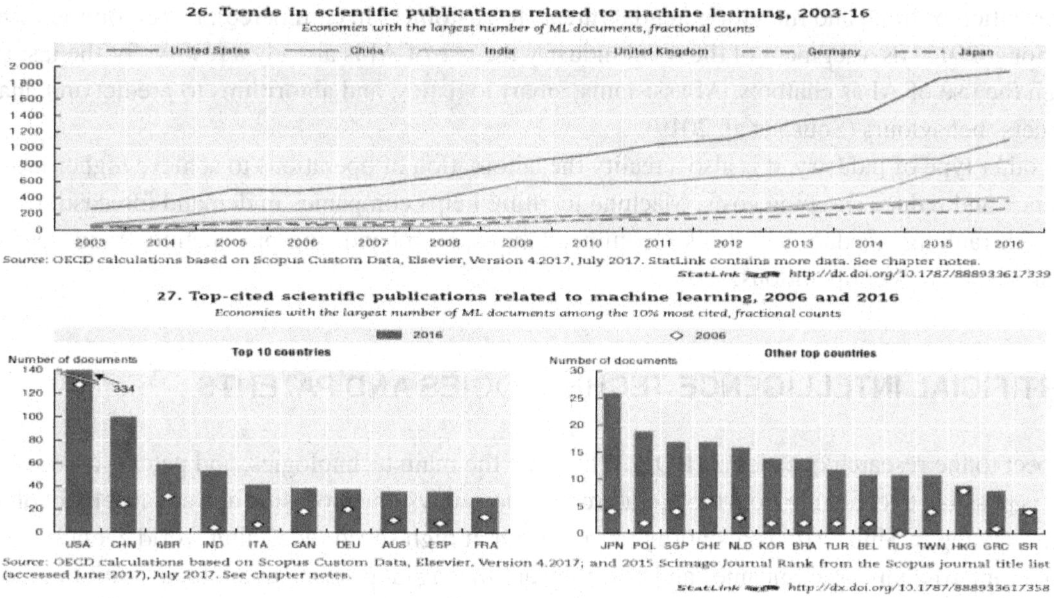

These publications give indications about the patterns of the research and about the applications of the AI and related technologies, which will be analysed in the following sections.

4. ARTIFICIAL INTELLIGENCE APPLICATIONS

To reply to research question 2 (RQ2) Which are the main AI applications? an analysis was made to the literature. The applications are enormous and can be found in almost every system in industry and in services (Dal Mas et al, 2019). Artificial Intelligence allows the development of algorithms called artificial neural networks working by modelling the human brain function and structure. Areas of Artificial intelligence technology, like computer vision, autonomous vehicles, automatic text generation, facial recognition (i.e. the use of facial recognition of iPhone as a digital password) and others, are the fields where machine learning and deep learning are more used. AI enabled applications (Murdoch, et al, 2019) much faster to be used in scenarios concerning computer vision, speech recognition, and natural language processing (Hengstler, Enkel, and Duelli, 2016).

Regarding the main sectors of application AI technologies have several implications on the Internet industry, Computer and Engineering, and in several other fields, like healthcare, manufacturing, agriculture, and automobile (Murdoch, et al, 2019). AI or machine learning is and will impact in the healthcare sector through the implementation of advanced technologies. The AI-based applications help understanding medical data and reaching the right diagnosis without direct human input. These applications are applied not only in the diagnosis processes, but also in the treatment protocol development, drug development, personalized medicine, and patient monitoring and care.

AI or machine learning also has a huge impact on the business and commerce of the banking industry. The implementation of these emerging technologies is used for the automation and of the bank operations (i.e. several banks use intelligent virtual assistant to improve their customer services; other example is the prevention of fraud and monitor potential threats to customers in commerce). For e-commerce business (Song, 2019) as a segment of the retail industry the use of AI is already a reality, for the last years through the use of AI as chatbots, AI assistants, smart logistics, and algorithms to predict and analyse customers' behaviours (Sousa et al, 2019).

On other type of industry, it is also a reality the automation of operations to achieve higher levels of efficiency and reduce shipping costs. Machine learning helps companies in demand forecasting, product search ranking, product and deals recommendations, merchandising placements, fraud detection, translations, and other operations.

5. ARTIFICIAL INTELLIGENCE TECHNOLOGIES AND PATENTS

In respect to the research question 3 (RQ3) Which are the main technologies, and patents associated to AI?, it is possible to conclude from the literature that, nowadays, the profusion and advancement of technologies (Wang & Shin, 2015) are enormous and occur at high speed redefining world economies and, in a more micro-analysis, companies and how they are managed, produce and interact with the market. The most important contemporary technologies (Aydin & Parker, 2018) have artificial intelligence (AI) incorporated, which is machines' ability to think as human beings - to have the power to learn, reason, perceive and decide rationally and intelligently. AI applications are numerous at the enterprise level in their digital transformation process, for example, virtual assistants or chatbots.

Also, big data and analytics technologies bring with it the ability to use new tools, architectures and methodologies to analyse new types of information (Holmström, et al. 2016; Melnyk, et al., 2018), such as sensors, audio, and video for which traditional information management platforms do not respond.

New advanced analytical tools are required that automatically identify business behaviours and forecasts, integrating analytical models into the business processes of companies, which play a central role in the design of business strategies, with a significant impact on the design of organizations where new functions emerge (Adebanjo, Teh & Ahmed, 2018).

Another critical technology for companies is the Internet of Things (IoT) as a network of billions of digitally connected devices that collect data and communicate with each other (Del Giudice, 2016). Its application to the various sectors of activity is an added value, as it allows greater efficiency and efficiency of the processes. The application of IoT is vast and intricate to define boundaries from the monitoring of the production process to identify problems with impact on the final quality of the products, allowing in real time to activate corrective actions, improve the efficiency of machines and other activities (Chandrasekaran, et al., 2015; Holmström, et al. 2016).

Moreover, Virtual Reality (VR) which replaces visual reality with a digital reality, while augmented reality (AR) overlaps digital elements with physical reality and both accelerates the learning of new competencies, the immediate resolution of tasks and the visual understanding of processes - contributing to greater effectiveness in the decision making. In addition, robots and drones can perform the work of a human through a programmed process - robotic process automation (Aydin, & Parker, 2018).

Furthermore, the application of drones is one of the emblematic elements of industry 4.0 and has revolutionized the way of monitoring equipment, locations, and specific situations. The adoption of drones in the industry allows greater precision and agility in the inspection of large equipment, obtaining evidence and data that help the decision making (McAdam et al., 2017).

3D Printing (or additive manufacturing) (Chan et al., 2018) is also redefining the way the production processes, equipment's, and materials are used to produce 3-dimensional object.

In the next figure (4), based on a study made by the World Economic Forum (WEF), it is presented the most frequent technologies, which are Image analysis, virtual assistants, predictive analysis, machine learning, and natural language processing, followed by self-driving technologies and robotics.

Figure 4. Technologies associated to AI
Source: WEF, 2018

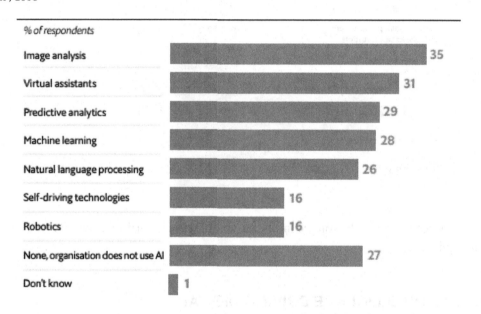

Regarding the main AI uses, the predictive analytics is the number-one AI use case that respondents feel has or will become relevant to their industry, cited by more than one in four respondents (26%). This involves the use of statistical algorithms to identify the likelihood of future outcomes (i.e. when is a delivery truck likely to break down, for example, and when might it hit traffic congestion or poor weather conditions, causing delays) (figure 5).

The applications of AI are innumerable at the level of the companies in their process of digital transformation, as in the marketing functions through the processing of a great number of data coming from purchases interactions, which allows to map more easily tendencies and behaviours of the consumers ; cybersecurity through greater ease in detecting security intrusions and threats to enterprise systems; in the service and customer service, through the generalization of the use of virtual Assistants (*chatboots*).

Some of the themes that are associated with Artificial Intelligence are the application of Robots to industry and services seek to improve citizen assistance (especially in the area of health), cooperation and coordination between machines / robots, intelligent sensors and robotics; autonomous transport, machine learning, and predictive systems.

Figure 5. Top AI Areas
Source: WEF, 2018

The next Figure (6) shows the top technologies combined with artificial intelligence, considering the field of application.

6. ARTIFICIAL INTELLIGENCE DRIVING DIGITAL TRANSFORMATION IN PORTUGAL

Notwithstanding the growing importance of AI, there are significant gaps in quantitative information when considering this reality applied to the Portuguese case. In turn, much of the existing information refers to data obtained through studies that are based on collecting information on the form of surveys from various stakeholders. As an example, CIONET Portugal conducted a study on the impact of AI on Portuguese companies and various sectors. One of the most relevant data from this study indicates that 34.6% of respondents will be using an AI solution in less than one year. Today, 39% of respondents say their organization is already using some type of AI tool in their daily operations. According to this study, respondents say that machine learning and chat bots will be the AI solutions that your organization will most often implement. Machine Learning is the most recognized AI tool by Portuguese companies; 94% of organizations report that they will apply this type of solution more often. At the same time, respondents say that Artificial Intelligence could have another kind of impact on their organizations, such as infra-structure automation, Internet of Things (IoT) AI, or even diagnostic support in a hospital, for example.

Figure 6. Top Technologies combined with artificial intelligence, by field of application

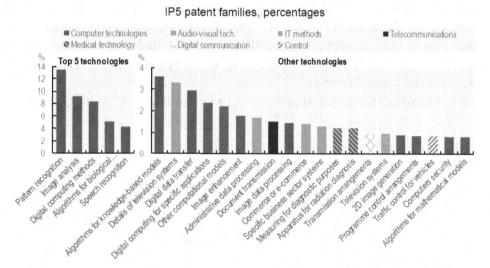

Top technologies combined with artificial intelligence, by field of application, 2012-16

IP5 patent families, percentages

Source: OECD, STI Micro-data Lab: Intellectual Property Database, http://oe.cd/ipstats January 2019. See chapter notes.

Figure 7. Patents for Top Technologies that embed AI, 2000-05 and 2010-15

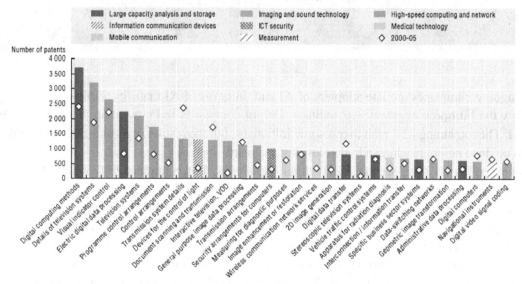

8. Patents for top technologies that embed artificial intelligence, 2000-05 and 2010-15

Number of IP5 patent families in AI by non-AI patent classes

Source: OECD, STI Micro-data Lab: Intellectual Property Database, http://oe.cd/ipstats, June 2017. StatLink contains more data. See chapter notes.

StatLink http://dx.doi.org/10.1787/888933616997

With the growth of AI, the uncertainty that jobs can shrink increases. The study also points out that I can have a positive impact of 15.1% on Portuguese employability. This list is a difference between the increase of posts status of work, allied to new actions and a loss of posts of work under this paradigm.

In another study of a sample of Portuguese companies (Artificial Intelligence in Europe: How Leading Companies Benefit from AI - Perspectives 2019 and Beyond) finds that Machine Learning and Smart Robotics technologies are a big expression in Portuguese companies, first (82%) and second (59%), both above the European levels (Figure 7).

Figure 8 allows you to analyse and position to track the different AI maturity states:

Figure 8. Maturity Levels of AI
Source: Microsoft and EY, 2018

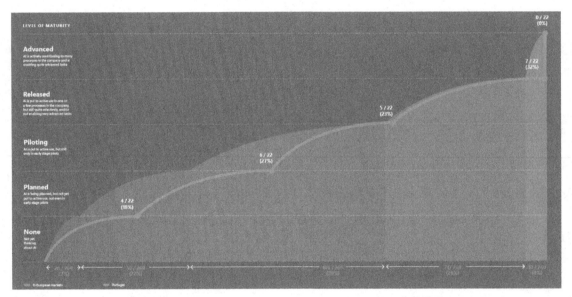

Portuguese companies are late adopters of AI and, in terms of AI maturity; companies in Portugal are below the European aggregate. In addition, 18% of companies in Portugal are not yet considering using AI. The remaining 82% plan to test some initiatives, but the results suggest that there is still some work to be done before reaching a higher level of maturity.

Looking at Figure 8, we see that the Technology, Media / Entertainment & Telecom (TMT) sector has the highest percentage of Released or Advanced companies.

The use of AI in Portugal is exhausted in some businesses / functions. However, in the companies that are part of the classification of this study, the use of an AI covers all business functions, however, it should be noted that 8 of the 22 companies in the measure do not use AI in their business / functions. Even so, the participation of Portuguese companies that use AI in their areas is distributed as follows: Technology and Digital (45%), Customer Service (36%) and R&D and Product Development (32%), in line with European trends (Figure 10).

Figure 9. AI Maturity for AI by Sector
Source: Microsoft and EY, 2018

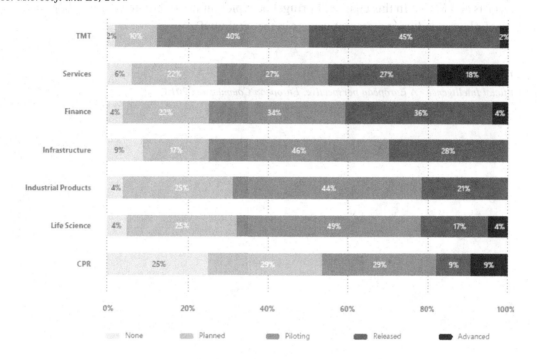

Figure 10. AI Application in Portugal
Fonte: Microsoft and EY, 2018

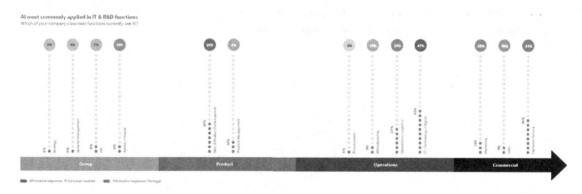

One of the main difficulties about the mediation aspect of the AI phenomenon is the difficulty in sector delimitation. In this context, a recent study promoted by the EC used a Techno-Economic Segment (TES) approach. The first step of the methodology was to define the TES limits (AI, in this case), identifying players that focus on AI as primary or secondary activity. These are defined as research centers, academic institutions and companies that have participated in one or more of the following activities: R&D processes, industrial production and marketing, specific AI related services (Syam, and Sharma, 2018). According to the data from this study (Figure 11) and in the EU context, it is the United Kingdom, Germany, France, Spain, Italy and the Netherlands that have the largest number of players in the area. In turn, and when weighted as a percentage of GDP, the focus is on countries such as Bulgaria, Estonia, Cyprus and Malta. In this chapter, Portugal occupies an intermediate position, both in terms of the number of players and its representativeness in the total GDP.

Figure 11. EU AI Players (GDP, 2009 - 2018)
Source: Artificial Intelligence - A European perspective, European Commission, 2018

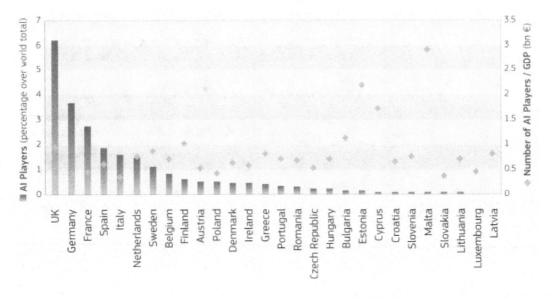

Figure 12. Distribution of players (%) in EU funded AI research projects, 2009-2018
Source: Artificial Intelligence A European perspective, European Commission, 2018

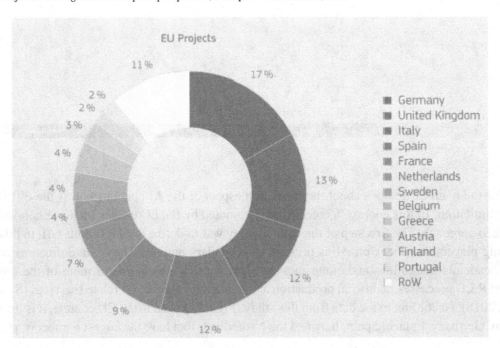

On the other hand, Figure 12 shows the distribution of players by country who participated in AI-related research projects under the FP7 and H2020 in the period 2009-2018. In this respect, there is a balanced distribution between the largest and most active countries in research, with emphasis on Germany, the United Kingdom, Italy, Spain, France and the Netherlands. In Portugal, only 2 of the AI players identified participated in this type of project being financed.

7. AI CASE STUDIES

a) Microsoft – Case 1

As Microsoft helps the industry move to a new world that is going to be made up of an intelligent cloud and an intelligent edge, we are one step closer to realizing the promise of AI in the manufacturing industry. Our approach to AI is about harnessing the explosion of digital data and computational power with advanced algorithms to enable collaborative and natural interactions between people and machines that extend the human ability to sense, learn, and understand.

The Microsoft intelligent cloud platform offers manufacturers a compelling partnership in your journey to adopt AI. Our business solutions allow you to use AI to drive transformation and automation with accelerators and practices. Our intelligent applications are infused into Microsoft products and services that are core to your productivity, communication, and business processes. Cortana Intelligence helps you turn data into intelligent action and iterative learning. Our investments in machine learning are transforming Azure into one of the most strategic analytics platforms for manufacturers.

For developers, we offer powerful AI tools and services through our collection of powerful Cognitive Services APIs that enable your apps to intelligently interpret the world and naturally engage your users. The Microsoft Bot Framework makes it easy for you to create new experiences and reach your users at scale. The Microsoft Cognitive Toolkit trains deep learning algorithms to learn like the human brain.

Manufacturers of all sizes are already leveraging the power of AI and the cloud to accelerate performance. Honeywell is a great example of a company that is bridging the physical and virtual worlds with AI to shift the value drivers from Honeywell's flagship devices to the data and insights they generate.

Jabil is using machine learning to detect and predict manufacturing failures of their circuit boards early in production. As a result, errors can be corrected prior to adding expensive electronic components, resulting in reduced scrapped materials and warranty costs, and an increase in customer satisfaction.

AI is helping the manufacturing industry move from mere predictive maintenance to a new level of predictive intelligence that allows manufacturers to maximize efficiency in a way that equipment rarely—or never—fails. We have seen manufacturers, such as Rolls Royce and Thyssenkrupp, leading with these AI-powered pre-emptive capabilities.

Security is another important application for AI. Uber is using the Face API in Cognitive Services to ensure that its one million drivers using the app match their accounts on file.

We believe humans and machines will work together to not only boost productivity, but also to create new jobs that are enhanced by AI. Microsoft is focused on infusing computers, equipment, and systems with the ability to reason, communicate, and perform with humanlike skill and agility. These applications span anomaly detection to cobots—autonomous robots capable of working together with humans in an office environment. Deep Microsoft investments in the field are advancing machine intelligence and perception, enabling computers that understand what they see, communicate in natural language, answer complex questions, and interact with their environment.

AI has the potential to make workers safer and more productive, but it doesn't replace people. People are essential. They manage factory floors and highly skilled tasks. They drive innovation and ingenuity. People solve challenges and they are still the most important front "customer service" line.

Over the past several years, customers such as Comau and Sandvik Coromant have reimagined their approach to manufacturing and are already seeing benefits from combining human and digital intelligence. These advancements include being able to better predict potential failures, keeping plant equipment running efficiently with longer uptime, and providing employees with better tools to manage quality across the manufacturing process.

Between collaborative robots, intelligent bots, drones, and augmented reality, we're only scratching the surface of what AI and human collaboration can help the manufacturing industry accomplish.

b) Microsoft – Case 2

Microsoft has developed the Smart Bot project for online shopping processes by creating a bot platform that allows you to initiate conversations with customers in natural language while they visit your site to try to complete their buying processes. Without that, the customer had to use any other communication channel (contact center or physical stores). In a healthcare project on Postoperative Rehospitalization Prediction, Microsoft created an information analysis platform using advanced data analysis (aka machine learning). The focus was on calculating a patient's likelihood of return based on their ability to analyze large volumes of information made up of a history of several years of data.

c) Vodafone

Vodafone has created a project called Machine learning at the service of the Customer to analyze customer satisfaction levels from social networks. To analyze the customer comments, we used the Phyton language that made the integration through the scikit-learn framework to implement the machine learning algorithms.

d) Altran

Move.IT is an initiative integrated into the Altran Group's E-Cockpit plan to contribute to the revolutionary development of autonomous driving technology. The development of numerous capabilities for sensing data captured by sensors using machine learning and deep learning techniques. These include the creation of a test scenario generation tool, lane line detection, pedestrian detection in different occlusion, background and lighting scenarios, and the calculation of visibility distance under meteorologically adverse. CGI uses artificial intelligence technology in the Digital Operations Transformation project for greater operational efficiency with regard to backoffice operations, supporting more than four million energy and service customers using large-scale automation. processes, enhancing and integrating technology in the labour ecosystem and providing a platform for managing integrated operation in real time. CTT has created an Advanced Routes Management AI project to optimize postal distribution centers, and currently mainland Portugal has about 4,000 routes that are daily travelled by postmen. This project considers traffic variation, terrain topology, and various other factors for route optimization. Another project CTT is developing is that of Robotics in non-standard format object handling operations, and the RestMail (RMS) robot has the capacity to handle over 90,000 objects per day and is prepared to respond to the new needs of the postal business, namely those arising from e-commerce. CTT, another project is the RPA - Robotic Process Automation, with the goal of process automation, reducing the performance of routine activities and without added value. For example, for collection scheduling, a process that took between 2 minutes and 30 seconds to 5 minutes and 22 seconds was reduced to 50 seconds in 77% of treated cases. Still in the case of CTT another project is the Use of AI / Bots in Contact Centers to improve customer service and information about their services, uses chat bots.

e) Deloitte

Deloitte has created a project that it calls Center of Excellence RPA, with a view to process robotization, with the objectives of reducing operating costs, improving process quality and auditability, better management of work peaks and above everything the liberation of human effort for tasks of higher added value.

f) Randstat

Randstat created the Machine learning empowering people consultants project to place data science at the service of clients in recruitment processes and using algorithms that perform real-time CV analysis. This technology is supported through natural language processing (NLP) algorithms.

8. FINAL REMARKS

The consequences of sudden and large-scale automation have become the centre of attention in recent years because of new developments in the field of so-called artificial intelligence. New algorithms in combination with the increasing processing power of computers have made it possible for machines to take care of tasks that until now only humans could do.

There is a relative maintenance of R&D levels, but the growth opportunities in this sector are real and very realistic, especially in new areas of artificial intelligence. It requires a new development path towards high value-added services and sophisticated solutions, especially for accessing external markets.

Looking ahead, less productive firms may lack the ability to adopt increasingly sophisticated technologies (e.g. artificial intelligence). In turn, the most productive firms may become more difficult to challenge, especially in a digital environment where intangible firm-specific assets (such as tacit knowledge, data, and algorithms) are an increasingly central source of value. This risk undermining business dynamism and competition and could ultimately affect productivity. Mounting signs of increasing mark-ups and industry concentration and declining firm entry and exit rates, especially in digital intensive sectors, are worrying in this respect.

Artificial Intelligence (AI) can help elaborate and analyse big data on workers skills and employment opportunities. Local labour market information and skills anticipation systems will be fundamental to guide individuals and workers in making well-informed career choices. At both the national and local level, employment and skills policies can respond to the future of work by better anticipating needs and preparing individuals with relevant competences that will be less vulnerable to automation.

REFERENCES

Adebanjo, D., Teh, P. L., & Ahmed, P. K. (2018). The impact of supply chain relationships and integration on innovative capabilities and manufacturing performance: The perspective of rapidly developing countries. *International Journal of Production Research, Taylor & Francis, 56*(4), 1708–1721. doi:10.1080/00207543.2017.1366083

Dal Mas, F., Piccolo, D., Cobianchi, L., Edvinsson, L., Presch, G., Massaro, M., & Skrap, M. (2019). The effects of Artificial Intelligence, Robotics, and Industry 4.0 technologies. Insights from the Healthcare Sector. In *Proceedings of the first European Conference on the impact of Artificial Intelligence and Robotics*. Academic Conferences and Publishing International Limited.

Del Giudice, M. (2016). Discovering the Internet of Things (IoT) within the business process management: A literature review on technological revitalization. *Business Process Management Journal, 22*(2), 263–270. doi:10.1108/BPMJ-12-2015-0173

Dwivedi, Y. K., Hughes, L., Ismagilova, E., Aarts, G., Coombs, C., Crick, T., Duan, Y., Dwivedi, R., Edwards, J., Eirug, A., Galanos, V., Ilavarasan, P. V., Janssen, M., Jones, P., Kar, A. K., Kizgin, H., Kronemann, B., Lal, B., Lucini, B., ... Williams, M. D. (2019). Artificial Intelligence (AI): Multidisciplinary perspectives on emerging challenges, opportunities, and agenda for research, practice and policy. *International Journal of Information Management*, 101994. doi:10.1016/j.ijinfomgt.2019.08.002

Hengstler, M., Enkel, E., & Duelli, S. (2016). Applied artificial intelligence and trust—The case of autonomous vehicles and medical assistance devices. *Technological Forecasting and Social Change, 105*, 105–120. doi:10.1016/j.techfore.2015.12.014

Huang, M. H., & Rust, R. (2018). Artificial Intelligence in Service. *Journal of Service Research, 21*(2), 155–172. doi:10.1177/1094670517752459

Jarrahi, M. H. (2018). Artificial intelligence and the future of work: Human-AI symbiosis in organizational decision making. *Business Horizons, 61*(4), 577–586. doi:10.1016/j.bushor.2018.03.007

Li, B. H., Hou, B. C., Yu, W. T., Lu, X. B., & Yang, C. W. (2017). Applications of artificial intelligence in intelligent manufacturing: A review. *Frontiers of Information Technology & Electronic Engineering, 18*(1), 86–96. doi:10.1631/FITEE.1601885

Mayo, R. C., & Leung, J. (2018). Artificial intelligence and deep learning – Radiology's next frontier? *Clinical Imaging, 49*, 87–88. doi:10.1016/j.clinimag.2017.11.007 PMID:29161580

Montes, G. A., & Goertzel, B. (2019). Distributed, decentralized, and democratized artificial intelligence. *Technological Forecasting and Social Change, 141*, 354–358. doi:10.1016/j.techfore.2018.11.010

Murdoch, W. J., Singh, C., Kumbier, K., Abbasi-Asl, R., & Yu, B. (2019). Definitions, methods, and applications in interpretable machine learning. *Proceedings of the National Academy of Sciences of the United States of America, 116*(44), 22071–22080. doi:10.1073/pnas.1900654116 PMID:31619572

Schmidhuber, J. (2015). Deep learning in neural networks: An overview. *Neural Networks, 61*, 85–117. doi:10.1016/j.neunet.2014.09.003 PMID:25462637

Song, X., Yang, S., Huang, Z., & Huang, T. (2019). The Application of Artificial Intelligence in Electronic Commerce. *Journal of Physics: Conference Series*, *1302*(3), 032030. Advance online publication. doi:10.1088/1742-6596/1302/3/032030

Sousa, M. J., Cruz, R., Rocha, Á., & Sousa, M. (2019). Innovation Trends for Smart Factories: A Literature Review. In Á. Rocha, H. Adeli, L. Reis, & S. Costanzo (Eds.), *New Knowledge in Information Systems and Technologies. WorldCIST'19 2019. Advances in Intelligent Systems and Computing* (pp. 689–698). Springer. doi:10.1007/978-3-030-16181-1_65

Syam, N., & Sharma, A. (2018). Waiting for a sales renaissance in the fourth industrial revolution: Machine learning and artificial intelligence in sales research and practice. *Industrial Marketing Management*, *69*, 135–146. doi:10.1016/j.indmarman.2017.12.019

Wan, J., Yang, J., Wang, Z., & Hua, Q. (2018). Artificial Intelligence for Cloud-Assisted Smart Factory. *IEEE Access: Practical Innovations, Open Solutions*, *6*, 55419–55430. doi:10.1109/ACCESS.2018.2871724

Wang, P. (2019). On Defining Artificial Intelligence. *Journal of Artificial General Intelligence*, *10*(2), 1–37. doi:10.2478/jagi-2019-0002

KEY TERMS AND DEFINITIONS

AI Software Platforms: Are used to build intelligent applications that provide predictions, answers, or recommendations. These applications automatically learn, adapt, and improve over time using information access processes combined with deep/machine learning.

Algorithm: Is a set of rules to solve a problem or carry out a routine or calculation.

Artificial Intelligence: Is software and hardware combined and that that attempts to simulate a human being.

Artificial Neural Network (ANN): Is an algorithm that attempts to replicate the operation of the human brain through the utilization of connected neurons which are organized in layers and send information to each other.

Bayesian Networks: Is a graph-based model representing a set of variables and their dependencies, focused on decision-making processes.

Big Data: Large amounts of structured and unstructured data that is too complex to be handled by standard data-processing software.

Chatbots: A chat robot that can converse with a human user through text or voice commands.

Clustering: Algorithm technique that allows machines to group similar data into larger data categories.

Computer Vision: How machines visually and interpret the world and understand it from images or videos.

Conversational AI Software Platforms: Are a subset of AI platforms specialized for the development of intelligent digital assistants and conversational chatbots. They use content analytics, information discovery, and other technologies to communicate with human beings.

Data Mining: The process of analyzing a large volume of data and bring out models, correlations and trends, in order to identify recurring patterns while establishing problem-solving relationships.

Data Science: Composed by mathematics, statistics, probability, computing, and data visualization to extract knowledge from a heterogeneous set of data (images, sound, text, genomic data, social network links, physical measurements, and others sources).

Deep Learning: Is a sub-discipline of machine learning that utilizes artificial neural network configured across multiple layers.

Keyword and Phrase Recognition: It is a system capacity to recognize specific words.

Knowledge Bases: Repositories of information organized as entities or intents linked together so that the application can find answers to questions or ambiguous references.

Machine Learning: Is scientific study of algorithms and statistical models that perform various functions without having to be programmed by a human, and without using explicit instructions, relying on patterns and inference. ML algorithms build a mathematical model based on sample data, known as "training data", in order to make predictions or decisions. Its application to business is referred as predictive analytics.

Machine Translation: An application of NLP used for language translation (human-to-human) in text- and speech-based conversations.

Natural Language Generation: Is the capacity to construct textual and conversational narratives from structured or semi-structured data.

Natural Language Processing (NLP): Focuses on the interactions between computers and human language in both the spoken and written form.

Optical Character Recognition (OCR): Conversion of images of text (typed, handwritten, or printed) either electronically or mechanically, into machine-encoded text.

Robotic Process Automation (RPA): Uses software with AI and ML capabilities to perform repetitive tasks.

Robotics: Focused on the design and manufacturing of robots that exhibit and/or replicate human intelligence and actions.

Unstructured Data: Raw data (i.e., audio, video, social media content).

Unsupervised Learning: A type of machine learning where an algorithm is trained with information that is neither classified nor labelled, thus allowing the algorithm to act without guidance (or supervision).

Voice and Speech Recognition: Are the translation of spoken or typed phrases into text to prepare it for analysis.

Section 2
Practical Cases, Application Reflections Over Digital Transformation, Security, and Privacy

Chapter 15

Digital Transformation for Businesses:
Adapt or Die! Reflections on How to Rethink Your Business in the Digital Transformation Context

Bruno de Lacerda
Chess Consultoria, Brazil

George Leal Jamil
(iD) https://orcid.org/0000-0003-0989-6600
Informações em rede Consultoria e Treinamento, Brazil

ABSTRACT

Digital transformation landed on organizational daily lives, whether businesspeople understand it or not. Adaptations and flexibility became strategic principles, along with new ways to comprehend how technology can really position a competitive advantage. Examining some open reflections and based on experiences, the authors of this chapter elaborate some scenarios, questions, and problems, which will motivate the reader on evaluating the actual turbulent context and understand precisely the achievements of their decisions regarding technology and novelty management contexts.

INTRODUCTION - MOTIVATION

As a matter of fact, the world was already showing us smooth signs of changes. We were all following our routines, concerned with daily life. Some scholars of trends, behavior, scenarios, and Foresight (discipline that studies future contexts through methodologies) presented us with situations of potential changes in the world.

The futurist Alvin Toffler (1980) shown, in his unforgettable *The Third Wave* in his exquisite and timeless approach, described the evolution of human society, from the predominance of agricultural

DOI: 10.4018/978-1-7998-4201-9.ch015

Copyright © 2021, IGI Global. Copying or distributing in print or electronic forms without written permission of IGI Global is prohibited.

activities, through the industrial phase, to the post-industrial era where we reached the information age, characterized by the "informational overload", an expression coined by him to indicate the excess of information produced and presented to any human being.

It turns out that we have a primitive brain living in a modern, post-digital world. The 4.0 world is no longer digital. We live in an era in which digital is ubiquitous, that is, it is present in all places and moments of our life. There is no more room to dissociate offline from online.

To our reader, we present a question: Do you know why few people can perceive and understand such signs of change in the world? Well, 98% of human history was built during the Agricultural Revolution, and only 2% in the various Industrial Revolutions we witnessed so far. Now, we are, by the way, in the 4th Industrial Revolution.

This data of our (re) evolution as a society corroborates our statement: We have a primitive brain living in a modern world! It took us decades to process changes. That is why there are geniuses who break the status quo, and think 20, 30 years ahead of their time. They are people who have an exponential view of the world and business, breaking the standards of linear thinking.

And what happened – until then – in these months of the world pandemic? Has the future been anticipated? COVID-19 was surely a future accelerator.

According to Brazilian Biologist Átila Iamarino, "Our lives are going to change a lot from now on, and someone who tries to maintain the 2019 status quo, has not yet accepted this new reality. Changes that the world would see decades to occur, which would take a long time to implement voluntarily, now have to be implemented in fright, in a matter of months."

We agree with this statement! Watching the Home Office trend: In Brazil, studies indicated that this type of remote work would only become a reality in the year 2030. Now, it is already a reality for countless companies. Several firms are just planning to make home office official among their collaborators, and, thus, make remote work a reality already in 2020, maybe without careful planning, but becoming a real decision.

Brazil, as a creative country, but not a leader in technology application and acceptance, present some facts which must be considered. After years of negotiation, and following a similar process held by Amazon in United States, the company Ifood – of food delivery using an Internet-based "app" – a leader in this sector in Latin America, received authorization from the National Civil Aviation Agency, for product deliveries via drones, even if it is on an experimental basis. It is certainly a milestone in the delivery market in Brazil. Interesting to think that Brazil shows an immense and challenging territory, which can serve as a good base for automated deliveries like it is proposed by Ifood drones.

As Covid-19 imposed severe restrictions on mobility and, consequently, for shopping, entrepreneurs had to adopt e-commerce and online stores solutions, resulting in an expressive growth for these solutions. Companies were forced to sell online as the only competitive survival, implementing this change, redesigning their business models completely in a matter of weeks.

This caused the Argentine e-commerce company Mercado Livre to surpass, on August 6, 2020, the Brazilian mining company Vale, and the also Brazilian oil company Petrobras, as the most valuable company in Latin America. Publicly traded on the American Nasdaq stock exchange, this Argentine company was one of the big winners in the second quarter, with its shares appreciating 101.8% between April and June. That left it only behind Tesla, which jumped 106.1%, among the 100 companies that are part of the technology index.

With the social distance imposed and adopted by customers, digital channels and platforms have become the only path to be followed. What was being procrastinated for the next few years, was suddenly anticipated, by the pound, overnight, without even time to plan and structure. A sarcastic dialogue was published in various Internet contexts, affirming that the pandemic was the main reason for digital transformation projects to be adopted!

And what can we expect for the future? Difficult to predict, to take any chances. A series of "million dollars answers". The big question is not about trying to predict the future, but rather, being open to reacting quickly to what lies ahead.

VUCA WORLD

The expression VUCA – from the acronym Volatility, Uncertainty, Complexity and Ambiguity – appeared in the 90s, in the Cold War scenario. It portrays exactly the characteristics of the world we live in today, with numerous challenges for organizations. Linear thinking no longer fits in this context. Looking at the world in a Cartesian way would be a very blurred, reductionist view when it comes to predict future scenarios.

The trend is that this apparent mess will increase even more. The question would not be how to resolve the impact of this world, since several actions take place in the field of the macro environment, which in most cases, is beyond our view.

It is important to mitigate impacts of these changes. Some skills, capabilities and aspects emerge to help this mitigation:

- Communication and connection skills.
- Facility to create, promote and work in networks.
- Align everyone around the organization's purpose and strategy.
- Empathy.
- Curiosity to see the world through the eyes of others.
- Avoid unconscious biases and filters that distort reality.
- See the world from different perspectives.
- Always question the status quo.
- Peripheral view and understand how the parts connect, interact.
- Capacity for innovation and adaptability.

An aspect of this amazing, turbulent, fast-moving world is the coexistence with risk, continuous learning, adaptations, and flexibility. Straightforward thinking is not an answer to all questions anymore. The VUCA scenario is where digital transformation is rolling out its main contribution and, likely, marking our lives forever.

DIGITAL TRANSFORMATION (DT) IMPACT ON BUSINESSES

A watchword currently within medium and large companies is: *We must carry out the digital transformation in our organization.*

However, this topic – Digital Transformation – is still misinterpreted in some executive levels. Digital transformation has become a practical synonym of technology, which is a wrong view for us to approach and guide the agenda. But, before defining DT, we need to understand what got us here.

We can understand that modern society was shaped by four revolutions, as briefly explained below:

- The 1st Industrial Revolution was based on steam power machines, triggered by urbanization, and energy production. The advance of industrialization produced a middle class of workers. Cities and industries grew rapidly, as the economy developed.
- The 2nd Industrial Revolution was marked by electricity. Some innovations began to emerge, such as the gasoline fueled engine, airplanes, by the improvement of scientific methods and mass production. Emblematic was the Ford T, a car with a gasoline engine built in large manufacturing lines.
- The 3rd Industrial Revolution was characterized by computing. The Internet gained scale. The advancement of electronics, computerized and robotic systems in manufacturing became real. The phenomenon of digitization and discussions about Artificial Intelligence came to the fore. Digital transformation began, albeit incipient and focused exclusively on technology.
- Here comes the 4th Industrial Revolution, also known as Industry 4.0, which arrives breaking paradigms through the convergence between the physical, digital and biological worlds. All integrated in favor of the new needs and habits of society.

The pioneer in this concept – 4th Industrial Revolution / Industry 4.0 – is the German engineer and economist Klaus Schwab (2018a), founder and chairman of the World Economic Forum and author of the book "The Fourth Industrial Revolution. For him, 4th Industrial Revolution is marked by four pillars:

- Technology - Access to emerging technologies.
- Speed – acceleration age.
- Exponentiality – To reach and produce great impact.
- Disruption – From new business models.

As technology constitutes a strong appeal for this context, Schwab (2018a) raised questions and challenges about the current wave of these new technologies. They came up with disruptive proposals and possibilities, subverting existing ways of feeling, calculating, organizing, relating, expressing, and making decisions.

This is where the tipping point comes in: The 4th Industrial Revolution is not just about technology. On the contrary. It is not even restricted to robotics and automation in the industry. When we talk about digital transformation, technology is not the protagonist, it is the consequence. The protagonism is centered on people, they are the ones who will in fact shape and modify the business world. Speaking of people, it is necessary to pause and warn: The future needs to be human and with extreme Governance about some technologies. The truth is that we are more BITS than ATOMS. This puts Society on a fine line between a fruitful world and a more unjust, less inclusive world.

Technologically less developed countries may lose competitiveness and social development. It is needed to work on skills to deal with this uncertain and chaotic future, which has everything to be extremely promising, but also severely dangerous.

Some Schwab (2018b) quotes, as presented in his text "Shaping the Fourth industrial revolution", brought here for a reflection:

"The benefits and challenges of digital transformation are similar; it is necessary to connect the points of the relationship between technology and its exponential opportunities."

"It is essential to understand the real human needs and how we can incorporate emerging technologies with genuine meaning."

"We also need to review the current governance models, with more agility and compatibility, including the private sectors, governments and regulatory institutions."

"Regulations and standards are being structured by this powerful array of innovative technology-based opportunities. It is up to us to work for a more evolutionary society."

Emerging technologies, such as Artificial Intelligence (AI), Internet of Things (IoT), Automation, Drones, 3D and 4D printing, Robotics, Blockchain, Machine Learning, Augmented Reality (AR), Virtual Reality (VR), etc., are fantastic and reckless at the same time.

Here, three examples of the real danger of some of these technologies.

Artificial Intelligence (AI)

Studies indicate that, in a few years, computers will become smarter than humans.

Have you ever imagined robots manipulating an entire society? The algorithms will soon know us better than we know ourselves.

Our cognitive ability will increasingly disengage from our intelligence. We can become toys for robots more intellectually evolved than we humans.

It may seem surreal, but those apocalyptic films of machines / robots at war with humans could become something real.

Internet of Things (IoT)

There are several risks associated with IoT systems that affect not only companies but users and society in general.

Cybersecurity is a considerable risk.

Our devices and networks will be exposed to hackers. As companies / homes and devices will be connected to the Internet, a cyber-attack may have access to all data in your home.

Think of someone having access to all your devices and devices? Unfortunately, as we write this chapter, first cases of life threat due to possible hacker attacks are informed by the Press.

3D Printers

3D printing offers unprecedented freedom of creation and design, it can be used at almost any point in the value chain.

The printing facility can encourage printing weapons and more.

As the technology becomes more sophisticated, even 4D printing already exists, they will be able to add complex materials to the printed weapons, including chemicals, cells, and biological tissues.

Bioprinting will become a reality. New regulatory issues will be essential.

Soon it will be possible for entire organs to be printed on demand. Is it possible to imagine the black market for organ sales? Is it possible to reach human DNA "printing"?

Empathy, communication, active listening, creativity, helpful leadership, and collaboration are some of the characteristics for us to make a difference in building a more humane future. The point is that there is no way we can stay out of the game. Today, technology is ubiquitous, that is, it is everywhere - and in abundance - in our daily lives. All new technologies need to make sense and difference in people's lives and in business, it is a basic principle of digital transformation that many have not yet reached.

As it was mentioned, digital transformation goes far beyond technology. A concept in which can be defined, from previous experiences on teaching and lecturing for students and attendees:

"Digital transformation is not necessarily technology. It is strategic thinking, a change of mindset. It is to rethink and redefine companies, through changes on organizational culture, processes, digitalization and innovation, which must be centered on people."

There are three basic pillars for the digital transformation process:

Business models - Digital transformation is directly linked to business strategy. It is important to restructure the organization's processes, gaining productivity and absorbing a digital and innovative culture.

Technology - New technologies are increasingly present in our lives. For organizations it means increased productivity, operational efficiency, and competitive advantage.

People - the ultimate sense of digital transformation is to make a difference for people, whether employees, customers or society. Every process needs to be human-centered, increasing value delivery.

The focal point of digital transformation is to change the mindset. For instance, it could be asked, comparing different views for mindset approaches, in an hypothetical case of a firm: "What is the objective of talking about agility, with offices and rooms full of frameworks and posts nailed to the walls, since the company lacks behavior, an agile attitude?" Digital transformation must go through cultural transformation. It is a top-down approach. It needs to come from managers, directors and executives. For those who do not have the will on changing their minds, concepts and ideas, digital transformation could become just a proposal, just a theoretical ideal. And it is worth making it clear: Culture is not a "thing" to be implanted, it spreads! It is the role of leadership to disseminate cultural transformation within the environment and associated network.

Another question to be reflected about is "What is the rationale of discussing *Exponential Organizations (ExO) and Scale-ups* if the mentality follows the linear and Cartesian model?" As the world is becoming full of ideas and technologies, we need an innovative business model to break paradigms and the status quo of things. Startups, for example, are already born within the concept of digital transformation, it is endogenous for this type of organization. Digital technologies and platforms are just the means to transform or even create new business models and even create new markets.

Traditional companies, with rigid, classic, business models, are facing troubles during the process. Metaphorically speaking, they are big ships because they have extreme difficulty for changes, modifying their paths toward the future. They are slow, bureaucratic, with excessive control and predictability. This type of company follows military models, as they can be regarded as monolithic institution.

It is impossible to achieve digital transformation when the decision makers companies seek the future by looking in the rear view. It will not be digital transformation, the factor which will drive the organization into the new world, of the post-digital economy, or "world 4.0". It is necessary to be open to errors, to fail quickly and cheaply, to test new possibilities. Calculated error should bring learning, continuous improvement and innovation which goes beyond the incremental.

To achieve digital transformation, it is needed to travel between chaos and order. Sometimes, with stricter processes and controls, otherwise with tests and learning in a risky scenario. It is important to consider that robust companies need to work with a risk factor for their decisions, which is calculable, leading to a better planning ability. Uncertainty is when one works in the "dark", a scenario usually feasible only for startups, as proposed in this innovative model. It is opportune to recall the metaphor of the basic states of matter (*gaseous, solid and liquid*). Chaos would be the gaseous state, totally uncontrollable, even at very high risk, depending on the situation. The order, on the other hand, would be the solid state. Extremely predictable, with methods and control, where everything is based on previous experiences. Still considering this useful metaphor, it is the case to think within the liquid state, with flexibility and evolution. Several things can emerge from there. Liquid structures are often more surprising.

Three characteristics are important for those who may be wondering where to start a digital transformation process:

Start small but think big - Entrepreneurial histories say that some big companies started in a small room or even in the garage. Apple and Amazon are perhaps the greatest examples. Have a big business dream, but modesty to know that everything in life has a beginning, and it is usually not at all glamorous. The important thing is to reach, at your start with your (Minimum Viable Product - MVP).

Act with bimodal structures - Some issues cannot or should not be changed. Compliance, governance and laws often prevent new possibilities and tests. Keeping the focus on situations where there is scope, possibilities for change is challenging, but proficuous. Work in parallel to gradually contaminate other areas and sectors of the company. This composes a lean model.

Fail fast and cheap - Anyone who is not willing to test and fail will never achieve Digital Transformation and business innovation. The LMA (Leadership / Management / Accountability) Startup model is an excellent option. Build product / service / business ideas. Measure public acceptance. Finally, act.

Finally, applying "pivot" techniques, as to adopt new ideas, review some concepts and also change and review value positioning is available, with inexpensive costs, at this time of business thinking. Otherwise, to change when the business is just operating, revisions can be dramatic and impactant.

THE PRINCIPLES OF EXPERIMENTATION

In times of digital transformation, companies and institutions looking for novelties as well as adding more value to their business, need to work on the culture of experimentation. Testing new ideas, products or even a business model leads to experimentation. Testing becomes a critical task, to be valued by managers all the time, even when a level of a customer problem solution comprehension is achieved. As changes happen in an accelerated and complex way, impacting all sectors and mainly the production chain, experimentation becomes increasingly necessary as a means of mitigating uncertainties, assumptions and, mainly, accelerating the process of digital transformation.

It is true that applying experimentation to a company is not an easy task. In order to create more value for your innovation projects, some principles are fundamental.

From Rogers (2017), we can learn seven principles of experimentation. This model, presented and discussed below, was based on the observation, by the author of innovative companies on competitive actions. It is worth remembering that these seven principles are applied to any business, resulting in a useful guiding model.

1. **Learn early:** The first principle is to start experimenting from the beginning of the innovation initiative, so that one can learn as early as possible during the process. It must be recalled that innovation requires processes, eventually the innovation management process. Through experimentation, ineffective ideas must fail as soon as possible in the development process, long before the product reaches the public, and while the cost of changing the course is much lower. Learning is assured when this cycle is treated like a process.

2. **Be fast and iterative:** The second principle of experimentation is speed. The principle pillar must be reinforced: "Fail fast, fail cheap!" Learn quickly from mistakes and cycle iteratively, instead of waiting long periods, like weeks or months. The Minimum Viable Product is studied, tested to transform ideas into products / services so that the prototype is tested as soon as possible. The first version does not need to be the most complete. On the contrary, we are talking about a product with the least possible resources, as long as its solution function to solve the problem for which it was created, configures a product to be used, even if in a prototype shape.

3. **Fall in love with the problem, not with the solution:** This is a classic phrase quoted by Waze co-founder, Uri Levine. The passion for the problem keeps him focused on the customer and his needs. By forcing yourself to understand the customer's problem first, you take an important step towards ensuring that the innovation process focuses on customer value. The focus on the problem and not on the solution encourages us to consider more than one possible solution. A solution, that at first seems promising, may prematurely interrupt more efficient choices, avoiding the best alternative to be selected.

4. **Receive reliable feedback:** After designing solutions, it is critical to gather *feedback* related to your ideas. That credibility starts with the people you talk to, those you interact when learning about the problem and exercising solutions. They must be chosen from real or potential customers, not you, your colleagues, or bosses. Develop prototypes and present them to those who will use them. Get the most reliable opinions, feelings and estimates about the testing sample. Analyze these answers carefully - they help one achieve the best solution - for your customer!!!

5. **Measure what matters now:** It is especially important to make measurements in any experiment. But what to measure? One of the solutions may be to work with the OKR methodology, which relates to Objectives and Key Results. This sets the definition of (an objective) and key results (measured by). One of its main differentials is precisely the agility in measuring these objectives and results. OKR's logic is to be dynamic, with shorter target cycles, usually every three months, allowing managers, customers and other innovation agents to get knowledge efficiently from "the field", real recognition about problem solutions and its effective value for the customer.

6. **Test your assumptions:** While it is essential to reduce risk in many new ventures, this principle is especially important in innovations that take the company to uncharted territories. If you do not feel secure with your product or business, experiment with real customers. An idea based on a simple assumption can generate bias and make the entrepreneur waste a lot of time and money. Companies who act based on classical models, accustomed to operating in their own territory, tend to ignore the assumption testing phase, when they are looking for innovation. There are methods to efficiently identify and test these assumptions.

7. **Fail with intelligence:** We have reached the last principle of experimentation and one thing is certain: failure is inevitable, it always happens! We can define failure as something that did not work out the way we planned. This is obviously not the goal of digital transformation, but it is an immovable part of the innovation process. The challenge of a failure is precisely to fail with

intelligence, or, detailing, bringing outcomes of learning which can be useful, not only to correct that specific proposal, but to understand and review the whole process that generated the failure, allowing us to correct and improve a bigger managerial context.

- ○ At the end, some questions can - and should - be raised, from this process:
- ○ What did you learn from the test failure?
- ○ Did you apply what you learned to change the strategy, the plan?
- ○ Did the failure occur so early and was it as cheap as possible?
- ○ Did you share the failure with the team?

Intelligent failure is, in fact, an essential part of experimentation in the digital transformation process. It is necessary to eliminate bad options quickly, and this must be done based on learning from tests.

These seven principles integrate an integrated view of digital transformation production, implementation, from a managerial level, not restricted to a specific technology or infrastructure. It also provides an opportune guidance to start DT project formulation, proposition, and design.

A CRITICAL VIEW ON HOW TO MASTER DIGITAL TRANSFORMATION

From Rogers (2017), we collect a view about DT context, with five major aspects (or *domains*, as well defined by the author): Customers, Competition, Data, Innovation and Value. We will approach this interesting overall view to build our own analysis, aiming to clarify decision-making processes that usually occur in DT projects.

It is opportune to consider these domains as strategic arenas, all integrated in one view of value positioning. To improve our perception, we will develop our study around each domain, each aspect overlooking it from the strategic focus. As a first consideration, we must assess the way of selling products and services, as well as the relationship with your customers, which has changed significantly and will continue to be modified. The post-digital world presents us with a scenario of connectivity, mobility and value delivery. Today, the relationship between brand and customer perception of value is much more interactive and dynamic, it is a two-way road.

The customer must be viewed as inserted in a *continuum*, where he or she is a content producer and has an active voice through digital media. He / she spends much of the time connected and is extremely demanding, in addition to being more immediate and critical, having access to information and getting detailed product information. If our readers doubt this fact, just recall about your smartphone being connected to an internet provider, by some technical facility, all day long.

"Our" Customer 4.0 travels around 60% of the purchase journey even before talking to the company who is offering him or her some product. And it happens through the internet and search engines like Google and other social media environments. In 2009, Google itself created the concept ZMOT (*Zero Moment Of Truth*) based on changing the behavior of the digital customer. Previously, when the consumer had the incentive to buy something, he went straight to the store, checked the options, talked to the seller, negotiated the price and took it home. This was the remarkable "zero moment of truth". The customer will read articles, watch videos on Youtube, check social media posts - professional, social, autonomous - evaluate the competition, analyze other people's comments and, after this potentially rich process, the customer draws his / her own conclusions.

If the customer feels satisfied with the product, he will be able to post a photo on social media, carry out your evaluation and, thus, feedback the search engines that will serve as the ZMOT of the other users. This simple mechanism is immediately available, accessible, almost inexpensive and helps guide further actions by other customers.

The digital transformation has also changed the way organizations view their competition. It is no longer enough just to worry about direct competitors, and not to treat them as enemies. A strategic alliance can serve, for example, as a barrier to new market entrants, one of Porter's five strengths. Increasingly, asymmetric competitors are uncomfortable, as potential replacements of value positioned. The current competitor is the one who provides products and services that can be used at the same time as yours.

One example for our discussion: One teacher often gives workshops and training on Saturdays. A competitor in this business is not necessarily another workshop, training professional, but a TV show that will take place on the same day and time. Home office solutions brought this competition to any professional who was working this way before. We can understand it as an evolving competition.

Data has become the new oil in the world. There is no room for guessing anymore in the digital world. Businesses need to be data driven. Innovation became a matter of survival, going beyond competitiveness. Delivering customer experiences is delivering value. Any modern organization needs to be Customer Centric. We brought the five domains, approached in an integrated view, in the field of digital transformation. In the following, they will be discussed individually.

Customers

As it is fundamental to think about a Customer Centric conception, the first domain of digital transformation must be that of *customer* analysis. One question that immediately emerges is: Do we have to deal at any cost as to increase market share and insert all customers within the same base of analysis?

In the post-digital economy, customers are treated in a personalized way, including the process of creation of *personas* - avatars or human icons which detail several social aspects of typical customers - to help analyze their capabilities on developing ethical commercial relationships. Classical methods for the marketing segmentation process, demographic profiles no longer tell us precisely about the decision scenarios for marketing and sales. Through the creation of *personas, it* is possible to draw psychographic profiles and deliver products and services to a specific audience, avoiding a large, confused, myope of the market. This forces organizations to rethink their marketing strategies, their "funnels" to understand this new customer purchasing journey. The customer is multi-screen, connected to several devices simultaneously, with attention being called all time. The strategy needs to be cross-channel, integrating the most diverse digital channels and point of contact between company and customers.

Another important point is always be true. Attempting to trick customers, is a dangerous posture, along with an evident ethical issue. When it comes to social media, brands are vulnerable. A Facebook post or a tweet unmasking something untrue in your organization could go viral on the internet and ruin the brand's reputation. In a few seconds, the company's reputation is exposed, being criticized if any false affirmation is used to compete.

Competition

It is quite common for business players to see competition and cooperation as a binary, diametrically opposed situation. The competitor is in the same sector, which sells products or services in a very similar way. It turns out that, as I mentioned, the new economy is moving towards a much more collaborative world of cooperation between - until then - considered rivals. Within the digital transformation process, it is wise to identify opportunities with your competitors, and sometimes to exercise mutual collaboration. The market is getting more and more troubled, challenged and finding your "blue ocean" will help you differentiate yourself and create an ever-greater displacement of your competitors.

The competition game is much more about the dispute for influence, purpose, and legacy. With a well-positioned business model, each organization will look for customization, experiences, and connection with your consuming public.

Data

The third domain for digital transformation is data, how organizations generate, manage and use their data contexts, in order to produce knowledge. In the past, data was deliberately handled through customer surveys and physical inventories. Currently, we face a flood of data. We have two types of data, structured and unstructured, thinking about it is presented, collected, and stored. Every minute, thousands of conversations are generated on social media. There is so much information that we live in the era of what many call *infoxication*.

According to Noah (2015), we lose more and more awareness of human intelligence, which causes non-conscious intelligence to develop at high speed, forcing us, humans, to actively upgrade our minds if we want to stay as active players and agents. In some occasions, humans give up to authority instead of the free market, the wisdom of the crowds and external algorithms prevail in part because they cannot cope with the flood of data. The excess of information and data is so expressive that we do not have time to absorb and decide what is important, what in fact we will add to knowledge. We need to work with the two aspects in synergy, "dataism" and humanism.

Never in the history of our society so much content has been produced as in the past two years, whether in photos, videos or texts. In the face of information overload, we need tools to mine data and not become a real "bunch of data." Big Data tools provide conditions for organizations to have new possibilities for forecasting, discover unexpected patterns in new businesses and create new value propositions. Data is increasingly becoming a powerful strategic asset for business.

Buckminster Fuller, a futurist thinker, developed the concept of the "Knowledge Duplication Curve" some decades ago. For him, until the year 1900, human knowledge doubled every century. At the end of World War II, knowledge was already doubling every 25 years. For our era, Fuller said that just 12 months are needed for an individual to double his knowledge capacity.

Decision making needs to be anchored on data. This way, we can affirm: the age of "guessing", just having an opinion which will base one decision, is over. Strategic dashboards, consolidating a plethora of indicators, values, and conditions, took on the role of the old Excel spreadsheet, becoming a de facto analytical tool. But it is important to state one conceptual difference: Information is not knowledge. Data serves to build information. Information is a basic element of knowledge. Each of these steps presents a more stable level for decision-making, building a superior level of detail. The correct interpretation of the information and data in which we collect needs to be applied strategically in business. It has to generate value, according to its potential.

Innovation

Innovation happens when ideas are successfully developed, tested and implemented in the market. It builds from inventions, which are the first attempt, addressing a possible problem, but not precisely identifying what are the structure, profiles, costs and other practical, to-the-market aspects for the solution to be implemented and offered for the final customer. This product / service is innovation. There are basically six types of innovation: Products, processes, new markets, new supplies, new business models and new ways to compete. There are two forms of impact; Incremental innovation happens when there are improvements in the product, process, or business. Radical innovation happens when it is disruptive, totally breaking the status quo of how we know things.

For a long time, innovation conceived exclusively on the finished products. Tests were costly, difficult to perform. The cost of failure was high, and everyone was really afraid to fail. Today, failure is considered one of the best ways of learning. Companies that are not open to error (with a certain margin) are unable to innovate. Innovation needs to be seen within the context of continuous learning and rapid experimentation. It is a new approach to understand innovation, from the perspective of testing and building the minimum viable product, to launch this proposal as soon as possible on the market, gaining in learning and reducing costs. A mantra widely used mainly within startups is the following done perfect, maybe better. But do not do it wrong! (So, a perfect solution must be so to solve the problem, not eventually the best technical or technological, essentially).

Value

The last actor in the field of digital transformation is the value that your business generates for customers, that is, the value proposition. The value proposition was long-lasting and already defined by the sector, but it is perceived by the final customer. Sometimes ago, the reigning thought was: "it is only necessary to execute the current proposal and value and that's it, there are customers who would be satisfied". This statement does not work this way anymore.

In the new economy, the value proposition is defined by the business and the offer evolution, according to the needs of the customers. It is a search for new opportunities to create value. Value is changeable and varies according to the characteristic and moment of life of the public. Organizations need to focus efforts on emerging opportunities and new fronts of competitive advantage. Value must be evaluated, analyzed, negotiated, and positioned dynamically. The value proposition is much more linked to the wishes of the consumer market. The secret is not to find customers for your products, but to search products (solutions) for customers.

COMPANIES WHO TOOK THE "RED PILL" (from the Matrix movie)

The film The Matrix (1999) was certainly a watershed in cinema. A totally timeless classic. In addition to the innovative special effects for the time, a trilogy was set and an interesting and provocative context was also started. Metaphors from this movie are now related to different areas of study. Since life often imitates art, and art imitates life, the relationship between the Matrix and digital transformation can be explored, just to define DT outcomes, limits, and motivations.

When the mysterious Morpheus asks Neo between taking the blue pill and continuing in life of appearances, boredom and illusion, or ingesting the red pill, which actually finds the real, unknown and risky world, he decides on the red pill. This way, the history leading character meets the Matrix, a powerful computer network system capable of enslaving humans through intelligent machines. The moment, in that story, is urgent for this choice. The digital transformation - which here would be Morpheus - is showing us both options: or we stay in the same environment, waiting for everything to pass and return as it was before, or we accept to discover a new world, full of uncertainties but that will show us how things really are.

It may seem obvious a choice for the red pill, but the truth is that many companies prefer to do more of the same, with small adaptations out of obligation, but the *status quo* and inertia reign. The blue pill, eventually characterized as a routine, standards, affirmation of a strong culture, bureaucratic structures and various other pressures, is taken daily without any additional perception.

Analyzing this metaphorical "pill decision", there are ways to identify which side is chosen and consequences of this choice. In the following, we develop the metaphor, wondering about three features of companies that decided to take the red pill from Matrix show:

Adaptability

There is a widespread notion, in the business environment, that we, somehow, reinstated the basic principle of Charles Darwin theory: "Adapt or die". When this remarkable scientist observed species around the world, he also perceived this factor, which guaranteed species survival and evolution.

In the business scenario, it can be reviewed as "whoever does not understand the movement of the market, changes in consumer behavior, new forms and sales channels, will be out of the game". Cultural changes, started from market evidence, with continuous analytical abilities, are demanded for organizations to thrive, compete, and win.

The good old theory of myopia in Marketing, debated by authors such as Theodore Levitt, is more present and relevant than ever. Adaptation has become synonymous with survival in the market. We need to explore different possibilities, validate new business models, experience new technologies with our customers. Predictability leads to boredom, and boredom leads to the loss of new discoveries and solutions.

Agility

Klaus Schwab's (2018b) famous phrase reflects the importance of companies being more agile and flexible: "Today it is no longer the biggest fish that eats the smallest, but the fastest fish that eats the slowest." Being more agile does not necessarily mean rushing and making the wrong decisions. Agility is much more linked to unlocking the organization, mitigating waste, breaking silos, reducing bureaucracy, decentralized and horizontal administration, with autonomy for people. Agility has a strong relationship with efficiency. A company must avoid giving up on quality and sticking to outdated methods that no longer work. Usual principle, nowadays, is: "Do the simple and well done in an agile way", enabling the organization to become increasingly efficient.

The *buzzword* of this moment is *Business Agility*, which means involving the entire company in making decisions and more agile deliveries. Agility has to be part of the organizational culture. An agile organization may be able to adjust quickly and take advantage of emerging opportunities in an ever-changing environment.

Change of Mindset

No change will happen in a genuine way if people do not change the way they think. Irish playwright, George Bernard Shaw said, once: "It is impossible to progress without change, and those who do not change their minds cannot change anything."

We need to unlearn and learn all the time, deconstruct post-truths. Companies planned for the past decade are doomed to fail in today's world.

If your company chose the "blue pill" way, it is certainly working within the *Fixed Mindset*, with numerous limitations and excuses for any and all different situations that escape the comfort zone. However, if the option was for the "red pill", it is most likely navigating in the context *of the Growth Mindset*, open to the unknown, new learnings and discoveries. Bernard Shaw phrase interpretation can lead us to a belief that obstacles exist to be overcome. They are driven by the challenge. One thing is for sure: Whatever the choice, companies that decide on the red pill will be ahead in the digital transformation process.

CULTURAL TRANSFORMATION IN ORGANIZATIONS

The importance of cultural transformation in the digital transformation process must be addressed for any interested professional. Transformation is much more about changing mentality than technology itself, it is the cause and not the consequence. Technology changes occur frequently, and can be negotiated, planned, and tested in a more reasonable way than profound changes in organizational culture.

Cultural transformation happens and reverberates in digital transformation. This way, we need to manage organizations within a more updated, evolved, and analytical approach. More lucid, participative, and active leaders are demanded, but it is needed also to go further. A new order to rethink in a more innovative way, leading more humane companies and aware of their role in the face of postmodern society is required, both from social and commercial perspectives.

Belgian corporate leader Frederic Laloux presented us with a beautiful work - Laloux (2014) - on breaking paradigms and organizational models of the past, present and future. He describes organizational environment from the perspective of five stages - in fact, ways of collaborating in organizational environments - based on different perspectives from around the world. They are: *Impulse-Red, Conformist-Amber, Director-Orange, Pluralist-Green and Teal (Integrals)*.

A new model of organization is born. These are new company concepts for the near future, just ahead of us. These companies will dictate references in the market, capable of substantially increasing productivity and competence, adapting to the challenging changes that digital transformation. Every transition to a new stage of consciousness has led to a new era of humanity and we are going through yet another. At every juncture, at every evolution step / portal, everything changed: society (from tribes and groups to modern families, companies and states), the economy (from exploration to horticulture, agriculture and industrialization), power structures, the role of religion, among other factors.

Organizations, as we know them today are simply expressions of our current worldview, our present stage of development as a society. It is a fact that there have been other models previously, and all the evidence indicates that more is yet to come. Laloux presents the ancient and current organizational models, based on human history. It also points to the next stage, the "Teal organizations". We will discuss these steps in the following:

Reactive-Infrared Paradigm

This is the first stage of development of humanity, which covers approximately the period from 100,000 BC to 50,000 BC, when we lived in small family groups. There was a constant effort of power by the troop chief. Fear is the government alignment of the organization, which was highly reactive, focusing on the short term. Extremely tactical vision that thrives in chaotic environments.

Division of labor and autocracy was significantly demarked. We can make a metaphor with packs (flocks). Unfortunate examples, which are only cited for an exercise, are criminal organizations, which relate their efforts by similar means, according to descriptions which can be understood from the policial literature and press.

Conformist-Amber Paradigm

This was a paradigm which emerged as the unavoidable "new possibility", from the rudimentar, initial "infrared" stage. When the Conformist-Amber consciousness appeared, the world has evolved from a tribal world to the era of agriculture, civilizations, institutions, bureaucracies and religion. So, fundamental organizations were formed.

Amber organizations have highly formal roles, centered on hierarchy. Command and control, *top-down* to *bottom-up*. Stability above all, following rigorous processes. Here, the future is a repetition of the past (so, predictive plans started to be adopted by some of our ancestors). This metaphor applies to armed forces, religious institutions, government agencies, and public school systems, among other existent definitions.

Director-Orange Paradigm

The orange stage had a new feature: It no longer kept a fixed universe model, governed by immutable laws, otherwise orchestrated by the complex mechanism of a clock, in which the inner workings and natural laws can be investigated and understood, bringing insights from rationality, producing future scenarios and related analysis. The goal here is to win and beat the competition at any cost. It aims only at profit and growth. Management centered on financial objectives.

The machine would be a metaphor. As examples we have, multinational companies and autonomous schools.

Pluralist-Green Paradigm

This level of awareness in organizations is highly sensitive to people's emotions. There is a base where all perspectives deserve the same respect and care. It seeks justice, equality, harmony, community, cooperation and consensus. Within the structure of the classic pyramid, it focuses on values-driven culture and empowerment to achieve employee motivation. This paradigm intends a clear purpose.

The metaphor for "green" ones would be the family. We can cite as examples, companies such as Starbucks, Patagonia and Mercur.

Evolutionary Teal Organizations: Teal Paradigm

This type is founded on three pillars: clear purpose, integral environment, without hidden features and self-managed structures, without bosses and much less command and control. Centralized and hierarchized capitalism loses space for networked relationships, co-creation, and collaboration. These are changes never seen before, a big impact on the business world.

It integrates with emerging technologies (nanotechnology, robotics, artificial intelligence, drones, 3D printers, internet of things, biotechnology, automation, augmented and virtual realities, among others), being different in relation to Pluralist-Green when they adopt technological advances with principles like self-management, clear purpose and commitment. Leadership is more situational, focused on trust and decentralization of powers. Decisions follow the consultative process, with the advice of specialists. Decisions happen even without common consensus.

As typical evolutionary, Teal organizations are organic, that is, they are living organisms, which constantly evolve and have a life on their own. They do not seek to foresee and control the future, as chaotic as we advance in the VUCA World. It is much more about listening and understanding the organization's purpose and the real environment in which Teal are inserted. The focus of the processes is on constant discoveries, analysis of environments and continuous evolution.

They are environments that favor the integrality of employees. Empowers individuals in the fields of emotional, spiritual, and rational intelligence. It provides employees with the most of their technical and emotional skills. Great examples of Teal organizations are the Dutch companies Buurtzorg and the American Morning Star.

CONCLUSION

At the end of this chapter, we leave a question for you: Is your company prepared for cultural transformation and reaching the fullness of digital transformation? And it is not because your organization is small that it will not suffer the impact of digital transformation, do not believe that it is a fad, one more term.

We presented, in an invitational format, a discussion and reflection focused on the turbulent days we face now and ahead, long journeys of learning and understanding business environment phenomena, market survival and evolution, unexpected sources of competition and time restrictions to fully comprehend reasons, implications and outcome from our business actions, strategies and plans.

Examples of companies and professionals who thrive and win, are perceived along with errors and risks, which emerge all the time, from different and unprecedent sources, demanding analytical behaviors and postures from entrepreneurs. And, as it usually happens nowadays, we do not see an end, a stable level in this process, we feel, all the time, that we are in the beginning or, at maximum, in the middle of a complex, not completely perceived journey. We must keep our minds open all the time, learning, analyzing, understanding, and registering facts which occur, actions which are successful and not, attempting to develop our preparation towards new levels of complexity in the future.

There are several challenges that must be faced to keep the business competitive. To act with the logic of the past is to modify everything you have built up to now. The digitalization of products and services, consumer behavior, the relationship between people and new businesses only prove that the future has arrived, and we are the ones who created it, but, unfortunately, it does not reach everyone.

REFERENCES

Laloux, F. (2014). *Reinventing Organizations: A Guide to Creating Organizations Inspired by the Next Stage of Human Consciousness*. Nelson Parker Publishing.

Rogers, D. L. (2017). *The digital transformation playbook: rethink your business for the digital age*. Columbia University Press.

Schwab, K. (2018a). *The Fourth Industrial Revolution*. Edipro.

Schwab, K. (2018b). *Shaping the fourth industrial revolution*. Excerpts from the World Economic Forum, Switzerland.

Toffler, A. (1980). *The third wave*. William Morrow.

Chapter 16
Analytical Technology Tools Against Corruption and Internal Frauds

Rafael Velasquez Saavedra Silva
Techbiz Forense Digital, Brazil

Matheus Felipe Saavedra da Silva
Enterprise Registry Solutions, Ireland

ABSTRACT

In Brazil, organized crime, unfortunately, finds a fertile field that allows its growth and development due to several different aspects. Also, the vast and continental dimension of the Brazilian territory, the evident social inequality, and in many cases, the lack of synergy and collaboration among municipal, provincial, and federal levels are problems. It is important to mention that, in recent times, via its main institutions—executive, legislative, and judiciary—Brazil has been organizing itself and trying to tackle corruption on different fronts, with the use of advanced technology, new procedures of criminal investigation, an increased collaboration between different players and internal cooperation, the celerity in the process of penal persecution, and the revision of laws related to the theme. This chapter aims at displaying technological innovations that have helped law enforcement to act with rigor, speed, and assertiveness in the production of evidence from digital evidence, while respecting the Brazilian Constitution, individual rights, and guarantees of every citizen.

INTRODUCTION

With the advance of technology, financial institutions have made their national and international movements more impersonal, agile and confidential, available to their clients, making the authorities' investigation work more difficult. Thus, it has become necessary for the institutions to adopt compliance policies as a way of private cooperation in investigating such crimes.

DOI: 10.4018/978-1-7998-4201-9.ch016

Copyright © 2021, IGI Global. Copying or distributing in print or electronic forms without written permission of IGI Global is prohibited.

The matter of corruption in public administration has never been more in evidence than in recent times. Whether due to the definitive sensitivity of its impacts on politics and the economy, or due to international pressures, the importance of revisiting the mechanisms by which the State organizes itself to face and repress certain behaviors of public and private agents is indisputable. These, benefiting from public capital, exercise their influence to illegitimate political decisions, acts and administrative contracts before society, with damage to the development of the country, according to the fundamental objectives of article 3 of the Federal Letter (building of a free, fair and equalitarian society; guarantee of national development; eradication of poverty and marginalization; reduction of inequalities; promotion of the common good).

In Brazil, the prevention and fight against money laundering has its legal base established initially in the Federal Law n. 9.613/98, which has been replaced by the Federal Law n. 12.683/12 and also by the Normative SARB n. 11.13.[1] (Andrade, R. F. (2018 julho 13).

The Money Laundering Law (Law n. 9.613/98) has created the Council for Financial Activities Control (COAF - Conselho de Controle de Atividades Financeiras) which, at the time, was under the scope of the Ministry of Economy, which granted even more responsibility to financial and economical intermediaries, but, due to the revision of the Federal Law n. 12.683/12, the legislation has become more rigorous.

In 2013, new laws were published: the Anti-Corruption Law (Law n. 12.846/13) and the Organized Crime Law (Law n. 12.850/13), offering mechanisms capable of improving the fight against money laundering in the country. In 2016, Brazil has gained a law that regulates the crime of terrorism financing (Federal Law n. 13.260/16).

Recently published, the Law n. 13.964/19 has significantly refined the penal legislation and the penal procedure, describing also in its details the chain of custody process.

It is important to mention that, under the national scope, there are organizations that support the prevention and combat against crimes of money laundering and corruption, and those organizations are:

a)   COAF[2] (Secretaria Especial da Fazenda. (n.d.). – Conselho de Controle de Atividades Financeiras –, council created under the scope of the Ministry of Economy, currently associated with the Central Bank, was established by the Law n. 9.613, in 1998; acts prominently in the prevention and in the combat against money laundering and the terrorism financing. The competencies of CFAC are defined in the articles 14 and 15 of the aforementioned law, as the following:
   ◦   Receive, examine and identify suspicions occurrences of illegal activities;
   ◦   Report inconsistencies to the competent authorities for the beginning of appropriate procedures in the event that the Council concludes by the existence or substantiated evidence of crimes of money laundering, concealment of assets, rights and values, or of any other illegal act;
   ◦   Coordinate and propose mechanisms for cooperation and information exchange that enable quick and efficient actions to the combat of concealment of assets, rights and values;
   ◦   Discipline and apply administrative penalties.
b)   Federal Police, Public Prosecution Service of the Union and the States, Civil Police of the States and Courts specialized in financial crimes and money laundering – organizations that are responsible for investigations, arrests, processing and decisions of suspicions and crimes committed against the financial system in Brazil.
c)   ENCCLA[3] (2020)– Estratégia Nacional de Combate à Corrupção e à Lavagem de Dinheiro (ENCCLA), created in 2003, is the main articulation network for the arrangement and discussions

alongside with a variety of organizations in the Executive, Legislative and Judiciary branches at federal and state levels and, in some cases, municipal, as well as the Public Prosecutor's Office of different spheres, and for the formulation of public policies and solutions aimed at fighting those crimes.

d) DRCI[4] (DRCI)– Departamento de Recuperação de Ativos e Cooperação Jurídica Internacional is responsible for:

I. articulate, integrate and propose actions between the organs of the Executive and Judiciary powers and the Public Prosecutor's Office to confront corruption, money laundering and transnational organized crime, also under the scope of Enccla;

II. coordinate the National Network of Technology Laboratories Against Money Laundering – Rede-Lab;

III. structure, implement and monitor government actions, in addition to promoting the articulation of the organs of the Executive and Judicial powers and the Public Prosecutor's Office in the following areas: international legal cooperation in civil and criminal matters, including matters of international food provision; international child abduction; international adoption; extradition; transfer of convicted persons and transfer of execution of the sentence; asset recovery;

IV. exercise the function of central authority, through the coordination and instruction of active and passive requests for international legal cooperation in the areas referred to in item III, by delegation from the Minister of State, unless there is a specific designation stating otherwise;

V. exercise the function of central federal authority in matters of international adoption of children, in accordance with the provisions of Law n. 8.069, of July 13th, 1990;

VI. negotiate international legal cooperation agreements in the areas referred to in item III and those related to other matters within its competence, in addition to exercising the functions of point of contact, linkage and similar in the international cooperation network and assets recovery;

VII. act in procedures related to the action of assets unavailability, rights or values as a result of the resolution of the United Nations Security Council, in accordance with the provisions of Law n. 13.170, of October 16th, 2015.

At the international level, we can mention the Financial Action Task Force (FATF/GAFI)[5], which is an intergovernmental entity established in 1989, as an initiative of OECD (Organização para a Cooperação e Desenvolvimento Econômico) country members and other associates. The representation is led by COAF alongside with the international areas of the Ministry of Economy, Central Bank of Brazil, Securities and Exchange Commission (CVM – Comissão de Valores Monetários), Superintendence of Private Insurance (SUSEP – Superintendência de Seguros Privados), Ministry of Justice (MJ – Ministério da Justiça), Federal Police (PF – Policia Federal), Attorney General Office (AGU – Advogacia Geral da União), among others.

The FATF's activities seek to establish standards and to promote the effective implementation of laws, regulations and operational actions to tackle money laundering, terrorist financing and other threats to the integrity of the international financial system.

Currently, FATF has a list of 40 recommendations that should be implemented in the countries' regulatory framework. They were recently modified with the assistance of CVM.

Nowadays, we live what scholars call "network life" – one that is extremely connected with the extensive use of computers, notebooks, smartphones, Internet, communication through apps (for example, WhatsApp, Messenger), use of social media tools (Facebook, Instagram, among others) and cloud computing, for instance. This environment has brought several benefits to people and companies, such as quick knowledge and information exchange, efficient commercial and financial transactions and agility in the creation of collaborative environments between people.

According to the research done by the Brazilian Institute of Geography and Statistics (IBGE – Instituto Brasileiro de Geografia e Estatística)[6], 70.5% of Brazilian households started to have access to the internet in 2017. This means 49.2 million connected households, with residents accessing the internet even more often via their mobile phone, since 92.7% of households already have at least one person who has an active mobile line. Internet access is preferably done on mobile phones, according to 69% of the respondents, who said they were connected to the network via a smartphone.

A survey conducted on social medias[7] (Rock Content 2019)has identified that 92.1% of the internet users in Brazil have access to social media apps such as Facebook and Instagram; YouTube is used by 72.3% of respondents, and 91.3% of internet users access their social media apps daily, with a considerable part of them (38.3%) spending, on average, more than 4 hours a day browsing these apps.

As for the Public Security aspect, especially regarding crimes related to corruption and money laundering, this environment has brought new factors. If, on one hand, it created a favorable space for the expansion of electronic crimes and international money laundering – those who use technology for criminal reasons –, on the other hand, it provides law enforcement with an environment that allows obtaining new evidences that can assist in identifying the perpetrators of crimes, methods they use, schedules they have and possible victims.

The collaboration of international economic and financial intermediaries has been a valuable aid in identifying people, assets and the destination of financial resources originated from money laundering, terrorism financing, international drug dealing and psychoactive substances.

However, a major concern of the public security authorities whose work is focused on fighting corruption is with the fact that this massive use of technology leads to a tremendous amount of information to be analyzed. According to statistics from the Federal Bureau of Investigation (FBI), in the United States,[8] (Ruan,, Carthy,, Kechadi,, & Crosbie. (2014). cases involving analysis of information in digital media have shown an average annual increase of 35% in the amount of digital information analyzed. As an example, an average digital forensic case that, in 2003, had an amount of information of 83GBytes, in 2007 it had 277GBytes. On a forecast for 2019, this case would have had a total amount of information of 10,000GBytes.

According to the article of the American researcher Cynthia Murphy,[9] in recent years, investigators have seen a spike in number of requests received for the analysis of mobile devices as they are, currently, a major source of evidence for criminal investigation. She points out a challenge of the wide variety of mobile devices commercially available, operating systems, all types of files and applications that need to have their extraction and analysis solutions continuously updated.

The development of information and communication technologies requires the permanent updating of methods and procedures, forcing anti-corruption agencies – with regard to the security of sensitive data processing, storage and protection systems – to safeguard the assets of cybernetic attacks and other harmful actions, increasingly focused on the econot-echnological area.

The increasing interdependence of productive processes and the control of information and communication technology systems raises concerns with regards the security of the State and society, due to the vulnerability to cyberattacks, requiring permanent attention of the Intelligence in its protection.

The application of the technological paradigm[10] (Conjur 2016)as an anti-corruption strategy is basically to lead to a greater capacity for processing available information, with the bias of transparency and social or state control. The first premise is that auditing, inspecting, controlling or investigating are tasks essentially linked to the ability to access and process information. The more transparent the information is and the easier it is to access it, the more information technology can be used as a tool in the fight against corruption.

It is the duty of all bodies involved in tackling corruption to face organized crime with the use of technology, intelligence, national and international cooperation, ensuring a swift and effective communication process that favors the integrated and coordinated action of these bodies. In recent years, Brazil has been developing methods and public policies and heavily using technology to combat this evil that plagues the country.

FACING CORRUPTION AND MONEY LAUNDERING

As the technological evolution moves fast (either with electronic equipment and software, the emergency of new mobile applications and systems on the Internet and also with the exponential increase in information generated by this channel), anti-corruption institutions need to be continuously updated and trained. Such updates may occur, in particular, in relation to new products, software and forensic solutions that have the capability to handle, quickly, large volumes of data, correlating information from various sources, both from electronic devices and data stored in the cloud to obtain evidences, thus helping to elucidate crimes.

Despite the enormous effort of the anti-corruption agencies to seek the best results, it is necessary to recognize that the sophistication of the way in which crimes are carried out, associated with other factors, has also demanded incessant actions in order to provide better technological equipment for institutions that act directly or indirectly in the fight against corruption and other crimes.

The sophistication of criminal organizations is singular, as they use various subterfuges, such as professional money launderers, middlemen, national and international drug dealing and offshore companies, aiming at trying to hide the money originated from corruption as hard as possible.

The Getúlio Vargas Foundation (FGV, 2016)[11] presents pivotal approaches in the fight against corruption:

- *Fighting corruption via repression of conducts*: the most traditional way of repressing conducts, the most common one within the public opinion, in favor to the aggravation of sanctions, and undoubtedly the criminalization of certain conducts, punishing with restrictions of freedom individual acts that undermine certain legal assets chosen by the legislator. Since the Constitution of 1824, the legislation in Brazil had already foreseen ways to punish the administrator who dishonored the management of public assets and resources, via criminal proceedings.
- *Fighting corruption via transparency in public management*: in view of the inherent limitation of the repressive system – which entails, as mentioned, that the conduct must be identified, investigated and repressed with a penalty at the expense of the treasury itself –, transparency, by applying

the advertising principles in its highest degree, is another way that Brazil has been using to harden the corruption in the public administration.

- *Fighting corruption via private sector collaboration*: the most innovative solution adopted by the Anti-Corruption Law. Without neglecting other forms of confronting corruption – the repression of misconducts and transparency in management –, the new law stimulated the creation of certain mechanisms, within the private sector itself, whose primary purpose is to expunge malpractice under penalty of contaminating all the "network" that may be related to the illegal act.

Within the horizon of fighting corruption in the private sector, there has been, in recent years, a revolution in the systems of corporate governance, internal audit, compliance and internal policies for preventing and tackling money laundering.

Large corporations and public bodies have reviewed several internal processes, such as: supplier registration purchase processes, evaluation of politically exposed personnel, in addition to the creation of specialized sectors in internal investigations and the creation of denunciation channels and structuration of defense lines. Still on the concept of lines of defense,[12] there is a clear definition of each line:

- First Line of Defense – the business and support areas ensure adherence to compliance in all business practices (compliance with standards).
- Second Line of Defense – the legal-advisory area interprets the rules, advises administrators and employees on compliance with the regulatory environment and assists compliance in the performance of their activities. Together with the Corporate Compliance area, the legal area formulates the principles and guidelines of compliance, develops methods, processes, tools and disseminates the compliance culture, while the Compliance and Risk Officers areas implement, execute and disseminate the activities carried out by corporate compliance.
- Third Line of Defense – the audit area periodically assesses compliance risks and the effectiveness of the risk officers' corporate compliance activities.

According to the 2020 report by the *Association of Certified Fraud Examiners* (ACFE)[13] in Latin America / Caribbean, the main cause of workplace fraud for 51% of respondents is corruption, and the main source of fraud detection is still the formal complaint, mentioned by 55% of respondents.

ANALYTICAL TOOLS APPLIED TO FIGHT CORRUPTION

The change in the police investigation process is notorious, because nowadays it is essential, for the elucidation of crimes, to have a vast range of technological resources: search for information in open sources, access to data extracted from mobile devices, access to data extracted from computers, telephone and/or telematics interception, access to cloud data, CCTV's and, specially, access to the public security systems themselves.

Technology is a great ally in the fight against corruption and can be used in several ways, for example, to:

- allow the public to access government data easily (in accordance with the Access to Information Law);

- create digital identification or, in other words, have a unique registration ID for access to public services, thus preventing fraud;
- promote the evolution of bidding systems/controls with artificial intelligence and data mining resources, allowing the analysis of patterns and eventual abnormalities in the event, for example, of direction and cartel formation;
- implement, on a larger scale, the blockchain, which various sectors have been testing and which governments can actively use in auditing public accounts and contracts with service providers. The blockchain allows you to control and track all transactions made by any public or private entity. It is as if it created a stamp for every existence cent and updated its record and location with each new move. As a result, in the event of a hypothetical attempt at embezzlement, it would be quickly discovered and reported by the network.

Currently, the areas of financial intelligence and anti-corruption of numerous agencies and entities receive numerous requests, provided it is followed by judicial authorizations, involving analysis in electronic devices, such as computers, notebooks, mobile phones, tablets and external hard drivers. In fact, the popularization of portable computing devices, such as smartphones and tablets, has been responsible for a radical change in the demand for investigations in the IT areas of these players, making such equipment represent already, in general, most of the production of these areas, generating a huge volume pending for examination and, naturally, with an increasing tendency.

In addition, in parallel to this growing volume of information of interest for criminal investigation stored directly on mobile devices, a new aggravation has been observed, thanks to the widespread storage of data on remote servers on the Internet (the so-called cloud). Besides, more and more seized devices are blocked by personal user passwords, which, in most cases, prevents the extraction of data through traditional tools available to intelligence agents.

Annually, the company Cellebrite publishes the Annual Digital Intelligence Benchmark Report: Law Enforcement,[14] which presents a series of information related to digital investigation involving law enforcement.

One of the numbers presented in this report asks respondents about the frequency with which the following sources of evidence appear in their investigations (Figure 1).

According to Jorge (2019, p. 181), "Due to these new perspectives, it is necessary that the police officer ahead of the criminal investigation be prepared to face the challenges proposed by the technological society and, above all, to be able to use technology to assist in the investigation of crimes".

There are several challenges faced by the police today to conduct technological criminal investigation, including:

Figure 1.
Source: CELLEBRITE REPORT, 2020.

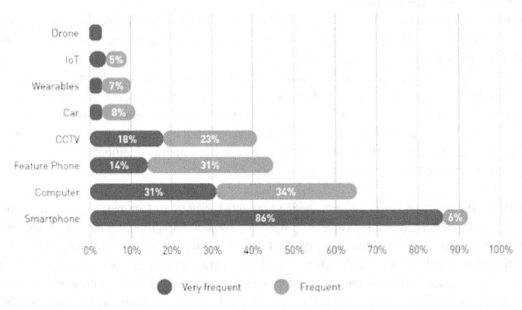

1) expressive increase in the volume of data to be analyzed;
2) ability to cross-reference (linkage) numerous data sources (computers, mobile devices – cell phones and tablets, data in the cloud, Internet of Things (IOT),[15] information provided from non-confidentiality, Public Security systems);
3) lack of training and investment in the Public Security forces;
4) lack of collaboration from service providers (cloud data);
5) lack of centralized information databases;
6) difficulty in accessing the State Transparency Portals, as recommended by the Access to Information Law;
7) lack of collaboration of some countries in sharing information about companies and people;
8) different realities in a continental country.

According to Vecchia (2019, p. 95), "one of the most important characteristics in computer forensics is the guarantee of the integrity of the evidence obtained to prevent reports from being invalidated due to doubts about possible manipulation or contamination of the material questioned".

Obtaining digital evidence must follow important steps for it to be considered valid in court.

TECHNOLOGIC SOLUTIONS

The great challenge of technology applied to fight corruption is to keep up with the rapid evolution of the different types of models, brands, operating systems and applications in mobile devices.

Every day, the use of smartphones becomes more of a reality for most Brazilians. According to the National Telecommunications Agency (Anatel 2020),[16] in May 2019, Brazil registered 228.640 million mobile lines in operation, demonstrating the widespread use of this device. The criminals also usee the same network to combine and commit crimes, especially with the messaging apps WhatsApp and Telegram. One of the greatest challenges today for the judiciary police, public prosecutors and criminal institutes is to, besides obtaining judicial authorization to access the device, be technically able to unblock and extract information.

Criminality is installed on various levels and segments of the Brazilian society; a fact that has resulted in the generalized feeling of insecurity for the population, which demands more effective actions from the State. Without considering the proper way to handle the real factors that influenced the growth of criminality, technology and collaboration are the main alternatives to fight it.

Typical sources of information used in the investigation focused on fighting corruption:

- Cloud
- Open Source Information
- Brazil Transparency Portal
- International Collaboration
- Computers / Servers
- Smartphones / Tablets
- TELCO and Banks information
- Public Security Systems
- Social Networks

One of the greatest technological challenges of the anti-corruption agencies is the time and effort spent to ascertain and consolidate the information of targets and/or companies, as there are several databases; and to link information from social medias, systems police, records of police reports, employment contracts, files from breach of tax and banking secrecy, criminal record, data extraction from smartphones, records of commercial boards, among other data. All this is, undoubtedly, one of the greatest difficulties in this fight.

Outlined below are some examples of tools available in the financial market that make it possible to link different sources of information:

a) Techbiz SNAP[17] (manufacturer: Techbiz Forense Digital): a tool that allows multiple databases to be connected with each other, providing links analysis between the researched entities, enriching the data of a specific research or target in a simple and visual way. SNAP is already used by the Civil Police of the State of São Paulo in the Intelligence Department (DIPOL).

This solution is composed of synapses, which are the connections responsible for obtaining data from different data sources. Synapses are the intelligence engine that allows new bases to be connected to others in order to enrich the information needed to solve the cases studied. Examples:

- Paterva – platform on which SNAP is based to perform synoptic integrations between different data sources.
- CrediLink – credit information and personal data system.
- Social Links – information system for social networks and dark web.
- Portal da Transparência – portal for information on payment and use of government resources.

Figure 2.
Source: Elaborated by the author (2020).

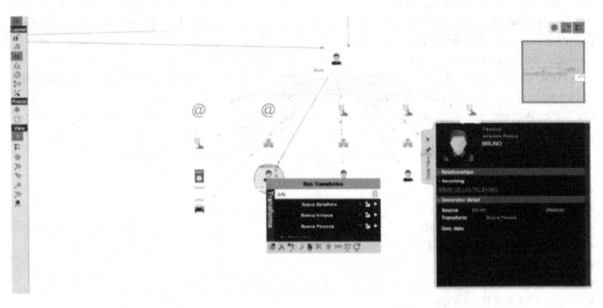

- Registro.br – Internet domain information system.
- JUSCESP – business activity registration system.
- Google Maps – addresses information system, telephone etc.
- Diário Oficial – portal containing official publications of the Federal Government.
- Consulta Operadora – telephony information system.
- Consulta IMEI – telephony information system.
- Consulta CNPJ – legal entity registration information system.
- OLX – merchandise sales portal.
- Mercado Livre – merchandise sales portal.
- OCR – extraction of texts and entities from images and documents pdf, doc, docx etc.

With the aforementioned solution, it is possible to consolidate all this information in a single interface (Figure 4) so that the intelligence analyst can conduct the investigation and produce the knowledge necessary to be recorded in the reports, as well as allowing integration with any other databases and automated imports of CDR files, bank secrecy files, integration with public security systems (SIMBA, INFOSEG, among other solutions).

With SNAP, it is possible to conduct searches using CPFs, CNPJs, identify the corporate relationship, locate profiles on social medias, correlate information from the dark web and link them to public security databases.

The following example is the query based on a name or a unique identifier (CPF -Cadastro de Pessoa Física), and the solution returns a variety of company information, emails and phones. If integrated with public security systems, it is possible to return information about vehicles, passport, criminal record, history in the prison system and labor relations.

Figure 2 – Search by name and CPF

Figure 3. Search on the Portal da Transparência
Source: Elaborated by the author (2020).

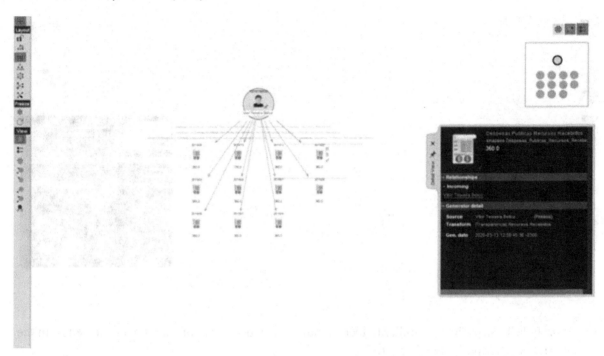

Figure 4. Search on social medias
Source: Elaborated by the author (2020).

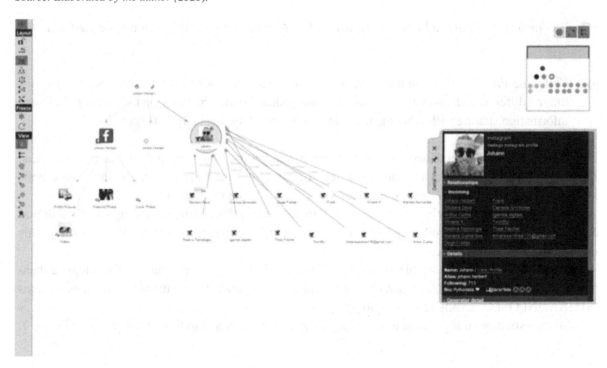

Figure 5. E-commerce search (Mercado Livre and OLX)
Source: Elaborated by the author (2020).

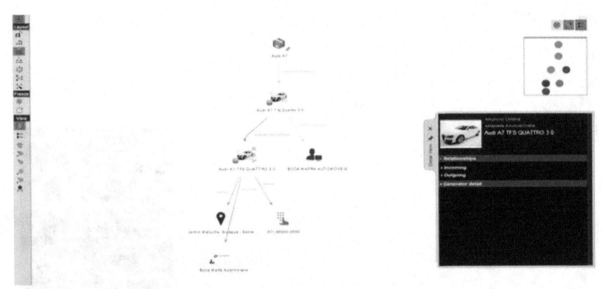

- Portal da Transparência – ability to locate, transform and present information originated from the Portal da Transparência (Figure 6).

- Social medias – ability to locate, transform and show information from social networks.

- E-commerce – ability to locate, transform and show information from e-commerce platforms.

b) Cellebrite Pathfinder[18] (manufacturer: (Cellebrite 2020): this solution has advanced features for linking different sources of information, including identification features via facial recognition and information sharing with other agents, allowing to speed up the analysis (Figure 9).

It is possible to add several identifiers, sometimes contradictory, from various data sources to suspects. That is the secret to map the suspicious journey. It reveals insights from seemingly unrelated events, locations and relationships to help researchers know what is to be focused on.

Digital data can no longer be ignored in current investigations. Due to the increasing variety of digital devices and cloud sources producing large volumes of data, investigators need tools to benefit from this important source of evidence.

With this solution, it is possible to: carry out an analytical study of text and media, integrate databases, import CDR files, bank breach of secrecy files and integrate them with public security systems (SIMBA, INFOSEG, among other solutions).

With this solution, it is possible to visualize the information on a map format, as shown in Figure 7.

Figure 6. Cellebrite Pathfinder
Source: Elaborated by the author (2020).

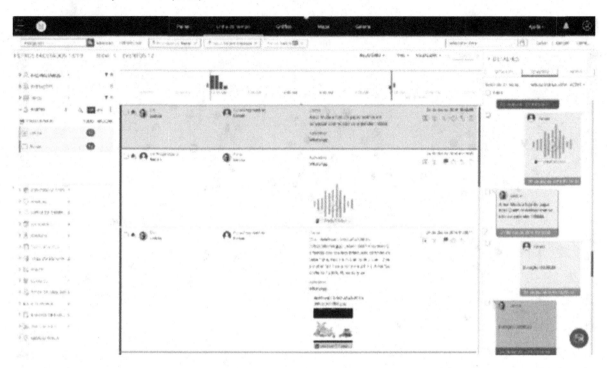

Figure 7. Viewing the summarized locations
Source: Elaborated by the author (2020).

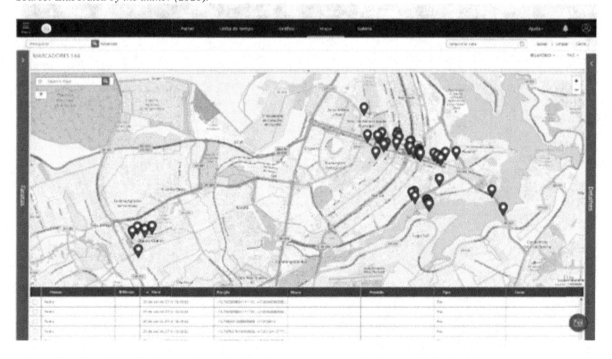

Figure 8. Applying filters and graphically viewing the relationships.
Source: Elaborated by the author (2020).

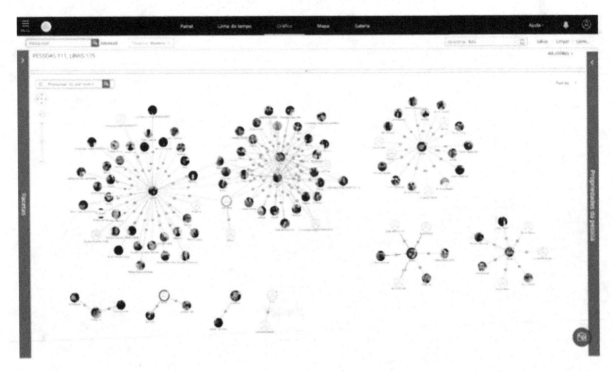

Figure 9. Viewing the media categories
Source: Elaborated by the author (2020).

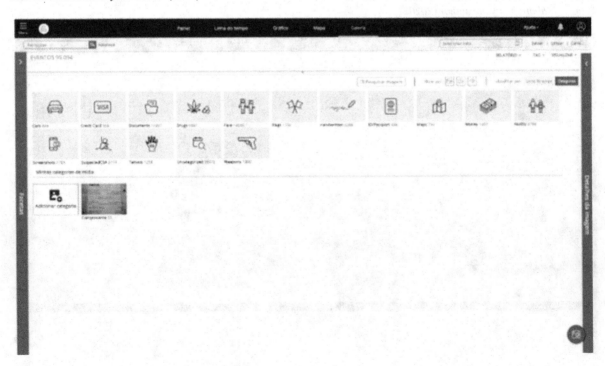

c)   Nuix Investigate[19] (Nuix): This solution provides end-to-end electronic discovery capabilities so that investigators and analysts can get to the truth more quickly.

It was the official solution used by law enforcement in the famous Panama Papers[20] case, as it was the only solution that managed to index and link the volume of data seized in the operation.

There are several benefits of one of the best processing services, daily analysis and intelligent review on a single platform. With Nuix, it is possible to process a large volume of information from different sources.

Figure 10. Nuix (Dashboard)
Source: Elaborated by the author (2020).

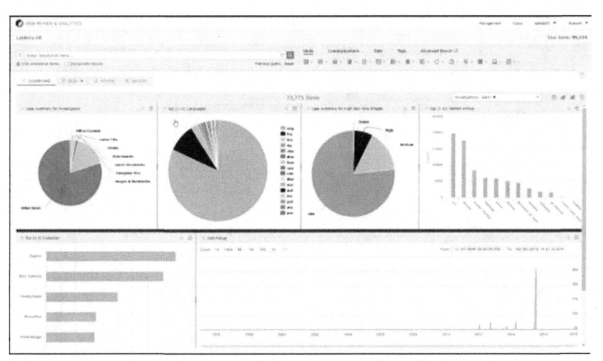

Using Nuix, it is possible to link several emails in an objective and simple way.

Nuix also makes it is possible to locate information related to credit cards, CNPJ[21], CPF[22], company names, quotes of monetary values, telephones, IP addresses and suspicious email information.

(Figure 12), terrific help in fighting corruption and money laundry.

Figure 11. Email analysis
Source: Elaborated by the author (2020).

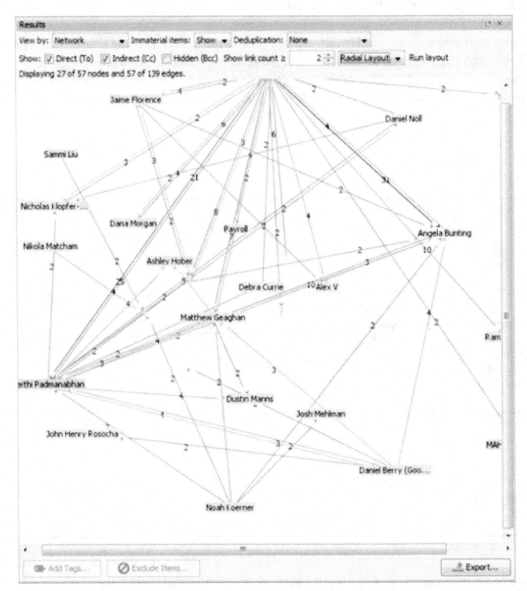

CONCLUSION

As presented in this article, tackling corruption is everyone's duty, and nowadays Brazil has a set of specific laws that have evolved over the years. For the private market, several anti-corruption guides and procedures are also available.

It should be noted that operations concerning the Lava Jato help public opinion to understand how important the work of institutions is in fighting this evil that plagues the country.

Figure 12.
Source: Elaborated by the author (2020).

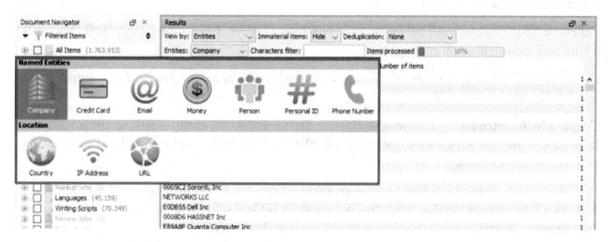

In recent years, via the DRCI and the bodies linked to the Ministry Foreign Affairs, there have been significant advances in the international collaboration, with the sharing of information of people and companies with suspicious movements of assets abroad.

Today, in Brazil, there are several solutions and technologies available to tackle corruption, but it takes political will, investment and a desire to innovate in investigative practices and procedures in this new scenario.

Investment in training and care for human capital are still one of the pillars of public security, as it is not enough to have access to the most advanced technologies without the proper training of public agents.

REFERENCES

Acfe. (2020). *Report to the Nations*. https://www.acfe.com/report-to-the-nations/2020/

Andrade, R. F. (2018 julho 13). *O combate à lavagem de dinheiro*. Legiscompliance. https://www.legiscompliance.com.br/colunistas/renata-andrade/79-o-combate-a-lavagem-de-dinheiro#:~:text=O%20crime%20de%20lavagem%20de%20dinheiro%20foi%20tipificado%20no%20Brasil,Lei%20n%C2%B0-%209.613%2F98.&text=Tal%20crime%20se%20d%C3%A1%20ao,ou%20indiretamente%2C%20de%20infra%C3%A7%C3%A3o%20penal

Barreto, A. (2019). *Deep Web: Investigação no submundo da internet*. Brasport.

Brasil, I. I. A. (2019 junho). *Três linhas de defesa*. https://global.theiia.org/translations/PublicDocuments/3LOD-IIA-Exposure-Document-Portuguese.pdf

Brasil. Anatel. (2020, Março 3). *Brasil registra 228,64 milhões de linhas móveis ativas em maio de 2019*. https://www.anatel.gov.br/institucional/noticias-destaque/2310-brasil-registra-228-64-milhoes-de-linhas-moveis-ativas-em-maio-de-2019

Cardoso, D. M. (2015). *Criminal compliance na perspectiva da lei de lavagem de dinheiro*. LiberArs.

Cellebrite. (2019). *Cellebrite industry trend survey: Law enforcement.* https://www.cellebrite.com/en/insights/industry-survey/. *Trend*

Cellebrite. (2020). *Annual digital intelligence benchmark report: Law enforcement.* https://www.cellebrite.com/en/insights/industry-report/

Cellebrite. (n.d.). *Encontre o caminho para o insight por meio de montanhas de dados.* https://www.cellebrite.com/pt/analytics-2/

Conjur. (2016, Setembro 14). *Suporte a litígios: Tecnologia serve como aliada na prevenção e no combate à corrupção.* https://www.conjur.com.br/2016-set-14/suporte-litigios-tecnologia-serve-aliada-prevencao-combate-corrupcao#1

Drci. (n.d.). *Departamento de Recuperação de Ativos e Cooperação Jurídica Internacional.* Ministério da Justiça e Segurança Pública. https://www.justica.gov.br/Acesso/institucional/sumario/quemequem/departamento-de-recuperacao-de-ativos-e-cooperacao-juridica-internacional

Enccla. (n.d.). *Últimas notícias.* http://enccla.camara.leg.br/

Estadão. (n.d.). *Dados de 200 mil offshores do Panama Papers serão publicados.* Estadão. https://politica.estadao.com.br/noticias/panama-papers,dados-de-200-mil-offshores-dopanama-papers-serao-publicados,10000049693

Fatf-Gafi. (n.d.). *GAFI (FATF).* Comissão de Valores Mobiliários. http://www.cvm.gov.br/menu/internacional/organizacoes/gafi.html

Fgv. (n.d.a). *Cadernos.* https://fgvprojetos.fgv.br/publicacao/cadernos-fgv-projetos-no27-lei-anticorrupcao-transparencia-e-boas-praticas

Fgv. (n.d.b). Lei Anticorrupção: Transparência e Boas Práticas [Versão Eletrônica]. *Cadernos FGV Projetos*, n. 27. Ibge. *Pesquisa nacional por amostra de domicílios contínua.* https://biblioteca.ibge.gov.br/visualizacao/livros/liv101631_informativo.pdf

Jorge, H. V. N. (2019a). *Investigação criminal tecnológica* (Vol. 1). Brasport.

Jorge, H. V. N. (2019b). *Investigação criminal tecnológica* (Vol. 2). Brasport.

Murphy, C. (2013). *Developing process for mobile device forensics.* http://www.mobileforensicscentral.com/mfc/documents/Mobile%20Device%20Forensic%20Process%20v3.0.pdf

Nuix. (n.d.). *Master Investigations With Forensic Precision.* https://www.nuix.com/products/nuixinvestigate

Rock Content. (2019, Fevereiro 8). *Social Media Trends: Panorama das empresas e dos usuários nas redes sociais.* https://inteligencia.rockcontent.com/social-media-trends-2019-panorama-das-empresas-e-dos-usuarios-nas-redes-sociais/

Ruan, K., Carthy, J., Kechadi, T., & Crosbie, M. (2014). *Cloud forensics: An overview.* Dublin: Centre for Cybercrime Investigation, University College Dublin. Snap. Snap: Suas investigações na Era Digital. http://snapdesktop.com.br/

Secretaria Especial da Fazenda. (n.d.). *Conselho de Controle de Atividades Financeiras – Coaf*. Ambiente em Migração – Ministério da Economia. https://www.fazenda.gov.br/acesso-a-informacao/institucional/estrutura-organizacional/conselho-de-controle-de-atividades-financeiras-coaf

Vecchia, E. D. (2019). *Perícia digital, da investigação à análise forense* (2. ed.). Campinas, SP: Millennium.

ENDNOTES

[1] Andrade, R. F. (2018 julho 13). *O combate à lavagem de dinheiro*. Legiscompliance. https://www.legiscompliance.com.br/colunistas/renata-andrade/79-o-combate-a-lavagem-de-dinheiro#:~:text=O%20crime%20de%20lavagem%20de%20dinheiro%20foi%20tipificado%20no%20Brasil,Lei%20n%C2%B0%209.613%2F98.&text=Tal%20crime%20se%20d%C3%A1%20ao,ou%20indiretamente%2C%20de%20infra%C3%A7%C3%A3o%20penal.

[2] Secretaria Especial da Fazenda. (n.d.). *Conselho de Controle de Atividades Financeiras – Coaf*. Ambiente em Migração – Ministério da Economia. https://www.fazenda.gov.br/acesso-a-informacao/institucional/estrutura-organizacional/conselho-de-controle-de-atividades-financeiras-coaf.

[3] Enccla. *Últimas notícias*. http://enccla.camara.leg.br/. 2020.

[4] Drci. *Departamento de Recuperação de Ativos e Cooperação Jurídica Internacional*. Ministério da Justiça e Segurança Pública. https://www.justica.gov.br/Acesso/institucional/sumario/quemequem/departamento-de-recuperacao-de-ativos-e-cooperacao-juridica-internacional.

[5] Fatf-Gafi. *GAFI (FATF)*. Comissão de Valores Mobiliários. http://www.cvm.gov.br/menu/internacional/organizacoes/gafi.html.

[6] Ibge. *Pesquisa nacional por amostra de domicílios contínua*. https://biblioteca.ibge.gov.br/visualizacao/livros/liv101631_informativo.pdf.

[7] Rock Content. (2019 fevereiro 8). *Social Media Trends: Panorama das empresas e dos usuários nas redes sociais*. https://inteligencia.rockcontent.com/social-media-trends-2019-panorama-das-empresas-e-dos-usuarios-nas-redes-sociais/.

[8] Ruan, K., Carthy, J., Kechadi, T., & Crosbie, M. (2014). *Cloud forensics: An overview*. Dublin: Centre for Cybercrime Investigation, University College Dublin.

[9] A Det. Cynthia A. Murphy pertence ao Departamento de Polícia de Wisconsin, nos Estados Unidos, e é especialista em análise forense digital, instrutora forense no Madison College de Wisconsin e no Instituto SANS. É autora do artigo "Developing Process for Mobile Device Forensics". Murphy, C. (2013). *Developing process for mobile device forensics*. http://www.mobileforensicscentral.com/mfc/documents/Mobile%20Device%20Forensic%20Process%20v3.0.pdf.

[10] Conjur. (2016 setembro 14). *Suporte a litígios: Tecnologia serve como aliada na prevenção e no combate à corrupção*. https://www.conjur.com.br/2016-set-14/suporte-litigios-tecnologia-serve-aliada-prevencao-combate-corrupcao#1.

[11] Fgv. *Cadernos*. https://fgvprojetos.fgv.br/publicacao/cadernos-fgv-projetos-no27-lei-anticorrupcao-transparencia-e-boas-praticas.

[12] IIA Brasil. (2019 junho). *Três linhas de defesa*. https://global.theiia.org/translations/PublicDocuments/3LOD-IIA-Exposure-Document-Portuguese.pdf.

[13] Acfe. (2020). *Report to the Nations*. https://www.acfe.com/report-to-the-nations/2020/.

[14]   Cellebrite. (2020). *Annual digital intelligence benchmark report: Law enforcement*. https://www.cellebrite.com/en/insights/industry-report/.

[15]   Tradução da expressão em inglês *Internet of Things*, que trata de redes de comunicação, dispositivos e sistemas de controle, ou seja, a conectividade entre os objetos utilizados pelas pessoas.

[16]   Brasil. Anatel. (2020 março 3). *Brasil registra 228,64 milhões de linhas móveis ativas em maio de 2019*. https://www.anatel.gov.br/institucional/noticias-destaque/2310-brasil-registra-228-64-milhoes-de-linhas-moveis-ativas-em-maio-de-2019.

[17]   Snap. Snap. http://snapdesktop.com.br/.

[18]   Cellebrite. (2020). *Annual digital intelligence benchmark report: Law enforcement*. https://www.cellebrite.com/en/insights/industry-report/.

[19]   Nuix. (n.d.). Master Investigations With Forensic Precision. https://www.nuix.com/products/nuix-investigate.

[20]   Estadão. *Dados de 200 mil offshores do Panama Papers serão publicados*. Estadão. https://politica.estadao.com.br/noticias/panama-papers,dados-de-200-mil-offshores-dopanama-papers-serao-publicados,10000049693.

[21]   CNPJ - National Register of Legal Entity

[22]   CPF – Security Number

Chapter 17
Digital Transformation, Public Policies, and the Triple Helix:
A Case Study of the City of Salvador

Ivan Euler Paiva
SENAI CIMATEC, Brazil

Sérgio Maravilhas
https://orcid.org/0000-0002-3824-2828
SENAI CIMATEC, Brazil & UNIFACS, Salvador University, Brazil

Flavio Souza Marinho
SENAI CIMATEC, Brazil

Renelson Ribeiro Sampaio
SENAI CIMATEC, Brazil

ABSTRACT

This exploratory and descriptive study aims to analyze the impacts and effectiveness of a public innovation policy promoted by a city hall in a Brazilian state capital involving startups, large companies, and a scientific and technological institution between 2017 and 2019; the purpose of this study is to promote economic development and address urban problems common to large metropolises. The strategy adopted, inspired by the propositions of the Triple Helix, was able to bring together startups, large companies, a city hall, and an important representative of academia. The results indicate the evolution of indicators of entrepreneurship in the city and present important lessons for the formulation of municipal innovation policies in Brazil.

DOI: 10.4018/978-1-7998-4201-9.ch017

Copyright © 2021, IGI Global. Copying or distributing in print or electronic forms without written permission of IGI Global is prohibited.

1. INTRODUCTION

Technological revolutions trigger abrupt changes even in public policies. The digital revolution is a catalyst for change capable of altering various aspects of contemporary society. Hyperconnectivity, the levers of digital change, and the impact of collaborative society are some of the main dimensions of this digital revolution and have opened up opportunities for cities to overcome some of their historical challenges (CUNHA; PRZEYBILOVICZ; MACAYA, & BURGOS, 2016). At the same time that new technologies present alternatives to the solution of old urban problems, they impose the need to update instruments that promote digital transformation, including through startups, which are new actors that have been recognized for their importance in the global innovation ecosystem.

Still without consensus to date, the adopted definition of a startup is "an organization built to find a repeatable and scalable business model" (BLANK, & DORF, 2012) and "a human institution designed to deliver a new product or service under conditions of extreme uncertainty" (RIES, 2011). Therefore, given their temporary nature, startups can be understood as organizations designed to promote transformation.

Given its importance for innovation and the economy, an important system of institutions to support new ventures since its early days has been increasingly fostered in several countries and regions, including risk investors, incubators and accelerators, shared work spaces and government-funded support programs (WEIBLEN, & CHESBROUGH, 2015). A fertile field flourishes, therefore, from the possibility of creating public policies that combine the promotion of innovation and entrepreneurship, which directs the use of new digital technologies to solve challenges common to large Brazilian and global cities.

A model of an innovation system that promotes regional development through innovation and entrepreneurship was named the "triple helix" by Etzkowitz and Leydesdorff (1996). The authors argue for the growing articulation between the university, the private sector, and the government for the development of knowledge and innovation.

University-industry-government interactions, which form a "triple helix" of innovation and entrepreneurship, are the key to knowledge-based economic growth and social development. The government is one of the primary institutional spheres, which has its relevance regarding the funding of research, programs, and projects (ETZKOWITZ, & ZHOU, 2017).

This exploratory and descriptive study aims to analyze the impacts and effectiveness of a public innovation policy promoted by a city hall of a Brazilian state capital involving startups, large companies, and a scientific and technological institution (STI) between 2017 and 2019 with the purpose of promoting economic development and addressing urban problems common to large metropolises.

This chapter has seven sections, in addition to this introduction. The next section contains a brief review of the literature on the development of policies to support innovation. In the following sections, the methodology and the case study are described. The subsequent section presents an analysis of the problem-situation and the main lessons learned and proposals for the problems presented. Finally, the results are analyzed, and the final considerations are made.

2. LITERATURE REVIEW

According to the Oslo Manual, a central document widely used in public policies to stimulate technological innovation, innovation is the implementation of a new or significantly improved product (good or service), or a process, or a new marketing method, or a new organizational method in business practices, workplace organization or external relations (OECD, 2006).

According to Potts and Kastelle apud Brandão, S.M. and Bruno-Faria M.F. (2013), from the economic point of view, there are three reasons to stimulate innovation in the public sector: the first is that, in most countries of the Organization for Economic Cooperation and Development (OECD), the public sector is a significant component of macroeconomics, and contributes with a significant portion (between 20 and 50%) of the Gross Domestic Product (GDP). The second is that the public sector is responsible for providing services to citizens and businesses, and innovation can achieve better results through new ways of solving problems. The third is that the public sector is responsible for fostering innovation in the private sector.

Public policies are understood as:

The set of programs and government actions that necessary and sufficient, integrated and articulated for the provision of goods or services to society, endowed with budgetary resources or resources derived from waiver of revenue and benefits of a financial and credit nature (IPEA, 2018, p 13).

According to the Oslo Manual (OECD, 2006), for the development of policies to support innovation, a better understanding of several critical aspects of the innovation process is necessary, such as innovation activities that are not included in R&D and interactions between the various actors of the innovation system. The Manual also states that innovation is important for the public sector and that broad knowledge of the information system can help reduce uncertainty in the formulation of innovation policies and plays a key role in economic progress.

Given its importance for innovation and the economy, an important system of institutions to support new ventures since its early days has been increasingly fostered in several countries and regions, including even by risk investors, incubators and accelerators, spaces for co-working and government-funded support programs (WEIBLEN, & CHESBROUGH, 2015). Therefore, a fertile field flourishes from the possibility of creating public policies that combine the promotion of innovation and entrepreneurship and directs the use of new digital technologies to solve common challenges in large Brazilian and global cities.

According to Cavalcante and Cunha (2017), innovation processes in the public sector have intensified in the last twenty years and gained a strategic dimension in contemporary states and played a role in driving economic development and modernization of public administration. Since the beginning of the 21st century, the area of innovation research in the public sector has gained more support, as evidenced by the increase in the number of publications on the subject in scientific journals, books and conferences. However, innovation in public management should be further investigated, and studies based on empirical evidence are still lacking (CAVALCANTE, & CAMÕES, 2017).

According to Vries, Bekkers and Tummers apud Oliveira and Junior (2017), of 210 articles found during the literature review on innovation in the public sector conducted in 2016, only 84 articles, approximately 40%, refer to consequences of innovation adoption and those who mention this aspect. Many focuses exclusively on the positive effects of innovations and neglect their negative effects, as if innovating by itself was a positive value to be pursued.

Cunha (2017) presents a new fact regarding the documents produced by national governments or international organizations, which is that the greatest concern refers to the institutional aspects internal to the state structures, with few promoting any link with their exterior, that is, with the innovation ecosystem.

There are many funding sources for innovation that were classified by the Oslo Manual as:

(i) own funds; (ii) funding originating from affiliated (subsidiary or associated) companies; (iii) financing from other (nonfinancial) companies; (iv) funding from financial companies (bank loans, risk capital, etc.); (v) government funding (loans, grants, etc.); (vi) funding from supranational or international organizations; (vii) other sources (OECD, 2006, p. 119).

Corder and Salles-Filho apud Maçaneiro and Cherobim (2011) note that "due to uncertainties and great risks, the largest source of resources for the initial investments of small innovative companies should come from the public sector because larger investors prefer later, safer phases". Therefore, it can be stated that public policies are extremely important to support and encourage companies, which boost the country's economy.

Economic subsidies are one of the main instruments of the government's policy of promoting innovation and are operated according to the rules of the World Trade Organization (WTO) (FINEP, 2010). This practice is old in developed countries, such as the United States, which created a financing program for technology-based companies in 1982, and Spain, which created a public entity in 1986 to promote and support innovation and the technological development of Spanish companies. However, in Brazil, it began to be effectively used in 2006, when the Innovation Law, Federal Law no. 10.973/2004, was regulated by Decree no. 5.798/2006 (BORGES, 2015).

The economic subsidy consists of the direct contribution of public resources to companies to carry out innovative projects. The objective of this instrument, which is used in several countries, is to expand innovation activities and increase the competitiveness of companies and the economy of the country. The grant can be applied to the cost of research, technological development, and innovation activities in Brazilian companies (FINEP, 2010).

The study conducted by the partnership between the Center for Management and Strategic Studies (CGEE, for its acronym in Portuguese) and the National Association of Research and Development of Innovative Enterprises (ANPEI, for its acronym in Portuguese) presented a balance of the experience in applying new instruments to support innovation. It showed that the instrument of the economic subsidy is cited by the surveyed companies as the most powerful mechanism to stimulate innovation, since the government provides nonrefundable public money for high technological risk projects (CGEE & ANPEI, 2009).

After analyzing the data from the FINEP survey, Costa, Szapiro and Cassiolato (2013) present some criticisms to the public call notices: (i) the notices support research and development activities in companies that have a low innovative character and, with this, generate negligible impacts on the market - a fact that should not occur in regard to nonrefundable resources directed to companies; (ii) the notices are focused on supporting innovative projects and their results, and not on projects in stages of research and development or innovation strategy of the company; (iii) it is observed that companies were created as a function of the project financed by the economic subsidy instrument, and for these companies to be able to maintain their activities after receiving all the resources from the financed project, it will be necessary for them to obtain new revenues through new government instruments to support innovation.

The results presented for micro and small enterprises point to the impact that the instrument of economic subsidies exerts on these companies. Although these data indicate that innovation is being encouraged as these companies wish, the reality may not be this. Problems of poor management of resources and lack of physical and organizational infrastructure may lead the company to not honor its commitments with the funding entity and with the staff hired for the project. According to Costa, Szapiro and Cassiolato (2013), this problem tends to worsen as delays occur in the disbursement schedule of projects and companies do not have other financial resources to maintain the progress of activities.

The fact that small companies do not invest in research and development, as large companies do, does not mean that they are not innovative or that they do not generate significant impacts to the market (BALDWIN, & GELLATLY, 2003).

The result of the study by Costa, Szapiro and Cassiolato (2013) was that the notices for proposals for the economic subsidy to innovation program were not effective considering its main objective of supporting innovation, which should benefit the introduction of a new product in the market. However, this does not mean that the economic subsidy instrument cannot or should not be used in different program designs that aim to finance research and development without the main concern in the distribution to the market, especially when considering projects of high technological risk. Other types of innovation may have happened to companies, such as process, marketing, or organizational innovation (OECD, 2006). They are intangible innovations, difficult to observe, and mainly directly measured.

According to the authors Andrade (2009) and Costa, Szapiro and Cassiolato (2013), the main weakness of public calls for tenders as an option for operationalization of the economic subsidy instrument is the difficulty that this alternative causes for its integration with other instruments, such as refundable financing, while creating competition between them. As the analyses of the projects to be financed through each of the instruments occur independently, the companies can request nonrepayable loans or receive refundable resources, through the grant, for the same project or for similar activities.

Andrade (2009) presents another criticism to the Notices, that FINEP does not adopt the technological risk criterion to select the subsidized projects, and uses a single criterion that is the framework to the themes of the public calls that, in addition to being disjointed from the needs of Government purchases, are often broad and little specific.

Maçaneiro and Cherobim (2011) performed an analysis of the empirical data collected from the public calls of the Program of Economic Subsidy to Innovation (Programa de Subvenção Econômica à Inovação) and information collected in the interviews conducted with the Micro and Small Enterprises (MSE) of the State of Paraná that had projects approved by the Program.

The authors also demonstrate the same problems for micro and small enterprises because the results of the study indicated that MSEs have difficulties in meeting the physical and financial schedule of the approved project, meeting deadlines, not exceeding costs, being able to be accountable to the project's funding institution, in addition to the fear of not executing and meeting the proposed objectives. (MAZANEIRO, & CHEROBIM, 2011).

CGEE & ANPEI (2009) also identified a low level of professionalization and formalization of innovation management, as many of them do not have qualified personnel to manage the access and use of funding instruments; thus, they are even more precarious in small businesses.

Public policies for innovation were implemented through incentive programs for startups. Two of these programs are based on the incentive to entrepreneurship and technological development: Start-up Brazil and InovApps. Start-up Brazil was the first public initiative aimed at accelerating startups in the country. The Program was launched in 2012 by the Ministry of Science, Technology, and Innovation (MCTI) to encourage and increase the success rate of startups through the contribution of financial resources to attract talent and assistance in accessing the market. InovApps was launched by the Ministry of Communications in 2014 to promote innovation and the development of new technologies and increase competition and market efficiency (RONCARATTI, 2017).

According to Roncaratti (2017) and Pinto (2017), the main innovation of the Start-up Brazil program was the construction of an organizational arrangement between public and private entities to accelerate startups, which offers direct and nonrefundable financial resources up to BRL 200 thousand in the form of research grants paid by the National Council for Scientific and Technological Development (CNPq) to the partners of the startups and/or fellows indicated in the project.

The Start-up Brazil program, through accredited accelerators, also offered training, mentoring, training and connection with investors and potential customers. In this arrangement, the accelerators act as co-investors in the supported startups and are remunerated only when the shareholding of the company is sold in the future (ZORTEA, & MALDANER. 2018).

In the period from 2013 to 2015, the Start-up Brazil program supported four classes in two editions, with public funds totaling BRL 34 million. The program received 2,855 applications from twenty-four states and more than fifty-seven countries and selected 183 companies from seventeen states and thirteen countries (RONCARATTI, 2017).

An important innovation element in the InovApps program was the possibility of incorporating public utility solutions in equipment more accessible to the end customer (citizen) and sharing the rights to use the solutions developed with the State, which is not common in promotion initiatives in Brazil. In the first edition, in 2014, the total investment was BRL 4.5 million, and the contest (InovApps) received 2,464 projects, of which 865 were qualified and fifty public utility applications were selected for awards in the amount of BRL 100 thousand each. In 2015, there were 933 applicants, of which 529 were qualified and one hundred utility applications were awarded in the amount of BRL 50,000, totaling an investment of BRL 5 million. (RONCARATTI, 2017).

The InovApps promoted a tender of applications of public interest, in which the winners would receive a fixed cash prize. The acquisition of the application was based on the tender modality according to the bidding law (law No. 8.666, of June 21, 1993), which allows the citizen to provide services to the government without the need to form a company (SWIATEK, 2019).

3. METHODOLOGY

To conduct this study, a qualitative exploratory and descriptive study was used through the strategy of a single case study. According to Yin (2015), a case study is an appropriate strategy when applied to a set of events that is not controlled by the researcher, there is little knowledge about the topic addressed, and it is developed in a delimited territory. In this case, in the accelerator of the SENAI CIMATEC.

The single-case study method was used as a research strategy because it is a subject little discussed. The case study was conducted between 2017 and 2019 through the agreement between the PMS and the SENAI CIMATEC. According to Yin (2015), a case study is an empirical investigation that investigates a contemporary phenomenon, especially when there is no clear definition between the phenomenon and the context.

To prepare the literature review, a search was conducted in the database of university library collections through e-books, scientific articles, dissertations, theses, books and technical scientific journals.

According to Lima and Mioto (2017), bibliographic research is a methodological procedure that is important in the production of scientific knowledge, which offers the researcher the possibility to search for answers to his research problem. The literature review goes beyond the simple observation of data contained in the researched sources, and it reproduces the critical understanding of the meaning it contains.

Finally, situation analysis and final considerations were performed based on the reflection of the author and the research conducted in the database.

4. CASE PRESENTATION

The adopted public policy consists of the selection and support of the development and testing of digital transformation solutions proposed by startups. This is a pioneering initiative in Brazil, which was carried out through a public notice that also involved large companies that acted in the specification and validation of the requirements of the proposals presented by the startups and supported the performance of the proofs of concept of the generated prototypes.

4.1 The Municipality of Salvador

Salvador, which was founded in 1549, is the first capital of Brazil and was intended to be the Iberian administrative center in America and the South Atlantic. The city was born cosmopolitan and destined to be a national and international reference. Its first name was São Salvador da Bahia de Todos os Santos. Currently, it is the fourth largest Brazilian state capital and is a rising metropolis, where modernity and avant-garde are combined with history, creativity, and diversity.

According to the Strategic Planning of Salvador from 2017 to 2020, Salvador has an economy concentrated in a few sectors, such as public administration, trade, administrative activities, and construction, which are responsible for 60% of jobs and 65% of the wage bill. This reality is not new; the Salvador's GDP performance in 2016 was BRL 61 billion, which is ranked in 9th place among the capitals, while the GDP per capita, which is BRL 20.6 thousand/year, was the lowest among the 10 largest Brazilian capitals.

Considering the interest of the Salvador City Hall (PMS, for its acronym in Portuguese) in innovative technological solutions developed by startups to contribute to the economic and social development of the city and to the development of new tools and technologies that improve the provision of public services to promote transparency and expand social participation, the City Hall designated the Municipal Secretariat of Sustainability, Innovation and Resilience (SECIS, for its acronym in Portuguese) as responsible for the execution and coordination of the agreement with the National Service for Industrial Training of Bahia state (SENAI/DR/BA, for its acronym in Portuguese).

The SECIS, an organ of the PMS organizational structure, aims to formulate, plan, coordinate, execute, monitor and evaluate the municipal policy of sustainable development, promote innovation in the city, execute studies and plans for environmental promotion, and formulate and implement a resilience strategy.

In the organizational structure of SECIS, there is an Innovation Directorate with the function of planning, guiding, and managing the activities focused on innovation in the city of Salvador, as well as promoting the entrepreneurial culture in the municipality. The SECIS innovation director had the responsibility of supervising and managing the execution of the agreement, along with the manager of technology and innovation of SENAI CIMATEC.

4.2 The SENAI CIMATEC unit

SENAI - was created by Decree-Law No. 4.048 of January 22, 1942, and its Rules of Procedure was approved by Decree-Law No. 494 of January 1, 1962 and updated by Decree-Law No 6635 of November

05, 2008. The Bahia Regional Department was established on April 1st, 1945 and amended provisions of the regulation by Decree-Law No. 6635 of November 5, 2008.

SENAI is a Brazilian nonprofit, private institution of public interest with legal personality under private law and is outside the public administration. It was named by the United Nations (UN), in 2014, as one of the main educational institutions of the Southern Hemisphere. It makes up the so called Third Sector.

In Brazil, there are approximately 1022 SENAI units, of which 518 are fixed units and 504 are mobile units. Of these 28 units are registered as the Executing Operational Unit in the Innovation Notice.

The mission of SENAI-BA is to promote professional and technological education, innovation, and the transfer of industrial technologies, which contributes to increasing the competitiveness of the industry in Bahia. Among its areas of expertise are vocational and higher education, the provision of technical and technological services, consulting, applied research and innovation.

SENAI-BA has 21 units, and SENAI CIMATEC is the only unit with the competence to execute the Innovation Notice in Bahia. The SENAI CIMATEC is linked to the National SENAI, the educational branch of the National Industry Confederation System (CNI, for its acronym in Portuguese). In Bahia, it is part of the Bahia State Industries Federation System (FIEB, for its acronym in Portuguese).

SENAI CIMATEC is a nonprofit STI private entity which, in a few years of existence, has occupied a prominent place in its different areas of activity, and contributes to scientific and technological production and innovation in Brazil. It has one of the most advanced centers of education, technology, and innovation in the country, and integrates a university center, a technological center, and a technical school, thus becoming the largest technological center of the North-Northeast.

In 2011, SENAI CIMATEC was indicated as one of the three institutions in the operation of the pilot project of the EMBRAPII Program in the areas of Integrated Manufacturing and Automation. EMBRAPII was created to support technological development projects with companies in the industrial sector to enhance their competitive strength.

The SENAI CIMATEC has the first accelerator in Bahia accredited by the Start-up Brazil Program of the MCTI and offers training and support to entrepreneurs for the development and generation of high-impact businesses.

4.3 The first municipal initiative linked to the Industrial Innovation Notice

With the agreement signed between the PMS and the SENAI/DR/BA in 2017, it was possible to carry out the first municipal initiative linked to the Notice of Industry Innovation. The City Hall made a financial contribution of BRL 1,000,000.00 (one million Brazilian reais) as scholarship for entrepreneurs and staff, and the institutions promoting the call for tenders (SENAI, SEBRAE, and SESI) made the economic counterpart of BRL 2,000,000.00 (two million Brazilian reais).

According to the Notice of the 2017 Industry Innovation, for each BRL 1 (one) invested by the City Hall, the SENAI, SEBRAE and SESI complemented with BRL 2 (two) for projects supported with a value of up to BRL 150,000.00 (one hundred and fifty thousand Brazilian reais).

The resources provided by SENAI, SEBRAE and SESI are economical and nonrefundable and are intended for the developmental phase of the projects. It primarily covers technical hours, raw materials, and inputs, whereas the resources provided by the PMS are financial but also of nonrefundable nature. The rules for the use of economic resources are described in the Notice of 2017 Industry Innovation, and the rules for financial resources are defined by the City Hall in the proposal of the thematic notice.

According to the Notice of 2017, the economic resources will be made available in the form of technical hours of specialists and use of infrastructure (machine hours, existing facilities) of SENAI CIMATEC.

According to the calls, the financial resources from the PMS will be allocated to the selected projects through grants up to BRL 50,000.00.

To develop the activities foreseen in the so-called thematic, each startup receives an investment of up to BRL 150 thousand through grants, technological services, and infrastructure necessary for the development of the projects. With the Notice, two very important things happen for the movement of the innovation ecosystem in Salvador: first, there is a contribution to economic development by stimulating the creation of new companies (startups) with challenging technological solutions and with great potential for innovation. growth. Then, there is helping to develop innovative solutions to problems of public interest, such as the digital transformation of processes.

The City Hall, framed as an anchor institution of the Industrial Innovation Notice, made three thematic calls in partnership with three large companies: i) smart city, in partnership with the Electronic Governance Company of Salvador (COGEL, for its acronym in Portuguese), ii) resilient city, in partnership with Resource IT Solutions, iii) sustainable city, in partnership with Civil Construction. The resources of the Industrial Innovation Call can only be accessed through the formalization of a thematic call proposal made by an industrial activity company (CNAE industrial primary).

Table 1. Calls, Period and Number of selected startups

THEMATIC CALL	PERIOD	SELECTED STARTUPS
SMART CITY	Jan/18 to Jan/19	10
RESILIENT CITY	Jul/18 to Jun/19	5
SUSTAINABLE CITY	Nov/18 to Oct/19	5
TOTAL		20

Source: prepared by the author, according to the technical report of the thematic calls made between 2017 and 2019 by SENAI CIMATEC (2020)

The agreement made it possible to contract 20 (twenty) innovative projects for the city and for the citizen. Most of the startups selected by the Notice presented digital technological solutions with great potential for scalability and market acceptance, which drew the attention of society. The selected startups went through an acceleration process of 12 (twelve) in the accelerator of SENAI CIMATEC, called Acelera Cimatec (Accelerates Cimatec).

The City Hall, as an anchor institution, had some obligations: (i) to present proposals for the thematic calls to be launched in the Public Notice, according to the guidelines contained in the website http://www.editaldeinovacao.com.br; (ii) articulate and detail the specific rules for the thematic call to be proposed together with SENAI CIMATEC (accredited Operational Unit); (iii) make financial resources available; participate and monitor the implementation of projects approved in the context of the thematic call; (iv) comply with the supply agreements that can be signed with the companies within the scope of the Category C thematic calls, which refer to the products/processes resulting from the approved projects; (v) provide access to a relevant testing environment.

The responsibilities of SENAI CIMATEC as the Operational Unit of the Industry Innovation Notice are as follows: (i) implement the object of the Agreement; (ii) submit the selected projects in the thematic calls to the Industry Innovation Notice through the platform http://www.editaldeinovacao.com.br; (iii) perform the activities under its responsibility, ensuring the good quality of the activities and services provided, seeking to achieve efficiency, effectiveness, and economy in its activities and according the principles that govern Public Administration; (iv) mandatorily invest the funds of the agreement in federal public financial institutions and, when not used, in savings accounts of an official financial institution if their use is expected to be in one month or more than one month; (v) general management of the approved projects in which it is involved; (vi) contribution of economic and financial compensation; (vii) accountability to SENAI-DN and all those involved in the project, in addition to being the provider of information about the project; (viii) transfer of financial resources for the approved projects, if there is (ix) acceleration of the approved projects.

The medium or large company (call demand) defined for each thematic call had an obligation: to provide at least one (01) technical person responsible for monitoring and participating in the technological development to be performed by SENAI CIMATEC. The startups also had obligation of a minimum financial counterpart of BRL 15,000.00 (fifteen thousand reais), which is 10% of the value of the financial support.

The economic and financial counterparts must be proven by means of invoices and payment receipts, according to the items presented in Appendix 10 of the Regulation of the Industry Innovation Notice of 2017.

The definitions of intellectual property, participation and use rights were described in the Thematic Calls. For the purposes of understanding intellectual property and participation rules, the following was defined:

- Project: joint development process between Startup, SENAI CIMATEC, Municipality of Salvador, and the Large Company (requesting the call).
- Product: technology developed by Startup obtained before the start of the project.
- Final Product: technology developed through the project.
- Solution: developed technology containing the Final Product and the product (if any) that will be the object of commercialization and economic exploitation of the parties.

According to the definitions above, the intellectual property and participation rules are:
For the SENAI CIMATEC:

- Coownership of up to 20% of the Intellectual Property of the Final Product agreed upon by evaluating the maturity of the Product (if any) and the technological contributions necessary for the development of the Final Product
- *Royalties* of 1% on the gross revenue from the commercialization of the Solution, for a period of five (05) years, counted from the first year after the completion of the Project.

For the municipality of Salvador:

- Right of use without cost, without exclusivity, free of *royalties*, for a period of up to five (05) years since the Solution.

For large companies (requesting the call):

- Right of use without cost, without exclusivity, free of *royalties*, for a period of up to five (05) years since the Solution.

The thematic calls allowed us to bring together startups, large companies, public managers, and a state-of-the-art technology center (SENAI CIMATEC) to solve relevant problems that are common to large Brazilian cities and, at the same time, have the potential to generate future companies.

The acceleration methodology for the business development of SENAI CIMATEC is formed by three (03) stages, called "tranche". At the end of each tranche, the companies present the evolution of the business up to that moment to a multidisciplinary board, where they must show all committed deliveries.

The activities of each tranche are divided as follows:

1st TRANCHE: Information alignment and survey; immersion in the problem; business modeling; and planning of prototype construction;

2nd TRANCHE: Development of the prototype (MVP[1]) and refinement of the business model; development of the test plan.

3rd TRANCHE: Conducting tests and refining the feasibility study (business case); Consolidation of learning.

During the execution of the acceleration process, the projects were periodically evaluated by the SENAI CIMATEC team, the City Hall, and the company requesting the call. The projects only advanced upon a positive opinion on the performance presented in the boards held at the end of each tranche. The financial resource was only made available through the advance of the projects in the challenge phases.

Of the twenty startups selected by the three calls, two (02) patents were requested, eight (08) products launched to the market and three (03) did not complete the acceleration process: one in the so-called sustainable city, which did not even sign the cooperation agreement, and two in the so-called smart city, which had their contracts terminated.

This initiative to launch thematic calls by the Industrial Innovation Notice has a relevant role in the innovation ecosystem in Salvador. The city invests to attract startups and, at the same time, becomes the laboratory where innovative technological solutions for urban challenges will be developed.

5. ANALYSIS OF THE PROBLEM-SITUATION AND PROPOSAL

According to the researchers and scholars cited in the literature review, little is known about the innovation process in the public sector. Many studies must still be done to study innovation and develop a framework for the collection of innovation data in the public sector. Several important questions about the measurement of innovation, especially about the impact or effects of innovations in the public sector, remain unanswered.

Currently, it is understood that the private sector already adopts innovative practices and processes but, in public administration, it is a relatively new topic that needs to advance substantially.

In public administration, the need for innovation is more latent in the municipal instance. Most people (84.72%)[2] live in the urban areas of the municipality and, according to the Federal Constitution, municipal management has the role of providing social welfare to the citizen. Constitutional Amendment No. 85/2015 assigned the municipality the responsibility of promoting and encouraging scientific development, research, scientific and technological training, and innovation.

The monitoring and evaluation of the application of the Industry Innovation Notice of 2017 in partnership with the PMS are essential to guide the application of new thematic calls and ensure its effectiveness. It is natural that, at the beginning of the agreement signed between PMS and SENAI/DR/BA, problems arise from the learning process. An identification of the deficiencies that emerged deserves attention from both institutions, allowing them to take measures that enable the improvement and maturation of internal processes and procedures.

The study conducted by CGEE & ANPEI (2009) mentions that the interviewed companies questioned whether the areas and themes chosen in the economic grant notices reflect strategic options of the federal government. In this sense, this criticism is void for the application of the Industry Innovation Notice in the case study of the PMS because the themes of the thematic calls were in agreement with the municipal public policies, and even enabled environments for public and private tests.

The problem of the low level of professionalization and formalization of innovation management, identified by the authors CGEE & ANPEI (2009) during the interviews, was minimized by the team of technicians of SENAI CIMATEC during the acceleration process, and guided how to manage resources and train them in accountability. SENAI CIMATEC tried its best to provide a set of important information so that the startup can make the most appropriate decision for the technological development of the selected projects.

The same authors of the study claim that the performance of funding institutions can be characterized as passive, as both are limited to making an initial evaluation of the proposals submitted by the companies, performing the procedures provided for in the Notice for hiring those selected and formally following up the execution of projects and accountability (CGEE & ANPEI, 2009). This situation did not occur in the application of the Industry Innovation Notice by the PMS and SENAI CIMATEC because the startups had weekly monitoring of their activities by the SENAI CIMATEC and monthly monitoring by the City Hall. The startups presented their difficulties, and the entities linked to each thematic call gave great support in the search for solutions.

The criticism of public calls for tenders that a single project or activity can be financed more than once by different economic subsidy instruments presented by Costa, Szapiro and Cassiolato (2013) was resolved in the 2017 Industry Innovation Notice. According to the Notice, one cannot support projects of a company whose scope and objectives are similar to those of other projects already executed or under execution by this company in other lines of support and/or promotion of innovation projects.

The traditional format of economic grant notices aims to directly finance companies without integration with academia or with the government itself, that is, the "triple helix" does not occur. The thematic calls of the PMS, through the Industry Innovation Notice, allowed this integration (municipal government, companies, and academia). The triple helix builds a true innovation ecosystem and takes the model of interaction between the actors a step further, towards new innovation strategies and practices resulting from this cooperation (ETZKOWITZ, & ZHOU, 2017). It can be stated that one of the strengths of the PMS thematic calls was the construction of the "triple helix".

5.1 Main Lessons Learned and Proposals

5.1.1 Delimitation of Call Topics

The three thematic calls (smart city, resilient city, and sustainable city) adopted a strategy to define a central theme, divided into lines of interest. It is observed that, despite evidence regarding the lessons learned in the formulation of the themes throughout the three calls, the strategy adopted to delimit the themes and show them to potential startups presents opportunities for improvement. The thematic calls were based on indicating topics that illustrate solutions desired by the City Hall within broad fields. It is observed that this alternative can result in a directional bias that restricts the set of solutions presented and generate a certain induction of the creative process.

Thus, adopting the strategy of establishing themes based on the problems faced by the City Hall or by society, in contrast to the indications of possible solutions, can result in unexpected projects and better results.

It is observed that the thematic calls promoted by the City Hall had a ratio of 7.7 projects received for each vacancy, against 18.2 projects received from other similar calls promoted by SENAI CIMATEC in the same period in partnership with other companies, as illustrated in Figure 01.

Figure 1. Ratio of the number of projects x number of vacancies per thematic call
Source: prepared by the author, according to the technical report of the thematic calls made between 2017 and 2019 by SENAI CIMATEC (2020)

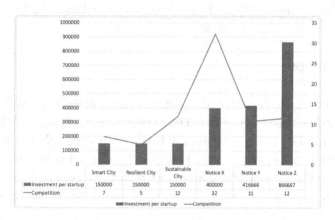

It is inferred that, with an approach based on the presentation of problems, it is possible to attract more and better qualified candidates, which tends to result in better options.

As the effort to survey and describe the problems to be solved requires greater dedication from the technicians and managers involved and greater effort of disclosure, one should evaluate and restrict future calls to a maximum of five well-characterized challenges.

Additionally, it is recommended that the test environments and the departments or public agencies that will be customers of the solutions be defined in advance, serving to illustrate the opportunity to potential stakeholders. The existence of a person who acts as a representative of the needs of the solution customer, and a focal point to direct the startup about what needs to be done, what is a priority and what should be left aside, can serve to optimize the development time, avoid reworking, and make it more aligned with the demands.

5.1.2 Project Selection Strategy

For each thematic call (smart city, resilient city, and sustainable city), a different strategy for selecting the projects to be supported was adopted. The learning curve for the selection process was very good. In the first call (smart city), the selection method was through the evaluation and analysis of the Business Model Canvas (BMC)[3], the registration form and a pitch[4] in video for each submitted project. In the second call, an interview (in person or online) with some preselected projects was included to remove some doubts that remained after analysis of the BMC, registration form, and pitch, which allowed us to better understand the team responsible for the submitted project. In the third call, this selection process was further improved by inviting the semifinalists to participate in a one-day workshop at SENAI CI-MATEC to inform the person responsible for the project how the entire acceleration process will take place and what the obligations and rights that they will have after signing the acceleration contract; after the workshop they made a pitch for a panel of evaluators, with the intention of the panel selecting the startups that will be accelerated for 12 months.

The submitted projects were scored according to the criteria described in the thematic calls (capacity, adherence, relevance, team, innovation, market) and presented on the platform of the Industry Innovation Notice. The assignment of scores on the platform helps in structuring the evaluation on a more objective and transparent basis. However, the interlocutions of the results of these evaluations received criticism for not efficiently and clearly translating feedback to the unselected startups. Therefore, this point needs to be evaluated and improved to make new calls.

5.1.3 Maturity of Startups

Approximately 68% (sixty-eight percent) of the startups selected in the PMS calls did not have a preliminary prototype that could be tested or that could be improved and subsequently tested. Comparatively, other similar calls promoted by other companies in partnership with SENAI CIMATEC selected 89% of the projects that already had prototypes that needed to be adapted to the intended applications. It is concluded, therefore, that this is a point to be evaluated, which contrasts with the investments necessary for startups with or without prototypes and a possible increase in the chances of success.

5.1.4 Investments

In the first calls, the investment made by the PMS and the Industry Innovation Notice was 74% lower than the average of other similar calls - BRL 150 thousand, on average in calls from the City Hall, against BRL 561,110.00 of the other three calls made by SENAI CIMATEC in the same period. Thus, the restriction of resources, added to the low maturity of the projects, may explain the number of projects that failed to obtain conclusive tests on their adequacy by the City Hall and other partners involved.

However, it is understood that the proposal of the PMS to reach a greater number of supported startups was assertive, since the innovation ecosystem of Salvador in 2017 was still nascent, there were few active startups, and few of them exceeded the level of ideation and validation (PRADO, et al., 2020).

It is believed that the thematic calls of the City Hall contributed to the strengthening of the local ecosystem and to the increase in the number of startups in Salvador, which went from 110 to 198 startups between 2017 and 2019.

According to data from the Brazilian Association of Startups (ABStartups, for its acronym in Portuguese), in 2019, Salvador became the first city in the Brazilian North-Northeast and the eighth in Brazil with the largest number of startups in operation. In 2017, Salvador was 18th in the national ranking, behind Manaus, Recife, and Fortaleza.

6. RESULTS OBTAINED

From the observed results and the evolution of entrepreneurship indicators of the city, it is inferred that, in addition to the effective generation of digital solutions for historical urban problems, the Notice contributed positively to stimulating the creation of innovative startups in the city of Salvador.

The results obtained in the public-private partnership, through the Industry Innovation Notice, were significantly satisfactory. However, it could be seen that the process of improving the application of the Notice to support innovation is complex and subject to risks. When promoting innovation-driven growth, it is essential to understand the importance of the roles of the public and private sectors and understand the value of each actor and what this can contribute to the local innovation ecosystem.

It is known that the investments made by the City Hall should be justified by some logic, so a way to measure the economic and social returns from financing for the development of innovative projects by startups is suggested for the next agreements. The indicators of job creation, increase in tax revenue and better quality of life for citizens are difficult to measure because the projects selected for the acceleration process in this case study were in the ideation phase or in the construction of the prototype. Perhaps if they were already in the operation or traction phase, these indicators could have been measured.

According to Hansen and Birkinshaw (2007), to identify the possible bottlenecks that exist in the complex web of innovation, it is essential to monitor the performance of the entire innovation value chain. For Adams (2006), innovation should be monitored from the point of view of process management, not only with metrics focused on its final results.

Entrepreneurship and innovation are considered global phenomena resulting from profound changes in international relations between nations and companies (MUNIZ, 2008). Innovation introduces uncertainty regarding the results and low integration among departments, and almost always become incompatible with the structures and bodies of the Brazilian public administration (BRANDÃO, & BRUNO-FARIA, 2017). In addition, innovation in public management produces time-consuming effects over time, and they are not always perceptible or measurable in a clear, comprehensive, and immediate manner.

The application of the Industry Innovation Notice by the PMS in partnership with SENAI CIMATEC achieved some indirect benefits, such as (i) encouraged scientific development, research, scientific and technological training, and innovation in compliance with Article 218 of the Federal Constitution; (ii) mobilized some public and private institutions, strengthening the innovation ecosystem of Salvador; (iii) trained the technicians of the City Hall in the activity of fostering innovation, through expertise in accelerating start-ups of the SENAI CIMATEC; and (iv) trained potential entrepreneurs.

The direct benefit would be the use of the products developed in the acceleration program, at no cost, within five years, but no solution was used by the PMS.

The implemented actions were able to bring together startups, large companies, a city hall, and an important representative of the academia. A public-private partnership is characterized through the Industry Innovation Notice with significantly satisfactory results.

7. CONCLUSION

In Brazil, the economic subsidy modality is one of the most common forms of innovation funding established by the Innovation Law (Federal Law no. 10.973/2004). The economic subsidy program of the federal government began to be operated in 2006 through public calls for tenders. The funds for the Program operated by the Financiadora de Estudo e Projetos (Study and Project Financing Agency, FINEP) come from the Fundo Nacional de Desenvolvimento Científico e Tecnológico (National Fund for Scientific and Technological Development, FNDCT) (COSTA; SZAPIRO, & CASSIOLATO, 2013).

Additionally, the partnership agreement, which is provided in Article 9 of the Innovation Law, is a legal instrument that allows the joining of efforts of the Institutions of Scientific and Technological Research (STR), with public institutions and private companies to perform activities that seek the development of technology, product, or process. This agreement allows a partnership between the university, private companies, and the government, a "triple helix", without creating a legal entity of its own, to promote the development of technological innovation (BARBOSA, 2011)

According to Andrade (2009), the economic subsidy may represent one of the most powerful instruments to induce the innovation process in companies and, at the same time, serve public interests. This is because, through public policy decisions, themes can be selected for the projects to be promoted that have high technological content to be researched and developed or of high interest to the country. The same does not occur with the other public modalities of support for innovation: credit repayable at favorable interest rates; tax incentives for Research and Development (R&D), and risk capital through equity holdings through venture capital funds (IPEA, 2012).

This paper analyzes a case of public policy established by the Municipality of Salvador in 2017, which was able to integrate resources and knowledge of STI, large companies, and startups by using a private instrument of public interest – the Industry Innovation Notice.

The policy consists of selecting and supporting the development and testing of digital transformation solutions proposed by startups. This is a pioneering initiative in Brazil, carried out through a public notice that also involved large companies that acted in the specification and validation of the requirements of the proposals presented by the startups; they also support the performance of proofs of concept of the prototypes generated. The STI played the role of supporting the validation and refinement of proposals, planning, execution of technological development actions and tests in relevant environments, as well as business modeling and its acceleration process.

The actions were implemented in the city of Salvador, which was the first capital of Brazil. It was founded in 1549 with the objective of being the Iberian administrative center in America and the South Atlantic. Currently, it has the fourth largest population in the country, where problems common to large metropolises coexist - such as those related to health, education, mobility, safety, citizenship, and environmental aspects - with cultural traits characteristic of a diverse environment, population with a high degree of miscegenation, historical richness, cultural and artistic identity, and creativity recognized worldwide.

The City Hall invested approximately BRL 1 million for the development of the activities, which was contributed through research grants totaling up to BRL 150 thousand per project, in addition to a complementary investment of BRL 2 million, which was made possible by the Industry Innovation Notice through resources from SENAI and SEBRAE and aimed at providing technological services and infrastructure necessary for the development of projects.

Three public calls were made for the selection of projects involving digital technologies and related to themes of smart cities, sustainable cities, and resilient cities. Innovative projects proposed by 20 (twenty) startups were selected, which also involved 3 large companies that acted as applicants. Finally, two patents and eight products launched on the market were requested.

From the observed results and the evolution of entrepreneurship indicators of the city, it is inferred that, in addition to the effective generation of digital solutions for historical urban problems, the Notice contributed positively to stimulating the creation of innovative startups in the city of Salvador. According to ABSTARTUPS, the city reached the first position among the capitals of the northeast region in 2019. Additionally, it is possible to note that the actions generated other impacts, among which the following stand out: (i) encouraged scientific development, research, scientific and technological training, and innovation; (ii) mobilized some public and private institutions, which strengthened the innovation ecosystem of Salvador; (iii) trained the technicians of the City Hall in the activity of fostering innovation; and (iv) trained potential entrepreneurs.

The implemented actions were able to bring together startups, large companies, a city hall, and an important academic representative. A public-private partnership is characterized through the Industry Innovation Notice with significantly satisfactory results.

Given the evaluations performed, it is also possible to point out opportunities for improvement of the mechanics and practices adopted. Although complex due to its nature, the opportunity to improve the practices of evaluating the impact of the implemented policy and the investments made stands out. As postulated by Hansen and Birkinshaw (2007), to identify the possible bottlenecks that exist in the complex web of innovation, it is essential to monitor the performance of the entire innovation value chain. For future initiatives, inspired by Adams (2006), it is recommended to monitor innovation from the point of view of process management, not only with metrics focused on its final results.

In turn, it must be recognized that entrepreneurship and innovation are considered global phenomena due to profound changes in international relations between nations and companies (MUNIZ, 2008). Innovation introduces uncertainty regarding the results and low integration among departments, and almost always becomes incompatible with the structures and bodies of the Brazilian public administration (BRANDÃO, & BRUNO-FARIA, 2017). In addition, innovation in public management produces time-consuming effects over time, and they are not always perceptible or measurable in a clear, comprehensive, and immediate manner.

The legal framework and public policies related to technology and innovation in Brazil are relatively recent and are in the process of maturing when compared to other developing countries. Innovation should enter the usual public administrative activity and be a way to promote more effective and efficient public policies. The aim of the present study is to contribute to systematizing the learning results of the analyzed practice and to guide new forms of stimulating entrepreneurship and digitization as alternatives to economic, social and environmental development.

As postulated in the literature, it is concluded that the economic subsidy instrument is recent and lacks specific studies, still raises doubts and debates regarding its proper use and results (BORGES, & HOFFMAN, 2017). In the practical case, however, the PMS used innovative policies and instruments, but similarly to the postulates of the Triple Helix (ETZKOWITZ, & LEYDESDORFF, 1996), a fact that characterizes a public policy that stimulates entrepreneurship and unique innovation among Brazilian municipalities by promoting digital transformation and involving a rich ecosystem formed by STI, large companies, startups, and public initiative.

The legal framework and public policies related to technology and innovation in Brazil are relatively recent and are in the process of maturing when compared to other developing countries.

Innovation should enter into the usual administrative activity and not be seen as a purpose of niche or specific sectors of public administration. Innovation in government can be a way to promote more effective and efficient public policies.

This study sought to present important information to support the proposition of actions aimed at improving this innovation support instrument, the Industry Innovation Notice, Category C. The intention was to contribute to SENAI by promoting the use of this instrument to foster innovation in Brazil.

It is hoped that the results obtained, along with future studies, will contribute to systematizing the learning results of the analyzed practice and guide new forms of stimulating entrepreneurship and innovation as alternatives to economic, social and environmental development.

REFERENCES

ABStartups. (2019). https://startupbase.com.br/c/community/all-saints-bay

Adams, R., Bessant, J., & Phelps, R. (2006). Innovation management measurement: A review. *International Journal of Management Reviews*, *8*(1), 21–47. doi:10.1111/j.1468-2370.2006.00119.x

Andrade, A. Z. B. (2009). *Estudo comparativo entre a Subvenção Econômica à Inovação operada pela FINEP e Programas correlatos de subsídio em países desenvolvidos* (Dissertação de Mestrado em Administração Pública). Escola Brasileira de Administração Pública e de Empresas da Fundação Getúlio Vargas, Rio de janeiro.

Bahia, D. S. (2019). *Pesquisa e desenvolvimento, capital de conhecimento e estrutura produtiva: Os efeitos do Programa de Subvenções Econômicas à inovação no Brasil (Tese de Doutorado em Economia)*. Universidade Federal de Juiz de Fora.

Baldwin, J., & Gellatly, G. (2003). *Innovation strategies and performance in small firms*. E. Elgar. doi:10.4337/9781781009703

Barbosa, D. B. (2011). O direito da inovação (2nd ed.). Rio de Janeiro: Lúmen Júris.

Blank, S., & Dorf, B. (2012). *The Startup Owner's Manual: The Step-By-Step Guide for Building a Great Company*. K & S Ranch.

Borges, D. B. (2015). *A subvenção econômica como instrumento de fomento à cooperação tecnológica: uma análise sob a perspectiva do setor empresarial* (Dissertação de Mestrado em Ciências da Administração) Universidade do Estado de Santa Catarina, Florianópolis.

Borges, D. B., & Hoffman, M. G. (2017). A subvenção econômica como instrumento de fomento à inovação: Análise sob a perspectiva de empresas de TIC da Grande Florianópolis. *Revista Brasileira de Gestão e Inovação*, *5*(1), 50–73. doi:10.18226/23190639.v5n1.03

Brandão, S. M., & Bruno-Faria, M. F. (2013). Inovação no setor público: análise de produção científica em periódicos nacionais e internacionais da área de administração. *Revista de Administração Pública*, *47*(1), 227-248.

Brandão, S. M., & Bruno-Faria, M. F. (2017). Barreiras à inovação em gestão em organizações públicas do governo federal brasileiro: análise da percepção de dirigentes. In *Inovação no setor público: teoria, tendências e casos no Brasil* (pp. 145–164). Enap/Ipea.

Brasil. (1942). *Decreto-Lei nº 4.048, de 22 de janeiro de 1942*. Cria o Serviço Nacional de Aprendizagem dos Industriários (SENAI). https://www2.camara.leg.br/legin/fed/declei/1940-1949/decreto-lei-4048-22-janeiro-1942-414390-publicacaooriginal-1-pe.html

Brasil. (2008). *Decreto nº 6.635, de 5 de novembro de 2008*. Altera e acresce dispositivos ao Regimento do Serviço Nacional de Aprendizagem Industrial - SENAI, aprovado pelo Decreto no 494, de 10 de janeiro de 1962. http://www.planalto.gov.br/ccivil_03/_Ato2007-2010/2008/Decreto/D6635.htm

Brasil. (2009). *Decreto nº 6.938, de 13 de agosto de 2009*. Aprova a Estrutura Regimental e o Quadro Demonstrativo dos Cargos em Comissão e das Funções de Confiança do Ministério da Ciência, Tecnologia, Inovações e Comunicações, remaneja cargos em comissão e funções de confiança, transforma cargos em comissão do Grupo-Direção e Assessoramento Superiores - DAS e substitui cargos em comissão do Grupo-Direção e Assessoramento Superiores - DAS por Funções Comissionadas do Poder Executivo - FCPE. http://www.planalto.gov.br/ccivil_03/_Ato2019-2022/2019/Decreto/D9677.htm#art9

Brasil. (2018). *Decreto nº 9.282, de 07 de fevereiro de 2018*. Altera o Decreto nº 8.889, de 26 de outubro de 2016, que aprova a Estrutura Regimental e o Quadro Demonstrativo dos Cargos em Comissão e das Funções de Confiança da Casa Civil da Presidência da República, e o Decreto nº 8.955, de 11 de janeiro de 2017, que aprova a Estrutura Regimental e o Quadro Demonstrativo dos Cargos em Comissão e das Funções de Confiança do Instituto Nacional de Colonização e Reforma Agrária - INCRA, e remaneja cargos em comissão e funções de confiança. http://www.planalto.gov.br/CCIVIL_03/_Ato2015-2018/2018/Decreto/D9282.htm

Cavalcante, P., & Camões, M. R. S. (2017). *Public Innovation in Brazil: an overview of its types, results and drivers*. Ipea.

Cavalcante, P., & Cunha, B. Q. (2017). É preciso inovar no governo, mas por quê? In *Cavalcante, P. et al. (Orgs.). Inovação no setor público: teoria, tendências e casos no Brasil* (pp. 15–32). Enap/Ipea.

CGEE. (2009). Os novos instrumentos de apoio à inovação: uma avaliação inicial. Brasília: Autores.

Costa, A. C., Szapiro, M., & Cassiolato, J. E. (2013). Análise da operação do instrumento de subvenção econômica à inovação no Brasil. Conferência Internacional LALICS.

Cunha, B. Q. (2017). Uma análise da construção da agenda de inovação no setor público a partir de experiências internacionais precursoras. In *Inovação no setor público: teoria, tendências e casos no Brasil*. Enap/Ipea.

Cunha, M. A., Przeybilovicz, E., Macaya, J. F. M., & Burgos, F. (2016). *Smart cities: Transformação Digital de cidades* (Vol. 16). Centro de Estudos em Administração Pública e Governo - CEAPG. doi:10.1016/S0264-2751(98)00050-X

Etzkowitz, H., & Leydesdorff, L. (1996). The Triple Helix: University, Industry, Government Relations: A Laboratory for Knowledge Based Economic Development. The Triple Helix of University, Industry, and Government Relations: The Future Location of Research Conference.

Etzkowitz, H., & Zhou, C. (2017). Hélice Tríplice: Inovação e empreendedorismo universidade-indústria-governo. *Estudos Avançados*, *31*(90), 23–48. doi:10.15900103-40142017.3190003

FINEP - Financiadora de Estudos e Projetos. (2010). *Manual do Programa de Subvenção Econômica à Inovação Nacional*. Academic Press.

Hansen, M. T., & Birkinshaw, J. (2007). The innovation value-chain. *Harvard Business Review*, *85*(6), 121–130. PMID:17580654

IPEA. (2012). A Subvenção Econômica cumpre a função de estímulo à inovação e ao aumento da competitividade das empresas brasileiras? In Brasil em Desenvolvimento 2011: Estado, Planejamento e Políticas Públicas (Vol. 2). IPEA.

IPEA. (2018). Avaliação de políticas públicas: guia prático de análise ex ante. Casa Civil da Presidência da República, Instituto de Pesquisa Econômica Aplicada. IPEA: Brasília.

Lima, T. C. S., & Mioto, R. C. T. (2007). Procedimentos metodológicos na construção do conhecimento científico: A pesquisa bibliográfica. *Revista Katálysis*, *10*(spe), 35–45. doi:10.1590/S1414-49802007000300004

Maçaneiro, M. B., & Cherobim, A. P. M. S. (2011). Fontes de financiamento à inovação: Incentivos e óbices às micro e pequenas empresas – estudo de casos múltiplos no Estado do Paraná. *Organizações & Sociedade*, *18*(56), 57–75. doi:10.1590/S1984-92302011000100003

Muniz, C. N. S. M. (2018). *Atitude Empreendedora e suas dimensões: Um estudo em micro e pequenas empresas* (Dissertação de Mestrado em Administração). Universidade de Brasília. Brasília.

National Institute of Standards and Technology. Technology Innovation Program. (2010). A Guide for Preparing and Submitting White Papers to the Technology Innovation Program. U.S. Department of Commerce.

OCDE – Organização para Cooperação e Desenvolvimento Econômico; Eurostat – Gabinete de Estatísticas da União Europeia. (2006). *Manual de Oslo*: *Diretrizes para coleta e interpretação de dados sobre inovação*. Publicado pela FINEP (Financiadora de Estudos e Projetos), 3ª Edição.

Oliveira, L. F., & Junior, C. D. S. (2017). Inovações no setor público: uma abordagem teórica sobre os impactos de sua adoção. In *Inovação no setor público: teoria, tendências e casos no Brasil* (pp. 33–42). Enap/Ipea.

Pinto, F. M. S. (2017). *A construção de um modelo de acompanhamento da evolução de startups digitais em contexto de aceleração: o caso Start-Up Brasil* (Dissertação de Mestrado em Economia, Administração e Contabilidade). Universidade de São Paulo, São Paulo.

Planejamento Estratégico de Salvador. Período de 2017 a 2020. (2019). http://www.salvador.ba.gov.br/images/PDF/arquivo_planejamento.pdf

Prado, V. J., Bezerra, K. D. R., Esteves, E. S. J., & Souza, L. N. (2020). O ecossistema de inovação da cidade de Salvador: Um diagnóstico do nível de maturidade. *Research. Social Development, 9*(3), 51–66.

Ries, E. (2011). *The Lean Startup: how today's entrepreneurs use continuous innovation to create radically successful businesses* (1st ed.). Crown Publishing.

Rogers, D. (2017). *Transformação Digital: Repensando o seu negócio para a era digital*. Autêntica Business.

Roncaratti, L. S. (2017). Incentivos a startups no brasil: os casos do Startup Brasil, InovAtiva e InovApps. In *Inovação no setor público: teoria, tendências e casos no Brasil* (pp. 215–229). Enap/Ipea.

Schumpeter, J. A. (1982). *Teoria do desenvolvimento econômico: uma investigação sobre lucros, capital, crédito, juro e o ciclo econômico*. Nova Cultural.

Senai Cimatec. (2020). *Campus Integrado de Manufatura e Tecnologia do Serviço Nacional de Aprendizagem Industrial*. Relatório técnico das chamadas temáticas entre 2017 e 2019.

Serviço Nacional de Aprendizagem Industrial (SENAI). (2019). *Edital de Inovação da Indústria 2017*. https://docente.ifsc.edu.br/alexandre.zammar/MaterialDidatico/Biotecnologia/edital-de-inovacao-para-a-industria-2017.pdf

Surdak, C. (2018). *A Revolução Digital: Os 12 Segredos Para Prosperar na Era da Tecnologia*. DVS Editora.

Swiatek, D. C. (2019). Inovando na relação da administração pública com Tecnologia: o mobilab e a contratação de startups pela prefeitura de São Paulo. In *Inovação e políticas: superando o mito da ideia* (pp. 296–312). Ipea.

Weiblen, T., & Chesbrough, H. W. (2015). Engaging with Startups to Enhance Corporate Innovation. *California Management Review, 57*(2), 66–90. Advance online publication. doi:10.1525/cmr.2015.57.2.66

Yin, R. K. (2015). *Estudo de caso: Planejamento e métodos* (5th ed.). Bookman.

Zortea, C. G. C., & Maldaner, L. F. (2018). Startups Accelerator Programs: A Comparative Analysis of Acceleration Mechanisms from Start-Up Brazil and Start-Up Chile Program. *Revista Eletrônica de Estratégia & Negócios, 11*(3), 29–53.

KEY TERMS AND DEFINITIONS

Digital Transformation: The digital transformation is the adoption of digital technological tools, which is forcing people to change their lifestyle. It is the virtualization of organizational operations, allowing to streamline processes and maximize results.

Economic Subsidy: The economic subsidy consists of a direct contribution of public resources to companies to carry out innovative projects.

Entrepreneurship: Entrepreneurship is directly associated with innovation. Entrepreneurship means solving problems, developing solutions, and investing resources in creating something new.

Innovation: Innovation is an invention that became a business, generating jobs and income.

Public Innovation Policy: Public innovation policies are governmental actions to promote activities in the area of science, technology and innovation that can result in satisfactory results of growth and development of the country at the federal, state and local levels.

Startup: Startup is a young organization built to find an innovative, scalable, and repeatable business model.

Triple Helix: Triple Helix is an articulation between three social actors—the university, the private sector, and the government—with the aim of generating regional development in the area of innovation.

ENDNOTES

[1]   MVP - Minimum Viable Product is the simplified version of a Final Product.

[2]   National Research by Household Sample (Pesquisa Nacional por Amostra de Domicílios - PNAD) 2015.

[3]   Business Model Canvas (BMC) – is a strategic management tool that allows developing and drafting new or existing business models.

[4]   Pitch – is a fast presentation of a product or business with the intent of "selling" an idea to investors, clients, associates, or partners.

Chapter 18
Preventive Maintenance as a Critical Success Factor in Industry 4.0

Pedro Fernandes da Anunciação

iD https://orcid.org/0000-0001-7116-5249

Instituto Politécnico de Setúbal, Setúbal, Portugal

Vitor Dinis

CIBERSUR, Setúbal, Portugal

Francisco Madeira Esteves

Instituto Politécnico de Setúbal, Setúbal, Portugal

ABSTRACT

In an economy that tends to operate in real time, where companies reduce stocks and value the customization of products and services according to the needs of their customers, information systems and technologies assume a predominant role. Equipment maintenance proves to be critical in supplying markets and meeting consumer needs. Regarding the maintenance of equipment, most managers are faced with the technical indications of suppliers, serving as a reference for the respective interventions. However, these indications often do not contemplate the contingency of certain situations, excessive hours of operation, or temperatures higher than those indicated. Preventive maintenance assumes an important role in the maintenance area by allowing interventions that are more appropriate to the wear and tear of the equipment. The technological potential associated with the internet of things or analytics allows the generation of economic value by guaranteeing the adequate conditions of the equipment and by avoiding disruptions in supply to the markets.

DOI: 10.4018/978-1-7998-4201-9.ch018

Copyright © 2021, IGI Global. Copying or distributing in print or electronic forms without written permission of IGI Global is prohibited.

INTRODUCTION

In this context of industrial development, management and managers are stimulated to read and act in the challenge of digital context. The necessary skills are not only technological but, above all, organizational and management (Anunciação, 2014). Modern societies, although technological, are organizational economies, based on the relationship of activities and sharing resources and knowledge, and where the growth of organizations will be carried out by the quality of management. This quality is the biggest professional challenge in the management field, because the speed of innovation results in a fast rupture with the past, requiring responsiveness, adjustment and development of new management models and tools to provide a reduction in complexity, risk, and instability. Organizations that fail to adapt and manage change will face competitive difficulties in the short term.

Two examples of the relevant technological innovations, looking at the challenges they provide to management and organizations, are Internet-of-Things (IoT) and Artificial Intelligence. Internet of Things (IoT) offers a network of billions of connected digital devices, adopted in homes, cars, clothing, that generate a need of urbanized information systems (Anunciação & Zorrinho, 2006) to support and improve the relationship between economic organizations.

This new digital world don`t require only the connection of a multiplicity of devices and objects that communicate with each other and act according to specific parameters or instructions. But this movement reflect a new economic and social order in which people and organizations develop their activities and their relationships. The digital world needs management.

The multiplicity of electronic devices requires the extension of information systems and technologies and the perception of the sphere of influence of people, through the satisfaction of their needs (personal, professional, economic, and social) wherever they are. The integration of a multiplicity of devices, systems, requirements, activities, processes, users, among other aspects, challenges the aim of architecture. These challenges bring architecture to another level and introduces the concept of urbanism in the domain of economy and society (Anunciação & Zorrinho, 2006) (Anunciação, 2016) (Anunciação, 2015).

The second example is Artificial Intelligence (AI). AI has had, on all sectors, the need for a more aggressive approach concerning digital transformation to compete (Tiersky, 2017). The impacts of AI are not only technological. The effects are mainly sociological since we will face new social and human order and that will correspond to the possibility of human being to rethink himself, and, consequently, the economy and society.

Specially in the scope of industry, we are living the era of «Industry 4.0». This designation was first used in 2011, in the Centrum der Büro und InformationsTechnik, Center for Office and Information Technology (Cebit), the largest information technology trade show in the world targeted to industry professionals, and was referred as one key initiative in the High-Tech Strategy announced by the German federal government in planning perspective to 2020. The following year, the Working Group on Industry 4.0 presented the recommendations for its implementations (Kagermann & Wahlster, 2013) (Kagermann, Wahlster & Helbig, 2013). Since then, Industry 4.0 is a subject of many academic publications, and many conferences have focused on this topic (Drath & Horch, 2014).

As Herman and Pentek state, there are two main reasons for the fascination with Industry 4.0 (Herman, Pentek & Otto, 2016). First, this change can revolutionize the industry, and it can be predicted rather than observed "a posteriori", which gives industry and enterprises the possibility to shape the future actively. Secondly, it is predicted that the economic effect of this change will be huge, by increasing the operational effectiveness and defining new models of business, products and services (Kagermann, Wahlster & Helbig, 2013) (Lasi et al., 2014) (Herman, Pentek & Otto, 2016).

Drawing on the review of academic literature and practical background, the authors Herman, Pentek and Otto identified six design principles for implementing Industry 4.0, that are (Herman, Pentek & Otto, 2015):

- Interoperability – the ability of Cyber-Physical System (CPS), Smart Factory (SM) and Humans to communicate via the Internet of Things (IoT) and the Internet of Services (IoS).
- Virtualization – the creation and support of virtual copies (digital twins) of the Smart Factory and of each Cyber-Physical System by linking the data from monitoring of the physical process with the data in the simulation models.
- Decentralization – the ability of making decisions independently by Cyber-Physical Systems and Smart Factories.
- Real-time capability – the capability of Smart Factory to collect, analyze and provision data in real time.
- Service orientation – Smart Factory and Cyber-Physical Systems services can be offered via the Internet of Services.
- Modularity – the ability of Smart Factory modules to flexibly adapt to changing requirements by replacing or expanding individual modules based on standardized software and hardware interfaces. New modules are identified automatically and can be utilized immediately via the Internet-of-Services.

In this movement, industrial organizations face some problems with the high complexity of market demands and the levels of consumption in the economy. Industrial organizations integrate complex process networks and value chains with countless stakeholders, physical material flows, energy resources and technologies convergence. Through IoT technologies, manufacturers can integrate the demand and supply chains, allow them to engage with end-customers in a unique and unprecedented way.

The core of Industry 4.0 is based on highly intelligent as well as connected systems that create a fully digital value chain. Industry 4.0 is also referred as the Industrial Internet of Things (IIoT) (Haddara & Elragal, 2015) and the great challenge is that the production processes assumes a significant complexity and a reliability in the economic activity to meet growing demand and reflect a strong dependence on technologies with a high criticality of the production systems.

Currently, most industrial companies do not produce for stock but seeks to guarantee an immediate supply to the market. These complexity and criticality are two economic requirements that result from models of society and economy in which markets and consumers condition the production. These are some characteristics of the designated Fourth Industrial Revolution, which happens with the introduction of cyber-physical systems (CPS).

Industry 4.0 is described as a fourth industrial revolution since the first industrial revolution in the late 18th century (Xu; Xu & Li, 2018), and describes the increasing digitalization of the industrial environment, or associated with it, through the creation of value chains that allow communication between products, their environment and business partners (Lasi *et al.* 2014) (Dallasega, Rauch & Linder, 2018).

We are in the digital factory (Agis *et al.*, 2010). It highlights three determining dimensions:

- Innovative communication, computational and data exploration technologies,

- The completeness of the supply and value chain for each product or component, and
- Not least, the management and decision-making capacity resulting from the two previous dimensions.

Industry 4.0 is mainly represented by CPS, IoT and Cloud Computing (Jasperneite, 2012) (Kagermann, Wahlster & Helbig, 2013) (Lasi *et al.*, 2014.) (Hermann, Pentek & Otto, 2016) (Moeuf *et al.*, 2017).

Figure 1. Industry 4.0 technologies (Boston Consulting Group, 2015)

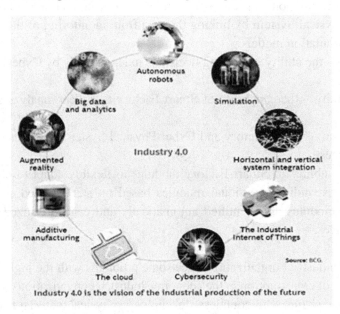

The high technological context of industrial enterprises challenge managers to a new management method. The economic dependence of digital factories, that can be seen and felt in the pressures on production systems, resulting from customization, horizontal integration through value networks, end-to-end digital integration of engineering across the entire value chain, vertical integration and networked manufacturing systems, among others, changed the industrial traditional environment. This new reality requires new business management tools answering to the criticality of the operation of industrial systems in the generation of economic value to the markets (Kagermann & Wahlster, 2013).

THE ROLE OF INFORMATION SYSTEMS GOVERNANCE

The criticality of the industrial systems operationality affects the time-to-market consumption and the availability of products, conditioning the entire value chain and respective stakeholders. The industry will continue to be a central "piece" in the economy and market functioning. In addition, it will also continue to leverage the creation of wealth in society, evolving to meet the demands of consumers and society. The governance of information systems is today a critical factor for the success of organizations. The Information Systems Governance must ensure the best conversion of the enterprise strategy into adequate system architectures, the robustness of processes and the constitution of effective teams. All that conditions will be more decisive in the future.

The current industry is at the centre of an ecosystem of suppliers of physical materials and informational resources, and the efficient and effective of logistics chain depends on the full harmony between the stakeholders, systems, means and internal and external dynamics. The most successful organizations will be those with the highest levels of maturity in the governance and urbanity of information systems and those that are best able to adapt to environment changes.

In the industry of the future, success will continue to be determined by excellence of coordination in an "urban" context of a broader economy, where governance of information systems will be essential as is essential the human organism's cognitive system in coordination of the different organs and elements (Gonçalves, Pimenta & Anunciação, 2019). The main factors that can be highlighted are:

- The coordination of external processes, supported by information systems, will go beyond the physical limits of factories in the logistics integration of suppliers and other stakeholders, ensuring the safeguarding of innovative experiences for customers and the sustainability of the economic ecosystem in which it operates;
- The depth of automation and its sophistication (artificial intelligence, IoT, autonomous robotics) will depend even more on advanced external information systems (IBM Watson, Google IoT and Tensor Flow, etc.) that will blur the frontier of internal / external information systems;
- The attraction of good professional talents will require the establishment of multidisciplinary teams, in wider geographies and with more fluid communication. The teams will tend to be small and / or with variable geometry over time, requiring a more careful management of the knowledge generated and its maintenance in the information systems;
- Anticipate signs of a reorganization of global power in which the new economic blocs will compete in the digital dimension (business systems supported on the Internet, manipulated news, mobile devices and applications, encryption and advanced combat systems) beyond the 4 classic and traditional dimensions (land, air, sea and space). As in the past, conflicts will affect civil society and industry will be one of the main targets, so the security of information systems will have a greater preponderance in corporate governance.

All this future condition justifies the relevance of the scientific study of Industry 4.0. The relevance and the criticality on economic balance justify the analysis of preventive maintenance, as a critical success factor in industry 4.0.

The context of preventive maintenance of industrial systems assumes an important preponderance in guaranteeing the operability of the entire value chain. This type of maintenance is part of the set of systematic actions for the control and monitoring of equipment to reduce or prevent failures in the respective performances. Preventive maintenance allows to increase the reliability of industrial equipment and systems, seeking to guarantee a performance close to ideal conditions.

INDUSTRY 4.0 AND PREVENTIVE MAINTENANCE

Along with the imminent changes Industry 4.0 and new technologies are expected to bring to industries, an excellent opportunity rises in the field of improving company's maintenance performance by reducing costs and assuring higher production uptime and higher profitability, through integration and development of preventive maintenance practices within the industry 4.0 adopting companies.

To contextualize, we introduce the industry 4.0 standard architectural model, followed by the vision of preventive maintenance in industry 4.0, and then we will proceed to define and study the domains involved in this area.

We use the Reference Architectural Model for Industry 4.0 (RAMI4.0), a widespread architecture for the Industry 4.0 framework, which is a proposed standard as IEC PAS 63088:2017.

Figure 2. RAMI4.0 (Gayko, 2018) (IEC, 2017) (Plattform Industrie 4.0, 2016) (ZVEI, 2016) (Plattform Industrie 4.0, w.d.)

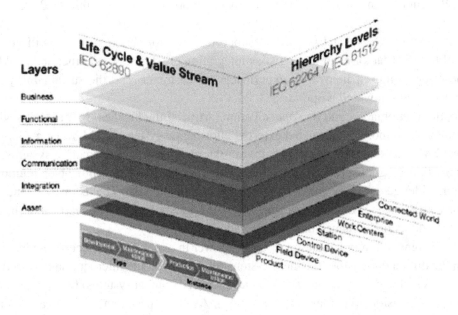

RAMI4.0 is a three-dimensional model of a service-oriented architecture describing the end-to-end engineering throughout the value-stream life cycle of the product. The left horizontal axis describes the life cycle value stream of products and facilities, the right horizontal axis describes the factory hierarchy levels, and the vertical axis describes the IT layers of a business idea into its aggregation levels, structured layer by layer, i.e., the virtual mapping of a product business.

The innovative concept of Industry 4.0 is the Cyber-Physical System (CPS), which is any system or product who has knowledge of its own, its creation, status, purposes, final destination, and so on, allowing other systems to communicate with it and be aware of that information (Smart Products are CPS's by definition). An extension of this concept are the Cyber-Physical Production Systems (CPPS) which results from the integration of the physical equipment and operator with applications designated as Digital Twins that control all aspects of its operation, maintenance needs, and security / prevention requirements, allowing the CPPS to control its own state and adapt to changing environments through modelling and simulation as well as supporting the human supervision. Digital Twins are essential to Industry 4.0 implementation and they must exist both at the CPPS level and at the Smart Factory level.

OBJECTIVES AND METHODOLOGY

The main objective of this study is to analyze the importance of preventive maintenance in competitive capability of economic organizations and propose an architecture to manage it in the context of industry 4.0. As referred before, the criticality of industrial information system (IIS), and the strong dependence of them, reveals the importance of a continuum well-functioning of productive systems in economic organizational performance. Without well-designed IIS and adequate levels of operational reliability it was difficult for companies to satisfy the economic dynamics that are supported by a just-in-time supply.

Given the importance of industrial equipment reliability in just-in-time economic activities, the authors decided to analyze, in the first part of the study, the managers sensibility about this issue and understand the economic impact of the preventive maintenance. This analysis was developed through the focus group technique, where different managers analyzed relevant topics associated with this subject. The adoption of the focus group methodology resulted from the search for objectivity and the possibility of interaction and sharing of participants' views, knowledge and experiences (Berg, 2001) (Morgan, 1996) (Queirós & Lacerda, 2013) (Ivanoff & Hultberg, 2006); the provision of psychological and sociocultural characteristics (Berg, 2001); the generation of a consensus on ideas, issues, themes and solutions due to the synergistic effect (Berg, 2001); or the generation of comparative data between experiences and points of view rather than individual data (Morgan, 1996), were some of the benefits sought with this methodology and that justified the adoption.

In the second part of the study, the authors try to estimate the economic results obtained from the application of preventive maintenance policies. The introduction of technological innovation in the context of industrial companies must be accompanied by an economic and financial analysis to assess the real gains obtained with the change.

In the third part, the authors try to present a model to support preventive maintenance management in the context of industry 4.0.

The study was developed, in the first part, using the focus group technique and 4 managers responsible for production in different sectors of economic activity were invited. Thus, the focus group integrated a Production director of an Oil refinery, Production director of an Auto factory, Production director of a Cement factory, and Production director of a Coffee factory. They analyzed the main issue related to preventive maintenance and evaluate these dimensions in your own enterprise. In the second part, the authors try to analyze and estimate the economic results of a possible adoption of preventive mainte- nance in a coffee production enterprise in Portugal. The relevance of this case study results from the fact that in Portugal the per capita consumption of coffee is high and takes permanent social characteristics, corresponding to an usual and daily behavior of the great majority of Portuguese people. Coffee con- sumption is made in different places such as restaurants, bars, companies, as well as in people's homes, which requires a strong and well-articulated distribution network. Given the cultural characteristics and considering the dependence of most of the Portuguese population, eventual breaks in the supply of this food good would have significant economic and social impacts.

Finally, in the third part, based on the elements collected, an attempt will be made to present a model proposal for the management of preventive maintenance within the framework of industry 4.0.

THE PORTUGUESE COFFEE CASE STUDY

Portuguese espresso coffee is part of the Portuguese culture and is seen as a national gastronomic product. Its characteristics, bitterness (sensation identified at the bottom of the tongue and throat that provides balance on the palate and depends on the degree of roasting of the beans and the preparation of the drink), aroma (odor exhaled by the coffee and felt through the nose through inhalation of the vapors still hot), acidity (characteristic perceived by the tongue and desirable if it is natural and if it does not refer to sour), sweetness (characteristic that results from the caramelization process that occurs in ripe grains), body (characteristic corresponding to the persistence of the drink in the taste), integrate the culture of most Portuguese coffee lovers.

This taste for coffee led AICC (Industrial and Commercial Coffee Association in Portugal) to create an institutional brand for coffee ("Portuguese Coffee - a blend of stories®") that constitutes a seal attributed to high quality processed coffee in Portugal and tradition. Being a different coffee, with its own unique characteristics, recognized by different markets, both national and international, as a specific and differentiated product, the objective associated with the creation of the seal was to allow the consumer to clearly identify the origin and transformation of this product and thus increase its valuation and demand, providing national companies with an increase in their exports in different markets (AICC, w.d.).

In Portugal, 80% of daily coffee consumption is made in the form of "espresso". On average, each Portuguese person drinks 2.5 cups of coffee per day, which corresponds to an average (national) consumption of coffee of 4.73 kg, per person and per year. The European countries that most consume coffee are the following: Finland (11.7 kg), Norway (9.4 kg), Denmark (8.5 kg), Sweden (8.1 kg) and Switzerland (7.5 kg) (AICC, w.d.). In Europe only 20% of coffee consumption is made outside the home and 80% is made at home. While in Portugal this trend is reversed. Our consumption is mostly outside the home.

With an average European coffee consumption of 6.4 kg (per person and per year) and 1.3 kg (per person and per year) worldwide, this sector of activity assumes significant economic relevance in the daily lives of European citizens. In Portugal more Espresso coffee is consumed, while outside Portugal, coffee consumption is generally made in bag or filter coffee, which implies larger quantities. Regarding the number of points of sale, in Portugal there is approximately one establishment for every 160 inhabitants, while the European average is around 400 inhabitants.

Portuguese coffee is thus "a drink obtained in an espresso machine, from a blend of roasted coffee, with an average volume between 35ml ± 5ml and with hazelnut cream, dense and persistent. Organoleptically it is a velvety drink, with an accentuated and well-balanced body, which is characterized by an enormous aromatic complexity, a soft acidity, a remarkable balance of flavors and a pleasant and persistent finish" (AICC, w.d.).

Coffee with these characteristics is distinguished by "portugalidade" (cultural heritage), historical tradition, consumption habit, slow process, diversity and richness of the raw material, biodiversity - very different origins, cream, emotional history around Portuguese espresso, and differentiating experience.

The maintenance of these very specific characteristics in coffee depends largely on the equipment associated with its production. The perception of the importance of these can even be evidenced in each of the characteristics previously described. With regard to bitterness, for example, the existence of a very intense bitterness may possibly be related to the fact that the beans have had a darker roast or the coffee powder has been in more prolonged contact with the water, resulting in an inferior drink. Regarding odor, for example, a lighter roasting of the grains allows for aromas of almonds, walnuts, and chestnuts. A medium roasting allows to obtain aromas of caramel and chocolate.

However, a darker roast can give rise to more intense aromas, providing odor of spices and even burning. This means that, considering that drinks with superior quality tend to have the most pronounced and pleasant aromas, deficiencies in the equipment or control of it can cause the loss of odors, passing unnoticed, or even generating unpleasant odors, such as the smell of ash.

These are small examples of the importance of the equipment and its maintenance in the quality of the final product. To better understand the technical parameters of the equipment necessary for a good Portuguese espresso, the following requirements are presented in table 1.

Table 1. Technical parameters to be considered when extracting the Espresso drink from a professional machine (AICC, w. d.)

Parameter	Portuguese Express
Roasted ground coffee mass (serving)	6 – 7g
Water pressure through the coffee serving	9 bar
Water temperature at the outlet of the machine	90° ± 2°C
Extraction time	25s ± 5s
Drink volume (including cream)	35 ml ± 5ml
Cream color	Hazelnut

Another relevant aspect related to production is highlighted. Portuguese coffee generally combines coffee from different origins, thus forming the so-called "blends" and roasting in Portugal is less intense compared to dark roasting, giving it less acidity and more aroma, more body, and more sweetness.

Figure 3. Industrial value chain of a coffee enterprise

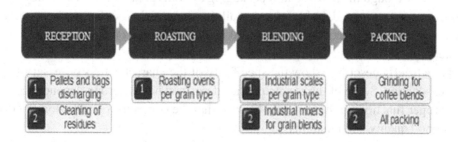

Coffee production has several areas and critical equipment. Coffee beans need to undergo an extensive conversion process to be able to reach our cups, in the form of an energizing and revitalizing drink. The different processes for obtaining coffee have a great effect on its quality and, therefore, vary the final price applied to the sellers.

In general, the coffee production process starts at the harvest stage. Harvesting can be done using the manual method, better known as picking, through which the ripe fruits are selected and picked manually, one by one. This method is mostly used for high quality coffee. However, the harvest can also be carried out mechanically, or striping, through which the fruits are captured and selected by machines. This method is usually used for the production of low-quality coffee.

After the harvest, the coffee is dried. This marks the second phase of the process towards coffee production. Drying can be carried out using two methods: the dry method and the water method. In the dry method, the fruits are left outdoors to dry for 100 days, and it is necessary to stir them continuously. During the night, to protect from the cold and humidity, the fruits are protected by being covered. After drying, the fruits are crushed allowing the seeds and the film surrounding them to dissociate. In the water method, which apparently appears to be contradictory to the drying phase, the fruits are placed in containers filled with water, where they remain for fermentation for a brief period. After this treatment, the coffee beans are dried and separated, to release them from the coffee film.

Roasting is the next stage. This constitutes a critical phase for the quality of the final product as it conditions most of the critical characteristics to the final product, previously mentioned. In the past, grains were roasted by hand and the result was quite irregular and unpleasant, presenting a mixture of raw and burnt grains. Today, through industrialization and technological evolution, the beans are roasted inside metal cylinders that rotate continuously, to guarantee a uniform and perfect roasting.

The roasting process and temperature used vary depending on the variety of coffee used, the country of origin and the roasting country, as consumer consumption profiles are different. However, in general, at 100°C, the grains become yellow; at 150°C they become light brown and double the volume, beginning to emanate the typical "aroma of coffee"; at 200 the process is completed.

After the roasting process is complete, the mixing phase follows. The blend is the most important part of the entire production process as it must guarantee the harmonious combination of the body, aroma, and flavor of the coffee. To be balanced, it must contain sweeter and stronger coffees; with aroma of chocolate and fruity; and more acidic, one of these characteristics having to prevail in superiority, to give personality to the mixture. It is in the blend that a final product suitable for different market segments regarding coffee consumption must be guaranteed.

After the mixing phase, grinding is carried out. Once roasted and ground, the coffee immediately begins to oxidize. Although the new vacuum packaging systems delay this process, they cannot prevent it. It is for this reason that it is advisable, to enjoy all the characteristics of a good coffee, to proceed to grinding at the time of consumption. It should also be noted that the preparation of coffee can be customized by adopting its own type of grinding.

These phases briefly described show the specificity of the characteristics necessary for each of the phases of its production. Some of the characteristics described have a strong dependence on the equipment and its proper functioning. It can easily be seen that the continuous production of coffee requires equipment of good quality and reliability.

In this context of continuous production and in the Portuguese case under analysis, we can assume that the criticality of the equipment is more evident in the phases of the blend's roasting. Note that in industrial units the phases may correspond to industrial organizational areas given the specificity of the equipment and necessary conditions. This criticality results from the fact that it is in the roast that the best qualities of each type and origin of coffee beans can be valued and in the fact that it is in the blend that the "secret" of the formula of each batch is that the brand makes available to the customer. market and customers. In the latter case, it is at this stage that a effort by the factory is required in the strict control of its organoleptic characteristics (body, flavor and aroma).

Thus, the critical equipment in the Roasting phase corresponds to the roasting ovens, which must be in the best technical and technological conditions to guarantee the desired characteristics for the final product. In the case of Blend, it is the precision of the industrial weighing scales that to weigh the toasted coffees for the constitution of each batch that assumes a significant importance.

MAIN RESULTS

Regarding the first part of the study, as referenced in the objectives and methodology chapter, the authors used the focus group technique to identify the main subjects associated with preventive maintenance. As said before, the focus group integrated high level production professionals with responsibilities in four economic sectors: Oil refinery, Auto factory, Cement factory, and Coffee factory.

It was proposed to the focus group members the analysis of the main dimensions in three perspectives traditionally considered in the field of management analysis:

- Vision and approach – which reflects management's understanding, knowledge and perspective on the topic under study;
- Management approach – which reflects the approach that managers adopt, in their practices, regarding the topic under study;
- Organizational model – which highlights the practices adopted by managers in managing the dimensions under study.

This three dimension of analysis was considered because, according to information systems governance literature (Gonçalves, Pimenta & Anunciação, 2019) and experience of the authors, the existence of maintenance management systems and computers does not, by itself, implies that maintenance management problems were solved. There must be a correct integration of different kinds of organizational resources, such as human resources, procedures, and objectives, to integrate organizational functioning with economic demand. This integration demands management competency in preventive maintenance and requires business and technological knowledge of the different processes.

The focus group members considered those main dimensions in three applied perspectives:

- Preventive maintenance vision and approach – maintenance philosophy, maintenance reliability, maintenance organization, and maintenance structure;
- Preventive maintenance management approach – quality checks, audits and evaluation of practices, reports and indicators;
- Maintenance organizational management model - Functioning budget, nature and evolution of costs, weight of preventive maintenance budget on the overall maintenance budget.

Table 2. Preventive maintenance vision and approach

Preventive maintenance vision and approach:	Yes	No
o Does organization have a maintenance department?	100%	0%
o Does organization have a maintenance philosophy?	100%	0%
o Is organization's main maintenance objective reliability?	100%	0%
o Does organization have a preventive maintenance plan?	25%	75%

Based on these dimensions, the focus group was presented with the following questions for analysis in the case study phase. In each dimension previously referenced, the main questions to study were the following:

- Preventive maintenance vision and approach:
    ◦ Does organization have a maintenance department?
    ◦ Does organization have a maintenance philosophy?
    ◦ Is organization's main maintenance objective reliability?
    ◦ Does organization have a preventive maintenance plan?
- Preventive maintenance management approach:
    ◦ Does organization implement regular quality checks on works performed, stimulates improved practices usage, and evaluates responsibilities?
    ◦ Does organization have automatic and continuous practices in place for maintenance performance evaluation, as well as for the determination of that evaluation capacity?
    ◦ Does organization have maintenance auditing practices defined as well as their frequency?
    ◦ Does organization have maintenance software systems to register, support and document its activities, produce regular reports, actual performance, and knowledge performance indicators, and provide for historically available reporting in activities and equipment's?
- Maintenance organizational management model:
    ◦ Is the preventive maintenance plan provided with its own budget?
    ◦ Does organization maintenance department own and manages its budget?
    ◦ Are maintenance costs valued as a cost center or as a profit center?
    ◦ What is the percentage weight of this preventive maintenance budget on the overall maintenance budget, related with conservation maintenance operations?
    ◦ How has preventive maintenance budget value evolved in the past three years?
    ◦ What was the nature of the costs contemplated?
    ◦ Has organization related preventive maintenance costs with reliability and overall profitability?
    ◦ Does organization maintenance department have policies and practices in place to redistribute service costs through other departments?

Then, it was proposed to the focus group members to answer the questions in view of their organization and responsibility. The results were the following:

As we can see in table 2, the results show that all the members consider important a maintenance philosophy and their organizations have a maintenance department, with objectives of reliability. However, the majority don't have a preventive maintenance plan.

Table 3. Preventive maintenance management approach

Preventive maintenance management approach:	Never	Sometimes	Always
o Does organization implement regular quality checks on works performed?		75%	25%
o Does organization implement regular improved practices usage?		50%	50%
o Does organization implement regular evaluations of responsibilities?	50%		50%
o Does organization have continuous and automatic maintenance performance evaluation?	50%	25%	25%
o Does organization have continuous and automatic maintenance performance evaluation capacity?	50%	50%	

The results of preventive maintenance management approach show a weak adoption of management practices associated with it (table 3).

Table 4. Preventive maintenance management approach (continuation)

Preventive maintenance management approach	Yes	No	don't know / don't answer
o Does organization have maintenance auditing practices defined?	100%		
o Does organization have maintenance auditing frequency defined?	75%	25%	
o Does organization have maintenance management software systems?	50%	50%	
o Does the maintenance software provide registration of activities?	50%	25%	25%
o Does the maintenance software provide support to activities?	50%	25%	25%
o Does the maintenance software provide documentation to activities?	50%	25%	25%
o Does the software provide for regular report of activities?	50%	25%	25%
o Does the software provide information about actual performance and / or KPI's of activities?	25%	50%	25%
o Does the software provide for historical reporting of activities and equipment's?	50%	25%	25%

Generally, half of the institutions do not adopt regular management practices associated with preventive maintenance and do not define or evaluate responsibilities or capacities (table 4).

Relatively to maintenance organizational management model, the authors complement the questions previously presented with five questions about the weight of the preventive maintenance in the overall maintenance budget; the weight of the preventive maintenance used in operations of conservation maintenance; the evolution of the preventive maintenance budget; and the nature of the main costs contemplated in the preventive maintenance budget. The answers were the follow:

Table 5. Maintenance organizational management model

Maintenance organizational management model	Yes	No
o Preventive maintenance has its own budget?	25%	75%
o Has organization related Preventive Maintenance costs with reliability and overall profitability?	25%	75%
o Does organization maintenance department have policies and practices in place to redistribute service costs through other departments?	100%	

- Maintenance costs are valued as a Profit center or as a Cost center? 75% cost center and 25% profit center;
- What is approximately the percentage weight of the Preventive Maintenance in the overall maintenance budget (10% or 30% or 50% or 70%)? 75% don't know / don't answer and 25% answer 70%.
- What is approximately the percentage weight of the Preventive Maintenance used in operations of Conservation Maintenance (10% or 30% or 50% or 70%)? 75% don't know / don't answer and 25% answer 30%.
- What has approximately the evolution of the Preventive Maintenance budget in the last three years? 75% don't know / don't answer and 25% answer the cost raised.
- What was the nature of the main costs contemplated in the Preventive Maintenance budget in the last three years (Replace or Upgrade or New)? 75% don't know / don't answer and 25% answer Upgrade.

After the first phase of the study was completed, the authors tried, in the second phase of the study, estimate the economic results of an adoption of preventive maintenance. To do this study, the analysis of the history of costs associated with the maintenance of equipment at the factory was carried out and it was found that the most critical sections associated with production are roasting and blending. A stoppage in production caused by a failure or equipment failure forces the company to bear high costs. This high volume of costs is associated, on the one hand, with equipment repair costs and, on the other hand, with loss of production. In addition, it is also important to consider the opportunity costs associated with unrealized sales as well as the market costs associated with uncertainties regarding the timely availability of products at sales points.

In the roasting section, the critical equipment is the roasting oven (designated as F01 and F02). Its production condition is evaluated following the degradation of the oven insulation by measuring the average temperature of the external wall over time.

In the blending section, the critical equipment is the industrial scale (designated as B01 and B02). Its operational status is assessed through the regular recording of calibration deviations and corresponding corrections.

As we can see, the standard individual equipment procedures recommended by their suppliers when adopted do not allow, in due time, to prevent failures or unscheduled stops of the respective equipment, since they do not allow management to monitor the degradation of the equipment. This analysis, although important, is limited to the extent that it presupposes the need for a phase of analysis of the recorded values and the ability to react to the verified scenario.

Adopting preventive maintenance allows the monitoring of the degradation of critical equipment from more reliable technological devices and, thus, with greater precision to predict the acceptable limits of the measured properties and the respective need for intervention. This information is automatically made available to those responsible for maintenance, allowing foreseeing, according to the production rate, the reach of the limit values as well as predicting the occurrence of equipment failures with greater accuracy.

The availability of this information, which is continually updated, and the recalculation of parameters in the expected periods of operation allow the definition of a clear trend of degradation, both for ovens and for industrial scales. This opportunity facilitates decision-making and the development of precise preventive maintenance actions, compared to the conditional maintenance recommended by equipment suppliers.

Based on the historical cost database of a coffee roasting production line, the authors looked to calculate the cost economy in the maintenance costs. For that purpose, a scenario was drawn in which the possibility was placed of an anticipated knowledge / decision of the intervention moment, of the specificity of the intervention to perform (time, materials, components, and so on), as well as the associated costs. Synergetic gains associated with the possibility of several conjugated and simultaneous maintenance interventions on the various equipment's were not considered, having in consideration the reduction in lost production time and costs, as well as reduction of maintenance costs, which reflects themselves also in productivity gains and profit.

Table 6. Typical programmed versus preventive number of interventions and order of magnitude for maintenance costs, at equipment's nominal capacity

Equipment	Programmed / y	Costs / y (€)	Preventive / y	Costs / y (€)
F01 (robust)	1	20 K	0.8	16 K
F02 (arabic)	1	20 K	0.6	12 K
B01 (robust)	8	1 K	4	0.5 K
B02 (arabic)	8	1 K	6	0.75 K
Total costs	-	42 K	-	29.25 K

These results are in line with expectations, and can be adjusted if we consider that:

- the maintenance carried out is based on the nominal parameters indicated by the furnace suppliers, ignoring the frequency of use of the equipment;
- some ovens operate at a higher temperature than other similar ones, according to the type of coffee they roost, and with a more intense use, which can accelerate the deterioration of the insulation of these ovens;
- the variation in the final mixtures of coffee, depending on the type of beans, may lead to the need for greater frequency in the calibration of some of the industrial scales comparing with others.

Again, above table does not include the effect of having simultaneous preventive maintenance activities, for instance doing a recalibration of scale B01 at the time of repairs at insulation of oven F01, which will further reduce all costs by avoiding one additional production line stopping for recalibration.

PREVENTIVE MAINTENANCE MODEL PROPOSAL

To propose a model for preventive maintenance functions in the framework of Industrie 4.0 we base it on RAMI 4.0 (Reference Architecture Model Industrie 4.0), mentioned before.

The RAMI 4.0 focused industrial production model is being applied to process industries to achieve a holistic integration of automation, business information, and manufacturing execution functions to improve all aspects of production and commerce across process industry value chains for greater efficiency. The RAMI 4.0 is a reference model to give companies a framework for developing future products and business models.

RAMI 4.0 is a three-dimensional map showing how to approach the deployment of Industry 4.0 in a structured manner. A major goal of RAMI 4.0 is to make sure that all participants involved in Industry 4.0 discussions and activities have a common framework to understand each other (Lydon, W.D.).

However, based on RAMI 4.0, the authors propose to model preventive maintenance at the starting point of the initial life time of the product, reducing then the model to a two dimensional one, aggregating those components in functional vertical modules, and distributing the different required applications by modules at the functional level, as presented in Figure 4.

Figure 4. Components, layers, modules and applications of a Preventive Maintenance implementation as per RAMI 4.0 (Cibersur, 2019)

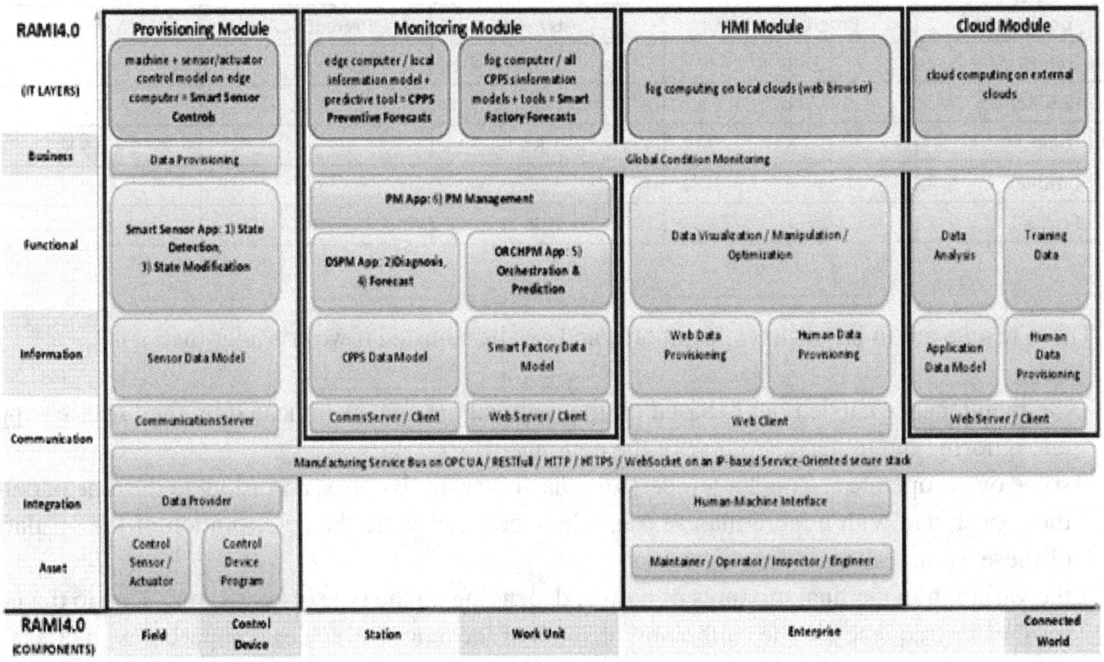

The represented architecture of a preventive maintenance system distinguishes four modules:

Figure 5. Preventive Maintenance Model (Cibersur, 2020)

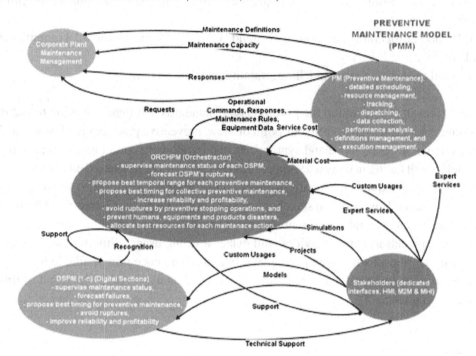

- a provisioning module, operating with the field and the control devices, being it smart sensors and devices, or not, and relying on a local edge computer for the control and state detection and modification,
- a monitoring module, with one "classical PM" (classical preventive maintenance, as per ISA-95/ IEC 62264) and two different digital twins for managing operations, one at the CPPS level (DSPM, digital section preventive maintenance), and another at the Smart Factory level (ORCHPM, orchestrator preventive maintenance):
- the PM, as a local cloud in datacenter, is fulfilling the classical preventive maintenance management functions, such as:
  1. for higher level systems - maintenance definitions, capabilities, requests and responses,
  2. for maintenance itself - detailed scheduling, resource management, tracking, dispatching, data collection, performance analysis, definitions management and execution management, and
  3. to lower levels - operational commands and responses, specific maintenance rules and equipment specific data,
- the DSPM, as an edge computing at the CPPS level to control the unitary operation and dialogs with each smart product (CPS) that uses its services, responsible for diagnosis and forecast functions for local preventive maintenance and protection operations, as well to communicate and dispatch between CPPS's,
- the ORCHPM, as a fog computing distributed through the complete production line and functioning as an intelligent and collaborative orchestrator to manage and optimize the activity of all DSPM's needed to produce a certain product, or to dispose of their services to third parties, and

aggregating, forecasting and recommending preventive maintenance actions for the entire production line,

- an HMI module operating as both a fog and a local computing for all communications and visualizations,
- and a Cloud module for data modelling, training and data analytics.

Our model takes in consideration the past industrial standards and their evolution to Industry 4.0 in terms of adding the indispensable, from our point of view, preventive practices to classical maintenance procedures as drawn in detail above and synthetized in the following model proposal in Figure 5.

This model is built taking in consideration established standard practices as maintenance definitions, capacity, responses and requests information rendering to corporate maintenance software, as well as all the relevant information flow between stakeholders and digital twins (orchestrator and digital sections), includes the man as an integral and essential partner at all level activities, integrates newly possible different business models as expert services, and makes a strong usage of models, simulations, custom usages and projects as results from the manageability and intelligence now available to all systems.

This model will be the base for future industrial tests and analysis and is the result of this research and of industry experience.

CONCLUSION

As main conclusions we can mention that the preventive maintenance assumes a strategic importance in the context of the real time operation of the current economy. This is highlighted by the production managers of the four sectors analyzed. However, although they assume this relevance, when asked whether they adopt this policy, the vast majority respond in the negative. As it was not possible to study the reasons for this apparent contradiction, the opportunity in future works is to investigate the reasons for such a position.

In the second part of the study, after verifying the relevance of the topic and studying the case of the largest coffee producing company in Portugal, it was possible to show that there are economic gains associated with the adoption of preventive maintenance. This study may in the future be extended to all coffee production lines to be able to estimate the gains in each of them. The case study analyzed is an excellent example of the importance of preventive maintenance due to the importance of coffee in Portuguese society and economy. An eventual difficulty in the daily supply of coffee to most Portuguese society would have significant repercussions, due to the cultural weight of this food good and the importance for the psychological stability of each person.

Finally, the authors sought to present a model to identify the most relevant dimensions in preventive maintenance and to facilitate its adoption by production managers. This model, which was based on RAMI 4.0 and ISA-95, is based on the reality of industry 4.0 and the potential of information technologies.

Since there was no opportunity to test it, it constitutes another challenge for the technical and scientific development of this work, the development of a proof of concept, in order to be able to validate its applicability.

REFERENCES

Agis, D.; Bessa, D.; Gouveia, J. & Vaz, P. (2010). *Wearing the future – Micro trends for the textile, clothing and fashion industries by 2020*. Portuguese Textile and Clothing Association.

AICC - Industrial and Commercial Coffee Association. (n.d.). Retrieved September 13, from www.aicc.pt

Anunciação, P. F. (2016). Organizational Urbanism: A Value Proposal for the Generation of Organizational Intelligence to Healthcare Institutions – The Case of a Portuguese Hospital Center. Handbook of Research on Information Architecture and management in Modern Organizations, 458-486.

Anunciação, P. F. (2015). Organizational Change through Information Systems: Metavision-Project Management Model in Internet Banking. Handbook of Research on Effective Project Management through the Integration of Knowledge and Innovation, 450-465.

Anunciação, P. F., & Zorrinho, C. (2006). *Organizational Urbanism – How to manage technological shock*. Sílabo Publishing.

Anunciação, P. F. (2014). *Ethics, Sustainability and the Information and Knowledge Society*. Chiado Publishing.

Lorenz, M., Rubmann, M., Waldner, M., Engel, P., Harnish, M., Justus, J., & the Boston Consulting Group. (2015). *Industry 4.0: The Future of Productivity and Growth in Manufacturing Industries*. https://www.bcg.com/publications/2015/engineeried_products_project_business_industry_4_future_productivity_growth_manufacturing_industries

Berg, B. L. (2001). Focus group interviewing. In B. L. Berg (Ed.), *Qualitative research methods for the Social Sciences* (Vol. 4, pp. 111–132). Pearson.

Dallasega, P., Rauch, E., & Linder, C. (2018). Industry 4.0 as an enabler of proximity for construction supply chains: A systematic literature review. *Computers in Industry, 99*, 205–225.

Drath, R., & Horch, A. (2014). Industrie 4.0 – hit or hype? *IEEE Industrial Electronics Magazine, 8*(2), 56–58.

Gayko, J. E. (2018). *The Reference Architectural Model RAMI4.0 and the Standardization Council as an element of Success for Industry 4.0*. Retrieved September 15, from https://www.din.de/resource/blob/271306/340011c12b8592df728bee3815ef6ec2/06-smart-manufacturing-jens-gayko-data.pdf

Gonçalves, F., Pimenta, J., & Anunciação, P. F. (2019). Information Systems Governance and New industrial Paradigms. Information Systems Governance – Concepts, best practices and case studies, 117-136.

Gonçalves, F., Pimenta, J., & Anunciação, P. F. (2019). Information Systems Governance and New industrial Paradigms. Information Systems Governance – Concepts, best practices and case studies, 211-212.

Haddara, M., & Elragal, A. (2015). *The Readiness of ERP Systems for the Factory of the Future*. Conference on ENTERprise Information Systems / International Conference on Project MANagement / Conference on Health and Social Care Information Systems and Technologies, CENTERIS / ProjMAN / HCist 2015.

Hermann, M., Pentek, T., & Otto, B. (2016). Design Principles for Industrie 4.0 Scenarios. *Proceedings of 2016 49th Hawaii International Conference on Systems Science.*

IEC PAS 63088. (2017). *Publicly Available Specification – Pre-Standard, Smart manufacturing – Reference architecture model industry 4.0 (RAMI4.0).* Retrieved July 22, from https://webstore.iec.ch/preview/info_iecpas63088%7Bed1.0%7Den.pdf

Ivanoff, S. D., & Hultberg, J. (2006). Understanding the Multiple Realities of Everyday Life: Basic Assumptions in Focus Group Methodology. *Scandinavian Journal of Occupational Therapy*, 13.

Jasperneite, J. (2012). Was Hinter Begriffen Wie Industrie 4.0 Steckt. *Computers and Automation*, *12*, 24–28.

Kagermann, H. & Wahlster, W. (2013). *Securing the future of German manufacturing industry. Recommendations for implementing the strategic initiative INDUSTRIE 4.0.* Final report of the Industrie 4.0 Working Group. Acatech – National Academy of Science and Engineering.

Kagermann, H., Wahlster, W., & Helbig, J. (2013). Recommendations for Implementing the Strategic Initiative Industrie 4.0. Final Report of the Industrie 4.0 Working Group. Acatech-National Academy of Science and Engineering.

Lasi, H., Peter, F., Thomas, F., & Hoffmann, M. (2014). Industry 4.0. *Business & Information Systems Engineering*, *6*(4), 239–242.

Lydon, B. (n.d.). *RAMI 4.0 Reference Architectural Model for Industrie 4.0, ISA's Flagship Publications.* Retrieved July 20, from https://www.isa.org/intech-home/2019/march-april/features/rami-4-0-reference-architectural-model-for-industr

Moeuf, A., Pellerin, R., Lamouri, S., Tamayo-Giraldo, S., & Barbaray, R. (2017). The Industrial Management of SMEs in the Era of Industry 4.0. *International Journal of Production Research*, (September), 8.

Morgan, D. L. (1996). Focus Groups. *Annual Review of Sociology*, 22. Retrieved May 8, from http://www.jstor.org/stable/2083427

Plattform Industrie 4.0. (n.d.). *A reference framework for digitalization.* Retrieved July 22, from https://www.plattform-i40.de/PI40/Redaktion/EN/Downloads/Publikation/rami40-an-introduction.pdf?__blob=publicationFile&v=7

Plattform Industrie 4.0. (2016). *Security in RAMI4.0.* Retrieved July 25, from https://www.plattform-i40.de/PI40/Redaktion/EN/Downloads/Publikation/security-rami40-en.pdf?__blob=publicationFile&v=7

Queirós, P., & Lacerda, T. (2013). The importance of interview in qualitative research. In I. Mesquita & A. Graça (Eds.), *Qualitative research in sport* (Vol. 2). Center for Research, Training, Innovation and Intervention in Sport, Faculty of Sport, Porto University.

Tiersky, H. (2017). The 5 key drivers of digital transformation today. *CIO.*

Xu, Xu, & Li. (2018). Industry 4.0: State of the art and future trends. *International Journal of Production Research*, *56*(8), 2941–2962.

ZVEI. (2016). *ZVEI explains RAMI 4.0*. Retrieved September 2, from https://www.zvei.org/en/subjects/industrie-4-0/

Chapter 19

A Novel Ripple and Cyber Bullies Data Disclose (RACYBDD) Framework to Protect Images on Social Media

Bhimavarapu Usharani
Koneru Lakshmaiah Education Foundation, India

Raju Anitha
Koneru Lakshmaiah Education Foundation, India

ABSTRACT

Due to the advancement in internet technology, everyone can connect to anyone living anywhere in this world who is far away from us by using social media. Social media became a public place to share everyone's personal photos and videos. These photos or videos are viewed, shared, and even downloaded by their respective friends, someone from their friends' profiles, and even unrelated persons also without their permission. One of the risks from the social media is the cyber bullying or online harassment. Cyber bullies perpetrate either through denigration or doxing. The cyber bullies are anonymous, and it is very difficult for us to catch and punish them. The main aim of this chapter is to provide the privacy and security to the photos that are sharing on social media. This chapter proposes a novel algorithm to keep the photos safe that are uploading on social media and the extension of the novel algorithm to reveal the details of the cyber bullies those who performed morphing on the photos that were downloaded from social media.

I. INTRODUCTION

Now a days we are using social media to communicate with the family and friends who are miles away from us. These days social media play a major role in the lives of the people. Many are addicted to this social media and it seems a prestigious issue to create a social media account. Whenever friends,

DOI: 10.4018/978-1-7998-4201-9.ch019

Copyright © 2021, IGI Global. Copying or distributing in print or electronic forms without written permission of IGI Global is prohibited.

family members or colleagues meet in auspicious occasion, they will first ask about their social media account id's. If any person does not maintain any social media id, remaining friends, family members or colleagues suggest them about creating account on social media. Apart from this, if anyone gets less likes for their posted photos or videos on social media, they are becoming sad and worrying just like they miss or lose one billion dollars. However, many are spending rest less lives and sleepless nights due to this social media.

The internet users are 4.021 billion and the social media users are 3.19 billion in 2018(Nathan Mcdonald 2018) .The internet users are 16 million in Dec 1995 but in Dec 2017 the internet users are 4,156 million (Internet world stats).The face book active users are just a million in 2004 but in 2018 it becomes to 1.49 billion daily active users and 2.27 billion monthly active users (newsroom.fb).The world population in 2017 is 7519 million, the internet users are 3885 million and the face book users are 1978 million (Internet World Stats, Usage and Population Statistics).When compared to other social media, face book have the most daily active users, so face book remains the most widely used social media these days. In united states 2018, the usage of social media by men is 65% where as women is 73% (Horst Stipp,2018). When compared to men internet users, women internet users reveal more personal information on social media. Women internet users uses social media to connect to their family members, friends and colleagues but men internet users use social media to gather information, contacts, status etc. Women internet users get in touch with friends, colleagues, family through social media is 69% and only 54% male internet users are communicating through social media (Iris Vermeren,2015). In general, women internet users disclose more personal information on social media in the form of personal photo albums, presenting themselves in profile photo.

Social Media is using by all types of people even criminals also. Dr.Daniela Sincek research work on " Gender Differences in Cyber Bullying"(Dr.Daniela Sincek,2014) reveals that men commits more cyber bulling, cyber stalking, Doxing, online shaming, cyber violence, cyber aggression, cyber forgery by presenting themselves as a some other person or through hidden identity. These days abuse of photos that are taking from social media especially from face book comes to light and the complaints (India Today, Times of India, Johanna Deeksha,2017) against the morphing and abuse of photos that are appearing on social media are increasing day by day. There is an immense need to provide the privacy and security for the photos that are publishing on social media. In the present era, we are seeing the news that are related to morphing of photos, because of this there is no security for personal lives and even the victim families are also suffering a lot. In this paper, we are enhancing the privacy and security to photos that are publishing on social media.

1.1 Problem

Social Media plays a crucial role in connecting the people to their family members, friends and colleagues to share every activity. Many of us are uploading their personal videos or photos onto social media to share their memorable movements with their family members or friends. In this computer era, it's become crazy to share one's photos and experiences on social media. The photos that are publishing on social media will be saving by someone and abuses these photos intentionally. Once the photos are uploaded on social media, no one can't stop anyone to take these photos from social media and the possibilities of abuse these photos are endless. Privacy is the essential human right, so there is the need to minimize the disclosure of personal information especially photos on the social media such as face book, Instagram, twitter, WhatsApp etc. It is to be identified that everyone should protect themselves from the cyber bullies. Many are unreported their online harassment or abuse even to their adult family members, friends or colleagues. This is nothing but encouraging the cyberbullies and they themselves complicating the matters and they must face dire consequences.

Because of this cyber bulling many people are suffering from depression and committing suicide(shaheen sheriff,2008). The victims should consult family members or friends when they are harassing by the cyberbullies (Robert Slonje,2008). Cyber Bullying Inventory (CBI) was studied by examining the Psychometric characteristics (Topcu,Erdur Baker,2010). To determine cyberbullies Cyber Victimisation scale was developed by questionnaires and surveys (Yavuz Akbulut et al,2010). Cyber Bullying Inventory and cyber victimisation scale are inadequate measures to prevent the intended harm by the cyber bullies. To stay safe on social media there is the need of strict privacy settings, restrict the access of the personal online profiles by the unrelated persons and limiting the disclose of the innocent person's personal information (Tolga Aricak et al,2008).Reduction of Cyber Bulling perpetration is explained by self-regulation(Amanda P.Williford,2013).Cyberbullying can be prevented by giving the knowledge of risks and strategies to defend victims (Enrique Chaux,M.V,2016).The cyberbullying can be prevented through socio-ecological framework through VISC program to the school students.(Petra Gradinger,Dagmar Strohmeier,2018).All the approaches that are discussed till now are only giving some sort of training to the school students for awareness and risks in cyberbullying.

Hence it is understood that, there must be an approach to stop the perpetration performed by the cyber bullies. This paper proposes a new approach called RACYBDD to enhance the privacy and security for the photos that are posting on the social media. RACYBDD extracts the information about the cyber bullies those who are saving or sharing or downloading the personal photos of other persons. When these cyber bullies try to upload these downloaded or saved photos on the internet RACYBDD framework publishes the complete information about the cyber bullies. This information helps to catch these cyber bullies and punish them. The solutions that are given by the other authors up to now are only just giving training to the school students and giving some sort of knowledge or awareness about cyberbullying characteristics, but this RACBIR framework will invoke automatically when someone is trying to save or share the photos that are already uploaded in the social media.

The rest of the paper is organised as follows: Section 2 discusses the preliminaries. Section 3 describes the RACYBDD system architecture. Section 4 introduces the Replica algorithm. Section 5 introduces the Cyber Bullies Reveal Algorithm. Section 6 discusses our experiments and results. Finally, the conclusion and future work are given.

II. PRELIMINARIES

2.1 Quantum Cryptography

Quantum Cryptography is a cryptography which stores the sensitive data across insecure networks. Quantum Cryptography is based on the classical cryptography and extends with the law of quantum mechanics. Quantum Cryptography was first proposed by Stephen Weisner in his work in "Conjugate Coding"(Stephen Wiesner,1983).Quantum Cryptography guarantees the privacy from the cyber bullies.C.Bennett and G.Brassard used weisners idea and developed first protocol in quantum cryptography (Charles .H.Bennett,G.Brassard,1984).Quantum Cryptography is more secure because quantum methods depend on the law of physics and it is impossible to solve. One of the primary features of quantum cryptography is it is impossible to generate perfect copies(clones).

No Cloning Theorem: It is impossible to create an identical copy of an arbitrary state.

The term clone is first coined by W.K.Wootters and W.H Zurek in their paper "A Single quantum cannot be cloned"(William.K.Wootters,Wojciech.H.Zurek,1982).

In this paper we are using the no cloning theorem that is part of the quantum cryptography.

2.2 Steganography

The term "Steganography" (J.Trithemius,1606) was coined by Johhannes Trithemius in 1499 in his book called "Steganographia". By using Steganography, we can transmit the data which internally contains some hidden data.

Image steganography is a process of hiding the secret message in the cover image which produces a stego image. The cover image i.e. original image and the stego image are almost similar. At the receiver side the hidden image in the stego image can be extract with or with out stego key.

III.RACYBDD FRAMEWORK

3.1 Architecture

Cyber bullies may be the known or unknown people. Even the known people, they perpetrate their dislike or enemy persons through fake ids, so they are the unrelated to the victims. This architecture helps us to catch the cyber bullies when they tried to upload the morphed photos that are downloaded from the social media. When the unrelated profile visits some others profile and want to share, save or download their personal photos a replica algorithm is invoked, and cyber bullies want to upload the morphed photos what they have uploaded a Cyber Bully Information Reveal Algorithm is invoked. The key components of RACBIR framework is ripple algorithm and CYBDD algorithm. RACYBDD architecture is shown in Fig 1 .

Figure 1. RACBIR Framework

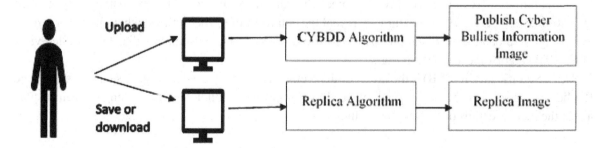

This section describes the main technologies that we are using for our Ripple and Cyber Bullies Information Reveal (RACBIR) framework.

IV. RIPPLE ALGORITHM

This paper mainly focuses on providing the privacy to the personal photos that are sharing on the social media. We are using the No Cloning theorem at the time of copying the photos form the social media. We proposed an algorithm called "Replica Algorithm" to not make the exact copy of the photos when cyber bullies are trying to save or share others profile personal photos from the social media. The detailed view of Replica algorithm is shown in Fig 2.

Algorithm 1: Ripple Algorithm

```
Input: Original Image
Output: Replica Image
1.When the option Save, or Share is choosing.
2.Go to (0,0) Pixel in the digital image
3.for each pixel in the image
      outpixel=originalpixel+(0.999*originalpixel)
   End
4.Apply the no cloning principle to the outpixel
5.Go to step 3 until no more pixels in the digital image
6.Extract the profile id and location of the cyber bully and embed this infor-
mation to the image that was generated at step (5)
```

At step 3 we are changing the intensity of the pixel. Due to change of intensity, there is the chance of accompany some blur to the photo. At step 5 we are using the no cloning theorem to each pixel. This step doubles the number of the pixels in the photo and finally the photo gets zoomed and blurred. The downloaded photo is unclear, worse and this photo is unfit to perform morphing. At step (6) we embed the details of the cyber bullies in the image using different steganographic techniques (W.Bender,D et al,1996, Zhicheng Ni,YunQ et al 2004, Joshua R.Smith,Barrett O.Comiskey 1996, N.K.Abdulaziz,K.K.Pang 2000).

Cyber bullies affect all ages of people, especially women. We proposed the extension to the Replica algorithm called "CYBDD Algorithm" to reveal the details of the cyber bullies, when the cyber bullies are trying to upload the morphed photos which was downloaded from social media. The detailed view of CYBDD algorithm is shown in Fig 3.

Least Significant Bit (LSB) is the most common embed technique used for digital steagonograph.The Replica image seems to be the original image. The Human eyes cannot detect any thing or even suspect about the hidden details of these cyber bullies.

Figure 2. Original Image and the Ripple Image

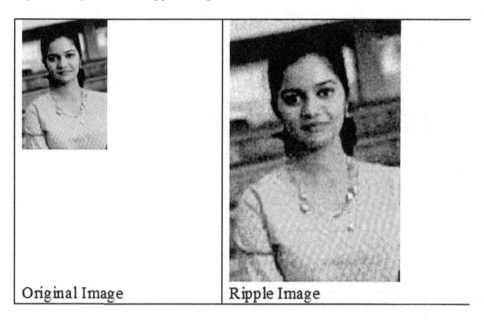

| Original Image | Ripple Image |

V.CYBDD (CYBER BULLIES DATA DISCLOSE) ALGORITHM

Algorithm 2: CYBDD Algorithm

```
Input: Morphed Replica Image
Output: Cyber Bullies Information Display Image
1.Check for the hidden message on the morphed photo.
2.Extract the details from the morphed photo
3.Upload the image and display the extracted cyber bully details as the fore-
ground text on the uploaded image.
```

At step (2) to extract the hidden information from the replica image use any steganographic technique. There are many steganographic techniques to extract the hidden text data from the image. One of the best extraction techniques used in the digital steganography is the LSB steganography. The flow for algorithm 2 is shown in Fig 4 . When CYBDD algorithm is applied to the fig2 then cyber bully information is extracted and displayed as shown in Fig 5 .

When people accept the unknown friend requests on social media the work of the cyber bullies are much easier to do perpetration. Even in such cases this CBIR algorithm protect the privacy and security of the personal photos on social media. The CBIR algorithm solves the issues of violating the rights of the victims, interest as well as privacy and builds the harmonious society.

VI. PERFORMANCE EVALUATION

The original image and the replica image are shown in figure 2:

Figure 3. Flow chart for Ripple Algorithm

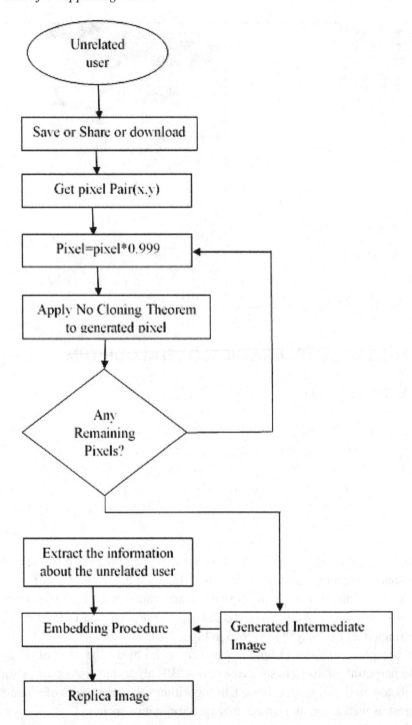

The quality measures included in this paper are listed below in table 1. These measures give the closeness between two images by exploiting the difference in the pixel values. O(i,j) denotes original image and R(i,j) denotes the replica image.

Figure 4. CYBDD Algorithm flow

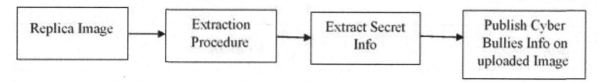

The first metric is the MSE (mean square error). This metric measures the average of the square of the errors for the estimated and what is to be estimated. The value of MSE is always non-negative and it includes both the variance and the bias. MSE tells how close a fitted line is according to the data points.

As the training data goes on increasing the mean square error values will be worsened. More bias and variance are more so the curve will be down if the training data goes on increasing. The lower value of MSE indicates low error.

Another metric is peak signal to noise ratio (PSNR), used to check the quality of the image. PSNR is used to compare the squared error between the original image and the Replica image. Higher PSNR value indicates that the reconstructed image is of high quality. The low value of PSNR tells the image is of low quality. High PSNR value indicates that less error is introduced in the reconstructed image.

Image Fidelity is the accuracy of the brightness of the reconstructed Replica image. Image Fidelity give the information about the loss of data in the reconstructed image.

Cross correlation indicates that the similarity between the two images.

Figure 5. Replica Image and Cyber Bullies Information Image

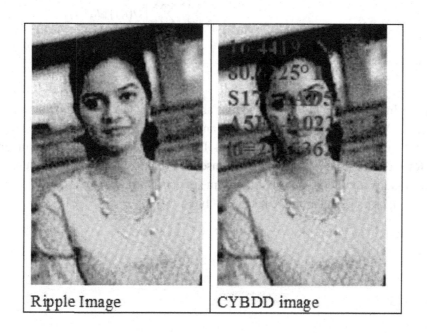

Table 1. Image Metric and the corresponding formulae

Metric	Formulae
Mean Square Error	$\sum_{i=0}^{M}\sum_{j=0}^{N}\left[O(i,j)-R(i,j)\right]^2$
Average Difference	$\dfrac{1}{M*N}\,[R(i,j)-O(i,j)]$
Peak signal to noise ratio (PSNR)	$10*\log_{10}\left(\dfrac{Max\,Intensity\,of\,R(i,j)}{MSE}\right)$
Max Difference	$Max(R(i,j)-O(i,j))$
Structural Content	$\dfrac{\sum_{i=0}^{M}\sum_{j=0}^{N}\left[O(i,j)\right]2}{\sum_{i=0}^{M}\sum_{j=0}^{N}\left[R(i,j)\right]2}$
Correlation Quality	$\dfrac{\sum_{i=0}^{M}\sum_{j=0}^{N}\left[O(i,j)*R(i,j)\right]}{\sum_{i=0}^{M}\sum_{j=0}^{N}\left[O(i,j)\right]}$
Image Fidelity	$1-\dfrac{\sum_{i=0}^{M}\sum_{j=0}^{N}\left[O(i,j)-R(i,j)\right]2}{\sum_{i=0}^{M}\sum_{j=0}^{N}\left[O(i,j)\right]2}$
Peak Mean Square Error	$\dfrac{1}{M*N}\dfrac{\sum_{i=0}^{M}\sum_{j=0}^{N}\left[O(i,j)-R(i,j)\right]2}{Max\left(O(i,j)\right]2}$
Cross Correlation	$\dfrac{\sum_{i=0}^{M}\sum_{j=0}^{N}\left[O(i,j)*R(i,j)\right]}{\sum_{i=0}^{M}\sum_{j=0}^{N}\left[O(i,j)\right]2}$

The results for Image shown in Fig:4 by using Table 1 formulae's is listed in table 2. We have taken 15 sample images. We have applied the CYBDD and replica algorithm to the 15 sample images and later calculated the metrics that was listed in table1.The calculated metrics is listed in table 3 and table 4.The results for different images for parameters mse, avg diff, psnr, mae, max difference are listed in table 3. The results for sample 15 images for parameters structural content, correlation quality, image fidelity, peak mean, cross correlation are listed in table 4.

Table 2. Results for Image shown in Fig:4 by using Table 1 formulae's

Metric	Result
Mean Square Error	2.4794886225422427E12
Avg Differnce	1347246.523497918
PSNR	0.6763975237412
Max Difference	2768918.0
Structural Content	0.31640482853147694
Correlation Quality	7.4121682965278336E17
Image Fidelity	0.8933667343863996
Peak Mean Square Error	4.50801519931088E-23
Cross Correlation	3.1605080258770983

Table 3. Results for different images for parameters mse, avg diff, psnr, mae, max difference

	MSE	AVGDIFF	PSNR(negative valus)	height	MAE	Max Difference
image1	2.4425467457394287E12	1356994.8904761905	9223372036854775646	168	1356994.8904761905	2655155.0
image2	1.7390681168219646E12	1137598.2239183218	9223372036854775646	259	1137598.2239183218	2292836.0
image3	1.786415718902424E12	1154076.0116865078	9223372036854775646	300	1154076.0116865078	2284848.0
image4	1.6006738916101003E12	1093898.6008730158	9223372036854775646	224	1093898.6008730158	2183983.0
Image5	2.073636663768338E12	1243591.4691306509	9223372036854775646	275	1243591.4691306509	2506559.0
Image6	1.9366239005675962E12	1194954.339206349	9223372036854775646	300	1194954.339206349	2407036.0
Image7	2.1126340375964062E12	1256170.2725561303	9223372036854775646	267	1256170.2725561303	2517945.0
Image8	1.8946622571583782E12	1188465.085925926	9223372036854775646	270	1188465.085925926	2384032.0
Image9	1.911379726727683E12	1191469.158887233	9223372036854775646	275	1191469.158887233	2428656.0
image10	1.8373743477594292E12	1168873.5066896593	9223372036854775646	201	1168873.5066896593	2341698.0
image11	1.7495765464824304E12	1139706.3779753086	9223372036854775646	225	1139706.3779753086	2345484.0
image12	1.748068465917633E12	1149126.7811357495	9223372036854775646	233	1149126.7811357495	2297426.0
image13	1.7493365667305974E12	1141291.6757126977	9223372036854775646	257	1141291.6757126977	2308849.0
image14	2.0648420823235E12	1239067.5015956077	9223372036854775646	251	1239067.5015956077	2497627.0
image15	1.9440316585652588E12	1198888.0774608834	9223372036854775646	170	1198888.0774608834	2453022.0

Table 4. Results for different images for parameters structural content, correlation quality, image fidelity, peak mean, cross correlation

	Structural Content	correlation Quality	Image Fidelity	Peak mean	width	cross correlation
image1	0.16148281426541283	4.57283315100385E19	0.9833289960120545	4.479396990182484E-26	300	6.192609439890005
image2	0.16230828428973143	4.155697654036708E19	0.9870451181378654	3.822498580502389E-26	194	6.161114969430219
image3	0.16563729065999544	7.545403478897523E19	0.9927960202749148	1.1436716596283186E-26	168	6.037287835459138
image4	0.18787755881850898	1.5393280789427206E19	0.9721049401376556	1.9137740494569477E-25	225	5.322615464500509
Image5	0.18252138567781295	4.108351978540939E19	0.9860833391013867	3.6878212297228024E-26	183	5.4788100379930365
Image6	0.19374580902490773	2.260342161460976E19	0.9777120912514463	1.0097928278538618E-25	168	5.161401968036589
Image7	0.17489603507983154	6.101886602867256E19	0.9900102817026019	1.85496653720654E-26	189	5.717682505172565
Image8	0.17394746856742663	4.454200972283339E19	0.9881155208855141	3.1561378330573843E-26	180	5.748862045740974
Image9	0.18011127328048637	2.502159155174028E19	0.9786560432624595	9.410990206956069E-26	183	5.552123316804857
image10	0.15139991938390454	3.0586711245469778E19	0.979982538560109	8.568026373338501E-26	251	6.605023332042215
image11	0.1757544371356959	5.523722702604812E19	0.9908765348391408	1.8563361206599695E-26	225	5.68975677824807
image12	0.16446991551417536	5.2796332308529816E19	0.9898684034460977	2.3183446116565365E-26	216	6.080139318329083
image13	0.16368552105529258	2.518001031234538E19	0.9786205563158112	1.029771899709573E-25	196	6.109275845248416
image14	0.1949174310777507	2.8842912211913093E19	0.9814703662813079	6.532918926024781E-26	201	5.130377485844812
image15	0.1775289711896273	6.181728873523111E19	0.9910560468779559	1.6141539530387495E-26	297	5.632883429104377

CONCLUSION

With the increase in the usage of internet, the tendency of sharing to something is increasing day by day. This paper mainly focuses on providing the privacy to the social media users, who are very curious on sharing their personal photos on social media. There is an immense need to protect the privacy as well as security in this digital world. We proposed a novel algorithm called "Replica Algorithm", to make impossible to provide the exact copy of the images that are saving on social media. we proposed an extension to replica algorithm called "CYBDD Algorithm" to reveal the details (profile id and location) of the cyber bully who performed morphing on the downloaded photos and trying to place these morphed photos in the internet. The main advantage of these two algorithms is not only providing the security to the photos but also, we can catch the cyber bully who are intentionally trying to defame the persons who have respect for their personal lives in the society.

REFERENCES

Mcdonald, N. (2018). *We are social*. Available on: https://wearesocial.com/us/blog/2018/01/global-digital-report-2018

Stats, I. W. (n.d.). *Usage and Population Statistics*. Available on: https://www.internetworldstats.com/emarketing.htm

Stats, I. W. (n.d.). *Usage and Population Statistics*. Available on: https://www.internetworldstats.com/facebook.htm

Stipp. (2018). *Percentage of adults in the Unites states who use social networks as of January 2018 by gender*. Available on:https://www.statista.com/statistics/471345/us-adults-who-use-social-networks-gender/

Vermeren, I. (2015). *Men Vs Women: Who is More Active on Social Media?* Available on: https://www.brandwatch.com/blog/men-vs-women-active-social-media/

Sincek. (2014). Gender Differences in Cyber-Bullying. *International Multidisciplinary Scientific Conferences on social sciences and arts*, 1-8.

Today, I. (2018). *Bengal Woman streams suicide on Facebook Live for boyfriend*. Available on: https://www.indiatoday.in/india/story/woman-commits-suicide-streams-act-on-facebook-live-1257898-2018-06-12

Today, I. (2016). *Salem: Morphed Facebook images drive woman to suicide*. Available on: www.indiatoday.in/india/story/morphed-images-on-facebook-drive-salem-woman-to-suicide-16741-2016-06-28

Times of India. (2014). *Girl kills self over Facebook harassment*. Available on: https://timesofindia.indiatimes.com/city/kolkata/Girl-kills-self-over-Facebook-harassment/articleshow/37211521.cms

Deeksha, J. (2017). *Revenge porn drives DU student to suicide: Hers's what you need to do online and at the police station to ensure abscene pics of you don't go viral*. Available on:www.edexlive.com/live-story/2017/apr/13/the-dark-net-and-its-crimes-329.html

Today, I. (2017). *Delhi: Cyber crooks stealing, morphing social media photos to extort victims*. Available on: https://www.indiatoday.in/mail-today/story/delhi-cyber-crooks-stealing-morhphong-photos-porn-sites-extrotion-966463-2017-03-20

Wiesner, S. (1983). Conjugate Coding. *SIGACT, Volume, 15*(1), 78–88.

Bennett & Brassard. (1984). Quantum cryptogramphy: Public key distribution and coin tossing. *Proceedings of IEEE international conference on computers, systems and signal processing, 1*, 175-179.

Wootters & Zurek. (1982). A Single quantum cannot be cloned. *Nature, 299*, 802–803.

Trithemius, J. (1606). Steganographia (secretwriting). Germany, Darmbstadil, Bibliop, Francop, Anno M.DC.XXI, 1-270.

Bender, Gruhl, Morimoto, & Lu. (1996). Techniques for data hiding. *IBM Systems Journal, 35*(3-4), 313-336.

Ni, Shi, Ansri, Su, Sun, & Lin. (2014). Robust Lossless Image Data Hiding. *IEEE International Conference on Multimedia and Expo*, 2199-2202.

Smith, J. R., & Comiskey, B. O. (1996). Modulation and Information Hiding in Images. *Proceedings of the first Information Hiding Workshop, 1174*, 1-21.

Abdulaziz & Pang. (2000). Robust Data Hiding for Images. *Proceedings for Communication Technology*, 380-383.

Sheriff. (2008). *Cyber Bullying: Issues and solutions for the school, the class room and the home.* Routledge.

Slonje & Smith. (2008). Cyberbullying:Another main type of bullying? *Scandinavian Journal of Psychology, 49*, 147-154.

Topcu. (2010). The Revised Cyber Bullying Inventory(RCBI):validity and reliability studies. *Procedia Social and Behavioral Sciences, 5*, 660-664.

Akbulut, Sahin, & Eristi. (2010). Development of a scale to investigate cybervictimization among online social utility members. *Contemporary Educational Technology, 1*(1), 46-59.

Aricak. (2008). Cyber bullying among Turkish adolescents. *CyberPsychology & Behavior, 11*(3), 253-261.

Chandramouli & Memon. (2001). Analysis of LSB based image steganography techniques. *Proceedings on International Conference on Image Processing, 3*, 1019-1022.

Quach, T. T. (2014). Extracting hidden messages in steganographic images. *Digital Forensic Research Conference*, 540-545.

Williford, A. P., & Jessica, E. (2013). Childrens Engagement with in the preschool classroom and their development of self-regulation. *Early Education and Development, 24*, 162–187.

Enrique Chaux, M. (2016). Effects of the cyberbullying prevention program media heroes(Medienhelden) on Traditional Bullying. *Wiley Periodicals,Inc,Volume, 42*(2), 157–165.

Gradinger & Strohmeier. (2018). Cyber Bullying preventon with in a socio-ecological framework: The Visc social competence program. *Reducing Cyberbullying in Schools, 1*, 189-202.

Chapter 20
Challenges in Risk Analysis in Pharmaceutical Process Control for Data Security in the Health Sector

Maria Tereza Sousa Silva
Bio-Manguinhos, Fiocruz, Brazil

Erica Louro da Fonseca
Bio-Manguinhos, Fiocruz, Brazil

Zulmira Hartz
Institute of Hygiene and Tropical Medicine (IHMT), Global Health and Tropical Medicine (GHMT), University NOVA of Lisbon, Portugal

Jorge Magalhães
iD https://orcid.org/0000-0003-2219-5446
Institute of Hygiene and Tropical Medicine (IHMT), Global Health and Tropical Medicine (GHMT), University NOVA of Lisbon, Portugal

ABSTRACT

The informational and digital era of big data brings with it the challenge of knowledge management. There is a need for better management, protection, and security of these data, as well as the respective validation. It is imperative to develop new technologies for data security and their respective implementation in any organizations. In this way, this chapter presents a blueprint in a pharmaceutical industry with the aim at proposing a risk analysis of digital data use during quality control. It is worth mentioning the age of knowledge, the intellectual capital plays an important role in economics and business. A key to competitiveness and, therefore, to economic development in technology runs through a robust process that demonstrates perpetual security for its digital transformation and the respective control in a process ensured by quality assurance. Thus, this implies that time and human resources in organizations are not infinite.

DOI: 10.4018/978-1-7998-4201-9.ch020

Copyright © 2021, IGI Global. Copying or distributing in print or electronic forms without written permission of IGI Global is prohibited.

INTRODUCTION

The 21st century is marked by the exponential era of data available daily on the web. This era of knowledge is characterized by the pressing need for new technologies to manage the brutal amount of data. This huge amount of data on the Web, characterized as Big Data, requires new approaches and perspectives for knowledge management. Big Data drives a new generation of methodologies developed to extract economic and strategic value from a large and varied volume of data (structured and unstructured), allowing high speed of capture and analysis ("Gray, J. and Chambers, L. and Bounegru, L., The Data Journalism Handbook, O'Reilly Media, 2012; O'Reilly, 2007).

Big Data refers to the third generation of the information age (Magalhaes, JL & Quoniam, L, 2015; Raghupathi & Raghupathi, 2014). Initially, this exponential volume of data met the criteria of the 3Vs: Volume, Variety and Velocity (Laney, 2001); subsequently, 2 Vs were added: the attributes of Veracity and Value. Some authors even attribute the last 3 Vs, such as Veracity, Versatility and Viability, where the combination of all "Vs" generates the "V" of Value (ALEIXO & DUARTE, 2015a). According to Minelli et al (2013), Big Data is divided into a perfect data storm, a perfect convergence storm and a perfect computing storm, the latter resulting from 4 phenomena: Moore's law, mobile computing, social networks and computing in cloud computing. This data collection must be treated to present information searched selectively and objectively to increase business intelligence, in addition to allowing an improvement in the decision-making process (Minelli, M., Chambers, M., & Dhiraj, A., 2013).

In the health area it is no different: scientific and technological information needs to be identified, extracted, treated and the essential information available for decision making. In the pursuit of research and development for health, the pharmaceutical industry generates more than US $ 1 trillion annually. Health is considered as a global public good: that it is not exclusive, that is, that no one or any community is excluded from its possession or consumption; and that its benefits are available to everyone. There is also the apparent consensus that health is not competitive, and that there is no rivalry, that is, the health of a person cannot be at the expense of excluding other people (Buse & Waxman, 2001; Haines et al., 2009; Z. M. A. Hartz, 2012; Vance, Howe, & Dellavalle, 2009).

In the health spectrum, it carries challenges and opportunities in the globalization process, which is the catalyst for the evolution of the term "Global Health". Global health can be understood, at the same time, as a condition, an activity, a profession, a philosophy, a discipline, or a movement. However, it must be considered that there is no consensus on what Global Health is, nor a single definition. Its field of action has imprecise limits (Fortes & Ribeiro, 2014), however it is indisputable that we live health in times of globalization (Koplan et al., 2009).

In the context of health, the pharmaceutical market is highly regulated, and it is subject to national and international inspections periodically. In Brazil, the pharmaceutical industry is regulated by the National Agency for Sanitary Surveillance (ANVISA), which is responsible to establish the minimum requirements to be followed to comply with Good Manufacturing Practices (GMP). The current resolution of Medicinal products for human use is RDC No. 301 published in 2019, republished in April 2020, where new concepts were included in the regulation for medicines in the country, among them, the validation and risk analysis (ANVISA, 2019).

In 2010, ANVISA also made available the Guide to Computer Systems Validation (GVSC - critical qualification) that guides a set of criteria to perform the validation of critical systems. In general, a system can be considered critical for validation if it offers patient risk, product quality and data integrity.

In this context of criticality, Enterprise Resource Planning (ERP) systems are widely used in industries (BRASIL. Ministério da Saúde. Agência Nacional de Vigilância Sanitária., 2010).

Project risk management and digital transformation are ways of addressing the risks that pharmaceutical processes are entailed, since actions are defined in Anvisa's RDC 301/2019 and others international guidelines. They were responsibilities established by a company that must "identify, analyze, evaluate, monitor and treat. " "risks" or the set of risk management activities (ANVISA, 2012).

According to Haddad (2013), in the panorama of the pharmaceutical industries, management by processes is disseminated through the implementation of the Quality Management System and aims to control processes. In the same sense, the management of the information inherent in each stage of the process is essential to have reliable and validated data, so that, in times of Big Data, digital data is ensured with the proper quality, security and effectiveness (Jorge Lima de Magalhães et al., 2019).

In areas of high density, such as pharmaceuticals, aerospace and telecommunications, among others of equal weight and impact, knowledge becomes the most important asset and, therefore, the need to better manage this knowledge (Lastres, HMM & Sarita, A, 1999; J. Magalhães, Hartz, Temido, & Antunes, 2018). So, considering the relevance of the Pharmaceutical Industry and the urgent need to adapt its production processes to the current legislation and their respective updates, it is necessary to comply with the requirements of RDC 301/2019, regarding the validation of computerized systems and the respective risk analysis that goes through data security.

INFORMATION AND KNOWLEDGE MANAGEMENT

Information is a data or set of data articulated to construct a meaningful message. The way to organize the data is an intention. It is therefore partially subjective. The information implies a transmitter and a receiver but also a media whose nature is far from neutral (Kira TARAPANOFF (org.), 2015).

These poles suppose the existence of an aptitude, in the form of selective understanding, to extract the meaning of the information from the surrounding noise. Information is therefore a set of data placed in a context, mainly organizational for what interests us here, and bearing a meaning. Again, the concept has given rise to considerable developments in the information system and the development of protocols to make information systems as efficient as possible. Three notions are generally associated: that of information system (with the question of its economic performance), that of quantity of information (with the tension that appears between the amount of information made available and the super information) and ambiguity (which opens the question of relevance, a question linked to the imprecise notion of "quality" of information) (Pesqueux, 2005).

Information is a condition for survival, given that it expands the context of communication, rescuing and preserving social memory. Its value is intangible and resists all mechanisms of forgetfulness and destruction, since the collection of information reconstruction allows the cognitive evaluation and the knowledge of a certain reality in question ((Gavirneni, Kapuscinski, & Tayur, 1999).

In the 21st century, thanks to the evolution of the Web, the speed of information generation is unprecedented and unprecedented even in the world. The world's per capita technological capacity to store information has almost doubled every 40 months since the 1980s. The Internet evolved from a purely static platform and assumed to be dynamic and an interactive role (Minelli, M. et al., 2013), allowing users to exchange large amounts of information instantly.

Once the proliferation of data and information through the internet and the flow of information is established and there are no restrictions on distance and availability, the big question that arises is the ability to screen, interpret and convert this volume of information into knowledge. The identification and analysis of the amount of information of a given area, whether scientific, technological or business; identify their state of the art and their respective correlations have become hard work (ALEIXO & DUARTE, 2015b; J.L. Magalhães & Quoniam, 2013).

Therefore, it is necessary a management analysis to integrate actions and to provide the effectiveness actions to generate technological innovation and, consequently, wealth of the country. Thus, a better management for information architecture, also known as business architecture, encourage a new understanding (Ross, Weill, & Robertson, 2006).

Knowledge Management requires the involvement and support of all the company's stakeholders to preserve, transmit and develop knowledge. Indeed, it is the individuals who are at the center of the creation of value and who hold the keys to the success of such a project. The management of the knowledge and know-how of the company is therefore not universal, it depends strongly on the culture of the country in which it is practiced (Balmisse, 2006).

To motivate individuals to share their knowledge, it is important to consider cultural and human factors, and not just tools and procedures define "culture" as the set of values, norms, habits, and customs specific to a society that will influence the personality of the individual (Pesqueux & Ferrary, 2011).

According to Morin (1982), it is necessary to elevate the concept of "system" of this theoretical level to the paradigmatic level. A paradigm, for the author, is the set of fundamental relationships of association and/or opposition between a small number of "master concepts" that command/control all existing knowledge in all the speeches and theories. Thus, to sustain the action cycle (application) of the knowledge to the action progress, it is necessary to try to identify/define what are these notions, featuring the new paradigm and to resume as the (re)definition of the system where the logic of complexity in modeling the actual performance interact with a posture of the researcher and the actors involved in evaluative process ((Z. M. de A. Hartz, 1997; PIAGET & GARCIA, 1983).

THE PHARMACEUTICAL INDUSTRY AND QUALITY CONTROL

Ensuring the quality of your services in compliance with regulatory orders is paramount. Thus, for the pharmaceutical sector, it is no different. Health products must comply with the pillars of quality, safety, and effectiveness. Therefore, pharmaceutical companies should seek alternatives that result in greater effectiveness and quality in the execution of their processes in agreement with the health regulatory agencies (ABNT, 2019).

The health control of the Brazilian pharmaceutical industries is carried out through current legislation issued by the National Health Surveillance Agency (ANVISA) whose main mission is:

"Protect and promote the health of the population through intervention in the risks arising from the production and use of products and services subject to health surveillance, in a coordinated and integrated action within the scope of the Unified Health System (SUS)"(ANVISA, 2019).

The production of medicines requires special care to guarantee quality, safety and efficacy. In this context, Good Manufacturing Practices (GMP) have a fundamental factor as they are applied to all stages of the product's life cycle, from experimental drugs, technology transfer, commercial manufacturing to product discontinuation (BRASIL. MS., 2019).

As recommended by RDC 301/2019, the pharmaceutical industry must achieve the quality objective reliably, being necessary to have a comprehensive Pharmaceutical Quality System, correctly implemented, incorporating good manufacturing practices and quality risk management (BRASIL. MS., 2019). In this perspective, PAIM et al. (2009) state that the process improvement attitude is a basic action on the part of organizations to respond to constant changes in their operating environment while maintaining the competitive production system. Therefore, improving processes is a critical factor for the institutional success of any organization, whether public or private, if it is carried out in a systematic way and is understood by everyone in the company (PAIM, CARDDOSO, CAULLIRAUX, & CLEMENTE, 2009).

According to RDC 301/2019, in Article 8, a suitable Pharmaceutical Quality System for the manufacture of medicines must guarantee continuous improvement through the implementation of appropriated quality actions to the level of knowledge of the process and the product. Likewise, article 22 defines risk assessment based on scientific knowledge and experience with the process as one of the principles of quality risk management and, ultimately, is linked to patient protection (BRASIL. MS., 2019). Furthermore, the Brazilian General Data Protection Law (LGPD) nº 13,709, of August 14, 2018) provides for the processing of personal data, including in digital media, by a natural person or a legal person under public or private law, with the objective of protecting the fundamental rights of freedom and privacy and the free development of the personality of the natural person (BRASIL, Presidência da República, 2018).

In Brazil, there are private pharmaceutical companies and the Official Pharmaceutical Laboratories (LFO) considered public. These LFO's are distributed throughout the national territory and comply with the country's sanitary legislation with equal rigor. They also seek technological innovation with investments to achieve continuous improvement in their Quality System. Among these LFO's, we can highlight the Marine Pharmaceutical Laboratory, the Pharmaceuticals Technology Institute (Farmanguinhos), the Immunobiological Technology Institute (Bio-Manguinhos), investing in the development and production of medicines, vaccines, biopharmaceuticals to meet the programs promoting the health of the Brazilian population. The challenges are intrinsic to each of these programs, which together aim to meet the demands of public health and seek excellence in expanding society's access to strategic health inputs. In line with ANVISA's regulatory requirements, the improvement of these laboratories is mandatory ("Bio-Manguinhos/Fiocruz ‖ Inovação em saúde - Bio-Manguinhos/Fiocruz ‖ Inovação em saúde ‖ Vacinas, kits para diagnósticos e biofármacos", 2020).

According to PAIM et al. (2009), to improve the process, the study and understanding of management enables the reduction of the time between the identification of a performance problem and the implementation of the necessary solutions. However, to reduce this time, the actions of modeling and analysis of processes must be well structured, allowing a quick diagnosis and facilitating the identification of solutions, which therefore allows the execution of the process in the shortest possible time and cost (PAIM et al., 2009).

In this context, there are analytical inspections, where the results must be considered satisfactory or not as specified. For example, timely records that demonstrate all the productive stages of the batch in accordance with the defined instructions and previous procedures. These must be quantifiable and traceable, and their records must be posted in validated systems. It is worth mentioning that, if there are deviations during the production process, they must be investigated with identification of the root cause and corrective actions must be implemented. Nevertheless, evaluation of the impact on product quality, as well as records that allow the tracking and history of the batch in question (BRASIL. MS., 2019).

In view of the above, it is urgent to reflect on the batch release process in Process Control - its intrinsic steps and risks. This is a meticulous and time-consuming activity. This should be more agile while maintaining its effectiveness, so that the expected deadlines for the distribution of lots in compliance with the demand of the programs are met. It should be noted that the process must be identified and mapped from end to end, in order to enable an assessment of the imminent risks, as well as to define critical parameters and the time of completion of each step (measurement of lead time). Likewise, the provision of data must be considered, in the sense of proposing improvement actions aimed at reducing the time of the activities performed. This can be characterized as a just in time process - a leaner process, however, more robust from the point of view of product quality and safety.

The concern with quality guides the quality management system to provide better functioning of its processes to obtain products manufactured with quality and guarantee consumer satisfaction. The system is based on sets of management concepts, practices and tools that employees are strategically concerned with managing, guiding and raising awareness among the sectors of the organization, aiming at the quality of processes and, in the end, customer approval (Shan et al., 2017) .

RDC 301/2019 of ANVISA recommends that the quality management system must be comprehensive and correctly implemented, incorporating Good Manufacturing Practices and Quality Risk Management. Also it must guarantee that the product design is achieved through design, planning, implementation, maintenance and continuous improvement that allows the consistent manufacture of products with appropriate quality attributes (BRASIL. MS., 2019).

According to Nunes Pinheiro (2017), in the pharmaceutical industries many quality management practices described in ISO 9001 are employed, among them: evidence-based risk management, quality by design, corrective and preventive actions, continuous improvement practices such as: PDCA, lean manufacturing, among others (Shan et al., 2017). According to RDC 301/2019, good manufacturing practice is the part of quality management that ensures that products are consistently produced and controlled, in accordance with appropriate quality standards for the intended use and required by the health record, authorization for use in clinical trial or product specifications. Good manufacturing practices include guidelines for the entire product processing chain, including the acquisition of materials, production, quality control, release, storage, shipping of finished products and related controls (BRASIL. MS., 2019).

Every quality management system can incorporate the PDCA cycle and the risk mindset to facilitate the planning and interaction of its processes, ensuring sufficient resources that effectively managed corroborate with the identification of opportunities for improvement and taking actions. Therefore, an adequate quality management system answers specific questions, so that the quality objective is fully achieved. Concerning the pharmaceutical industry, the appropriate management and minimization of the risks involved in the manufacture of medicines, with the objective of guaranteeing the quality, efficacy and safety of the finished product, GMPs appear as a compulsory and technical regulatory tool (Vogler, Gratieri, Gelfuso, & Cunha Filho, 2017).

RISK MANAGEMENT IN THE PHARMACEUTICAL INDUSTRY

The quality of products and their inputs have been increasingly demanded and to correspond to such levels, processes, equipment and professionals must be evaluated at each production stage. To assess these levels of quality in products and services, quality risk management is an integral part, and the quality risk management system is now internalized in regulatory authorities, compulsory to the pharmaceutical industries (Sindicato da Indústria de Produtos Farmacêuticos no Estado de São Paulo, 2012).

According to Geyer (2018), the implementation of risk-based approaches contributes to prioritizing inspections of high-risk installations. The ISO 9001: 2015 standard enables an organization to use the process approach, combined with the PDCA cycle and the risk mindset, considering risk as an effect of uncertainty. A positive deviation from a risk can offer an opportunity, but not all positive risk effects result in opportunities (Geyer, Sousa, & Silveira, 2018).

RISK MANAGEMENT IN THE LIGHT OF LEGISLATION:

1. According to RDC 301/2019:
   - Art. 21 Quality Risk Management is a systematic process of assessing, controlling, communicating, and reviewing risks to the quality of the medication. Quality Risk Management can be applied proactively and retrospectively. All new processes in the pharmaceutical industry must be governed by risk management, and these new processes must be analyzed proactively.
   - Art. 22 defines risk assessment based on scientific knowledge, experience with the process as one of the principles of quality risk management and, ultimately, is linked to patient protection and in addition, the level of effort, formality and documentation of the Quality Risk Management process must be compatible with the level of risk.
2. According toQ9 – Quality Risk Management (ICH, 2005):
   - Risk is defined as the combination of the probability of damage occurring and the severity of that damage. Risk management is a systematic process for assessing, controlling, communicating, and reviewing quality risks throughout the drug's life cycle. Thus, it seeks to guarantee a high-quality medicine for the user, being a proactive way to identify and control quality problems during its development and manufacture. In addition, risk management helps in decision making when a quality problem arises. To start a risk management process, it is necessary to define the Problem Tree – tools such as *smart* or *masp* for troubleshooting, the maximum gathering of information about the defined problem, through an established leadership (ICH, 2005). In this sense, to carry out the process, it is necessary to:
     1. Assess the Risk: Risk identification, Risk analysis and Risk control
     2. Control Risk: it is the decision-making process to reduce and / or accept risks. The purpose of risk control is to reduce risks to an acceptable level.
     3. Communicate Risk: it is the sharing of information between all stakeholders, where the parties communicate at any stage of the quality and risk management process. The product / result of the quality and risk management process must be effectively communicated and documented.
     4. Review the Risk: it is the ongoing part of the process as a mechanism to review or monitor events. The result of the quality and risk management process must be reviewed to consider new knowledge and experiences. Once a quality and risk management process is initiated, this process should continue to be used for events such as reviews, inspections, audits or product change controls that may have an impact on the original quality

management decision with risk-based. The frequency of reviews should be based on the level of risk and may include reconsidering risk acceptance decisions.

It is worth mentioning the Risk Management Tools used to carry out the risk assessment. Table 1 highlights the main risk management tools according to ICH (2005):

Table 1. Key Risk Management Tools

MAIN RISK ANALYSIS TOOLS		
TOOL	**DEFINITION**	**OBJECTIVE**
FMEA *Failure Mode Effects Analysis*	Failure Mode and Effects Analysis	Define, identify, and eliminate potential failures
FMECA *Failure Mode, Effects and Criticality Analysis*	Analysis of Mode Criticality and Failure Effects	Estimate the severity of failure modes; The probability of failure modes occurring; analyze the criticality
FTA *Fault Tree Analysis*	Fault Tree Analysis	It addresses a failure system, as it combines its multiple causes
HACCP *Hazard Analysis and Critical Control Points*	Hazard Analysis and Critical Control Points	Conduct a hazard analysis; Identify preventive measures for each stage of the process; Determine critical control points; Establish critical limits; Establish a system to monitor critical control points; Establish corrective actions to be taken; Establish a system to verify that HACCP is efficient and; Establish a record-keeping system
HAZOP *Hazard Operability Analysis*	Analysis of Operational Hazards	Qualitative, systematic, and structured approach through the appropriate use of guide words applied to critical points related to the process under analysis
PHA *Preliminary Hazard Analysis*	Preliminary Hazard Analysis	Identify future hazards so that preventive measures can be estimated before a process, system or product enters its operational phase
Risk Ranking and Filtering	Risk Classification and Filtering	Compare and classify risks

Source: Adapted from (International Council for Harmonisation of Technical Requirements for Pharmaceuticals for Human Use, 2016, p. 9; Sindicato da Indústria de Produtos Farmacêuticos no Estado de São Paulo, 2012)

IDENTIFY PROCESS RISKS TO ENSURE DATA SECURITY

The careful and systematic investigation of the processes through modeling, the improvement of theoretical knowledge and the use of the guidelines applied at the institute provided elements that highlighted the dangers and the critical control points. The listed items were discussed in focal meetings with multidisciplinary and focal teams through the Brainstorming tool. The meetings held in four moments aimed at confirming the identification of critical points, carrying out the analysis and classification.

There is also the question of Failure Mode Effect Analysis (FMEA) provides a perspective of the evidence that failure to manage supply chain risks can effectively have a significant negative impact on organizations. They are consequences of a failure to manage risks effectively. These include not just only financial losses, but also, reduction in product quality, damage to property and equipment, loss of reputation in the eyes of customers, suppliers and the wider public, and delivery delays. There is evidence that economic, political and social developments over the past decade appear to be increasing the risk of supply chain disruptions as supply chains get longer and more complex involving more partners due to the increase in global sourcing (Kumar, Dieveney, & Dieveney, 2009).

Given the above, it can be concluded that for effective Quality Management and Statistical Process Control with risk analysis are provided goals of focusing on their implementation. So, this implementation is presented in several areas like the philosophical and behavioral requirements, the statistical monitoring, and the statistical design (Gershon, 1991; Kumar et al., 2009; Werkema, 1995; Wu, Khan, & Hussain, 2007).

FINAL CONSIDERATIONS

The pharmaceutical industry is an extremely important sector for the health sector. Its research, development and innovation provide mankind with medicines and treatments aiming at a better quality of life and health promotion. On the other hand, the government policies of each country, combine the promotion, attention, diagnosis, data security and access to all its population in order to improve their quality of life.

The quality control tools associated with risk analysis for data security in the pharmaceutical industry, characterize many benefits and quality intrinsic to the process, such as: increased automation and reduced human intervention, reduced rework, scrap (process losses) and, consequently, increasing the productive capacity and data security.

The intelligent use of process control technologies in production, through risk analysis as an aspect of total quality, has beneficial effects far beyond the traditional aspects of traditional assured quality. Therefore, not only does it comply with sanitary standards and LGPD, it also increases your profits and consumer confidence.

Humanity's constant search for a better quality of life are efforts made, worldwide, by all sectors of the economy. Health is no different, which translates into constant challenge. This challenge involves constant updates of safety and efficacy, whether in technologies for new drugs and medications, as well as for the protection of this data, data security, analysis of these risks for both in-process control and for the population that will use these products.

REFERENCES

ABNT. (2019). *ABNT - Associação Brasileira de Normas Técnicas*. Recuperado 31 de março de 2019, de http://www.abnt.org.br/

Aleixo, J. A., & Duarte, P. (2015). Big data opportunities in healthcare. how can medical affairs contribute? *Revista Portuguesa de Farmacoterapia*, 7, 230–236.

ANVISA. (2012). *Agência Nacional de Vigilância Sanitária*. Recuperado 18 de fevereiro de 2013, de Lista de Estatísticas website: http://portal.anvisa.gov.br/wps/portal/anvisa/anvisa/home/medicamentos/!ut/p/c4/04_SB8K8xLLM9MSSzPy8xBz9CP0os3hnd0cPE3MfAwMDMydnA093Uz8z00B_A_cgQ_2CbEdFADghJT0!/?1dmy&urile=wcm%3Apath%3A/anvisa+portal/anvisa/inicio/medicamentos/publicacao+medicamentos/lista+de+estatisticas+-+genericos

ANVISA. (2019). *Agência Nacional de Vigilância Sanitária*. Author.

Balmisse, G. (2006). *Guide des Outils du Knowledge Management: Panorama, choix et mise en oeuvre.* Recuperado de https://www.leslivresblancs.fr/informatique/applications-pro/knowledge-management/livre-blanc/outils-du-km-panorama-choix-et-mise-en-oeuvre-62.html

Bio-Manguinhos/Fiocruz. (2020). Recuperado 3 de setembro de 2020, de Bio-Manguinhos/Fiocruz || Inovação em saúde || Vacinas, reativos para diagnósticos e biofármacos website: https://www.bio.fiocruz.br/index.php/br/

Brasil. Ministério da Saúde. Agência Nacional de Vigilância Sanitária. *RESOLUÇÃO - RDC Nº 17, DE 16 DE ABRIL DE 2010.*, (2010).

Brasil. MS., A. *Boas Práticas de Fabricação—RDC Nº 301, DE 21 DE AGOSTO DE 2019.*, Pub. L. No. RDC Nº 301 (2019).

Brasil, Presidência da República. *Lei Geral de Proteção de Dados Pessoais (LGPD)—13709.*, (2018).

Buse, K., & Waxman, A. (2001). Public-private health partnerships: A strategy for WHO. *Bulletin of the World Health Organization, 79*(8), 748–754. doi:10.1590/S0042-96862001000800011 PMID:11545332

Fortes, P. A. de C., & Ribeiro, H. (2014). Saúde Global em tempos de globalização. *Saúde e Sociedade, 23*(2), 366–375. doi:10.1590/S0104-12902014000200002

Gavirneni, S., Kapuscinski, R., & Tayur, S. (1999). Value of Information in Capacitated Supply Chains. *Management Science, 45*(1), 16–24. doi:10.1287/mnsc.45.1.16

Gershon, M. (1991). Statistical Process Control for the Pharmaceutical Industry. *PDA Journal of Pharmaceutical Science and Technology, 45*(1), 41–50. PMID:2007968

Geyer, A. R. C., Sousa, V. D., & Silveira, D. (2018). Quality of medicines: Deficiencies found by Brazilian Health Regulatory Agency (ANVISA) on good manufacturing practices international inspections. *PLoS One, 13*(8), e0202084. doi:10.1371/journal.pone.0202084 PMID:30089162

Gray, J., Chambers, L., & Bounegru, L. (n.d.). *The Data Journalism Handbook.* O'Reilly Media. Recuperado 6 de março de 2014, de http://www.infovis-wiki.net/index.php?title=Gray,_J._and_Chambers,_L._and_Bounegru,_L.,_The_Data_Journalism_Handbook,_O%27Reilly_Media,_2012

Haines, A., McMichael, A. J., Smith, K. R., Roberts, I., Woodcock, J., Markandya, A., Armstrong, B. G., Campbell-Lendrum, D., Dangour, A. D., Davies, M., Bruce, N., Tonne, C., Barrett, M., & Wilkinson, P. (2009). Public health benefits of strategies to reduce greenhouse-gas emissions: Overview and implications for policy makers. *Lancet, 374*(9707), 2104–2114. doi:10.1016/S0140-6736(09)61759-1 PMID:19942281

Hartz, Z. M. A. (2012). Meta-evaluation of health management: Challenges for "new public health". *Ciencia e Saude Coletiva, 17*(4), 832–834. doi:10.1590/S1413-81232012000400004

Hartz, Z. M. de A. (1997). *Avaliação em saúde: Dos modelos conceituais à prática na análise da implantação de programas.* Editora FIOCRUZ. Recuperado de http://books.scielo.org/id/3zcft

International Council for Harmonisation of Technical Requirements for Pharmaceuticals for Human Use. (2016, julho 20). *ICH Official web site: ICH*. Recuperado 20 de julho de 2016, de ICH harmonisation for better health website: https://www.ich.org/home.html

Kira, T. (Org.). (2015). *Analise da Informacao para Tomada de Decisao Desafios e Solucoes* (Vol. 1). Brasil: Editora Intersaberes. Recuperado de https://www.estantevirtual.com.br/b/kira-tarapanoff/analise-da-informacao-para-tomada-de-decisao-desafios-e-solucoes/158550962

Koplan, J. P., Bond, T. C., Merson, M. H., Reddy, K. S., Rodriguez, M. H., Sewankambo, N. K., & Wasserheit, J. N. (1993–1995). Consortium of Universities for Global Health Executive Board. (2009). Towards a common definition of global health. *Lancet, 373*(9679), 1993–1995. Advance online publication. doi:10.1016/S0140-6736(09)60332-9

Kumar, S., Dieveney, E., & Dieveney, A. (2009). Reverse logistic process control measures for the pharmaceutical industry supply chain. *International Journal of Productivity and Performance Management, 58*(2), 188–204. doi:10.1108/17410400910928761

Laney, D. (2001). *3D Data Management: Controlling Data Volume*. Velocity, and Variety. Recuperado de http://blogs.gartner.com/doug-laney/files/2012/01/ad949-3D-Data-Management-Controlling-Data-Volume-Velocity-and-Variety.pdf

Lastres, H. M. M., & Sarita, A. (1999). *Informação e Globalização na Era do Conhecimento*. Editora Campus Ltda.

Magalhães, Igarashi, Hartz, Antunes, Macedo, Magalhães, … Macedo. (2019). *Project Management in Risk Analysis for Validation of Computer Systems in the Warehouse System*. Recuperado 11 de maio de 2020, de Http://services.igi-global.com/resolvedoi/resolve.aspx?doi=10.4018/978-1-5225-9993-7.ch008

Magalhães, J., Hartz, Z., Temido, M., & Antunes, A. (2018). Gestão do conhecimento em tempos de big data: Um olhar dos desafios para os sistemas de saúde. *Anais do Instituto de Higiene e Medicina Tropical, 17*, 7–16. doi:10.25761/anaisihmt.256

Magalhães, J. L., & Quoniam, L. (2013). Perception of the Information Value for Public Health: A Case Study for Neglected Diseases. In *Rethinkin the Conceptual Base for New Practical Applications in Information Value and Quality* (p. 345). IGI Global. Recuperado de https://www.igi-global.com/chapter/perception-information-value-public-health/84218

Magalhaes, J. L., & Quoniam, L. (2015). Percepção do valor da informação por meio da inteligência competitiva 2.0 e do Big Data na saúde. In Análise da Informação para Tomada de Decisão: Desafios e soluções (p. 365). Brasil: Kira Tarapanoff.

Minelli, M., Chambers, M., & Dhiraj, A. (2013). *Big Data, Big Analytics*. John Wiley & Sons, Inc. Recuperado de https://books.google.com.br/books/about/Big_Data_Big_Analytics.html?hl=pt-BR&id=Mg3WvT8uHV4C

O'Reilly, T. (2007). *What is Web 2.0: Design Patterns and Business Models for the Next Generation of Software* (SSRN Scholarly Paper Nº ID 1008839). Rochester, NY: Social Science Research Network. Recuperado de Social Science Research Network website: https://papers.ssrn.com/abstract=1008839

Paim, R., Carddoso, V., Caulliraux, H., & Clemente, R. (2009). *Gestão de Processos: Pensar, Agir e Aprender eBook: Paim, Rafael, Cardoso, Vinicius, Caulliraux, Heitor, Clemente, Rafael: Amazon.com. br: Loja Kindle*. Bookman. Recuperado de https://www.amazon.com.br/Gest%C3%A3o-Processos-Pensar-Agir-Aprender-ebook/dp/B018KGC3F0

Pesqueux, Y. (2005). Management de la connaissance: Un modèle organisationnel? *Management de la connaissance : un modele organisationnel?* Recuperado de https://halshs.archives-ouvertes.fr/halshs-00004005/document

Pesqueux, Y., & Ferrary, M. (2011). Management de la connaissance (2o ed). Economica. Recuperado de /Entreprise/Livre/management-de-la-connaissance-9782717860153

Piaget, J., & Garcia, R. (1983). Article. *Psychogenèse et Histoire des Sciences. 19*(1), 304.

Raghupathi, W., & Raghupathi, V. (2014). Big data analytics in healthcare: Promise and potential. *Health Information Science and Systems, 2*(1), 3. Advance online publication. doi:10.1186/2047-2501-2-3 PMID:25825667

Ross, J. W., Weill, P., & Robertson, D. (2006). *Enterprise Architecture as Strategy: Creating a Foundation for Business Execution*. Harvard Business Review Press.

Shan, C., Muruato, A. E., Nunes, B. T. D., Luo, H., Xie, X., & Medeiros, D. B. A. (2017). A live-attenuated Zika virus vaccine candidate induces sterilizing immunity in mouse models. *Nature Medicine*. Advance online publication. doi:10.1038/nm.4322 PMID:28394328

Sindicato da Indústria de Produtos Farmacêuticos no Estado de São Paulo. (2012). *Sindusfarma*. Recuperado 15 de fevereiro de 2013, de Syndicate of pharmaceutical industries in the State of Sao Paulo website: http://www.sindusfarmacomunica.org.br/indicadores-economicos/

Vance, K., Howe, W., & Dellavalle, R. P. (2009). Social Internet Sites as a Source of Public Health Information. *Dermatologic Clinics, 27*(2), 133–136. doi:10.1016/j.det.2008.11.010 PMID:19254656

Vogler, M., Gratieri, T., Gelfuso, G. M., & Cunha Filho, M. S. S. (2017). As boas práticas de fabricação de medicamentos e suas determinantes. *Vigilância Sanitária em Debate, 5*(2), 34. doi:10.22239/2317-269x.00918

Werkema, M. C. C. (1995). *Ferramentas estatisticas basicas para o gerenciamento de processos*. Universidade Federal de Minas Gerais. Escola de Engenharia. Fundacao Christiano Ottoni.

Wu, H., Khan, M. A., & Hussain, A. S. (2007). Process Control Perspective for Process Analytical Technology: Integration of Chemical Engineering Practice into Semiconductor and Pharmaceutical Industries. *Chemical Engineering Communications, 194*(6), 760–779. doi:10.1080/00986440601098755

Chapter 21
Digital Transformation of the Real Estate Segment With Big Data and Marketing Analytics:
A Case Study From QUOT

Luciano Barbosa

UFPE, Brazil

Sérgio Ricardo Goes Oliveira

UFBA, Brazil

Joao Rocha Jr.

UEFS, Brazil

Emanuele Marques

UFC, Brazil

Sérgio Maravilhas

iD https://orcid.org/0000-0002-3824-2828

SENAI CIMATEC, Brazil & UNIFACS, Salvador University, Brazil

ABSTRACT

In this chapter, the birth of a Brazilian start-up is analyzed against the background of the digital transformation of the real estate segment. First, the authors describe the economic importance of the sector and its operation. Then they present the platform that makes use of advanced techniques in the areas of artificial intelligence, visualization, management, and data processing. This platform helps to capture wealth and amount of data in real-time, demonstrating the revolutionary potential of the era of big data and consumer analytics. The text explores the changes that the platform imposes on the traditional real estate model while detailing how the decision-making process in this sector is impacted.

DOI: 10.4018/978-1-7998-4201-9.ch021

Copyright © 2021, IGI Global. Copying or distributing in print or electronic forms without written permission of IGI Global is prohibited.

INTRODUCTION

It is undeniable that access, processing and analysis of data have assumed a central importance within the competitive business context. The growing production of information, migration of business from the real world to the virtual world and technological development has presented companies with problems and opportunities. This data growth occurs in parallel with the attempt to develop tools that cannot only store such data, but also analyze it. In the case of the business area, it is expected that access to these data and their analysis capacity will provide organizations with competitive capabilities that favor them in the competitive scenario.

Apparently, there is a disconnect or, at least, a mismatch between the development of the academic and analytical world in the area of marketing and of information technology regarding new forms, tools and technologies for data storage and analysis. Wedel and Kannan (2016) discuss, precisely, the evolution of the capacity for marketing analysis within data-rich environments. The authors hope that the next evolution of the analytical capacity of marketing within the digital economy will take place through the development of models that can generate diagnostics and support for real-time decisions arising from what we call "Big Data".

The term Big Data has been used a lot inappropriately in relation to supporting marketing decisions. Sanders (2016) points out that Big Data without analysis (analytics) is nothing more than the massive use of data. As well as the use of analytics without Big Data is just statistical applications. That is, the combination of Big Data, analytics and all the growing computational power is what can transform data into intelligence.

It is important what Sanders (2016) calls attention. According to the author, in the still incipient marketing and retail literature on the use of Big Data, the weight or importance relative to the capacity of analysis (analytics) is little found. For example, Reis et. al (2016) discuss the theme of relationship marketing and the possibilities of adding value through Big Data. Although the text provides a clear presentation of the concept of Big Data, the capacity for analysis is treated as something underlying and secondary. When, in fact, they are important complements so that the analysis capacity generated, defended through Big Data, can add the value proposed by the authors in the study.

MARKETING AND BIG DATA

The articles related to the discussion on the debate on the use of Big Data to support marketing decisions generally present a conceptual introduction and highlight the five main characteristics that comprise it, namely: volume, speed, variety, truthfulness

and value (Reis et. al, 2016; Sanders, 2016).

Therefore, we will not enter this conceptual presentation since the references in the previous paragraph do so in a very competent manner. What is most relevant in relation to the use of Big Data to support marketing decisions is that the current statistical and econometric models used in the marketing literature do not handle large volumes of data efficiently. With regard to structured data, the recent advances in marketing analysis are able to face great challenges, however with regard to unstructured data there are still major advances to be made. Future solutions for Big Data analysis must be able to diagnose, predict and prescribe approaches to analyze massive amounts of unstructured data. There are already solutions related to unstructured data analysis for data mining in text format and approaches with learning machines (Sanders, 2016; Sivarajah et al., 2017).

The present study seeks to present a possible solution in this sense. In other words, it presents a decision support tool with a focus on unstructured data analysis approach.

Decision Support Systems

Decision support systems (SSD) are applications that help users to make decisions more easily in a given domain, topic or within an organization. SSDs have been used in several areas such as medicine, agriculture, transport, among others.

In the retail context, there are few tools that help customers make decisions in the process of purchasing a product. For this reason, a usual way for the user to find out about the market value of a desired product is, for example, by browsing Web sites that market that product.

In this paper, we present the case of the QUOT platform, an SSD tool to provide users interested in the process of buying and / or selling real estate, useful information to help them in this process. Several users can benefit from the analyzes provided. People interested in buying / selling / renting or real estate brokers and realtors can use the tool to understand the real estate market in a given city and, for example, be able to identify the market value of the property to be sold. Another example of a potential user is city halls, which can update property taxes based on updated data provided by the tool.

A great highlight of the tool is the quality and comprehensiveness of the data on which the analyzes are carried out. This data is constantly obtained from several Brazilian real estate websites using techniques that are state-of-the-art in the area of Web Crawling. The fact that data from several sites are used helps to mitigate possible problems of bias in the analyzes, which can happen, for example, if data from a single site are used (Olston and Najork, 2010).

BRAZILIAN REAL ESTATE MARKET

The Brazilian real estate market is in an accelerated state of change, not only due to the delicate economic issues that affect Brazil, but also due to the effects of digital transformation that affect the sector. According to data from the business consulting company EY (2017), 785 thousand residential units were delivered in Brazil, which represented a turnover of R $ 104 billion in 2017. The same company estimates that, in 2035, these numbers will reach 971 thousand residential units with a turnover of R $ 273 billion.

Basically, this market consists of buying and selling new and used units. Usually, the sale is intermediated by a real estate broker or professional broker. The realtor has specialized training to evaluate the property, determine prices and conduct the entire marketing process. Although it is allowed in Brazil that this sale takes place directly between the individual owner of the property and third parties, which ends up happening very often.

Even having specialized knowledge, the broker ends up conducting research today, just as the layman does to price his property and put it up for sale or rent. A commonly used way to estimate the price of a given property is to look for similar properties on ad sites available on the Internet, performing a comparative analysis. Thus, using the desired property profile, a scan can be carried out for similar properties that are for sale in the region (eg neighborhood) of interest. In addition to being quite laborious, this approach presents serious problems, such as the difficulty in finding properties with similar profiles to the desired one in the place of interest. It was precisely within this scenario that a group of entrepreneurs with technological expertise and knowledge of the real estate market started the development of the real estate pricing platform called Quot.

WHAT IS QUOT?

Quot is a web tool with the objective of helping in the property pricing process and in understanding the price panorama of an area (city, region and / or neighborhood). For this, Quot provides a graphical interface in which the user can carry out exploratory queries on real estate prices from a given profile of interest. Through this query interface, it is possible to obtain information of the price of different property profiles. In addition, the tool is capable of estimating the price of a property (sale or rent), given an address and the profile of the property (number of rooms, area, etc.). The statistics and estimates presented in the Quot are performed using an ad base obtained through the collection on Brazilian real estate websites. For this, it makes use of well-established statistical models in the area of spatial interpolation to, from a set of geo-referenced properties data, infer the market value of a given property based on its location and profile. To provide all these functionalities, Quot uses advanced techniques in the areas of artificial intelligence, data visualization and big data for data collection, storage, visualization and analysis.

It is important to note that Quot was developed with resources to support innovation from the Brazilian Government and the Government of the State of Bahia. The resources were made available through a public notice of support for innovation promoted and supported by the Foundation for the Support of Research of the State of Bahia (FAPESB), Secretary of Science and Technology and Innovation (SECTI) of the Government of the State of Bahia, Financier of Studies and Projects (FINEP) and the National Council for Scientific and Technological Development (CNPq), which is an entity linked to the Ministry of Science, Technology, Innovations and Communications to encourage research in Brazil.

Data Collection Process

The ad base used by Quot is built using a collector of web pages or web crawler. For this, from a list of real estate sites, the collector, or crawler, navigates the links on the pages of those sites and, when visiting a page, he identifies if this is an ad. If so, the attributes of the property are extracted and inserted into the ad base. To perform the collection, the collector uses Machine Learning / Artificial Intelligence techniques that make the collector as efficient as possible, while at the same time obtaining good ad coverage from the sites.

The Quot ad base is built from ads from thousands of Brazilian websites. The geographic distribution of the sites used in our database is shown in Figure 1. In general, more populous states have a greater number of sites: São Paulo is the state with the most real estate sites, while the states in the North region have a very small number .

Figure 1. Geographic distribution of real estate websites based on the Quot.
Source: Quot

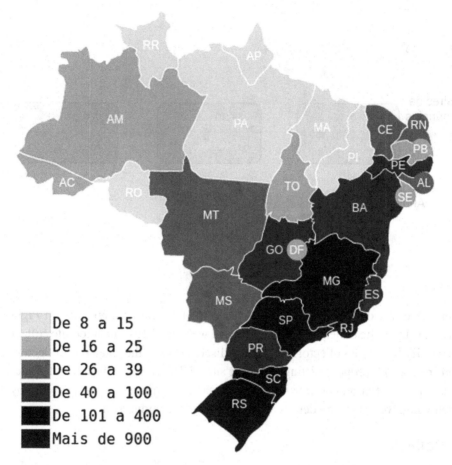

All the ads collected are georeferenced, that is, they have information on the property's latitude and longitude. In addition to the spatial information, the following attributes are extracted from the property listing page: number of bedrooms, area, number of bathrooms, number of parking spaces, sale or rent value and its type (apartment or house).

In order to efficiently manage this data, Quot uses cutting-edge data modeling techniques. For example, to deal with the geographical information of the ads (latitude and longitude), Quot uses spatial indexes as data replication and spatial indexes like R-Tree (Beckmann et al. 1990). These structures allow a quick result for a user's query: the average return time for a Quot query is around 100ms.

Web data collectors, or web crawlers, are applications that collect web pages (Olston and Najork, 2010). The most common and popular use of Web crawlers is made by search engines to collect pages to populate their databases. Web crawlers have been used in other domains that also benefit from data collected from the Web. For example, collectors have been proposed for the Natural Language Processing domain (Barbosa, Bangalore, 2011), Database (Barbosa, Freire, 2005) and local search (Ahlers, Boll, 2009).

Figure 2. Architecture of the proposed solution
Source: Quot

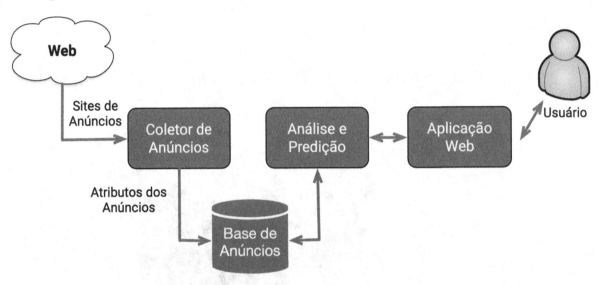

To collect real estate data, we implemented the collector strategy presented in Figure 2. Its main components are: I) Inter-site collector: given real estate website URLs, the inter-site collector finds other real estate sites. II) Intra-site collector: from sites discovered by the inter-site collector, the intra-site collector finds pages with property listings on these sites. III) Extractor: the attributes and values of real estate (such as square meter and price) on ad pages are extracted from pages identified by the intra-site collector. Following, we give more details about each of these components.

Inter-Site Collector

Traditional techniques of focused collectors follow page outlinks to browse the Web graph in search of relevant content. There are cases, however, in which the use of this strategy alone can lead to poor performance, for example, in domains where the pages are sparsely distributed in the Web graph. To deal with this problem, based on the work of Barbosa et al. (2011), we propose a focused collector that uses, in addition to outlinks, links that point to real estate sites to locate other relevant sites. More specifically, the collector exploits a graph whose nodes are pages that point to real estate sites already discovered (backlink pages), and pages pointed to by backlink pages (outlink pages). The main assumption of this strategy is that there are backlinks pages that have links to various real estate sites, called hubs. Hubs are therefore a rich source of links to real estate websites. Examples of real estate hubs are company pages that produce software specifically for real estate. These sites usually list real estate websites that use their software.

Intra-Site Collector

The intra-site collector aims to collect pages that contain pages with real estate ads on real estate sites. To prevent the collector from visiting unproductive regions of a website, it is important that it explores regularities in the link structure of the websites. For this, the collector explores the link patterns on these sites. Usually, the Uniform Resource Locator (URL) of the real estate listings on the same site have common standards. The Link Classifier is the component of the collector that given tokens from a URL predicts whether that URL points to an ad page. This prediction is made through models of supervised learning.

Extractor

The extractor receives a page with an advertisement for a property and extracts from that page the attributes of the property such as price, number of rooms and square meter. The great challenge of performing this task is that HTML pages are designed for human consumption and, therefore, do not have a common pattern. Given a page containing a real estate ad, the extractor first detects nodes in the DOM tree of the HTML page containing base attributes for the domain, such as bedrooms, area and bathrooms. From these attributes, it detects regions of the tree containing structured information about the attributes of the property. For this, it uses the ancestors common to the identified nodes. In the next step, identify the attributes present on the page, from the text on nodes that have a path similar to the nodes containing the base attributes. Finally, the extractor segments the texts contained in the subtree children of the roots of the detected regions, and identifies the attribute-value pairs from the segmented texts.

The extractor is able to extract attributes close to the HTML page. Some attributes such as price, latitude and longitude usually appear in isolation in the HTML of the page. So, in order to extract them, we created rules based on pattern matching. For example, for price we check in the text where R $ appears followed by a number.

The result of the extractor is the data of the properties with the following attributes: price, latitude, longitude, number of rooms, number of parking spaces, bathrooms and suites.

Analysis and Prediction Module

Analyzes based on real estate ads are carried out by the Analysis and Prediction module. In it, various information about the ads collected is calculated, for example, price history, average prices in a given region and price estimate for a given property. These analyzes are generated by data analysis models (descriptive and predictive statistics).

Supervised learning algorithms are a group of Machine Learning techniques that infer a function from data examples (training set) to predict classes (classification) or values (regression) (Mitchell, Michalski, & Carbonell, 2013). Once created, this function is used to estimate values for new examples. For the specific price estimation task for real estate, our examples are real estate and we are particularly interested in regression to estimate prices.

The algorithm used in our solution for price prediction was Random Forest (Liaw and Wiener, 2002). In general, this algorithm builds several decision trees and joins them together to create a more accurate model. A decision tree basically consists of a set of yes or no questions about the characteristics that lead to the result of the prediction. For example, a possible rule would be if the area of a property is greater than 100 square meters and the number of bedrooms is equal to 3, the estimated value of the property is 800,000 reais. These rules are created automatically from the examples passed in the training set. For the construction of this set of trees, two basic concepts are used: creation of decision trees from: 1) random sampling of training instances, and 2) random subsets of characteristics. The final prediction value is the average of the estimated values for each tree.

The tool used to carry out the experiments was Caret (Kuhn et al., 2008), a software package written in the R language. This package was chosen because it has the implementation of several regressors. In addition, it allows the search for the best values of the hyper-parameters existing in these models.

The user interacts with the system through the Web application (Figure 3). This component is responsible for the interface with the Analysis and Prediction module, transforming user interactions into queries and displaying results in graphs and visualizations.

Figure 3. WEB panel
Source: Quot

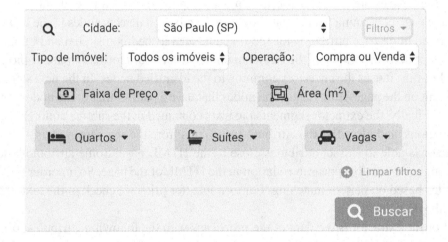

The color map used (Figure 4) is a segmented sequential color map, ranging from the least saturated color (lowest price) to the most saturated color (highest price). This choice is based on data visualization principles and color theory (Muzner, 2014) and allows for easier comparison and identification of price value ranges by color saturation.

Price Estimate

Another different feature of the Web application is the request for price estimation. Accessing the price estimation panel through the toolbar (Figure 3), the user can provide the parameters of the property to calculate the estimate, as shown in Figure 5a. The result of the estimate is shown just below the form (Figure 5b) and also contains the degree of certainty for that result. This indicator is important to inform the user about the quality of the estimate, that in the case of the example, the quality is high (70%).

The indicator shown uses a segmented categorical color map, ranging from shades of red (low quality), through yellow (medium quality), to shades of green (high quality).

For a more in-depth analysis of property prices, the user can view details of the price distribution for the different attributes of the property. To do this, he accesses the Detailed View panel, available from the toolbar (Figure 4d).

Figure 4. Screen capture of the Quot Web application showing the city of São Paulo.
a) Interactive thematic map of average price per m², using a sequential color map. b) Filter bar. c) Details of the price variation across the city. d) Toolbar for price estimation and detailed visualization features.
Source: Quot

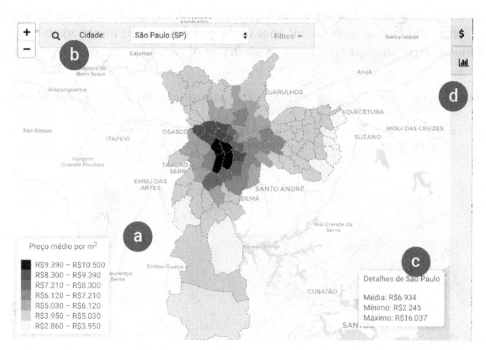

Figure 5. Price Estimation Panel.
Source: Quot

Using Quot

We will illustrate the use of Quot with a case study in which a user wants to estimate the price of a property located in the Pinheiros neighborhood, in the city of São Paulo. In addition to just getting a numerical value, that user would also like to understand what factors are influencing the estimate price. In the scenario described below, we will show all the steps of the analysis made by the user to obtain the estimate.

Figure 6 shows some price statistics for the Pinheiros neighborhood in São Paulo. For example, it is possible to obtain information about the m² price of the properties in the neighborhood, separating by number of rooms (Figure 6a), area (Figure 6b) and number of parking spaces (not shown in the figure).

Figure 6. Detailed View Panel showing property price statistics for the Pinheiros neighborhood in São Paulo.
a) Average price of m² (above) and property (below) by number of rooms. b) Average price of m² (above) and property (below) by area. c) Variation in the average m² price for the chosen neighborhood and city.
Source: Quot

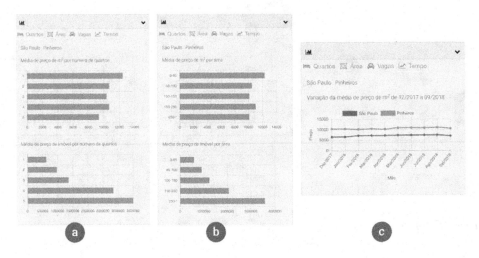

In addition, it is possible to access a graph that compares the price variation of the property in the selected neighborhood with the price of the property in the city over time (Figure 6c), allowing to identify whether the price of properties in the region is in an upward trend or low. All charts are interactive, and users can get accurate price values by hovering over the bars and lines.

He starts by accessing the Quot web application and chooses the city of São Paulo on the map. Initially, he gets an overview of the average price of m² per neighborhood (Figure 4). From this overview, he observes in the thematic map (Figure 4a), and, according to the legend of colors, that Pinheiros and three other neighborhoods in the surroundings are the most valued neighborhoods in the city, with an average price of m² between R $ 9,390 and R $ 10,500. He also notes that this range is well above the average price (R $ 6,934) per m² for the city of São Paulo (Figure 4c).

To get a little more detail about the price variation within the Pinheiros neighborhood, the user clicks on the Pinheiros neighborhood on the map. At that moment, he notes that the average is R $ 10,476, but within the neighborhood it has a high variation, with minimum and maximum prices equal to R $ 2,688 and R $ 15,989, respectively. He clicks on the other neighborhoods in the surroundings and can also see that they have average and price variation similar to Pinheiros. At this point, the user wonders whether this variation also occurs within the property profile for which he wishes to estimate. To answer this question, he activates the filter panel (Figure 4b) and specifies in the search form, apartment as a type of property, one bedroom and one parking space. The result is shown in Figure 7.

Figure 7. Web application viewing results of applying filters, with the Pinheiros neighborhood highlighted
Source: Quot

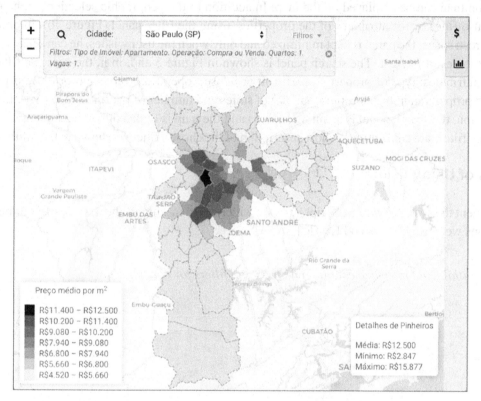

The user immediately sees that the profile he selected is not present in the entire city (due to the number of neighborhoods in gray), and that Pinheiros is the most valued neighborhood for this profile. When selecting Pinheiros, he notes that the average is the highest, R $ 12,500, but a large variation in the price of m² is still present.

After this initial analysis, the user decides to observe the detailed view for the different properties. It clears the search filters, but still leaves the Pinheiros neighborhood selected, and activates the detailed view panel (Figure 6). He notes that one-bedroom apartments have the cheapest average property price when compared to apartments with a larger number of rooms, but, in compensation, they have the most expensive m² value. Smaller apartments (up to 65m²) also have the most expensive m². Regarding the behavior of the average price over time (Figure 6c), there is a slight increase in the average value in the middle of the year, followed by a slight decrease in the month of September, but the average value is still higher than at the beginning of 2018.

After the analysis is completed, the user decides to request the price estimate for the desired property. He opens the price estimate panel, fills in the form with the information (Figure 5a) and then obtains the amount of R $ 592,627 (Figure 5b). He also notes that his estimate has a degree of certainty of 70%, indicating that the estimate has a high quality.

After accessing the data overview, the user can browse the map, selecting different neighborhoods. When selecting a neighborhood, the details box (Figure 4c) is adjusted to show the average, minimum and maximum price values for the selected neighborhood. This allows the user to have access to more information than can be displayed on the map. In addition to the geographic selection on the map, the user can also filter by the attributes of the properties, using the filter panel (Figure 4b). In order not to take up screen space, the panel is kept minimized and only when the user wishes, he can select the values for the attributes of interest. The search panel is shown in Figure 3 and, in it, the user can filter by the following attributes: type of property (apartment or house), operation (buy / sell or rent), price range, area of the property, number of rooms, number of suites and number of parking spaces. By clicking the Search button, the search panel is again minimized and the map is updated to reflect the search parameters. If any filters are configured, a short description of the chosen filters is shown in the minimized bar.

Results of Using Quot

To implement the system, two JavaScript libraries widely used to support the development of interactive applications were used: D3.js and Leaflet.

Figure 8. Initial Quot interface containing a map and filters for consultation.
Source: Quot

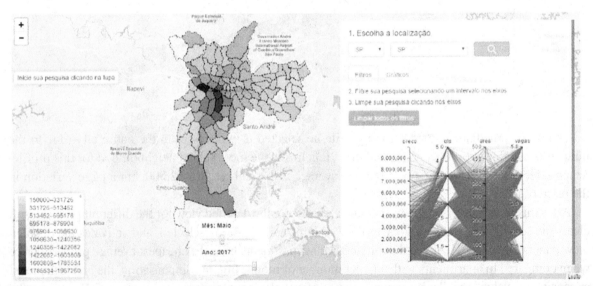

Figure 9. Graphs showing the evolution of neighborhood prices.
Source: Quot

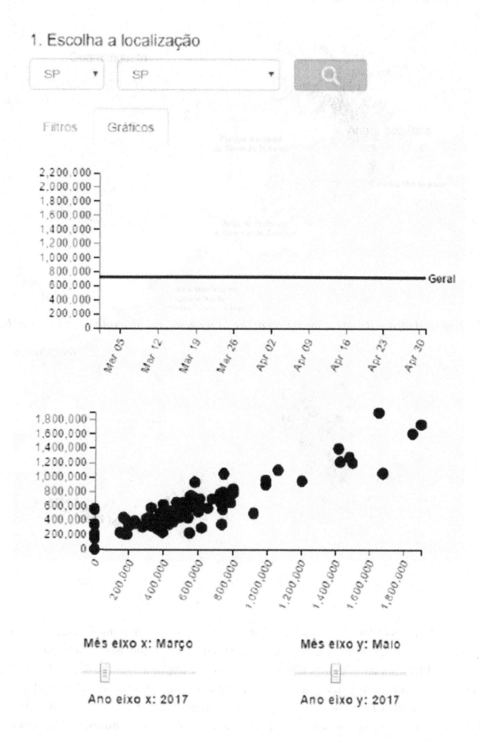

Figure 10. Distribution of median prices in the neighborhoods of São Paulo based on the selection made in the filters of parallel coordinates.
Source: Quot

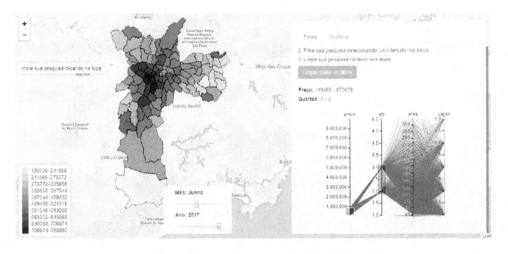

Figure 11. Graphs showing the price evolution of the Moema neighborhood from March to June 2017.
Source: Quot

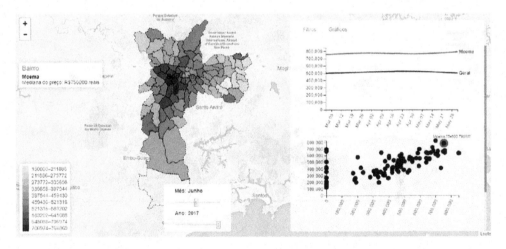

The interface consists of four features. The first consists of a map showing the distribution of median prices according to the region pre-selected by the user. The second consists of visualizing the property data in the form of parallel coordinates, allowing filters to be applied over the data. The third is a graph showing a time series of the average prices of the regions through a multiline chart and the fourth is a scatterplot graph, where it is possible to analyze the average price of each region in different periods defined by the user. Illustration 2 shows the map and parallel coordinate features, and Illustration 3 shows the time series and scatterplot features.

We will explain how each feature works through a case study. We carried out a case study on data obtained for the city of São Paulo using the data collection strategy described in the previous section.

These data have about 26 thousand properties collected in the period from March to June 2017. Consider the scenario presented in Figure 7, where a user wants to analyze June 2017 values of properties between 120 thousand and 875 thousand reais and 2 or 3 bedrooms . To do this, the user selects these values in the right coordinate filter on the interface. The map shows the distribution of the median price of properties with this profile. It is possible to observe through the color scale reflected in the map that the central neighborhoods of the map (for example Pinheiros, Moema and Jardim Paulista) have a higher average price of properties compared to other neighborhoods in the city of São Paulo.

Now, the user wants to observe the historical evolution of property prices with this profile. To do this, he clicks on the graphics tab of the interface. Two charts are presented for him.

The graph at the top shows a line, called general, indicating the price variation for the entire city of São Paulo for properties with the selected profile. If the user places the mouse over one of the neighborhoods in the city, the line with the price variation for that neighborhood will be plotted in red in this graph. This allows the user to compare the price evolution of the desired neighborhood with that of the city. In the example in Figure 9, the price evolution of the Moema neighborhood is compared with the general one. Clearly, it is seen that the value of real estate for this neighborhood is greater than for the entire city, and that there is not much difference in the variation of the history of both.

The second illustration, that of dispersion, allows us to visualize the evolution of the median price of the properties of the neighborhoods in relation to two months specified on the x-axis and the y-axis of the graph, where each point on the graph corresponds to a neighborhood. With this, the user can perceive which neighborhoods in the city had a drop or price increase in the period of the analyzed months. The user can interact with the graph by manipulating the mouse over the graph points, which represent the desired neighborhoods for analysis. In illustration 5, for example, the x-axis represents prices for the month of March 2017 and the y-axis for June 2017. By placing the mouse over the Moema neighborhood on the map, the user can see which point on the scatterplot corresponds to that neighborhood, and verify that there was not much variation in the price of its properties in this period.

Similar Solutions on the Web

Currently, there are some sites on the Web that provide services similar to Quot. Zap Imóveis, for example, has a service that estimates the sale or rental price of a property, called Quanto Vale (What is the value). A report containing the estimate is delivered to the user after 24 hours. In addition to the estimate, this report contains the minimum and maximum price of the property. When compared to Quot, the service offered by Zap Imóveis has some limitations: I) Price estimation for a few cities: through a consultation with Zap Imóveis, we found that they only estimate real estate in the city of São Paulo and some regions of the city of Rio de Janeiro. In the current version, Quot estimates the price of eight (8) Brazilian capitals. II) Possibly biased database: the estimates presented by Zap Imóveis are made on the basis of the website's own ads. This can lead to a possible bias in the data because, for example, Zap Imóveis currently only accepts paid advertisements, which are often carried out by brokers or real estate agents and not individuals. Quot tries to mitigate this problem by collecting ads from a large number of Brazilian Web sites. III) Limited data exploitation: although Zap Imóveis presents some graphs showing, for example, real estate price history in several cities, there is no interface in which the user can explore the data in various ways. Quot provides a series of statistical data for analysis that helps better understand what is behind the price of a property, such as statistics of property prices in a given region of the city, price history, property prices by area, number suites, parking spaces, among others.

Another site that provides a service similar to Quot is Valutare. He has available a service called How Much Does Your Property Cost which, as its name says, estimates the price of a property. Similar to Zap Imóveis, Valutare has a low coverage of cities, and is limited to the city of São Paulo.

In addition, it does not have statistics on real estate in a given region (neighborhood). The pricing service is currently free and, in order to obtain the price estimate, the user must submit a form and wait to receive an email message with it, unlike the Quot in which the price estimate is made in real time.

The third similar solution is InfoProp. This site has a base of real estate sales prices, not ad prices. The user can explore statistics on this data, but the functionality for viewing the data is very simple. Some statistics, for example, are presented in tables and not in graphs. As shown on the website, they do not have a price estimation service and the data is restricted to the city of São Paulo.

ANALYSIS OF THE PROPOSAL'S IMPACT WITH THE TRADITIONAL MODEL OF THE REAL ESTATE MARKET

Although the production of studies on Big Data is not something so new, as of 2014 the publication of studies gained a strong acceleration. Still, use for the business area focuses on descriptive analysis (what happened to the business?), predictive analysis (what is likely to happen in the future?) and prescriptive analysis (what do I do now?) (Sivarajah et al., 2017). In its report, Quot is able to identify properties in the vicinity of the address searched and display its prices (descriptive), it is able to estimate a price for the property with the characteristics surveyed (prescriptive) and gather statistical information about the property, such as value per square meter and its evolution in the last 12 months compared to the neighborhood / city average.

Quot is currently available in eight Brazilian capitals: Belo Horizonte, Curitiba, Florianópolis, Porto Alegre, Recife, Rio de Janeiro, Salvador and São Paulo.

The impact of Quot in the real estate market can reach several interested parties. The main ones are: I) Buyer / Seller; II) Realtor / Real estate; III) Builders; IV) Financing banks and insurance companies; V) Government; VI) Fintechs; VII) Construtechs.

Buyer / Seller

In Brazil, the owner is allowed to advertise and conduct the entire buying / selling process without the help of intermediaries. In this case, the tool can help the seller have a better estimate of the market price of his property, as well as help those who want to buy to determine if the advertised price of a particular property is within market conditions.

Realtor / Real Estate

It is estimated that there are about 400 thousand brokers in Brazil and more than 40 thousand real estate companies in active status. This number does not consider the effects of the COVID-19 pandemic and is present in different journalistic sources from the end of 2019.

The realtor has the competence to carry out a property evaluation that goes beyond the price. The tool can assist the professional in terms of automation of his work, since he evaluates and researches the market price of numerous properties. As it is also consulted by candidates for buyers / sellers of real estate. Even though, the owners contact these professionals just to know the price of the property, the Quot platform provides a report that can be used by the broker to promote their professional services, in addition to the agility in the return. The tool can also assist the professional broker in expanding his area of expertise due to the coverage of the tool. To cover a larger territory, the broker would have to physically move to the location of the property. All of these advantages apply to real estate companies that are formed by brokers.

Builders / Developers

According to a document from the Ministry of Cities (Givíziez and Oliveira, 2018), the need to build 1,235 million housing units per year in Brazil, by 2030, is estimated for the entire country, already considering a reduction in the housing deficit, obsolescence of real estate and demographic variables.

Builders need to set sales prices for their properties, evaluate competing offers and, in some cases, estimate the price of properties that are given as a guarantee for purchases of new units, or even as part of the payment. This research process that can take days using Quot becomes more agile and accurate.

Developers can systematically search for properties in areas of interest and thus determine places where there are attractive prices for acquisitions and the potential for launching new real estate businesses.

Financing Banks and Insurance Companies

According to data from the Brazilian Association of Real Estate Credit and Savings Entities (Abecip, 2020) in 2019 a total of 297,961 properties were financed.

Banks and insurance companies have products aimed at the real estate market, such as financing and insurance. The products need an estimate of the market price of the properties to calculate the value of the service, assess risks and other technical and transactional issues. For this, they have a series of service providers that provide such a service in a matter of days or weeks. Thus making the process time-consuming and often costly, the use of Quot can dramatically speed up the processes for financing and calculating property insurance policies.

Government

Governments can also benefit from using Quot to update their indicators and tax rates for property-related taxes and fees. It is common for the indicators used by governments to make such charges to be out of date. Using Quot can make such charges more up-to-date and fairer.

Fintechs

There are a multitude of Finthecs coming up with different innovative proposals. Some representatives of a category of Finthecs have appeared and sought Quot to build some kind of partnerships. In essence, these institutions do credit intermediation by means of the contractor having their own property to provide as collateral. The market value of the property ends up being the most important variable to define the value to be borrowed and the rate.

Construtechs

There are also different companies in the construction / real estate sector that currently operate as a database of purchase and sale announcements, intermediaries of purchase / sale / rental contracts and other business models that move with the property as the central element and the market price of this property is the most important variable in the process. These business models estimate the price of the property as something important to have in terms of precision and agility.

CONCLUSION

As well described by Davenport et al (2020), the use of Artificial Intelligence (AI) not only influences changes in the processes of organizations, but it also influences changes in consumer behavior. Quot is a good example of how AI can influence an industry's business processes. For example, a bank to finance a property needs to estimate its market price. Current processes take a few days to weeks, employing different service providers and with incredible bias potential. Quot does this in real time, which has the potential to streamline analysis processes while offering greater security for estimating property value.

Despite the significant potential for profound transformations in marketing activities, provided by AI, Big Data and the full range of analytical capabilities, many organizations fail to use such technologies to create competitive advantages (Yerevelles, Fukawa, & Swayne, 2016). In the case of the real estate sector, to ignore the creation of value related to pricing is to bet on the delay. It is important to highlight that there are class organizations that pressure the National Congress for laws that favor such classes, which can bring difficulties for technological transformations to consolidate.

As stated by Sanders (2016), there are still a series of questions that challenge marketing academics to seek new solutions to the new reality brought about by information technologies and mainly by all the transformations that man in society has developed. The practical implications for the development of research in marketing, especially with regard to Big Data analysis, include not only the partnership with other areas of knowledge, but also the rethinking of education itself for those working with analysis and marketing decision support.

REFERENCES

Ahlers, D., & Boll, S. (2009). Adaptive geospatially focused crawling. In *Proceedings of the 18th ACM conference on Information and knowledge management*, (pp. 445–454). ACM. 10.1145/1645953.1646011

Barbosa, L., & Bangalore, S. (2011). Focusing on novelty: a crawling strategy to build diverse language models. *Proceedings of the 20th ACM international conference on Information and knowledge management*, 755–764. 10.1145/2063576.2063687

Barbosa, L., Bangalore, S., & Sridhar, V. K. R. (2011). Crawling back and forth: Using back and out links to locate bilingual sites. *Proceedings of the 5th International Joint Conference on Natural Language Processing*, 429–437.

Barbosa, L., & Freire, J. (2005). Searching for hidden-web databases. *Proceedings of the 8th ACM SIGMOD International Workshop on Web and Data-bases*, 1–6.

Beckmann, N., Kriegel, H. P., Schneider, R., & Seeger, B. (1990, May). The R*-tree: an efficient and robust access method for points and rectangles. In *Proceedings of the 1990 ACM SIGMOD international conference on Management of data* (pp. 322-331). 10.1145/93597.98741

Davenport, T., Guha, A., Grewal, D., & Bressgott, T. (2020). How artificial intelligence will change the future of marketing. *Journal of the Academy of Marketing Science*, *48*(1), 24–42. doi:10.100711747-019-00696-0

Davenport, T., & Harris, J. (2007). *Competição Analítica: Vencendo Através da Nova Ciência*. Elsevier.

Erevelles, S., Fukawa, N., & Swayne, L. (2016). Big Data consumer analytics and the transformation of marketing. *Journal of Business Research*, *69*(2), 897–904. doi:10.1016/j.jbusres.2015.07.001

Givisiez, G., & Oliveira, E. (2018). *Demanda futura por moradias: demografia, habitação e mercado*. Ministério das Cidades.

Kuhn, M. (2008). Building predictive models in R using the caret package. *Journal of Statistical Software*, *28*(5), 1–26. doi:10.18637/jss.v028.i05

Liaw, A., & Wiener, M. (2002). Classification and regression by randomForest. *R News*, *2*(3), 18–22.

Mitchell, R. S., Michalski, J. G., & Carbonell, T. M. (2013). *An artificial intelligence approach*. Springer.

Munzner, T. (2014). *Visualization analysis and design*. CRC Press. doi:10.1201/b17511

Olston, C., & Najork, M. (2010). Web crawling. *Foundations and Trends in Information Retrieval*, *4*(3), 175–246. doi:10.1561/1500000017

Reis, A. C., Iacovelo, M. T., Almeida, L. B. B., & Costa Filho, B. A. (2016). Marketing de Relacionamento: Agregando Valor ao Negócio com *Big Data*. *Revista Brasileira de Marketing*, *15*(4), 512–523. doi:10.5585/remark.v15i4.3379

Rogers, D. (2017). *Transformação Digital: Repensando o seu negócio para a era digital*. Autêntica Business.

Sanders, N. R. (2016). How to use big data to drive your supply chain. *California Management Review*, *58*(3), 26–48. doi:10.1525/cmr.2016.58.3.26

Sivarajah, U., Kamal, M. M., Irani, Z., & Weerakkody, V. (2017). Critical analysis of Big Data challenges and analytical methods. *Journal of Business Research*, *70*, 263–286. doi:10.1016/j.jbusres.2016.08.001

Surdak, C. (2018). *A Revolução Digital: Os 12 Segredos Para Prosperar na Era da Tecnologia*. DVS Editora.

Wedel, M., & Kannan, P. K. (2016). Marketing Analytics for Data-Rich Environments. *Journal of Marketing*, *80*(6), 97–121. doi:10.1509/jm.15.0413

KEY TERMS AND DEFINITIONS

Artificial Intelligence: It is the area of computer science responsible for building machines capable of learning for themselves with the objective of replicating the human cognitive process.

Big Data: It is considered an area of knowledge that studies how to obtain, process, and analyze data and information considering a large magnitude of structured and unstructured data.

Digital Transformation: Incorporation of digital technology in organizations with the digitization of processes and tasks to solve problems and increase competitiveness.

Marketing Analytics: Process of measuring, analyzing, and managing data in order to optimize marketing investments.

Pricing: Pricing process for a particular product or service.

Real Estate: Market that includes the sale of new and used properties.

Realtor: Trained and certified professional prepared to attend the entire process of buying and selling real estate.

Chapter 22
Protection Study in the EPS, Electrical Power System:
Use of the Powerworld® Software

Gustavo Vinicius Duarte Barbosa
Faculdade Pitágoras, Brazil

José Ronaldo Tavares Santos
Centro Universitário UNA, Brazil

ABSTRACT

Electrical power systems are susceptible to faults caused, for example, by storm, pollution, vandalism, lightning, salt spray, etc. The unscheduled interruption in the supply of electricity to consumers, whether industrial, residential, or commercial, entails severe fines for the transmission utility and/or electricity distributor, imposed by the regulatory agency. Thus, the EPS must have a well-dimensioned protection system, capable of identifying the fault, which is characterized by a single-phase, two-phase, three-phase short circuit, among others, and interrupt the missing section in the minimum time so that the effects of this lack are as small as possible for the SEP, especially with regard to its integrity and operational security.

1. INTRODUCTION

In this work, an Electric Power System (EPS) composed of four buses will be presented, with the respective levels of short circuit, as shown in Figure 1.

An unscheduled interruption in the supply of electricity can result in excessive costs due to the interruption of a process in the industry, for example, as well as social costs that are difficult to measure. Therefore, it must be ensured that the EPS is reliable and safe with regard to the regular supply of electricity to final consumers. Notwithstanding, the EPS is subject to failures, caused by numerous factors, making it necessary to design an effective protection system with a prompt response to these unpredictable events.

DOI: 10.4018/978-1-7998-4201-9.ch022

Copyright © 2021, IGI Global. Copying or distributing in print or electronic forms without written permission of IGI Global is prohibited.

Figure 1. Basic scheme of an electricity transmission system
Source: Simulation at PowerWorld®, 2020.

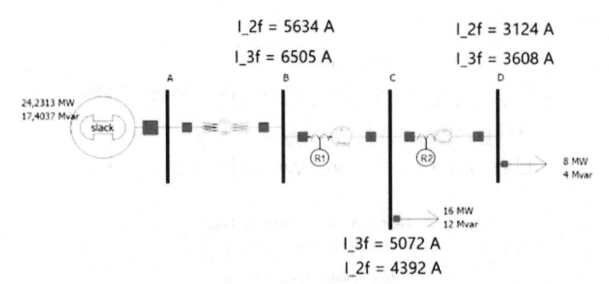

The EPS illustrated in Figure 1 is composed of two load buses (Power Utilities) with nominal voltages of 50 kV, interconnected by electric power transmission lines. Circuit breakers and protection relays, with the respective current transformers (CTs), are also shown in this figure.

It should be noted that for a fault occurring in the CD section of the EPS above, the relay R2 must trip the circuit breaker and de-energize the transmission line corresponding to that missing section. Thus, only the load connected to bus D will be without power supply for a certain period of time, until the transmission concessionaire's maintenance team moves to the defect location and corrects the cause of the defect (corrective maintenance).

From the above, if relay R1 operates before R2, the supply of electricity will be interrupted for a greater number of consumers, by de-energizing the transmission line corresponding to the BC section, after "trip" on the circuit breaker commanded by relay R1. This, in turn, characterizes a failure in the coordination / selectivity of the protection relays.

Therefore, it is up to the EPS Protection Engineer to carry out protection studies in the system in order to ensure the coordination and selectivity of the protection relays. A well-dimensioned protection system has the advantage of guaranteeing continuity in the supply of electricity, thereby avoiding the extrapolation of continuity indicators imposed by the regulatory agency, as well as increasing the operational safety of the system and, therefore, the levels of quality of the electric energy delivered to the final consumers.

2. METHODOLOGY FOR ADJUSTING 51F / 50F FUNCTIONS (PHASE OVERCURRENT)

Figure 2 below illustrates a block diagram showing the basic arrangement of a protection system, indicating the transducers of electrical quantities (CTs and PTs), as well as the protection relay responsible for the trip in the circuit breaker.

Figure 2. Basic arrangement of a protection system
Source: Coury et al., 2012

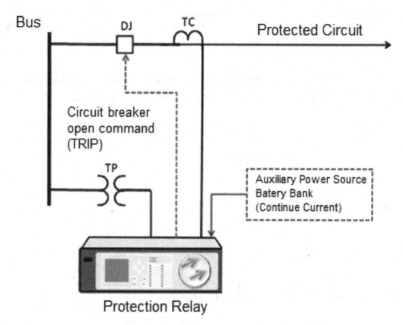

In addition to the task of identifying and "clearing" the fault, the protection also has resources capable of locating the fault, making it possible to quickly restore the system once the corrective maintenance team will be moved to the defect location with the maximum speed, avoiding inspecting the entire length of a transmission line, considering routes that in Brazil reach 2,000 km in some cases (connection of the 500 kV line connecting the plants of the river Madeira complex with the country's Midwest) (G.V.D.B et al, 2019).

2.1 The Location of the Fault Point

In this section, the principles concerning the fault location technique are demonstrated using the three-phase fundamental voltage and current phasors collected from two transmission line terminals, as discussed in Girgis et al (1992), based on the equation of voltages and currents at the point of occurrence of the fault and using the TL series impedance matrix. In the presentation, the TL described in Figure 3 will be considered..

Figure 3. Single-line LT fault used in the algorithm equations
Source: Adapted from Girgis et al., 1992

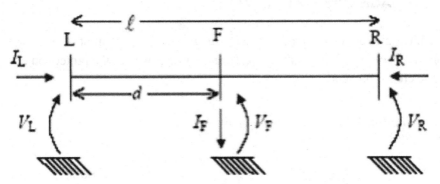

Once the three-phase voltage and current phasors are synchronized on the L and R buses, the three-phase voltage vectors can be represented as a function of the current vectors as follows:

$$[V_F] = [V_L] - d[Z_{a,b,c}][I_L] \tag{1}$$

$$[V_F] = [V_R] - (\ell - d) \cdot [Z_{a,b,c}] \cdot [I_R] \tag{2}$$

Matching (1) and (2),

$$[V_L] - [V_R] + \ell \cdot [Z_{a,b,c}] \cdot [I_R] = d \cdot [Z_{a,b,c}] \cdot ([I_R] + [I_L]) \tag{3}$$

Equation (3) can be expressed as follows:

$$Y = M \cdot d \tag{4}$$

$$Y = [V_L] - [V_R] + \ell \cdot [Z_{a,b,c}] \cdot [I_R] \tag{5}$$

$$M = [Z_{a,b,c}] \cdot ([I_R] + [I_L]) \tag{6}$$

Using the least squares method, one can discover the value of the unknown d in (4):

$$d = (\overline{M}^T \cdot M)^{-1} \cdot \overline{M}^T \cdot Y \tag{7}$$

Being $\overline{M}^T$ the transposition of the matrix M with its conjugated elements, $[V_R]$ and $[I_R]$ the fundamental three-phase voltage and current vectors collected at the LT remote terminal, $[V_L]$ and $[I_L]$ the fundamental three-phase voltage and current vectors measured at the local terminal of the line, $[Z_{a,b,c}]$ the series impedance matrix of TL and d the fault distance. Therefore, the above method adopts simple calculations and is not influenced by factors such as fault incidence angles, types of faults and fault resistances. Therefore, the method does not consider the line capacitance, so its application is only acceptable with satisfactory levels of accuracy in short lines, where the capacitive effect can be neglected. The value of the distance found, d, is a complex number, where only the real part of that number is considered.

As explained in Aguirre (2004), the matrix $(\overline{M}^T \cdot M)^{-1} \cdot \overline{M}^T$ is the least squares matrix, also called the pseudo-inverse matrix.

2.2 Use of PowerWorld® Software to Determine Power Flows and Short-Circuit Current Levels on EPS Buses

The PowerWorld® has a student version, available free of charge, which allows power flow studies to be carried out and short circuit levels to be determined in a EPS with a limited number of bars. For the purposes of our protection study, it was very useful with regard to the purpose of raising the levels of short-circuit currents in the EPS of Figure 1.

PowerWorld® presents a very friendly interface, allowing the construction of a EPS for simulating power flows, as shown in Figure 4. In this example, a synchronous generator, two transmission lines and a 100/50 kV – 100 MVA step-down transformer were used and, subsequently, the power flows in that EPS were simulated. In addition to obtaining the power flows in the LTs, losses and voltage levels of the bars were raised, as seen in Figure 5 and Figure 6.

Figure 4. EPS simulated in the PowerWorld®
Source: Simulation at PowerWorld®, 2020

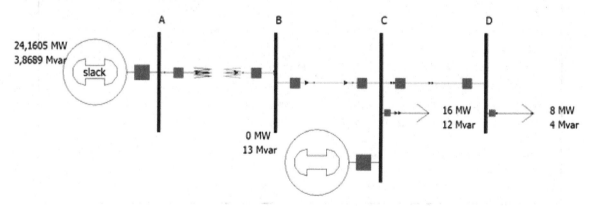

Figure 5 shows the active and reactive power flows obtained through simulation in PowerWorld®, which is based on the Newton-Raphson method for solving the non-linear equations that model the problem of non-linearized power flow. It is also observed the calculation of active and reactive losses in this section of the EPS, which should be minimized as far as possible. The technical losses in the

EPS constitute non-invoiced, non-distributed energy and engineering solutions should be implemented, such as the reconduction of the stretch, aiming at increasing the LT's ampacity, as well as the insertion of capacitive shunt compensation or the use of synchronous compensators, such as engineering solutions capable of minimizing these losses and allowing the EPS to remain in its normal operating regime.

Figure 5. Power Flow and Losses in the BC Section
Source: Simulation at PowerWorld®, 2020.

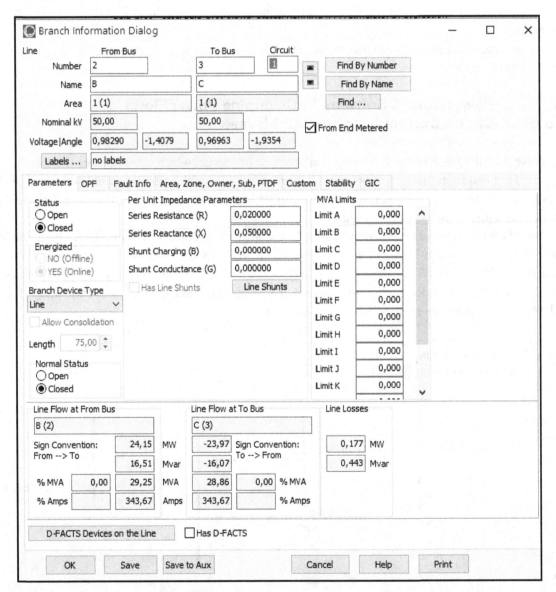

Figure 6 shows the voltage in Bus C resulting from the flow of active and reactive power in the BC section of EPS of Figure 4. A voltage of approximately 48.5 kV is perceived in this bus, that is, there was a voltage drop of approximately 1.5 kV resulting from the power flow (active and reactive) in the

TL connecting buses B and C. Considering the injection of 13 MVAr by the synchronous compensator in Bus C of this EPS, it is observed that there will be less reactive power flowing in the AB section and, therefore, less voltage drop in this TL, according to the result obtained and shown in Figure 7 below. In this case, the voltage at Bar C was regulated to a level of approximately 49.5 kV, demonstrating the importance of EPS supervision and control with the use of a powerful simulation tool for conducting EPS expansion studies, as well as within the scope operation.

With this simulation tool, in the perspective of planning the expansion of the EPS, it is possible to determine the best point of operation of the system in view of the expected growth of the load in the medium to long term horizon, from the proposal of measures to control the power flows in TLs, such as the diversion of these active power flows, by alternative routes, using lagging transformers in order to relieve the load demand on a given transmission line, as well as the adoption of capacitive shunt compensation or the installation of voltage regulators, with tap variation, to control the tension in the system bars.

This fact characterizes the subject in question in a context of digital transformation, as the computational methods currently available greatly facilitate the EPS engineer in protection studies, as well as in determining future scenarios regarding the analysis of changes dynamics imposed on the electric power system over the years, assisting the planner in making decisions that optimize the allocation of financial resources. Therefore, from the analysis of future scenarios, it is even possible to postpone investments in the expansion of the system and, consequently, gain revenue in the short term, which may be strategic in some circumstances within the scope of the optimal investment capitalization policy of the electricity transmission company.

Therefore, the importance of using the PowerWorld® Software in power flow studies at EPS is perceived, as well as in determining the levels of short circuit currents (single phase, two phase, three phase, among others) for dimensioning the protection, as shown in Figure 8. These levels of short-circuit currents are presented in pu or directly in Ampères. This simulation tool greatly facilitates the work of the EPS Protection Engineer, as well as streamlines protection studies in terms of coordination and selectivity.

With the PowerWorld® fault analysis feature, the short-circuit current levels were obtained in the EPS in Figure 1, which is the object of the protection study presented in this work. As shown in the figure above, the intensities of the short-circuit currents at different points in the EPS can be determined.

Analyzing Figure 8, it can be seen that a three-phase short circuit in the C-Bus of the EPS of Figure 1 imposes voltage sags in the other EPS buses, according to the results presented above.

In addition, using the short-circuit simulation tool available on PowerWorld®, the system's Y_{Bus} matrices are automatically measured in zero, positive and negative sequences, as shown in Figure 9 below.

2.3 Protection Coordination (Function 51F - Phase Overcurrent - Timed Curves)

In this part of the work, a procedure for dimensioning the protection (function 51 F - timed curves) will be demonstrated for the EPS illustrated in Figure 1, obtaining at the end of the same, the coordinogram from this protection study, which was generated through MATLAB ®.

First, the levels of the load current circulating through the transmission lines are determined, according to the calculation shown below. These currents can also be obtained directly from the simulation in PowerWorld®, without the need for the calculation shown below.

Figure 6. Voltage at Bus B without synchronous compensator
Source: Simulation at PowerWorld®, 2020.

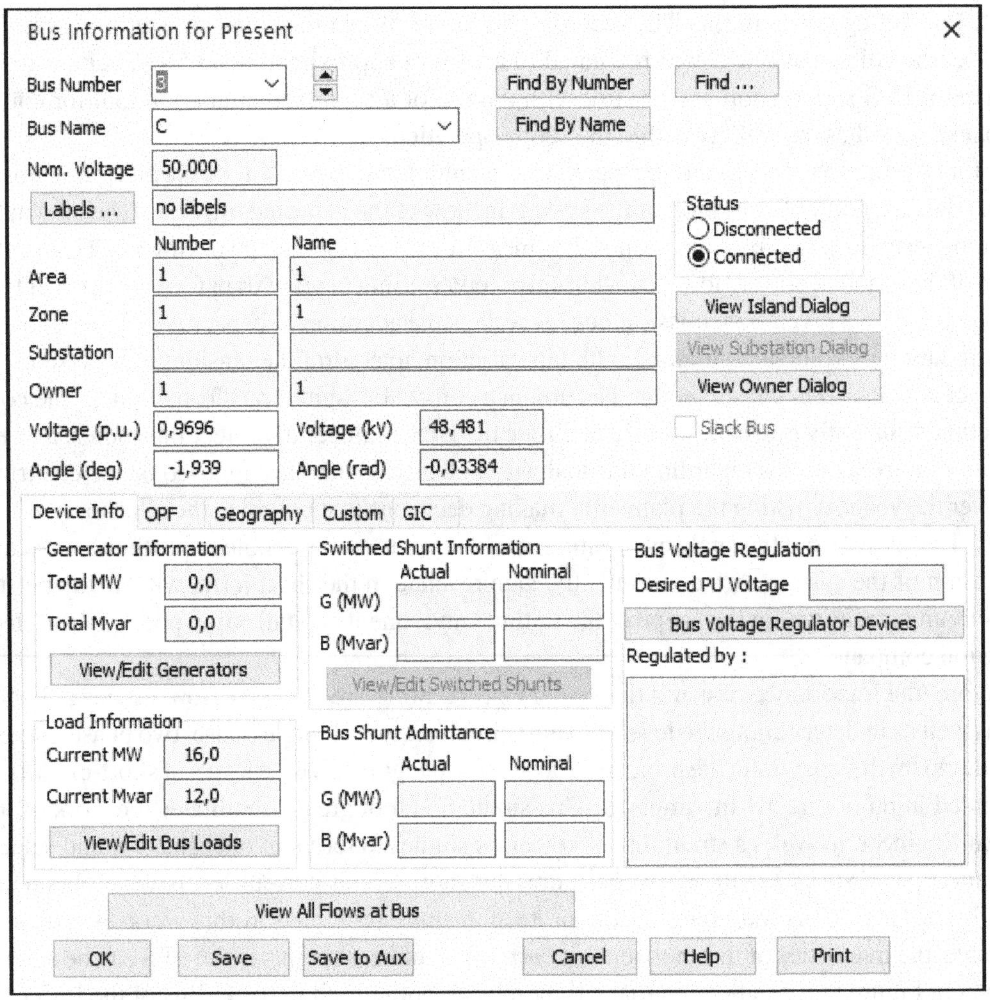

$$S_1 = \sqrt{(16)^2 + (12)^2} = 20\,MVA$$

$$S_2 = \sqrt{(8)^2 + (4)^2} \approx 8,94\,MVA$$

$$I_{L1} = \frac{20MVA}{\sqrt{3} \cdot 50kV} = 231A$$

$$I_{L2} = \frac{8,94MVA}{\sqrt{3} \cdot 50kV} = 103A$$

Subsequently, CTs (Current Transformers) are dimensioned, based on two premises:

$$I_{NOM} > I_{trecho}$$

Figure 7. Influence of the synchronous compensator on the voltage at bus B
Source: Simulation at PowerWorld®, 2020

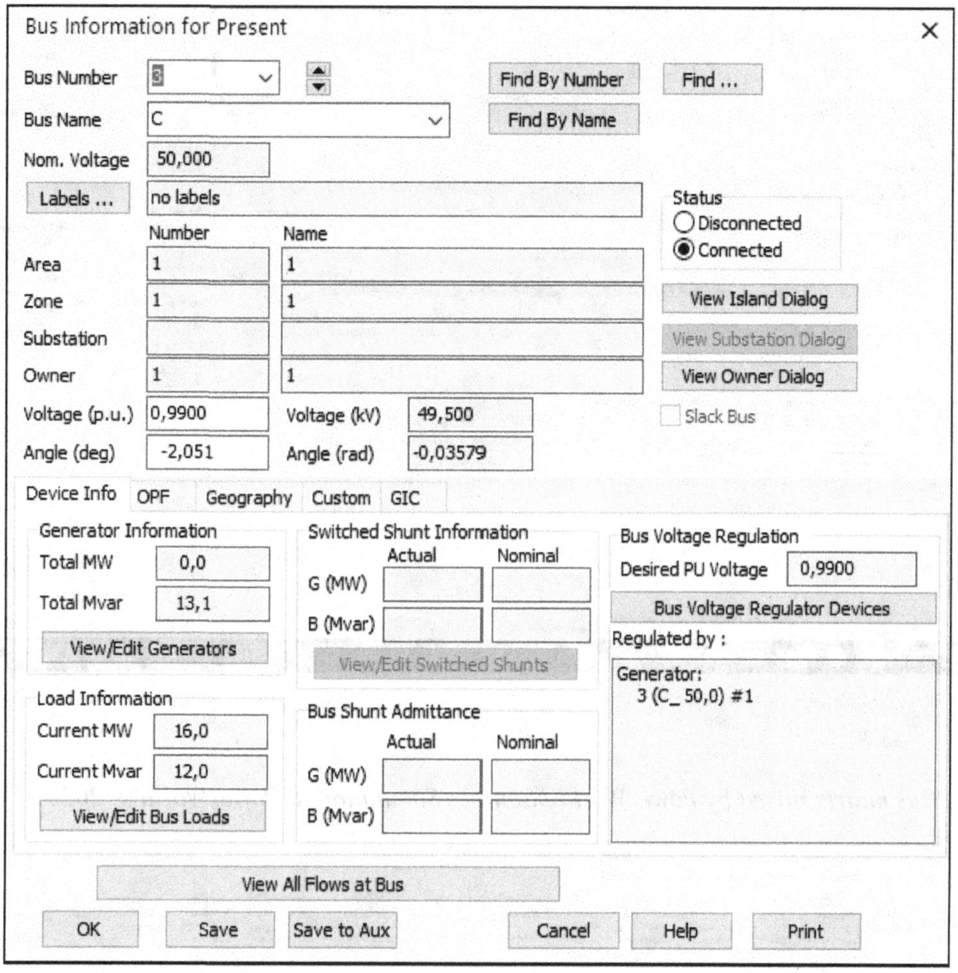

$$I_{PMAX} > I_{CC3\varphi},$$

so that IPMAX = 20.INOM to avoid CT saturation for three-phase short circuit current.

These criteria are used to determine the RTC of the CTs, as indicated in Table 1 below.

Regarding the minimum operating current, the following premise must be obeyed:

$$\frac{I_{NOM} \cdot F_C}{RTC} < I_{MINAT} < \frac{I_{CC2\varphi\,endofthestretch}}{RTC} \tag{8}$$

In Equation (8), Fc is an overload factor that is estimated at around 30%, that is, Fc = 1.3. With the aforementioned equation, the minimum relay setting current can be determined, as shown in Figure 9 below. In other words, for the nominal current of the section the relay must not operate, according to the time curve of function 51F (phase overcurrent).

Figure 8. PowerWorld® Fault Analysis
Source: Simulation at PowerWorld®, 2020

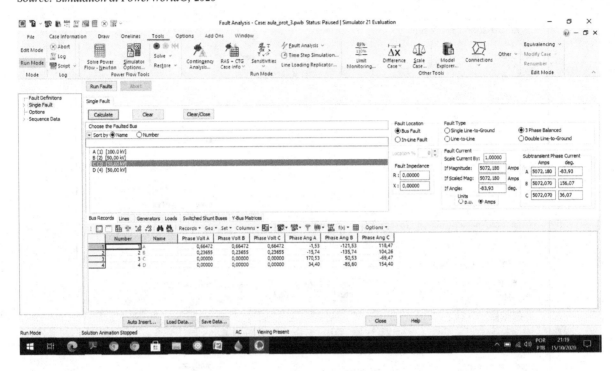

Figure 9. YBus matrix raised by PowerWorld®Source: Simulation at PowerWorld®, 2020

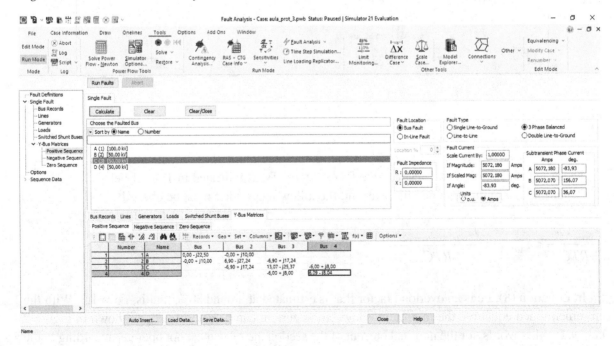

Figure 10. Inverse time curve with the minimum adjustment current value
Source: Prepared by the authors, 2020.

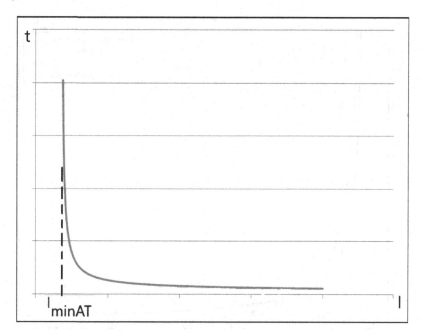

Analyzing Figure 9, it can be seen that the relay will act according to the time curve for function 51F, which obeys Equation (9), as shown below:

$$t = \frac{TMS \cdot \beta}{\left(\dfrac{I}{I_{ajuste}}\right)^{\alpha} - 1} \tag{9}$$

The curve implemented in software for a relay is given by Equation (9), where TMS is a multiplicative constant that adjusts the height of the curve in the coordinogram, with β and α being slope coefficients of the curve (MI, NI and EI), as shown in Figure 10.

To define the type of curve in the protection coordinogram, the following values are used for the constants β and α present in Equation (9), as defined below:

§ **β = 0,14 e α = 0,02: (normally reverse curve);**
§ **β = 13,5 e α = 1: (very reverse curve); and**
§ **β = 80 e α = 2: (extremely reverse curve).**

2.4 Coordination Example Between Relays R1 and R2 of EPS in Figure 1-Procedure

Based on Figure 11, there are minimum settings for the actuation currents of relays R1 and R2.

Figure 11. Variation of inverse time curves as a function of β and α
Source: *Rodrigues, J.M., 2013*

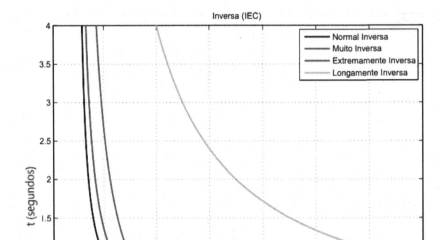

Therefore, the following steps must be performed to ensure coordination between R1 and R2 with respect to function 51F (phase overcurrent). Such steps are embodied according to the step-by-step procedure suggested below:

Figure 12. Coordination between relays R1 and R2 of the EPS in Figure 1
Source: *Prepared by the authors, 2020.*

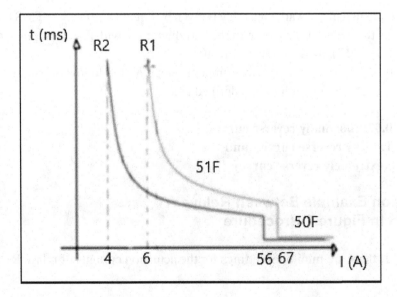

1°) Any current point greater than 6 A is chosen on the R1 curve to ensure coordination between the curves (chosen 15 A in this example);

2°) The primary current of the CT1 connected to R1 is calculated:

IP = 15 * RTC1 = 18 * 100 = 1200 A

3°) It is verified in the secondary of the CT2 which current corresponds to 1200 A in the primary:

$$I_{STC2} = \frac{1200}{RTC2} = \frac{1200}{70} = 17,14\,A$$

4°) The time it takes for relay R2 to act on this current is determined:

$$t_{R2\,para17,14A} = \frac{TMS \cdot \beta}{\left(\dfrac{I}{I_{ajuste}}\right)^{\alpha} - 1}$$

5°) A TMS for R2 is determined: (TMS between 0.1 and 1): Chosen 0.1

$$t_{R3\,para22,5A} = \frac{(0,1)\cdot(0,14)}{\left(\dfrac{17,14}{4}\right)^{0,02} - 1} = 0,47s$$

6°) The TMS of the curve of relay R1 is calculated to ensure that in this current Relay R1 operates with a time greater than R3 (premise = 0.5 s)

$$t_{R1} = t_{R2} + 0.5s$$

$$(0,47+0,5) = \frac{(TMS_1)\cdot(0,14)}{\left(\dfrac{15}{6}\right)^{0,02} - 1}$$

$$TMS_1 = 0.1281$$

$$TMS_2 \, ^3\, 0.1281$$

$$TMS_2 = 0.18$$

However, the initial setting point of the 50F instantaneous function must be determined in the protection coordinate. For example, in the case of the relay R1 of the EPS in Figure 1, this setting is specified as follows:

$$I_{ATINST} \geq \frac{I_{CC_{3\varphi \text{ to 80\% of end of stretch}}}}{RTC1}$$

$$I_{k3\varphi\, 80\%} = 6505A - (6505 - 5072)A \cdot (0,8)$$

$$I_{k3\varphi\, 80\%} = 5358,6A$$

$$I_{ATINST} \geq \frac{5358,6}{80}$$

$$I_{ATINST}\, {}^{3}\, 66.98A$$

$$I_{ATINST} = 67A$$

The three-phase short circuit current up to 80% of the end of the section considered can be determined using a proportionality rule, taking the values of the short circuit levels in the terminal bars, as developed in the above calculation, as well as through simulation in the short circuit calculation tool available in the PowerWorld® environment.

The settings of the 50F function (instantaneous curve of the Figure 9 coordinogram) can be determined for the other relays in the EPS of Figure 1 by establishing a procedure similar to the one discussed above, being summarized in Table 1.

3. RESULTS

Table 1 shows the adjustments from the protection study developed in this research work.

Table 1. Summary of adjustments made with the EPS protection study

Relé	I_{aj_min} Função 51F	I_{aj_min} Função 50F	RTC	TMS
1	6	67	400/5 - 80	0,1
2	4	56	350/5 - 70	0,18

Source: Prepared by the authors, 2020.

The coordinogram resulting from this protection study, with respect to function 51F, is illustrated in Figure 11 below, whose inverse time curves were obtained with the MATLAB® script available in the Appendix.

In Figure 13 of this research work there is an alternative to the use of MATLAB to survey the 51F protection coordinate for the EPS in Figure 1, which in this case was generated in Excel, applying Equation 9 previously mentioned in this approach.

Analyzing Figure 11, it is observed that the system is coordinated and selective, confirming the accuracy of the calculations obtained through simulation in the PowerWorld® environment, which is established as a powerful tool to support EPS protection studies.

4. CONCLUSION

This research work presented a proposal dedicated to support EPS protection studies with the use of a powerful simulation tool, used both for determining the power flows in the transmission lines, as well as for calculating the different types of absences that may affect this system.

PowerWorld® is a free simulator for academic purposes and many of the concepts regarding the supervision and control of the EPS, as well as regarding the studies of operation and expansion of the Electric Power System, are easily understood by simulating different scenarios, depending on the changes topological features in the EPS configuration due to maneuvers and / or performance of protection devices in situations of unscheduled contingencies.

Therefore, with regard to protection studies, PowerWorld® allows the modeling of the EPS by inserting the altimetric data of the transmission lines and the specifications of the other equipment, providing a tool for the calculation of the short-circuit currents, as shown in Figure 8. Furthermore, this simulation software is established as a resource of extreme relevance and feasibility in teaching the concepts inherent to protection studies, as well as in power flow studies for the simulation of future scenarios.

From the above, it is clear that the adoption of PowerWorld®, as well as MATLAB®, in the study of concepts linked to the planning and operation of the EPS, makes the teaching-learning process developed within disciplines such as EPS Protection more efficient and dynamic, since such computational resources allow the analysis of systems not yet built and the study of the dynamic response of existing systems in the face of disturbances that manifest in the Electric Power System.

REFERENCES

Aguirre. (2004). *Introdução a identificação de sistemas: técnicas lineares e não-lineares aplicadas a sistemas reais*. UFMG.

Hoidalen, H. (n.d.). *ATPDraw*. SINTEF Energy Research – Norwegin University of Science and Technology.

Girgis, A. A., Hart, D. G., & Peterson, W. L. (1992, January). A New Fault Location Technique For Two- and Three-Terminal Lines. *IEEE Transactions on Power Delivery*, 7(1), 98–107. doi:10.1109/61.108895

MATLAB, User´s Guides. (n.d.). The MathWorks Inc.

Parmar, S. (2015). *Fault location algorithms for electrical power transmission lines - Methodology, design and testing. Intelligent electrical power grids.* EWI.

Stevenson, W. Jr. (1982). *Elements of Power System Analysis* (4th ed.). Academic Press.

APPENDIX

```
% script para plotagem de três curvas de t x I para função 51F
% Prof. MSc. Eng. Gustavo Vinicius Duarte Barbosa
% Prof. MSc. Eng. José Ronaldo Tavares Santos

TMS1 = 0.18;
TMS2 = 0.1;

Iaj1 = 6;
Iaj2 = 4;

beta = 0.14;
alfa = 0.02;

I1 = (6.5:0.1:70);
size(I1)
I2 = (4.5:0.1:60);
size(I2)

%size(I)
for ii = 1:636
    t1(ii) = (beta*TMS1)/ (((I1(ii)/Iaj1).^alfa) - 1);
end

for ii = 1:556
    t2(ii) = (beta*TMS2) / (((I2(ii)/Iaj2).^alfa) - 1);
end


% Plotagem das curvas de corrente versus tempo para a função 51F

plot(I1,t1,'Color','b','LineWidth',2.0);
hold on;
plot(I2,t2,'Color','g','LineWidth',2.0);
xlabel(' Corrente elétrica');
ylabel('Tempo de Atuação');
title('Curva T x I Relé 51F');
legend('TMS1 = 0.18', 'TMS2 = 0.1');
grid on;
hold off;
```

Figure 13.

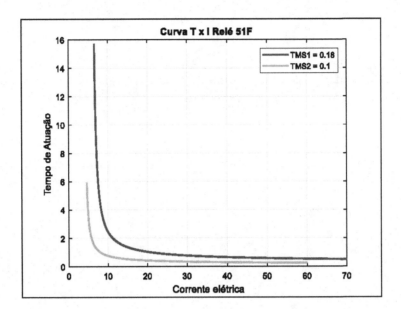

Chapter 23
Digital Transformation in Local Administration:
Case Study of União das Freguesias de Setúbal, Portugal

Miraldina Ximenes Duarte

Escola Superior de Ciências Empresariais, Instituto Politécnico de Setúbal, Portugal

ABSTRACT

Information disseminated through digital networks has a fundamental impact on social welfare, given the range of opportunities offered by the digital economy and the new information and communication technologies, with profound impacts in several areas, namely work, education,and increase the quality and efficiency of public services.The creation of a more efficient, effective, more transparent public administration capable of providing public services with a higher quality level and in an integrated way to the citizen is one of the great objectives and at the same time one of the great challenges that the professionals of public administration face. The state has the social role of avoiding info-exclusion by applying measures directed at the population at risk. Such measures should be able to be applied in the governmental organs closest to the target population. The objective of this study will focus on the analysis of the transition of municipalities to the digital society.

1. THEORICAL FRAMING

Based on Innovation, using the Digital Transformation in Public Administration, which is called E-government, facing Resistance to Change.

1.1 The Inovation

Innovation has become common sense, a kind of Oasis or Holy Grail of the corporate world. Any manager is always looking for some idea that can revolutionize the operation of the business and open doors to a

DOI: 10.4018/978-1-7998-4201-9.ch023

Copyright © 2021, IGI Global. Copying or distributing in print or electronic forms without written permission of IGI Global is prohibited.

new level of results. The problem is that, in the midst of this frenzy, the understanding of what innovation really means, the real importance of business innovation is lost.

Why is innovation so important to businesses?

"Innovation seems an abstract term, but its definition is clear. It is a process of implementing new ideas, aiming to generate value for an organization. It may involve the creation of a new service, product, system, or process, but it can also be summarized in the improvement of an existing one." [1]

And, the OECD Oslo Handbook (2005) has refined the definition in which Innovation is the *"... implementation of a new or significantly improved product, good or service, or a new process, or a new marketing method, or a new organizational method in business practices, workplace organization or external relations. "*

As Van de Ven & Engleman, (2004) points out, innovation results from a new combination of ideas that already existed, but whose reformulation brings something new, something that defies the current environment.

Contrary to general opinion, innovation - especially business innovation - is not limited to a moment of solitary genius. It is not a revolutionary idea that appears in a "tear" of various thoughts. Rather, it is a consistent process of formulating new proposals after direct contact with what one intends to innovate. It offers companies the advantage to penetrate more rapidly into existing markets, connect with developing markets, or create their own markets.

If a company does not innovate, it puts itself in a position vulnerable to any obstacles that may occur in the market in which it operates. It should not depend on a single market segment. It is enough for this segment to fail, to do without or to change products/services that the company has been directed to, that the company itself has no possibility of continuity.

The importance of business innovation is mostly focused on the survival and growth of the company itself, resulting in long-term dividends.

Organizational innovation capacity depends on a number of factors that trigger and sustain new ideas - the external environment, which includes the history of the site, culture and competitors; - the internal structure of the organization, which includes leadership, its management systems, as well as the improvement of financial performance and investment in employees, with the necessary competencies to perform their functions, being able to participate in the innovation process.

In this way, they can generate new opportunities for their survival in the future. Having the main benefits, medium and long term:

- the **improvement of financial performance**, where increased revenue and, necessarily, the reduction of costs through the acquisition of raw materials or the implementation of more efficient processes, will positively influence the profit margin;
- **differentiation** by the provision of a product/service distinct from the main competitors. For example, in customer service, the company is concerned with satisfying the request also taking into account the cost. Thus, companies that offer a better customer experience and are at an advantage against major competitors are able to achieve better results;
- **productivity**, which triggers the growth of an organization. Any idea that allows to develop the performance of the company, will result in the real opportunity of growth of the same;

- **investment in human resources,** with the necessary skills to develop the organization, should be taken into account. They are the ones who deal with the main problems and failures and are the ones who identify opportunities for improvement.

In relation to financial investment, there needs to be flexibility and method. On the one hand, it is inappropriate for a company not to be open to investing in new ideas that arise, as it may lose great opportunities. On the other hand, it is also harmful that it accepts to invest in all the ideas, because not all will produce returns that justify this same investment. The riddle, therefore, is to establish a process and/ or method in order to filter ideas and identify which innovations have the potential of greater impact. In this way, it is possible to maximize returns and reduce the risk inherent in any new project.

It is not enough just to create new products or services, it is also possible to innovate in other areas, even in the management of human resources. Therefore, employees need to be encouraged to develop and present ideas. There are numerous methods, but none will work if the manager does not foster an open management style. Managers who demonstrate a need to centralize work and a narcissistic perspective do not offer encouragement to spontaneous collaborations.

Employees should be assured that their innovations will be recognized, and more importantly, that recognition will not be taken by others. After all, nothing is so frustrating than presenting an idea and observing that it is used for the benefit of the company and not receiving the credit deserved.

In the Public Sector, innovation is imperative to become a basic concept, contributing to the development of a third generation innovation policy - promoting the knowledge-based economy.

Innovation is the beginning of transformation, contributing decisively to the realization of a development model based on knowledge. To do this, it is necessary to flex the bureaucratic system in order to facilitate innovation, impelling it to change because it challenges pre-established ideas, resulting in the development of solutions and the detection of opportunities for new products and services.

Fonseca, (2006) argues that, since the process of change is a phenomenon common to most modern western democracies, this method was, in some countries, called "reinvention of government", in others by "new public management" and in others by "modernization or reform of the state". The promotion of a culture of innovation has been one of the most used methodologies. However, the new context in which public organizations move has been demanding profound changes in this administrative *status quo*. It is known that for an organization to be innovative, it must be flexible, manage knowledge in order to generate new knowledge, create teams in order to develop new coordination mechanisms. On the contrary, the emergence of innumerable innovations, both political and organizational, of structures and methods of administrative management. At times they are small discrete and incremental innovations, i.e small legislative changes in the management framework, real fundamental innovations that translate into new products or services or new ways of providing them.

The focus shifted from the act of innovation to the process of innovation, which is considered an interactive process, in which policymakers, managers, employees and the citizens themselves participate, establishing quality standards. Therefore, it is necessary to evaluate performance in order to promote learning and continuous improvement.

1.2 Digital Transformation

Bounfour, (2016) defines that "... digital transformation is a new development in the use of digital tools, systems and symbols in and around organizations. Although the term does not have a clear definition, it covers several dimensions. "

In a McKinsey paper (2017), it has been reported that over the past 70 years the world has advanced, since the use of the electronic valve, through the transistor, semiconductor, and mainframe processing to the minicomputer, then to the personal computer, and then the Internet. Such innovations were introduced in the industry by IT departments - Information Technology. Each of them managed to catch the attention of the CIO - Chief Information Officer, who were responsible for adopting the technology. The Chief Executive Officer (CEO), for his part, received periodic briefings on the results and associated costs.

Software has evolved from bespoke, custom-built programming to enterprise software application packages, and then to software as a service, with cloud solutions. Among the benefits, we can mention the increase in productivity and profit, resulting from the decrease in operating costs, aiming at economic growth. Supported by Bell (1973), that over the last 30 years many of the cycles of technology adoption have come with the promise of performance improvements and increased productivity. This, a sociologist at Harvard University, had anticipated the advent of the Information Age, long before the Internet or the personal computer became commonplace and present everywhere. According to him, the resulting structural change in the global economy would be in the same order as the Industrial Revolution. For the next four decades, the dynamics of Moore's Law[2] and the associated technological advances, such as minicomputers, relational databases, computers, the internet, and smartphones, have created an increasingly successful US\$ 2 trillion information technology industry - well in the line predicted by Bell.

In the 21st century, Bell's dynamics have been stimulated with the introduction of new disruptive technologies, including Big Data; Artificial Intelligence (AI); cloud logging (Cloud); the Internet of Things (IoT) and the Smart Grid are a striking example of these forces in motion.

Michael Porter, (2015) of the Harvard Business School, speculates that the new world of intelligent and integrated equipment represents a paradigm shift in the fundamental dynamics of competition. Porter suggests that IOT (Internet of Things) is not simply a matter of competitive advantage, it is existential. With a more pessimistic view, Cisco Systems' John Chambers predicts that 40 percent of today's business will fail over the next 10 years; 70% will try to become digital, but only 30% will succeed.

Bughin and Manyika, (2012) provide an analysis of the impact of the Internet on each country's economic growth, depending on its position and potential. Of the thirteen countries they analyzed, they concluded that the Internet contributed 3.4 per cent to GDP[3], where the United States leads the procurement system. In Europe, the United Kingdom and Sweden are revolutionaries, while France and Germany are very influential in terms of use. The position of India and China is rapidly developing, unlike two of the BRICs (Brazil and Russia) along with Italy, which are still in the early stages.

In Portugal, the power of IoT (Internet of Things), cloud computing (Cloud) and AI (Artificial Intelligence) enabled the digital transformation of the segment of public service providers. Where the intervention of political power has opened new perspectives on the dynamics of digital transformation.

"The Europe 2020 Strategy, as a framework for growth and jobs, aims to create the conditions for the smart, sustainable and inclusive growth of the European Union (EU) during the current decade in order to overcome structural deficiencies in the economy, improve competitiveness and productivity, ensuring a sustainable social market economy."[4]

It was in the RCM - Resolution of the Council of Ministers no. 33/2016, on June 3, in which the project group called CTIC - Council for Information and Communication Technologies in Public Administration was set up. Where Digital Transformation in Public Administration was recognized with the approval of the Information and Communication Technologies (ICT) 2020 Strategy, through the Resolution of the Council of Ministers no. 108 in 2017.

Project created with the aim of providing the Public Administration with a global strategy that promotes better management of Information and Communication Technologies (ICT) as a support for administrative simplification, providing citizens with a better quality of life, and a more efficient delivery of its services.

The measures/actions envisaged under the ICT 2020 Strategy are based on three specific axes: (i) Integration and interoperability; (ii) Innovation and competitiveness and (iii) Sharing of resources. Its main objectives are to Make digital services simpler, more accessible and more inclusive; Enhance the adherence to digital services by citizens and businesses; Ensure sustainable development in digital transformation.

And, as guiding principles, (i) Security, resilience and data protection[5], in order to ensure the safeguarding of information held by the Public Administration; (ii) the Usability and inclusion of public services, in order to make them more accessible and easier to use; (iii) Reinforcement of the digital competencies of PA employees and (iv) Sharing of resources, in order to achieve greater efficiency in their use.

It should be noted that the bureaucratic - pyramidal model - still predominant in local public administration, suffocates the change. This type of organization, with a rigid chain of command, depersonalized functions, managed by formal rules and procedures and functionally specialized agents (the same long-term task), does not have an organizational environment favorable to innovation, i.e the introduction of new ideas, methods, processes and/or layouts, even when already tested by other entities.

On the opposite level, true larger systemic or transformational innovations that incite new work dependencies, new organizational structures, and significant performance changes - such as the implementation of e-government on a global scale, with all associated changes.

1.3 e-Government / Local e-Government

For Zweers & Planqué, (2003) cit in Lima, (2003) *e-government* is an emerging concept that intends to provide or make available information, services or products, by means of computer science, from or through public organisms, to any moment, place and citizen, in order to generate value to all the actors involved with the public sphere. For Ferrer, (2003) it can be called - e-government - the set of services and access to information that the State allows to the different actors of civil society by electronic means. This means that e-government is a much more comprehensive concept than a computerized government. This type of management aims to be a Public Administration computerized, open and agile in the capacity to receive information, respond and create interaction with a view to a better society. This increases citizenship, reduces bureaucracy, increases transparency in management and appropriates citizen participation in the oversight of public power.

Mateus, (2008) argues that the implementation of e-government, that is, the computerization of Public Administration, is one of the current concerns of the governments of several developed countries, being seen as the main vector for the promotion and fomentation of the new paradigm of information society. Increasingly, government officials have shown interest, willingness and verification of the need to implement improvements in the transformation of the functioning of the various Public Administration services, making them more efficient, effective, transparent and more oriented to citizens' needs. These improvements result in improved serviceability, improving quality levels. In this context, Information Technology (IT) is an important highlight and a decisive role, and the need for reform and transformation of the public sector that, over the last few years, has been recognized as essential to evolution and modernization, if any, have in some sectors a long way to go.

Considering the need to approach citizens' decision making, when they assume the role of citizen / customer, the concept of local e-government (Dias et al, 2003) or Local Public Administration emerges. Khosrow-Pour, (2006) argues that the concept of e-government is a natural consequence, local e-government inherits its characteristics, but at the local level, associated with a region/parish, with greater proximity to communities.

Still, Gouveia, (2004) assumes that Local Public Administration, with the local e-government, has the opportunity to restructure services, through the stimulation of initiatives that reach the individual's demand in relation to local power, making services more accessible and adapted to the needs of the community. He also argues that in several countries local e-government initiatives are seen as opportunities for change and dynamism for local democracy and for the transformation of services provided by Local Public Administration. Initiatives at the local level should be seen as a complement to measures at the central level, and e-government and local e-government can and should desirably be associated, forming part of the same trend in which the objective common is the provision of quality services to the citizen. Thus facilitating the relation of the citizen to the decision-making power, within the scope of public participation with the local power, as an individual exercising rights and duties, covering the duties of contribution.

Local e-government initiatives are the local complement, ensuring community participation and awareness of the potential of technological communication with the Public Administration.

Portugal, a Case of Success

E-government is a project that aims to empower the public sector to meet the current challenges of the new digital age and new needs. In order to do so, it will have to transform the provision of services in order to reach the expectations of citizens who are increasingly informed and therefore demanding. Enabling the renewal of local democracy, through the creation of mechanisms that allow and encourage citizen participation in decision making, allowing local power to be more participatory, encouraging accountability and the ability to lead the community itself. Consequently, by promoting local economic capacity, by fostering a digital relationship with its citizens, where it will have to provide itself and offer better technological infrastructures, while fostering the development of skills in this area of digital.

Over the years, IT has been seen as a catalyst for the transformation and modernization of Public Administration, and so several initiatives have been launched in this direction over the years. With the creation in 1999 of the first *Loja do Cidadão*, in Lisbon, that later was extended to the capitals of District. A space that under the same roof brought together various services provided by public and private entities. Later in 2004, the launch of the Citizen Portal reinforced the provision of electronic public services, but also the access of citizens and businesses to information.

Among the most representative initiatives is the SIMPLEX program, which consists of a program of administrative and legislative simplification, aimed at bringing the State closer to civil society, facilitating the contact of citizens and companies in their relationship with the Public Administration and, simultaneously, contributing to increase the internal efficiency of public services.

Since the launch in 2006, with the creation of citizen card, the company on time, simplified business information or zero licensing. After a first edition that lasted until 2011, the program was relaunched in 2016 under the name SIMPLEX (+). The new version of the program contemplates, for example, the possibility of merchants being able to issue electronic invoices, exempting paper printing. The impact that this type of policies has on the good performance of the country in terms of digital transformation of the Public Administration can be proven through two important international indices. In the United Nations Ranking of the United Nations E-Government Survey (2018), the United Nations World Survey on Digital Services provided by Portugal, in two years, moved from the 38th to the 29th position, thus integrating the list of 11 new countries that joined the High Performance Group this year.[6]

A recent study by the European Commission (EC), CAPGEMINI, (2017) which analyzes the implementation of digital public services in Europe, indicates that Portugal is at the top of the ranking alongside Malta, with the best performance in relation to the provision of services through the internet and adapted to mobile devices.

Smartphones and tablets are increasingly present equipment in the lives of citizens and mostly used in interactions with the Public Administration. In this sense, Portugal stands out by its policies of digital transformation of the Public Administration - e-government -, making its services more accessible and easy to use.

In both reports, the SIMPLEX Program is singled out as an example of good practice.

Gouveia, (2004) argues that responsibility for the development of the local e-government belongs to those who govern and manage the territory of the community, that is, it is the responsibility of local authorities. Therefore, for a structured development of local e-government, it will be necessary to consider the existence of an e-autarchy, or digital autarchy, and digital cities.

1.4 Resistance to Change

Administrative reform has come a long way, in which governments have consistently struggled with incompetence and inefficiency since the government bureaucracy existed.

It is in the 90s, of the last century, that arises a great enthusiasm around the development of e-government or digital government, driven not only by the globalization of the economy and the proliferation of the internet, but especially due to a new attitude of the political class face to the use of Information Technologies in Public Administration. Until that date, the role of IT in public bodies was reduced to replacing procedures that were done manually by digital data-processing systems. The English term, e-government, is born by analogy to words such as e-commerce and e-business that were recurrently used in the private sector, where the implementation of IT was already much more advanced.

At present, the Information Society has a considerable emphasis and a determining role, which is now recognized by politicians and used by public administration professionals as a key instrument for the implementation of digital governance and, consequently, for the modernization, reform and transformation of the public sector. However, if, on the one hand, the level of its use is higher in private entities, and public entities are less inclined to use it fully and to resist the use of new procedures, on the other hand there is a great difficulty of the use of the new tools by a large majority of the population, especially the older and less educated. Gouveia, (2004).

In relation to the management of change, Michael Crisp, (1991) points out some guidelines for the positive reach of it.

- there should be a good reason for making the change, i.e., changes are usually delicate because they remove people from the so-called "comfort zone". The manager must take seriously the difficulties he faces in implementing them, and make sure that the employee understands the reason and the reasons why the change must be carried out;
- involve people in change. It's a great way to influence people to resist change less, including them in the process of change so they feel essential. Being part of the planning and transition process gives the person a sense of control. As the company improves its skills on change management, it can solve problems by taking advantage of new opportunities beneficial to both parties: customers, employees and the company's own partners;
- a respected person must be chosen to carry out the change process. Any kind of change needs a leader. The organization must select someone for whom the team has high regard and respect. However, sometimes someone who is not internal to the organization can be more easily accepted;
- provide training in new values and behaviors. People need guidance in order to understand what the "new way" means and why it is most desirable. The training keeps the groups together and allows them to express their concerns, as well as to reinforce newly acquired competencies;
- create symbols of change by encouraging the development of newsletters, new logos or slogans and/or promoting events that evidence change and help celebrate it;
- thank and value people. Once the change begins to take effect, the organization needs to recognize the value of the people who contributed to it.

Alexandre Real, in his article (2017) argued that there is a mistake regarding the subject of resistance to change, that is, some people argue that to internalize and automate a change requires at least sixty days.

It is an organizational classic, to consider that people are resistant to change. This statement is a fraud, because effectively no one is resistant to change, there are badly formulated and improperly planned change management processes.

When one thinks of change one must first assume a paradox: stability is important for day-to-day productivity and social peace, only that change is a survival imperative, that is, if the individual does not change, national competition and worldwide will surpass it. In this context, and in order to overcome the initial paradox, it will be fundamental to elaborate a starting point:

- What is gained and lost with the change?

After elaborating the relationship between what is earned and what is lost, it is suggested that a balance be drawn in order to ascertain whether the proposed change has a positive, negative or even zero impact.

After resolving the trade-off issue, it is critical to outline and implement a communication plan for all direct and indirect recipients of the change. This communication strategy should contemplate several items, such as, equating what is gained with the change; what are the main constraints that may occur with the implementation of the process; to alert to the possibility of the emergence of new constraints that can not be determined or predicted in the planning phase; the timing of implementation and evaluate the external threats to the fact that the individual does not accept the change.

It is very important that in outlining the process of change one must be cautious about predicting the various constraints that will arise, and it is essential that the implementation of the change be time-consuming. It is often in the urgency of changing that the idea arises that "people are resistant to change".

Change requires that people know why they are changing and the "biological clock of change" must be respected. We all have the so-called "neural motorways" that are embodied in our habits, for example when we go to work and do a certain itinerary every day, from some time we act on "autopilot", that is, we act without thinking about the itinerary we are going to carry out. This automatism of actions is intrinsic to a set of daily tasks both personally and professionally.

In this sense, it can be affirmed that the change is not determined by the will of the people, but by a biological process that takes time and that must be respected.

2. STUDY OF SETÚBAL'S PARISHES UNION

Setúbal's Parishes Union: 36,76 km^2 of territorial área

Figure 1.

With a territorial area of 36,76 km and more than 38 thousand inhabitants[7], UFS - Union of Parishes of Setúbal in Portugal was created in 2013, within the scope of an administrative reorganization, as a result of Law no. 56/2012, of November 8, and of Law no. 11-A / 2013, of January 28[8].

With the administrative reorganization of 2013, Santa Maria da Graça, São Julião and Nossa Senhora da Anunciada, joined the Union of Parishes of Setúbal. Gathering the areas of the county have been inhabited the longest.

The purpose of this study, explained with statistical data and information on the internal dynamics of the Entity, illustrates why this study is so essential and what is making it difficult for the citizen when addressing UFS.

Based on the law of the Constitution of the Republic, some concepts related to the subject to be studied, such as administrative procedures in public administration, will be exemplified, taking into account the legal code that defines them and their application.

The problem of the profitability of computing means will also be addressed as it is a key medium for any administrative process. Also the need to insert public administration in the information society, making this as acquired, the new e-government.

It was characterized the entity of local power, namely its area and population. Statistical data were presented to better understand the number of people who may need UFS services.

2.1 Administrative Procedures

In an ever-changing society, it is essential that the public administration adapt to this same transformation. To do this, it should have facilitating methods when constantly being approached by national and / or foreign citizens.

One of the main services performed at UFS is the "Testimonial" - that is, the services certify that the citizen, whether national or international, lives alone or with his family at the address indicated, which must be in the area bounded to UFS. And for this there are certain Procedures.

Immigrants, to reside in Portugal, must have a residence permit, granted by the SEF - Foreign and Borders Service. To do this, it is imperative to obtain the documents - proof of residence and/or household - from the parish board of the residence where they chose to live - in order to obtain the said temporary authorization in how they hold a fixed address.

In order to acquire these certificates, you can go to the Pole of Nossa Senhora da Anunciada or to the Headquarters - Santa Maria da Graça. However, there are differences in obtaining the same documents, such as:

- who does not have a voter registration in the ISMEC - Information System and Management of the Electoral Census - has to obtain the signature of two people who are voters in UFS, so that they can be witnesses (sign the internal file of the services). Only in this way can the services accept the document. However, if you request the Testimonial at the Pole and after a short time you go to Headquarters, you have to repeat the process, and witnesses, again;
- at the end of the calendar year, the Polo of the citizen/customer is used for the following year (there is a field for this renewal). At Headquarters everything begins again;
- In the computer system there is no document attached or scanned in the file of the citizen/customer, so that the administrative officer can have access in any UFS body.

It is on the basis of these difficulties that in the future it will be necessary to propose improvements in order to facilitate the day-to-day life, first of all of the citizens and consequently of the employees, by the standardization of procedures and profitability of the computer system.

In order to provide the various services it is mandatory to follow the Code of Administrative Procedure[9], of which there is the definition that "the administrative procedure is the formal mode of acts and through which administrative action occurs to achieve a purpose." The goal is the mission of an administrative act.

The obligation to comply with strict legal formalities guaranteeing citizens' safety distinguishes public action from private activity. This guarantee is given by the legal order and the security of knowing that information can only be disclosed among public institutions.

Thus, the administrative procedure is in some way the guarantor of administrative action, it can not be arbitrary or discriminatory and must comply with the rules of administrative procedure.

The administrative process covers four key principles:

- **Unit,** claims that the procedure is a single process that has a beginning and an end;
- **Contradiction**, in which the resolution of the case is based on facts and foundations of the law, through the verification of facts and evidence;

○ **Impartiality**, guarantees that the action will occur without favoritism or enmity. Employees should refrain from personal interests in the event, relationship or a certain friendship / aversion or even if they are part of the witnesses;

○ **Legality**, requires that the procedure be developed within the premises during all stages.

Globalization has transformed societies by facilitating the mobility of people in various parts of the world, whether by seeking a better life or by adversities beyond their control. The countries and societies that host these populations have the duty to design infrastructures so as to provide services that can answer their doubts and help them solve problems regarding their daily living in that country and/or city.

Table 1. Foreign population with legal residence status

Resident Population due Census Migrations					
Territory		Resident Population			
		Total	Unchanged population	Immigrants from another municipality	Immigrants from another country	Emigrants went to another municipality
Location	Years	2011	2011	2011	2011	2011
Setúbal County		121 185	116 043	2 828	806	x
Resident population by migration according to Census – individual Data Sources: NIS - X, XII, XIV and XV Population Census Source: PORDATA Latest update: 2015-06-26 **Data obtained at** www.pordata.pt **on 30-07-2019**						

Nowadays there are times of global mobility, such as in Portugal, where people from various parts of the world are arriving, such as French, Brazilians, Nepalese, Chinese, Indians, Angolans, Mozambicans, among other nationalities mentioned in the following table.

Table 2. Immigrant Population for the County of Setúbal

Years	Total	Nationality																		
		Europe							Africa						America		Asia			
		Total	Spain	France	Moldova	United Kingdom	Romania	Ukraine	Total	Angola	Cape Verde	Guinea-Bissau	Mozambique	S. Tomé and Principe	Total	Brazil	Total	China	India	Nepal
2014	390 113	153 936	9 092	6 541	8 458	16 559	31 505	37 609	98 948	19 478	46 565	17 729	2 513	10 028	94 392	85 286	42 492	21 042	6 372	3 543
2015	383 769	195 137	10 019	8 440	6 945	17 230	30 523	35 782	93 583	18 068	38 346	16 817	2 787	9 405	89 738	80 515	44 969	20 815	6 852	4 795
2016	392 969	166 414	11 133	11 293	6 113	19 384	30 429	34 428	88 157	16 876	36 193	15 306	2 823	8 640	89 462	79 569	48 963	21 953	7 142	5 829
2017	416 682	182 694	12 526	15 319	5 207	22 431	30 760	32 420	85 887	16 764	34 706	14 051	2 814	8 478	94 108	83 061	53 652	22 698	7 901	7 436
2018	477 472	202 298	14 066	19 771	4 834	26 445	30 908	29 197	89 771	18 310	34 444	15 960	2 999	9 623	117 965	104 504	66 941	24 858	11 340	11 487

Data Sources: NIS / FSB / MHA - Foreign Population with resident Legal Status - (individual)
Source: PORDATA
Last updated: 2019-07-01
Data obtained at https: www.w.pordata.pt on 11-06-2019

2.2 Monetization of Computer Resources

The development of the electronical government or e-government, as it is often termed. It expresses the creation of a computerized Public Administration, since the end of the 1990s, the central concerns and priorities of successive governments have been seen as the primary vectors for the promotion and fomentation of the new paradigm of society known as - Society of Information. Since that time, the willingness and need to transform the functioning of public administration, making it more efficient, effective, transparent, more citizen-oriented and more capable of providing services with better quality levels, have begun to focus considerable attention on the development and implementation of strategies to achieve this desired transformation. It is here that the Municipalities, within the scope of their attributions of promotion of development, education and culture, play an active role in the Town Councils, insofar as they represent the most decentralized government organ and closest to the local communities.

It is in this context that the urgent need to make computer resources more profitable, namely Fresoft - a software program directed at local authorities -, which consists of a process management resource taking advantage of the continuous technological progress, making it possible to access online through platforms functioning within and/or outside the organization (intranet and internet).

It develops innovative IT solutions, specifically targeted at local authorities, allowing optimization of response times, increasing productivity, reducing costs and, in real time, obtaining data crucial to the decision-making process, facilitating citizens' day-to-day lives, employees and decision-makers.

In order to help unlock the progressive development of UFS, there is the possibility of implementing a continuous training plan for employees, namely administrative employees.

3. CONCLUSION

With digital transformation in the 21st century, the adoption cycle has reversed. Global business transformations are initiated and encouraged by visionary CEOs, who are today the engines of massive change unprecedented in the history of information technology, possibly unprecedented in the history of world trade. Today, Digital Transformation is on all the top management agendas of organizations, already part of the CEO's strategic plans.

In a globalized world, countries wishing to have a competitive position must foster innovation, including in their public administrations. Always bearing in mind that any innovation has to be thought in terms of repercussions on the fundamental values of the State.

Fonseca, (2006) mentions that innovation policy in the public sector is the set of guidelines and strategies defined by the government in order to stimulate and support innovation in a traditionally adverse context. However, there are barriers to innovation, of which the following stand out: the lack of competition and incentives; Aversion to risk; Inadequate/maladaptive systematic procedures to existing technologies; Short-term planning and budgeting; and, Resistance to change by employees.

The digital transformation and modernization of Public Administration has been one of the central concerns of successive governments and the virtual trend can not stop now that citizens live in the digital era. That is why political power has been developing strategies aimed at simplifying access to services by electronic means, focusing on the **citizen (user-centricity)**, making them increasingly mobile friendly (58% of the portuguese access to the internet by mobile phone, according to Marktest), developed in co-creation with the users, personalizing according to their needs; in **transparency and accountability**, promoting effective public management, the results of which are measurable and easily scrutinized. Many countries are implementing *open data government* projects, providing citizens with online information about the public sector (in Portugal through the portal *dados.gov*), as well as e-procurement initiatives, using digital platforms to restructure their hiring processes and public procurement; Finally, **e-participation**, as a process of co-creation of new policies, allows the citizen to access services and consult data and / or projects (such as participatory budgeting in Portugal). In decision-making processes, such as online voting in local and national elections, there is still a long way to go.

Innovation ultimately germinates in the management of human resources, because innovation does not depend so much on investment in technology as on the human capacity to use resources - both tangible and / or intangible - available to innovate.

Like the concept of e-government, the concept of local e-government is not an end in itself, but rather refers to the use of ICTs to provide citizens and organizations in a given territory with services and conditions for the promotion of democracy and quality of life, through the exchange of electronic information. Over the last decades, the attention and interest of the political power by the digital has evolved, nowadays there is a widespread recognition of the importance of IT as an instrument of transformation and modernization of Public Administration.

The Modernization of Local Democracy is achieved through the creation of mechanisms that allow and encourage citizen participation in decision making, i.e., that it is more open to the community, increasing its accountability and its ability to lead the community itself. With a fully integrated network, utilities can aggregate, evaluate and correlate the connections of a huge amount of data from all types of equipment. In addition to generating information in real time.

The creation of a more efficient, more effective and transparent public administration capable of providing public services with a higher level of quality and in an integrated way to the citizen is one of the great objectives and at the same time one of the great challenges facing them the professionals of the Public Administration.

On the civil society side, there is also a greater demand for quality, accessibility, efficiency and transparency in the services provided by the State. The strategic challenge for Public Administration is thus to provide digital services of high quality and usability, in order to match the level offered by private sector services.

In addition to the efficiency gains at the administrative level, the use of IT has been seen as an opportunity to change the paradigm of an institution-centered Public Administration to a more citizen-centric and business-oriented one, capable of providing quality information and services, accessible at any time, and according to the needs of those who seek them. It is here that the development of competencies in the so-called digital transformation, with the investment in human capital, will be necessary to demonstrate the importance of the valorization of talent management, aiming to combat the digital skills gap. Where the role of active citizenship spaces is important, so as to bridge digital literacy. Therefore, there is a need for public entities to broaden their learning networks through citizen participation.

Not forgetting the training of the professionals of the PA bodies, namely in the Union of Parishes of Setúbal, in Portugal, where there was an urgent need to adapt to the needs of their residents/customers in order to facilitate the implementation of requests made by them. For existing gaps to be diminished or even annulled, it presupposes a consistent bet on two main vectors: leadership and technology. Primarily, it assumes that the bet is not exclusive to either case.

A digital leader is one who can not fear change. He caresses and promotes it. That it enables its collaborators to believe in it and themselves to become agents that promote change.

We are in an era where technology has made great strides and is becoming more powerful, becoming a vehicle for facilitating its users, but also because the speed of transformation of organizations is far from following technological developments. This applies to the State, Government and institutions of central power, and also to local power.

From the point of view of new technologies, it is clear that any country will only become competitive if it is able to compete on a global scale by taking the lead in research and development in areas such as "Cloud Computing", Data Security, "Big Data, "or the new forms of Artificial Intelligence, such as sensors that can make a city a SmartCity, or Machine Learning Systems that can automate simpler service systems. Any of these technologies can become fundamental in a city, at the service of the citizen; of the holders of political power; improvement in the quality of care; transparency and process monitoring, resulting in a better quality of decision making.

In Portugal, the last years have been fertile in modernization initiatives, where the major challenge is to achieve a cultural transformation, in the way citizens, elected representatives, leaders and civil servants conceive of their mission in the governance of a State in the 21st century. Portugal needs this change. The future that is now being drawn across Europe has this transformation at the forefront. We do not produce cheaper or more, so we have to innovate in technology. This premise should make Portugal more competitive and also more attractive if the evolution is placed in the day-to-day of the citizens and in their relationship with the State.

Leaders responsible for defining the strategies of the official entities with whom the companies contact have a vision to embark on this revolution - which has already begun, but almost in silence!

The promotion of the local economic capacity, especially of the Town Councils, derives not only from the fact that they respond to the governmental structure with more proximity and visibility to the residents / customers, but also the real knowledge of the specificities of its population, allowing to guide the measures of the central government and adapt them to its inhabitants, so that they do not stay out of the digital revolution and are not excluded in the development of the country.

REFERENCES

Bell, D. (1973). *The Coming of Post-Industrial Society: A Venture in Social Forecasting*. New York, NY: Basic Books.

Bounfour, A. (2016). *Digital Futures, Digital Transformation, From Lean Production to Acceluction*. Academic Press.

Bughin & Manyika. (2012). https://www.mckinsey.com/

Crisp, M. (Ed.). (1991). Rate Your Skills as a Manager. Crisp Publications.

Dias, S., Santos, L., & Amaral, L. (2003). *Portuguese Local E-Government*. ICEIS.

Gouveia, L. B. (2004). *Local e-government: Digital governance in the municipality*. OPorto, SPI Editions.

Porter & Heppelmann. (2015). How Smart, Connected Products are Transforming Competition. *Harvard Business Review*.

Khosrow-Pour, M. (2006). *Encyclopedia of E-Commerce, E-Government and Mobile Commerce*. Idea Group Reference.

Likert, R. (1961). *New Patterns of Management*. McGraw-Hill.

Lima, R., & Cavalcanti, M. (2003). *Efficient Brazil, Brazil citizen: Technology at the servisse of social justice*. https://books.google.pt

Mateus. (2008). The Electronic Government, its bet in Portugal and the importance of Communication Technologies for its strategy. *Journal of Polytechnic Studies, 6*(9), 23-48.

OCDE. (2014). Oslo Manual: Innovation Data Colletion and Interpretation Guidelines (3rd ed.). FINEP.

Van de Ven, A. H., & Engleman, R. M. (2004). Event- and outcome-driven explanations of entrepreneurship. *Journal of Business Venturing, 19*(3), 343-358. doi:10.1016/S0883-9026(03)00035-1

ENDNOTES

1. OECD. Oslo Manual. Guidelines for collecting and interpreting innovation data. 3rd ed. Rio de Janeiro: FINEP (2004).

2. It emerged in 1965 through a concept established by Gordon Earl Moore (co-founder of Intel), which said that computer processing power would double every 18 months.

3. GDP - Gross Domestic Product, corresponds to the set of all goods and services produced within the borders of a region or country, during a year.

4. www.tic.gov.pt– Portugal 2020.

5. Corrigendum to Regulation (EU) 2016/679 of the European Parliament and of the Council of 27 April 2016 on the protection of individuals with regard to the processing of personal data and on the free movement of such data and repealing Directive 95/46/EC (General Regulation on Data Protection). Applicable from the 25.05.2018.

6. https://www.portugal.gov.pt

7. Data from the National Institute of Statistics - Census 2011.

8. Data from the Diário da República, of 28-02-2013.

9. Decree Law 442/91, 15 November. As amended by the following legal acts: Statement of Rectification 265/91, 31 December; Statement of Rectification 22-A / 92, February 29; Decree Law 6/96, 31 January.

Chapter 24
Business Games in the Development of Competencies of the Navy Supply Officers

Igor Oliveira
Brazilian Navy, Brazil & UNIFACS, Salvador University, Brazil

Sérgio Maravilhas
ⓘ https://orcid.org/0000-0002-3824-2828
SENAI CIMATEC, Brazil & UNIFACS, Salvador University, Brazil

Sérgio Ricardo Goes Oliveira
UFBA, Brazil

ABSTRACT

The Brazilian Navy encourages the adoption of active learning methodologies aiming the development of competencies in the military. This research aims to analyze the contributions of the game Simulador para Treinamento em Administração (Simulator for Training in Administration) in the development of competencies of the Supply Officers who accomplished the Curso de Aperfeiçoamento em Intendência para Oficiais (CAIO). This research has a qualitative approach and an exploratory-descriptive nature. A questionnaire was used to investigate the participants' perception and semi-structured interviews were conducted to understand the expectation of the Centro de Instrução Almirante Newton Braga (CIANB) regarding the application of business games for the development of competencies. The results show that the participants positively perceive the use of business games as a teaching-learning strategy. Finally, it was possible to map the competencies developed with the application of the STA and verify that the intended objectives with the use of the methodology were met.

DOI: 10.4018/978-1-7998-4201-9.ch024

Copyright © 2021, IGI Global. Copying or distributing in print or electronic forms without written permission of IGI Global is prohibited.

INTRODUCTION

The origin of Business Games is strongly associated with war games and the military context. The Armed Forces use games and simulations in order to reproduce, in a controlled environment, an approximation of reality (Motta & Quintella, 2012).

The present research is developed in the challenges of the military professional training of the Supply Officers, that is, military linked to the management area of the Brazilian Navy specifically to the *CAIO* participants in 2018, at the *CIANB*. The preparation of these officers aims to meet a demand from the institution, since they occupy managerial or even command functions. However, the increasing complexity of the problems faced by military organizations demands competencies that must be developed in the several courses taken in their careers.

The competencies that need to be developed are described in the profile of the Intermediate Officers of the *Corpo de Intendentes da Marinha* (CIM), and are present in the CAIO curriculum, namely: leadership, ethics, responsibility, spirit of cooperation, coherent attitudes, initiative, decision-making capacity, holistic view, negotiation, among others (Brazil, 2019).

Regarding the training of managers, it is worth highlighting the difficulty of full learning in academic or corporate environments. In this context, experiential learning methods, especially the Business Games, are presented as alternatives for the development of competencies (Oliveira &Sauaia, 2011). Competency is understood as the gathering of knowledge, skills and attitudes that, mobilized, generate value for the individual and for the organization in which it operates (Zucatti, Silveira, Abbad& Flores, 2019).

It is from this perspective, that the relevance of using Business Games for the development of skills is verified. During the games, it is possible to notice the behavior and interaction of the participants, as well as offering training in order to simulate reality in different scenarios (Schmitz, Alperstedt, Van Bellen, & Schmitz, 2015).

Considering what has been exposed, this research aims to address the following question: What are the contributions of the Simulator for Trainning in Administration (STA) for the development of competencies in the Supply Officers who accomplished CAIO? As a result of this question, the general objective of analyzing the contributions of the Business Games in the development of competenciess of the Brazilian Navy Supply Officers who accomplished the CAIO is reached. In order to answer the general objective, an assessment was made of the perception of CAIO's Supply Officers regarding the contribution of Business Games to the development of competencies; mapping of the competencies developed in the application of the STA game; the understanding of CIANB's expectations regarding the use of Business Games concerning the development of competencies in the professional-military training of Supply Officers.

Thus, this research is justified by the growing relevance of the experiences provided by the Business Games and its effectiveness in the development of competencies (Melo, Sardinha, & Menezes, 2017). As well as the possibility of stimulating in the Brazilian Navy, as well as in other Armed Forces, the use of Business Games in professional-military training courses.

To answer the presented objectives, initially, a documentary research in the CAIO curriculum and in the STA game manual was carried out in order to identify the assumptions of the expected profile of the improved Supply Officer. In continuity, a questionnaire was applied to the CAIO´s 2018 class to collect data regarding the perception of the students, obtaining 43 responses from the 71 (total enrolled) questionnaires sent. There were also three semi-structured interviews: with the person responsible for coordinating the course, with the teacher responsible for the application of STA and with a specialist in Business Games.

Based on this introduction, the article is structured in 5 more sections. Section 2 presents the theoretical framework, which will address the main concepts and theories that underlie the research. Section 3 discusses the methodology used in the study. Then, the results are presented in section 4, and in section 5 these results are discussed and, finally, in section 6, the article is concluded.

THEORETICAL FRAMEWORK

To facilitate the understanding of this theme, this section is organized into three subtopics: competencies development, experiential learning and business games. In order to synthesize the theoretical framework, the graphic scheme of figure 1 is presented.

Figure 1.

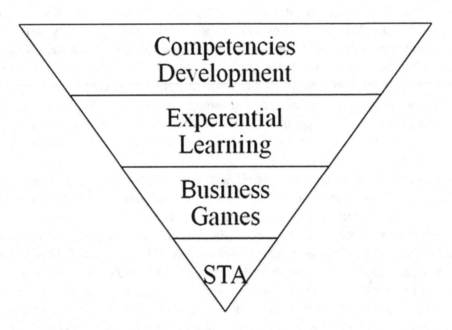

Such figure seeks, in a summarized way, to present a drawing of the present research, covering from the theoretical framework to the object of study of this research (the "Simulador para Treinamentoem-Administração - STA game).

Competencies Development

The concept of competency relates to the individual's ability to successfully perform the proposed activities. It is a continuous and articulated process of formation and development of knowledge, skills and attitudes in which the person has the responsibility for its self-development and, interrelating with other people, aiming at the improvement of its training, adds value to individual and collective activities. (Bitencourt, 2004; Bonotto, &Felicetti, 2014).

Competency can be understood as the ability to act effectively in a given kind of situation, supported by knowledge, however without being limited to them. Competency enables professionals to use more than one resource to solve problems in an innovative way at a necessary moment, or it is the existence of cognitive structures that allow the use of knowledge, skills and attitudes in an integrated manner, performing a competent action (Perrenoud, 2004; Zabala & Arnau, 2015).

Competency can also be known as the gathering of knowledge, skills and attitudes that, when triggered, generate value for the individual and for the organization in which it works (Zucatti et al., 2019). The development of competencies, in turn, is a process in which, in an interrelated way, the subject uses the attitudinal, conceptual and procedural components (Zabala & Arnau, 2007).

In this sense, organizations were pressured by changes in society with regard to the demand for professionals who, in addition to the traditional characteristics contained in job descriptions, have solid individual capabilities and professional competencies (Alver, Cabral, Penha, dos Santos & Personal, 2013; Neves & Alberton, 2017).

In order to meet the needs of organizations in the challenges of their daily lives that the teachings in the field of management find real meaning. Combining practice with theory is fundamental for the training of managers, since learning and development takes place optimally when it occurs through experience (Mintzberg, 2006). Increasingly, managers are required to have the ability to make a critical and innovative decision in a constantly changing environment, which demands constant learning and continuous training, in addition to the competence to learn (Silva, 2013).

Competencies can be divided into two large groups. They are technical skills (hard skills) and behavioral skills (soft skills) that, due to the peculiarities of each one, require different ways for their development. The literature indicates that soft skills are more difficult to develop (Oliveira, 2014). Therefore, the holistic, interpersonal and interdisciplinary character of Business Games contributes to the development of competencies, since it covers the different competency groups (Arbex, 2005).

In view of the managerial challenges existing in the 21st century, it is possible to observe in the literature, studies listing the necessary competencies for the professional's performance in the job market. The most relevant and demanded competencies by organizations today are presented in Figure2.

Figure 2.

Author	Competencies
González-Morales (2010)	Team work; leadership; responsibility; autonomous learning; ethical and professional morals; negotiation; oral communication; interpersonal skills; creativity; Ability to apply knowledge in the workspace; Critical thinking and problem solving; and Ability to learn new skills.
National Research Council (2012)	Team work; leadership; communication (oral and written); creativity; innovation; systemic view; initiative; critical thinking; ability to solve problems; decision making; flexibility; adaptability; conflict resolution; productivity; negotiation; continuous learning; integrity; and managerial capacity.
Swiatkiewicz (2014)	Availability; responsibility; capacity for initiative; punctuality; motivation; organization; zeal for quality; social relationships; flexibility; Communication capacity; and teamwork.
Andrade (2016)	Team work; Communication capacity; empathy; self knowledge; Proactivity; and Systemic vision.

Through its reading, it is possible to identify similarity between the different studies carried out. The competencies, such as "teamwork" and "communication", are highlighted, which are mentioned in all works. The terms "leadership", "responsibility", "negotiation", "initiative", "systemic vision" and "ability to solve problems" also appear frequently in the referred figure.

Experiential Learning

The Experiential Learning Theory (ELT) is inspired by authors, like John Dewey and Kurt Lewin, among others who gave centrality to the issue of experience in the learning process, considering the student as the center of the educational system. The ELT is a dynamic view of learning based on a learning cycle driven by the resolution of the dual dialectic of action / reflection and experience / abstraction (Kolb & Kolb, 2017).

In experiential education, learning is understood as a process in which the production of knowledge is carried out through the transformation of experience. Thus, the fact that knowledge is understood as a cyclical process of transformation, continuously created and recreated, not a finished process, which must be acquired or transmitted (Kolb, 1984) is highlighted. Thus, we seek to learn by doing, with practice, demonstrating the learning result.

In the context of experiential learning, it is possible to highlight the development of individual, behavioral and social competencies in order to contribute to the development of the organization (Oliveira, 2014).

It is in this sense that this study deals with adult education, specifically in the professional-military teaching environment, in which the institution expects the effective action of the individual or team that, endowed with the necessary knowledge and attitudes, interfere adequately in the solution of the problems and challenges faced by the organization. Group dynamics, games, simulations and experiences are relevant instruments of this educational style.

The use of experiential education through the use of Business Games allows a closer approximation to reality, as the game is an important instrument to assist the development of competencies in students, since it allows simulating different situations (Cidral, 2003).

Business Games

With the end of the conflicts that marked the first half of the 20th century, the games, initially designed to simulate situations of war, expanded their scope and underwent adaptations. This geopolitical change enabled other applications for war games, such as, for example, the Business Games, changing the "battlefield" for the business environment (Rosas &Sauaia, 2006).

The use of business games in the training of administrators began in the 1950s in the USA, with the game Top Management Simulation, made by the American Management Association (AMA), as well as with the RAND Corporation, which developed an exercise of simulation called Monopologs, developed for US Air Force logistics. The objective of the game was to encourage participants to make decisions about inventory management without risk. (Jungles, de Souza Rodrigues, & Garcia, 2019; Motta &Quintella, 2012; Rosas &Sauaia, 2006).

The Brazilian Navy is a pioneer in the country in the application of simulations for learning and for decision making at a strategic level. The institution has been developing and promoting didactic and analytical games for several decades, these with the core in the area of defense and national security (Souza, 2008). The *Escola de Guerra Naval* was the first educational institution in Latin America to use the method of games, employing it since 1914. (da Silva, 2017).

The adoption of Business Games as a focus on stimulating and developing managerial competencies is indicated in the specialized literature, as the Business Games would be an experiential activity in which, through a controlled reality, with the possible use of simulators, they are projected sectors and / or companies, offering management tools so that those involved can test decision making under uncertainty (Oliveira & Sauaia, 2011).

Business Games provide participants with a learning method that comprises the three formative dimensions of competency: knowledge by contextualizing the problem situation of the game and the factors of the process dynamics, the skill developed by the practical action of playing and interacting with the other members and the attitude generated by virtue of competition and cooperation (Freitas & Santos, 2005).

Among the advantages inherent to the Business Games, the development of managerial competencies, the integration of knowledge guaranteeing a systemic vision of the organization, the possibility of reducing the gap between theory and practice and the development of competencies and behaviors in issues stand out that require leadership and teamwork. It should be noted, however, that, under no circumstances, the use of games will reach the reality in all its levels of complexity and possible situations (Oliveira & Sauaia, 2011).

Business Games can be classified according to several characteristics. The main games are explained in Figure 3.

Figure 3.

Categories	Features
The means of examining results	Computerized and manuals
Regarding the skills involved	Behavioral games and procedural games
As for the interaction between the teams	Interactive and non-interactive
Regarding the economy sector	Industrial, commercial, financial and services
As for the response time	In real time, by correspondence and by remote processing
About the basic nature of the game	Systemic games, human games and mixed games
Regarding the functional areas	General games, specific games, sector games, and functional games

It is possible to verify that there are different perspectives and possibilities for classifying business games. It should also be noted that such categories do not exhaust all aspects.

Regarding the analysis of the number of publications in the area of business games in the country, it is observed that there has been a growth on the theme (Barcante & Beltrão, 2013). In a synthesis of Brazilian studies that analyze publications in the area of simulations, Mrtvi, Westphal, Bandeira-de-Mello, and Feldmann (2017) analyzed 184 articles, dividing the simulations into two main categories regarding the approach: simulations as environment research and simulations as the object of research.

This study found that research that deals with simulations as an object of study represents the majority in relation to those that use simulations as a research environment. In addition, there was a predominance of studies related to the development of simulators followed, respectively, by studies on teaching-learning and the use of games.

Simulator for Trainning in Administration (STA)

In relation to the functional area, the game can be characterized as being general and covers different areas of the company, such as financial, commercial and production. It simulates realism of the competitive environment and allows to test the decision-making capacity and teamwork.

STA brings students' theoretical knowledge closer to everyday life and can be defined like a highly dynamic training exercise, which uses a computer model of a competitive situation between companies that manufacture the same type of product and sell it in an oligopolistic market. The management of each of the companies is in charge of a group of participants of the game who work as a team. Executives make strategic and operational decisions very similar to the ones they have to make in real life. Using a mathematical model of the reality developed, such decisions are processed, producing reports on the performance of each team.

After the decisions have been made by the participants, the referee processes them on the computer, producing performance reports. After analyzing the reports, the players make the decisions for the next period, allowing the student to test the result of the choices made without having the possible burdens of real life, allowing for learning and reflection in a controlled environment that approaches reality.

The STA is coordinated by a referee with the functions of forming the teams, presenting the rules of the game, clarifying doubts, conducting the dynamics of the game and directing the final plenary session which, in turn, is carried out from the activity and the winning team is announced. Negotiations may also take place with the other participants in the game and fines imposed by the referee on the players.

The next topic will address the methodological procedures followed to carry out this work, presenting the research classification, the sample selection, the data collection instruments, among other aspects related to the method.

METHODOLOGY

This topic aims to characterize the present research in relation to the various methodological aspects. The purpose of the article was to analyze the contributions of the STA game to the development of competencies of the Supply Officers who performed the CAIO.

This study is an applied research with a qualitative and exploratory-descriptive approach. It seeks to familiarize itself with the investigated phenomenon, discovering a new type of approach to the subject, since the use of games for teaching in the Navy is already used for war games.However, the adoption of business games for the training of Suppply Officers started at CIANB in 2015. The research also seeks to describe the characteristics of a given population or phenomenon (Prodanov & Freitas, 2013).

The importance of the chosen case is due to the fact that all the Brazilian Navy Supply Officers from 2015, necessarily, when carrying out CAIO, participated in the application of the STA Game, object of study of this research. Initially, a documentary research was carried out on the CAIO menu and in the STA Game Manual. Then, a bibliographic survey was carried out that helped in the construction of the theoretical framework that supports this work.

In order to mitigate the possible effects of forgetfulness, the selected sample was the CAIO 2018 group, composed of 71 Supply Officers, of whom 43 responded to the virtual questionnaire which made available on a link through a web form prepared from Google Forms.

The questionnaire, containing 17 questions, was adapted from Melo et al. (2017), being divided as follows: three questions make it possible to obtain data on the interviewee and his familiarity with the game of companies; twelve questions on the Likert scale made it possible to verify the opinion about the game applied in the discipline, as well as the participants' satisfaction, and two questions address opinion about the contribution of the game in the development of competencies, one of which is free to comment and the other to mention among the options previously established according to the literature.

The survey was based on a seven-level Likert scale, increasing in degree of agreement with the following milestones: I totally disagree (1), neutrality point (4), I totally agree (7). On this scale, the basic properties of reliability, validity and sensitivity are highlighted (Cummins & Gullone, 2000).

To understand the expectations and objectives of the CIANB in relation to the STA game, individual interviews were carried out, following a semi-structured script with the STA game instructor, the CAIO coordinator and a company games specialist. The interviews were recorded and transcribed for analysis and interpretation (Vergara, 2006).

Figure 4 was designed to demonstrate the link between the data collection instruments used and the research objectives.

Figure 4.

Specific objectives	Data collection instrument
Evaluate the perception of the CAIO 2018 Supply Officers regarding the contribution of business games to the development of skills.	Questionnaire
Map the skills developed in the application of the STA game.	Questionnaire / Interview / Literature Review
Understand the expectation of CIANB on the use of business games regarding the development of competencies in the professional-military training of Supply Officers.	Interview / Documentary Research

With the use of collection instruments mentioned in Figure 4, it was possible to obtain answers that, after being analyzed, contributed to a better understanding of the phenomenon studied. The next topic will present the analysis of the results of this study.

RESULTS

This section analyzes the results obtained that contributed to the achievement of the objectives intended by this work. It is divided into three subtopics, namely: analysis of the questionnaire, analysis of the interviews and discussion of the results.

Questionnaire analysis

By sending a questionnaire to CAIO´s 2018 participants, it was possible to obtain 43 responses out of a total of 71 (60%). As for the characterization of the student officers who answered the questionnaire, it can be seen that 79% of the respondents are men, while 21% are women. The 43 respondents are in the age group between 28 and 35 years old and 65% of them had participated in a business game before.

Regarding the statements "the STA game challenged my managerial capacity", "the game stimulated teamwork" and "I would like to participate in a game again", it was possible to verify that the student officers agree with the statements in significant percentages. A total of 93% of the participants understand that the game challenges management competency, 95.4% agree that STA encourages teamwork and 83.7% would like to participate again in a business game. Such percentages indicate that, in the perception of student officers, the use of the game is attractive, bringing management challenges and contributing to the collaboration between team members.

Figure 5.

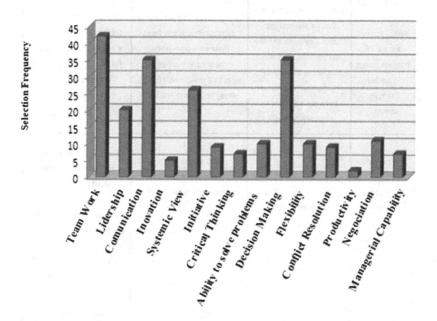

With regard to the statements "the STA game provided the application of knowledge acquired throughout CAIO", "the STA game provided the integration of knowledge acquired throughout CAIO" and "the STA game provided the acquisition of new knowledge", 53.5% agreed with the first statement, demonstrating that they perceived the application of knowledge acquired in CAIO in the decisions of the game. However, it is noteworthy that, for this statement, there was a division in the responses, since 46.5% of the respondents disagreed or remained neutral. 65.1% of the military, on the other hand, agreed with the second statement on the integration of knowledge, while 76.8% understood that the game provided the acquisition of new knowledge.

When analyzing the results obtained with the statements "the STA game enabled the analysis of problems", "the STA game allowed the practice of decision making", "the STA game allowed the practice of results control", "the game promoted adaptation to new situations "," the game made it possible to search for explanation of results" and "the STA game made it possible to make analogies with work", it was possible to observe that for the six statements the percentage of agreement was higher than 79%. It is noteworthy that, in the perception of student officers, the practice of decision-making was more prominent, with the agreement of 93% of respondents.

Figure 6.

Interview script	Interviewed		
	Course coordinator	Professor responsible for STA	Games Specialist
1) What are the intended objectives with the use of business games as a teaching-learning strategy?	"one of the goals is for students to become aware that the subjects that students have learned are not isolated, they mix, they serve as a whole" "[...] I want students to have the initiative to actively learn."	"Allow participants the opportunity to learn from their own experience, without having to pay the price that would result from a wrong decision in real life."	"The basic objective is to provide an experience of what he may face in the future [...] to prepare the student for decision making."
2) What are the main challenges and difficulties regarding the use of business games?	"Having a qualified teacher to teach this subject [...]"	"Eventually there may also be relationship difficulties between the members of a group" [...] "The error in understanding the rules or the data provided can be frustrating for the participant."	"There is a great difficulty in winning over the student [...]" "A second challenge is the role of the teacher, in this type of discipline the center is the student, the teacher becomes a facilitator [...]"
3) In your opinion, what are the main competencies developed in the application of a game?	"[...] the Supply Officer has to have an overview of the problem [...] You will be managers of a higher level, you have to know how to look at the problem as a whole."	"The STA game works mainly with the competencies of systemic vision, assessment and decision making, teamwork and technical knowledge."	"In a team game, there is a very important relational side, conflict management is worked on ... Business games work on analytical capacity, decision making in an uncertain scenario [...]".
4) What changes regarding the application of a business game in a military teaching environment?	"It is an opportunity to bring to our institution the good practices that are used abroad, making us grow [...]"	"[...] the purpose of STA for this specific application (officers in charge), is not purely military. On the contrary, it seeks in this case to bring to the intendant a more detailed understanding of the business variables that were discussed in disciplines offered by others instructors in the earlier stages of the course."	"This is a very interesting change, the Navy is not a company. In essence, the Navy has other objectives. The Navy has no profit [...]" "We adapt the scenario and the game with the reality that will be useful for the public [...]"

In question 16, the following question was asked to the student officers: "In your opinion, of the competencies listed below, which are developed in the STA game? Select up to five options". It is noteworthy that the listed competencies were removed from the literature review and are present in Figure 2 of this article. Figure 5 shows the frequency of selection of competencies by respondents:

When analyzing graph 1, it is concluded that in the perception of the Student Officers, the main competencies developed in the STA game are: teamwork, leadership, communication, systemic vision and decision making. It is worth mentioning that other competences were also mentioned, but less frequently.

Finally, respondents were asked to express themselves freely about the use of STA to develop competencies. From the responses obtained, two stand out: "Seeing the situation as a whole, developing several plans to reach the goal" and "I found it interesting, but it doesn't have much to do with the functions we perform at the Brazilian Navy".

Thus, it is possible to observe again the relevance of the development of the systemic vision with the use of STA. On the other hand, the second statement reflects on the need to customize the game for the performance of activities performed by a Brazilian Navy Supply Officer.

Interview Analysis

Three interviews were carried out, containing four questions with the following interviewees: CAIO coordinator, professor responsible for the application of STA and a professor specialized in business games. Figure 6 presents a summary of the most relevant points of each interview, thus enabling a comparative analysis of responses.

When asked about the intended objectives with the use of business games as a teaching-learning strategy, it was possible to perceive a convergence in opinions. For the interviewees, the game allows the student to actively learn through experience, corroborating with the understanding of the literature referenced in this work. In addition, the Course Coordinator emphasized that the game makes it possible to challenge the student regarding the integration of the knowledge acquired throughout the course, since the game works in multidisciplinary situations.

As for the main challenges mentioned by the interviewees for the use of games, it is clear that the most prominent challenge is the role of the teacher, cited by both the course coordinator and the games specialist. In addition to needing specific training to apply the game, the teacher must position himself as a facilitator, ceasing to be the protagonist of the learning process. For the person responsible for the STA application, two difficulties can occur during the game, they are: relationship problems between the members of the groups, motivated by the different opinions about the decisions to be taken and wrong understanding of the rules of the game by the students, causing frustration with the results obtained.

When asked about the competencies developed with the application of business games, the interviewees scored the following: systemic view, decision making, teamwork, technical knowledge, conflict management and managerial capability. Such competencies are present in table 1 of this paper, which deals with the competencies required for the 21st century.

Thus, it is possible to perceive an alignment between the opinion of the interviewees and those of the main authors on the topic. Based on the interviews carried out, the exercise of decision-making and the systemic view stand out as the main competencies developed through games.

The last question asked to the interviewees was: "What changes regarding the application of company games in a military environment?". Faced with this questioning, each interviewee answered from a perspective.

For the course coordinator, the use of business games in a military environment is a benchmarking opportunity, bringing to the Brazilian Navy the good practices existing in the market. For the person in charge of STA, the game integrates the business knowledge acquired during the course by the student-officer, therefore, it is not a purely military objective, having more relationship with the retention of the knowledge obtained in other disciplines.

And finally, in the vision of the game specialist, it is necessary to customize the games to be applied in a military environment, so that they get closer to the challenges that will be encountered by the military in the exercise of their functions.

DISCUSSION

After analyzing the responses to the questionnaire and the interviews, it was possible to establish a connection between the results obtained by these different data collection instruments. Such results contributed to the achievement of the objectives outlined in this article as indicated in Figure 4.

As for the assessment of the perception of the Supply Officers of the CAIO's class of 2018 with regard to the contribution of business games to the development of competenciess, the results indicate that students positively perceive the use of business games as a teaching-learning strategy. This point is supported by the academic studies that supported this research.

Regarding the identification of the competencies developed in the application of the STA, after crossing the results of the interviews and the questionnaire with the course curriculum in the light of the theoretical framework, it was possible to map the following competencies: "decision making", "systemic view", "Communication", "leadership", "managerial capacity", "technical knowledge" and "conflict management".

Regarding the CIANB's expectation about the use of business games for the development of competenciess, it is concluded that the use of such an active teaching methodology meets both the requirements described in the curriculum menu on the competenciess present in the profile of the improved Supply Officer as well as expected by the course coordinator, that is, that students actively learn, exercising leadership, teamwork and decision making, in simulated environments, integrating the knowledge acquired throughout CAIO.

CONCLUSION

This work is part of the theme of teaching in Administration and aimed to analyze the contributions of the STA Game in the development of competencies of the Supply Officers who accomplished CAIO. The game is an extracurricular activity, applied as one of the last activities in the academic calendar, in order to integrate the knowledge discussed at CAIO.

It was observed, from the obtained data, that the dynamics carried out with the students provided a reflection, in a more comprehensive and integrated way, besides stimulating them in the development of competencies that are not usually worked in a traditional class.

Regarding the perceptions of the Student Officers about the use of the STA game as a tool for learning, it was concluded that the students understood the main objective of the simulation in which they participated, which was to make it possible to experience the management process without their decisions incur real consequences.

Through the intersection between the theoretical framework, the competencies described in the course curriculum and the results obtained with the collection instruments used in this article, it was possible to map the competencies developed by STA, which can be highlighted: "decision making", "Systemic vision", "communication", "leadership", "managerial capacity", "technical knowledge" and "conflict management".

It is noteworthy that other competencies perceived by the students, and highlighted by the interviewees, were also mapped. However, they were not highlighted because they were mentioned less frequently.

It is also noticed a connection of the competencies mapped with the characteristics "spirit of cooperation", "decision-making capacity", "holistic view", "negotiation" expected from an Intermediate Supply Officer, according to the profile contained in the course curriculum.

In addition, it is clear that the expectations of teachers and CIANB were reached regarding the use of games as a teaching-learning strategy, indicating that the desired effect was achieved. Both teachers and students perceived competencies development through this teaching-learning strategy.

Thus, according to the results of the study, it is possible to state that the STA game, as described in its application, was effective in the development of competencies. However, it is emphasized that this statement is true in the context studied, since the active methodology makes it possible to develop in students' relevant competencies for their professional-military practice.

It is concluded that the use of STA contributed greatly to the development of competencies of the Student Officers who performed the CAIO in 2018. The conclusion is in line with the studies referenced in this article, corroborating with the understanding that the use of business games as a teaching-learning strategy it is beneficial for students. Developing competencies in a simulated environment is a way to prepare students for future challenges in a more dynamic and attractive way for students.

As noted in this article, the game integrates the knowledge obtained in the various disciplines taught throughout the course. Therefore, in order to enhance the effect of competencies development through the use of games, it is recommended to use the integrated classroom between conventional and experiential learning.

Regarding the limitations present in this article, it is noteworthy that it was not possible to collect the answers to the questionnaire with all 71 Official Students of the CAIO class of 2018. Another limitation was the lack of access to data from classes of previous years, as that CIANB has applied Business Games since 2015. This would enable a more accurate analysis to be made by comparing the data. Lastly, another limitation is found in the fact that the data obtained on the studied sample came from self-assessment, which can cause distortion in the results.

This research does not intend to exhaust the subject, therefore, as a suggestion for future work, the possibility of a serial study with the next classes of Supply Officers is observed, with a view to proving the results of this study. The use of other research methods, such as a quantitative study or even the use of Mixed Methods Research, could reveal other evidence not indicated in this work. It is also suggested to study about the need for customization or the proposal to create a game specifically for the Brazilian Navy Officers, so that the decisions made by the participants are even closer to the reality to be faced by an Intermediate Officer of the CIM.

This research encourages new discussions regarding the contributions of experiential learning, specifically in the use of business games, for the process of developing competencies in a military environment, with the alignment between theory and practice as its guide.

REFERENCES

Alver, R. A., Cabral, A. C. A., Penha, E. D. S., dos Santos, S. M., & Pessoa, M. N. M. (2013). *Relações entre estilos de aprendizagem e a autopercepção de competências profissionais em alunos concludentes do curso de graduação em Administração da UFC*. Paper presented at the IV Encontro de Ensino e Pesquisa em Administração e Contabilidade Brasilia, DF. http://www.anpad.org.br/admin/pdf/2013_EnEPQ229.pdf

Andrade, C. S. L. d. (2016). *A influência das soft skills na atuação do gestor: a percepção dos profissionais de gestão de pessoas* (Mestre em Administração). Fundação Getúlio Vargas, Rio de Janeiro, RJ. https://bibliotecadigital.fgv.br/dspace/bitstream/handle/10438/17711/Dissertac%CC%A7a%CC%83o%20Final%202016.pdf?sequence=1&isAllowed=y

Arbex, M. A. (2005). O valor pedagógico dos jogos de empresa na aprendizagem de gestão de negócios. *Revista da FAE, 8*(2), 9. https://scholar.google.com/citations?user=3Kc6gxMAAAAJ&hl=pt-BR&oi=sra

Barcante, L. C., & Beltrao, K. I. (2013). *40 years of Brazilian S&G-Analysis and Perspectives*. Paper presented at the Developments in Business Simulation and Experiential Learning: Proceedings of the Annual ABSEL conference, Oklahoma City. https://absel-ojs-ttu.tdl.org/absel/index.php/absel/article/view/54/52

Bitencourt, C. C. (2004). A gestão de competências gerenciais e a contribuição da aprendizagem organizacional. *Revista de Administração de Empresas, 44*(1), 58–69. doi:10.1590/S0034-75902004000100004

Bonotto, G., & Felicetti, V. L. (2014). Habilidades e competências na prática docente: perspectivas a partir de situações-problema. *Educação por escrito, 5*(1), 17-29. doi:10.15448/2179-8435.2014.1.14919

Brasil. (2019). *Currículo do Curso de Aperfeiçoamento de Intendência para Oficiais (CAIO)*. Rio de Janeiro, RJ: Marinha do Brasil. Recuperado em 17 agosto, 2019, de https://www.ead.marinha.mil.br/moodle/pluginfile.php/78753/mod_resource/content/1/Of10-93-2019-DEnsM-AnA-Curriculo-CAIO-063.2%281%29.pdf

Cidral, A. (2003). *Metodologia de aprendizagem vivencial para o desenvolvimento de competências para o gerenciamento de projetos de implementação de sistemas de informação* (Doutorado). Universidade Federal de Santa Catarina - UFSC, Florianópolis. https://repositorio.ufsc.br/xmlui/handle/123456789/8540

Cummins, R. A., & Gullone, E. (2000). Why we should not use 5-point Likert scales: The case for subjective quality of life measurement. *Proceedings, second international conference on quality of life in cities*. https://www.researchgate.net/file.PostFileLoader.html?id=586e1b0bed99e1fee15524a1&assetKey=AS%3A447110639296516%401483610891715

da Silva, J. C. B. L. (2007). Definição dos objetivos para um jogo de guerra. *Revista da Escola de Guerra Naval, 10*, 36. https://revista.egn.mar.mil.br/index.php/revistadaegn/article/view/422

Freitas, S. C. d., & Santos, L. P. G. (2005). *Os benefícios da utilização das simulações empresariais: um estudo exploratório*. Paper presented at the Encontro Anual da Associação dos Programas de Pós Graduação em Administração, Brasília, DF. http://www.anpad.org.br/diversos/down_zips/9/enanpad2005-epqb-2364.pdf

González-Morales, D., De Antonio, L. M. M., & García, J. L. R. (2011). *Teaching "Soft" skills in software engineering*. Paper presented at the 2011 IEEE Global Engineering Education Conference (EDUCON). https://www.academia.edu/18007251/Teaching_and_x201C_soft_and_x201D_skills_in_Software_Engineering

Jungles, B. F., de Souza Rodrigues, J., & Garcia, S. F. A. (2019). Desenvolvimento de competências com jogos de empresas: pesquisa de opinião em um experimento com alunos do ensino técnico. *Gepros: Gestão da Produção, Operações e Sistemas, 14*(3), 194. https://revista.feb.unesp.br/index.php/gepros/article/view/2619

Kolb, A. Y., & Kolb, D. A. (2017). Experiential learning theory as a guide for experiential educators in higher education. *Experiential Learning & Teaching in Higher Education, 1*(1), 7-44. https://learningfromexperience.com/downloads/research-library/experiential-learning-theory-guide-for-higher-education-educators.pdf

Kolb, D. (1984). *Experiential learning: Experience as the source of learning and development*. Prentice Hall.

Melo, N. H. S., Sardinha, I. N., & Menezes, E. O. d. (2017). Aprendizagem vivencial: a contribuição dos jogos de empresas no desenvolvimento de competências. *Revista Lagos, 5*(2). https://www.lagos.vr.uff.br/index.php/lagos/article/view/241

Mintzberg, H. (2006). *MBA? Não, obrigado: Uma visão crítica sobre a gestão eo desenvolvimento de gerentes*. Bookman.

Motta, G. S., & Quintella, R. H. (2012). A utilização de jogos e simulações de empresas nos cursos de graduação em administração no estado da Bahia. *REAd. Revista Eletrônica de Administração (Porto Alegre), 18*(2), 317-338.https:// doi:10.15901413-23112012000200002

Mrtvi, V. O., Westphal, F. K., Bandeira-de-Mello, R., & Feldmann, P. R. (2017). Jogos de empresas: Abordagens ao fenômeno, perspectivas teóricas e metodológicas. *Revista de Administração Contemporânea, 21*(1), 19–40. doi:10.1590/1982-7849rac2017150212

National Research Council. (2012). *Education for life and work: Developing transferable knowledge and skills in the 21st century* (J. W. Pellegrino & M. L. Hilton Eds.). Washington, DC: National Academies Press. http://www.sebrae.com.br/Sebrae/Portal%20Sebrae/Anexos/Education_for_Life_and_work.pdf

Neves, F. S., & Alberton, A. (2017). Jogos de empresas: o que os alunos aprendem? Um estudo com alunos de graduação e pós-graduação. *Revista Espacios, 38*(45), 17. http://www.revistaespacios.com/a17v38n45/a17v38n45p14.pdf

Oliveira, M. A., & Sauaia, A. C. A. (2011). Impressão docente para aprendizagem vivencial: um estudo dos benefícios dos jogos de empresas. *Administração: ensino e pesquisa, 12*(3), 355-391.. doi:10.13058/raep.2011.v12n3.159

Oliveira, S. (2014). *Educação Vivencial em Administração: seriam jogos e simulações alternativas?* Paper presented at the XVII SEMEAD Seminários em Administração, São Paulo, SP. https://www.researchgate.net/publication/316253816_Educacao_Vivencial_em_Administracao_seriam_jogos_e_simulacoes_alternativas

Perrnoud, P. (2004). *Diez nuevas competencias para enseñar: invitación al viaje*. Barcelona: Graó.

Prodanov, C. C., & Freitas, E. C. d. (2013). Metodologia do trabalho científico: métodos e técnicas da pesquisa e do trabalho acadêmico (Segunda Edição ed.). Novo Hamburgo, RS: Editora Feevale. doi:10.1017/CBO9781107415324.004

Rosas, A. R., & Sauaia, A. C. A. (2006). Jogos de empresas na educação superior no Brasil: Perspectivas para 2010. *Enfoque: Reflexão Contábil, 25*(3), 72–85. doi:10.4025/enfoque.v25i3.3489

Schmitz, L. C., Alperstedt, G. D., Van Bellen, H. M., & Schmitz, J. L. (2015). Limitações e dificuldades na utilização da abordagem experiencial no ensino de gerenciamento de projetos em um curso de graduação em administração. *Administração: ensino e pesquisa, 16*(3), 537-569. . doi:10.13058/raep.2015. v16n3.283

Silva, M. A. (2013). *Laboratório de gestão: jogo de empresas com pesquisa para a formação crítica em administração* (Doutorado Doutorado). Universidade de São Paulo, São Paulo, SP. https://teses.usp. br/teses/disponiveis/12/12139/tde-20082013-150104/pt-br.php

Souza, A. J. N. d. (2008). A anatomia de um jogo de guerra didático. *Revista da Escola de Guerra Naval, 12*, 17. https://revista.egn.mar.mil.br/index.php/revistadaegn/article/view/404

Swiatkiewicz, O. (2014). Competências transversais, técnicas ou morais: um estudo exploratório sobre as competências dos trabalhadores que as organizações em Portugal mais valorizam. *Cadernos EBAPE. BR, 12*(3), 633-687. http://bibliotecadigital.fgv.br/ojs/index.php/cadernosebape/article/view/12337

Vergara, S. C. (2006). *Projetos e relatórios de pesquisa*. Atlas.

Zabala, A., & Arnau, L. (2015). *11 ideas clave: cómo aprender y enseñar competencias*. Graó.

Zucatti, A. P. N., Silveira, L. M. O. B., Abbad, G. S., & Flores, C. D. (2019). Criação de uma Simulação para o Desenvolvimento de Competências em um Hospital. *Psicologia: Ciência e Profissão, 39*. Advance online publication. doi:10.1590/1982-3703002102017

KEY TERMS AND DEFINITIONS

Brazilian Navy: Is the branch of the Brazilian Armed Forces responsible for conducting naval operations.

Business Game: A learning method that allows participants to play managerial roles in fictitious companies that, through a controlled reality, with the possible use of simulators, test decision making under conditions of uncertainty.

Competency: Ability to act effectively in a given type of situation, supported by knowledge, however without being limited to them.

Competency Development: It is a continuous and articulated process of formation and development of knowledge, skills and attitudes in which the person has the responsibility for its self-development and, interrelating with other people, aiming at the improvement of its training, adds value to individual and collective activities.

Experiential Learning Theory (ELT): Is a dynamic view of learning based on a learning cycle driven by the resolution of the dual dialectic of action / reflection and experience / abstraction.

Improvement Course in Intendency for Officers (CAIO): Course with the objective of updating and expanding the knowledge necessary for the performance of positions and the exercise of functions of intermediate and higher hierarchical degrees in the career of the Officer of the Corps of Intendents.

Navy Supply Corps Officer: The Navy supply corps officer is the corps of officers of the Brazilian Navy who hold positions related to the application and preparation of Naval Power, aimed at attending to logistical activities and those related to the economy, finances, assets, administration and internal control.

Simulator for Training in Administration (STA): A highly dynamic training exercise, which uses a computer model of a competitive situation between companies that manufacture the same type of product and sell it in an oligopolistic market.

Chapter 25
The Importance of Defining a Roadmap for a Digital Transformation:
A Case Study of a Large Civil Construction Company in Portugal

Marta Lamelas Costa
Polytechnic Institute of Setúbal, Portugal

João Loureiro
Tecnovia Sociedade de Empreitadas S.A., Portugal

Catarina Gata
Tecnovia Sociedade de Empreitadas S.A., Portugal

ABSTRACT

The transition from a traditional organizational logic to a digital one is not immediate as it forces a re-adjustment of processes, Information Systems and even organizational structures. The company selected for analysis belongs to the civil construction sector. The case study consists of identifying and detailing operational procedures in the field of information systems and consequent diagnosis of the transition to a digital scenario, preparing it for new global competitiveness scenarios, as well as analyzing the intra and extra-organizational dimensions that should be considered in the process of transformation. The operational management of the company is based on traditional procedures, where data recording is mostly handwritten. It would be beneficial to use knowledge management systems, preparing the company for an increasingly widespread trend, such as the digital economy. This would allow an increase in the efficiency and productivity of processes, through the improvement of production, archive, and knowledge management in the scope of its operations.

DOI: 10.4018/978-1-7998-4201-9.ch025

Copyright © 2021, IGI Global. Copying or distributing in print or electronic forms without written permission of IGI Global is prohibited.

INTRODUCTION

This study appears in the current economic context, in which the theme of digital transformation is increasingly present, as most business leaders agree that digital transformation, a wave of business innovation fueled by technology, is interrupting their business or will do so soon enough. Although even less than half have adopted a digital strategy (Olavsrud, 2017), it is becoming extremely important for companies to define a strategy and a roadmap for digital change. They should seek to adapt their traditional business models to the potential of the digital context, bearing in mind that the simple introduction of new technologies, such as tablets, smartphones, cloud, among others, does not, by itself, guarantee a transition to this new context (Anunciação & Esteves, 2019).

With the exception of technology in products, technology does not add value to the business (Westerman, 2017). In truth, technology allows you to do business differently, and that is how it adds value. As referred by Westerman (2017) "e-commerce is not about the Internet; it is about selling differently. Analytics is not about databases and machine language algorithms, it is about understanding customers better, or optimizing maintenance processes, or helping doctors diagnose cancer more accurately. IoT is not about RFID tags it is about radically synchronizing operations or changing business models" (Anunciação & Esteves, 2019).

Therefore, the transition to digital logic assumes a broader vision, involving innovation in the business, consolidating commercial relations with customers and observing the development of their behavior, observing the practices of counterparts in the main international markets, developing new internal and external dynamics and the training of employees at IS level, among other examples.

As no company goes digital instantly, it is important that the process is planned and managed, so that the transition is controlled and without unforeseen events. There must be a sharing of responsibility among the entire organization, starting with top management.

This wave of change encompasses all economic and social organizations, whether public or private and this study included a private economic organization in the construction sector. This sector was chosen as it maintains a very traditional technological culture, where some resistance to change persists, with low levels of preparation in the face of technological developments and because it is one of the most relevant sectors in the Portuguese economy. In addition to its relevance in the national economy, the civil construction sector is strategic for the European Union, having in recent years faced several challenges in terms of market competition, human capital, environmental requirements and regulations. As a result of the financial crisis that Portugal went through, the sector lost about 30 thousand companies and more than 260 thousand workers (Pinto, 2019). However, it is expected that the sector will have a marked growth globally. Chinese companies, which dominate the global ranking of players in the construction sector, will contribute to this growth, with Australia being a great opportunity for foreign investment, due to the public investment policy in the public works sector (Deloitte, 2018).

The company chosen for this study started its activity in the 60s, in the area of earthworks, roads and urbanization, together with the exploration of quarries for their own production of aggregates, ready-mixed concrete and bituminous mixtures. For over almost 60 years, the company has diversified its area of operation, currently operating in all fields of public and private construction. The Industry Area, dedicated to the exploration of quarries and the production of construction materials also grew and became one of the company's business areas. Currently, the company operates 9 industrial production centers distributed throughout Portugal, constituting itself as a certified and reference supplier of aggregates, bituminous mixtures and ready-mixed concrete. In addition to Portugal, its internationalization strategy, which began in the early 1990s, has been present in African and Central and Latin American countries.

In light of the current economic context, the company has felt the need to modernize and introduce information technologies and systems with the goal of generating value (results center) and not just from a cost center perspective.

Given the size of the company, in this analysis, a greater focus was given to the process of Quarries Exploration and Production of Aggregates, which is carried out using its own resources in its regular activity, without resorting to subcontracting. Its operational management is based on traditional processes, where data recording is mostly handwritten. In this way, it would be beneficial to use knowledge management systems, in order to prepare for a digital economy, an increasingly widespread trend.

It is expected that the use of these systems will increase the efficiency and productivity of operations by improving production, archiving and knowledge management within the scope of its operations. Innovation brings speed to organizations, forcing a break with the past, requiring agility, adequacy and development of new models and management tools that reduce complexity, risk and instability (Anunciação & Esteves, 2019).

Considering these aspects, this work intends to present a new model of management of the digital transformation process, in which the investment in new information technologies should not only be considered but also in alignment with the business, which requires economic-financial analyzes of returns. The larger the company, the greater the importance attributed to the management of these processes, since information technologies only constitute competitive advantages when properly inserted in business and organizations. For this reason, this work provides a real economic study of the costs and benefits associated with a digital transformation process. Works of this nature must always be accompanied by an analysis of the economic and financial viability associated with the respective investments.

To achieve the objectives presented, the work is developed throughout six chapters: chapter 2 pertains to the description of the internship, characterizing the company where the case study is inserted, referring to the various aspects of its business, its history, its organizational structure, mission, values, responsibilities and certifications. This chapter also refers to the characterization of the IS Department, the Industry Area and the Technical Area.

The third chapter is dedicated to the choice of the studied process and in chapter 4 the methodology of the research process used is mentioned, which is essential to the development of knowledge as a constructive and continuous process, increasing with research and interpretation. The methodological approach chosen was developed in two phases, using direct observation, bibliographic research and semi-structured interviews to collect information.

In chapter 5, the case study is approached through the description of the current situation of the company and the key problems identified and the proposed Roadmap for the company is presented. Chapter 6 presents the expected results in the scope of the study, based on the improvement proposal presented.

The last chapter is the conclusion of the work, in which a summary of the work is made, highlighting the importance of the solutions presented in view of the problems identified and considering the internal and external environment in which the company operates.

2. THEORETICAL FRAMEWORK

2.1. Characterization of the Civil Construction Sector

In order to carry out this work, the civil construction sector was chosen, which is strategic for the European Union, because it moves several sectors upstream and downstream on its production chain and produces the necessary buildings and infrastructures for the rest of the economy and society (Campos, 2013). It is the largest economic activity and the largest industrial employer in Europe (Campos, 2013) and its value chain includes the production, supply and sale of construction materials, especially quarrying, where some companies have their main activity, given their complementarity with the civil construction sector. The value chain also includes the supply of equipment and machinery, the provision of services related to research, among others. This value chain ends with the execution of construction and delivery to the customer, with the final product being made in different geographies and with different teams. These teams are usually large, which requires rigorous planning and coordination.

The demand directed at the civil construction sector depends on the country's economic situation, being, therefore, a cyclical activity that is, for this reason, considered one of the main indicators of the national economy.

Among the various challenges that this sector faces, the market, environmental requirements, regulation and the loss of assets in the labor market stand out. In this sector it is difficult to retain human capital, as there is a high turnover, high job insecurity, low pay, high accident rate, strong technicality and little investment in training, among other critical factors. The economic context in Europe in recent years has forced European companies to invest in internationalization, with the consequence of the need to operate in different cultures, adapt to different languages and different legal and fiscal realities.

Regarding the information generated by the companies in this sector, it appears that it is generally dispersed, and there is often no integration between the operational and administrative aspects. The information is quite varied and on a large scale, which requires great efficiency in its collection, in order to avoid delays in responding to stakeholder questions and problems. The adaptation of these companies to new contexts and the characteristics of the information generated, implies that the IS accompany all these needs, as the information is indispensable for decision making and is considered a strategic resource.

The civil construction sector is known for its very traditional technological culture, with little flexibility and preparation in the face of technological developments and resistance to transformation.

2.2. Company Characterization

The company in question positions itself as one of the most important construction companies in Portugal. Its core business is civil construction, public works and the supply of construction materials in more than 20 Industrial Centers in Portugal and other countries.

This company started operating in Portugal, having later followed an internationalization strategy focusing its efforts on Africa and Central and Latin America. In the mainland Portuguese market, the company has about 650 employees, organized in the following areas: Commercial and Technical Production, Industry, Human Resources, Technical, Procurement and Subcontracting, Equipment, Legal, Financial and Administrative. The Commercial and Technical Production area is oriented towards presentation proposals and project execution. The Industry Area is dedicated to the production of materials and the rest are support and services. Each area is led by a Director and structured in Departments that are coordinated by Managers who have at their disposal the necessary resources for the development of their activity.

2.2.1. Characterization of the IS / IT Department

The IS/IT Department is the responsibility of the Administrative and Financial Area. Its main mission is to provide support to the company's IS, at headquarters and at various branches, in different parts of Portugal and Cape Verde, ensuring the operationality of the support systems for operational and management activities.

Among the various IS systems and infrastructures, servers, network infrastructures, Microsoft operating systems, computers, the internet and various peripherals stand out. These components must be addressed as a whole, requiring a proactive and coordinated development between technology, company processes and people.

As far as hardware is concerned, there are currently around 200 employees using computers for professional purposes. The assignment and characteristics of this material depends on the professionals' needs, that is, the applications they need for their tasks.

In this Department, the main processes are the management and maintenance of network infrastructure and services and the helpdesk. Among these, the Assisted Weighing System (SPA) stands out as it is used in the scales of the company's quarries. SPA is a modular software application, designed to work seamlessly with weighing equipment, facilitating the management of weighing movements, loads and unloads. Its integration with the Primavera logistics module allows commercial transactions to be made based on the weight of the product, complementing the ERP Primavera with a document editor with specific features for weighing operations.

2.3. Characterization of the Industry Area

The Industry Area is responsible for the management of nine Industrial Centers where the company explores and manages quarries; crushing plants; concrete production plants; bituminous mixtures production plants; handling and loading equipment; clear spaces; scales; workshops and laboratories.

For all quarries there is a Local Quarry Officer, whose functions are the mastery of crushing, washing and drilling equipment; knowledge of equipment maintenance; the coordination and management of work teams; the coordination of equipment within the quarries; the preparation of exploration areas; and ensuring the quality of the materials produced, among other responsibilities.

2.3.1. Characterization of the Company's Quarries

In this company, the main raw material for the manufacture of aggregates is acquired in quarries, where the company has an exploration license from north to south of the country. The productive circuit of the manufacture of aggregates begins with planning the type of drilling and the disassembly method used in the massif. The next step is drilling, which aims to prepare the rock mass for dismantling, in order to place explosive material through the holes. It is followed by the dismantling, which consists of the extraction of the mineral mass using explosive material.

After being detached from the rock mass, the materials are loaded by an excavator or loader and transported in a dumper to the Crushing Plant. In this Central, the blocks are crushed and selected until the desired dimensions are obtained. Then, the aggregates are stored in stocks and/or purchased by internal or external customers.

2.4. Characterization of the Quality Department

The Quality Department is concerned with improving the company's processes and is responsible for the production control of aggregates, from the quality of the raw material to the finished product and market placement. It is transversal to all departments of the company as it validates and formalizes all procedures.

This department guarantees the improvement of quality levels through the Quality Management System (QMS), which is documented in five levels: Quality Manual; Law Suit; Procedures; Work instructions; Monitoring Plans, Forms and Records, whose formal description and validation is the concern of those responsible for the respective Area and the Quality Department.

Among these processes, procedures, forms and records, those analyzed in this work are the responsibility of the Industry Area.

The Quality Department also has the responsibility to ensure that all employees from the different Industrial Centers are aware of these documents and that they try to comply with them. This Department is also responsible for ensuring that products are in compliance with European legislation. For this purpose, tests are carried out in the company's laboratories.

The Laboratory Analyst is accountable for the company's production control and records the Conformities and Non-Conformities of the aggregates, which are sent to the Quarry Exploration Manager and to the Local Quarry Manager by email.

3. CHOICE OF THE PROCESS STUDIED

The company in question has sought to adapt to the context in which it operates, embracing different challenges, such as the dematerialization of information, in a logic of digital transformation. This objective arose due to the way the company's operational management is carried out, based on traditional processes where the data recording is mostly handwritten.

Considering these objectives, the manager of the Quality Department suggested the study of this Area. This was proposed because this Area has a complementary role to the construction sector when managing the production of the materials used in the construction.

The process chosen for an in-depth study was the Quarry Exploration and Aggregate Production, which is the responsibility of the Industry Area.

Among the various procedures, "Aggregate Production Control" and "Crushing Plant Equipment Maintenance" were chosen for this work, as they are procedures that originate and manage data that indicate the performance of the business and have enough impact on the company's efficiency. The objective of this choice was to seek solutions to optimize processes and acquire knowledge about the company's daily performance, preparing it for new global competitiveness scenarios.

The analysis logic used for this work can later be passed on to other processes from other departments of the company.

4. METHODOLOGY

The methodological options chosen for the preparation of this work were interviews, bibliographic research and direct observation, through a top-down approach, in which we sought to collect information from the manager of the Quality Department and Manager of Quarrying.

We also sought to collect other information through interviews with other employees directly linked to the processes studied, namely, the Person Responsible for the Technical Area, the Local Responsible for Quarries, the Administrative and Operators of the Industry Area.

With this data, the proposal to support the activity was elaborated, supported by information technologies. This proposal was validated by the Quality Department from a conceptual point of view.

The interview was one of the methods chosen, as it is one of the most used in organizational diagnosis and the most valid for accessing information. The interview is part of the qualitative technique, in which the reality investigated, according to Terence and Filho (2006), is subjective and complex and its procedure seeks to examine the context and interact with the participants, with a tendency to be descriptive. In the literature, interviews can be structured, semi-structured and unstructured. For the present study, we opted for the semi-structured interview as its characteristics are advantageous, given the context analyzed.

According to what was mentioned by Barañano (2004) regarding semi-structured interviews, we tried to conduct the interviews imposing some limits on the subject through the presentation of a theme and the different areas interviewees should address. Considering what is referred in the literature about this type of interviews, there was always a concern for establishing an interaction and proximity between the interviewer and the interviewee, in order to favor spontaneous responses, similar to an informal conversation (Boni & Quaresma, 2005).

Another methodological option chosen was bibliographic research through the analysis of a series of documents related to the case study such as: printed forms filled out by different employees who work in the company's quarries; reports generated from these forms, company charts, manuals; and internal policies and standards.

The collection of this information was complemented by direct observation, which, in turn, resulted in capturing aspects related to the behavior of people in their daily activities, the relationship between human resources and the cultural aspects of the organization.

5. CASE STUDY

5.1. Description of the Current Situation

The procedures analyzed in this work are the "Control of Production of Aggregates" and "Maintenance of Equipment of the Crushing Plant". These are part of the "Quarry Exploration and Aggregate Production" process, in the "Quarry Exploration" area, managed by the Industry Department, according to the following hierarchy:

Table 1. Framework of the procedures studied in its process and area (DI, 2018).

Area	Process	Procedure
Quarrying	Quarrying and Aggregate Production	Production Control of Aggregates
		Crushing Plant Equipment Maintenance

These procedures present objective and clear work instructions and their interconnection with other processes constitutes the organizational routine, in which, each employee performs his tasks following a sequential logic. To manage, plan and visually describe this workflow, there are several tools. Among these, the process flowchart stands out, which shows a series of events that produce a final result, presenting who and what is involved in each process. These workflows explain the productive steps developed by each employee and how each of these steps relates to the work of others in the process. Considering these aspects, the procedures "Control of Production of Aggregates" and "Maintenance of Crushing Plant Equipment" were transformed, in visual representation, through the elaboration of workflows, since this type of documentation did not exist in the company. In this way, we sought to facilitate the identification of the main axes to be improved.

The "Aggregate Production Control" procedure begins with filling in the Ref. I.DE. 25b/2 (Tables 2 and 3) made by the drivers of excavators / loaders.

The "Aggregate Production Control" procedure (Figure 1) also begins with the filling out of the following forms by the dumpers/truck drivers (Tables 2 and 3): Ref. I.DE. 25a/2 and Printed Ref. IR.DE.06/2.

Figure 1. "Aggregate Production Control" procedure which starts with the driver of the dumper/truck.

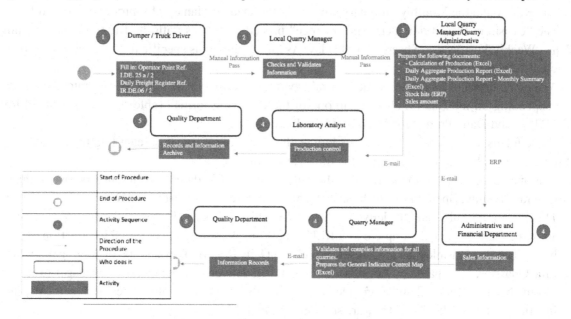

The "Aggregate Production Control" procedure also begins with the filling of the following forms by the Crushing Plant Operators (Tables 2 and 3): Printed Ref. I.DE. 1/25; Printed Ref. IR.DE.06/2; Daily Sheet - Primary; Registration of Daily Installation Production.

The Daily Freight Register Ref: IR.DE.06/2 serves to specify the type of material being transported and also for the RLP to verify if the material load entering the Primary (registered by the Crushing Center Operator in their Operator Point/Daily Sheet-Primary/Daily Log Shipping, depending on the Quarries) is equal to the load indicated by the Dumper Driver.

Of the six forms mentioned above, there are three that are not completed in all Quarries: Daily Freight Register, Daily Sheet – Primary and Registration of Daily Installation Production.

In general, the procedure starts with the excavator/loader driver loading the material detached from the rock mass into the dumper/truck. Then, it transports the material to the Crushing Plant, unloading it to the Primary, following the desired circuit inside the Crushing Plant to obtain the desired dimensions.

At the end of the day, the completed forms are handed over to the respective Local Quarry Officer RLP for validation. As there are several RLPs responsible for two Quarries, this means that they have to travel several times a week, with the printed materials not being checked on some days in some of these Quarries. These forms are then digitized and filed by the administrative or RLP for 5 years. Administrative officers provide administrative support to the various people responsible for the activities carried out in the industrial area in which they operate. These, or the RLPs, have the responsibility to use the information on the forms, after their respective validation, to prepare the following documents (Table 3): Calculation of Production, Daily Aggregate Production Report (RDPA), Daily Aggregate Production Report - Monthly Summary.

The information on the forms is also used to make stock adjustments. Stock adjustments are the adjustment of the stocks that physically exist in the quarry and the stocks indicated in the company's ERP.

These documents are finally sent to the Quarry Manager who compiles the information for all quarries and produces a document with that information that he sends to the Quality Department.

The RDPA and the Monthly Summary are sent to the Quarry Manager for production control.

The "Crushing Plant Equipment Maintenance" procedure begins with the filling of the Crushing Plant's Weekly Verification Sheets every Friday. As this document is specific to each Central, there are different versions of it.

At the beginning of this process, the Central Operator also fills in the Ref.I.DE Operator Point. 25/1 and depending on the Quarry, also fills in one of the following forms (Tables 2 and 3): Printed Ref. I.DEP.11/1 and Daily Production Record of Installation.

These forms are also part of this procedure as they contain information regarding the maintenance of the crushing plant, as can be seen in the following Tables.

This analysis allowed us to identify that the same forms are filled out by different employees, that is, the Central Crushing Operator fills in the same forms as the Excavator/Loader and Dumper/Truck drivers.

These forms are subsequently delivered to the RLP which checks and assesses the need to request the repair of the plant through the Impreto Ref. IR.DE. 12/1 or ask for Internal Material Requisition to do so (Table 3). The Responsible then prepares, in Excel, the Daily Report of Production of Aggregates which, in some Quarries, is prepared by Administrators and then delivered to the Quarries Manager (Table 3). The forms listed in Tables 2 and 3 provide information for the creation of a series of documents, their designation and who fills them. They are summarized in Table 3.

Table 2. Data filled in the forms of the "Aggregate Production Control" and "Crushing Plant Equipment Maintenance" procedures.

Forms	Main Information of Back of sheet	Responsible for writing the Data
1 - Operator Point Ref: I.DE.25/1	-	Central Crushing Operator
2 - Operator Point Ref: I.DE.25a/2	Weekly Verification Sheet Record of Weekly Occurrences	Dumper Operator *and* Truck Operator
3 – Operator Point Ref: I.DE.25b/2	Weekly Verification Sheet Record of Weekly Occurrences	Loader Operator or Backhoe Operator and Drilling Car Operator
4 - Daily Freight Register Ref: IR.DE.06/2	-	Dumper conductor and Central Crushing Operator
5 - Daily Sheet - Primary	-	Central Crushing Operator
6 - Daily Installation Production Record	-	
7 - Crushing Plant Weekly Checks Sheet	-	

Table 3. Data filled in the forms of the "Aggregate Production Control" and "Crushing Plant Equipment Maintenance" procedures.

Document	Responsible for writing the Data
8 - Daily Aggregate Production Report	Local Quarry Manager/Administrative Quarry
9 - Daily Aggregate Production Report - Monthly Summary	
10 - Production Calculation	Administrative
11 - Consumption Map	
12 - Internal Requisition	Local Quarry Manager
13 - Repair Request	

5.1.1. Key Issues Identified

The diagnosis was made from detailed knowledge of the sequence of activities. The purpose of which was to recommend solutions, considering the objectives of the analyzed business area, having identified the following key problems:

- Repetition of Data: In several Quarries it was found that there are several forms to be filled in with the same information. In some cases, this duplication exists to justify the crossing of information, in order to verify whether the Operators have tampered with the data. However, this system can be fallible, as Operators can talk and decide to change the information together.

- Different Terminologies and Incomplete Justifications: The "Reasons for stopping the Crushing Plants" are filled out daily in each quarry by the Operators, in three different forms, all of them with different terminologies.

It was also verified that there is no correspondence of terms between the forms and the Report originated.

- Absence of History and Traceability: It appears that much of the information is out of date and inconsistent, due to the need for data to be entered several times in different documents.

There is no organized, updated and always available history of satisfied and pending Repair Requests. Another history related issue is the lack of traceability, that is, when the resolution of a certain problem is requested regarding repairs/revisions, it is difficult to understand if it is still being solved, if it has already been solved, or if someone has yet to start resolving it. Regarding the breakdowns of the Crushing Plant, which may occur in the middle of the week, these may run the risk of not being registered in the Weekly Verification Sheets, as this form is only completed on Friday.

- Standardization of Procedures: There is no uniform filling of forms between the various quarries, with quarries in which certain fields of the forms are filled out and others in which they are not. This divergence between the procedures can be explained by the relative autonomy of the Local Officers in each Quarry.
- Excess of Paper Documentation: The company has five Local Quarry Officers responsible for seven Quarries, which means that two of them are responsible for two quarries each.

Each Local Quarry Officer (RLP) has to check several forms per month making a total of, approximately, 1254 forms in the 6 Quarries. For this calculation, all forms analyzed by the RLP were accounted for, including those completed by employees who are directly involved in the two procedures analyzed and those who are not directly involved. These data are relative, since the equipment, the number of employees and the procedures vary between quarries and in the same quarry, depending on weather conditions or orders. For this reason, the amount of completed documents can also vary depending on daily requests.

- Delays in Procedures: The fact that all forms are filled out by hand can increase the delay in the circulation of information and, the fact that it circulates on paper, can facilitate its loss and increase the delay in solving problems.

An example of these problems is visible when the Crushing Plant remains idle for several hours, without production, because the Local Quarry Officer has yet to check the forms where maintenance-related issues are indicated.

The time spent by those responsible for checking all forms varies between 15 to 30 minutes.

- Parts' Wear Control: The wear of the parts of the Crushing Plants is controlled through direct observation of the RLP and Operators and also through the analysis of the laboratory results of the aggregates produced.

For example, when laboratory tests begin to detect mixtures of particle sizes, which give rise to Non-Conformities, one of the possible causes is the wear of the Nets. When products that do not comply with the established requirements are identified, a methodology is applied, which prevents their use or involuntary delivery. However, if this delivery occurs, there may be complaints and damage to the company's image with customers.

- Minimum Stock: The stock of parts varies depending on their value and the speed of wear.

Information on the need to replace these parts can be found in the Weekly Crushing Sheets of the Crushing Plant which, being on paper, can be lost or forgotten. The consequence of this action is only detected later, during the laboratory tests, which aim to control the quality of the aggregates. In these, you can obtain various results that are not in accordance with the limits required by European standards, without checking the conformity that certifies that the product meets the necessary requirements of the applicable directives.

Nonconformities have numerous harmful consequences for the company, such as cancellation of orders, verification in external audits, among others.

- Inventory of Parts: In most Quarries, it is not easy to access the inventory of parts that make up a plant and their respective reference. This reference would make it possible to know where the material is, since there are often parts that are ordered and when the order arrives at the Central Warehouse, whoever receives the order no longer remembers who ordered it. This creates a lot of confusion with orders not being met on a first come, first served basis.
- Inaccuracy in Aggregate Production Information: The information regarding aggregate production in all Quarries is not accurate, as these quantities are calculated from the number of daily freights carried out by the dumpers and the maximum capacity of each of these vehicles. Inaccuracy can arise if, among other aspects, there are mistakes in filling the number of freights (Operator Point and Daily Freight Record), if the dumper is not loaded to its maximum capacity or if the dumper is loaded with material that disperses along the production path.
- Decision Support Information: One of the characteristics of the information analyzed is its dispersion, due to the use of independent systems, with often no integration between the operational and administrative aspects.

It appears that all forms are filled out manually, with a greater likelihood of errors occurring. The fact that all information is dispersed on paper, in Excel files or does not exist, makes the process more susceptible to human error. This fact also does not allow the process to be easily analyzed, such as analyzing decision support data and acting preventively at critical points, aiming at improving effectiveness and efficiency.

Regarding the real stock adjustments mentioned above, it is common to have some confusion regarding the actual quantities, with the values not coinciding with what is indicated in the ERP used by the company. Another example is information related to the production of aggregates in all Quarries, which is not available at any time to the Quarry Manager.

5.2. Solution Design

One of the biggest challenges of the Information Systems is to ensure the availability of information and the good management of the organization, quickly, reliably and with little probability of errors occurring.

Considering this premise and taking into account the current difficulties identified, we propose a business model with flexible partners to accompany the company's growth, adopting the best technologies. Thus, we tried to outline the improvement proposal through workflows (Figures 2) and in different topics, in order to answer the main key problems identified in chapter 5.1.1., namely:

- **Improved access to decision support information**

Regarding the "Aggregate Production Control" procedure, it is suggested that the information on the quantities of material entering the Primary be recorded automatically by passing the dumpers/trucks over set of scales which will be installed before the Primary. This proposal is outlined in Figure 2. In the proposed solution, the RLP will have to validate the tons of material that enter the Primary daily and enter in the software information about the products produced that day. It would calculate the approximate quantities of each product using pre-defined formulas for each Central of crushing (Figure 2). The Laboratory Analyst will receive a notification in the software which he will also have access to, telling him/her when it is necessary to collect samples (Figure 2). Regarding the "Crushing Plant Maintenance" procedure, the improvement proposal involves ensuring that the information currently contained in the Weekly Verification Sheets will be filled in on a smartphone or tablet by the Crushing Plant Operator. The Quarry Manager, like the RLP, will have access to the sum of the quantities produced and the eventual need for repair of the Crushing Plant using the software. This monitoring and follow-up of the results' evolution can be done from dashboards, in real time, at the end of the day, week or at the end of the month.

The Laboratory Analyst will also have access to this information, as will the Quality Manager and the Administrative and Financial Department (Figures 2).

The proposal designed to respond to the "Crushing Plant Equipment Maintenance" procedure involves software that ensures maximum management efficiency, being a solution for planning and controlling the activities of maintenance. This software will allow that, in case there is a need to repair the Central, the RLP can make a Request for Repair in the software, which, depending on the severity, sends it to the Quarry Manager or to the Maintenance Team or the person Responsible of the Quarry Workshop. After solving the problem, those involved indicate that it is solved through the "Closing" of the order, to which the RLP will have access through automatic notification. This solution will provide information on the current status and evolution of maintenance costs.

- **Traceability, Repairs and Maintenance**

Regarding Repairs and Maintenance, it is proposed that the system ensures their traceability, being the RLP who should make the Repair Request and confirm its execution.

- **Construction of a history of repairs and "reasons for stopping" crushing plants**

Figure 2. Proposed "Aggregate Production Control" procedure that starts with the driver of the dumper/ truck.

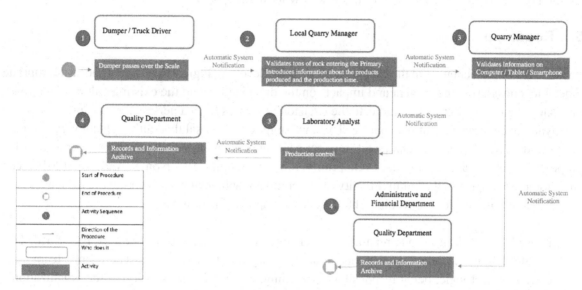

The absence of a history of repairs and of the "Reasons for stopping crushing plants" can be overcome by introducing information into software adopted for this purpose. This would allow for the construction of a history where it is easy to search for information as well as the centralization of information, allowing modifications in one place, avoiding incompatibilities between several versions of the same information, guaranteeing access to data in different ways and avoiding the delay in the process.

- **Correct completion of the justification for the "reasons for stopping"**

To guarantee the correct filling in of the reasons for the Stop Reasons, the software must allow the Operators to select pre-defined "justifications".

- **Equipment wear control**

Considering the poor wear control of the equipment that is in force, it is proposed that the system automatically alert the RLP when the Plant Maintenance period is approaching, integrating the proposed software with the software that currently controls the hours of operation of each equipment of the Central. This ensures data from these two different systems are available for analysis and management of the quarry as a whole.

- **Referencing Central Crushing Parts**

In order to facilitate communication between the different heads of the workshop and the various local heads of quarry, it is suggested that lists be created with the parts of each plant and their respective reference. This reference will facilitate communication when it is necessary to order new parts, which may be indicated in the part guide and thus facilitate the correspondence between the part and the order.

It is also recommended that there be a minimum stock of parts that register greater wear and that can be repaired quickly with the know-how of those who work in the quarry.

5.3. Roadmap

To guide the implementation of the change, it is crucial to develop a logical action plan and an appropriate timetable, considering the content and impacts on the organization and the existing culture. The Roadmap should guide the action and indicate the decision processes from a perspective of a process model of a dynamic and transformational nature. Thus, we suggest a proposal that, although not very detailed, is believed to present some fundamental steps for a change process to be adopted by the company. This proposal, which is based on the life cycle proposed by the authors Anderson & Anderson (2010), can and should be adapted to the cultural reality of the company with a view to adopting the most appropriate cycle to obtain the desired results. Thus, the following cycle is proposed:

- Phase I - Identification and preparation for change - the team for the change must be formed. This should delimit the "case" of the change and identify the desired results. The change team must obey a project logic, being responsible for reading, evaluating and specifying the organizational capacity for the change, the global strategy to be followed and the identification of the support infrastructure;
- Phase II - Creation of the vision, commitment and organizational capacities - this phase involves the construction of an organizational "understanding" of the changing situation, vision and strategy of change, identifying the expected benefits, namely, by specifying the new increments in organizational capacity;
- Phase III - Survey and assessment of the current situation - this phase comprises of the survey and assessment of the current situation. Its objective is to evaluate the way of functioning in order to identify the change requirements that should support the new operating architecture;
- Phase IV - Architecture of the desired state - definition and design (architecture) of the new (desired) state, which should resolve or correct the problems or situations identified in the previous phase;
- Phase V - Impact assessment - this phase comprises of the analysis and assessment of the impact of the desired state, allowing decision making regarding the identified hypotheses of change;
- Phase VI - Planning and organization of implementation - comprises of the development of a master plan for operationalizing change and organizational preparation to support implementation;
- Phase VII - Course learning and correction - comprises the evaluation/correction of the system for continuous improvement, strengthening of learning and consolidation of best practices.

For change to be managed efficiently and effectively, it is important that it is developed as a project, that is:

- with a perfectly defined scope, understandable and accepted by top management;
- based on feasible planning in accordance with the defined objectives and existing organizational constraints;
- supported by a feasibility analysis, which makes the estimated gains and return on investment evident;

- supported by top management;
- evident of the individual results of the changes proposed to the various stakeholders;
- accompanied by a multidisciplinary team, led by an executive-level staff.

6. EXPECTED RESULTS WITHIN THE STUDY

The improvement proposal, developed from the information collected and its systematization, aims to achieve a series of benefits for the organization. In general, this proposal aims to increase the monitoring of processes by improving their control, with the aim of producing and supplying the requested products in a timely manner, in the most efficient way possible. These solutions also seek to meet the dematerialization of information and the reduction of bureaucracy. It allows managers to know the company's daily performance by giving them access to the results achieved and the possibility of comparing them with the defined goals. The results can also be compared with the values of the sector and it may be possible to know the evolution and trend over time.

The fact that the proposal translates into an increase in tools that support the work of Local Quarry Officers makes the sudden absence of any of these employees less painful for the company. With the proposed solution, it will be simpler for new employees to understand how the process is carried out. There will be an opportunity to improve existing procedures and irrelevant operations may be reduced, also, information will circulate more quickly and in a more accessible manner and, therefore, there will be greater data sharing. The fact that there is uniformity in the introduction of information is important to compare the results between the different quarries.

Other advantages for the proposed suggestion include improving the quality of information. In general, there will be a reduction in administrative work, as there are fewer human resources allocated to filling and verifying several forms per week and filling out Excel reports. Thus, the process becomes more agile because, after inserting the data, the tool will process it, generating daily, weekly and monthly reports that can be consulted at any time. In this way, managers will have greater control over the company's operation, a total view of the business and access to performance indicators (KPI) which, when evaluated, allow for comparative analysis.

In addition to the aforementioned, in the "Aggregate Production Control" procedure, in particular, the solution will also allow for a better analysis of the causes of Non-Conformities and Product Performance, planning the amount of dumpers needed to supply the Primary considering its distance to the front of the dismantling. This would ensure that there are no interruptions in the supply of rock to the Crushing Plant.

The proposed tools will also support parts' inventory, ensuring stock availability, through an integrated inventory management. These will also make it possible to know: the data related to each failure, which are recorded in the system, as well as the entire workflow related to the repair request; the details of each failure, their frequency, symptoms and causes, and also the actions taken, materials consumed and subcontracted; stopping time; the average repair time; and the related costs, among other information. Consequently, it would be possible to act in a preventive logic manner about them. They will also make it possible to know the average stoppage time of the Plant, in order to assess the weight of the stoppage of production for repairs/maintenance, with the high values being able to indicate problems in the equipment, related to its age or bad usage practices and anticipate the purchase of parts where there is greater wear. This avoids production stoppages whilst waiting for the arrival of these parts and avoids non-conformities through the use of inappropriate networks, as well as helping to forecast the necessary amount of fuel for the time of operation of the Crushing Plant. The proposed solution will decrease the response time to intervention requests and increase productivity by reducing the crushing plant downtime through optimizing maintenance and generally improving the company's quarries efficiency.

CONCLUSION

Information is essential to the decision-making process of the managers or agents responsible for this function in organizations. It is already known that the greater and better the information available, the greater the success of the decision-making process. Considering this need, it was essential to develop systems that would allow the management of this knowledge, and it is essential, nowadays, for managers and other employees to use technologies and IS efficiently.

Therefore, organizations must adapt, changing structures, procedures and behaviors that allow them to improve performance, guaranteeing business objectives and generating competitive advantage over competitors, in order to survive in a world where there is little room to fail.

Based on the analysis of organizational systems (processes, activities, procedures, information systems, etc.) it was possible to identify the lack of process coherence, the inexistence of procedures and the poor quality of information. It was also possible to prioritize and understand inefficiencies that interfere downstream in the value chain and that may not be detected on a daily basis, during the repetition of the tasks performed. Out these a few stand out: absence of data history, repetition of data, lack of standardization in some procedures, excess of paper documentation, delay in procedures and scarce decision support information available at any time, among other difficulties.

Taking into account the main key problems identified, it was clear the importance of economic and business digital transformation. Therefore, a proposal to support the activity based on a new digital paradigm and translated into flowcharts that outline the process was elaborated. This proposal, which is supported by information technologies, aims to provide the organization with tools to reduce red tape and duplicate tasks in daily operations, giving organizational management more time to perform in a creative and innovative way. They must now consider the automatization of processes to increase organizational and employee performance in the areas considered. The analysis was facilitated and the processes improved through the integration of objectives and performance indicators. This solution went against the profitability of resources and the dematerialization of information, translating into real and sustainable economic and financial results.

To guide the change, a Roadmap was suggested, in which the proposal presented is implemented, in a phased manner, over eight phases. This work can be seen as the beginning of a larger digital transformation project, which can be passed on to other processes in the area concerned or in other areas, developed in future works.

REFERENCES

Anderson, D., & Anderson, L. (2010). *Beyond Change Management. How to Achieve Breakthrough Results Through Conscious Change Leadership* (2nd ed.). Pfeiffer.

Anunciação, P., & Esteves, F. (2019). Challenges to Business Models in the Digital Transformation Context. Handbook of Research on Business Models in Modern Competitive Scenarios, 11, 197 – 210.

Anunciação, P., & Zorrinho, C. (2006). *Urbanismo Organizacional, Como Gerir o Choque Tecnológico nas Empresas* (1st ed.). Edições Sílabo.

Baganha, M., Marque, J., & Góis, P. (2002). O Sector da Construção Civil e Obras Públicas em Portugal: 1990-2000. *Oficina do Centro de Estudos Sociais*, (173), 1-39. Disponível em: 11, novembro, 2018, em: https://iconline.ipleiria.pt/bitstream/10400.8/1041/1/outras_publicações_2002.pdf

Barañano, A. (2004). *Métodos e Técnicas de Investigação em Gestão, Manual de apoio à realização de trabalhos de investigação*. Edições Silabo.

Boni, V., Quaresma, J. (2005). Aprendendo a entrevistar: como fazer entrevistas em Ciências Sociais. *Revista Eletrónica dos Pós-Graduandos em Sociologia Política da UFSC, 2*(1), 68-80.

Caldeira, J. (2012). *100 Indicadores da Gestão, Key Performance Indicators*. Lisboa: Conjuntura Actual Editora, S.A.

Campos, A. (2013). *Competitividade da Construção* (Tese de Mestrado, Escola de Engenharia, Universidade do Minho). Disponível em: 10, novembro, 2018, em: https://repositorium.sdum.uminho.pt/bitstream/1822/36278/1/Dissertação%20-%20José%20Silva%20-%202014.pdf

Carrasqueira, L. (2018). Três perguntas a.... *Indústria Revista de Empresários e Negócios, 108*, 12-13. Disponível em: 10, novembro, 2018, em: http://cip.org.pt/wp-content/uploads/2018/09/IND_115_LRv2.pdf

Carvalho, J. (2010). *Logística e Gestão da Cadeia de Abastecimento*. Edições Sílabo.

Claranet. (2018). *Beyond Digital Transformation, Reality check for European IT and Digital leaders* (Claranet research report 2018). Disponível em: 15, dezembro, 2018, em: https://br.claranet.com/sites/all/assets/br/Claranet%20research%20report%202018_2.pdf

Clough, P., & Nutbrown, C. (2007). *A student's guide to Methodology* (2nd ed.). Sage Publications Ltd.

Correia, B. (2018). Três perguntas a.... *Indústria Revista de Empresários e Negócios, 108*, 12-13. Disponível em: 10, novembro, 2018, em: http://cip.org.pt/wp-content/uploads/2018/05/IND_115_LR.pdf

Deloitte. (2018, Dezembro). *Plano Estratégico de Inovação e Competitividade 2030 para o Setor AEC*. 7º Fórum Estratégico PTPC, Lisboa.

Estrela, S. (2014). *A Gestão da Informação na Tomada de Decisão das PME da Região Centro um estudo exploratório e de multicasos no âmbito da Ciência da Informação (Tese de Mestrado)*. Faculdade de Letras da Universidade de Coimbra.

Federação Portuguesa da Indústria da Construção e Obras Públicas. (2018). *Construção cresce 3,5% em 2018*. Disponível em: 10, fevereiro, 2019, em: http://www.fepicop.pt/index.php?id=22

Ferreira, A., & Martinez, L. (2008). *Manual de Diagnóstico e Mudança Organizacional* (1st ed.). Editora RH.

Gandhi, P., Khanna, S., & Ramaswamy, S. (2016). Which industries are the most digital. *Harvard Business Review*. Disponível em: 5, março, 2019, em: https://www.mckinsey.com/mgi/overview/in-the-news/which-industries-are-the-most-digital

Guerra, I. (2006). *Pesquisa Qualitativa e Análise de Conteúdo*. Princípia Editora.

Kotter, J. P. (2017). *Liderar a mudança: porque falham os esforços de mudança. HBR 10 Artigos Essenciais, Gerir a Mudança*. Conjuntura Actual Editora.

Laudon, K. C., & Laudon, J. P. (2016). *Management Information Systems, Managing the Digital Firm* (14th ed.). Pearson Education Limited.

Neves, P. (2011). *Sucesso e Mudança nas Organizações: Uma Questão de Confiança* (1st ed.). Editora RH.

Ngúvulo, S. (2016). *Conceção de um sistema informático de gestão do pessoal do ISCED – Cabinda* (Tese de Mestrado, Universidade Fernando Pessoa). Disponível em: 10, março, 2019, em: https://bdigital.ufp.pt/bitstream/10284/5480/1/DM_Sebastião%20Ngúvulo.pdf

Nova SBE & EY. (2018) *Estudo da Maturidade Digital das empresas portuguesas*. Disponível em: 17, maio, 2019, em: https://www.ey.com/Publication/vwLUAssets/ey-estudo-da-maturidade-digital-das-empresas-portuguesas/$FILE/ey-estudo-da-maturidade-digital-das-empresas-portuguesas.pdf

Olavsrud, T. (2017). *Digital disruption is coming but most businesses don't have a plan*. CIO.

Pinto, I. (2019). Construção perde 14 mil trabalhadores apesar do boom do imobiliário. *Jornal Dinheiro Vivo*. Disponível em: 11, abril, 2019, em: https://www.dinheirovivo.pt/economia/construcao-perde-14-mil-trabalhadores-apesar-do-boom-do-imobiliario/

Rego, A., Gomes, J. F., Cunha, R. C., Cardoso, C. C., Marques, C. A., & Cunha, M. P. (2015). *Manual de Gestão de Pessoas e do Capital Humano*. Edições Sílabo.

Rogers, D. (2016). *The Digital Transformation Playbook: Rethink your business for the digital age*. Columbia University Press.

Rosini, A. M., & Palmisano, A. (2003). *Administração de Sistemas de Informação e a Gestão do Conhecimento*. Thomson.

Santos, N. (2018). Três perguntas a.... *Indústria Revista de Empresários e Negócios, 108*, 12-13. Disponível em: 10, novembro, 2018, em: http://cip.org.pt/wp-content/uploads/2018/05/IND_115_LR.pdf

Saraiva, A. (2018). Identificar as oportunidades e antecipar as dificuldades. Transformação Digital. *Indústria Revista de Empresários e Negócios, 108*, 3. Disponível em: 6, dezembro, 2018, em: http://cip.org.pt/wp-content/uploads/2018/05/IND_115_LR.pdf

Tabrizi, B., Lam, E., Girard, K., & Vernon, I. (2019). Digital Transformation Is Not About Technology. *Harvard Business Review*. Disponível em: 21, janeiro, 2019, em: https://hbr.org/2019/03/digital-transformation-is-not-about-technology

Terence, A., & Filho, E. (2006). Abordagem quantitativa, qualitativa e a utilização da pesquisa-ação nos estudos organizacionais. *XXVI ENEGEP – Fortaleza*, 1-9. Disponível em: 23, dezembro, 2018, em: http://www.abepro.org.br/biblioteca/enegep2006_tr540368_8017.pdf

Westerman, G. (2017). Your Company doesn't need a digital strategy. *MIT Sloan Management Review*, (October), 25.

Chapter 26
The Digital Transformation in a Distribution Editorial Center:
One of the Oldest in Portugal

Sofia Carujo

Plátano Editora, Portugal

ABSTRACT

Digital transformation is a current challenge for all companies; it cannot be seen as a trend but as a necessity. Normally, when we hear about digital transformation, we associate it with a technological integration in the processes. But its scope is more comprehensive, as it implies a dematerialization of all resources and processes, a redesign of the material processes hitherto practiced that requires a structural transformation of the company with direct repercussions on its culture. We can even talk about digital literacy. The impact of this transformation in companies can be comparable to the impact of the industrial revolution, which will bring companies greater competitiveness; however, not all of them are qualified for this process because, in addition to financial capacity, there must be capable human capital.

«With great powers, great responsibilities»

Ben Parker

Digital transformation is a current challenge for all companies; it cannot be seen as a trend but as a necessity. Normally, when we hear about Digital Transformation, we associate it with a technological integration in the processes. But its scope is more comprehensive, as it implies a dematerialization of all resources and processes, a redesign of the material processes hitherto practiced that requires a structural transformation of the company with direct repercussions on its culture. We can even talk about digital literacy. The impact of this transformation in companies can be comparable to the impact of the Industrial

DOI: 10.4018/978-1-7998-4201-9.ch026

Copyright © 2021, IGI Global. Copying or distributing in print or electronic forms without written permission of IGI Global is prohibited.

Revolution, which will bring companies greater competitiveness, however, not all of them are qualified for this process because, in addition to financial capacity, there must be capable human capital.

If companies are empowered with technological tools, they will surely achieve a more advantageous proximity to customers, and internally decision making will be more sustained. Sysorex, a company specialized in data analysis, released data confirming that if companies do not assume a digital transformation, they will be overtaken by competitors who have already done so.

This transformation implies several challenges for storage logistics, starting with the warehouse layout, inventory management, adoption of management support technologies, product traceability and the dematerialization of documents and processes.

For Boyson et al. (1999, apud Di Serio et al., 2007), the evolution of logistics is divided into four distinct stages:

1. Undeveloped logistics: until the 1970s, logistics activities focused on the efficiency of physical distribution within transport, warehousing, inventory control, order processing and shipping activities.
2. Incipient logistics: in the 1980s, the focus was on integrating the logistics functions in order to maximize their efficiency. This stage emphasizes transport and storage.
3. Integrated internal logistics: in the 1990s, new distribution channels and new concepts of the production process emerged. In that decade, there was a search for competitiveness by adoption of quantitative methods of quality control, offering services to customers, in the formulation of internal cross-functional teams and in the segmentation of the base of the chain.
4. Integrated external logistics: since the beginning of the 21st century, there has been a greater concern with the interfaces between the members of the supply chain. The focus is on improving demand forecasting and collaborative planning between links in the supply chain, and increasing investments in information sharing systems to manage the links in the chain.

For Santos (2004), "an efficient logistic management can help the company well positioned in the market, in terms of product or service differentiate itself through the reduction of operational costs or a well done service, superior to the competition, or still both in a specific segment of customers, products or even geographic area". These generic strategies are identified by Porter (1986) as being: leadership in total cost, differentiation and focus.

The warehouse in the supply chain has the function of bringing consumer goods to points of sale, it is the link between the supply channel and the distribution channel.

If until a while ago it (warehouse) was seen only as a "necessary evil" for organizations, today, it is seen as strategic for the potential growth of the organization. In parallel with the evolution of the market, we have, consequently, an evolution in storage management techniques.

We can define the warehouse as a service unit in an organic and functional structure of a commercial or industrial company, with well-defined objectives for the storage, conservation, control and supply of materials and products (Richards, 2014).

The warehouse plays a pivotal role in the entire supply chain, and will continue to do so, even due to the impact of the financial cost it represents for organizations, with a percentage between 2-5% of the total costs (Frazelle, 2002). It is also a means to enhance and increase the organization's competitiveness, ceasing to be seen as a necessary evil for the organization and only a cost generator, and becomes a link department in the organization.

Its main function is the storage and dispatch of articles for the supply chain. Warehousing can be defined as the process where three main functions occur: receiving products from a source, storing the products for the necessary time until they are requested by a customer (internal or external) and removing the products when they are requested (Queirolo et. al., 2002).

The management of the warehouse's operational processes must be a process of continuous improvement, using information technologies simultaneously with the necessary physical systems, as the technology alone will not be sufficient to achieve excellence in the process.

In most cases, warehouse management is seen only as a necessary cost associated with the product and not as a strategic factor that can be decisive throughout the chain.

Warehouse management encompasses a set of functions such as: reception, storage, preservation of finished or semi-finished products, shipping, etc. With the current technological advances in the area of warehousing and physical distribution of products and the robotization and computerization of these products, these spaces have become one of the most productive areas within a company's logistics chain.

The functions and activities of a warehouse are:

1. Receiving goods receiving and checking the goods received, a quantitative and qualitative validation is carried out according to the order form to the supplier.
2. Storage - optimized storage so that access is made easier using fixed storage equipment, such as racks, and internal cargo handling equipment, such as forklifts.
3. Conservation and maintenance: it is maintained in accordance with the appropriate conservation and safety standards.
4. Stock management and control: the product is available in the right quantity and at the right time, reducing the cost of storage.
5. Shipping of goods - initiated by the receipt of the order, and must respect the agreed packaging and shipping criteria.

But in order for the functions to be fulfilled, they must take into account the fundamental principles for an efficient organization: optimization of the available space; minimize handling operations and internal transportation of products, efficient storage. These objectives, which can be achieved through an appropriate layout, appropriate identification signs in the different areas of the warehouse, storage according to the product's rotation and respective positioning. The warehouse's internal and external infrastructure affects two very important factors: productivity and safety.

The layout is the way the warehouse areas are organized, with the objective of optimizing the entire existing space and coordination between the various operators, equipment and space. If it is not well defined, it can lead to an increase in costs, loss of productivity and an eventual increase in internal risk for logistics operators. It, also, must be flexible and modular because it must meet current needs as well as future needs.

Inventory is one of the most valuable assets of companies. The stock is an investment in articles for future use and is expected to exist in the right quantity, at the right time, in the right place and at the lowest possible cost. The efficient management of the inventory gives the company a competitive advantage over its competitors, both externally and internally. It confers, among other things, a cost reduction because the stock has a high cost of the financial and storage cost, for one hand an overstock is not desired, on the other hand, too, situations of stock shortages are not intended. To answer this need, we have, as a solution, the adoption of technologies to support storage management, so that management is efficient, because not all companies work with Just in time production, where the stock corresponds to real needs storage and, when it exists, it is in cross-docking.

Information means "action to form", as Carvalho (2012: 383) describes: "information emerges as the process of transmitting knowledge associated with the (thing) form it informed. The evolution of the concept gradually established the separation between form (matter) and the mind, and the information becomes something capable of containing, storing knowledge, regardless of the subject and the form ".

However, information, when analyzed in the business context, is the most valuable resource for organizations, and can be traded. Because only with the use of it is it possible for managers to make a conscious decision.

For Richards (2014), the introduction of new technologies in the operation not only improves its competitiveness in a challenging market, but it can also be fundamental to meet the increasing needs of customers.

The technologies significantly improve the productivity of the warehouse. The process becomes more effective and efficient, as well as the internal communication with the other departments, such as the financial, commercial and marketing department, leading to a higher level of service and at a lower cost. In terms of storage logistics, our technological focus is on the adoption of a WMS - Warehouse Management System. These can be used vertically or integrated in an ERP and supported by other technologies such as automation, RFID, or voice recognition. The company's strategy must be understood so that its needs, current and future, are met with the appropriate choice of a WMS solution.

The poor location of products in the warehouse can lead to inefficiency in the shipping process, which will consequently be reflected in the entire process in the supply chain and an increase in operating costs. A correct and visible location is essential in the daily activity of the warehouse, as well as the way they are arranged. Both, the location and the definition of product, delivery flows can be optimized with the use of a technological solution. The importance of product traceability is also essential at the external level, following the product's path along the chain to its final destination assumes an increasing importance in customer loyalty. With the proliferation of digital commerce, the market for companies has expanded and diversified and, as a consequence the level of consumer demand has increased, they are more knowledgeable, requiring more information in real time. A few years ago, when we made a purchase with shipping, it was not expected that we would receive the tracking number to be able to track it in real time. Today, it is mandatory.

With the dematerialization of documents and processes, it is expected: cost reduction, increased productivity, greater efficiency, quick access and sustainability. However, we can only reach this level with the support of technologies, such as ERP - Enterprise Resource Planning, EDI + Electronic Data Interchange, CRP - Continuous Replenishment Program, ECR - Efficient Consumer Response, WMS, DMS - Distribution Manager System, identification systems automatic identification, capture and sharing of data on products, goods and people, among many other technologies. As we are talking about technologies, we run the serious risk that next year what is new at that time may be obsolete.

Today, the goal for some companies is still the implementation of a WMS. But there are companies that are already betting on the application of artificial intelligence, implementation of robotization systems in warehouses: the case of Amazon, the use of Drones for delivery of orders, in the near future, or the lot- Internet of Things, which translates into the use of intelligent sensors that can perform, among other functions, traceability, control and product management.

Finally, the omnichannel experience, the customer as mentioned above, is increasingly demanding and moves through different channels, physical store, virtual store or APP, but the expectation at the time of purchase it is the same, regardless of the chosen channel, which means that technological integration is vital, from the moment of ordering, through storage and ending in distribution. The last mile can even be considered the most demanding moment of the entire logistics operation, the barometer of the entire operation, if the customer is not satisfied, risks and high costs may occur.

THE BOOK SECTOR IN PORTUGAL

The book sector includes two major components: publishing and retailing. The book sector, and in particular the book trade, is going through a period in which great challenges, in addition to those arising from the conjuncture of deep crisis that, since 2011, the country has been going through.

In the context of an economic crisis, particularly acute in Portugal after 2011, the public protection (central and local) of culture has been decreasing dramatically (Garcia et al., 2014).

Private consumption and investment worsened the declines observed in 2011, and public consumption fell slightly less than in the same period last year. From then on, the contraction of the book sales market, which did not return to sales in the years prior to the economic crisis, has also not escaped the concentration of small and medium-sized publishers in large publishing groups in the last few cycles. Publishers whose activity is increasing in innovative ways: quality titles, short print runs, innovative distribution.

Today, Portugal presents a Complex educational situation. On the one hand, after a very positive evolution, we have reached reasonable educational levels in the young population, both in terms of access and quality, and in terms of equity, indicating good recovery capacity in almost all areas. On the other hand, reflecting a past of great backwardness, weak qualification rates of the old population persist, which worsen dramatically as they progress to higher age groups. This situation demands extra attention to the recovery of the less qualified population, without losing the educational gains obtained by the youngest in recent years.

The growth of book readers in the country, in a context already marked in several others by the reverse movement, had on the ongoing processes of reconfiguration of Portuguese society, particular the increase in school qualifications (at the various levels of education) and the growth of new ones, middle classes (and their feminization), some of the main explanatory factors (Neves, 2011).

In this period of profound financial and economic crisis, there was a drop in the levels of cultural participation in the various areas in the EU-27, a drop that is particularly noticeable in Portugal, with an emphasis, precisely, on reading books and going to the cinema (both with 10 percentage points less, cinema for 29%) and visiting public libraries (9 points less for 15%).

The predominant social profile of book readers refers to qualification in terms of education and socio-professional activity, for the youngest (students in particular) and for the female predominance. The higher the reading levels of individuals, the more these attributes are reinforced.

Another factor of great relevance for the book trade, particularly for independent bookstores, is that of the consumption habits of the Portuguese who pass mainly through shopping centers (first openings in the early 1980's) and, therefore, through bookstores located there. (Santos et al, 2007: 142) and hypermarkets and supermarkets (opening of the first in 1985), to a large extent also located in shopping centers.

Education is a decisive, but difficult, bet for the future of Portuguese, and it is essential that the whole of society is committed to improving the quality and equity conditions that are offered to raise the qualifications of the Portuguese and that it is possible to build the necessary consensus for the sustainability of the reforms to be carried out.

In recent times, digital books, known as e-books, and their readers have been gaining importance, changing the way reading is viewed and gaining followers.

Numbers of the e-book sales are not known in Portugal, but if there is one thing we can easily verify: it is the scarcity of supply and the absence of consistent policies for the promotion of the digital market by publishers.

Changes in the book chain due to the dematerialization of the book trade particularly affect the traditional commerce sector since electronic commerce (and e-commerce) is done, as mentioned above, on platforms and in e-distributors, and where the bookstore is just one among other commercial locations. On the publishing side, the bet on the e-book by the most important publishers in terms of volume of editing is only a few years old and favors joint editing on both media. It also privileges software that does not require dedicated readers (e-readers).

Portugal follows the set of countries in which regulation on book prices is in impose by law, an option that is part of the dominant international trend. The existence of the law does not appear to be the subject of dispute today. This does not mean that changes are not equable. One of them refers, following what other countries have already done, to the inclusion of the e-book. Although it is not known in what sense, the tutelage of the culture has already expressed its willingness (and even the taking of initiative) to change it.

There is unanimous distrust of the State's manifest inability to ensure compliance with the legal framework in force.

In this regard, on December 5, 2013, APEL took a position clearly in favor of LPFL, thus noting that its members (among them some of those targeted by the aforementioned position of independent booksellers) are cohesive as to the existence of the law and, therefore, to your application.

Regarding public cultural policies, the current trend seems to be the absence of measures of protection.

Among the aspects of public policies that apply to book trade (VAT currently reduced in the printed book 6%, normal rate in the e-book 23%; competition law). The other has to do with illegal copying (Dionísio and Leal, 2012), which mainly affects the technical book, and refers to the legislation on Copyright and especially that of Private Copying because the inadequacy of some rules and the lack of inspection by IGAC (General Inspection of Cultural Activities) harms, even more indirectly, book trade.

There is currently an interesting debate in Portugal on the legislation that regulates authors' rights; its promoters seem to want to safeguard the interests of the authors but, apparently, forget the rights of publishers, booksellers and other professionals in the sector.

The main emerging changes in the book sector and, in particular, with regard to the case of illicit duplication of books, can be associated with several trends:

- Reaction from society in general and from inspection to the practice of illicit duplication (photocopies and digitization study books);
- Proliferation of e-books, with multiple possibilities for multimedia use in the case of technical books;
- Revitalization of Portuguese city centers, as a result of changes in rental policies, with an inevitable impact on leisure supply and demand.

Regard to the problem of various forms of illegal copying, the book sector, alongside the phonographic are, probably, the most affected by the impact of digital media and technologies. On the other hand, most people - in particular the youngest - find it difficult for copyright to apply to intellectual property, accustomed to being free to copy in digital media.

In addition to the challenges presented above, the sector suffers yet another clash, the introduction of gratuity and the reuse of school manuals, initially to students of the 1.º Cycle and 2.º Cycle school and subsequently extended to students of the 3.º Cycle and Ensino Secundário school.

The current world is experiencing an abnormal situation, COVID 19, and Portugal is no exception. In the last months we have lived 11 pre-covid weeks, 10 weeks of confinement and currently a new reality, which for the book market was more of a struggle. Due to the confinement, bookstores were forced to close during this period, most of them do not have online sales, so the activity was null. In a study released in October 2020 by APEL Portuguese Association of Editors and Booksellers, prepared by GfK on the Portuguese Book Market, we found that the market had a variation of -57.6 € compared to the same period in confinement and -15.8% in the period of new normality, representing in units -1.2 million and -.08 million units respectively, in value for the first period there was a loss of 16.1 M € and in the second period of 7.4 M € .

Perhaps this is yet another alert to the need for digital transformation and how the need for it is transversal to all markets.

The Case of Grupo Editorial Plátano, One of the Oldest in Portugal

Francisco Prata Ginja founder of Grupo Editorial Plátano, new arrived in Lisbon from a village in Castelo Branco, started working at Didáctica Editora, Lda, going through all departments. Later, he left the job and, in 1972, founded Plátano Editora Lda, dedicated to the school books. His entrepreneurial vision of the market led him to acquire the publishing house where he started his professional career. Years later, and in order to face the group's strategy, he founded Paralelo Editora in 1979 which would be the group's distributor for general editions, stopping editing only school editions. The internationalization of the group began in 1976 with the Angolan market as a priority destination and, since 2010, there publishers were set up to operate in the Angolan market.

Currently, the group is managed by the second generation, two sons who together continue the project started in 1944 when Didáctica Editora was founded. In 2006, they take the first step towards digital transformation with the creation of a digital content platform for students and teachers, called Booka.

The passing of testimony did not alter the group's DNA, the priority remains modernization and the anticipated response to the needs of such a specific editorial market, and for this reason digital transformation is a priority.

Grupo Editorial Plátano owns three publishers, Plátano Editora, SA, Didáctica Editora, SA and Paralelo Editora, SA. It operates in the market in two business areas: school books and general editions, for each of the business areas it has a distributor; for school edition Plátano Editora, SA and for general editions Paralelo Editora SA, although each has independent legal personality all share human and physical resources.

«Plátano Editora was created in 1972, dedicated to the edition of school books. Since its early days, its editions have been imposed on the Portuguese educational landscape and, especially, the manuals dedicated to basic education. A company with a family-based structure, where the strong character, will and constant concern for the quality of its founder, combined with the strong entrepreneurial spirit, which have in half a dozen years become a reference in the Portuguese publishing market.

Present

Following the philosophy that presided over its foundation, - publishing and distributing school textbooks - Plátano Editora, now, has a very wide range of authors, covering the vast majority of subjects from the 5th to the 12th year of schooling. With a consolidated position in the school market, it faces the future with optimism. Against the backdrop of meeting the real needs of education in Portugal, these past years have revealed major changes in the production structure of this company. New authors, improvement of the graphic and pedagogical characteristics of the manuals, widespread use of new technologies dictate the strategic plan that coordinates the different sectors. Anyone who presents themselves with a valid project for a textbook or other type of edition is traditionally well received. We believe that a good book is an irreplaceable learning experience. In the process, Plátano Editora is equipped with the most advanced technology in the field of graphic arts, being able to do all phases of the book with the exception of printing and finishing. Multimedia products and school textbooks, for the simple fact of adapting to new learning trends, are part of everyday priorities.

Didáctica Editora was founded in 1944, being one of the oldest publishers in Portugal. Since its birth, it directed all its editorial activity towards school books, counting, for this, with some of the most prestigious authors of several subjects, among which Júlio Martins, Alves de Moura, Óscar Lopes and Palma Fernandes. In 1979, the majority of its share capital was acquired by Plátano Editora SA, where it remains today, becoming Grupo Editorial Plátano.

Present

Its editorial line begins to diversify into other areas, namely technical and general interest books, while maintaining a strong component in the production of school books. The entire development of its activity over the years has been guided by strong financial strength and strict management. In this context, the future looks like a lot of work, but at the same time challenging».

Paralelo Editora, SA distributor of the "Edições Gerais" segment of Grupo Editorial Plátano sells directly and resells to different segments of the book market. Distribution is national and international. Exports to the main CPLP countries.

In the last two years, the company has innovated in the ordering process through the creation and continuous development of the Portal for Booksellers

«This portal is intended for all professionals of resale of school editions - Plátano Editora - and of Edições Gerais - Paralelo Editora - objective of becoming an instrument of work and communication and, at the same time, the Virtual Dedicated Seller for all those who develop their activity in this sector. Available 24 hours a day and 365 days a year! »

To access its contents and features, the user will have to make his registration request, where he can place orders; obtain information about our editorial news; know the campaigns in progress; read the circulars. All of this is available on the Portal just a click away.

In addition to the portal for B2B, there is another portal for B2C, the two are linked, via EDI, to the billing system and latter, to the software of the logistics operator, allowing a quick order processing and tracking.

The company has two distributors and three publishers, carrying out an internal procurement process between them. The ERP Primavera is used for this management, which, for inventory control needs, can generate some errors.

Figure 1. Internal supply flow

Human resources, although part of each company, in practice, work as one whole and are shared.

In the daily activity of the warehouse, there is a picking line for each of the distributors, as well as different warehouses and storage areas for each of them.

In terms of storage management, in addition to the daily challenges across all warehouses, the following challenges were identified as being specific to this organization:

a) Finding a Picking solution, since the existing one will stop working when migrating from ERP Primavera V.103;
b) Difficulty in inventory management, given the limitations of ERP Primavera in the inventory module for the internal management of three warehouses and the flows between them;
c) Treatment of compound articles;
d) Optimization of internal flows in terms of receiving and storing articles, order separation and preparation of management reports.

With the development and investment made for the integration, via EDI - Electronic Data Interchange, of the purchases made on the websites destined for B2B and B2C with the ERP, it became clear the need for this efficiency and effectiveness verified in the last mile. The process of delivering the goods to the customer is the last process, but it is also the most demanding, any incidence verified may question the customer's return and generate additional costs.

In a market study published last September by Aplog in partnership with the consultancy Delloite entitled «Online shopping experience and last mile operations», mentioned above, we can also verify that

54% of virtual purchases do not continue due to the costs of delivery, on average the Portuguese pay € 4.2 for each delivery order, for the leisure and entertainment category the value is € 4.90, free delivery of purchases is one of the attributes highly valued by the buyer. However, only 1 in every 5 companies it offers this free of charge. Another option valued by the customer is the choice of delivery location, and one of the options is collection in store and here only 54% of operators offer this possibility and 20% at a collection point.

OBJECTIVES AND METHODOLOGY

This work has as main objective the presentation of a proposal for study and eventual adoption of a Warehouse Management System (WMS) applied to a bookstore company.

According to Banzato (2004), a WMS is a software management system that improves warehouse operations, through efficient information management and task completion, with a high level of control and inventory accuracy. And he adds: the implementation of a WMS enables cost reduction, which is obtained by improving the efficiency of the workforce, which leads to a reduction in the workload, the need for overtime and the correction of errors in the checkpoint.

In the current context of competitiveness, companies are often pressured by technological attractiveness, which due to the pandemic context in which we operate is the new trend of the coming times as an urgent response to the low touch economy. This acceleration has as a goal the desire to obtain competitive advantages through the respective acquisition, which in many cases this added value may be more than a differentiation factor, it may even be the survival factor. However, as several authors refer, the introduction of technologies, in itself, does not provide the automatic generation of competitive advantages. It is important that the respective decision is based on an economic and financial analysis that highlights the potential benefits or gains associated with the technologies.

The phases proposed for this study are as follows:

- Identification of market challenges;
- Evaluation of the opportunity by Top Management;
- Identification of commercially available solution;
- reduction + Identification and quantification of the benefits and associated costs;
- Viability study.

The first WMS solutions emerged in the 1970's. This system allows integrated control over all warehouse activities, upstream and downstream of the supply chain and in the company. Through this solution, it is possible to view the inventory levels in real time and to know the exact location of the products, which allows for a more efficient daily operation, such as put away and picking (Hill, 2003).

- The main characteristics indicated and considered were the following:
- Multi-warehouse;
- Database independent (vertical solution);
- System that operates in real time;
- Decision support information in real time;
- Integration with ERP

- And the general characteristics:
- Picking;
- Inventory;
- Graphic design of the warehouse;
- Document type management;
- Physical and logical definition of the layout;
- Article management;
- Traceability
- Customer and supplier management;
- Order management;
- Route management;
- Radio frequency terminals:
- Operations management;
- Reverse logistics;
- Among others.

All of them are adaptable to all sectors of activity.

Analysis the results, regarding the first phase, the identification of current challenges in this market were described in the previous chapters, such as the drop in sales, aggravated by the pandemic. The importance that eBooks have been gaining in the market access the free use of school books, the digital transformation that the market started and which now has the new normality as an accelerator, among others.

Regarding the second phase, in an interview with the Chief Executive Officer of Grupo Editorial Plátano, we sought to assess, in the first place, the main challenges in the management of warehouse operations. The most evident concerns were the following:

- Inventory management, as in any other distributor, namely trying to avoid situations of overstock or breakage of articles, as both represent cost increases;
- Implementation of a correct layout and simplification of processes, evident in a clear recognition of the need to use technologies in order to streamline continuous improvement processes. The company's view is that this practice is directly related to increasing its competitiveness vis-à-vis the rest of the market players;
- Rearrangement of the business to face the challenges because they are in a «market in constant change, not only through the buying habits of the customer, but mainly through the omnichannel experience, regardless of the channel chosen by him, the optimization of stocks will be vitally important» ;
- Importance of adopting a WMS, so that the level of service of excellence to the customer can be guaranteed and, not forgetting, that with this solution there will be a guarantor of the «agility and rigor of our storage operations and providing our employees with a tool that will allow them to be more efficient and effective in their daily work ».

The CEO consider that a WMS solution would allow a decrease in the average order preparation time, as well as a simplification in the process of locating 1300 One of goods and an optimization of the storage space which, in the end, provide employees with an increase productivity diary.

The expected benefits are as follows:

- Optimization of storage space;
- Permanent and real-time inventory;
- Traceability of articles from receipt to end consumer;
- The Reduction of shipping and shipping errors;
- Reduction of time in internal logistics flows;
- Reduction of logistical costs;
- Increased productivity in carrying out all logistical operations;
- Decision support information in real time;
- Adaptation to e-commerce needs;
- Omni-channel operations management.

In view of the mentioned benefits, greater agility and rigor in warehousing operations is expected and to provide employees with a tool that can enable them to achieve greater efficiency and effectiveness in their daily lives, constituting a critical success factor for the company's competitiveness. . However, digital transformation is also carried out by people and in a family-owned company, and where on average employees have been working for more than seventeen years, resistance to change can be an obstacle. The project must include the sharing of objectives with employees in a SMART way, as well as training and monitoring them throughout the process. The digital transformation to happen has to be disruptive, that is, it has to interrupt the usual follow-up of a process, the pencil and the printed order will be replaced by a PDA. And it doesn't happen just in one department but in all departments, it requires a restructuring of processes, internal and external.

According to the Warehouse Director, the solution of a WMS will be a relevant factor for the continuity of the business, where the online channel is more and more preferred, and for the level of service to be maintained there is a need to decrease the average time of the order cycle. Information sharing along the chain and with the current ERP, which have limitations, are enormous, not only in the integrated management of the warehouse, but also in terms of stock control and picking process. Leading to an absence of optimized aviation routes, this point is fundamental for the reduction of the order cycle time and for the perfect order. According to the interviewee, the warehouse area that will benefit the most is picking, followed by the reception and conference of goods. This Logistics Center, which houses three publishers and two distributors with more than six thousand SKU's, kites school and promotional products, intra-group purchases, among others, so a WMS solution would end up benefiting across the activity.

He stated the main objectives to be achieved: excellent customer service, increased efficiency in deliveries, optimization of storage space, decreased shipping time, increased productivity, simplified process and reduced time in annual inventory counts. This decrease will have an enormous impact since they force a stop in the daily activity of dispatch.

In addition to the costs, directly associated with the purchase and implementation of the solution, it was pointed out as another possible obstacle to resistance to change on the part of logistics operators. It will be a disruptive change in processes and practices, but that has prepared a training process that will make the integration a success.

In the third phase of the study, the solutions on the market were identified. The following solutions were identified, as those that best fit the specificity of the company:

- Eye Peak - WMS Primavera System - This solution is developed by Primavera, a company with more than 20 years of experience in developing solutions innovative management to business. This WMS system promises a centralized management of all processes and faster operations. The track and trace of the merchandise is automated, from reception, through storage, to dispatch. This will allow significant improvements in the daily management of the warehouse. The solution provides a service layer that ensures integration with automatisms and robotic systems, allowing you to obtain the outputs of these machines and automatically integrate them into the WMS. In this way, the information is updated immediately, mirroring in the system the processes that are performed by machines and robots. Another feature is the extensibility that allows you to communicate with other systems.

- xLog - Tecnibite - Tecnibite is a company, with over 30 years of experience, that provides services in the area of information technologies, such as the analysis and development of software solutions, systems integration, design and implementation of engineering solutions and outsourcing of IT services. It operates in areas such as: logistics, aviation, and pharmaceutical, among others. XLog is a WMS developed by Tecnibite to respond to companies in the logistics sector and companies that need to manage their own warehouses. The XLog Gold Edition allows you to manage a warehouse and supports the most modern identification and filling technologies, namely barcode, datamatix, RFID, radio frequency and voice picking.

The criteria identified for evaluating the solutions were: security, a WMS is an operating system any interruption in the system calls into question the functioning of the warehouse which, in the event of a stop causes losses, there must be an evaluation of the performance indicators of the solution and a verification of measures in case of operational incidents; functionality, must be flexible to market developments and future needs; Integration with ERP, if not, an integrator will have to be developed; ease of use, in order to facilitate use by current and future operators; Compatibility with other technologies used, or in the future, is a need. Maintenance is vital for optimizing the solution in all operational and documentary activities and the cost, not only of the software but of the remaining costs associated with its implementation and maintenance.

Table 1.

Solution	Security	Functionality	Integration Compatibility	intuitive ease of use	Compatibilidade	Maintenance	Cost
Eye Peak	4	4	5	4	4	4	4
xLog	2	4	3	4	4	4	2

After analyzing the solutions, the choice falls on the Eye Peak solution, given the characteristics related to the direct integration with the ERP Primavera, an adequate platform for the immediate and future objectives of the company, configuration flexibility and the total cost of the project.

With regard to quantification, it is estimated that the main benefits with the adoption of the WMS are the following: reduction in personnel, decrease in order cycle time, increase in dispatches sent and, consequently, a daily increase in sales and decrease in the time of completion of the annual inventory. X, RHO.

On the other hand, it is estimated an increase in costs in the following areas: acquisition of the license and WMS implementation project, necessary hardware, annual maintenance contract, Wifi network and consumables.

Last but not least, the project's success is also due to the implementation project, which must respect 4 stages:

1. Detailed survey of documentary processes and flows, audit of operations for an analysis of current and future needs.
2. Design of the solution according to the specifications resulting from phase 1.
3. Implementation to validate the solution.
4. On-the-job training. 4. Support to operators at the start of the project.

CONCLUSION

A year ago, digital transformation was a strategic priority. Today, it is an emergency for the survival of any company and regardless of the sector in which it operates. The book market is struggling with several changes: changing consumer habits, low literacy rates, the sharp closure of independent bookstores, the proliferation of book sales other than just bookstores, increased online sales at the expense of space physicist. More than an article, today, sell a service; the last mile is the barometer of the supply chain.

Companies that do not invest in this technological transformation will not be able to follow and differentiate themselves in the market, with consumers increasingly informed, with a market without borders, increasingly need to have information in real time.

However, the process is not easy, in addition to the financial factor. It is necessary to change processes, management paradigms, corporate culture, and change is not always seen as an ally, quite the contrary. A learning process, transversal to all departments, is necessary, in which the result may not be immediately or immediately qualified. Financially, technological modernization will mean huge investment, and must be planned in a careful way taking into account the current and future needs of the company.

Grupo Editorial Plátano, a group with more than 50 years' operating in the market, family management, with presence in the African market since the 70's, is one of the four groups in Portugal with school editions bet on technological transformation from an early age as a need for continuity. The book market is a changing market. How many years have they not bought a dictionary? The drop in sales of dictionaries, in proportion, almost resembles the drop in sales of audio CDs when the emergence of other free music platforms. Without this equipping of solutions that allow us to provide an excellent service to the customer, it is not just delivering the book to the address, it is delivering it to the right address, at the right time, in the shortest time and at the lowest possible cost. For the logistical objective to be achieved, it is necessary to adopt technologies that can optimize the order cycle, minimize storage costs, reduce errors, and enable integration with different partners and the sharing of information in real time along the supply chain. One of the effects, almost immediate, of the pandemic crisis that we are experiencing was the increase in sales on the online channel. The effect is to stay, the fear of digital purchases was overcome by the need, proof is in the solutions that appeared, developed by logistics operators such as CTT to respond to the need for small businesses to have an online presence.

Due to the benefits presented above and in view of the costs, the eventual adoption of a WMS will increase the group's competitive advantage in such a peculiar market.

REFERENCES

Arbache, F. S. (2004). *Gestão de Logística, distribuição e trade marketing* (4th ed.). Editora FGV.

Donald, B. J., Closs, D. J., Cooper, M. B., & Bowersox, J. C. (2013). *Supply Chain Logistics Management* (4th ed.). The McGraw-Hill Global Education Holdings, LLC.

Geyer, F. (2020). *The definitive Guide to B2B Digital Transformation.*

Geyer & Ballou. (1993). *Logística empresarial: transportes, administração de materiais e distribuição física.* Atlas Editora.

Richards, G. (2011). *Warehouse Management.* London: Kogan Page Limited.

Ross, D. (2011). *Introduction to Supply Chain Management Technologies.* Taylor and Francis Group.

Serrano, M. J. (2009). *Logística de Almacenamiento* (2nd ed.). Paraninfo.

Tejero, J. J. A. (2011). Logística integral. La gestión operativa de la empresa (4th ed.). Madrid: ESIC Editorial.

Torres, M. (2013). *Sistemas de Almacenaje y Picking.* Diaz de Santos.

Vieira, D., & Roux, M. (2011). *Projeto de Centros de Distribuição, fundamentos, metodologia e prática para a moderna cadeia de suprimentos.* Campus / Elsevier Editora Ltda.

Westerman, G. (2016). *Liderando na Era Digital.* M. Books.

Chapter 27
Scaling Agile at Enterprise to Enable and Accelerate the Digital Transformation

Luciano Ricardo Faustinoni da Silva
IBM, Brazil

ABSTRACT

One of the great mistakes some companies or business leaders do when thinking about their digital transformation is to start by technology. Frequently, it is common to hear from companies that they would like to do a project using artificial intelligence (AI), or they would like to have a blockchain or even use internet of things (IoT). There is nothing wrong on thinking and knowing about technologies and their potential. However, the digital transformation is broader than it. So, the question that comes immediately is: How to start? What should organizations think about when planning a digital journey? There are several frameworks to help to start.

One of the great mistakes some companies or business leaders do when thinking about their digital transformation is to start by technology. Frequently, is common to hear from companies they would like to do a project using Artificial Intelligence (AI), or they would like to have a Blockchain or even use Internet of Things (IoT). There is nothing wrong on thinking and knowing about technologies and their potential. However, the digital transformation is broader than it.

Accordingly to the Harvard Business Review article "Why So Many High-Profile Digital Transformations Fail"(by Thomas H. Davenport and George Westerman, March 09, 2018) one of the errors is "digital is not just a thing that you can you can buy and plug into the organization. It is multi-faceted and diffuse, and doesn't just involve technology. Digital transformation is an ongoing process of changing the way you do business".

Companies should think about a journey. A journey that includes components such as organization culture, capabilities and business value. All of it with the purpose to provide the best experience to the clients. Internal (inside the company) and External (outside market). External because companies should reinvent their business model digitally in order to provide the best experience to the clients, in a way

DOI: 10.4018/978-1-7998-4201-9.ch027

Copyright © 2021, IGI Global. Copying or distributing in print or electronic forms without written permission of IGI Global is prohibited.

they have the same great experience if they go digital or physical. Internal because companies must be digital inside. It will have a complete transformational journey if it also changes the mindset and the way the business operates, aligning the new business models created with the digital transformation to the outside world.

So, the question that comes immediately is: how to start? What should organizations think about when planning a digital journey? There are several frameworks to help to start. The Digital Reinvention Operation Environment from IBV (IBM Institute of Business Value) describes well the key elements needed to be considered when executing the digital journey.

The Mackinsey article Unlocking success in digital transformations (October 29, 2018), one of the 5 categories in order to have a successful transformation: "having the right digital-savvy leaders in place; building capabilities for the workforce of the future; empowering people to work in new ways; giving day-to-day tools a digital upgrade and communicating frequently via traditional and digital methods".

Fact is that, as stated in the introduction of this chapter, digital transformation is not about a single element but understanding the multi components that if put together in a proper way successfully forms the puzzle required to shift the companies to a different stage. These elements could be consolidated into:

- New business models – what are the business models to be changed to connect physical and digital, using exponential technologies, to deliver a great experience to your customers.
- New ways of working – how the company is prepared to the new business models being pursued (IT architect, devops, process efficiency and data).
- Culture and capabilities – how the organization is aligned with the new ways of working and if the employees are prepared with the skills of future and new business models.

Notice that each of the elements are interconnected and should coexist aligned with the strategy and purpose of the organization. A disconnect between the elements may incur on waste of effort and investment.

Another key factor to consider is how to measure the success of this transformation. Companies usually tend to create too many metrics, some of them valuable but several not really meaningful. This usually causes increment of workload and frustration. Defining what really matters to measure during the transformation is also important to evaluate progress and improvement areas. Think about what matters to your organization.

For this chapter, the components to be highlighted for the digital transformation journey are new ways of working and culture and capabilities. How to create an agile environment where the teams are able to deliver fast, collaborate, bringing value and innovation to the enterprise.

During the past years, on several workshops and presentations with different clients or companies, it has been common hearing from their technology leaders the question on how to start this agile journey. There are usually a lack of understanding or confusion regarding the methodology versus the cultural change. It is hard sometimes to visualize that Agile techniques, Design Thinking and lean are all embedded on Agile transformation.

Not uncommon as well to hear about obstacles such as lack of executive support, complex environment and organization, lack of skills and others. The question is: how to do it?

First, Agile is not a method, but a cultural change. This is a key element to understand to achieve the goal to scale agile at enterprise level. Culture does not change in a day. It takes time and, most important, if companies want to scale agile, their leaders (in all levels) must be agile.

THE REAL CASE

Six years ago, a large technology (IT) corporation started their agile journey. A centenary traditional IT environment, where leading was about driving results through command and control. IT teams were segregated into transformation (new projects) and sustain (IT support), resulting in separate silos, several control points, excessiveness processes and documentation, lack of innovation and collaboration and, not surprisingly, disengagement.

In addition, teams were spread in too many different locations driving increase of waiting time, fragmented knowledge, lack of interaction and distance from leadership.

From an IT landscape, as a centenary company, several legacy applications were old, with lack of documentation and knowledge inside the team. The environment was complex, changes used to take a lot of time and, by the time they were completed, the value add was really low.

As a result, the IT area delivered low business value and was seen as a passive back-office support department. A place where talents did not like to be.

This is a real example, but not unique and very common to find on several other companies in the industry.

Making a change was key not only for the IT department, but also to reflect the need to transform the entire company to follow the time to market and new business models being required. A market which was urging for speed, innovation and better experience with clients. A bold move was necessary.

To shift the direction of this Titanic, and avoid the iceberg, this organization focused on few items which were mandatory to begin the move:

- New ways of working
- Reorganize the department to provide autonomy and accountabilities to the teams (self-direction and business driven teams)
- Leadership change to a new mindset
- A new strategy for work environment
- Create a culture of continuous learning and enabling a diversity and inclusive environment that would foster collaboration and innovation.

THE METHOD

Cultural changes sometimes can get fuzzy, so having clarity to the team on purpose and a tangible goal to be achieved is also a key element to help to drive the transformation. In addition, in a scenario of a large and complex organization, breaking the challenge into smaller pieces is a good way to start.

Think big and start small. Aligned with this principle, the first action was the development of a plan considering which were the teams that could gain faster traction to the new mindset and techniques and, through a continuously iteration process, improve and scale it.

The following principles were defined:

- Teams should be formed as small squads, collocated in the same workplace and cross functional. Being accountable for design, build, test, deploy and support the application inside their respective scope.

- Backlog prioritization would be defined by a Product Owner. A professional from business area with accountability for making decisions
- Clear agile principles and values
- Multiple squads would be grouped as Tribe, within the same goal or scope
- Guilds would connect the squads with same interest to collaborate and share knowledge
- Clear measurement process focused on improvement would be clear to everyone.

An interactive and continuous process was created. With the support of agile coaches, some hired from outside the company and some formed inside, the squads were being built in a collaborative approach, understanding for each of them how it would make more sense to organize. For example, the teams supporting the billing systems organized themselves on couple squads forming a Billing Tribe. The taxes team, due to some specific characteristics decided that the best would be to organize the squads by system features or functionalities. Every fifteen days a certain group of new squads were created with the benefit to receive the insights and learning from the squads that were already operating under the new model and mindset.

As a matter of fact, agile is about continuous improving. The best way to learn and improve is through the practice. As the iterations were progressing, the squads were practicing and sharing what was going well and what was not through the retrospective ceremony. Practice, Practice and Practice.

Along with practice, a development plan was in place. A well structure training digital platform was in place to support the team to acquire knowledge and capabilities. Face to face classes were also implemented to leadership and squads.

With the method well defined and being executed, measuring the progress was crucial to understand improvement. Establishing a way to measure how each squad was progressing with the intent to always get better is a key element on scaling agile. One critical principle was also defined: measurement was about how to get better and not comparing one squad with another. The intention was to understand specifically what the maturity level of each squads, challenges and areas for improvement were.

Measuring how to get better and retrospective are important as well to establish a relationship of trust and connecting the teams and leadership with the new culture. Understanding the purpose of both practices (either in the squad level but, most important, on leadership level) is essential to relief the tension that usually surround metrics.

NEW WAYS OF WORKING

How to enable an IT landscape strategy which is aligned with the new business model in a complex environment with old legacy applications, manual processes, shadow IT spread over different business units and lack of velocity to deliver new projects?

First step was really to understand how the architecture was defined and aligned with the business strategy. This is an important topic when thinking about a digital transformation. Understanding how your IT environment is prepared, not short term only, but mid and long term to support the business considering velocity and scalability, is fundamental to create the basis of an IT strategy. In this company, this was not different.

Three major actions were considered:

1.   Simplifying the IT landscape:

Finding synergy points within the IT organization is an interest dynamic. The first reaction companies may face during this exercise is "self-protection". IT teams fighting against themselves to convince the organization that, although there are potential (sometimes very clear) synergies between some of the scope, they had to maintain the system, otherwise something critical to the business will break. Specific for this organization reaction was not different. Fear is a common feeling along with changes and in order to break resistance adopting clarity and transparency is a great medicine.

First action was to provide the real purpose of the assessment which was to simplify the IT landscape to generate value to the organization, deliver cost reduction on infrastructure and free-up more capacity from the team to delivery new demands.

Second, was to evaluate on which team the scope would make sense to be allocated. For this company, to align with the concept of having self-direct squads (this concept will be detailed in this chapter), the strategy was to consolidate scope within the teams instead of having it distributed among several different ones.

Third, was to define a strategy for reskilling for the teams receiving or losing scope. One of the major goals was free-up capacity inside the squads for new demands, so providing new capabilities and skills to the team was a success factor to execute this strategy.

As the team started to see the training investment on new skills to the teams together with business results and recognition, conflicts and resistance were replaced by engagement and self-motivation.

2.   Redefining IT priorities:

When the IT organizations are divided by silos, with low synergy and integration with the business, it is common to face lack of prioritization and strategic view of the IT landscape. Everything seems to be important and the result is usually bad investment of time and money. This scenario usually reflects on team morale and increment of low value processes and controls. It was common to see in the organization, professionals hiding themselves on useless processes with the false feeling of empowerment.

To change this scenario, a bold decision was made. Aligned with the business goals and strategy, a detailed application inventory and mapping was conceived, establishing which were the IT systems that should be considered as investment, maintain or sunset. This initiative was strategic in order to help the organizations define where to prioritize, invest on capacity and allocate the budget properly. Working together with the business, after several rounds of mapping and validation, more or less 10% of the overall IT landscape was considered as investment application to the organization. A vision of priority was defined, and the team had a much clear view where they should focus and what skills would be required.

Another aspect that the organization started to notice was the proximity with the business areas. A different atmosphere started to be created whit a much more strategic IT area being consolidated.

3.   Strategic and long-term mindset:

Consolidating the bases of the IT department through a simplification view of architecture and redefining the priorities allowed the organization to think forward. Three major points were listed as critical to have an IT organization that was capable to support the business strategy long term:

- Scalability: have an IT environment capable of adhering to the frequently market demand changes in the velocity required.
- Enable IT teams capable of continue to delivery within a secure environment
- Innovation and modernization by allowing the development teams to have access of modern technologies and an experimentation environment.

Based on the topics above, the path defined was Hybrid Cloud environment. A clear plan was created to migrate one hundred percent of the applications to a hybrid cloud environment within 2 years. A huge challenge considering the complexity of the business and IT applications. A roadmap was created having a clear view of the strategy to migrate for each of the application. An architecture board also was created to understand the challenges of infrastructure and applications and a detailed plan was created and executed by the teams.

It was clear that changing the way of working was a key factor for the major digital transformation being proposed. Aligning the IT landscape, with a solid short and long term view focused on business strategy reinforced the purpose of the organization, enhanced the capabilities of the team and was also a starting point for the cultural change.

THE LEADERSHIP CHANGE TO A NEW MINDSET

To change leadership mindset, it is important to provide clarity on what are the principles and outcomes being pursued. For this case the principles were:

- Clarity over certainty
- Course correct over perfection
- Innovation for everyone over selected few
- Talent density versus process density
- Empowered teams over command control.

Setting the principles properly is important to make sure leadership understand what changes are required. It also helps to start an important process which is to make sure the proper leaders are selected for the organization. In this example, in addition to the principles, there was also a board to interview the top-level leadership to understand if they understood what was being proposed and also if they were fit to the new culture being pursued.

Sometimes, complacency can kill an organization. There is no easy choice. If the leadership is not aligned with the future state, it is better to change it quickly.

Another action, very successful in this case, was to bring some leaders from outside. Find professionals from other companies that are adherent to the culture being proposed and already is established and doing it well is a great way to introduce agents of change to the organization.

A critical point of attention regarding setting the proper leadership is the middle management layer. Usually, the top-level or first layer of leaders are very exposed, so it is easier to identify the ones that are not aligned with new culture. The major challenge is the mid-level or middle management. They impact directly the team, since they are usually working closer in a daily basis, and also it is easier for these leaders to present themselves as if they have the new mindset to the top level and act differently (with the old mindset) to the bottom of the pyramid. To avoid this to happen, it is critical for the top management to also be closer to the team.

Make sure engagement surveys are running in all levels of organization, but also have a direct contact to identify potential disruption or disengagement from the team. Working closer to the middle management and make sure they receive the proper training are also fundamental. Recommending the team to look to outside (what are the companies that works the best in that area) it is also a good way to provoke and make sure the team is continuously improving.

"The bad apple dynamic": As leadership begins to change and reflect it direct to the team, it is common to see the bad apples becoming more evident. As the team starts to engage in the new culture, there is no more space for the ones that are only pretending or are not really a fit. This is a positive and natural selection process.

SELF-DIRECT AND BUSINESS VALUE DRIVEN SQUADS

Being Self-direct does not mean that leadership doesn't play a role with the team. Actually, it is the opposite. Leaders must be present and know even more their craft.

As described in the example of this company, the environment was split in silos, with heavy processes and procedures to make sure the work was being done properly. This used to result in a false sense of progress. Excessiveness controlling incurred on fear a lack of confidence to the team. It also concentrated the decision and accountability to the leaders, and the team was frequently passive, waiting for the direction instead of assuming certain risks to execute with speed or to attempt to innovate. Fear defeats new ideas.

The first step to change this scenario was breaking the silos. An organization change was required and the reference model used to do it was the Spotify approach (https://www.youtube.com/watch?v=4 GK1NDTWbkY&list=PLVoXxzMVwkZ0vndMplV_rhwMHyS199vr1).

Transformation (new projects) and Sustain (IT support) were reorganized into cross functional end to end squads (the new name for the teams). Each squad would have maximum of 6 to10 professionals and should be physically located in the same working area. Cross functional squads would now be responsible to understand a requirement, deliver and support it through the product life cycle. They should also have the skills to do it. The initial result could not be better. Existing processes to handle work between teams did not make sense anymore. Why having it if now everyone were accountable to the end to end work? Innovation now was not an exclusive opportunity for the transformation team. Talents from the sustain teams, that were hidden resolving problems behind the tickets, could now use their skills to develop or suggest new ideas. Being located in the same place, increased exponentially the collaboration and problem resolution inside the squads. Squad backlogs, from years, were being executed and delivered without any additional investment. Only using the squad capacity and prioritization.

Becoming business driven squads was also a key value to the cultural change process. In the beginning, these teams were used to execute IT projects without really understanding the business value behind. The intention was positive, but results were a disaster. Years of projects and financial investments were usually thrown in the trash, either because the requirement changed, or the business was asking for something much simpler.

Introducing concepts like product life cycle, design thinking, value stream mapping, user experience or user centric approach were game changers to deliver value to the organization. In addition, the introduction of the role of Product Owner, as a person from the business to define priorities and work very close to the squads, was key to shift the organization from IT projects to business value driven approach.

Leadership role was also fundamental in the process to establish self-direct teams. These squads were held accountable to their work and could not fear to commit mistakes.

Fail fast and course correct it is an important learning process for the team but mostly to the leaders. There is no innovation without taking risk. Letting the team to take risk leads to great results. Being a servant leader, that support the teams to resolve blockers and also to quickly find alternatives in case of the need to change route, it is crucial to root the new mindset. Leading by example it is not just a motivational speech.

IMPROVING THE WORKPLACE ENVIRONMENT

Workplace environment sometimes may be left as secondary priority, but it is not. People spend most of the time of their life at work. Would you like to spend this time in a non-attractive work environment?

Having a great place to work does not only bring engagement, but also enables the team to collaborate and it is a great differentiator to attract talents from other great companies.

During the transformation, all the strategic workplace locations were remodeled to fit in the new culture being paved. A place where the team could easily to collaborate, connecting digital and physical tools (e.g. wall board, post it, collaborative rooms, digital tools for code sharing, etc.). Having the squads work backlogs exposed was also an interest process to provide clarity and learning to the other teammates and squads on what was being executed.

Prior to the workplace transformation, the level of occupancy in the site was around 50%. After few months after sites being renewed, a request for expansion was being made.

Physically changing the work environment was also important to concretize and provide a real sense of change to the organization. The squads could see and feel the changes, creating a great sense of belonging.

CONTINUOUS LEARNING

If people are the great asset of any company, their knowledge is how much they value. Having the proper skills is a key driver to any change. During this transformation, this company worked on different actions to provide capabilities to the team. In order to make the agile change, external help was pursued, and few Agile consultants were hired to structure and initiate the work. As the work progressed, not all the agile coaches were from outside. Internal professionals, hungry to learn and be part of the transformation, were selected and trained to become the new agile agents or coaches, and bringing this balancing was key to enable capability inside the team and also create an organic environment for change.

People from inside the organization sometimes may not be completely skilled but, usually, they have a great knowledge of the processes and organization. With some training, the right professionals can become great allies to influence the others to pursue the new goals.

Professionals with previous different skills that showed interest for this role were selected, trained and act as Agile coach and agent of transformation.

Digital and physical approach for training were also defined. A web platform with all the contents related to the proposed change (strategy, goals, clear vision, methodology and trainings) was made available to the team on a self-service model.

Face to face training sessions with the agile coaches were established and provided to all the team, starting from the leadership. The idea of incrementally creating other agents or agile coaches internally in the team also helped spread the sense of continuous learning approach.

More and more, the digital platform was filled with new trainings and the teams were stimulated to consume the content. A gamification approach and also the use of AI to personalize the experience in the platform were a boost to embed this new culture of learning inside the organization.

Having the most capable organization as part of the overall strategy reinforced the importance of this goal and provided the clarity to each of individual on what the IT department was aiming for.

ENABLING INNOVATION THROUGH A DIVERSE AND INCLUSIVE ENVIRONMENT

After almost two years of transformation, the organization had changed. It was much more mature and structured in the proposed Agile model. The teams were already advancing on Devops, automation and other techniques to gain velocity and time to market. Culture was much more solid within the teams and among leadership. However, innovation was still shy and not following the same pace.

Once again, having the proper mindset for change was required and leadership understood that, in order to enable innovation, it was also required different ideas. The question to answer by this company was: how to have different ideas if the majority of professionals have the same background? The same life experiences. How to diverge? The answer was clear and a call to action for inclusion was done.

The organization demography was cleared mapped to identify where to focus on. A clear plan, based on the forecast of new positions, was done in order to create opportunities for People with Disabilities (PwD), technical women and black community. A work to educate and raise awareness to the leadership was continuously in place. Initiatives using external specialized companies were defined to accelerate the inclusion process. One example was the neurodiversity program where, in the first years, twelve professionals with Autism Spectrum Disorder (ASD) were selected to compose the squads in the IT department.

The results were outstanding. Collaboration and engagement within the team increased double digit. Improvements on IT applications accessibility were identified and fixed. Enhancements on tools and agile ceremonies were adapted to include all the population and the number of innovative projects and patents were also relevant increased.

From an inclusion perspective, the IT department of this company became a reference and led the way for the change.

EXPERIMENTATION AND NEW TECHNOLOGIES

In the begging of this chapter, it was made clear the digital transformation is not about technology, but business value. However, it was also made clear that knowing technology it is a key element to identify the potential of possibilities to be explored to help resolve business problems and reinvent business models.

As the transformation in the company was progressing, squads were formed and becoming more and more mature and self-directed. Few automations were already implemented helping the teams free-up capacity and leadership was much more onboarded with the new mindset.

The sense of freedom to innovate and take risks without the fear of being penalized by any mistake was consolidating inside the organization. Trust was overcoming command control.

Artificial Intelligence: In one of the discussions with the business a problem was raised. One of the largest business unit responsible to manage client infrastructure and services brought the challenge of having a better process to manage and allocate the tickets properly. Maintenance services were being delayed, as consequence service level agreement were being lost driving to financial penalties. It was a complex problem to be resolved. IT environment supporting this process had multiple sources of data (millions of tickets), manual processes and tickets were not always documented in a structured format.

Prior to this agile transformation, this request would likely die in the first discussion. Problem would be too complex to resolve, project would be too large and take too much time to be deployed and cost tones of dollars.

After few discovery sessions, using design thinking techniques the squad comes with a proposal. The idea was to implement a solution, using Artificial Intelligence to ingest millions of structured and non-structured data in order to provide the support team insights for problem resolution. An ambitious project considering that by the time nobody in the squad had a really profound knowledge on Artificial Intelligence.

The challenge was still evident. Among millions of tickets, there were thousands of problems versus solution possibilities and, not knowing technology, could lead the team to spend too much time and investment to fail.

In the spirit of Agile, one of the squad members come with a proposal to break the problem into smaller pieces. Why don't start selecting one of the problems to quickly pilot and find how it works? Something unthinkable few years prior to transformation. In two months, the squad released the pilot into production. Benefits were incredible. The squad developed a mechanism to ingest millions of data using Artificial Intelligence including ticket transcripts, enriching the data and insights. The squad improved their skills on the new technology. Business could quickly identify if the value being delivered would worth the case and what improvements had to be made for the following iterations. This became a successful case inside the company with formal recognitions to the squad.

Blockchain

Managing IT assets such as computers, cell phones and others were a pain point inside the company. Lack of historical data on asset maintenance, hand over between vendors supporting the process led the company to lose track of the asset life cycle and take bad decisions on asset maintenance or replacement. The result: bad experience to the end user and waste of money.

In a company with more than three hundred thousand employees spread all over the globe, challenge become even more complex. The squad supporting this process was formed by professionals in average over 20 years of company. Professionals that in the past were used to stay reacting to tickets being raised due to system failure or maintenance.

The relationship between the squads and business was getting more mature. There was a better understanding from IT and business of the role of the Product Owner (PO - a person from the business working close to the squads to prioritize the demand based on business value). This was a key factor driving new projects in the IT area. Business value and user experience were the center of discussion, but technology the enabler.

During one of the planning sessions with the PO raises the problem described above. Three major challenges:

- Enhance the experience to the users to open requests for asset maintenance or replacement
- Provide a way for the support team to capture and track the life cycle of the asset with historical information to support business decisions
- Trust in the processes for handling asset among different vendors

After few sessions of discovery, the squad developer raises her hand and say: "why don't we create a digital platform running over a Blockchain solution"? By the time, Blockchain was even newer than AI for business. Once again, the team broke a complex problem on couple and continuous iterations. As the team was deploying functionalities to production, the Product Owner was able to experiment and provide feedbacks for improvements. The concept of launching a minimum value product (MVP) to few users called friends and family approach was also implemented to collect additional feedbacks and improve the product. As a result, this was the first internal Blockchain project implemented in Latin America, also resulting the team to be formal recognized by the organization.

Machine Learning Algorithmics and Internet of Things (IoT)

How to create an intelligent service desk to support field services to external clients? This question was raised during one of the iterations with the business unit. The scenario was not good. Once again, manual processes, lack of data and intelligence leading the team to take bad decisions on ticket assignment to field service technicians to resolve client issues. Client dissatisfaction, service level agreement and financial loss.

The problem was also very complex. More than thousands of technicians in the field, having to support a large geographic location with remote locations. In addition, the lack of skill of these professionals would incur in several calls to the reduced service desk team to resolve simple questions. Last, but not least, logistic of components and parts to be used for equipment replacement during maintenance were also an important element to execute the service. Frequently, tickets were assigned to the technician that was not the most skilled to the problem or was distant from the location or even had to wait for the component to arrive.

The problem was broken into pieces:

- First. Reduce the number of calls from the technicians to the service desk for simple problem resolution
- Second. Develop a digital platform to enable ticket assignment and monitor real time service level agreement for each client (by location)
- Third. Enhance the platform with machine learn algorithms and IoT to enable intelligence and automation to recommend service desk support on ticket assignment based in the following components: technicians' skills, machine parts availability, geo localization and service level agreement information.

This project was interested on several aspects when thinking about digital transformation. First, the capability of the IT and business team to collectively focus on a user centric approach to identify the personas and pain points to drive a solution. Second, the capability of breaking the problem into smaller pieces and different technology solutions. And third, drove to the squad the need of self-develop on multiple skills such as data science, AI and IoT.

The first solution delivered was a chatbot with AI embedded to enable the field service technicians to resolve simple problems instead of calling the service desk team. This helped reduce number of calls and, by consequence, increase capacity from service desk team to focus on other critical tasks. Video interaction, with demo on how to resolve certain type of issues, was also embedded in the solution to create a better experience.

Second was the development of a digital platform to replace the manual process including a real time board where the service desk team could easily see the service level agreement (SLA) status for each client. A first seed of intelligence was also implemented in this solution with predictive analytics showing, by client, which SLA could still be achieved or not.

Third, and most complex one, was a 360-degree view of the client. Presenting to the service desk team a view of the client status, and also recommending to the attendant what would be the best ticket assignment based on technicians' skills, machine parts availability, geo localization and service level agreement information.

In addition to the phases described above, the solution was also deployed incrementally by region. Taking into consideration number of tickets, size and complexity of the region, etc. This allowed the squads and users to experiment each of the functionality being deployed and improve with the continuous feedback process.

The examples above reinforces the fact that a new culture was being adopted. Having the squads and business cocreating and collaborating with a user centric approach were a great result of this change. The experimentation process and continuous feedback were essential for being able to deliver innovation.

CONCLUSION

Scaling Agile to the enterprise is fundamentally about cultural change. Most of companies, especially large corporations, tend to give up even prior to start due to its complexity and sometimes due to top level executives having other priorities.

One of the mantras of Agile manifesto is: "Think big start small". This is very valuable and useful as well to make this cultural move. A great way is to start with simple questions:

- What are the areas or teams inside a business unit where this new culture can be well accepted and quickly adopted?
- Is this area will deliver business value associated to this change?
- Do you have the proper skills to make this change?
- What if a specific team inside of a department is selected to pilot this change?
- Who are the sponsors to influence for this change?
- What are the companies that are already doing or done with this change that could be benchmark?

Finding a place to begin is important to get traction and also start to organically see the changes. A good cultural change happens from the top to the bottom but also from the bottom to the top.

Second step, after selecting a good area to start, is to define your cultural values or principles. In the Forrester report "Scaling Agile: What The Spotify Approach Can Do For You" (Diego Lo Giudice with Christopher Mines, Andrew Dobak, Kara Hartig), the authors paraphrase the guru Peter Ducker stating: "Culture eats process for lunch".

In the article, it also highlights few tips that should be considered when thinking about your value principles:

- "Culture counts more than process"
- "Culture without transparent and accepted principles produces bad behavior"
- "A framework should fit the culture you want, not the one you have".

As described in the article, companies should think about principles they want to achieve, and not their current values.

Third step is to find sponsors and leaders inside the company that are really committed to the change. Of course, as much sponsorship from the executive level, more it will be the priorities and results. However, it is important to remind that changes are also made from bottom to the top. As the organization starts to get traction, the trend is to organically and positively infect other areas with the new changes.

Fourth step is to find professionals inside the company that are looking for new challenges and align their skills to the new culture being pursued. Training these professionals and making them agents of transformation are really helpful to engage other employees and use the internal workforce.

In the beginning of this article, it was made clear that digital transformation is not a short run. It is more a long run or a marathon. It requires a clear understanding of what is the enterprise strategy as well what are the business drivers, internal and external, to be resolved to make sure the company provides the same experience to their clients in the physical and digital world. As most of the long runs, sometimes it gets easy to give up in the middle, lose traction or motivation. Celebrate each step, every important mile achieved, is also key to maintain the organization moving.

Having the proper agile culture in the organization is the fuel required to accelerate the change and take the enterprise to the next level.

REFERENCES

Davenport, T., & Westerman, G. (2018). *Why So Many High-Profile Digital Transformations Fail.* Harvard Business Review. https://hbr.org/2018/03/why-so-many-high-profile-digital-transformations-fail

Kniberg, H. (2014) *Spotify Engineering Culture.* https://blog.crisp.se/2014/03/27/henrikkniberg/spotify-engineering-culture-part-1 https://www.youtube.com/watch?v=4GK1NDTWbkY&list=PLVoXxzMVwkZ0vndMplV_rhwMHyS199vr1

Lo Giudice, D., Mines, C., Dobak, A., & Hartig, K. (2020). *Scaling Agile: What The Spotify Approach Can Do For You.* Forrester. https://www.forrester.com/report/Scaling+Agile+What+The+Spotify+Approach+Can+Do+For+You/-/E-RES144558?objectid=RES144558

Posner, B., & Kouzes, J. (2012). *The Leadership Challenge* (5th ed.). Jossey-Bass.

Rifkin, J. (2015). *The Zero Marginal Cost Society*. Palgrave Macmillar.

The Agile Manifesto. (2001). https://agilemanifesto.org/

The Digital Reinvention Operation Environment from IBV (IBM Institute of Business Value). (n.d.). https://www.ibm.com/thought-leadership/institute-business-value

The Mackinsey article Unlocking success in digital transformations. (2018). https://www.mckinsey.com/~/media/McKinsey/Business%20Functions/Organization/Our%20Insights/Unlocking%20success%20in%20digital%20transformations/Unlocking-success-in-digital-transformations.ashx

Compilation of References

Abdulaziz & Pang. (2000). Robust Data Hiding for Images. *Proceedings for Communication Technology*, 380-383.

ABNT ISO/IEC 27.001 – Information technology - Security Techniques - Information security management systems — Requirements. 2013

ABNT ISO/IEC 27.002 - Code of Practice for Information Security Controls, 2013.

ABNT. (2019). *ABNT - Associação Brasileira de Normas Técnicas*. Recuperado 31 de março de 2019, de http://www.abnt.org.br/

ABStartups. (2019). https://startupbase.com.br/c/community/all-saints-bay

Accessnow. (2018). *Human Rights in the Age of Artificial Intelligence*. Retrieved Mar 13, from https://www.accessnow.org/cms/assets/uploads/2018/11/AI-and-Human-Rights.pdf

Acfe. (2020). *Report to the Nations*. https://www.acfe.com/report-to-the-nations/2020/

Acha, V., & Brusoni, S. (2008). The changing governance of knowledge in avionics. *Economics of Innovation and New Technology*, *17*(1-2), 43–57. doi:10.1080/10438590701279284

Acquisti, A., & Gross, R. (2007). *Privacy risks for mining online social networks*. In *NSF Symposium on Next Generation of Data Mining and Cyber-Enabled Discovery for Innovation (NGDM'07)*, Baltimore, MD.

Adams, P. Brusoni, S. & Malerba, F. (2010). The long-term evolution of the knowledge boundaries of firms: Supply and demand perspectives. *The Third Industrial Revolution in Global Business*.

Adams, P., Brusoni, S., & Malerba, F. (2010). The long-term evolution of the knowledge boundaries of firms: Supply and demand perspectives. *The Third Industrial Revolution in Global Business*.

Adams, R., Bessant, J., & Phelps, R. (2006). Innovation management measurement: A review. *International Journal of Management Reviews*, *8*(1), 21–47. doi:10.1111/j.1468-2370.2006.00119.x

Adebanjo, D., Teh, P. L., & Ahmed, P. K. (2018). The impact of supply chain relationships and integration on innovative capabilities and manufacturing performance: The perspective of rapidly developing countries. *International Journal of Production Research, Taylor & Francis*, *56*(4), 1708–1721. doi:10.1080/00207543.2017.1366083

Agis, D.; Bessa, D.; Gouveia, J. & Vaz, P. (2010). *Wearing the future – Micro trends for the textile, clothing and fashion industries by 2020*. Portuguese Textile and Clothing Association.

Agiwal, M., Roy, A., & Saxena, N. (2016). Next generation 5G wireless networks: A comprehensive survey. *IEEE Communications Surveys and Tutorials*, *18*(3), 1617–1655. doi:10.1109/COMST.2016.2532458

Aguirre. (2004). *Introdução a identificação de sistemas: técnicas lineares e não-lineares aplicadas a sistemas reais*. UFMG.

Ahlers, D., & Boll, S. (2009). Adaptive geospatially focused crawling. In *Proceedings of the 18th ACM conference on Information and knowledge management*, (pp. 445–454). ACM. 10.1145/1645953.1646011

AICC - Industrial and Commercial Coffee Association. (n.d.). Retrieved September 13, from www.aicc.pt

Aiyebelehin, A. J., Makinde, B., Odiachi, R., & Mbakwe, C. C. (2020). Awareness and Use of Cloud Computing Services and Technologies by Librarians in Selected Universities in Edo State. *International Journal of Knowledge Content Development & Technology, 10*(3), 7–20.

Akbulut, Sahin, & Eristi. (2010). Development of a scale to investigate cybervictimization among online social utility members. *Contemporary Educational Technology, 1*(1), 46-59.

Alaba, F. A., Othman, M., Hashem, I. A. T., & Alotaibi, F. (2017). Internet of Things security: A survey. *Journal of Network and Computer Applications, 88*, 10–28. doi:10.1016/j.jnca.2017.04.002

Alaerds, R., Grove, S., Besteman, S., & Bilderbeek, P. (2017). *The Foundations of our Digital Economy*. Wouter Pegtel & Splend.

Albrechtslund, A. (2007). Ethics and technology design. *Ethics and Information Technology, 9*, 63–72. Retrieved Mar 22, from https://www.researchgate.net/publication/225493059_Ethics_and_technology_design

Aleixo, J. A., & Duarte, P. (2015). Big data opportunities in healthcare. how can medical affairs contribute? *Revista Portuguesa de Farmacoterapia, 7*, 230–236.

Alexa. (2018). *The top 500 sites on the web*. Retrieved from https://www.alexa.com/topsites

Al-Jarrah, O. Y., Al-Jarrah, P. D., Yoo, S. M., Karagiannidis, G. K., & Taha, K. (2015). *Efficient Machine Learning for Big Data: A Review. In Big Data Research*. Elsevier. doi:10.1016/j.bdr.2015.04.001

Alnajrani, H. M., Norman, A. A., & Ahmed, B. H. (2020). Privacy and data protection in mobile cloud computing: A systematic mapping study. *PLoS One, 15*(6). doi:10.1371/journal.pone.0234312 PMID:32525944

Alon, U. (2006). *An introduction to systems biology: design principles of biological circuits*. Chapman and Hall/CRC. doi:10.1201/9781420011432

Alver, R. A., Cabral, A. C. A., Penha, E. D. S., dos Santos, S. M., & Pessoa, M. N. M. (2013). *Relações entre estilos de aprendizagem e a autopercepção de competências profissionais em alunos concludentes do curso de graduação em Administração da UFC*. Paper presented at the IV Encontro de Ensino e Pesquisa em Administração e Contabilidade Brasilia, DF. http://www.anpad.org.br/admin/pdf/2013_EnEPQ229.pdf

Alves, A., & Barbosa, R. R. (2010). Influences and barriers to information sharing: A theoretical perspective. *Ciência da Informação*.

Alves, A., & Barbosa, R. R. (2010). Influences and barriers to information sharing: A theoretical perspective. *Information Science*.

Amin, A., & Cohendet, P. (2011). *Architectures of Knowledge: Firms, Capabilities, and Communities. Architectures of Knowledge: Firms*. Capabilities, and Communities.

Anand, A. (2018, May 31). *ITIL in a world of digital transformation*. Retrieved from Axelos Global Best Practice: https://www.axelos.com/news/blogs/may-2018/itil-in-a-world-of-digital-transformation

Anandakumar, H., & Umamaheswari, K. (2017). Supervised machine learning techniques in cognitive radio networks during cooperative spectrum handovers. *Cluster Computing, 20*(2), 1505–1515. doi:10.100710586-017-0798-3

Anderson, M., Anderson, S., & Armen, C. (2004). *Towards machine ethics*. AAAL-04 workshop on agent organizations: theory and practice, San Jose, CA.

Anderson, D., & Anderson, L. (2010). *Beyond Change Management. How to Achieve Breakthrough Results Through Conscious Change Leadership* (2nd ed.). Pfeiffer.

Andrade, A. Z. B. (2009). *Estudo comparativo entre a Subvenção Econômica à Inovação operada pela FINEP e Programas correlatos de subsídio em países desenvolvidos* (Dissertação de Mestrado em Administração Pública). Escola Brasileira de Administração Pública e de Empresas da Fundação Getúlio Vargas, Rio de janeiro.

Andrade, C. S. L. d. (2016). *A influência das soft skills na atuação do gestor: a percepção dos profissionais de gestão de pessoas* (Mestre em Administração). Fundação Getúlio Vargas, Rio de Janeiro, RJ. https://bibliotecadigital.fgv.br/dspace/bitstream/handle/10438/17711/Dissertac%CC%A7a%CC%83o%20Final%202016.pdf?sequence=1&isAllowed=y

Andrade, R. F. (2018 julho 13). *O combate à lavagem de dinheiro*. Legiscompliance. https://www.legiscompliance.com.br/colunistas/renata-andrade/79-o-combate-a-lavagem-de-dinheiro#:~:text=O%20crime%20de%20lavagem%20de%20dinheiro%20foi%20tipificado%20no%20Brasil,Lei%20n%C2%B0%209.613%2F98.&text=Tal%20crime%20se%20d%C3%A1%20ao,ou%20indiretamente%2C%20de%20infra%C3%A7%C3%A3o%20penal

Andriole, S. (2017). Five Myths About Digital Transformation Vol58 No 3. *MIT Sloan Management Review*, 1–5.

Antonelli, C., & Amidei, F.B. (2011). *The dynamics of knowledge externalities: Localized technological change in Italy*. Academic Press.

Antonelli, C., & Teubal, M. (2010). Venture capitalism as a mechanism for knowledge governance. *The Capitalization of Knowledge: A Triple Helix of University-Industry-Government*.

Antonelli, C., Amidei, F.B., & Fassio, C. (2014). The mechanisms of knowledge governance: State owned enterprises and Italian economic growth, 1950-1994. *Structural Change and Economic Dynamics*.

Antonelli, C., Amidei, F.B., & Fassio, C. (2015). Corrigendum to "The mechanisms of knowledge governance: State owned enterprises and Italian economic growth, 1950-1994". *Structural Change and Economic Dynamics*.

Antonelli, C. (2006). The business governance of localized knowledge: An information economics approach for the economics of knowledge. *Industry and Innovation, 13*(3), 2006. doi:10.1080/13662710600858118

Antonelli, C. (2007). Technological knowledge as an essential facility. *Journal of Evolutionary Economics, 17*(4), 451–471. doi:10.100700191-007-0058-4

Antonelli, C. (2008). The new economics of the university: A knowledge governance approach. *The Journal of Technology Transfer, 33*(1), 1–22. doi:10.100710961-007-9064-9

Antonelli, C. (2013). Knowledge Governance: Pecuniary Knowledge Externalities and Total FactorProductivity Growth. *Economic Development Quarterly, 27*(1), 62–70. doi:10.1177/0891242412473178

Antonelli, C. A. (2016). Schumpeterian growth model: Wealth and directed technological change. *The Journal of Technology Transfer, 41*(3), 395–406. doi:10.100710961-015-9410-2

Antonelli, C., & Calderini, M. (2008). The governance of knowledge compositeness and technological performance: The case of the automotive industry in Europe. *Economics of Innovation and New Technology, 17*(1-2), 23–41. doi:10.1080/10438590701279243

Antonelli, C., & Fassio, C. (2014). The heterogeneity of knowledge and the academic mode of knowledge governance: Italian evidence in the first part of the 20th century. *Science & Public Policy, 41*(1), 15–28. doi:10.1093cipolct030

Antonelli, C., & Fassio, C. (2016). Globalization and the Knowledge-Driven Economy. *Economic Development Quarterly*, *30*(1), 3–14. doi:10.1177/0891242415617239

Antonelli, C., Patrucco, P. P., & Quatraro, F. (2008). The governance of localized knowledge externalities. *International Review of Applied Economics*, *22*(4), 479–498. doi:10.1080/02692170802137661

Anunciação, P. F. (2015). Organizational Change through Information Systems: Metavision-Project Management Model in Internet Banking. Handbook of Research on Effective Project Management through the Integration of Knowledge and Innovation, 450-465.

Anunciação, P. F. (2016). Organizational Urbanism: A Value Proposal for the Generation of Organizational Intelligence to Healthcare Institutions – The Case of a Portuguese Hospital Center. Handbook of Research on Information Architecture and management in Modern Organizations, 458-486.

Anunciação, P. F., Esteves, F. M., & Gonçalves, F. M. (2019). Analytics, Intelligence and Ethics. In Business Intelligence (BI): Advances in Research and Applications. Nova Publishers.

Anunciação, P., & Esteves, F. (2019). Challenges to Business Models in the Digital Transformation Context. Handbook of Research on Business Models in Modern Competitive Scenarios, 11, 197 – 210.

Anunciação, P. F. (2014). *Ethics, Sustainability and the Information and Knowledge Society*. Chiado Publishing.

Anunciação, P. F., & Zorrinho, C. (2006). *Organizational Urbanism – How to manage technological shock*. Sílabo Publishing.

Anunciação, P., & Zorrinho, C. (2006). *Urbanismo Organizacional, Como Gerir o Choque Tecnológico nas Empresas* (1st ed.). Edições Sílabo.

ANVISA. (2012). *Agência Nacional de Vigilância Sanitária*. Recuperado 18 de fevereiro de 2013, de Lista de Estatísticas website: http://portal.anvisa.gov.br/wps/portal/anvisa/anvisa/home/medicamentos/!ut/p/c4/04_SB8K8xLLM9MSSzPy8 xBz9CP0os3hnd0cPE3MfAwMDMydnA093Uz8z00B_A_cgQ_2CbEdFADghJT0!/?1dmy&urile=wcm%3Apath%3A/ anvisa+portal/anvisa/inicio/medicamentos/publicacao+medicamentos/lista+de+estatisticas+-+genericos

ANVISA. (2019). *Agência Nacional de Vigilância Sanitária*. Author.

Arbache, F. S. (2004). *Gestão de Logística, distribuição e trade marketing* (4th ed.). Editora FGV.

Arbex, M. A. (2005). O valor pedagógico dos jogos de empresa na aprendizagem de gestão de negócios. *Revista da FAE*, *8*(2), 9. https://scholar.google.com/citations?user=3Kc6gxMAAAAJ&hl=pt-BR&oi=sra

Aricak. (2008). Cyber bullying among Turkish adolescents. *CyberPsychology & Behavior, 11*(3), 253-261.

Arnaboldi, V., Conti, M., Passarella, A., & Pezzoni, F. (2012). Analysis of ego network structure in online social networks. In *2012 International Conference on Privacy, Security, Risk and Trust and 2012 International Conference on Social Computing* (pp. 31–40). IEEE. 10.1109/SocialCom-PASSAT.2012.41

Ashton, K. (2009). That 'internet of things' thing. *RFID Journal, 22*(7), 97-114.

Associates, M. (2019). *Manhattan Associates*. Retrieved from https://www.manh.com/

Assumpção, T. (2008). Systemic vision relates knowledge and intangible assets. *Fnq*. Available from: www.fnq.org.br/ site/ItemID=1032/369/default.aspx

Assumpção, T. (2008). *Visão sistêmica relaciona conhecimento e ativos intangíveis*. FNQ. Disponível em: www.fnq. org.br/site/ItemID=1032/369/default.aspx

AWS – Amazon Web Cloud services. (2020). *Free Tier for cloud computing services.* Available at https://aws.amazon.com/products/storage/?nc2=h_ql_prod_st

Axelos. (n.d.). Retrieved from https://www.axelos.com/: https://www.axelos.com/

Babar, S., Mahalle, P., Stango, A., Prasad, N., & Prasad, R. (2010). *Proposed security model and threat taxonomy for the Internet of Things (IoT).* Paper presented at the International Conference on Network Security and Applications. 10.1007/978-3-642-14478-3_42

Backstrom, L., Dwork, C., & Kleinberg, J. (2007). Wherefore art thou r3579x?: anonymized social networks, hidden patterns, and structural steganography. In *Proceedings of the 16th international conference on World Wide Web* (pp. 181–190). ACM. 10.1145/1242572.1242598

Bada, M., & Nurse, J. (2020). The Social and Psychological Impact of Cyber-Attacks. In V. Benson & J. McAlaney (Eds.), *Emerging Cyber Threats and Cognitive Vulnerabilities* (pp. 73–92). Academic Press. doi:10.1016/B978-0-12-816203-3.00004-6

Baganha, M., Marque, J., & Góis, P. (2002). O Sector da Construção Civil e Obras Públicas em Portugal: 1990-2000. *Oficina do Centro de Estudos Sociais,* (173), 1-39. Disponível em: 11, novembro, 2018, em: https://iconline.ipleiria.pt/bitstream/10400.8/1041/1/outras_publicações_2002.pdf

Bahia, D. S. (2019). *Pesquisa e desenvolvimento, capital de conhecimento e estrutura produtiva: Os efeitos do Programa de Subvenções Econômicas à inovação no Brasil (Tese de Doutorado em Economia).* Universidade Federal de Juiz de Fora.

Baldwin, J., & Gellatly, G. (2003). *Innovation strategies and performance in small firms.* E. Elgar. doi:10.4337/9781781009703

Balmisse, G. (2006). *Guide des Outils du Knowledge Management: Panorama, choix et mise en oeuvre.* Recuperado de https://www.leslivresblancs.fr/informatique/applications-pro/knowledge-management/livre-blanc/outils-du-km-panorama-choix-et-mise-en-oeuvre-62.html

Barañano, A. (2004). *Métodos e Técnicas de Investigação em Gestão, Manual de apoio à realização de trabalhos de investigação.* Edições Silabo.

Barbosa, D. B. (2011). O direito da inovação (2nd ed.). Rio de Janeiro: Lúmen Júris.

Barbosa, L., & Bangalore, S. (2011). Focusing on novelty: a crawling strategy to build diverse language models. *Proceedings of the 20th ACM international conference on Information and knowledge management,* 755–764. 10.1145/2063576.2063687

Barbosa, L., Bangalore, S., & Sridhar, V. K. R. (2011). Crawling back and forth: Using back and out links to locate bilingual sites. *Proceedings of the 5th International Joint Conference on Natural Language Processing,* 429–437.

Barbosa, L., & Freire, J. (2005). Searching for hidden-web databases. *Proceedings of the 8th ACM SIGMOD International Workshop on Web and Data-bases,* 1–6.

Barcante, L. C., & Beltrao, K. I. (2013). *40 years of Brazilian S&G-Analysis and Perspectives.* Paper presented at the Developments in Business Simulation and Experiential Learning: Proceedings of the Annual ABSEL conference, Oklahoma City. https://absel-ojs-ttu.tdl.org/absel/index.php/absel/article/view/54/52

Barreto, A. (2019). *Deep Web: Investigação no submundo da internet.* Brasport.

Becker & Mota. (n.d.). *Arbitration leaks: a segurança da informação no procedimento arbitral.* Available at https://www.jota.info/opiniao-e-analise/artigos/arbitration-leaks-a-seguranca-da-informacao-no-procedimento-arbitral-18042018

Beckmann, N., Kriegel, H. P., Schneider, R., & Seeger, B. (1990, May). The R*-tree: an efficient and robust access method for points and rectangles. In *Proceedings of the 1990 ACM SIGMOD international conference on Management of data* (pp. 322-331). 10.1145/93597.98741

Bell, D. (1973). *The Coming of Post-Industrial Society: A Venture in Social Forecasting.* New York, NY: Basic Books.

Bell, S. C., & Orzen, M. A. (2012). *Lean IT: Enabling and Sustaining Your Lean Transformation.* BP Trends.

Bender, Gruhl, Morimoto, & Lu. (1996). Techniques for data hiding. *IBM Systems Journal, 35*(3-4), 313-336.

Bennett & Brassard. (1984). Quantum cryptogramphy: Public key distribution and coin tossing. *Proceedings of IEEE international conference on computers, systems and signal processing, 1*, 175-179.

Bento. (n.d.). *A nova lei de proteção de dados no Brasil e o general data protection regulation da União Europeia* [The Brazilian New Data Protection Law and the General Data Protection Regulation from European Union]. Available at https://www.migalhas.com.br/dePeso/16,MI289555,11049-A+nova+lei+de+protecao+de+dados+no+Brasil+e+o+g eneral+data+protection

Berg, B. L. (2001). Focus group interviewing. In B. L. Berg (Ed.), *Qualitative research methods for the Social Sciences* (Vol. 4, pp. 111–132). Pearson.

Bessa, L. R. (2019). *Nova Lei do Cadastro Positivo.* Thomson Reuters.

Beth, S., David, N., & Burt, W. C. (2003). Supply Chain Challenges: Building Relationships. *Harvard Business Review.*

Bhagat, S., Cormode, G., Krishnamurthy, B., & Srivastava, D. (2009). Class-based graph anonymization for social network data. *Proceedings of the VLDB Endowment International Conference on Very Large Data Bases, 2*(1), 766–777. doi:10.14778/1687627.1687714

Bhardwaj, A. (2020). 5G for Military Communications. *Procedia Computer Science, 171*, 2665–2674. doi:10.1016/j.procs.2020.04.289

Bianchi, M., Casalino, N., Draoli, M., & Gambosi, G. (2012). *An innovative approach to the governance of E-government knowledge management systems. Information Systems: Crossroads for Organization, Management, Accounting and Engineering: ItAIS.* The Italian Association for Information Systems.

Bianchi, M., Casalino, N., Draoli, M., & Gambosi, G. (2013). *An innovative approach to the governance of e-government knowledge management systems. Information Systems: Crossroads for Organization, Management, Accounting and Engineering: ItAIS.* The Italian Association for Information Systems.

Bio-Manguinhos/Fiocruz. (2020). Recuperado 3 de setembro de 2020, de Bio-Manguinhos/Fiocruz ‖ Inovação em saúde ‖ Vacinas, reativos para diagnósticos e biofármacos website: https://www.bio.fiocruz.br/index.php/br/

Biometric. (2020). *Aadhaar's architect discusses what went into world's biggest biometric repository.* Retrieved Mar 18, from https://www.biometricupdate.com/202003/aadhaars-architect-discusses-what-went-into-worlds-biggest-biometric-repository

Bitencourt, C. C. (2004). A gestão de competências gerenciais e a contribuição da aprendizagem organizacional. *Revista de Administração de Empresas, 44*(1), 58–69. doi:10.1590/S0034-75902004000100004

Bkassiny, M., Li, Y., & Jayaweera, S. K. (2012). A survey on machine-learning techniques in cognitive radios. *IEEE Communications Surveys and Tutorials, 15*(3), 1136–1159. doi:10.1109/SURV.2012.100412.00017

Blank, S., & Dorf, B. (2012). *The Startup Owner's Manual: The Step-By-Step Guide for Building a Great Company.* K & S Ranch.

Blocki, J., Blum, A., Datta, A., & Sheffet, O. (2013). Differentially private data analysis of social networks via restricted sensitivity. In *Proceedings of the 4th conference on Innovations in Theoretical Computer Science* (pp. 87–96). ACM. 10.1145/2422436.2422449

Boni, V., Quaresma, J. (2005). Aprendendo a entrevistar: como fazer entrevistas em Ciências Sociais. *Revista Eletrónica dos Pós-Graduandos em Sociologia Política da UFSC, 2*(1), 68-80.

Bonotto, G., & Felicetti, V. L. (2014). Habilidades e competências na prática docente: perspectivas a partir de situações-problema. *Educação por escrito, 5*(1), 17-29. doi:10.15448/2179-8435.2014.1.14919

Borges, D. B. (2015). *A subvenção econômica como instrumento de fomento à cooperação tecnológica: uma análise sob a perspectiva do setor empresarial* (Dissertação de Mestrado em Ciências da Administração) Universidade do Estado de Santa Catarina, Florianópolis.

Borges, D. B., & Hoffman, M. G. (2017). A subvenção econômica como instrumento de fomento à inovação: Análise sob a perspectiva de empresas de TIC da Grande Florianópolis. *Revista Brasileira de Gestão e Inovação, 5*(1), 50–73. doi:10.18226/23190639.v5n1.03

Borghi, V. (2006). Tra cittadini and istituzioni. Riflessioni sull'introduzione di dispositivi partecipativi nelle pratiche istituzionali locali. In *Rivista delle politiche sociali, n°2*. Ediesse.

Borghi, V. (2006). Tra cittadini e istituzioni. Riflessioni sull'introduzione di dispositivi partecipativi nelle pratiche istituzionali locali. In *Rivista delle politiche sociali, n°2*. Ediesse.

Bounfour, A. (2016). *Digital Futures, Digital Transformation, From Lean Production to Acceluction*. Academic Press.

Boyd, D., & Crawford, K. (2012). Critical questions for big data: Provocations for a cultural, technological, and scholarly phenomenon. *Information Communication and Society, 15*(5), 662–679. doi:10.1080/1369118X.2012.678878

Brandão, S. M., & Bruno-Faria, M. F. (2013). Inovação no setor público: análise de produção científica em periódicos nacionais e internacionais da área de administração. *Revista de Administração Pública, 47*(1), 227-248.

Brandão, S. M., & Bruno-Faria, M. F. (2017). Barreiras à inovação em gestão em organizações públicas do governo federal brasileiro: análise da percepção de dirigentes. In *Inovação no setor público: teoria, tendências e casos no Brasil* (pp. 145–164). Enap/Ipea.

Brasil, I. I. A. (2019 junho). *Três linhas de defesa*. https://global.theiia.org/translations/PublicDocuments/3LOD-IIA-Exposure-Document-Portuguese.pdf

Brasil, Presidência da República. *Lei Geral de Proteção de Dados Pessoais (LGPD)—13709.*, (2018).

Brasil. (1942). *Decreto-Lei nº 4.048, de 22 de janeiro de 1942*. Cria o Serviço Nacional de Aprendizagem dos Industriários (SENAI). https://www2.camara.leg.br/legin/fed/declei/1940-1949/decreto-lei-4048-22-janeiro-1942-414390-publicacaooriginal-1-pe.html

Brasil. (2008). *Decreto nº 6.635, de 5 de novembro de 2008*. Altera e acresce dispositivos ao Regimento do Serviço Nacional de Aprendizagem Industrial - SENAI, aprovado pelo Decreto no 494, de 10 de janeiro de 1962. http://www.planalto.gov.br/ccivil_03/_Ato2007-2010/2008/Decreto/D6635.htm

Brasil. (2009). *Decreto nº 6.938, de 13 de agosto de 2009*. Aprova a Estrutura Regimental e o Quadro Demonstrativo dos Cargos em Comissão e das Funções de Confiança do Ministério da Ciência, Tecnologia, Inovações e Comunicações, remaneja cargos em comissão e funções de confiança, transforma cargos em comissão do Grupo-Direção e Assessoramento Superiores - DAS e substitui cargos em comissão do Grupo-Direção e Assessoramento Superiores - DAS por Funções Comissionadas do Poder Executivo - FCPE. http://www.planalto.gov.br/ccivil_03/_Ato2019-2022/2019/Decreto/D9677.htm#art9

Brasil. (2018). *Decreto nº 9.282, de 07 de fevereiro de 2018*. Altera o Decreto nº 8.889, de 26 de outubro de 2016, que aprova a Estrutura Regimental e o Quadro Demonstrativo dos Cargos em Comissão e das Funções de Confiança da Casa Civil da Presidência da República, e o Decreto nº 8.955, de 11 de janeiro de 2017, que aprova a Estrutura Regimental e o Quadro Demonstrativo dos Cargos em Comissão e das Funções de Confiança do Instituto Nacional de Colonização e Reforma Agrária - INCRA, e remaneja cargos em comissão e funções de confiança. http://www.planalto.gov.br/CCIVIL_03/_Ato2015-2018/2018/Decreto/D9282.htm

Brasil. (2018). *Lei 13.709 de 14 de agosto de 2018*. Available at http://www.planalto.gov.br/ccivil_03/_ato2015-2018/2018/Lei/L13709.htm

Brasil. (2018). *Lei Geral de Proteção de Dados Pessoais (LGPD)*. Retrieved from http://www.planalto.gov.br/ccivil_03/_ato2015-2018/2018/lei/L13709.htm

Brasil. (2019). *Currículo do Curso de Aperfeiçoamento de Intendência para Oficiais (CAIO)*. Rio de Janeiro, RJ: Marinha do Brasil. Recuperado em 17 agosto, 2019, de https://www.ead.marinha.mil.br/moodle/pluginfile.php/78753/mod_resource/content/1/Of10-93-2019-DEnsM-AnA-Curriculo-CAIO-063.2%281%29.pdf

Brasil. Anatel. (2020, Março 3). *Brasil registra 228,64 milhões de linhas móveis ativas em maio de 2019*. https://www.anatel.gov.br/institucional/noticias-destaque/2310-brasil-registra-228-64-milhoes-de-linhas-moveis-ativas-em-maio-de-2019

Brasil. Ministério da Saúde. Agência Nacional de Vigilância Sanitária. *RESOLUÇÃO - RDC Nº 17, DE 16 DE ABRIL DE 2010.*, (2010).

Brasil. MS., A. *Boas Práticas de Fabricação—RDC Nº 301, DE 21 DE AGOSTO DE 2019.*, Pub. L. No. RDC Nº 301 (2019).

Brazil. (n.d.a). *Constituição Federal*. Available at: http://www.planalto.gov.br/ccivil_03/constituicao/constituicao.htm

Brazil. (n.d.b). *Lei Geral de Proteção de Dados*. Available at: http://www.planalto.gov.br/ccivil_03/_ato2015-2018/2018/lei/L13709.htm

Brazil. (n.d.c). *Lei 8.078 – Código de Defesa do Consumidor*. Available at: http://www.planalto.gov.br/ccivil_03/leis/l8078.htm

Brazil. (n.d.d). *Lei 12.965 - Marco Civil da Internet*. Available at: http://www.planalto.gov.br/ccivil_03/_ato2011-2014/2014/lei/l12965.htm

Bronk, C., Krüger, J., Nickolay, B., & Gaycken, S. (2013). *The secure information society: ethical, legal and political challenges*. Spinger.

Bughin & Manyika. (2012). https://www.mckinsey.com/

Burlamaqui, L. (2011), Knowledge Governance: An Analytical Approach and its Policy Implications. In Knowledge Governance -Reasserting the Public Interest. Anthem Press.

Burlamaqui, L. (2011). Knowledge Governance: An Analytical Approach and its Policy Implications. In Knowledge Governance-Reasserting the Public Interest. Anthem Press.

Burlamaqui, L. (2010). *Knowledge Governance Innovation and Development. Political Economics Magazine* (Vol. 30). Printed.

Burlamaqui, L. (2010). *Knowledge Governance Innovation and Development. Revista de Economia Política* (Vol. 30). Impresso.

Burlamaqui, L., Castro, A. C., & Kattel, R. (2011). *Knowledge Governance –Reasserting the Public Interest.* Anthem Press.

Burnes, B. (2017). *Managing Change* (7th ed.). Pearson Education Limited.

Buse, K., & Waxman, A. (2001). Public-private health partnerships: A strategy for WHO. *Bulletin of the World Health Organization, 79*(8), 748–754. doi:10.1590/S0042-96862001000800011 PMID:11545332

BV. O. S. (2015). *Optimus Sorter.* Retrieved 2020, from http://www.optimussorters.com/en/sorters/optisorter-horizontal

Byrd, T.A., Markland, R.E., Karwan, K.R., & Philipoom, P.R. (1966). *An object-oriented rule-based design structure for a maintenance management system.* Academic Press.

Cabrita, R. (2004). Intellectual capital: the new wealth of organizations. *Digital Magazine of the Banking Training Institute.* Available at: www.ifb.pt/publicacoes/info_57/artigo03_57.htm

Cabrita, R. (2004). *O capital intelectual: a nova riqueza das organizações. Revista Digital do Instituto de Formação Bancária.* European Distance Education Network. Disponível em: www.ifb.pt/publicacoes/info_57/artigo03_57.htm

Cadbury, A. (1992). *The Financial Aspects of Corporate Governance. The Committee on the Financial Aspects of Corporate Governance and Gee and Co. Ltd.* Committee on the Financial Aspects of Corporate Governance.

Cadwalladr, C., & Graham-Harrison, E. (2018). Revealed: 50 million Facebook profiles harvested for Cambridge Analytica in major data breach. *The Guardian.*

Caldeira, J. (2012). *100 Indicadores da Gestão, Key Performance Indicators.* Lisboa: Conjuntura Actual Editora, S.A.

Campan, A., & Truta, T. M. (2008). Data and structural k-anonymity in social networks. In *International Workshop on Privacy, Security, and Trust in KDD* (pp. 33–54). Springer.

Campos, A. (2013). *Competitividade da Construção* (Tese de Mestrado, Escola de Engenharia, Universidade do Minho). Disponível em: 10, novembro, 2018, em: https://repositorium.sdum.uminho.pt/bitstream/1822/36278/1/Dissertação%20-%20José%20Silva%20-%202014.pdf

Candès, E. J., Li, X., Ma, Y., & Wright, J. (2011). Robust principal component analysis? [JACM]. *Journal of the Association for Computing Machinery, 58*(3), 1–37. doi:10.1145/1970392.1970395

Capurro, R. (2010). Desafíos téoricos y prácticos de la ética intercultural de la información. In Conferencia inaugural en el I Simpósio Brasileiro de Ética da Informação, João Pessoa (Vol. 18). Academic Press.

Cardoso, D. M. (2015). *Criminal compliance na perspectiva da lei de lavagem de dinheiro.* LiberArs.

Carrasqueira, L. (2018). Três perguntas a.... *Indústria Revista de Empresários e Negócios, 108*, 12-13. Disponível em: 10, novembro, 2018, em: http://cip.org.pt/wp-content/uploads/2018/09/IND_115_LRv2.pdf

Carr, N. (2003). IT does not matter anymore. *Harvard Business Review*, (5), 41–49. PMID:12747161

Cartlidge, A., Hanna, A., Rudd, C., Macfarlane, I., Windebank, J., & Rance, S. (2007). *An Introductory overview of ITIL.* The UK Chapter of the itSMF.

Carvalho, J. C. (2017). *Logística e Gestão da Cadeia de Abastecimento.* Edições Sílabo.

Carver, J. (2001). *On Board Leadership. Jossey-Bass Wiley.*

Castells, M. (1996). *The Rise of the Network society, the Information Age: Economy, society and Culture* (Vol. 1). Blackwell Publishers.

Castells, M. (2000). The Rise of the Network Society: Economy. *Society and Culture*, 1.

Cavalcante, P., & Camões, M. R. S. (2017). *Public Innovation in Brazil: an overview of its types, results and drivers.* Ipea.

Cavalcante, P., & Cunha, B. Q. (2017). É preciso inovar no governo, mas por quê? In *Cavalcante, P. et al. (Orgs.). Inovação no setor público: teoria, tendências e casos no Brasil* (pp. 15–32). Enap/Ipea.

Cellebrite. (2019). *Cellebrite industry trend survey: Law enforcement.* https://www.cellebrite.com/en/insights/industry-survey/. *Trend*

Cellebrite. (2020). *Annual digital intelligence benchmark report: Law enforcement.* https://www.cellebrite.com/en/insights/industry-report/

Cellebrite. (n.d.). *Encontre o caminho para o insight por meio de montanhas de dados.* https://www.cellebrite.com/pt/analytics-2/

CGEE. (2009). Os novos instrumentos de apoio à inovação: uma avaliação inicial. Brasília: Autores.

Chandramouli & Memon. (2001). Analysis of LSB based image steganography techniques. *Proceedings on International Conference on Image Processing, 3,* 1019-1022.

Chang, Y., Li, W., & Yang, Z. (2017). *Network intrusion detection based on random forest and support vector machine.* Paper presented at the 2017 IEEE international conference on computational science and engineering (CSE) and IEEE international conference on embedded and ubiquitous computing (EUC). 10.1109/CSE-EUC.2017.118

Chan, L. (2002). Why Haven't we mastered alignment? The importance of the informal organization structure. *MIS Quarterly Executive, 1*(2), 97–112.

Chao, C. H. (2019). Ethics Issues in Artificial Intelligence. *2019 International Conference on Technologies and Applications of Artiðcial Intelligence (TAAI) Technologies and Applications of Artiðcial Intelligence (TAAI), 2019 International Conference on.*

Chen, L., & Fong, P. S. W. (2012). Revealing Performance Heterogeneity Through Knowledge Management Maturity Evaluation: A Capability-Based Approach. *Expert Systems with Applications, 39*(18), 13523–13539. doi:10.1016/j.eswa.2012.07.005

Chen, L., & Fong, P. S. W. (2013). Visualizing Evolution of Knowledge Management Capability in Construction Firms. *Journal of Construction Engineering and Management, 139*(7), 839–851. doi:10.1061/(ASCE)CO.1943-7862.0000649

Choo, C. W. (1998). *The knowing organization, how organizations use information to construct meaning, create knowledge and make decisions.* Oxford University Press.

Choo, C. W. (2008). *Social use of information in organizational groups, information management: Setting the scene* (A. Huizing & E. J. De Vries, Eds.). Elsevier.

Ciborra, C. (1997). From Profundis? Deconstructing the Concept of Strategic Alignment. *Scandinavian Journal of Information Systems, 9*(1), 67–82.

Cidral, A. (2003). *Metodologia de aprendizagem vivencial para o desenvolvimento de competências para o gerenciamento de projetos de implementação de sistemas de informação* (Doutorado). Universidade Federal de Santa Catarina - UFSC, Florianópolis. https://repositorio.ufsc.br/xmlui/handle/123456789/8540

Claranet. (2018). *Beyond Digital Transformation, Reality check for European IT and Digital leaders* (Claranet research report 2018). Disponível em: 15, dezembro, 2018, em: https://br.claranet.com/sites/all/assets/br/Claranet%20research%20report%202018_2.pdf

Clough, P., & Nutbrown, C. (2007). *A student's guide to Methodology* (2nd ed.). Sage Publications Ltd.

Collina, M., Bartolucci, M., Vanelli-Coralli, A., & Corazza, G. E. (2014). Internet of Things application layer protocol analysis over error and delay prone links. *2014 7th Advanced Satellite Multimedia Systems Conference and the 13th Signal Processing for Space Communications Workshop (ASMS/SPSC)*, 398-404. doi: 10.1109/ASMS-SPSC.2014.6934573

Conjur. (2016, Setembro 14). *Suporte a litígios: Tecnologia serve como aliada na prevenção e no combate à corrupção.* https://www.conjur.com.br/2016-set-14/suporte-litigios-tecnologia-serve-aliada-prevencao-combate-corrupcao#1

Consultoria, I. (n.d.). Fundamentos sobre classificadores ("sorters"). *Revista intraLOGÍSTICA.* Retrieved 2020, from https://www.imam.com.br/consultoria/artigo/pdf/fundamentos_sobre_classificadores_sorters.pdf

Conzon, D., Bolognesi, T., Brizzi, P., Lotito, A., Tomasi, R., & Spirito, M. A. (2012). *The virtus middleware: An xmpp based architecture for secure iot communications.* Paper presented at the 2012 21st International Conference on Computer Communications and Networks (ICCCN). 10.1109/ICCCN.2012.6289309

Cooper, K. A. (2015). *Security for the Internet of Things.* Academic Press.

Correia, B. (2018). Três perguntas a.... *Indústria Revista de Empresários e Negócios, 108*, 12-13. Disponível em: 10, novembro, 2018, em: http://cip.org.pt/wp-content/uploads/2018/05/IND_115_LR.pdf

Costa, A. C., Szapiro, M., & Cassiolato, J. E. (2013). Análise da operação do instrumento de subvenção econômica à inovação no Brasil. Conferência Internacional LALICS.

Cots, M., & Oliveira, R. (2019). *Lei Geral de Proteção de Dados Pessoais Comentada.* Thomson Reuters.

Crisp, M. (Ed.). (1991). Rate Your Skills as a Manager. Crisp Publications.

Cummins, R. A., & Gullone, E. (2000). Why we should not use 5-point Likert scales: The case for subjective quality of life measurement. *Proceedings, second international conference on quality of life in cities.* https://www.researchgate.net/file.PostFileLoader.html?id=586e1b0bed99e1fee15524a1&assetKey=AS%3A447110639296516%401483610891715

Cunha, B. Q. (2017). Uma análise da construção da agenda de inovação no setor público a partir de experiências internacionais precursoras. In *Inovação no setor público: teoria, tendências e casos no Brasil.* Enap/Ipea.

Cunha, M. A., Przeybilovicz, E., Macaya, J. F. M., & Burgos, F. (2016). *Smart cities: Transformação Digital de cidades* (Vol. 16). Centro de Estudos em Administração Pública e Governo - CEAPG. doi:10.1016/S0264-2751(98)00050-X

Curty, R. G. (2005). *O Fluxo Da Informação Tecnológica No Projeto De Produtos Em Indústrias De Alimentos.* 249 F. Dissertação (Mestrado Em Ciência Da Informação) –Programa De Pós-Graduação Em Ciência Da Informação, Universidade Federal De Santa Catarina. Florianópolis.

Curty, R. G. (2005). *The Flow of Technological Information in the Product Project In Food Industries* (Master's thesis). Graduate Program in Information Science, Federal University of Santa Catarina. Florianopolis.

Cutler, D. R., Edwards, T. C. Jr, Beard, K. H., Cutler, A., Hess, K. T., Gibson, J., & Lawler, J. J. (2007). Random forests for classification in ecology. *Ecology, 88*(11), 2783–2792. doi:10.1890/07-0539.1 PMID:18051647

CyberInsecurity. A New Protocol to Counter Cyberattacks in International Arbitration. (n.d.). Available at https://www.cpradr.org/news-publications/articles/2018-07-05-cyberinsecurity-a-new-protocol-to-counter-cyberattacks-in-international-arbitration

da Silva, J. C. B. L. (2007). Definição dos objetivos para um jogo de guerra. *Revista da Escola de Guerra Naval, 10*, 36. https://revista.egn.mar.mil.br/index.php/revistadaegn/article/view/422

Dal Mas, F., Piccolo, D., Cobianchi, L., Edvinsson, L., Presch, G., Massaro, M., & Skrap, M. (2019). The effects of Artificial Intelligence, Robotics, and Industry 4.0 technologies. Insights from the Healthcare Sector. In *Proceedings of the first European Conference on the impact of Artificial Intelligence and Robotics*. Academic Conferences and Publishing International Limited.

Dallasega, P., Rauch, E., & Linder, C. (2018). Industry 4.0 as an enabler of proximity for construction supply chains: A systematic literature review. *Computers in Industry, 99*, 205–225.

Danish Data Protection Act. (2018). *Law n. 502 (English version), 2018*. Retrieved from https://www.datatilsynet.dk/media/7753/danish-data-protection-act.pdf

Davenport, T., & Westerman, G. (2018). *Why So Many High-Profile Digital Transformations Fail*. Harvard Business Review. https://hbr.org/2018/03/why-so-many-high-profile-digital-transformations-fail

Davenport, T. (2014). *Big data @ work: Dispelling the myths, uncovering opportunities*. Harvard Press Review. doi:10.15358/9783800648153

Davenport, T. H., & Prusak, L. (1997). *Information Ecology: Mastering The information and Knowledge Environment*. Oxford UniversityPress.

Davenport, T., Guha, A., Grewal, D., & Bressgott, T. (2020). How artificial intelligence will change the future of marketing. *Journal of the Academy of Marketing Science, 48*(1), 24–42. doi:10.100711747-019-00696-0

Davenport, T., & Harris, J. (2007). *Competição Analítica: Vencendo Através da Nova Ciência*. Elsevier.

Day, W. Y., Li, N., & Lyu, M. (2016). Publishing graph degree distribution with node differential privacy. In *Proceedings of the 2016 International Conference on Management of Data* (pp. 123–138). ACM. 10.1145/2882903.2926745

De Hert, P., & Papakonstantinou, V. (2016). The new General Data Protection Regulation: Still a sound system for the protection of individuals? *Computer Law & Security Review, 32*(2), 179–194. doi:10.1016/j.clsr.2016.02.006

de Ven, A. V., & Hargrave, T. (2000). *Social*. Technical, and Institutional Change.

Declaração Universal de Direitos Humanos. (n.d.). Available at: https://nacoesunidas.org/wp-content/uploads/2018/10/DUDH.pdf

Deeksha, J. (2017). *Revenge porn drives DU student to suicide: Hers's what you need to do online and at the police station to ensure abscene pics of you don't go viral*. Available on:www.edexlive.com/live-story/2017/apr/13/the-dark-net-and-its-crimes-329.html

Defense News. (2016). *Chinese Businessman Pleads Guilty of Spying on F-35 and F-22*. Available at https://www.defensenews.com/breaking-news/2016/03/24/chinese-businessman-pleads-guilty-of-spying-on-f-35-and-f-22/

Del Giudice, M. (2016). Discovering the Internet of Things (IoT) within the business process management: A literature review on technological revitalization. *Business Process Management Journal, 22*(2), 263–270. doi:10.1108/BPMJ-12-2015-0173

Deloitte. (2017). *Five questions about applying analytics to risk management.* Available at https://www2.deloitte.com/content/dam/Deloitte/au/Documents/risk/deloitte-au-risk-risk-angles-applying-analyticsrisk- management-250215.pdf

Deloitte. (2018, Dezembro). *Plano Estratégico de Inovação e Competitividade 2030 para o Setor AEC.* 7º Fórum Estratégico PTPC, Lisboa.

Dias, S., Santos, L., & Amaral, L. (2003). *Portuguese Local E-Government.* ICEIS.

Din, I. U., Guizani, M., Kim, B.-S., Hassan, S., & Khan, M. K. (2018). Trust management techniques for the Internet of Things: A survey. *IEEE Access: Practical Innovations, Open Solutions, 7,* 29763–29787. doi:10.1109/ACCESS.2018.2880838

Donald, B. J., Closs, D. J., Cooper, M. B., & Bowersox, J. C. (2013). *Supply Chain Logistics Management* (4th ed.). The McGraw-Hill Global Education Holdings, LLC.

Donaldson, A., & Walker, P. (2004). Information Governance – a view from the NHS. *International Journal of Medical Informatics, 73*(3), 281–284. doi:10.1016/j.ijmedinf.2003.11.009 PMID:15066559

Doneda, D. (2019). *Da Privacidade à Proteção de Dados Pessoais – Elementos de Formação da Lei Geral de Proteção de Dados.* Thomson Reuters.

Dorai, R., & Kannan, V. (2011). SQL injection-database attack revolution and prevention. *J. Int'l Com. L. & Tech., 6,* 224.

Doteveryone. (2018). *People, Power and Technology.* The 2018 Digital Attitudes Report. Retrieved Feb 18, from https://www.doteveryone.org.uk/report/digital-attitudes/

Drahos, P. (2010). The Global Governance of Knowledge: Patent Offices and Their Clients. Academic Press.

Drahos, P. (2010). The Global Governance of Knowledge: Patent Offices and Their Clients. The Global Governance of Knowledge: Patent Offices and Their Clients.

Drath, R., & Horch, A. (2014). Industrie 4.0 – hit or hype? *IEEE Industrial Electronics Magazine, 8*(2), 56–58.

Drci. (n.d.). *Departamento de Recuperação de Ativos e Cooperação Jurídica Internacional.* Ministério da Justiça e Segurança Pública. https://www.justica.gov.br/Acesso/institucional/sumario/quemequem/departamento-de-recuperacao-de-ativos-e-cooperacao-juridica-internacional

Duan, Y., Wang, J., Kam, M., & Canny, J. (2005). Privacy preserving link analysis on dynamic weighted graph. *Computational & Mathematical Organization Theory, 11*(2), 141–159. doi:10.100710588-005-3941-2

Dutch General Data Protection Regulation Implementation Act. (2018). Retrieved from https://zoek.officielebekendmakingen.nl/stb-2018-144.html

Dvir, A., & Buttyan, L. (2011). *VeRA-version number and rank authentication in RPL.* Paper presented at the 2011 IEEE Eighth International Conference on Mobile Ad-Hoc and Sensor Systems. 10.1109/MASS.2011.76

Dwivedi, Y. K., Hughes, L., Ismagilova, E., Aarts, G., Coombs, C., Crick, T., Duan, Y., Dwivedi, R., Edwards, J., Eirug, A., Galanos, V., Ilavarasan, P. V., Janssen, M., Jones, P., Kar, A. K., Kizgin, H., Kronemann, B., Lal, B., Lucini, B., ... Williams, M. D. (2019). Artificial Intelligence (AI): Multidisciplinary perspectives on emerging challenges, opportunities, and agenda for research, practice and policy. *International Journal of Information Management,* 101994. doi:10.1016/j.ijinfomgt.2019.08.002

Dwork, C. (2006). Differential privacy. automata, languages and programming. *33rd International Colloquium on Automata, Languages and Programming JUL,* 10–14.

Dwork, C., McSherry, F., Nissim, K., & Smith, A. (2006). Calibrating noise to sensitivity in private data analysis. TCC, 3876, 265–284. doi:10.1007/11681878_14

Dwork, C. (2008). Differential privacy: A survey of results. In *International Conference on Theory and Applications of Models of Computation* (pp. 1–19). Springer.

Dwork, C., & Smith, A. (2010). Differential privacy for statistics: What we know and what we want to learn. *Journal of Privacy and Confidentiality, 1*(2), 2. doi:10.29012/jpc.v1i2.570

Earl, M. J. (1989). *Management Strategies for Information Technology.* Prentice Hall.

Echelmeyer, W., Kirchheim, A., & Wellbrock, E. (2008). International Conference on Automation and Logistics. *Robotics-Logistics: Challenges for Automation of Logistic Processes.*

Economist Intelligence Unit. (2008). *The Future of enterprise information Governance.* The Economist Intelligence Unit Limited.

Elder-Vass, D. (2015, Summer). The Moral Economy of Digital Gifts. *International Journal of Social Quality, 5*(1), 35–50.

Elder-Vass, D. (2018). Moral economies of the digital. *European Journal of Social Theory, 21*(2), 141–147.

Emami-Naeini, P., Dixon, H., Agarwal, Y., & Cranor, L. F. (2019). Exploring how privacy and security factor into IoT device purchase behavior. *Proceedings of the 2019 CHI Conference on Human Factors in Computing Systems.* 10.1145/3290605.3300764

Embalagem, E.-S. (2020). *Envolvimento com Filme Estirável.* Retrieved 2020, from https://www.embalcer.pt/pt/Categorias/Envolvimento-com-Filme-Estiravel

Enccla. (n.d.). *Últimas notícias.* http://enccla.camara.leg.br/

Enrique Chaux, M. (2016). Effects of the cyberbullying prevention program media heroes(Medienhelden) on Traditional Bullying. *Wiley Periodicals,Inc,Volume, 42*(2), 157–165.

Erevelles, S., Fukawa, N., & Swayne, L. (2016). Big Data consumer analytics and the transformation of marketing. *Journal of Business Research, 69*(2), 897–904. doi:10.1016/j.jbusres.2015.07.001

Estadão. (n.d.). *Dados de 200 mil offshores do Panama Papers serão publicados.* Estadão. https://politica.estadao.com.br/noticias/panama-papers,dados-de-200-mil-offshores-dopanama-papers-serao-publicados,10000049693

Estrela, S. (2014). *A Gestão da Informação na Tomada de Decisão das PME da Região Centro um estudo exploratório e de multicasos no âmbito da Ciência da Informação (Tese de Mestrado).* Faculdade de Letras da Universidade de Coimbra.

Etzkowitz, H., & Leydesdorff, L. (1996). The Triple Helix: University, Industry, Government Relations: A Laboratory for Knowledge Based Economic Development. The Triple Helix of University, Industry, and Government Relations: The Future Location of Research Conference.

Etzkowitz, H., & Zhou, C. (2017). Hélice Tríplice: Inovação e empreendedorismo universidade-indústria-governo. *Estudos Avançados, 31*(90), 23–48. doi:10.15900103-40142017.3190003

European Commission. (2013). Protection of Undisclosed Know-how and Business Information (Trade Secrets) Against their Unlawful Acquisition, Use and Disclosure. Brussels: COM (2013) 813.

European Commission. (2019). *Digital Economy.* Retrieved on September, 2020, from https://ec.europa.eu/jrc/en/research-topic/digital-economy

European Commission. (2019). *REGIOSTARS, Guide for applicants*. Retrieved Mar 21, from https://ec.europa.eu/regional_policy/sources/projects/regiostars/doc/regiostars/2019/regiostars2019_guide_applicants_en.pdf

European Commission. (2020). *Shaping Europe`s digital future, Economy & Policy, Dc Connect*. Retrieved Mar 22, from https://ec.europa.eu/digital-single-market/en/economy-society

European Defense Agency. (2019). *Inside the Engine Room Checking the EU's Defense Mechanics*. Available at https://eda.europa.eu/docs/default-source/eda-magazine/final-full-magazine-edm18-(pdf).pdf

European Parliament. (2016). *General Data Protection Regulation*. Retrieved from https://gdpr-info.eu/

European Union. (n.d.). *EU General Data Protection Regulation (GDPR)*. Available at https://eugdpr.org/

Europol. (2020). *European Cybercrime Centre - EC3*. Available at https://www.europol.europa.eu/about-europol/european-cybercrime-centre-ec3

Evans, D. (2011). *Internet of things: How the next Internet evolution changes everything*. Cisco Computers report. Available at https://www.cisco.com/c/dam/en_us/about/ac79/docs/innov/IoT_IBSG_0411FINAL.pdf

Evfimievski, A., Gehrke, J., & Srikant, R. (2003). Limiting privacy breaches in privacy preserving data mining. In *Proceedings of the twenty-second ACM SIGMODSIGACT-SIGART symposium on Principles of database systems* (pp. 211–222). ACM. 10.1145/773153.773174

Expresso. (2019). *Russia ponders 'temporarily disconnecting' from the world Internet*. Retrieved Mar 19, from https://expresso.pt/internacional/2019-02-11-Russia-pondera-desligar-se-temporariamente-da-Internet-mundial

Fama, E. F., & Jensen, M. C. (1983). Separation of ownership and control. *The Journal of Law & Economics*, 26(2), 1983. doi:10.1086/467037

Fanuc. (n.d.). *Robôs industriais*. Retrieved 2020, from https://www.fanuc.eu/pt/pt/rob%C3%B4s

Farris, I., Taleb, T., Khettab, Y., & Song, J. (2018). A survey on emerging SDN and NFV security mechanisms for IoT systems. *IEEE Communications Surveys and Tutorials*, 21(1), 812–837. doi:10.1109/COMST.2018.2862350

Fatf-Gafi. (n.d.). *GAFI (FATF)*. Comissão de Valores Mobiliários. http://www.cvm.gov.br/menu/internacional/organizacoes/gafi.html

FBI – Federal Bureau of Investigation. (2014). *Combating Economic Espionage and Trade Secret Theft*. Retrieved on September, 2020, from https://www.fbi.gov/news/testimony/combating-economic-espionage-and-trade-secret-theft

Federação Portuguesa da Indústria da Construção e Obras Públicas. (2018). *Construção cresce 3,5% em 2018*. Disponível em: 10, fevereiro, 2019, em: http://www.fepicop.pt/index.php?id=22

Fernandes. (2017). *Curso de Direito Constitucional* (9th ed.). Salvador: JusPOIVM.

Fernández-Caramés, T. M., & Fraga-Lamas, P. (2018). A Review on the Use of Blockchain for the Internet of Things. *IEEE Access: Practical Innovations, Open Solutions*, 6, 32979–33001. doi:10.1109/ACCESS.2018.2842685

Ferreira, A., & Martinez, L. (2008). *Manual de Diagnóstico e Mudança Organizacional* (1st ed.). Editora RH.

Ferris, K. (2018, October 8). Built on ITIL. *Digital Transformation*.

Fgv. (n.d.a). *Cadernos*. https://fgvprojetos.fgv.br/publicacao/cadernos-fgv-projetos-no27-lei-anticorrupcao-transparencia-e-boas-praticas

Fgv. (n.d.b). Lei Anticorrupção: Transparência e Boas Práticas [Versão Eletrônica]. *Cadernos FGV Projetos*, n. 27. Ibge. *Pesquisa nacional por amostra de domicílios contínua*. https://biblioteca.ibge.gov.br/visualizacao/livros/liv101631_informativo.pdf

Fields, B., Jacobson, K., Rhodes, C., d'Inverno, M., Sandler, M., & Casey, M. (2011). Analysis and exploitation of musician social networks for recommendation and discovery. *IEEE Transactions on Multimedia*, *13*(4), 674–686. doi:10.1109/TMM.2011.2111365

Filho. (n.d.). *A diretiva europeia sobre proteção de dados pessoais - uma análise de seus Aspectos Gerais*. Available at: http://www.lex.com.br/doutrina_24316822_A_DIRETIVA_EUROPEIA_SOBRE_PROTECAO_DE_DADOS_PESSOAIS__UMA_ANALISE_DE_SEUS_ASPECTOS_GERAIS.aspx

FINEP - Financiadora de Estudos e Projetos. (2010). *Manual do Programa de Subvenção Econômica à Inovação Nacional*. Academic Press.

Finland Data Protection Act - Tietosuojalaki. (2018). Retrieved from https://finlex.fi/fi/laki/ajantasa/2018/20181050

Floridi, L. (2003). On the Intrinsic Value of Information Objects and the Infosphere. *Ethics and Information Technology*, *4*(4), 287–304.

Floridi, L. (2009). Network Ethics: Information and Business Ethics in a Networked Society. *Journal of Business Ethics*, *90*, 649–659.

Floridi, L., & Sanders, J. W. (2004). On the Morality of Artiðcial Agents. *Minds and Machines*, *14*(3), 349–379.

Fong, P. S. W., & Chen, L. (2012). Governance Of Learning Mechanisms: Evidence From Construction Firms. *Journal of Construction Engineering and Management*, *138*(9), 1053–1064. doi:10.1061/(ASCE)CO.1943-7862.0000521

Ford, C. (2020). *U.S. Department of State: Responding to Modern Cyber Threats with Diplomacy and Deterrence*. Retrieved on November, 2020, from https://www.state.gov/responding-to-modern-cyber-threats-with-diplomacy-and-deterrence/

Fortes, P. A. de C., & Ribeiro, H. (2014). Saúde Global em tempos de globalização. *Saúde e Sociedade*, *23*(2), 366–375. doi:10.1590/S0104-12902014000200002

Forum, W. E. (2015, Setembro). *Deep Shift Technology Tipping Points and Societal Impact*. Retrieved from http://www3.weforum.org/docs/WEF_GAC15_Technological_Tipping_Points_report_2015.pdf

Foss, K., & Foss, N.J. (2009). Managerial Authority When Knowledge Is Distributed: A Knowledge Governance Perspective. *Knowledge Governance: Processes and perspectives*.

Foss, N. J., Husted, K., Michailova, S., & Pedersen, T. (2003). *Governing knowledge Processes: Theoretical Foundations and Research Opportunities*. Working paper No. 1, Center for Knowledge Governance, Copenhagen Business School.

Foss, N. J., Husted, K., Michailova, S., & Pedersen, T. (2003). *Governing knowledge Processes: Theoretical Foundations And Research Opportunities*. Working paper No. 1, Center for Knowledge Governance, Copenhagen Business School.

Foss, N.J. (2005). *The Knowledge Governance Approach*. Academic Press.

Foss, N.J., & Klein, P.G. (2008). The Theory of The Firm and Its Critics: A Stocktaking and Assessment. *New Institutional Economics: A Guidebook*.

Foss, N.J., & Klein, P.G., (2008). The Theory of The Firm and Its Critics: A Stocktaking And Assessment. *New Institutional Economics: A Guidebook*.

Foss, N.J., & Michailova, S. (2009). Knowledge Governance: What Have We Learned? And Where Are We Heading? *Knowledge Governance: Processes and perspectives.*

Foss, N. J. (2007). The Emerging Knowledge Governance Approach: Challenges And Characteristics. *Organization, 14*(1), 29–52. doi:10.1177/1350508407071859

Frazão, A. (2019). Capítulo 4 – Objetivos e Alcance da Lei Geral de Proteção de Dados. In G. Tepedino, A. Frazão, & M. D. Olivera (Eds.), *Lei Geral de Proteção de Dados Pessoais e Suas Repercussões no Direito Brasileiro* (pp. 99–130). Thomson Reuters.

Freire, P. S., Soares, A. P., Nakayama, K. M., & Spanhol, F. J. (2008). Processo de Profissionalização Com A Implantação De Boas Práticas De Governança Corporativa Para A Abertura de Capital (Ipo) Em Empresa Brasileira com Gestão de Tipo Familiar. In XXVIII Encontro Nacional de Engenharia de Produção, Rio de Janeiro.

Freire, P. S. (2013). *Aumente a Qualidade e Quantidade de Suas Publicações Científicas: Manual Para Projetos E Artigos Científicos.* Editora Crv. doi:10.24824/978858042815.5

Freire, P. S. (2013). *Increase the Quality and Quantity of Its Scientific Publications: Manual for Projects and Scientific Articles.* Crv Publishing House.

Freire, P. S. (2014). *Aumente A Qualidade E Quantidade De Suas Publicações Científicas: Manual Para Projetos E Artigos Científicos.* Editora Crv.

Freire, P. S. (2014). *Increase The Quality and Quantity of Your Scientific Publications: Manual for Projects and Scientific Articles.* Crv Publishing House.

Freire, P. S., Nakayama, K. M., & Spanhol, F. J. (2010). Compartilhamento Do Conhecimento: Grupo Colaborativo Um Caminho Para O Processo De Aprendizagem Organizacional. In *Gestão De Pessoas* (1st ed.). Pandion.

Freire, P. S., Nakayama, K. M., & Spanhol, F. J. (2010). Knowledge Sharing: Collaborative Group A Path to The Organizational Learning Process. In *People Management* (1st ed.). Pandion.

Freire, P. S., Soares, A. P., Nakayama, K. M., & Spanhol, F. J. (2008). Professionalization Process With The Implementation of Good Corporate Governance Practices For Ipo in A Brazilian Company with Family Type Management. In *XXVIII National Meeting of Production Engineering*, Rio de Janeiro.

Freitas, S. C. d., & Santos, L. P. G. (2005). *Os benefícios da utilização das simulações empresariais: um estudo exploratório.* Paper presented at the Encontro Anual da Associação dos Programas de Pós Graduação em Administração, Brasília, DF. http://www.anpad.org.br/diversos/down_zips/9/enanpad2005-epqb-2364.pdf

Frikken, K. B., & Golle, P. (2006). Private social network analysis: How to assemble pieces of a graph privately. In *Proceedings of the 5th ACM workshop on Privacy in electronic society* (pp. 89–98). ACM. 10.1145/1179601.1179619

Galbraith, J. (1997). Designing the Innovative Organization. In How Organizations Learn: Successful Reports From Large Organizations. Studies In Health Technology And Informatics.

Galbraith, J. (1997). Projetando a Organização Inovadora. In Como As Organizações Aprendem: Relatos De Sucesso Da Grandes Organizações. Studies In Health Technology And Informatics.

Galpin, T. J. (1996). *The Human Side of Change: A Practical Guide to Organization Redesign.* Academic Press.

Gandhi, P., Khanna, S., & Ramaswamy, S. (2016). Which industries are the most digital. *Harvard Business Review.* Disponível em: 5, março, 2019, em: https://www.mckinsey.com/mgi/overview/in-the-news/which-industries-are-the-most-digital

Garde, S., Knaup, P., Hovenga, E. J. S., & Heard, S. (2007). Towards Semantic Interoperability For Electronic Health Records: Domain Knowledge Governance For Openehr Archetypes. *Methods of Information in Medicine.*

Gartner Group. (2020). *Four trends impacting cloud adoption in 2020.* Available at https://www.gartner.com/smarterwithgartner/4-trends-impacting-cloud-adoption-in-2020/

Gavirneni, S., Kapuscinski, R., & Tayur, S. (1999). Value of Information in Capacitated Supply Chains. *Management Science, 45*(1), 16–24. doi:10.1287/mnsc.45.1.16

Gayko, J. E. (2018). *The Reference Architectural Model RAMI4.0 and the Standardization Council as an element of Success for Industry 4.0.* Retrieved September 15, from https://www.din.de/resource/blob/271306/340011c12b8592df728bee3815ef6ec2/06-smart-manufacturing-jens-gayko-data.pdf

Geada, N. (2020). Change Management in the Digital Economy. *International Journal of Innovation in the Digital Economy, 11*(3).

Geada, N., & Anunciação, P. (2020, March). Change Management Perceptions in Portuguese Hospital Institutions through ITIL. *International Journal of Healthcare Information Systems and Informatics.*

Geers, K. (2018). *Cyberspace and the Changing Nature of Warfare.* NATO Cooperative Cyber Defense Centre of Excellence. Available at https://ccdcoe.org/library/publications/cyberspace-and-the-changing-nature-of-warfare/

Gehrke, J., Lui, E., & Pass, R. (2011). Towards privacy for social networks: A zero-knowledge based definition of privacy. In *Theory of Cryptography Conference* (pp. 432–449). Springer. doi:10.1007/978-3-642-19571-6_26

Gerhardt, Silveira, & Tolfo. (2009). *Métodos de pesquisa.* Universidade Federal do Rio Grande do Sul. Available at: http://www.ufrgs.br/cursopgdr/downloadsSerie/derad005.pdf

German Data Protection Act - Bundesdatenschutzgesetz (BDSG). (2017). Retrieved https://www.gesetze-im-internet.de/englisch_bdsg/index.html

Gershon, M. (1991). Statistical Process Control for the Pharmaceutical Industry. *PDA Journal of Pharmaceutical Science and Technology, 45*(1), 41–50. PMID:2007968

Geyer & Ballou. (1993). *Logística empresarial: transportes, administração de materiais e distribuição física.* Atlas Editora.

Geyer, A. R. C., Sousa, V. D., & Silveira, D. (2018). Quality of medicines: Deficiencies found by Brazilian Health Regulatory Agency (ANVISA) on good manufacturing practices international inspections. *PLoS One, 13*(8), e0202084. doi:10.1371/journal.pone.0202084 PMID:30089162

Geyer, F. (2020). *The definitive Guide to B2B Digital Transformation.*

Giebels, D., & Teisman, G. R. (2015). Towards Ecosystem-Based Management for Mainports: A Historical Analysis of The Role of Knowledge in The Development of The Rotterdam Harbor from 1827 To 2008. *Ocean and Coastal Management.*

Giebels, D., & De Jonge, V. N. (2014). Making Ecosystem-Based Management Effective: Identifying and Evaluating Empirical Approaches to The Governance Of Knowledge. *Emergence.*

Giebels, D., Van Buuren, A., & Edelenbos, J. (2013). Ecosystem-Based Management in The Wadden Sea: Principles for The Governance of Knowledge. *Journal of Sea Research, 82*, 176–187. doi:10.1016/j.seares.2012.11.002

Giebels, D., Van Buuren, A., & Edelenbos, J. (2015). Using Knowledge in A Complex Decision-Making Process -Evidence and Principles from The Danish Hooting Project's Ecosystem-Based Management Approach. *Environmental Science & Policy, 47*, 53–67. doi:10.1016/j.envsci.2014.10.015

Giebels, D., Van Buuren, A., & Edelenbos, J. (2016). Knowledge Governance for Ecosystem-Based Management: Understanding Its Context-Dependency. *Environmental Science & Policy, 55*, 424–435. doi:10.1016/j.envsci.2015.08.019

Ginneken, J. Van (2009). The power of the Swarm, self Governance in an organization. *Business Contact.*

Ginneken, J. Van (2009). The power of the Swarm, self-Governance in an organization. *Business Contact.*

Girgis, A. A., Hart, D. G., & Peterson, W. L. (1992, January). A New Fault Location Technique For Two-and Three-Terminal Lines. *IEEE Transactions on Power Delivery, 7*(1), 98–107. doi:10.1109/61.108895

Givisiez, G., & Oliveira, E. (2018). *Demanda futura por moradias: demografia, habitação e mercado.* Ministério das Cidades.

Goldman, F. (2010). Governança Do Conhecimento E Gestão Do Conhecimento Organizacional. *Revista Gestão & Tecnologia, Pedro Leopoldo.*

Goldman, F. (2010). Knowledge Governance and Organizational Knowledge Management. *Management & Technology Magazine.*

Gomes. (n.d.). *Lei da União Europeia que protege dados pessoais entra em vigor e atinge todo o mundo; entenda.* Available at: https://g1.globo.com/economia/tecnologia/noticia/lei-da-uniao-europeia-que-protege-dados-pessoais-entra-em-vigor-e-atinge-todo-o-mundo-entenda.ghtml

Gomes, M. C. O. (2019). Para Além de uma "Obrigação Legal": o que a Metodologia de Benefícios nos Ensina Sobre o Papel dos Relatórios de Impacto à Proteção de Dados. In A. P. M. C. Lima, C. B. Hissa, & P. M. Saldanha (Eds.), *Direito Digital Debates Contemporâneos* (pp. 141–154). Thomson Reuters.

Gonçalves, F., Pimenta, J., & Anunciação, P. F. (2019). Information Systems Governance and New industrial Paradigms. Information Systems Governance – Concepts, best practices and case studies, 117-136.

Gonçalves, F., Pimenta, J., & Anunciação, P. F. (2019). Information Systems Governance and New industrial Paradigms. Information Systems Governance – Concepts, best practices and case studies, 211-212.

González-Morales, D., De Antonio, L. M. M., & García, J. L. R. (2011). *Teaching "Soft" skills in software engineering.* Paper presented at the 2011 IEEE Global Engineering Education Conference (EDUCON). https://www.academia.edu/18007251/Teaching_and_x201C_soft_and_x201D_skills_in_Software_Engineering

Gooderham, P., Minbaeva, D. B., & Pedersen, T. (2011). Governance Mechanisms for The Promotion of Social Capital for Knowledge Transfer in Multinational Corporations. *Journal of Management Studies, 48*(1), 123–150. doi:10.1111/j.1467-6486.2009.00910.x

Google. (2020). *Google Analytics.* Available at https://www.google.com/analytics/

Goshal, S., & Bartlett, C. (2000). *The Individualized Organization.* Rj: Campus. Corporate Governance & Ethics In Organizations. Academic Knowledge. Uniesp São Paulo Multidisciplinary Magazine: Uniesp.

Goshal, S., & Bartlett, C. (2000). *A Organização Individualizada. Rj.* Campus.

Gouveia, L. B. (2004). *Local e-government: Digital governance in the municipality.* OPorto, SPI Editions.

Governança Corporativa & Ética Nas Organizações. (2008). Saber Acadêmico. In *Revista Multidisciplinar Da Uniesp.* São Paulo: Uniesp.

Gradinger & Strohmeier. (2018). Cyber Bullying preventon with in a socio-ecological framework: The Visc social competence program. *Reducing Cyberbullying in Schools, 1*, 189-202.

Grandori, A. (2009). Poliarchic Governance and The Growth of Knowledge. *Knowledge Governance: Processes and Perspectives.*

Grandori, A. (2009). *Poliarchic Governance and The Growth of Knowledge. Knowledge Governance: Processes and Perspectives.* Academic Press.

Grandori, A. (2013). *Epistemic Economics and Organization: Forms of Rationality and Governance for a Wiser Economy.* Academic Press.

Grandori, A. (1997). Governance Structures, Coordination Mechanisms And Cognitive Models. *The Journal of Management and Governance, 1*(1), 29–42. doi:10.1023/A:1009977627870

Grandori, A. (2001). Neither Hierarchy nor Identity: Knowledge Governance Mechanisms And The Theory of the Firm. *The Journal of Management and Governance, 5*(3/4), 381–399. doi:10.1023/A:1014055213456

Grandori, A. F., & Ut Facias, M. F. (2009). Associational Contracts for Innovation. *International Studies of Management & Organization.* Advance online publication. doi:10.2753/IMO0020-8825390405

Granjal, J., Monteiro, E., & Silva, J. S. (2013). *Application-layer security for the WoT: Extending CoAP to support end-to-end message security for Internet-integrated sensing applications.* Paper presented at the International Conference on Wired/Wireless Internet Communication. 10.1007/978-3-642-38401-1_11

Granovetter, M. (2005). The impact of social structure on economic outcomes. *The Journal of Economic Perspectives, 19*(1), 33–50. doi:10.1257/0895330053147958

Gray, J., Chambers, L., & Bounegru, L. (n.d.). *The Data Journalism Handbook.* O'Reilly Media. Recuperado 6 de março de 2014, de http://www.infovis-wiki.net/index.php?title=Gray,_J._and_Chambers,_L._and_Bounegru,_L.,_The_Data_Journalism_Handbook,_O%27Reilly_Media,_2012

Griffith, T. L., Sawyer, J. E., & Neale, M. A. (n.d.). Virtualness and knowledge in teams: Managing the Lover triangle of organizations, individuals, and information technology. MIS Quarterly, 27(2), 265-287.

Grosz, B. J. & Stone, P. (2018). A century-long commitment to assessing artificial intelligence and its impact on society. *Communications of the ACM, 61*(12), 68-73.

Guerra, I. (2006). *Pesquisa Qualitativa e Análise de Conteúdo.* Princípia Editora.

Haddara, M., & Elragal, A. (2015). *The Readiness of ERP Systems for the Factory of the Future.* Conference on ENTERprise Information Systems / International Conference on Project MANagement / Conference on Health and Social Care Information Systems and Technologies, CENTERIS / ProjMAN / HCist 2015.

Haines, A., McMichael, A. J., Smith, K. R., Roberts, I., Woodcock, J., Markandya, A., Armstrong, B. G., Campbell-Lendrum, D., Dangour, A. D., Davies, M., Bruce, N., Tonne, C., Barrett, M., & Wilkinson, P. (2009). Public health benefits of strategies to reduce greenhouse-gas emissions: Overview and implications for policy makers. *Lancet, 374*(9707), 2104–2114. doi:10.1016/S0140-6736(09)61759-1 PMID:19942281

Hammer, M., & Champy, J. (1994). *Reengineering the Corporation: A manifesto for business revolution.* Nicholas Brealy.

Han, G., Xiao, L., & Poor, H. V. (2017). *Two-dimensional anti-jamming communication based on deep reinforcement learning.* Paper presented at the 2017 IEEE International Conference on Acoustics, Speech and Signal Processing (ICASSP). 10.1109/ICASSP.2017.7952524

Hansen, M. T., & Birkinshaw, J. (2007). The innovation value-chain. *Harvard Business Review, 85*(6), 121–130. PMID:17580654

Hartz, Z. M. A. (2012). Meta-evaluation of health management: Challenges for "new public health". *Ciencia e Saude Coletiva, 17*(4), 832–834. doi:10.1590/S1413-81232012000400004

Hartz, Z. M. de A. (1997). *Avaliação em saúde: Dos modelos conceituais à prática na análise da implantação de programas*. Editora FIOCRUZ. Recuperado de http://books.scielo.org/id/3zcft

Hassija, V., Chamola, V., Saxena, V., Jain, D., Goyal, P., & Sikdar, B. (2019). A survey on IoT security: Application areas, security threats, and solution architectures. *IEEE Access: Practical Innovations, Open Solutions, 7*, 82721–82743. doi:10.1109/ACCESS.2019.2924045

Hawkins, A. (2017). KFC China is using facial recognition tech to serve customers - but are they buying it? *The Guardian*. Retrieved Mar 17, from https://www.theguardian.com/technology/2017/jan/11/china-beijing-first-smart-restaurant-kfc-facial-recognition

Hay, M., Li, C., Miklau, G., & Jensen, D. (2009). Accurate estimation of the degree distribution of private networks. In *Data Mining, 2009. ICDM'09. Ninth IEEE International Conference on* (pp. 169–178). IEEE. 10.1109/ICDM.2009.11

Hay, M., Miklau, G., Jensen, D., Towsley, D., & Weis, P. (2008). Resisting structural reidentification in anonymized social networks. *Proceedings of the VLDB Endowment International Conference on Very Large Data Bases, 1*(1), 102–114. doi:10.14778/1453856.1453873

He, X., Vaidya, J., Shafiq, B., Adam, N., & Atluri, V. (2009) Preserving privacy in social networks: A structure-aware approach. In *Web Intelligence and Intelligent Agent Technologies, 2009. WI-IAT'09. IEEE/WIC/ACM International Joint Conferences on* (vol. 1, pp. 647–654). IET. 10.1109/WI-IAT.2009.108

Helou, A. R. H. A. (2009). *Integrated Risk Management Method In the Context of Public Administration. Dissertation* (Master's Thesis). Graduate Program in Engineering and Knowledge Management of The Federal University of Santa Catarina. Santa Catarina: Ufsc.

Helou, A. R. H. A. (2009). *Método De Gestão Integrada De Riscos No Contexto Da Administração Pública. Dissertação* (Dissertação De Mestrado). 208 F. Programa De Pós-Graduação Em Engenharia E Gestão Do Conhecimento Da Universidade Federal De Santa Catarina. Santa Catarina: Ufsc.

Henderson, J. C., & Venkatraman, N. (1993). Strategic Alignment: Leveraging Information Technology for Transforming Organizations. *IBM Systems Journal, 32*(1), 4–16. doi:10.1147j.382.0472

Hengstler, M., Enkel, E., & Duelli, S. (2016). Applied artificial intelligence and trust—The case of autonomous vehicles and medical assistance devices. *Technological Forecasting and Social Change, 105*, 105–120. doi:10.1016/j.techfore.2015.12.014

Hermann, M., Pentek, T., & Otto, B. (2016). Design Principles for Industrie 4.0 Scenarios. *Proceedings of 2016 49th Hawaii International Conference on Systems Science.*

Hirschheim, R., & Sabherwal, R. (2001). Detours in the Path toward Strategic Information Systems Alignment. *California Management Review, 44*(1), 87–108. doi:10.2307/41166112

Hoadley, D. (2020). *Artificial Intelligence and National Security Report updated by Kelley M. Sayler*. Congressional Research Service Report. Available at https://fas.org/sgp/crs/natsec/R45178.pdf

Hoebeke, L. (1990). Measuring in organizations. *Journal of Applied Systems Analysis, 117*, 115–122.

Hoebeke, L. (2006). Identity: The paradoxical nature of organizational closure. *Kybernetes, 35*(1/2), 65–75. doi:10.1108/03684920610640236

Hoehn, J., & Sayler, K. (2020). *National Security Implications of Fifth Generation (5G) Mobile Technologies Report.* Congressional Research Service Report. Available at https://crsreports.congress.gov/product/pdf/IF/IF11251

Hofmann, E., & Rüsch, M. (2017, April 13). Computers in Industry. Industry 4.0 and the current status as well as future prospects on logistics, 23-34.

Hoidalen, H. (n.d.). *ATPDraw.* SINTEF Energy Research – Norwegin University of Science and Technology.

Holsapple, S.W., & Singh, M. (2001). The Knowledge Chain Model: Activities For Competitiveness. *Expert Systems with Application.*

Hovenga, E., Garde, S., & Heard, S. (2005). Nursing Constraint Models for Electronic Health Records: A Vision for Domain Knowledge Governance. *International Journal of Medical Informatics, 74*(11-12), 886–898. doi:10.1016/j.ijmedinf.2005.07.013 PMID:16115795

Huang, M. H., & Rust, R. (2018). Artificial Intelligence in Service. *Journal of Service Research, 21*(2), 155–172. doi:10.1177/1094670517752459

Huizing & Bouman. (2002). Knowledge and Learning, Markets and Organizations: Managing the information transaction space. In The strategic management of intellectual capital and organizational Knowledge. Oxford University Press.

Huizing, A. (2007). The value of a rose: rising above Objectivism and subjectivism. In Information Management: Setting the Scene. London: Elsevier.

Huizing, A., & Bouman, W. (2002). Knowledge and Learning, Markets and Organizations: Managing the information transaction space. In The strategic management of intellectual capital and organizational Knowledge. Oxford University Press.

Hummen, R., Hiller, J., Wirtz, H., Henze, M., Shafagh, H., & Wehrle, K. (2013). 6LoWPAN fragmentation attacks and mitigation mechanisms. *Proceedings of the sixth ACM conference on security and privacy in wireless and mobile networks.* 10.1145/2462096.2462107

Husted, K., Michailova, S., Minbaeva, D. B., & Pedersen, T. (2012). Knowledge-Sharing Hostility and Governance Mechanisms: An Empirical Test. *Journal of Knowledge Management, 16*(5), 754–773. doi:10.1108/13673271211262790

Ibgc. (2014). *Introdução Às Boas Práticas De Governança Corporativa Para Organizações De Capital Fechado.* Disponível. Em: Http://Www.Ibgc.Org.Br/Userfiles/Files/Audpub.Pdf?__Akacao=1793926&__Akcnt=98ff2d07&__Akvkey=9c99&Utm_Source=Akna&Utm_Medium=Email&Utm_Campaign=Ibgc%3a+Audi%Eancia+P%Fablica+-+Caderno+De+Governan%E7a+Para+Empresa+De+Capital+Fechado

Ibgc. (2014). *Introduction to Good Corporate Governance Practices for Privately Held Organizations.* Http://Www.Ibgc.Org.Br/Userfiles/Files/Audpub.Pdf?__Akacao=1793926&__Akcnt=98ff2d07&__Akvkey=9c99&Utm_Source=Akna&Utm_Medium=Email&Utm_Campaign=Ibgc%3a+Audi%Eancia+P%Fablica+-+Caderno+De+Gove rnan%E7a+Para+Empresa+De+Capital+Fechado

IBM – International Business Machines – Blockchain. (2020c). *What is Blockchain technology?* Available at https://www.ibm.com/br-pt/blockchain/what-is-blockchain

IBM – International Business Machines – Cloud services. (2020). Available at https://www.ibm.com/br-pt/cloud

IBM – International Business Machines – Internet of Things. (2020b). Available at https://www.ibm.com/br-pt/cloud/internet-of-things

ICCA Launches Working Group on Cybersecurity in Arbitration. (n.d.). Available at https://www.arbitration-icca.org/news/2017/361/icca-launches-working-group-on-cybersecurity-in-arbitration.html

IEC PAS 63088. (2017). *Publicly Available Specification – Pre-Standard, Smart manufacturing – Reference architecture model industry 4.0 (RAMI4.0)*. Retrieved July 22, from https://webstore.iec.ch/preview/info_iecpas63088%7Bed1.0%7Den.pdf

Imai, M. (2006). *Gemba Kaizen*. MT Biznes.

Infolog Ptd, L. (2020). *Infolog Simplifying Logistics & Supply Chain*. Retrieved from https://www.infolog.com.sg/en/

International Council for Harmonisation of Technical Requirements for Pharmaceuticals for Human Use. (2016, julho 20). *ICH Official web site: ICH*. Recuperado 20 de julho de 2016, de ICH harmonisation for better health website: https://www.ich.org/home.html

International Organization for Standardization. (2018). *When it comes to keeping information assets secure, organizations can rely on the ISO/IEC 27000 family*. Available at https://www.iso.org/obp/ui/#iso:std:iso-iec:27000:ed-5:v1:en

INTERPOL. (2020). *Cybercrime: COVID-19 Impact*. Retrieved on October, 2020, from https://www.interpol.int/News-and-Events/News/2020/INTERPOL-report-shows-alarming-rate-of-cyberattacks-during-COVID-19

Investopedia. (n.d.). *Blockchain explained*. Available at https://www.investopedia.com/terms/b/blockchain.asp

IPEA. (2012). A Subvenção Econômica cumpre a função de estímulo à inovação e ao aumento da competitividade das empresas brasileiras? In Brasil em Desenvolvimento 2011: Estado, Planejamento e Políticas Públicas (Vol. 2). IPEA.

IPEA. (2018). Avaliação de políticas públicas: guia prático de análise ex ante. Casa Civil da Presidência da República, Instituto de Pesquisa Econômica Aplicada. IPEA: Brasília.

Irish Data Protection Act. (2018). Retrieved from http://www.justice.ie/en/JELR/Pages/Data_Protection_Act_2018

IT Governance Institute. (2003). *Board Briefing on IT Governance* (2nd ed.). Retrieved from: https://www.isaca.org/Content/ContentGroups/ITGI3/Resources1/Board_Briefing_on_IT_Governance/26904_Board_Briefing_final.pdf

Italian Data Protection Code. (2018). Retrieved from https://www.gazzettaufficiale.it/eli/id/2018/09/04/18G00129/sg

Ivanoff, S. D., & Hultberg, J. (2006). Understanding the Multiple Realities of Everyday Life: Basic Assumptions in Focus Group Methodology. *Scandinavian Journal of Occupational Therapy*, 13.

Jain, V., Wadhwa, S., & Deshmukh, S. (2009). Production Planning & Control: The Management of Operations. *Revisiting information systems to support a dynamic supply chain: issues and perspectives, 20*(1), 17–29.

Jamil, G. L., & Magalhães, L. F. C. (2015). Perspectives for big data analysis for knowledge generation in project management contexts. In *Handbook of research on effective project management research through the integration of knowledge and innovation*. IGI Global. doi:10.4018/978-1-4666-7536-0.ch001

Jamil, G. L., Santos, L. H. R., & Jamil, C. C. (2018). Market Intelligence as an Information System Element: Delivering Knowledge for Decisions in a Continuous Process. In *Handbook of Research on Expanding Business Opportunities With Information Systems and Analytics*. IGI Global.

Jamil, L. C., Vieira, A. A. P., & Xavier, A. J. D. (2018). Reflecting on Analytics Impacts on Information Architecture Contexts as a Source of Business Modelling for Healthcare Services. In *Handbook of Research on Expanding Business Opportunities With Information Systems and Analytics*. IGI Global.

Jarrahi, M. H. (2018). Artificial intelligence and the future of work: Human-AI symbiosis in organizational decision making. *Business Horizons*, *61*(4), 577–586. doi:10.1016/j.bushor.2018.03.007

Jasperneite, J. (2012). Was Hinter Begriffen Wie Industrie 4.0 Steckt. *Computers and Automation*, *12*, 24–28.

Jebran, L. (n.d.). *Learning about Internet governance, blockchain and cryptocurrency*. Available at the Internet Society information portal at https://www.internetsociety.org/blog/2018/08/blockchain-technologies-internet-governance/

Jimene. (2019). *LGPD: Lei Geral de Proteção de Dados Comentada*. Thomson Reuters Brazil.

Jing, Q., Vasilakos, A. V., Wan, J., Lu, J., & Qiu, D. (2014). Security of the Internet of Things: Perspectives and challenges. *Wireless Networks*, *20*(8), 2481–2501. doi:10.100711276-014-0761-7

Jorge, H. V. N. (2019a). *Investigação criminal tecnológica* (Vol. 1). Brasport.

Julien, Cuadra, William, Luke, & Harris. (2009). SECTION III-Information Use-Chapter 7-Information Behavior. Annual Review of Information Science and Technology, 43, 317-358.

Jungles, B. F., de Souza Rodrigues, J., & Garcia, S. F. A. (2019). Desenvolvimento de competências com jogos de empresas: pesquisa de opinião em um experimento com alunos do ensino técnico. *Gepros: Gestão da Produção, Operações e Sistemas*, *14*(3), 194. https://revista.feb.unesp.br/index.php/gepros/article/view/2619

Kagermann, H. & Wahlster, W. (2013). *Securing the future of German manufacturing industry. Recommendations for implementing the strategic initiative INDUSTRIE 4.0*. Final report of the Industrie 4.0 Working Group. Acatech – National Academy of Science and Engineering.

Kagermann, H., Wahlster, W., & Helbig, J. (2013). Recommendations for Implementing the Strategic Initiative Industrie 4.0. Final Report of the Industrie 4.0 Working Group. Acatech-National Academy of Science and Engineering.

Kahn & Blair. (2004). *Information Nation-seven keys to information management compliance*. AIIM.

Karwa, V., Raskhodnikova, S., Smith, A., & Yaroslavtsev, G. (2011). Private analysis of graph structure. *Proceedings of the VLDB Endowment International Conference on Very Large Data Bases*, *4*(11), 1146–1157. doi:10.14778/3402707.3402749

Kasem-Madani, S., & Meier, M. (2015). *Security and privacy policy languages: A survey, categorization and gap identification*. arXiv preprint arXiv:1512.00201.

Kathuria, A., Mann, A., Khuntia, J., Saldanha, T. J. V., & Kauffman, R. J. (2018). A Strategic Value Appropriation Path for Cloud Computing. *Journal of Management Information Systems*, *35*(3), 740–775. doi:10.1080/07421222.2018.1481635

Kaur, P., & Gurm, J. (2016). Detect and prevent HELLO FLOOD attack using centralized technique in WSN. *International Journal of Computer Science and Engineering Technology*, *7*(8), 379–381.

Khairi, A., Farooq, M., Waseem, M., & Mazhar, S. (2015). A Critical Analysis on the Security Concerns of Internet of Things (IoT). *Perception*, 111.

Khosrow-Pour, M. (2006). *Encyclopedia of E-Commerce, E-Government and Mobile Commerce*. Idea Group Reference.

Kifer, D., & Machanavajjhala, A. (2011). No free lunch in data privacy. In *Proceedings of the 2011 ACM SIGMOD International Conference on Management of data* (pp. 193–204). ACM. 10.1145/1989323.1989345

Kim, H. (2008). *Protection against packet fragmentation attacks at 6LoWPAN adaptation layer*. Paper presented at the 2008 International Conference on Convergence and Hybrid Information Technology. 10.1109/ICHIT.2008.261

Kim, S. W., & Narasimhan, R. (2002). Information System Utilization in Supply Chain Integration Efforts. *International Journal of Production Research*, 4585–4609. doi:10.1080/00207540210000022203

Kira, T. (Org.). (2015). *Analise da Informacao para Tomada de Decisao Desafios e Solucoes* (Vol. 1). Brasil: Editora Intersaberes. Recuperado de https://www.estantevirtual.com.br/b/kira-tarapanoff/analise-da-informacao-para-tomada-de-decisao-desafios-e-solucoes/158550962

Kleinberg, J. M. (2007). Challenges in mining social network data: processes, privacy, and paradoxes. In *Proceedings of the 13th ACM SIGKDD international conference on Knowledge discovery and data mining* (pp. 4–5). ACM. 10.1145/1281192.1281195

Kling, R., & Lamb, R. (1999, Setembro). IT and Organiacional Change in Digital Economies. *A Socio-Technical Approach*, 17-25.

Kniberg, H. (2014) *Spotify Engineering Culture*. https://blog.crisp.se/2014/03/27/henrikkniberg/spotify-engineering-culture-part-1 https://www.youtube.com/watch?v=4GK1NDTWbkY&list=PLVoXxzMVwkZ0vndMplV_rhwMHyS199vr1

Kolb, A. Y., & Kolb, D. A. (2017). Experiential learning theory as a guide for experiential educators in higher education. *Experiential Learning & Teaching in Higher Education, 1*(1), 7-44. https://learningfromexperience.com/downloads/research-library/experiential-learning-theory-guide-for-higher-education-educators.pdf

Kolb, D. (1984). *Experiential learning: Experience as the source of learning and development*. Prentice Hall.

Kooiman, J. (2007). Governing as governance. *Information governance: In search of the Forgotten Grail 21*.

Kooiman, J. (2007). *Governing as governance*. Sage Publications.

Kooiman, J. (Ed.). (2005). Fish for life, interactive governance for fisheries. Amsterdam University Press.

Koplan, J. P., Bond, T. C., Merson, M. H., Reddy, K. S., Rodriguez, M. H., Sewankambo, N. K., & Wasserheit, J. N. (1993–1995). Consortium of Universities for Global Health Executive Board. (2009). Towards a common definition of global health. *Lancet, 373*(9679), 1993–1995. Advance online publication. doi:10.1016/S0140-6736(09)60332-9

Korolova, A., Motwani, R., Nabar, S. U., & Xu, Y. (2008). Link privacy in social networks. In *Proceedings of the 17th ACM conference on Information and knowledge management* (pp. 289–298). ACM. 10.1145/1458082.1458123

Kotsiantis, S. B., Zaharakis, I., & Pintelas, P. (2007). Supervised machine learning: A review of classification techniques. *Emerging Artificial Intelligence Applications in Computer Engineering, 160*(1), 3-24.

Kotsiantis, S., & Kanellopoulos, D. (2006). Association rules mining: A recent overview. *GESTS International Transactions on Computer Science and Engineering, 32*(1), 71–82.

Kotter, J. P. (2017). *Liderar a mudança: porque falham os esforços de mudança. HBR 10 Artigos Essenciais, Gerir a Mudança*. Conjuntura Actual Editora.

Kuhn, M. (2008). Building predictive models in R using the caret package. *Journal of Statistical Software, 28*(5), 1–26. doi:10.18637/jss.v028.i05

Kulkarni, A., Pino, Y., & Mohsenin, T. (2016). *SVM-based real-time hardware Trojan detection for many-core platform*. Paper presented at the 2016 17th International Symposium on Quality Electronic Design (ISQED). 10.1109/ISQED.2016.7479228

Kumar, J., Rajendran, B., Bindhumadhava, B., & Babu, N. S. C. (2017). *XML wrapping attack mitigation using positional token*. Paper presented at the 2017 International Conference on Public Key Infrastructure and its Applications (PKIA). 10.1109/PKIA.2017.8278958

Kumar, S., Dieveney, E., & Dieveney, A. (2009). Reverse logistic process control measures for the pharmaceutical industry supply chain. *International Journal of Productivity and Performance Management, 58*(2), 188–204. doi:10.1108/17410400910928761

Kurnia, R., Mulyanti, B., & Widiaty, I. (2020) *IOP Conference on Services Materials for Science Engineering.* doi:10.1088/1757-899X/830/4/042098

Laloux, F. (2014). *Reinventing Organizations: A Guide to Creating Organizations Inspired by the Next Stage of Human Consciousness.* Nelson Parker Publishing.

Laney, D. (2001). *3D Data Management: Controlling Data Volume.* Velocity, and Variety. Recuperado de http://blogs. gartner.com/doug-laney/files/2012/01/ad949-3D-Data-Management-Controlling-Data-Volume-Velocity-and-Variety.pdf

Lasi, H., Peter, F., Thomas, F., & Hoffmann, M. (2014). Industry 4.0. *Business & Information Systems Engineering, 6*(4), 239–242.

Lastres, H. M. M., & Sarita, A. (1999). *Informação e Globalização na Era do Conhecimento.* Editora Campus Ltda.

Laudon, K. C., & Laudon, J. P. (2014). Managment Information Systems - Managing the Digital Firm (13th ed.). Pearson.

Laudon, K. C., & Laudon, J. P. (2016). *Management Information Systems, Managing the Digital Firm* (14th ed.). Pearson Education Limited.

Leonardi, M. (2019). *Fundamentos de Direito Digital.* Thomson Reuters.

Liaw, A., & Wiener, M. (2002). Classification and regression by randomForest. *R News, 2*(3), 18–22.

Li, B. H., Hou, B. C., Yu, W. T., Lu, X. B., & Yang, C. W. (2017). Applications of artificial intelligence in intelligent manufacturing: A review. *Frontiers of Information Technology & Electronic Engineering, 18*(1), 86–96. doi:10.1631/FITEE.1601885

Likert, R. (1961). *New Patterns of Management.* McGraw-Hill.

Li, L., Zhang, H., Peng, H., & Yang, Y. (2018). Nearest neighbors based density peaks approach to intrusion detection. *Chaos, Solitons, and Fractals, 110*, 33–40. doi:10.1016/j.chaos.2018.03.010

Lima, R., & Cavalcanti, M. (2003). *Efficient Brazil, Brazil citizen: Technology at the servisse of social justice.* https://books.google.pt

Lima, C. C. C. (2019). Capítulo II – Do Tratamento de Dados Pessoais. In V. N. Maldonado & R. O. Blum (Eds.), *LGPD Lei Geral de Proteção de Dados Comentada* (pp. 179–219). Thomson Reuters.

Lima, T. C. S., & Mioto, R. C. T. (2007). Procedimentos metodológicos na construção do conhecimento científico: A pesquisa bibliográfica. *Revista Katálysis, 10*(spe), 35–45. doi:10.1590/S1414-49802007000300004

Lindamood, J., Heatherly, R., Kantarcioglu, M., & Thuraisingham, B. (2009). Inferring private information using social network data. In *Proceedings of the 18th international conference on World wide web* (pp. 1145–1146). ACM. 10.1145/1526709.1526899

Lindsay, D. (2014). The 'right to be forgotten' by search engines under data privacy law: A legal analysis of the Costeja ruling. *Journal of Medicine and Law, 6*(2), 159–179. doi:10.5235/17577632.6.2.159

Lin, J., Yu, W., Zhang, N., Yang, X., Zhang, H., & Zhao, W. (2017). A survey on internet of things: Architecture, enabling technologies, security and privacy, and applications. *IEEE Internet of Things Journal, 4*(5), 1125–1142. doi:10.1109/JIOT.2017.2683200

Liu, T., & Lu, D. (2012). *The application and development of IoT.* Paper presented at the 2012 International Symposium on Information Technologies in Medicine and Education.

Liu, K., & Terzi, E. (2008). Towards identity anonymization on graphs. In *Proceedings of the 2008 ACM SIGMOD international conference on Management of data* (pp. 93–106). ACM. 10.1145/1376616.1376629

Liu, L., Wang, J., Liu, J., & Zhang, J. (2008). *Privacy preserving in social networks against sensitive edge disclosure. Tech. rep., Technical Report Technical Report CMIDAHiPSCCS 006-08.* Department of Computer Science, University of Kentucky.

Lo Giudice, D., Mines, C., Dobak, A., & Hartig, K. (2020). *Scaling Agile: What The Spotify Approach Can Do For You.* Forrester. https://www.forrester.com/report/Scaling+Agile+What+The+Spotify+Approach+Can+Do+For+You/-/E-RES144558?objectid=RES144558

Löffer, E., & Bovair, A.G. (2009). Public Managemente And Governance (2nd ed.). Nuc: Routledge.

Löffer. E., & Bovair, A.G. (2009). Public Management and Governance (2nd ed.). Nuc: Routledge.

Longhi, J. V. R. (2019). Marco Civil da Internet no Brasil: Breves Considerações Sobre Seus Fundamentos, Princípios e Análise Crítica do Regime de Responsabilidade Civil dos Provedores. In G. M. Martins & J. V. R. Longhi (Eds.), *Direito Digital Direito Privado e Internet* (pp. 123–154). Foco Jurídico.

Lorenz, M., Rubmann, M., Waldner, M., Engel, P., Harnish, M., Justus, J., & the Boston Consulting Group. (2015). *Industry 4.0: The Future of Productivity and Growth in Manufacturing Industries.* https://www.bcg.com/publications/2015/engineeried_products_project_business_industry_4_future_productivity_growth_manufacturing_industries

Lydon, B. (n.d.). *RAMI 4.0 Reference Architectural Model for Industrie 4.0, ISA's Flagship Publications.* Retrieved July 20, from https://www.isa.org/intech-home/2019/march-april/features/rami-4-0-reference-architectural-model-for-industr

MacAfee. (2018). *The Economic Impact of Cybercrime – No Slowing Down.* Retrieved on November, 2020, from https://www.mcafee.com/enterprise/en-us/solutions/lp/economics-cybercrime.html

Maçaneiro, M. B., & Cherobim, A. P. M. S. (2011). Fontes de financiamento à inovação: Incentivos e óbices às micro e pequenas empresas – estudo de casos múltiplos no Estado do Paraná. *Organizações & Sociedade, 18*(56), 57–75. doi:10.1590/S1984-92302011000100003

MacNeil, H. (1992). *Without consent: the ethics of disclosing personal information in public archives.* Academic Press.

Macwan, K. R., & Patel, S. J. (2017). k-degree anonymity model for social network data publishing. *Advances in Electrical and Computer Engineering, 17*(4), 117–224. doi:10.4316/AECE.2017.04014

Macwan, K. R., & Patel, S. J. (2018). k-NMF anonymization in social network data publishing. *The Computer Journal, 61*(4), 601–613. doi:10.1093/comjnl/bxy012

Macwan, K. R., & Patel, S. J. (2018). Node differential privacy in social graph degree publishing. *Procedia Computer Science, 143,* 786–793. doi:10.1016/j.procs.2018.10.388

Maes, R. (2007). Information Management: An integrative perspective. In A. Huizing & E. De Vries (Eds.), Information Management: Setting the Scene. London: Elsevier.

Maes, R. (2007). Information Management: An integrative perspective. In Information Management: Setting the Scene. London: Elsevier.

Magalhães, Igarashi, Hartz, Antunes, Macedo, Magalhães, ... Macedo. (2019). *Project Management in Risk Analysis for Validation of Computer Systems in the Warehouse System.* Recuperado 11 de maio de 2020, de Http://services.igi-global.com/resolvedoi/resolve.aspx?doi=10.4018/978-1-5225-9993-7.ch008

Magalhães, J. L., & Quoniam, L. (2013). Perception of the Information Value for Public Health: A Case Study for Neglected Diseases. In *Rethinkin the Conceptual Base for New Practical Applications in Information Value and Quality* (p. 345). IGI Global. Recuperado de https://www.igi-global.com/chapter/perception-information-value-public-health/84218

Magalhaes, J. L., & Quoniam, L. (2015). Percepção do valor da informação por meio da inteligência competitiva 2.0 e do Big Data na saúde. In Análise da Informação para Tomada de Decisão: Desafios e soluções (p. 365). Brasil: Kira Tarapanoff.

Magalhães, J., Hartz, Z., Temido, M., & Antunes, A. (2018). Gestão do conhecimento em tempos de big data: Um olhar dos desafios para os sistemas de saúde. *Anais do Instituto de Higiene e Medicina Tropical, 17,* 7–16. doi:10.25761/anaisihmt.256

Maggiolini, P. (2014, September-October). Deepening for the Concept of Digital Ethics. *PENSATA, Business Administration Journal, 54*(5), 585–591.

Mahnke, V., & Pedersen, T. (2003). *Knowledge Flows, Governance and The Multinational Enterprise: Frontiers in International Management Research.* Academic Press.

Mahnke, V., & Pedersen, T. (2003). Knowledge Governance and Value Creation. *Knowledge Flows, Governance and the Multinational Enterprise: Frontiers in International Management Research.*

Mahnke, V., & Pedersen, T. (2003a). Knowledge Flows, Governance and The Multinational Enterprise: Frontiers in International Management Research. Knowledge Flows. *Governance and The Multinational Enterprise: Frontiers in International Management Research.*

Mahnke, V., & Pedersen, T. (2003b). Knowledge Governance and Value Creation. Knowledge Flows. *Governance and the Multinational Enterprise: Frontiers in International Management Research.*

Maldonado, V. N. (2019). Capítulo III – Dos Direitos do Titular. In V. N. Maldonado & R. O. Blum (Eds.), *LGPD Lei Geral de Proteção de Dados Comentada* (pp. 220–244). Thomson Reuters.

Marconi, M. A., & Lakatos, E. M. (2009). *Fundamentals of Scientific Methodology.* Atlas.

Marconi, M. A., & Lakatos, E. M. (2009). *Fundamentos de Metodologia Científica.* Atlas.

Mateus. (2008). The Electronic Government, its bet in Portugal and the importance of Communication Technologies for its strategy. *Journal of Polytechnic Studies, 6*(9), 23-48.

Mathur, A., Newe, T., & Rao, M. (2016). Defence against black hole and selective forwarding attacks for medical WSNs in the IoT. *Sensors (Basel), 16*(1), 118. doi:10.339016010118 PMID:26797620

MATLAB, User´s Guides. (n.d.). The MathWorks Inc.

Mayer, K. J. (2006). Spillovers and Governance: An Analysis of Knowledge and Reputational Spillovers in Information Technology. *Academy of Management Journal.*

Mayo, R. C., & Leung, J. (2018). Artificial intelligence and deep learning – Radiology's next frontier? *Clinical Imaging, 49,* 87–88. doi:10.1016/j.clinimag.2017.11.007 PMID:29161580

Mc Kinsey. (2011). *Big Data: the next frontier for innovation, competition, and productivity.* Accessed at https://www.mckinsey.com/insights/business_technology/big_data_the_next_frontier_for_innovation

McAfee, A., & Brynjolfsson, E. (2012). Big data: The management revolution. *Harvard Business Review, 90*(10), 60–68. PMID:23074865

Mcdonald, N. (2018). *We are social*. Available on: https://wearesocial.com/us/blog/2018/01/global-digital-report-2018

Mearian, L. (2020). *Computerworld – What is Blockchain: A complete guide*. Available at https://www.computerworld.com/article/3191077/what-is-blockchain-the-complete-guide.html

Mecalux, S. (2020). *Armazéns verticais e carrosséis verticais ou horizontais*. Retrieved 2020, from https://www.mecalux.com.br/manual-de-armazenagem/sistemas-de-armazenagem/armazem-vertical-carrossel-horizontal

Melo, J. F., & Rockembach, M. (2019). Arquivologia e Ciência da Informação na Era do Big Data: Perspectivas de Pesquisa e Atuação Profissional em Arquivos Digitais. *Prisma. com*, (39), 14-28.

Melo, N. H. S., Sardinha, I. N., & Menezes, E. O. d. (2017). Aprendizagem vivencial: a contribuição dos jogos de empresas no desenvolvimento de competências. *Revista Lagos, 5*(2). https://www.lagos.vr.uff.br/index.php/lagos/article/view/241

Mendes, L. S. (2014). *Privacidade, Proteção de Dados e Defesa do Consumidor: Linhas Gerais de um Novo Direito Fundamental*. Saraiva.

Michailova, S., & Foss, N.J. (2009). Knowledge Governance: Themes and Questions. *Knowledge Governance: Processes and Perspectives*.

Michailova, S., & Sidorova, E. (2011). From Group-Based Work to Organizational Learning: The Role of Communication Forms and Knowledge Sharing. *Knowledge Management Research and Practice, 9*(1), 73–83. doi:10.1057/kmrp.2011.4

Microsoft Azure. (2020). Available at https://azure.microsoft.com/pt-br/

Microsoft. (2020). *New cyberattacks targeting U.S. elections*. Retrieved on November, 2020, from https://blogs.microsoft.com/on-the-issues/2020/09/10/cyberattacks-us-elections-trump-biden/

Millar, V. E., & Porter, M. E. (1985). *How Information Gives You Competitive Advantage*.

Minelli, M., Chambers, M., & Dhiraj, A. (2013). *Big Data, Big Analytics*. John Wiley & Sons, Inc. Recuperado de https://books.google.com.br/books/about/Big_Data_Big_Analytics.html?hl=pt-BR&id=Mg3WvT8uHV4C

Ministerio Público Federal do Distrito Federal e Territórios. (2020). *MPDFT ajuíza 1ª ação civil pública com base na LGPD*. Retrieved from https://www.mpdft.mp.br/portal/index.php/comunicacao-menu/sala-de-imprensa/noticias/noticias-2020/12384-mpdft-ajuiza-1-acao-civil-publica-com-base-na-lgpd

Mintzberg, H. (2006). *MBA? Não, obrigado: Uma visão crítica sobre a gestão eo desenvolvimento de gerentes*. Bookman.

Mishra, A. K., Tripathy, A. K., Puthal, D., & Yang, L. T. (2018). Analytical model for sybil attack phases in internet of things. *IEEE Internet of Things Journal, 6*(1), 379–387. doi:10.1109/JIOT.2018.2843769

Mitchell, R. S., Michalski, J. G., & Carbonell, T. M. (2013). *An artificial intelligence approach*. Springer.

Mitroff, I., Mason, R., & Pearson, C. (1994). *Frame break: The Radical Redesign Of American Business*. Jossey-Bass.

Mitrokotsa, A., Rieback, M. R., & Tanenbaum, A. S. (2010). Classifying RFID attacks and defenses. *Information Systems Frontiers, 12*(5), 491–505. doi:10.100710796-009-9210-z

Moeuf, A., Pellerin, R., Lamouri, S., Tamayo-Giraldo, S., & Barbaray, R. (2017). The Industrial Management of SMEs in the Era of Industry 4.0. *International Journal of Production Research*, (September), 8.

Montes, G. A., & Goertzel, B. (2019). Distributed, decentralized, and democratized artificial intelligence. *Technological Forecasting and Social Change, 141*, 354–358. doi:10.1016/j.techfore.2018.11.010

Moore, M. (2018). *Democracy Hacked. How Technology is Destabilising Global Politics*. Oneworld Publications.

Moreira & Schenini. (n.d.). *A lei de proteção de dados pessoais da União Europeia (GDPR) e sua aplicação extraterritorial às entidades e empresas brasileiras*. Available at: https://www.migalhas.com.br/dePeso/16,MI267772,81042-A+lei+de+protecao+de+dados+pessoais+da+Uniao+Europeia+GDPR+e+sua

Moreira, Becker, & Lameirão. (n.d.). Os incidentes cibernéticos e a advocacia. *Lex Machinæ*. Available at: http://www.lexmachinae.com/2017/09/25/os-incidentes-ciberneticos-e-advocacia/

Morgan, D. L. (1996). Focus Groups. *Annual Review of Sociology*, 22. Retrieved May 8, from http://www.jstor.org/stable/2083427

Mosenia, A., & Jha, N. K. (2016). A comprehensive study of security of internet-of-things. *IEEE Transactions on Emerging Topics in Computing, 5*(4), 586–602. doi:10.1109/TETC.2016.2606384

Motta, G. S., & Quintella, R. H. (2012). A utilização de jogos e simulações de empresas nos cursos de graduação em administração no estado da Bahia. *REAd. Revista Eletrônica de Administração (Porto Alegre), 18*(2), 317-338.https://doi:10.15901413-23112012000200002

Moura, B. d. (2006). *Logística – Conceitos e Tendências*. V. N. Famalicão: Centro Atlântico.

Mrtvi, V. O., Westphal, F. K., Bandeira-de-Mello, R., & Feldmann, P. R. (2017). Jogos de empresas: Abordagens ao fenômeno, perspectivas teóricas e metodológicas. *Revista de Administração Contemporânea, 21*(1), 19–40. doi:10.1590/1982-7849rac2017150212

Müller, R., Glückler, J., Aubry, M., & Shao, J. (2013). Project Management Knowledge Flows In Networks Of Project Managers and Project Management Offices: A Case Study in the Pharmaceutical industry. *Project Management Journal, 44*(2), 4–19. doi:10.1002/pmj.21326

Muniyandi, A. P., Rajeswari, R., & Rajaram, R. (2012). Network anomaly detection by cascading k-Means clustering and C4. 5 decision tree algorithm. *Procedia Engineering, 30*, 174–182. doi:10.1016/j.proeng.2012.01.849

Muniz, C. N. S. M. (2018). *Atitude Empreendedora e suas dimensões: Um estudo em micro e pequenas empresas* (Dissertação de Mestrado em Administração). Universidade de Brasília. Brasília.

Munzner, T. (2014). *Visualization analysis and design*. CRC Press. doi:10.1201/b17511

Murdoch, W. J., Singh, C., Kumbier, K., Abbasi-Asl, R., & Yu, B. (2019). Definitions, methods, and applications in interpretable machine learning. *Proceedings of the National Academy of Sciences of the United States of America, 116*(44), 22071–22080. doi:10.1073/pnas.1900654116 PMID:31619572

Murphy, C. (2013). *Developing process for mobile device forensics*. http://www.mobileforensicscentral.com/mfc/documents/Mobile%20Device%20Forensic%20Process%20v3.0.pdf

Nadai, F. C., & Calado, L. R. (2005). Knowledge as a Strategic Resource: Characterizing a Knowledge-Intensive Organization (oic). In *Viii Sowe-Seminars in Administration, 2005. Sao Paulo. Annals....* Fea-Usp.

Nadai, F. C., & Calado, L. R. (2005). O Conhecimento Como Recurso Estratégico: Caracterizando Uma Organização Intensiva. In *Viii Semead-Seminários Em Administração, 2005. São Paulo. Anais....* Fea-Usp.

Narayanan, A., & Shmatikov, V. (2008). Robust de-anonymization of large sparse datasets. In *2008 IEEE Symposium on Security and Privacy* (pp. 111–125). IEEE. 10.1109/SP.2008.33

National Institute for Standards and Technology. (n.d.). *The NIST definition of cloud computing.* Available at https://csrc.nist.gov/publications/detail/sp/800-145

National Institute of Standards and Technology. (2018). *Framework for Improving Critical Infrastructure Cybersecurity – Version 1.1.* Retrieved on November, 2020, from https://www.nist.gov/publications/framework-improving-critical-infrastructure-cybersecurity-version-11

National Institute of Standards and Technology. Technology Innovation Program. (2010). A Guide for Preparing and Submitting White Papers to the Technology Innovation Program. U.S. Department of Commerce.

National Research Council. (2012). *Education for life and work: Developing transferable knowledge and skills in the 21st century* (J. W. Pellegrino & M. L. Hilton Eds.). Washington, DC: National Academies Press. http://www.sebrae.com.br/Sebrae/Portal%20Sebrae/Anexos/Education_for_Life_and_work.pdf

NATO. (2008). Directive on Physical Security. NATO Security Committee. AC/35-D/2001-REV2, 7 January 2008. [s.l.]

NATO. (2015). Directive on Classified Project and Industrial Security. NATO Security Committee. AC/35-D/2003-REV5, 13 May 2015. [s.l.]

NATO. (2020). *Cyber Defense.* Retrieved on April, 2020, from https://www.nato.int/cps/en/natohq/topics_78170.htm

Naughton, J. (2017). Deep Thinking: Where Machine Intelligence Ends and Human Creativity Begins by Garry Kasparov – review. *The Guardian.* Retrieved Mar 17, from https://www.theguardian.com/books/2017/jun/04/deep-thinking-where-machine-intelligence-ends-human-creativity-begins-garry-kasparov-review

Neves, F. S., & Alberton, A. (2017). Jogos de empresas: o que os alunos aprendem? Um estudo com alunos de graduação e pós-graduação. *Revista Espacios, 38*(45), 17. http://www.revistaespacios.com/a17v38n45/a17v38n45p14.pdf

Neves, P. (2011). *Sucesso e Mudança nas Organizações: Uma Questão de Confiança* (1st ed.). Editora RH.

Ngu, A. H., Gutierrez, M., Metsis, V., Nepal, S., & Sheng, Q. Z. (2016). IoT middleware: A survey on issues and enabling technologies. *IEEE Internet of Things Journal, 4*(1), 1–20. doi:10.1109/JIOT.2016.2615180

Ngúvulo, S. (2016). *Conceção de um sistema informático de gestão do pessoal do ISCED – Cabinda* (Tese de Mestrado, Universidade Fernando Pessoa). Disponível em: 10, março, 2019, em: https://bdigital.ufp.pt/bitstream/10284/5480/1/DM_Sebastião%20Ngúvulo.pdf

Ni, Shi, Ansri, Su, Sun, & Lin. (2014). Robust Lossless Image Data Hiding. *IEEE International Conference on Multimedia and Expo*, 2199-2202.

Nissim, K., Raskhodnikova, S., & Smith, A. (2007). Smooth sensitivity and sampling in private data analysis. In *Proceedings of the thirty-ninth annual ACM symposium on Theory of computing* (pp. 75–84). ACM. 10.1145/1250790.1250803

Nonaka, I., & Takeuchi, H. (1997). *Creation of Knowledge in the Company* (5th ed.). Campus.

Nonaka, I., & Takeuchi, H. (1997). *Criação de Conhecimento na Empresa* (5th ed.). Campus.

Nonaka, I., Toyama, R., & Hirata, T. (2008). *Managing Flow: A Process Theory Of The Knowledge-Based Firm.* Palgrave Macmillan. doi:10.1057/9780230583702

Nooteboom, B. (2000). Learning by Interaction: Absorptive Capacity, Cognitive Distance and Governance. *Journal of Management and Governance.*

Nova SBE & EY. (2018) *Estudo da Maturidade Digital das empresas portuguesas*. Disponível em: 17, maio, 2019, em: https://www.ey.com/Publication/vwLUAssets/ey-estudo-da-maturidade-digital-das-empresas-portuguesas/$FILE/ey-estudo-da-maturidade-digital-das-empresas-portuguesas.pdf

Nuix. (n.d.). *Master Investigations With Forensic Precision*. https://www.nuix.com/products/nuixinvestigate

O'Brien, J., & Marakas, G. M. (2011). *Management Information Systems*. Mcgraw-Hill.

O'Reilly, T. (2007). *What is Web 2.0: Design Patterns and Business Models for the Next Generation of Software* (SSRN Scholarly Paper Nº ID 1008839). Rochester, NY: Social Science Research Network. Recuperado de Social Science Research Network website: https://papers.ssrn.com/abstract=1008839

O'Rourke, C., Fishman, N., & Selkow, W. (2003). Enterprise Architecture Using the Zachman Framework. Pennsylvania State University: Course Technology.

OCDE – Organização para Cooperação e Desenvolvimento Econômico; Eurostat – Gabinete de Estatísticas da União Europeia. (2006). *Manual de Oslo*: *Diretrizes para coleta e interpretação de dados sobre inovação*. Publicado pela FINEP (Financiadora de Estudos e Projetos), 3ª Edição.

OCDE. (2014). Oslo Manual: Innovation Data Colletion and Interpretation Guidelines (3rd ed.). FINEP.

OCDE. (2016). *Princípios De Governo Das Sociedades Do G20 E Da Ocde*. Éditions OCDE. Http://Dx.Doi.Org/10.1787/9789264259195-Ptpai

OECD. (2016). *Principles of Government Of Societies Of The G20 And OECD*. Http://Dx.Doi.Org/10.1787/9789264259195-Ptpai

Ohata, M. & Kumar, A. (2012, Sept.). Big Data: A Boom for Business Intelligence. *Financial Executive*.

Olavsrud, T. (2017). *Digital disruption is coming but most businesses don't have a plan*. CIO.

Oliveira, M. A., & Sauaia, A. C. A. (2011). Impressão docente para aprendizagem vivencial: um estudo dos benefícios dos jogos de empresas. *Administração: ensino e pesquisa, 12*(3), 355-391. . doi:10.13058/raep.2011.v12n3.159

Oliveira, S. (2014). *Educação Vivencial em Administração: seriam jogos e simulações alternativas?* Paper presented at the XVII SEMEAD Seminários em Administração, São Paulo, SP. https://www.researchgate.net/publication/316253816_Educacao_Vivencial_em_Administracao_seriam_jogos_e_simulacoes_alternativas

Oliveira, L. F., & Junior, C. D. S. (2017). Inovações no setor público: uma abordagem teórica sobre os impactos de sua adoção. In *Inovação no setor público: teoria, tendências e casos no Brasil* (pp. 33–42). Enap/Ipea.

Olston, C., & Najork, M. (2010). Web crawling. *Foundations and Trends in Information Retrieval, 4*(3), 175–246. doi:10.1561/1500000017

Origgi. (2017). *Reputation: What It Is and Why It Matters* (Reputação: o que é e por que importa, em tradução livre). Available at https://aeon.co/ideas/say-goodbye-to-the-information-age-its-all-about-reputation-now

Oriwoh, E., al-Khateeb, H., & Conrad, M. (2016). *Responsibility and Non-repudiation in resource-constrained Internet of Things scenarios*. Academic Press.

Overbeek, P. (2005). *Information Security under control: Ground rules, management, organization and technique*. FT Prentice Hall Financial Times.

Paim, R., Carddoso, V., Caulliraux, H., & Clemente, R. (2009). *Gestão de Processos: Pensar, Agir e Aprender eBook: Paim, Rafael, Cardoso, Vinicius, Caulliraux, Heitor, Clemente, Rafael: Amazon.com.br: Loja Kindle.* Bookman. Recuperado de https://www.amazon.com.br/Gest%C3%A3o-Processos-Pensar-Agir-Aprender-ebook/dp/B018KGC3F0

Paisley. (2017). It's All About the Data: The Impact of the EU General Data Protection Regulation on International Arbitration. *Fordham International Arbitration & Mediation Conference Issue.* Available at https://ir.lawnet.fordham.edu/cgi/viewcontent.cgi?article=2707&context=ilj

Pajouh, H. H., Javidan, R., Khayami, R., Ali, D., & Choo, K.-K. R. (2016). A two-layer dimension reduction and two-tier classification model for anomaly-based intrusion detection in IoT backbone networks. *IEEE Transactions on Emerging Topics in Computing.*

Paris Call. (2018). *For trust and security in cyberspace: Ensuring international cyberspace security.* Available at https://pariscall.international/en/

Pariser, E. (2011). The filter bubble: What the Internet is hiding from you. Penguin UK.

Park, S. H., Huh, S. Y., Oh, W., & Han, S. P. (2012). A social network-based inference model for validating customer profile data. MIS Quarterly, 36(4), 1217-1237.

Park, B. (2011). Threats and security analysis for enhanced secure neighbor discovery protocol (SEND) of IPv6 NDP security. *International Journal of Control and Automation, 4*(4).

Park, N., & Kang, N. (2016). Mutual authentication scheme in secure internet of things technology for comfortable lifestyle. *Sensors (Basel), 16*(1), 20. doi:10.339016010020 PMID:26712759

Parmar, S. (2015). *Fault location algorithms for electrical power transmission lines - Methodology, design and testing. Intelligent electrical power grids.* EWI.

Pastore. (n.d.). Practical approaches to cybersecurity in arbitration. *Fordham International Law Journal.* Available at https://ir.lawnet.fordham.edu/cgi/viewcontent.cgi?referer=https://www.google.com.br/&httpsredir=1&article=2658&context=ilj

Patino, B. (2019). *La civilisation du poisson rouge: petit traité sur le marché de l'attention.* Grasset. doi:10.5771/9783956504211-812

Peltokorpi, V., & Tsuyuki, E. (2007). Organizational Governance in Internal Hybrids: A Case Study of Maekawa Manufacturing Ltd. *Corporate Governance, 7*(2), 123–135. doi:10.1108/14720700710739778

Pemsel, S., & Müller, R. (2012). The Governance of Knowledge in Project-Based Organizations. *International Journal of Project Management, 30*(8), 865–876. doi:10.1016/j.ijproman.2012.02.002

Pemsel, S., Müller, R., & Söderlund, J. (2016). Knowledge Governance Strategies in Project-Based Organizations. *Long Range Planning, 49*(6), 648–660. doi:10.1016/j.lrp.2016.01.001

Pemsel, S., Wiewiora, A., Müller, R., Aubry, M., & Brown, K. (2014). A Conceptualization of Knowledge Governance in Project-Based Organizations. *International Journal of Project Management, 32*(8), 1411–1422. doi:10.1016/j.ijproman.2014.01.010

Peppard, J., & Ward, J. (1999). Mind the GAP: Diagnosing the relationship between THE IT Organisation and the rest of the business. *The Journal of Strategic Information Systems, 8*(1), 29–60. doi:10.1016/S0963-8687(99)00013-X

Permanent Court of Arbitration website goes offline, with cyber-security firm contending that security flaw was exploited in concert with China-Philippines arbitration. (n.d.). Available at https://www.iareporter.com/articles/permanent-court-of-arbitration-goes-offline-with-cyber-security-firm-contending-that-security-flaw-was-exploited-in-lead-up-to-china-philippines-arbitration

Perrnoud, P. (2004). *Diez nuevas competencias para enseñar: invitación al viaje.* Barcelona: Graó.

Pesqueux, Y. (2005). Management de la connaissance: Un modèle organisationnel? *Management de la connaissance : un modele organisationnel?* Recuperado de https://halshs.archives-ouvertes.fr/halshs-00004005/document

Pesqueux, Y., & Ferrary, M. (2011). Management de la connaissance (2o ed). Economica. Recuperado de /Entreprise/Livre/management-de-la-connaissance-9782717860153

Pessoa, C. R. M., Batista, C. L., & Marques, M. E. (n.d.). Internet of Things and Internet of All Things. In *Handbook of Research on Expanding Business Opportunities With Information Systems and Analytics.* IGI Global.

Pessoa. (2016). *Gestão da informação e do conhecimento no alinhamento estratégico em empresas de engenharia* (PhD thesis). Universidade Federal de Minas Gerais. Available at: https://repositorio.ufmg.br/handle/1843/BUOS-AMXG58?locale=pt_BR

Piaget, J., & Garcia, R. (1983). Article. *Psychogenèse et Histoire des Sciences. 19*(1), 304.

Pijpers, G. (2006). *Information usage behavior theory and practice.* Academic Service.

Pinto, F. M. S. (2017). *A construção de um modelo de acompanhamento da evolução de startups digitais em contexto de aceleração: o caso Start-Up Brasil* (Dissertação de Mestrado em Economia, Administração e Contabilidade). Universidade de São Paulo, São Paulo.

Pinto, I. (2019). Construção perde 14 mil trabalhadores apesar do boom do imobiliário. *Jornal Dinheiro Vivo.* Disponível em: 11, abril, 2019, em: https://www.dinheirovivo.pt/economia/construcao-perde-14-mil-trabalhadores-apesar-do-boom-do-imobiliario/

Piteira, M., Aparicio, M., & Costa, C. (2019). Ethics of Artificial Intelligence: Challenges. *2019 14th Iberian Conference on Information Systems and Technologies (CISTI) Information Systems and Technologies (CISTI), 2019 14th Iberian Conference.*

Planejamento Estratégico de Salvador. Período de 2017 a 2020. (2019). http://www.salvador.ba.gov.br/images/PDF/arquivo_planejamento.pdf

Plattform Industrie 4.0. (2016). *Security in RAMI4.0.* Retrieved July 25, from https://www.plattform-i40.de/PI40/Redaktion/EN/Downloads/Publikation/security-rami40-en.pdf?__blob=publicationFile&v=7

Plattform Industrie 4.0. (n.d.). *A reference framework for digitalization.* Retrieved July 22, from https://www.plattform-i40.de/PI40/Redaktion/EN/Downloads/Publikation/rami40-an-introduction.pdf?__blob=publicationFile&v=7

Pongle, P., & Chavan, G. (2015). Real time intrusion and wormhole attack detection in internet of things. *International Journal of Computers and Applications, 121*(9).

Porter & Heppelmann. (2015). How Smart, Connected Products are Transforming Competition. *Harvard Business Review.*

Portugal Data Protection Act. (2019). Retrieved https://dre.pt/application/conteudo/123815982

Posner, B., & Kouzes, J. (2012). *The Leadership Challenge* (5th ed.). Jossey-Bass.

Prado, V. J., Bezerra, K. D. R., Esteves, E. S. J., & Souza, L. N. (2020). O ecossistema de inovação da cidade de Salvador: Um diagnóstico do nível de maturidade. *Research. Social Development, 9*(3), 51–66.

Prodanov, C. C., & Freitas, E. C. d. (2013). Metodologia do trabalho científico: métodos e técnicas da pesquisa e do trabalho acadêmico (Segunda Edição ed.). Novo Hamburgo, RS: Editora Feevale. doi:10.1017/CBO9781107415324.004

Provan, K. G., & Kenis, P. (2008). Modes of network governance: Structure, management, and effectiveness. *Journal of Public Administration: Research and Theory, 18*(2), 229–252. doi:10.1093/jopart/mum015

Pu, C., & Hajjar, S. (2018). *Mitigating Forwarding misbehaviors in RPL-based low power and lossy networks.* Paper presented at the 2018 15th IEEE Annual Consumer Communications & Networking Conference (CCNC). 10.1109/CCNC.2018.8319164

Putnam, L. L. (1983). The Interpretative Perspective: An Alternative to Functionalism. In L. L. Putnam & M. E. Pacanowsky (Eds.), *Communication and Organizations: An Interpretative Approach* (pp. 31–54). Sage Publications.

Qiu, J., Wu, Q., Ding, G., Yuhua, X., & Feng, S. (2016). A survey of machine learning for big data processing. *EURASIP Journal on Advances in Signal Processing, 67*. Advance online publication. doi:10.118613634-016-0355-x

Quach, T. T. (2014). Extracting hidden messages in steganographic images. *Digital Forensic Research Conference*, 540-545.

Queirós, P., & Lacerda, T. (2013). The importance of interview in qualitative research. In I. Mesquita & A. Graça (Eds.), *Qualitative research in sport* (Vol. 2). Center for Research, Training, Innovation and Intervention in Sport, Faculty of Sport, Porto University.

Raban, D. R., & Rafael, S. (2003). *Subjective Value of Information: The Endowment Effect.* IADIS International Conference: E-Society 2003, Lisbon, Portugal

Raban, D. R., & Rafael, S. (2003). *Subjective Value of Information: The Endowment Effect.* In IADIS International Conference: E-Society 2003, Lisbon, Portugal.

Rafaeli, S., & Raban, D. (2003). Experimental Investigation of the Subjective Value of information in Trading. *Journal of the Association for Information Systems, 4*(1), 119–139. doi:10.17705/1jais.00032

Raghupathi, W., & Raghupathi, V. (2014). Big data analytics in healthcare: Promise and potential. *Health Information Science and Systems, 2*(1), 3. Advance online publication. doi:10.1186/2047-2501-2-3 PMID:25825667

Rashid, M. M., Hossain, E., & Bhargava, V. K. (2009). Cross-layer analysis of downlink V-BLAST MIMO transmission exploiting multiuser diversity. *IEEE Transactions on Wireless Communications, 8*(9), 4568–4579. doi:10.1109/TWC.2009.080513

Raza, S., Chung, T., Duquennoy, S., Voigt, T., & Roedig, U. (2010). *Securing internet of things with lightweight ipsec.* Academic Press.

Raza, S., Duquennoy, S., Höglund, J., Roedig, U., & Voigt, T. (2014). Secure communication for the Internet of Things—A comparison of link-layer security and IPsec for 6LoWPAN. *Security and Communication Networks, 7*(12), 2654–2668. doi:10.1002ec.406

Razzaque, M. A., Milojevic-Jevric, M., Palade, A., & Clarke, S. (2015). Middleware for internet of things: A survey. *IEEE Internet of Things Journal, 3*(1), 70–95. doi:10.1109/JIOT.2015.2498900

Reddy, R. V., Murali, D., & Rajeshwar, J. (2019). Context-aware middleware architecture for IoT-based smart healthcare applications. In *Innovations in Computer Science and Engineering* (pp. 557–567). Springer. doi:10.1007/978-981-13-7082-3_64

Reding, V. (2009). *Internet of the future: Europe must be a key player.* Speech to the Lisbon Council.

Rego, A., Gomes, J. F., Cunha, R. C., Cardoso, C. C., Marques, C. A., & Cunha, M. P. (2015). *Manual de Gestão de Pessoas e do Capital Humano.* Edições Sílabo.

Reis, A. C., Iacovelo, M. T., Almeida, L. B. B., & Costa Filho, B. A. (2016). Marketing de Relacionamento: Agregando Valor ao Negócio com *Big Data. Revista Brasileira de Marketing, 15*(4), 512–523. doi:10.5585/remark.v15i4.3379

Requeijo, J. F., & Pereira, Z. L. (2008). *QUALIDADE: Planeamento e Controlo Estatístico de Processos.* Prefácio.

Richards, G. (2011). *Warehouse Management.* London: Kogan Page Limited.

Ries, E. (2011). *The Lean Startup: how today's entrepreneurs use continuous innovation to create radically successful businesses* (1st ed.). Crown Publishing.

Rifkin, J. (2015). *The Zero Marginal Cost Society.* Palgrave Macmillar.

Ritta, C. O., & Ensslin, S. R. (2010), Investigação Sobre A Relação Entre Ativos Intangíveis E Variáveis Financeiras: Um Estudo Nas Organizações Brasileiras Pertencentes Ao Índice Ibovespa Nos Anos De 2007 E 2008. *10º Congresso Usp De Controladoria E Contabilidade, 2010.*

Ritta, C. O., & Ensslin, S. R. (2010). *Research on The Relationship Between Intangible Assets and Financial Variables: A Study In Brazilian Organizations Belonging to the Ibo vespa Index In The Years 2007 and 2008.* In 10th Usp Congress of Comptant and Accounting, 2010.Anais... São Paulo.

Robert, A., & Schultheis, M. S. (1998). Management Information Systems: The Manager's View. Irwin/McGraw Hill.

Rock Content. (2019, Fevereiro 8). *Social Media Trends: Panorama das empresas e dos usuários nas redes sociais.* https://inteligencia.rockcontent.com/social-media-trends-2019-panorama-das-empresas-e-dos-usuarios-nas-redes-sociais/

Rockembach, M. (2017). Inequalities in digital memory: Ethical and geographical aspects of web archiving. *International Journal of Information Ethics, 26,* 26. doi:10.29173/irie286

Rockembach, M. (2018). Arquivamento da Web: Estudos de caso internacionais e o caso brasileiro. *RDBCI: Revista Digital de Biblioteconomia e Ciência da Informação, 16*(1), 7–24.

Rockembach, M., & da Silva, A. M. (2018). Epistemology and Ethics of big data. In *Challenges and Opportunities for Knowledge Organization in the Digital Age* (pp. 812–819). Ergon-Verlag.

Rockembach, M., & Pavão, C. M. G. (2018). Políticas e tecnologias de preservação digital no arquivamento da web. *Revista Ibero-americana de Ciência da Informação. Brasília. UnB., 11*(1), 168–182.

Rogers, D. (2016). *The Digital Transformation Playbook: Rethink your business for the digital age.* Columbia University Press.

Rogers, D. (2017). *Transformação Digital: Repensando o seu negócio para a era digital.* Autêntica Business.

Rogers, D. L. (2017). *The digital transformation playbook: rethink your business for the digital age.* Columbia University Press.

Roncaratti, L. S. (2017). Incentivos a startups no brasil: os casos do Startup Brasil, InovAtiva e InovApps. In *Inovação no setor público: teoria, tendências e casos no Brasil* (pp. 215–229). Enap/Ipea.

Rosas, A. R., & Sauaia, A. C. A. (2006). Jogos de empresas na educação superior no Brasil: Perspectivas para 2010. *Enfoque: Reflexão Contábil, 25*(3), 72–85. doi:10.4025/enfoque.v25i3.3489

Rosenblum, D. (2007). What anyone can know: The privacy risks of social networking sites. *IEEE Security and Privacy*, *5*(3), 40–49. doi:10.1109/MSP.2007.75

Rosini, A. M., & Palmisano, A. (2003). *Administração de Sistemas de Informação e a Gestão do Conhecimento*. Thomson.

Ross, D. (2011). *Introduction to Supply Chain Management Technologies*. Taylor and Francis Group.

Ross, J. W., Weill, P., & Robertson, D. (2006). *Enterprise Architecture as Strategy: Creating a Foundation for Business Execution*. Harvard Business Review Press.

Ruan, K., Carthy, J., Kechadi, T., & Crosbie, M. (2014). *Cloud forensics: An overview*. Dublin: Centre for Cybercrime Investigation, University College Dublin. Snap. Snap: Suas investigações na Era Digital. http://snapdesktop.com.br/

Samarati, P., & Sweeney, L. (1998). Generalizing data to provide anonymity when disclosing information. PODS, 98, 188. doi:10.1145/275487.275508

Samarati, P., & Sweeney, L. (1998). *Protecting privacy when disclosing information: k-anonymity and its enforcement through generalization and suppression. Tech. rep., technical report*. SRI International.

Sanders, N. R. (2016). How to use big data to drive your supply chain. *California Management Review*, *58*(3), 26–48. doi:10.1525/cmr.2016.58.3.26

Santiago, Tamba, & Harumi. (n.d.). *Proteção de dados no Brasil: novo marco regulatório*. Available at: https://www.migalhas.com.br/dePeso/16,MI290866,91041-Protecao+de+dados+no+Brasil+novo+marco+regulatorio

Santiso. (2001). International Co-Operation for Democracy and Good Governance: Moving Towards a Second Generation? *European Journal of Development Research*.

Santos, N. (2018). Três perguntas a.... *Indústria Revista de Empresários e Negócios, 108*, 12-13. Disponível em: 10, novembro, 2018, em: http://cip.org.pt/wp-content/uploads/2018/05/IND_115_LR.pdf

Saraiva, A. (2018). Identificar as oportunidades e antecipar as dificuldades. Transformação Digital. *Indústria Revista de Empresários e Negócios, 108*, 3. Disponível em: 6, dezembro, 2018, em: http://cip.org.pt/wp-content/uploads/2018/05/IND_115_LR.pdf

Sartor, G. (2014). The right to be forgotten: dynamics of privacy and publicity. In *Protection of Information and the Right to Privacy-A New Equilibrium?* (pp. 1–15). Springer. doi:10.1007/978-3-319-05720-0_1

Satur, R. V., Dias, G. A., & da Silva, A. M. B. M. (2020). Direito autoral, plágio e coautoria. *Brazilian Journal of Information Science*, *14*(1), 57–87. doi:10.36311/1981-1640.2020.v14n1.04.p57

Schmidhuber, J. (2015). Deep learning in neural networks: An overview. *Neural Networks*, *61*, 85–117. doi:10.1016/j.neunet.2014.09.003 PMID:25462637

Schmitz, L. C., Alperstedt, G. D., Van Bellen, H. M., & Schmitz, J. L. (2015). Limitações e dificuldades na utilização da abordagem experiencial no ensino de gerenciamento de projetos em um curso de graduação em administração. *Administração: ensino e pesquisa, 16*(3), 537-569. . doi:10.13058/raep.2015.v16n3.283

Schneider, M., & Saldanha, G. (2015). Entrevista com Rafael Capurro (07-10-2015)| Interview with Rafael Capurro (10-07-2015). *Liinc em Revista, 11*(2).

Schomakers, E. M., Lidynia, C., Müllmann, D., & Ziefle, M. (2019). Internet users' perceptions of information sensitivity–insights from germany. *International Journal of Information Management*, *46*, 142–150. doi:10.1016/j.ijinfomgt.2018.11.018

Schumpeter, J. A. (1982). *Teoria do desenvolvimento econômico: uma investigação sobre lucros, capital, crédito, juro e o ciclo econômico*. Nova Cultural.

Schwab, K. (2018b). *Shaping the fourth industrial revolution*. Excerpts from the World Economic Forum, Switzerland.

Schwab, K. (2019). *2019 is the year to stop talking about ethics and start taking action*. Retrieved Mar 22, from https://www.fastcompany.com/90279512/2019-is-the-year-to-stop-talking-about-ethics-and-start-taking-action

Schwab, K. (2018a). *The Fourth Industrial Revolution*. Edipro.

Secretaria Especial da Fazenda. (n.d.). *Conselho de Controle de Atividades Financeiras – Coaf*. Ambiente em Migração – Ministério da Economia. https://www.fazenda.gov.br/acesso-a-informacao/institucional/estrutura-organizacional/conselho-de-controle-de-atividades-financeiras-coaf

Senai Cimatec. (2020). *Campus Integrado de Manufatura e Tecnologia do Serviço Nacional de Aprendizagem Industrial*. Relatório técnico das chamadas temáticas entre 2017 e 2019.

Senge, P. (2006). The fifth discipline, the art and practice of the Learning Organization. Random House.

Serrano, M. J. (2009). *Logística de Almacenamiento* (2nd ed.). Paraninfo.

Serviço Nacional de Aprendizagem Industrial (SENAI). (2019). *Edital de Inovação da Indústria 2017*. https://docente.ifsc.edu.br/alexandre.zammar/MaterialDidatico/Biotecnologia/edital-de-inovacao-para-a-industria-2017.pdf

Shan, C., Muruato, A. E., Nunes, B. T. D., Luo, H., Xie, X., & Medeiros, D. B. A. (2017). A live-attenuated Zika virus vaccine candidate induces sterilizing immunity in mouse models. *Nature Medicine*. Advance online publication. doi:10.1038/nm.4322 PMID:28394328

Shapiro, C., & Varian, H. R. (1999). *Information rules*. Harvard Business School Press.

Shelby, Z., Hartke, K., & Bormann, C. (2014). *The constrained application protocol (coap)(rfc 7252)*. Available online. http://www. rfc-editor. org/info/rfc7252

Sheriff. (2008). *Cyber Bullying: Issues and solutions for the school, the class room and the home*. Routledge.

Shi, C., Liu, J., Liu, H., & Chen, Y. (2017). Smart user authentication through actuation of daily activities leveraging WiFi-enabled IoT. *Proceedings of the 18th ACM International Symposium on Mobile Ad Hoc Networking and Computing*. 10.1145/3084041.3084061

Silva, M. A. (2013). *Laboratório de gestão: jogo de empresas com pesquisa para a formação crítica em administração* (Doutorado Doutorado). Universidade de São Paulo, São Paulo, SP. https://teses.usp.br/teses/disponiveis/12/12139/tde-20082013-150104/pt-br.php

Simonsson, M., & Johnson, P. (2006). Assessment of IT Governance-A Prioritization of Cobit. KTH, Royal Institute of Technology, Stockholm, Research report # 151.

Simonsson, M., & Johnson, P. (2006). Assessment of IT Governance-A Prioritization of Cobit. KTH, Royal Institute of Technology, Stockholm, Research report #151. Information Governance: In search of the Forgotten Grail 22.

Sincek. (2014). Gender Differences in Cyber-Bullying. *International Multidisciplinary Scientific Conferences on social sciences and arts*, 1-8.

Sindicato da Indústria de Produtos Farmacêuticos no Estado de São Paulo. (2012). *Sindusfarma*. Recuperado 15 de fevereiro de 2013, de Syndicate of pharmaceutical industries in the State of Sao Paulo website: http://www.sindusfarma-comunica.org.br/indicadores-economicos/

Singh, L., & Zhan, J. (2007). Measuring topological anonymity in social networks. In *2007 IEEE International Conference on Granular Computing (GRC 2007)* (pp. 770–770). IEEE. 10.1109/GrC.2007.31

Siqueira, A. H. A. (2019). Capítulo I – Disposições preliminares. In B. Feigelson & A. H. A. Siqueira (Eds.), *Comentários à Lei Geral de Proteção de Dados Lei 13.709/2018* (pp. 15–58). Thomson Reuters.

Sivarajah, U., Kamal, M. M., Irani, Z., & Weerakkody, V. (2017). Critical analysis of Big Data challenges and analytical methods. *Journal of Business Research, 70,* 263–286. doi:10.1016/j.jbusres.2016.08.001

Slonje & Smith. (2008). Cyberbullying: Another main type of bullying? *Scandinavian Journal of Psychology, 49,* 147-154.

Smith, J. R., & Comiskey, B. O. (1996). Modulation and Information Hiding in Images. *Proceedings of the first Information Hiding Workshop, 1174,* 1-21.

Smith, J. A. (1998). *The Warehouse Management Handbook.* Tompkins Press.

Snowden, E. (2019). *Permanent record.* Macmillan.

Solutions, D. F. (2020). *Paletizador Automático.* Retrieved 2020, from https://dsifreezing.com/pt/produtos/automacao/paletizador-automatico/

Solutions, E. L. (2020). *EXE Logistics Solutions LLC - Excellence in Execution.* Retrieved from https://exelogistics-solutions.com/

Sombra, T. L. S. (2019). Fundamentos da Regulação da Privacidade e Proteção de Dados Pessoais: Pluralismo Jurídico e Transparência em Perspectiva. São Paulo: Thomson Reuters.

Song, X., Yang, S., Huang, Z., & Huang, T. (2019). The Application of Artificial Intelligence in Electronic Commerce. *Journal of Physics: Conference Series, 1302*(3), 032030. Advance online publication. doi:10.1088/1742-6596/1302/3/032030

Sousa, M. J., Cruz, R., Rocha, Á., & Sousa, M. (2019). Innovation Trends for Smart Factories: A Literature Review. In Á. Rocha, H. Adeli, L. Reis, & S. Costanzo (Eds.), *New Knowledge in Information Systems and Technologies. WorldCIST'19 2019. Advances in Intelligent Systems and Computing* (pp. 689–698). Springer. doi:10.1007/978-3-030-16181-1_65

Souza, A. J. N. d. (2008). A anatomia de um jogo de guerra didático. *Revista da Escola de Guerra Naval, 12,* 17. https://revista.egn.mar.mil.br/index.php/revistadaegn/article/view/404

Spanish Organic Law 3/2018 for the Protection of Personal Data and for the granting of digital rights. (2018). Retrieved from https://www.boe.es/buscar/pdf/2018/BOE-A-2018-16673-consolidado.pdf

Srivastava, J., Ahmad, M. A., Pathak, N., & Hsu, D. K. W. (2008). Data mining based social network analysis from online behavior. *Tutorial at the 8th SIAM International Conference on Data Mining (SDM'08).*

SrlC. (2015). *Pick to Light.* Retrieved from https://www.cassioli.com.br/todos-os-produtos/pick-to-light/

Stamp, M. (2011). *Information Security: Principles and Practice* (2nd ed.). John Wiley & Sons. doi:10.1002/9781118027974

Stats, I. W. (n.d.). *Usage and Population Statistics.* Available on: https://www.internetworldstats.com/emarketing.htm

Stats, I. W. (n.d.). *Usage and Population Statistics.* Available on: https://www.internetworldstats.com/facebook.htm

Stein, M., Campitelli, V., & Mezzio, S. (2020). Managing the Impact of Cloud Computing. *The CPA Journal, 90*(6), 20–27. Retrieved October 2020, from http://search.ebscohost.com/login.aspx?direct=true&db=bsu&AN=144364480&lang=pt-br&site=ehost-live

Stephen, R., & Arockiam, L. (2017). Intrusion detection system to detect sinkhole attack on RPL protocol in Internet of Things. *International Journal of Electrical Electronics and Computer Science*, *4*(4), 16–20.

Stevenson, W. Jr. (1982). *Elements of Power System Analysis* (4th ed.). Academic Press.

Stipp. (2018). *Percentage of adults in the Unites states who use social networks as of January 2018 by gender.* Available on:https://www.statista.com/statistics/471345/us-adults-who-use-social-networks-gender/

STJ. (n.d.). *Compartilhamento de informações de banco de dados exige notificação prévia ao consumidor.* Available at: https://www.stj.jus.br/sites/portalp/Paginas/Comunicacao/Noticias/Compartilhamento-de-informacoes-de-banco-de-dados-exige-notificacao-previa-ao-consumidor.aspx

Stores, W. C. (2020). *WCS - Supply Chain Expertise. Delivered.* Retrieved from https://www.wwchainstores.com/

Sun Tzu. (1963). *The Art of War* (S. B. Griffith, Trans.). Oxford University Press.

Suo, H., Wan, J., Zou, C., & Liu, J. (2012). *Security in the internet of things: a review.* Paper presented at the 2012 international conference on computer science and electronics engineering. 10.1109/ICCSEE.2012.373

Surdak, C. (2018). *A Revolução Digital: Os 12 Segredos Para Prosperar na Era da Tecnologia.* DVS Editora.

Suresh, P., Daniel, J. V., Parthasarathy, V., & Aswathy, R. (2014). *A state of the art review on the Internet of Things (IoT) history, technology and fields of deployment.* Paper presented at the 2014 International conference on science engineering and management research (ICSEMR). 10.1109/ICSEMR.2014.7043637

Sveiby, K. E. (1998). *A nova riqueza das organizações: gerenciando e avaliando patrimônios de conhecimento.* Campus.

Sveiby, K. E. (1998). *The new wealth of organizations: managing and evaluating knowledge assets.* Campus.

Swamy, S. N., Jadhav, D., & Kulkarni, N. (2017). *Security threats in the application layer in IOT applications.* Paper presented at the 2017 International Conference on I-SMAC (IoT in Social, Mobile, Analytics and Cloud)(I-SMAC). 10.1109/I-SMAC.2017.8058395

Sweeney, L. (2002). k-anonymity: A model for protecting privacy. *International Journal of Uncertainty, Fuzziness and Knowledge-based Systems*, *10*(05), 557–570. doi:10.1142/S0218488502001648

Swiatek, D. C. (2019). Inovando na relação da administração pública com Tecnologia: o mobilab e a contratação de startups pela prefeitura de São Paulo. In *Inovação e políticas: superando o mito da ideia* (pp. 296–312). Ipea.

Swiatkiewicz, O. (2014). Competências transversais, técnicas ou morais: um estudo exploratório sobre as competências dos trabalhadores que as organizações em Portugal mais valorizam. *Cadernos EBAPE. BR*, *12*(3), 633-687. http://bibliotecadigital.fgv.br/ojs/index.php/cadernosebape/article/view/12337

Syam, N., & Sharma, A. (2018). Waiting for a sales renaissance in the fourth industrial revolution: Machine learning and artificial intelligence in sales research and practice. *Industrial Marketing Management*, *69*, 135–146. doi:10.1016/j.indmarman.2017.12.019

Systems, E. (n.d.). *Roller conveyors.* Retrieved 2020, from Roller conveyors: internal transport according to a modular design: https://easy-systems.eu/en/products/roller-conveyors/

Tabrizi, B., Lam, E., Girard, K., & Vernon, I. (2019). Digital Transformation Is Not About Technology. *Harvard Business Review.* Disponível em: 21, janeiro, 2019, em: https://hbr.org/2019/03/digital-transformation-is-not-about-technology

Tai, C. H., Yu, P. S., Yang, D. N., & Chen, M. S. (2011). Privacy-preserving social network publication against friendship attacks. In *Proceedings of the 17th ACM SIGKDD international conference on Knowledge discovery and data mining* (pp. 1262–1270). ACM. 10.1145/2020408.2020599

TASS – Russian News Agency. (2020). *Russian citizen sentenced for attempt to hand over classified data to CIA.* Retrieved on November, 2020, from https://tass.com/society/1225813

Tassa, T., & Cohen, D. J. (2011). Anonymization of centralized and distributed social networks by sequential clustering. *IEEE Transactions on Knowledge and Data Engineering, 25*(2), 311–324. doi:10.1109/TKDE.2011.232

Taylor, J. (2010). Google chief: My fears for Generation Facebook. *Independent.* Retrieved Mar 18, from https://www.independent.co.uk/life-style/gadgets-and-tech/news/google-chief-my-fears-for-generation-facebook-2055390.html

Tejero, J. J. A. (2011). Logística integral. La gestión operativa de la empresa (4th ed.). Madrid: ESIC Editorial.

Terence, A., & Filho, E. (2006). Abordagem quantitativa, qualitativa e a utilização da pesquisa-ação nos estudos organizacionais. *XXVI ENEGEP – Fortaleza*, 1-9. Disponível em: 23, dezembro, 2018, em: http://www.abepro.org.br/biblioteca/enegep2006_tr540368_8017.pdf

The Agile Manifesto. (2001). https://agilemanifesto.org/

The Digital Reinvention Operation Environment from IBV (IBM Institute of Business Value). (n.d.). https://www.ibm.com/thought-leadership/institute-business-value

The Mackinsey article Unlocking success in digital transformations. (2018). https://www.mckinsey.com/~/media/McKinsey/Business%20Functions/Organization/Our%20Insights/Unlocking%20success%20in%20digital%20transformations/Unlocking-success-in-digital-transformations.ashx

The world's most valuable resource is no longer oil, but data. (n.d.). *The Economist.* Disponível em https://www.economist.com/leaders/2017/05/06/the-worlds-most-valuable-resource-is-no-longer-oil-but-data

Tiersky, H. (2017). The 5 key drivers of digital transformation today. *CIO.*

Times of India. (2014). *Girl kills self over Facebook harassment.* Available on: https://timesofindia.indiatimes.com/city/kolkata/Girl-kills-self-over-Facebook-harassment/articleshow/37211521.cms

Today, I. (2016). *Salem: Morphed Facebook images drive woman to suicide.* Available on: www.indiatoday.in/india/story/morphed-images-on-facebook-drive-salem-woman-to-suicide-16741-2016-06-28

Today, I. (2017). *Delhi: Cyber crooks stealing, morphing social media photos to extort victims.* Available on: https://www.indiatoday.in/mail-today/story/delhi-cyber-crooks-stealing-morhphong-photos-porn-sites-extrotion-966463-2017-03-20

Today, I. (2018). *Bengal Woman streams suicide on Face book Live for boyfriend.* Available on: https://www.indiatoday.in/india/story/woman-commits-suicide-streams-act-on-facebook-live-1257898-2018-06-12

Toffler, A. (1980). *The third wave.* William Morrow.

Topcu. (2010). The Revised Cyber Bullying Inventory(RCBI):validity and reliability studies. *Procedia Social and Behavioral Sciences, 5,* 660-664.

Torres, M. (2013). *Sistemas de Almacenaje y Picking.* Diaz de Santos.

Trithemius, J. (1606). Steganographia (secretwriting). Germany, Darmbstadil, Bibliop, Francop, Anno M.DC.XXI, 1-270.

Tsai, C.-F., Hsu, Y.-F., Lin, C.-Y., & Lin, W.-Y. (2009). Intrusion detection by machine learning: A review. *Expert Systems With Applications, 36*(10), 11994-12000.

Tuna, G., Kogias, D. G., Gungor, V. C., Gezer, C., Taşkın, E., & Ayday, E. (2017). A survey on information security threats and solutions for Machine to Machine (M2M) communications. *Journal of Parallel and Distributed Computing*, *109*, 142–154. doi:10.1016/j.jpdc.2017.05.021

U.S. Cyber Command. (2020). *U.S. Cyber Command History*. Retrieved on October, 2020, from https://www.cybercom.mil/About/History/

Ultimation Industries. (2018). *Ultimation*. Retrieved from POWER AND FREE CONVEYORS: https://www.ultimationinc.com/products-conveyor-systems/power-and-free-conveyors/

UNICRI. (n.d.). *UNICRI Centre for Artificial Intelligence and Robotics*. Retrieved Mar 19, from http://www.unicri.it/in_focus/on/UNICRI_Centre_Artificial_Robotics

United Nations. (2013). *Report of the Group of Governmental Experts on Developments in the Field of Information and Telecommunications in the Context of International Security*. Available at https://undocs.org/A/68/98

United Nations. (2019). *United Nations Conference on Trade and Development – Digital Economy Report 2019*. New York: United Nations Publications. Available at https://unctad.org/system/files/official-document/der2019_overview_en.pdf

VAINZOF (n.d.). *World's Biggest Data Breaches & Hacks*. https://informationisbeautiful.net/visualizations/worlds-biggest-data-breaches-hacks/

Vale, M. (2004). Innovation, and knowledge driven by a focal corporation: The case of the Autoeuropa supply chain. *European Urban and Regional Studies*, *11*(2), 124–140. doi:10.1177/0969776404036252

Vale, M., & Caldeira, J. (2007). Proximity and knowledge governance in localized production systems: The footwear industry in the north region of Portugal. *European Planning Studies*, *15*(4), 531–548. doi:10.1080/09654310601134854

Vale, M., & Caldeira, J. (2008). Fashion and the governance of knowledge in a traditional industry: The case of the footwear sectoral innovation system in the northern region of Portugal. *Economics of Innovation and New Technology*, *17*(1-2), 61–78. doi:10.1080/10438590701279318

Van Buuren, A. (2009). Knowledge for governance, governance of knowledge: Inclusive knowledge management in collaborative governance processes. *International Public Management Journal*, *12*(2), 208–235. doi:10.1080/10967490902868523

Van de Ven, A. H., & Engleman, R. M. (2004). Event- and outcome-driven explanations of entrepreneurship. *Journal of Business Venturing*, *19*(3), 343-358. doi:10.1016/S0883-9026(03)00035-1

Van Grembergen, W. (2004). *Strategies for Information Technology Governance*. IDEA Group Publishing. doi:10.4018/978-1-59140-140-7

Van Grembergen, W., & De Haes, S. (2007). *Implementing IT governance: models, practices and cases*. IGI Global.

Van Haren Publishing. (2011). *ITIL Foundations - Best Practice*. Author.

Vance, K., Howe, W., & Dellavalle, R. P. (2009). Social Internet Sites as a Source of Public Health Information. *Dermatologic Clinics*, *27*(2), 133–136. doi:10.1016/j.det.2008.11.010 PMID:19254656

Varajão, L. A. (2007). *Planeamento de Sistemas de Informação*. FCA - Editora de Informática.

Vecchia, E. D. (2019). Perícia digital, da investigação à análise forense (2. ed.). Campinas, SP: Millennium.

Vergara, S. C. (2006). *Projetos e relatórios de pesquisa*. Atlas.

Vergílio, R. (2019). *Main ethical risks arising from the digital transformation of an energy company*. ISGec – Information System Governance European Clube.

Vermeren, I. (2015). *Men Vs Women: Who is More Active on Social Media?* Available on: https://www.brandwatch.com/blog/men-vs-women-active-social-media/

Vieira, D., & Roux, M. (2011). *Projeto de Centros de Distribuição, fundamentos, metodologia e prática para a moderna cadeia de suprimentos*. Campus / Elsevier Editora Ltda.

Vogler, M., Gratieri, T., Gelfuso, G. M., & Cunha Filho, M. S. S. (2017). As boas práticas de fabricação de medicamentos e suas determinantes. *Vigilância Sanitária em Debate, 5*(2), 34. doi:10.22239/2317-269x.00918

Wang, Y., Chakrabarti, D., Wang, C., & Faloutsos, C. (2003). Epidemic spreading in real networks: An eigenvalue viewpoint. In *22nd International Symposium on Reliable Distributed Systems, 2003. Proceedings* (pp. 25–34). IEEE.

Wang, D. W., Liau, C. J., & Hsu, T. (2006) Privacy protection in social network data disclosure based on granular computing. In *2006 IEEE International Conference on Fuzzy Systems* (pp. 997–1003). IEEE. 10.1109/FUZZY.2006.1681832

Wang, P. (2019). On Defining Artificial Intelligence. *Journal of Artificial General Intelligence, 10*(2), 1–37. doi:10.2478/jagi-2019-0002

Wan, J., Yang, J., Wang, Z., & Hua, Q. (2018). Artificial Intelligence for Cloud-Assisted Smart Factory. *IEEE Access: Practical Innovations, Open Solutions, 6*, 55419–55430. doi:10.1109/ACCESS.2018.2871724

Webb, A. (2019). The big nine: How the tech titans and their thinking machines could warp humanity. Hachette UK.

Wedel, M., & Kannan, P. K. (2016). Marketing Analytics for Data-Rich Environments. *Journal of Marketing, 80*(6), 97–121. doi:10.1509/jm.15.0413

Weiblen, T., & Chesbrough, H. W. (2015). Engaging with Startups to Enhance Corporate Innovation. *California Management Review, 57*(2), 66–90. Advance online publication. doi:10.1525/cmr.2015.57.2.66

Weick, K., & Quinn, R. (1999). *Organizational Change and Development*. Annual Revision Psychology.

Weill, P., & Ross, J. W. (2004). *It Governance – How top Performers Manage it Decision Rights for Superior Results*. Harvard Business SchoolPress.

Wellman, B. (1996). For a social network analysis of computer networks: a sociological perspective on collaborative work and virtual community. In *Proceedings of the 1996 ACM SIGCPR/SIGMIS conference on Computer personnel research* (pp. 1– 11). ACM. 10.1145/238857.238860

Welsh T., Benkhelifa E. (2020). On Resilience in Cloud Computing: A Survey of Techniques across the Cloud Domain. *ACM Computing Surveys, 53*(3), 59-59. doi:10.1145/3388922

Werkema, M. C. C. (1995). *Ferramentas estatisticas basicas para o gerenciamento de processos*. Universidade Federal de Minas Gerais. Escola de Engenharia. Fundacao Christiano Ottoni.

Westerman, G. (2016). *Liderando na Era Digital*. M. Books.

Westerman, G. (2017). Your Company doesn't need a digital strategy. *MIT Sloan Management Review*, (October), 25.

White House. (2013). *Presidential Policy Directive – Critical Infrastructure Security and Resilience*. Available at https://obamawhitehouse.archives.gov/the-press-office/2013/02/12/presidential-policy-directive-critical-infrastructure-security-and-resil

White House. (2018). *The Cost of Malicious Cyber Activity to the U.S. Economy*. Retrieved on November, 2020, from https://www.whitehouse.gov/wp-content/uploads/2018/03/The-Cost-of-Malicious-Cyber-Activity-to-the-U.S.-Economy.pdf

Wiesner, S. (1983). Conjugate Coding. *SIGACT, Volume, 15*(1), 78–88.

Wiggen, J. (2020). *The Impact of COVID-19 on Cyber Crime and State-Sponsored Cyber Activities*. Retrieved on November, 2020, from https://www.kas.de/documents/252038/7995358/The+impact+of+COVID-19+on+cyber+crime+and+state-sponsored+cyber+activities.pdf/b4354456-994b-5a39-4846-af6a0bb3c378?version=1.0&t=1591354291674

Williams, A. (2016). AMS - automotive manufacturing solutions. *AGVs encontram o seu caminho*. Retrieved 2020, from https://www.automotivemanufacturingsolutions.com/agvs-encontram-o-seu-caminho/35024.article

Williford, A. P., & Jessica, E. (2013). Childrens Engagement with in the preschool classroom and their development of self-regulation. *Early Education and Development, 24*, 162–187.

Womark, J. P., Jones, D., & Ros, D. (1990). *The Machine that Changed the World.* Macmillan Publishing Company.

Wootters & Zurek. (1982). A Single quantum cannot be cloned. *Nature, 299*, 802–803.

World Bank. (1992). *Governance and development.* Oxford University Press.

World Economic Forum. (2020). *Cybersecurity, emerging technology and systemic risk.* Available at http://www3.weforum.org/docs/WEF_Future_Series_Cybersecurity_emerging_technology_and_systemic_risk_2020.pdf

Wu, X., Zhu, X., Wu, G.Q., & Ding, W. (2014). Privacy preserving social network publication against mutual friend attacks. *IEEE Transactions on Data Privacy, 7*(2), 71–97.

Wu, H., Khan, M. A., & Hussain, A. S. (2007). Process Control Perspective for Process Analytical Technology: Integration of Chemical Engineering Practice into Semiconductor and Pharmaceutical Industries. *Chemical Engineering Communications, 194*(6), 760–779. doi:10.1080/00986440601098755

Wu, X., Ying, X., Liu, K., & Chen, L. (2010). A survey of privacy-preservation of graphs and social networks. In *Managing and mining graph data* (pp. 421–453). Springer. doi:10.1007/978-1-4419-6045-0_14

Xiao, L., Li, Y., Han, G., Liu, G., & Zhuang, W. (2016). PHY-layer spoofing detection with reinforcement learning in wireless networks. *IEEE Transactions on Vehicular Technology, 65*(12), 10037–10047. doi:10.1109/TVT.2016.2524258

Xu, Xu, & Li. (2018). Industry 4.0: State of the art and future trends. *International Journal of Production Research, 56*(8), 2941–2962.

Yang, Y., Wu, L., Yin, G., Li, L., & Zhao, H. (2017). A survey on security and privacy issues in Internet-of-Things. *IEEE Internet of Things Journal, 4*(5), 1250–1258. doi:10.1109/JIOT.2017.2694844

Ying, X., & Wu, X. (2011). On link privacy in randomizing social networks. *Knowledge and Information Systems, 28*(3), 645–663. doi:10.100710115-010-0353-5

Yin, R. K. (2015). *Estudo de caso: Planejamento e métodos* (5th ed.). Bookman.

Yu, W., Liang, F., He, X., Hatcher, W. G., Lu, C., Lin, J., & Yang, X. (2017). A survey on the edge computing for the Internet of Things. *IEEE Access: Practical Innovations, Open Solutions, 6*, 6900–6919. doi:10.1109/ACCESS.2017.2778504

Zabala, A., & Arnau, L. (2015). *11 ideas clave: cómo aprender y enseñar competencias.* Graó.

Zetes. (n.d.). *The benefits of voice picking.* Retrieved 2020, from https://www.zetes.com/pt/solucoes-para-armazem/picking-a-encomenda/vantagens-de-voice-picking

Zhang, Q., & Wang, X. (2009). *SQL injections through back-end of RFID system.* Paper presented at the 2009 International Symposium on Computer Network and Multimedia Technology. 10.1109/CNMT.2009.5374533

Zhang, K., Liang, X., Lu, R., & Shen, X. (2014). Sybil attacks and their defenses in the internet of things. *IEEE Internet of Things Journal, 1*(5), 372–383. doi:10.1109/JIOT.2014.2344013

Zheleva, E., & Getoor, L. (2008). Preserving the privacy of sensitive relationships in graph data. In *Privacy, security, and trust in KDD* (pp. 153–171). Springer. doi:10.1007/978-3-540-78478-4_9

Zhou, B., & Pei, J. (2008). Preserving privacy in social networks against neighborhood attacks. In *Data Engineering, 2008. ICDE 2008. IEEE 24th International Conference on* (pp. 506–515). IEEE. 10.1109/ICDE.2008.4497459

Zhou, B., Pei, J., & Luk, W. (2008). A brief survey on anonymization techniques for privacy preserving publishing of social network data. *SIGKDD Explorations*, *10*(2), 12–22. doi:10.1145/1540276.1540279

Zortea, C. G. C., & Maldaner, L. F. (2018). Startups Accelerator Programs: A Comparative Analysis of Acceleration Mechanisms from Start-Up Brazil and Start-Up Chile Program. *Revista Eletrônica de Estratégia & Negócios*, *11*(3), 29–53.

Zou, L., Chen, L., & Ozsu, M. T. (2009). K-automorphism: A general framework for privacy preserving network publication. *Proceedings of the VLDB Endowment International Conference on Very Large Data Bases*, *2*(1), 946–957. doi:10.14778/1687627.1687734

Zuboff, S. (2019). *The Age of Surveillance Capitalism: The Fight for a Human Future at the New Frontier of Power: Barack Obama's Books of 2019*. Profile Books.

Zucatti, A. P. N., Silveira, L. M. O. B., Abbad, G. S., & Flores, C. D. (2019). Criação de uma Simulação para o Desenvolvimento de Competências em um Hospital. *Psicologia: Ciência e Profissão*, *39*. Advance online publication. doi:10.1590/1982-3703002102017

ZVEI. (2016). *ZVEI explains RAMI 4.0*. Retrieved September 2, from https://www.zvei.org/en/subjects/industrie-4-0/

Zyngier, S. (2010). Governance of knowledge management. Encyclopedia of Knowledge Management.

Zyngier, S., Burstein, F., & Mckay, J. (2005). *Governance of strategies to manage organizational knowledge: A mechanism to oversee knowledge needs*. Case Studies in Knowledge Management. doi:10.4018/978-1-59140-351-7.ch006

About the Contributors

Pedro Anunciação is Professor of Information Systems at Polytechnic Institute of Setúbal Coordinator of Research Center in Business Administration General-Secretary of Information Systems Governance European Club Portuguese Chapter.

George Jamil is a professor of several post-graduation courses from Minas Gerais, Brazil. He has two post-doctoral titles (from Universidade do Porto, Portugal - market intelligence and from Univsersidad Politecnica de Cartagena, Spain - Entrepreneurship). PhD in Information Science from the Federal University of Minas Gerais (UFMG), Masters degree in Computer Science (UFMG) and undergraduated in Electric Engineering (UFMG). He got post-doctoral degrees from FLUP - University of Porto, Portugal - and from Universidad Politecnica de Cartagena, Spain. He wrote more than thirty books in the information technology and strategic management areas, with more than ten works in books as co-author and Editor. He works also as a business consultant and as an active ecossystem actor in business innovation and startups front in several countries. His main research interests are information systems management, strategy, knowledge management, software engineering, marketing and IT adoption in business contexts.

* * *

Ricardo de Sousa Correia of the Portuguese Air Force is 38 years old, married and father of a son. His experience was mainly developed on the logistics and financial areas, particularly in procurement, contracting, distribution, reception, staging and onward movement and logistics management – activities developed in military environment. His assignments include duty as logistics and financial Officer in several military missions and exercises in Europe and Africa. Captain Sousa Correia's military and civilian education includes First Degree of the Portuguese Air Force Academy in Military Technologies – Supply Management, Spanish Language Course, Logistics Functional Area Services Staff Officer Course, Principles and Guidelines for UN Peacekeeping Operations Course, European Security and Defence Policy Course and a Master's Degree in Logistics Management.

Marta Costa graduated in Information Mangement Systems by College of Business Administration (ESCE) of Polytechnic Institute of Setúbal (IPS). Marta has also a BSc and a MSc in Geological Engineering by NOVA University of Lisbon (QS World University Rankings 2014 and 2016).

Thiago R. Veloso Costa is Legal Manager - Norsk Hydro - Extrusion Brazil, Attending Master's Degree in Business Strategy at FIA - Business School (FIA) São Paulo - SP, having earned his LL.B. from the Pontifical Catholic University of Minas Gerais (PUC-MG) and a certificate degree in International Trade Relations from the same institution, as well as a certificate degree in Tax Law from Faculdade Milton Campos-MG. Certification in International Contracts from the Hague Academy of International Law, in Arbitration and International Contracts from the London School of Economics and Political Science, in addition to certifications in Brazil in Crisis Management and Reputation from Escola Superior de Propaganda e Marketing (ESPM), and in Data Protection and Privacy from Insper.

Md. Alimul Haque is currently working as Assistant Professor in the Department of Computer Science, Veer Kunwar Singh University, Ara, India. He received his Bachelor and Master degree in Computer Application in 2004 and 2008 respectively and the PhD. Degree on "Security and Privacy aspects on Wireless Communication Networks" from V. K. S. University, Ara, India in 2017. His research interests include cyber security, wireless communication networks, IoT and Artificial Intelligence. His research has led to publications of numerous papers in peer reviewed journals of the world. He has been Life member of ISCA, Kolkata, India.

Shameemul Haque did his M.C.A from Lalit Narayan Mishra Institute of Economic Development & Social Change, Patna in 2002and PhD in 2019 From Veer Kunwer Singh University, Ara. He is Assistant Professor at Al-Hafeez College Ara, He has worked at King Khalid University, Saudi Arabia from 2009 to 2019. He has published 8 research paper in peer reviewed Journals. He has also presented paper at many Conferences. He is Editorial Board member of many International Journals.

Kailash Kumar has more than 17 years of teaching experience in India and abroad. Presently, serving as an Assistant Professor and Chair-CCI Steering Committee in the College of Computing and Informatics, Saudi Electronic University, Riyadh, KSA since 2014. Previously, he served as Dean (Academics) in the department of Computer Science and Engineering from 2010 to 2014 in Modern Institute of Technology & Research Centre, India. He has vast experience of 17 years in teaching at national and international level. He has served as reviewer in many international journals such as International Journal of Web-Based Learning and Teaching Technologies (IJWLTT) - IGI Global, Elsevier and IEEE Sensors Journals. He has also delivered special talks in IEEE conferences and chaired various technical sessions in international conferences. He is associated with various technical societies of national and international repute. He has published various research papers in reputed journals. His research paper entitled "Bitcoin and its Modus Operandi" in Workshop/Conference conducted by Bank Albilad Chair of E-commerce (BACEC) is rewarded by cash prize of SAR 5000. He is a member of IEEE (#97049444), Life Member of Computer Society of India (CSI), Life member of Indian Society for Technical Education (ISTE), IAENG, Associate Member of Institute of Engineers (AMIE), Member of Computer Science Teacher's Association, International Society on Multiple Criteria Division Making and International Association of Computer Science & Information Technology. He has authored the book on "Theory of Computation" and contributed chapters in several books. His recent achievement includes Explorer Award - IoT Cloud Developer issued by IBM (https://www.youracclaim.com/go/4tUVU3pw1KMO8u3ufxhw4g) and Mastery Award - IoT Cloud Developer issued by IBM(https://www.youracclaim.com/badges/f15016e2-94b1-4c65-b335-c363e8cf639e/public_url). He is profoundly engrossed in the area of Data Science, Machine Learning, Artificial Intelligence, Blockchain Technology, E-commerce, Compiler Construction etc.

Bruno de Lacerda is a Consultant, Lecturer, Author, Professor and Researcher, working in Brazil with topics such as Professional and entrepreneurial use of Social Media, Startups and innovation processes, Social adoption of technologies. As a visionary leader, he is now responsible of mentoring several companies in Brazil over leadership and innovation management.

Kamal R. Macwan received his B.E. degree in Computer Engineering from D.D.I.T., Nadiad, India in 2010. Received his M.E. degree in Computer Engineering from B.V.M Engineering College, V.V. Nagar, India in 2013. Currently, he is pursuing Ph.D. in the Department of Computer Engineering, S V National Institute of Technology, Surat, India. His research interests include Information Security, Privacy Preservation techniques.

Jorge Magalhães postgraduated in Competitive Intelligence for Public Health. Doctor and Master in Sciences in Management and Technological Innovation. Has over 20 years of experience in strategic management in the pharmaceutical Industrial Operations and in the last 14 years to act in R, D & I for Public Health area at FIOCRUZ. Published 03 books, 9 book chapters and several articles in journals indexed. Actually work in Technology Innovation Center (NIT-Far) at FIOCRUZ. It is leader of the CNPq Research Group Knowledge Management and Prospecting Health. The emphasis of their research permeate the identification, extraction and analysis of essential information within the "Big data" for Health, regarding the Management and Technological Innovation. The topics covered are inherent in Global Health, in which involves the pharmaceutical industry, pharmochemical and public health. Investigations are carried out through the development of prospective and technological scenarios of information science tools, Competitive Intelligence and Knowledge Management. Included in this context the analysis of BIG DATA, Web 2.0, Health 2.0 Technological Trends, market, Patents and Knowledge Translation.

Armando Barreiros Malheiro da Silva is Associated Professor of the Faculty of Arts of the University of Porto and member of the coordinating committee of the Information Science degree taught by the Arts and Engineering Faculties of the University of Porto. Born in Braga, PdD in Contemporary History in the University of Minho, graduated in Philosophy by Philosophy Faculty of the Catholic University of Braga and in History by the Faculty of Arts of the University of Porto. He obtained the diploma of the course of Librarian-Archivist of the Faculty of Arts of the University of Coimbra. Is member of the Center for Studies in Technology, Arts and Communication Sciences (CETAC.Media) and shares his researches in areas such as the archivist and information science; the metanalysis; political and ideological History in Portugal in the XIX-XX century; Family history and local studies.

Sérgio Maravilhas is a Lecturer at SENAI/CIMATEC and UNIFACS, Brazil. More than 33 years of professional experience. With two Post-Docs, one from UFBA (Patents and innovation) and another from UNIFACS (FAB LABS), both with PNPD/CAPES Grants; PhD in Information and Communication in Digital Platforms (FCT Grant) from Porto and Aveiro Univs., Portugal; a Master Science in Information Management (FEUP + Sheffield University, UK); a Postgrad Course in ICT (FEUP); a Postgrad in Innovation and Technological Entrepreneurship (FEUP + North Carolina State University, USA); and a 5 years Degree in Philosophy, Educational Branch (FLUP). A Teacher since 1998, worked at ESE-IPP (Teacher/Supervisor - Internet@School project, 2002/2005), and a University Lecturer and Researcher since 2005 at Aveiro University, and since 2010 at ULP and IESFF in Masters and MBAs. Teaches Marketing, Research Methods, Creative Processes, Innovation, Intellectual and Industrial Property, Technology Watch, Information Management, Organizational Behaviour, ICT, Sales, and Neuro-Linguistic Programming. Publishes about Patent Information, Innovation, Marketing, Web 2.0, Web Radio, FAB LABS, Technology, and Sustainability.

Sérgio Oliveira graduated in Business Administration from the School of Business Administration of São Paulo FGV (1997), Master in Business Administration from the Federal University of Bahia (2000) and doctorate in Business Administration from the School of Business Administration of São Paulo - FGV (2007). He is currently an Adjunct Professor at the School of Administration at the Federal University of Bahia. He was a full professor in the Master's program in Administration at Universidade Salvador - Unifacs for 10 years. He coordinated graduate courses and undergraduate courses in administration. He worked as an executive in companies in the auditing, consulting, civil construction and education sectors. He developed numerous technological innovation projects, obtaining their approval in several economic grant notices. Developed the Change Management simulation Executive Change, an award-winning technological solution.

Felipe Palhares is the first Brazilian national to have been recognized as a Fellow of Information Privacy by the International Association of Privacy Professionals and is currently the only Brazilian national to have earned all privacy and data protection certifications issued by the IAPP. He is also a certified Data Protection Officer by Maastricht University. He holds an LL.M. degree in Corporate Law from the New York University and is admitted to practice law in Brazil and in New York State.

Sankita J. Patel received her B.E., M.Tech., and Ph.D. degrees in Computer Engineering from S V National Institute of Technology, Surat, India in 2002, 2008 and 2015, respectively. Currently, she is working as an Assistant Professor in the Department of Computer Engineering, S V National Institute of Technology, Surat, India. Her research interests include Information and Communication Security, Security and Privacy in Internet of Things, Privacy Preserving Data Publishing/Mining and Biometric Cryptosystem.

Jose Poças Rascão (PhD, ISCTE / ULI) is a Professor of Management Information Systems at the Polytechnic Institute of Setubal, Graduate School of Business Sciences, Portugal. It is research in the Research Unit in the development of enterprise (UNIDE) at the Lisbon University Institute (ISCTE / ULI). Since 2000 he has published 15 books and over 80 research papers in international scholarly academic journals, about on management strategy and management of information. Under his supervision, 17 Masters Theses have been successfully from 2007 to 2018. From 2010 to 2015 was Director of Course Management of Distribution and Logistics. From 2013 to 2014 was Coordinator of Research Center, Polytechnic Institute of Setubal, Graduate School of Business Sciences. From 2000-2004 was Information Systems Management Course Coordinator Polytechnic Institute of Setubal, Graduate School of Business Sciences. He also works the private Management Consultant for large and medium-sized enterprises. He worked the Management Consult at Price Waterhouse and Coopers & Lybrand between 1989 and 1995.

Alexis da Rocha Silva is a Brazilian researcher and IT Professional, working in the Munich, Germany IBM as a Software Engineer.

Matheus Felipe Silva is an expat living in Dublin, Ireland, working as QA Manager. BSc in Computer Science and a Master's degree in Project Management, ISTQB certified with 17 years experience working with IT - being 12 of them dedicated to Testing and Quality Assurance.

Rafael Velasquez Silva is a researcher of Forensic Technology, Computer Forensic Specialist and Partner of Techbiz Forense Digital Head of Sao Paulo office (branch) - Mission of develop a business plan and sales strategy for the market that ensures achievement of company sales goals and profitability. Responsible for performance and development of the growths in his territory – SP, MG, RS, SC and PR. Techbiz Mission: Help our customers to find the answers. IT Security and Forensic Solutions: Forensic Hardware (Bridges, Duplicators, Write Blockers, Computers), Mobile Extractions, Forensic Analyze software, SIEM, Packet Inspection, Endpoint Protection, Employee Monitoring and Behavior Monitoring. Solutions for Military Industries, Law Enforcement, Services, Judiciary, Government, Telecom, Banks and Industry markets.

Narendra Singh obtained his M.Sc. degree in Physics from Bihar University, Muzaffarpur, India in 1969 and Ph.D. in 1984 from Patna University, Patna. He was Professor and Ex- Head, University Department of Physics, V.K.S. University, Ara (India). He is the life member of different academic and Research Societies of India and abroad. He is a member of the Editorial Board of National Journal "ARJP". He has published over 97 research papers in peer reviewed journals of the world. He was a U.G.C. Visiting Associate at I.I.T. Kharagpur, India during 2001-2003. In span of 28 years of his research career, he has remained engaged in the preparation of fine ceramics, ferroelectric piezoelectric and non-Lead based materials. Presently, he was Principal Investigator of Major Research Project sponsored by DRDO, New Delhi and was engaged in synthesis and characterization of Lead free ferroelectricpiezoelectric systems for sensor applications.

Maria Tereza Sousa Silva is a Master's student in Management, Research and Development in the Pharmaceutical Industry at Fundação Oswaldo Cruz, FIOCRUZ (Farmanguinhos), Graduated in Biological Sciences postgraduate in Microbiology. I am currently a quality analyst at the Institute of Technology in Immunobiologicals. Experience in the area of Health, with emphasis on Public Health, working mainly in the release of products according to good practice legislation.

Gustavo Vinicius Duarte Barbosa is a Federal Public Servant belonging to the Civil Personnel of Higher Level of the Air Force Command, awarded by the Airspace Control Department (DECEA) for the position of Electrical Engineer of the DACTA 1301. Career Degree in Electrical Engineering from the Federal University of Minas Gerais (2003), taking a professional technical course in Electronics from the Technical College of the Pedagogical Center of the Federal University of Minas Gerais (1997). Master in Electrical Engineering from the Graduate Program in Electrical Engineering at the UFMG School of Engineering (2018).

Index

Recommended Reference Books

IGI Global's reference books are available in three unique pricing formats:
Print Only, E-Book Only, or Print + E-Book.

Shipping fees may apply.

www.igi-global.com

ISBN: 978-1-5225-9866-4
EISBN: 978-1-5225-9867-1
© 2020; 1,805 pp.
List Price: US$ 2,350

ISBN: 978-1-5225-8876-4
EISBN: 978-1-5225-8877-1
© 2019; 141 pp.
List Price: US$ 135

ISBN: 978-1-5225-7847-5
EISBN: 978-1-5225-7848-2
© 2019; 306 pp.
List Price: US$ 195

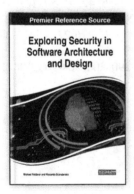

ISBN: 978-1-5225-6313-6
EISBN: 978-1-5225-6314-3
© 2019; 349 pp.
List Price: US$ 215

ISBN: 978-1-5225-1941-6
EISBN: 978-1-5225-1942-3
© 2017; 408 pp.
List Price: US$ 195

ISBN: 978-1-5225-0808-3
EISBN: 978-1-5225-0809-0
© 2017; 442 pp.
List Price: US$ 345

Do you want to stay current on the latest research trends, product announcements, news, and special offers?
Join IGI Global's mailing list to receive customized recommendations, exclusive discounts, and more.
Sign up at: **www.igi-global.com/newsletters.**

Publisher of Peer-Reviewed, Timely, and Innovative Academic Research

www.igi-global.com   Sign up at www.igi-global.com/newsletters   facebook.com/igiglobal   twitter.com/igiglobal   linkedin.com/igiglobal

Ensure Quality Research is Introduced to the Academic Community

Become an Evaluator for IGI Global Authored Book Projects

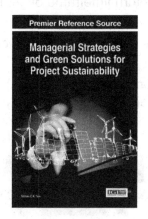

The overall success of an authored book project is dependent on quality and timely manuscript evaluations.

Applications and Inquiries may be sent to:
development@igi-global.com

Applicants must have a doctorate (or equivalent degree) as well as publishing, research, and reviewing experience. Authored Book Evaluators are appointed for one-year terms and are expected to complete at least three evaluations per term. Upon successful completion of this term, evaluators can be considered for an additional term.

If you have a colleague that may be interested in this opportunity, we encourage you to share this information with them.

IGI Global Author Services

Providing a high-quality, affordable, and expeditious service, IGI Global's Author Services enable authors to streamline their publishing process, increase chance of acceptance, and adhere to IGI Global's publication standards.

Benefits of Author Services:

- **Professional Service:** All our editors, designers, and translators are experts in their field with years of experience and professional certifications.

- **Quality Guarantee & Certificate:** Each order is returned with a quality guarantee and certificate of professional completion.

- **Timeliness:** All editorial orders have a guaranteed return timeframe of 3-5 business days and translation orders are guaranteed in 7-10 business days.

- **Affordable Pricing:** IGI Global Author Services are competitively priced compared to other industry service providers.

- **APC Reimbursement:** IGI Global authors publishing Open Access (OA) will be able to deduct the cost of editing and other IGI Global author services from their OA APC publishing fee.

Author Services Offered:

English Language Copy Editing
Professional, native English language copy editors improve your manuscript's grammar, spelling, punctuation, terminology, semantics, consistency, flow, formatting, and more.

Scientific & Scholarly Editing
A Ph.D. level review for qualities such as originality and significance, interest to researchers, level of methodology and analysis, coverage of literature, organization, quality of writing, and strengths and weaknesses.

Figure, Table, Chart & Equation Conversions
Work with IGI Global's graphic designers before submission to enhance and design all figures and charts to IGI Global's specific standards for clarity.

Translation
Providing 70 language options, including Simplified and Traditional Chinese, Spanish, Arabic, German, French, and more.

Hear What the Experts Are Saying About IGI Global's Author Services

"Publishing with IGI Global has been *an amazing experience* for me for sharing my research. The *strong academic production* support ensures quality and timely completion." – **Prof. Margaret Niess, Oregon State University, USA**

"The service was *very fast, very thorough, and very helpful* in ensuring our chapter meets the criteria and requirements of the book's editors. I was *quite impressed and happy* with your service." – **Prof. Tom Brinthaupt, Middle Tennessee State University, USA**

Learn More or Get Started Here:

For Questions, Contact IGI Global's Customer Service Team at cust@igi-global.com or 717-533-8845

IGI Global
PUBLISHER of TIMELY KNOWLEDGE
www.igi-global.com

www.igi-global.com

Celebrating Over 30 Years of Scholarly
Knowledge Creation & Dissemination

InfoSci®-Books

A Database of Nearly 6,000 Reference Books Containing Over 105,000+ Chapters Focusing on Emerging Research

GAIN ACCESS TO **THOUSANDS** OF REFERENCE BOOKS AT **A FRACTION** OF THEIR INDIVIDUAL LIST **PRICE**.

InfoSci®-Books Database

The **InfoSci®-Books** is a database of nearly 6,000 IGI Global single and multi-volume reference books, handbooks of research, and encyclopedias, encompassing groundbreaking research from prominent experts worldwide that spans over 350+ topics in 11 core subject areas including business, computer science, education, science and engineering, social sciences, and more.

Open Access Fee Waiver (Read & Publish) Initiative

For any library that invests in IGI Global's InfoSci-Books and/or InfoSci-Journals (175+ scholarly journals) databases, IGI Global will match the library's investment with a fund of equal value to go toward **subsidizing the OA article processing charges (APCs) for their students, faculty, and staff** at that institution when their work is submitted and accepted under OA into an IGI Global journal.*

INFOSCI® PLATFORM FEATURES

- Unlimited Simultaneous Access
- No DRM
- No Set-Up or Maintenance Fees
- A Guarantee of No More Than a 5% Annual Increase for Subscriptions
- Full-Text HTML and PDF Viewing Options
- Downloadable MARC Records
- COUNTER 5 Compliant Reports
- Formatted Citations With Ability to Export to RefWorks and EasyBib
- No Embargo of Content (Research is Available Months in Advance of the Print Release)

*The fund will be offered on an annual basis and expire at the end of the subscription period. The fund would renew as the subscription is renewed for each year thereafter. The open access fees will be waived after the student, faculty, or staff's paper has been vetted and accepted into an IGI Global journal and the fund can only be used toward publishing OA in an IGI Global journal. Libraries in developing countries will have the match on their investment doubled.

To Recommend or Request a Free Trial:

www.igi-global.com/infosci-books

eresources@igi-global.com • Toll Free: 1-866-342-6657 ext. 100 • Phone: 717-533-8845 x100

Printed in the United States
by Baker & Taylor Publisher Services